THE CONFESSIONS OF
JEAN JACQUES
ROUSSEAU

I

☆ B O N I B O O K S ☆

THE CONFESSIONS OF JEAN-JACQUES ROUSSEAU

Translated from the French by
W. CONYNGHAM MALLORY

☆ ALBERT & CHARLES BONI ☆

CONTENTS

BOOK I

THE
CONFESSIONS
OF
JEAN-JACQUES
ROUSSEAU

BOOK I

[1712–1728]

I HAVE begun on a work which is without precedent, whose accomplishment will have no imitator. I propose to set before my fellow-mortals a man in all the truth of nature; and this man shall be myself.

I have studied mankind and know my heart; I am not made like any one I have been acquainted with, perhaps like no one in existence; if not better, I at least claim originality, and whether Nature has acted rightly or wrongly in destroying the mold in which she cast me, can only be decided after I have been read.

I will present myself, whenever the last trumpet shall sound, before the Sovereign Judge with this

[3]

book in my hand, and loudly proclaim, "Thus have I acted; these were my thoughts; such was I. With equal freedom and veracity have I related what was laudable or wicked, I have concealed no crimes, added no virtues; and if I have sometimes introduced superfluous ornament, it was merely to occupy a void occasioned by defect of memory: I may have supposed that certain, which I only knew to be probable, but have never asserted as truth, a conscious falsehood. Such as I was, I have declared myself; sometimes vile and despicable, at others, virtuous, generous, and sublime; even as Thou hast read my inmost soul: Power Eternal! assemble round Thy throne an innumerable throng of my fellow-mortals, let them listen to my confessions, let them blush at my depravity, let them tremble at my sufferings; let each in his turn expose with equal sincerity the failings, the wanderings of his heart, and if he dare, aver, *I was better than that man.*"

I was born at Geneva, in 1712, son of Isaac Rousseau and Susannah Bernard, citizens. My father's share of a moderate competency, which was divided among fifteen children, being very trivial, his business of a watchmaker (in which he had the reputation of great ingenuity) was his only dependence. My mother's circumstances were more affluent; she was daughter of a Mons. Bernard, minister, and possessed a considerable share of modesty and beauty; indeed, my father found some difficulty in obtaining her hand.

The affection they entertained for each other was almost as early as their existence; at eight or nine years old they walked together every evening on the banks of the Treille, and before they were ten, could not support the idea of separation. A natural sympathy of soul confined those sentiments of predilection which habit at first produced; born with minds susceptible of the most exquisite sensibility and tenderness, it was only necessary to encounter similar dispositions; that moment fortunately presented itself, and each surrendered a willing heart.

The obstacles that opposed served only to give a degree of vivacity to their affection, and the young lover, not being able to obtain his mistress, was overwhelmed with sorrow and despair. She advised him to travel—to forget her. He consented—he traveled but returned more passionate than ever, and had the happiness to find her equally constant, equally tender. After this proof of mutual affection, what could they resolve?—to dedicate their future lives to love! the resolution was ratified with a vow, on which Heaven shed its benediction.

Fortunately, my mother's brother, Gabriel Bernard, fell in love with one of my father's sisters: she had no objection to the match, but made the marriage of his sister with her brother an indispensable preliminary. Love soon removed every obstacle, and the two weddings were celebrated the same day: thus my uncle became the husband of my aunt, and their children were doubly cousins german. Before a year was expired, both had the happiness to become fathers, but were soon after obliged to submit to a separation.

My uncle Bernard, who was an engineer, went to serve in the empire and Hungary, under Prince Eugene, and distinguished himself both at the siege and battle of Belgrade. My father, after the birth of my only brother, set off, on recommendation, for Constantinople, and was appointed watchmaker to the Seraglio. During his absence, the beauty, wit, and accomplishments * of my mother attracted a number of admirers, among whom Mons. de la Closure, Resident of France, was the most assiduous in his attentions. His passion must have been extremely violent, since after a period of thirty years I have seen him affected at the very mention of her name. My mother

---

They were too brilliant for her situation, the minister, her father, having bestowed great pains on her education. She was taught drawing, singing, and to play on the theorbo; had learning, and wrote very agreeable verses. The following is an extempore piece which she composed in the absence of her husband and brother, in a conversation with some person relative to them, while walking with her sister-in-law, and their two children:

> *Ces deux messieurs, qui sont absens,*
> > *Nous sont chers de bien des manieres;*
> *Ce sont nos amis, nos amans,*
> > *Ce sont nos maris et nos freres,*
> *Et les peres de ces enfans.*

> *These absent ones, who justly claim*
> *Our hearts, by every tender name,*
> > *To whom each wish extends:*
> *Our husbands and our brothers are,*
> *The fathers of this blooming pair,*
> > *Our lovers and our friends.*

had a defense more powerful even than her virtue; she tenderly loved my father, and conjured him to return; his inclination seconding his request, he gave up every prospect of emolument, and hastened to Geneva.

I was the unfortunate fruit of this return, being born ten months after, in a very weakly and infirm state; my birth cost my mother her life, and was the first of my misfortunes. I am ignorant how my father supported her loss at that time, but I know he was ever after inconsolable. In me he still thought he saw her he so tenderly lamented, but could never forget that I had been the innocent cause of his misfortune, nor did he ever embrace me, but his sighs, the convulsive pressure of his arms, witnessed that a bitter regret mingled itself with his caresses, though, as may be supposed, they were not on this account less ardent. When he said to me, "Jean Jacques, let us talk of your mother," my usual reply was, "Yes, father, but then, you know, we shall cry," and immediately the tears started from his eyes. "Ah!" exclaimed he, with agitation, "Give me back my wife; at least console me for her loss; fill up, dear boy, the void she has left in my soul. Could I love thee thus wert thou only *my* son?" Forty years after this loss he expired in the arms of a second wife, but the name of the first still vibrated on his lips, still was her image engraved on his heart.

Such were the authors of my being: of all the gifts it had pleased Heaven to bestow on them, a feeling heart was the only one that descended to me; this had been the source of their felicity, it was the foundation of all my misfortunes.

I came into the world with so few signs of life, that they entertained but little hope of preserving me, with the seeds of a disorder that has gathered strength with years, and from which I am now relieved at intervals, only to suffer a different, though more intolerable evil. I owed my preservation to one of my father's sisters, an amiable and virtuous girl, who took the most tender care of me; she is yet living, nursing, at the age of fourscore, a husband younger than herself, but worn out with excessive drinking. Dear aunt! I freely forgive your having preserved my life, and only lament that it is not in my power to bestow on the decline of your days the tender solicitude and care you lavished on the first dawn of mine. My nurse, Jaqueline, is likewise living, and in good health—the hands that opened my eyes to the light of this world may close them at my death. We suffer before we think; it is the common lot of humanity. I experienced more than my proportion of it. I have no knowledge of what passed prior to my fifth or sixth year; I recollect nothing of learning to read, I only remember what effect the first considerable exercise of it produced on my mind; and from that moment I date an uninterrupted knowledge of myself.

Every night, after supper, we read some part of a small collection of romances which had been my mother's. My father's design was only to improve me in reading, and he thought these entertaining works were calculated to give me a fondness for it; but we soon found ourselves so interested in the adventures they contained, that we alternately read whole nights together, and could not bear to give over until at the conclusion of a volume. Sometimes, in a morning, on hearing the swallows at our window, my father, quite ashamed of this weakness, would cry, "Come, come, let us go to bed; I am more a child than thou art."

I soon acquired, by this dangerous custom, not only an extreme facility in reading and comprehending, but, for my age, a too intimate acquaintance with the passions. An infinity of sensations were familiar to me, without possessing any precise idea of the objects to which they related—I had conceived nothing—I had felt the whole. This confused succession of emotions did not retard the future efforts of my reason, though they added an extravagant, romantic notion of human life, which experience and reflection have never been able to eradicate.

My romance reading concluded with the summer of 1719, the following winter was differently employed. My mother's library being quite exhausted, we had recourse to that part of her father's which had devolved to us; here we happily found some valuable books, which was by no means extraordinary, having been selected by a minister that truly deserved that title, in whom learning (which was the rage of the times) was but a secondary commendation, his taste and good sense being most conspicuous. The history of the Church and Empire by Le Sueur, Bossuett's Discourses on Universal History, Plutarch's Lives, the History of Venice by Nani, Ovid's Metamorphoses, La Bruyere, Fontenelle's World, his Dialogues of the Dead, and a few volumes of Moliere, were soon ranged in my father's closet, where, during the hours he was employed in his business, I daily read them, with an avidity and taste uncommon, perhaps unprecedented at my age.

Plutarch presently became my greatest favorite. The satisfaction I derived from the repeated readings I gave this author, extinguished my passion for romances, and I shortly preferred Agesilaus, Brutus, and Aristides, to Orondates, Artemenes, and Juba. These interesting studies, seconded by the conversations they frequently occasioned with my father, produced that republican spirit and love of liberty, that haughty and invincible turn of mind, which rendered me impatient of restraint or servitude, and became the torment of my life, as I continually found myself in situations incompatible with these sentiments. Incessantly occupied with Rome and Athens, conversing, if I may so express myself, with their illustrious heroes; born the citizen of a republic, of a father whose ruling passion was the love of his country, I was fired with these examples; could fancy myself a Greek or Roman, and readily give into the character of the personage whose life I read; transported by the recital of any extraordinary instance of fortitude or intrepidity, animation flashed from my eyes, and gave my voice additional strength and energy. One day, at table, while relating the fortitude of Scœvola, they were terrified at seeing me start from my seat and hold my hand over a hot chafing-dish, to represent more forcibly the action of that determined Roman.

My brother, who was seven years older than myself, was brought up to my father's profession. The extraordinary affection they lavished on me might be the reason he was too much neglected: this certainly was a fault which cannot be justified. His education and morals suffered by this neglect, and he acquired the habits of a libertine before he arrived at an age to be really one. My father tried what effect placing him with a master would produce, but he still persisted in the same ill conduct. Though I saw him so seldom that it could hardly be said we were acquainted, I loved him tenderly, and believe he had as strong an affection for me as a youth of his dissipated turn of mind could be supposed capable of. One day, I remember, when my father was correcting him severely, I threw myself between them, embracing my brother, whom I covered with my body, receiving the strokes designed for him; I persisted so obstinately in my protection, that either softened by my cries and tears, or fearing to hurt me most, his anger subsided, and he pardoned his fault. In the end, my brother's conduct became so bad that he suddenly disappeared, and we learned some time after that he was in Germany, but he never wrote to us, and from that day we heard no news of him: thus I became an only son.

If this poor lad was neglected, it was quite different with his brother, for the children of a king could not be treated with more attention and tenderness than were bestowed on my infancy, being the darling of the family; and what is rather uncommon, though treated as a beloved, never a spoiled child; was never permitted, while under paternal inspection, to play in the street with other children; never had any occasion to contradict or indulge those fantastical humors which are usually attributed to nature, but are in reality the effects of an injudicious education. I had the faults common to my age, was talkative, a glutton, and sometimes a liar; made no scruple of stealing sweetmeats, fruits, or, indeed, any kind of eatables; but never took delight in mischievous waste, in accusing others, or tormenting harmless animals. I recollect, indeed, that one day, while Madam Clot, a neighbor of ours, was gone to church, I made water in her kettle; the remembrance even now makes me smile, for Madam Clot (though, if you please, a good sort of creature) was one of the most tedious grumbling old women I ever knew. Thus have I given a brief, but faithful, history of my childish transgressions.

How could I become cruel or vicious, when I had before my eyes only examples of mildness, and was surrounded by some of the best people in the world?

My father, my aunt, my nurse, my relations, our friends, our neighbors, all I had any connections with, did not obey me, it is true, but loved me tenderly, and I returned their affection. I found so little to excite my desires, and those I had were so seldom contradicted, that I was hardly sensible of possessing any, and can solemnly aver I was an absolute stranger to caprice until after I had experienced the authority of a master.

Those hours that were not employed in reading or writing with my father, or walking with my governess, Jaqueline, I spent with my aunt; and whether seeing her embroider, or hearing her sing, whether sitting or standing by her side, I was ever happy. Her tenderness and unaffected gayety, the charms of her figure and countenance, have left such indelible impressions on my mind, that her manner, look, and attitude, are still before my eyes; I recollect a thousand little caressing questions; could describe her clothes, her head-dress, nor have the two curls of fine black hair which hung on her temples, according to the mode of that time, escaped my memory.

Though my taste, or rather passion, for music, did not show itself until a considerable time after, I am fully persuaded it is to her I am indebted for it. She knew a great number of songs, which she sung with great sweetness and melody. The serenity and cheerfulness which were conspicuous in this lovely girl, banished melancholy, and made all round her happy.

The charms of her voice had such an affect on me,

that not only several of her songs have ever since remained on my memory, but some I have not thought of from my infancy, as I grow old, return upon my mind with a charm altogether inexpressible. Would any one believe that an old dotard like me, worn out with care and infirmity, should sometime surprise himself weeping like a child, and in a voice querulous, and broken by age, muttering out one of those airs which were the favorites of my infancy? There is one song in particular, whose tune I perfectly recollect, but the words that compose the latter half of it constantly refuse every effort to recall them, though I have a confused idea of the rhymes. The beginning, with what I have been able to recollect of the remainder, is as follows:

Tircis, je n'ose
Ecouter ton Chalumeau
Sous l' Ormeau;
Car on en cause
Déjà dans notre hameau.

—— —— un Berger
s'engager
sans danger,
Et toujours l'épine est sous la rose.

I have endeavored to account for the invincible charm my heart feels on the recollection of this fragment, but it is altogether inexplicable. I only know, that before I get to the end of it, I always find my voice interrupted by tenderness, and my eyes suffused with tears. I have a hundred times formed the resolution of writing to Paris for the remainder of these words, if any one should chance to know them: but I am almost certain the pleasure I take in the recollection would be greatly diminished was I assured any one but my poor aunt Susan had sung them.

Such were my affections on entering this life. Thus began to form and demonstrate itself a heart at once haughty and tender, a character effeminate, yet invincible; which, fluctuating between weakness and courage, luxury and virtue, has ever set me in contradiction to myself; causing abstinence and enjoyment, pleasure and prudence, equally to shun me.

This course of education was interrupted by an accident, whose consequences influenced the rest of my life. My father had a quarrel with M. G——, who had a captain's commission in France, and was related to several of the Council. This G——, who was an insolent ungenerous man, happening to bleed at the nose, in order to be revenged, accused my father of having drawn his sword on him in the city, and in consequence of this charge they were about to conduct him to prison. He insisted (according to the law of this republic) that the accuser should be confined at the same time; and, not being able to obtain this, preferred a voluntary banishment for the remainder of his life, to giving up a point by which he must sacrifice his honor and liberty.

I remained under the tuition of my uncle Bernard, who was at that time employed in the fortifications of Geneva. He had lost his eldest daughter, but had a son about my own age, and we were sent together to Bossey, to board with the Minister Lambercier. Here we were to learn Latin, with all the insignificant trash that has obtained the name of education.

Two years spent in this village softened, in some degree, my Roman fierceness, and again reduced me to a state of childhood. At Geneva, where nothing was exacted, I loved reading, which was, indeed, my principal amusement; but, at Bossey, where application was expected, I was fond of play as a relaxation. The country was so new, so charming in my idea, that it seemed impossible to find satiety in its enjoyments, and I conceived a passion for rural life, which time has not been able to extinguish; nor have I ever ceased to regret the pure and tranquil pleasures I enjoyed at this place in my childhood; the remembrance having followed me through every age, even to that in which I am hastening again towards it.

M. Lambercier was a worthy, sensible man, who, without neglecting our instruction, never made our acquisitions burthensome, or tasks tedious. What convinces me of the rectitude of his method is, that notwithstanding my extreme aversion to restraint, the recollection of my studies is never attended with disgust; and, if my improvement was trivial, it was obtained with ease, and has never escaped memory.

The simplicity of this rural life was of infinite advantage in opening my heart to the reception of true friendship. The sentiments I had hitherto formed on this subject were extremely elevated, but altogether imaginary. The habit of living in this peaceful manner soon united me tenderly to my cousin Bernard; my affection was more ardent than that I had felt for my brother, nor has time ever been able to efface it. He was a tall, lank, weakly boy, with a mind as mild as his body was feeble, and who did not wrong the good opinion they were disposed to entertain for the son of my guardian. Our studies, amusements, and tasks, were the same; we were alone; each wanted a playmate; to separate would, in some measure, have been to annihilate us. Though we had not many opportunities of demonstrating our attachment to each other, it was certainly extreme; and so far from enduring the thought of separation, we could not even form an idea that we should ever be able to submit to it. Each of a disposition to be won by kindness, and complaisant, when not soured by contradiction, we agreed in every particular. If, by the favor of those who governed us he had the ascendant while in their presence, I was sure to acquire it when we were alone, and this preserved the equilibrium so necessary in friendship. If he hesitated in repeating his task, I prompted him; when my exercises were finished, I helped to write his; and, in our amusements, my disposition being most active, ever had the lead. In a word, our characters accorded so well, and the friendship that subsisted between us was so cordial, that during the five years we were at Bossey and

Geneva we were inseparable: we often fought, it is true, but there never was any occasion to separate us. No one of our quarrels lasted more than a quarter of an hour, and never in our lives did we make any complaint of each other. It may be said, these remarks are frivolous; but, perhaps, a similar example among children can hardly be produced.

The manner in which I passed my time at Bossey was so agreeable to my disposition, that it only required a longer duration absolutely to have fixed my character, which would have had only peaceable, affectionate, benevolent sentiments for its basis. I believe no individual of our kind ever possessed less natural vanity than myself. At intervals, by an extraordinary effort, I arrived at sublime ideas, but presently sunk again into my original languor. To be beloved by every one who knew me was my most ardent wish. I was naturally mild, my cousin was equally so, and those who had the care of us were of similar dispositions. Everything contributed to strengthen those propensities which nature had implanted in my breast, and during the two years I was neither the victim nor witness of any violent emotions.

I knew nothing so delightful as to see every one content; not only with me, but all that concerned them. When repeating our catechism at church, nothing could give me greater vexation, on being obliged to hesitate, than to see Miss Lambercier's countenance express disapprobation and uneasiness. This alone was more afflicting to me than the shame of faltering before so many witnesses, which, notwithstanding, was sufficiently painful; for though not over-solicitous of praise, I was feelingly alive to shame; yet I can truly affirm, the dread of being reprimanded by Miss Lambercier alarmed me less than the thought of making her uneasy.

Neither she nor her brother were deficient in a reasonable severity, but as this was scarce ever exerted without just cause, I was more afflicted at their disapprobation than the punishment. Certainly the method of treating youth would be altered if the distant effects, this indiscriminate, and frequently indiscreet method produces, were more conspicuous. I would willingly excuse myself from a further explanation, did not the lesson this example conveys (which points out an evil as frequent as it is pernicious) forbid my silence.

As Miss Lambercier felt a mother's affection, she sometimes exerted a mother's authority, even to inflicting on us, when we deserved it, the punishment of infants. She had often threatened it, and this threat of a treatment entirely new, appeared to me extremely dreadful; but I found the reality much less terrible than the idea, and what is still more unaccountable, this punishment increased my affection for the person who had inflicted it. All this affection, aided by my natural mildness, was scarcely sufficient to prevent my seeking, by fresh offenses, a return of the same chastisement; for a degree of sensuality had mingled with the smart and shame, which left more desire than fear of a repetition. I was well convinced the same discipline from her brother would have produced a quite contrary effect; but from a man of his disposition this was not probable, and if I abstained from meriting correction, it was merely from a fear of offending Miss Lambercier, for benevolence, aided by the passions, has ever maintained an empire over me which has given law to my heart.

This event, which, though desirable, I had not endeavored to accelerate, arrived without my fault; I should say, without my seeking; and I profited by it with a safe conscience; but this second, was also the last time, for Miss Lambercier, who doubtless had some reason to imagine this chastisement did not produce the desired effect, declared it was too fatiguing, and that she renounced it for the future. Till now we had slept in her chamber, and during the winter, even in her bed; but two days after another room was prepared for us.

Who would believe this childish discipline, received at eight years old, from the hand of a woman of thirty, should influence my propensities, my desires, my passions, for the rest of my life, and that in quite a contrary sense from what might naturally have been expected? The very incident that inflamed my senses, gave my desires such an extraordinary turn, that, confined to what I had already experienced, I sought no further, and, with blood boiling with sensuality almost from my birth, preserved my purity beyond the age when the coldest constitutions lose their sensibility; long tormented, without knowing by what, I gazed on every handsome woman with delight; imagination incessantly brought their charms to my remembrance, only to transform them into so many Miss Lamberciers. Even after having attained the marriageable age this odd taste still continued and drove me nearly to depravity and madness.

If ever education was perfectly chaste, it was certainly that I received; my three aunts were of exemplary prudence. My father, it is true, loved pleasure, but his gallantry was rather of the last than the present century. At M. Lambercier's a good maid-servant was discharged for having once made use of an expression before us which was thought to contain some degree of indelicacy. I entertained a particular aversion for courtesans, nor could I look on a rake without a degree of disdain mingled with terror. My aversion for lewdness went so far, since one day I walked through a hollow in the road at Petit Sacconez; I saw on both sides cavities in the earth and was told that it was there the people did their pairing. When I thought of it, it came to my mind, that I had seen dogs in a similar situation, and my heart revolted at the remembrance.

These prejudices of education, proper in themselves to retard the first explosions of a combustible constitution, were strengthened, as I have already hinted, by the effect the first moments of sensuality produced in me, for notwithstanding the troublesome ebullition

of my blood, I was satisfied with the species of voluptuousness I had already been acquainted with, and
sought no further. I never went to the other species
of voluptuousness and had no suspicion that I was
so near it. In my crazy fancies during my erotic passions and while I was committing extravagant acts, I
borrowed the help of the other sex in my imagination.

Thus I passed the age of puberty, with a constitution extremely ardent, without knowing or even wishing for any other gratification of the passions than
what Miss Lambercier had innocently given me an
idea of; and when I became a man, that childish taste,
instead of vanishing, only associated with the other
that I never could remove from my sensual desires.
This folly, joined to a natural timidity, has always
prevented my being very enterprising with women,
so that I have passed my days in languishing in silence
for those I most admired, without daring to disclose
my wishes.

To fall at the feet of an imperious mistress, obey
her mandates, or implore pardon, were for me the
most exquisite enjoyments, and the more my blood
was inflamed by the efforts of a lively imagination the
more I acquired the appearance of a whining lover.

It will be readily conceived that this mode of making love is not attended with a rapid progress or
imminent danger to the virtue of its object; yet,
though I have few favors to boast of I have not been
excluded from enjoyment, however imaginary. Thus
the senses, in concurrence with a mind equally timid

and romantic, have preserved my morals chaste, and feelings uncorrupted, with precisely the same inclinations, which, seconded with a moderate portion of effrontery, might have plunged me into the most unwarrantable excesses.

I have made the first, most difficult step, in the obscure and painful maze of my Confessions. We never feel so great a degree of repugnance in divulging what is really criminal, as what is merely ridiculous. I am now assured of my resolution, for after what I have dared disclose, nothing can have power to deter me. The difficulty attending these acknowledgments will be readily conceived, when I declare, that during the whole of my life, though frequently laboring under the most violent agitation, being hurried away with the impetuosity of passion I could never, in the course of the most unbounded familiarity, acquire sufficient courage to declare my folly, and implore the only favor that remained to bestow. That has only once happened, when a child, with a girl of my own age; even then it was she who first proposed it.

In thus investigating the first traces of my sensible existence, I find elements, which, though seemingly incompatible, have united to produce a simple and uniform effect; while others, apparently the same, have, by the concurrence of certain circumstances, formed such different combinations, that it would never be imagined they had any affinity; who would believe, for example, that one of the most vigorous springs of my soul was tempered in the identical source from whence luxury and ease mingled with my constitution and circulated in my veins? Before I quit this subject, I will add a striking instance of the different effects they produced.

One day, while I was studying in a chamber contiguous to the kitchen, the maid set some of Miss Lambercier's combs to dry by the fire, and on coming to fetch them some time after, was surprised to find the teeth of one of them broken off. Who could be suspected of this mischief? No one but myself had entered the room: I was questioned, but denied having any knowledge of it. Mr. and Miss Lambercier consult, exhort, threaten, but all to no purpose; I obstinately persist in the denial; and, though this was the first time I had been detected in a confirmed falsehood, appearances were so strong that they overthrew all my protestations. This affair was thought serious; the mischief, the lie, the obstinacy, were considered equally deserving of punishment, which was not now to be administered by Miss Lambercier. My uncle Bernard was written to; he arrived; and my poor cousin being charged with a crime no less serious, we were conducted to the same execution, which was inflicted with great severity. If finding a remedy in the evil itself, they had sought ever to allay my depraved desires, they could not have chosen a shorter method to accomplish their designs, and, I can assure my readers, I was for a long time freed from the dominion of them.

As this severity could not draw from me the expected acknowledgment, which obstinacy brought on several repetitions, and reduced me to a deplorable situation, yet I was immovable, and resolutely determined to suffer death rather than submit. Force, at length, was obliged to yield to the diabolical infatuation of a child, for no better name was bestowed on my constancy, and I came out of this dreadful trial, torn, it is true, but triumphant. Fifty years have expired since this adventure—the fear of punishment is no more. Well, then, I aver, in the face of Heaven, I was absolutely innocent: and, so far from breaking, or even touching the comb, never came near the fire. It will be asked, how did this mischief happen? I can form no conception of it, I only know my own innocence.

Let any one figure to himself a character whose leading traits were docility and timidity, but haughty, ardent, and invincible, in its passions; a child, hitherto governed by the voice of reason, treated with mildness, equity, and complaisance, who could not even support the idea of injustice, experiencing, for the first time, so violent an instance of it, inflicted by those he most loved and respected. What perversion of ideas! What confusion in the heart, the brain, in all my little being, intelligent and moral!—let any one, I say, if possible, imagine all this, for I am incapable of giving the least idea of what passed in my mind at that period.

My reason was not sufficiently established to enable

me to put myself in the place of others, and judge how much appearances condemned me, I only beheld the rigor of a dreadful chastisement, inflicted for a crime I had not committed; yet I can truly affirm, the smart I suffered, though violent, was inconsiderable to what I felt from indignation, rage, and despair. My cousin, who was almost in similar circumstances, having been punished for an involuntary fault, as guilty of a premeditated crime, became furious by my example. Both in the same bed, we embraced each other with convulsive transport; we were almost suffocated; and when our young hearts found sufficient relief to breathe out our indignation, we sat up in the bed, and with all our force, repeated a hundred times, Carnifex! Carnifex! Carnifex! Executioner, tormentor.

Even while I write this I feel my pulse quicken, and should I live a hundred thousand years, the agitation of that moment would still be fresh in my memory. The first instance of violence and oppression is so deeply engraven on my soul, that every relative idea renews my emotion: the sentiment of indignation, which in its origin had reference only to myself, has acquired such strength, and is at present so completely detached from personal motives, that my heart is as much inflamed at the sight or relation of any act of injustice (whatever may be the object, or wheresoever it may be perpetrated) as if I was the immediate sufferer. When I read the history of a merciless tyrant, or the dark and the subtle machination of a knavish designing priest, I could on the instant set off to stab the miscreants, though I was certain to perish in the attempt.

I have frequently fatigued myself by running after and stoning a cock, a cow, a dog, or any animal I saw tormenting another, only because it was conscious of possessing superior strength. This may be natural to me, and I am inclined to believe it is, though the lively impression of the first injustice I became the victim of was too long and too powerfully remembered not to have added considerable force to it.

This occurrence terminated my infantine serenity; from that moment I ceased to enjoy a pure unadulterated happiness, and on a retrospection of the pleasures of my childhood, I yet feel they ended here. We continued at Bossey some months after this event, but were like our first parents in the Garden of Eden after they had lost their innocence; in appearance our situation was the same, in effect it was totally different.

Affection, respect, intimacy, confidence, no longer attached the pupils to their guides; we beheld them no longer as divinities, who could read the secrets of our hearts; we were less ashamed of committing faults, more afraid of being accused of them: we learned to dissemble, to rebel, to lie: all the vices common to our years began to corrupt our happy innocence, mingle with our sports, and embitter our amusements. The country itself, losing those sweet and simple charms which captivate the heart, appeared a gloomy desert, or covered with a veil that concealed its beauties. We cultivated our little gardens no more: our flowers were neglected. We no longer scratched away the mold, and broke out into exclamations of delight, on discovering that the grain we had sown began to shoot. We were disgusted with our situation; our preceptors were weary of us. In a word, my uncle wrote for our return, and we left Mr. and Miss Lambercier without feeling any regret at the separation.

Near thirty years passed away from my leaving Bossey, without once recalling the place to my mind with any degree of satisfaction; but after having passed the prime of life, as I decline into old age (while more recent occurrences are wearing out apace) I feel these remembrances revive and imprint themselves on my heart, with a force and charm that every day acquires fresh strength; as if, feeling life flee from me, I endeavored to catch it again by its commencement. The most trifling incidents of those happy days delight me, for no other reason than being of those days, I recall every circumstance of time, place, and persons; I see the maid or footman busy in the chamber, a swallow entering the window, a fly settling on my hand while repeating my lesson. I see the whole economy of the apartment; on the right hand Mr. Lambercier's closet, with a print representing all the popes, a barometer, a large almanac, the windows of the house (which stood in a hollow at the bottom of the garden) shaded by raspberry shrubs, whose shoots sometimes found entrance; I am sensible the reader has no occasion to know all this, but I feel a kind of necessity for relating it. Why am I not permitted to recount all the little anecdotes of that thrice happy age, at the recollection of whose joys I even tremble with delight? Five or six particularly—let us compromise the matter—I will give up five, but then I must have one, and only one, provided I may draw it out to its utmost length, in order to prolong my satisfaction.

If I only sought yours, I should choose that of Miss Lambercier's backside, which, by an unlucky fall at the bottom of the meadow, was exposed to the view of the King of Sardinia, who happened to be passing by; but that of the walnut tree on the terrace is more amusing to me, since here I was an actor, whereas, in the above-mentioned scene I was only a spectator; and I must confess I see nothing that should occasion risibility in an accident, which, however laughable in itself, alarmed me for a person I loved as a mother, or perhaps something more.

Ye curious readers, whose expectations are already on the stretch for the noble history of the terrace, listen to the tragedy, and abstain from trembling, if you can, at the horrible catastrophe.

At the outside of the courtyard door, on the left hand, was a terrace; here they often sat after dinner; but it was subject to one inconvenience, being too much exposed to the rays of the sun; to obviate this defect, Mr. Lambercier had a walnut tree set there, the planting of which was attended with great solemnity. The two boarders were godfathers, and while the earth was replacing round the root, each held the tree with one hand, singing songs of triumph. In order to water it with more effect, they formed a kind of luson around its foot: myself and cousin, who were every day ardent spectators of this watering, confirmed each other in the very natural idea, that it was nobler to plant trees on the terrace than colors on a breach, and this glory we were resolved to procure without dividing it with any one.

In pursuance of this resolution, we cut a slip off a willow, and planted it on the terrace, at about eight or ten feet distance from the august walnut tree. We did not forget to make a hollow round it, but the difficulty was how to procure a supply of water, which was brought from a considerable distance, and we not permitted to fetch it: but water was absolutely necessary for our willow, and we made use of every stratagem to obtain it.

For a few days everything succeeded so well that it began to bud, and throw out small leaves, which we hourly measured, convinced (though now scarce a foot from the ground) it would soon afford us a refreshing shade. This unfortunate willow, by engrossing our whole time, rendered us incapable of application to any other study, and the cause of our inattention not being known, we were kept closer than before. The fatal moment approached when water

must fail, and we were already afflicted with the idea
that our tree must perish with drought. At length
necessity, the parent of industry, suggested an invention, by which we might save our tree from death,
and ourselves from despair; it was to make a furrow
underground, which would privately conduct a part
of the water from the walnut tree to our willow.
This undertaking was executed with ardor, but did
not immediately succeed—our descent was not skill-
fully planned—the water did not run, the earth falling in and stopping up the burrow; yet, though all
went contrary, nothing discouraged us, *Labor omnia
vincit labor improbus.* We made the basin deeper, to
give the water a more sensible descent; we cut the
bottom of a box into narrow planks; increased the
channel from the walnut tree to our willow, and laying a row flat at the bottom, set two others inclining
towards each other, so as to form a triangular channel; we formed a king of grating with small sticks
at the end next the walnut tree, to prevent the earth
and stones from stopping it up, and having carefully
covered our work with well-trodden earth, in a transport of hope and fear attended the hour of watering.
After an interval which seemed an age of expectation,
this hour arrived. Mr. Lambercier, as usual, assisted
at the operation; we contrived to get between him
and our tree, towards which he fortunately turned
his back. They no sooner began to pour the first pail
of water, than we perceived it running to the willow; this sight was too much for our prudence, and

we involuntarily expressed our transport by a shout of joy. The sudden exclamation made Mr. Lambercier turn about, though at that inſtant he was delighted to observe how greedily the earth, which surrounded the root of his walnut tree, imbibed the water. Surprised at seeing two trenches partake of it, he shouted in his turn, examines, perceives the roguery, and, sending instantly for a pick axe, at one fatal blow makes two or three of our planks fly, crying out meantime with all his ſtrength, *an aqueduct! an aqueduct!* His strokes redoubled, every one of which made an impression on our hearts; in a moment the planks, the channel, the basin, even our favorite willow, all were plowed up, nor was one word pronounced during this terrible transaction, except the above-mentioned exclamation. *An aqueduct!* repeated he, while deſtroying all our hopes, *an aqueduct! an aqueduct!*

It may be supposed this adventure had a still more melancholy end for the young architects; this, however, was not the case; the affair ended here. Mr. Lambercier never reproached us on this account nor was his countenance clouded with a frown; we even heard him mention the circumſtance to his siſter with loud burſts of laughter. The laugh of Mr. Lambercier might be heard to a considerable diſtance. But what is still more surprising, after the first transport of sorrow had subsided, we did not find ourselves violently afflicted; we planted a tree in another spot, and frequently recollected the catastrophe òf the former, repeating with a significant emphasis, *an aque-*

duct! an aqueduct! Till then, at intervals, I had fits of ambition, and could fancy myself Brutus or Aristides, but this was the first visible effect of my vanity. To have constructed an aqueduct with our own hands, to have set a slip of willow in competion with a flourishing tree, appeared to me a supreme degree of glory! I had a juster conception of it at ten, than Cæsar entertained at thirty.

The idea of this walnut tree, with the little anecdotes it gave rise to, have so well continued, or returned to my memory, that the design which conveyed the most pleasing sensations, during my journey to Geneva, in the year 1754, was visiting Bossey, and reviewing the monuments of my infantine amusement, above all, the beloved walnut tree, whose age at that time must have been verging on a third of a century, but I was so beset with company, that I could not find a moment to accomplish my design. There is little appearance now of the occasion being renewed; but should I ever return to that charming spot, and find my favorite walnut tree still existing, I am convinced I should water it with my tears.

On my return to Geneva, I passed two or three years at my uncle's, expecting the determination of my friends respecting my future establishment. His own son being devoted to engineering, was taught drawing, and instructed by his father in the elements of Euclid: I partook of these instructions, but was principally fond of drawing. Meantime they were irresolute, whether to make me a watchmaker, a lawyer, or a minister. I should have preferred being a minister, as I thought it must be a charming thing to preach, but the trifling income which had been my mother's, and was to be divided between my brother and myself, was too inconsiderable to defray the expense attending the prosecution of my studies. As my age did not render the choice very pressing, I remained with my uncle, passing my time with very little improvement, and paying pretty dear, though not unreasonably, for my board.

My uncle, like my father, was a man of pleasure, but had not learned, like him, to abridge his amusements for the sake of instructing his family, consequently our education was neglected. My aunt was a devotee, who loved singing psalms better than thinking of our improvement, so that we were left entirely to ourselves, which liberty we never abused.

Ever inseparable, we were all the world to each other; and, feeling no inclination to frequent the company of a number of disorderly lads of our own age, we learned none of those habits of libertinism to which our idle life exposed us. Perhaps I am wrong in charging myself and cousin with idleness at this time, for, in our lives, we were never less so; and what was extremely fortunate, so incessantly occupied with our amusements, that we found no temptation to spend any part of our time in the streets. We made cages, pipes, kites, drums, houses, ships, and bows; spoiled the tools of my good old grandfather by endeavoring to make watches in imitation of him;

but our favorite amusement was wasting paper, in drawing, washing, coloring, etc. There came an Italian mountebank to Geneva, called Gamber-Corta, who had an exhibition of puppets, that he made play a kind of comedy. We went once to see them, but could not spare time to go again, being busily employed in making puppets of our own, and inventing comedies, which we immediately set about making them perform, mimicking to the best of our abilities the uncouth voice of Punch; and, to complete the business, my good aunt and uncle Bernard had the patience to see and listen to our imitations; but my uncle, having one day read an elaborate discourse to his family, we instantly gave up our comedies, and began composing sermons.

These details, I confess, are not very amusing, but they serve to demonstrate that the former part of our education was well directed, since being, at such an early age, the absolute masters of our time, we found no inclination to abuse it; and so little in want of other companions, that we constantly neglected every occasion of seeking them. When taking our walks together, we observed their diversions without feeling any inclination to partake of them. Friendship so entirely occupied our hearts, that, pleased with each other's company, the simplest pastimes were sufficient to delight us.

We were soon remarked for being thus inseparable: and what rendered us more conspicuous, my cousin was very tall, myself extremely short, so that we exhibited a very whimsical contrast. This meager figure, small, sallow countenance, heavy air, and supine gait, excited the ridicule of the children, who, in the gibberish of the country, nicknamed him *Barna Bredanna;* and we no sooner got out of doors than our ears were assailed with a repetition of *"Barna Bredanna."* He bore this indignity with tolerable patience, but I was instantly for fighting. This was what the young rogues aimed at. I engaged accordingly, and was beat. My poor cousin did all in his power to assist me, but he was weak, and a single stroke brought him to the ground. I then became furious, and received several smart blows, some of which were aimed at *Barna Bredanna.* This quarrel so far increased the evil, that, to avoid their insults, we could only show ourselves in the streets while they were employed at school.

I had already become a redresser of grievances; there only wanted a lady in the way to be a knight-errant in form. This defect was soon supplied; I presently had two. I frequently went to see my father at Nion, a small city in the Vaudois country, where he was now settled. Being universally respected, the affection entertained for him extended to me; and, during my visits, the question seemed to be, who should show me most kindness. A Madam de Vulson, in particular, loaded me with caresses; and, to complete all, her daughter made me her gallant. I need not explain what kind of gallant a boy of eleven must be to a girl of two and twenty; the artful hussies know how to set these puppets up in front, to conceal more serious engagements. On my part, I saw no inequality between myself and Miss Vulson, was flattered by the circumstance, and went into it with my whole heart, or rather my whole head, for this passion certainly reached no further, though it transported me almost to madness, and frequently produced scenes sufficient to make even a cynic expire with laughter.

I have experienced two kinds of love, equally real, which have scarce any affinity, yet each differing materially from tender friendship. My whole life has been divided between these affections, and I have frequently felt the power of both at the same instant. For example, at the very time I so publicly and tyrannically claimed Miss Vulson, that I could not suffer any other of my sex to approach her, I had short, but passionate, assignations with a Miss Goton, who thought proper to act the schoolmistress with me. Our meetings, though absolutely childish, afforded me the height of happiness. I felt the whole charm of mystery, and repaid Miss Vulson in kind, when she least expected it, the use she made of me in concealing her amours. To my great mortification, this secret was soon discovered, and I presently lost my young schoolmistress.

Miss Goton was, in fact, a singular personage. She was not handsome, yet there was a certain something in her figure which could not easily be forgotten, and this for an old fool, I am too often convinced of. Her eyes, in particular, neither corresponded with her age, her height, nor her manner; she had a lofty imposing air which agreed extremely well with the character she assumed, but the most extraordinary part of her composition was a mixture of forwardness and reserve difficult to be conceived; and while she took the greatest liberties with me, would never permit any to be taken with her in return, treating me precisely like a child. This makes me suppose she had either ceased herself to be one, or was yet sufficiently so to behold us play the danger to which this folly exposed her.

I was so absolutely in the power of both these mistresses, that when in the presence of either, I never thought of her who was absent; in other respects, the effects they produced on me bore no affinity. I could have passed my whole life with Miss Vulson, without forming a wish to quit her; but then, my satisfaction was attended with a pleasing serenity; and, in numerous companies, I was particularly charmed with her. The sprightly sallies of her wit, the arch glance of her eye, even jealousy itself, strengthened my attachment, and I triumphed in the preference she seemed to bestow on me, while addressed by more powerful rivals; applause, encouragement, and smiles, gave animation to my happiness. Surrounded by a throng of observers, I felt the whole force of love—I was passionate, transported; in a *tête-à-tête,* I should have been constrained, thoughtful, perhaps unhappy. If Miss Vulson was ill,

I suffered with her; would willingly have given up
my own health to establish hers (and, observe, I
knew the want of it from experience); if absent, she
employed my thoughts, I felt the want of her; when
present, her caresses came with warmth and rapture
to my heart, though my senses were unaffected. The
familiarities she bestowed on me I could not have
supported the idea of her granting to another; I
loved her with a brother's affection only, but experienced all the jealousy of a lover.

With Miss Goton this passion might have acquired
a degree of fury; I should have been a Turk, a tiger,
had I once imagined she bestowed her favors on any
but myself. The pleasure I felt on approaching Miss
Vulson was sufficiently ardent, though unattended
with uneasy sensations; but at sight of Miss Goton,
I felt myself bewildered—every sense was absorbed
in ecstasy. I believe it would have been impossible to
have remained long with her; I must have been suffocated with the violence of my palpitations. I equally
dreaded giving either of them displeasure; with one
I was more complaisant; with the other, more submis-
sive. I would not have offended Miss Vulson for the
world; but if Miss Goton had commanded me to
throw myself into the flames, I think I should have
instantly obeyed her. Happily, both for her and myself, our amours, or rather rendezvous, were not of
long duration: and though my connection with Miss
Vulson was less dangerous, after a continuance of
some greater length, that likewise had its catastrophe;

indeed the termination of a love affair is good for nothing, unless it partakes of the romantic, and can furnish out at least an exclamation.

Though my correspondence with Miss Vulson was less animated, it was perhaps more endearing; we never separated without tears, and it can hardly be conceived what a void I felt in my heart. I could neither think nor speak of anything but her. These romantic sorrows were not affected, though I am inclined to believe they did not absolutely center in her, for I am persuaded (though I did not perceive it at that time) being deprived of amusement bore a considerable share in them.

To soften the rigor of absence, we agreed to correspond with each other, and the pathetic expressions these letters contained were sufficient to have split a rock. In a word, I had the honor of her not being able to endure the pain of separation. She came to see me at Geneva.

My head was now completely turned; and during the two days she remained here, I was intoxicated with delight. At her departure, I would have thrown myself into the water after her, and absolutely rent the air with my cries. The week following she sent me sweetmeats, gloves, etc. This certainly would have appeared extremely gallant, had I not been informed of her marriage at the same instant, and that the journey I had thought proper to give myself the honor of, was only to buy her wedding suit.

My indignation may easily be conceived; I shall

not attempt to describe it. In this heroic fury, I swore never more to see the perfidious girl, supposing it the greatest punishment that could be inflicted on her. This, however, did not occasion her death, for twenty years after while on a visit to my father, being on the lake, I asked who those ladies were in a boat not far from ours. "What!" said my father, smiling, "does not your heart inform you? It is your former flame, it is Madam Christin, or, if you please, Miss Vulson." I started at the almost forgotten name, and instantly ordered the waterman to turn off, not judging it worth while to be perjured, however favorable the opportunity for revenge, in renewing a dispute of twenty years past, with a woman of forty.

Thus, before my future destination was determined, did I fool away the most precious moments of my youth. After deliberating a long time on the bent of my natural inclination, they resolved to dispose of me in a manner the most repugnant to them. I was sent to Mr. Masseron, the City Register, to learn (according to the expression of my uncle Bernard) the thriving occupation of a scraper. This nickname was inconceivably displeasing to me, and I promised myself but little satisfaction in the prospect of heaping up money by a mean employment. The assiduity and subjection required completed my disgust, and I never set foot in the office without feeling a kind of horror, which every day gained fresh strength.

Mr. Masseron, who was not better pleased with my abilities than I was with the employment, treated me with disdain, incessantly upbraiding me with being a fool and blockhead, not forgetting to repeat, that my uncle had assured him I was a knowing one, though he could not find that I knew anything. That he had promised to furnish him with a sprightly boy, but had, in truth, sent him an ass. To conclude, I was turned out of the registry, with the additional ignominy of being pronounced a fool by all Mr. Masseron's clerks, and fit only to handle a file.

My vocation thus determined, I was bound apprentice; not, however, to a watchmaker, but to an engraver, and I had been so completely humiliated by the contempt of the register, that I submitted without a murmur. My master, whose name was M. Ducommon, was a young man of a very violent and boorish character, who contrived in a short time to tarnish all the amiable qualities of my childhood, to stupefy a disposition naturally sprightly, and reduce my feelings, as well as my condition, to an absolute state of servitude. I forgot my Latin, history, and antiquities; I could hardly recollect whether such people as Romans ever existed. When I visited my father, he no longer beheld his idol, nor could the ladies recognize the gallant Jean Jacques; nay, I was so well convinced that Mr. and Miss Lambercier would scarce receive me as their pupil, that I endeavored to avoid their company, and from that time have never seen them. The vilest inclinations, the basest actions, succeeded my amiable amusements, and even obliterated the very remembrance of them. I must have had, in spite of my good education, a great propensity to degenerate, else the declension could not have followed with such ease and rapidity, for never did so promising a Cæsar so quickly become a Laradon.

The art itself did not displease me. I had a lively taste for drawing. There was nothing displeasing in the exercise of the graver; and as it required no very extraordinary abilities to attain perfection as a watch-case engraver, I hoped to arrive at it. Perhaps I should have accomplished my design, if unreasonable restraint, added to the brutality of my master, had not rendered my business disgusting. I wasted his time, and employed myself in engraving medals, which served me and my companions as a kind of insignia for a new invented order of chivalry, and though this differed very little from my usual employ, I considered it as a relaxation. Unfortunately, my master caught me at this contraband labor, and a severe beating was the consequence. He reproached me at the same time with attempting to make counterfeit money, because our medals bore the arms of the Republic, though, I can truly aver, I had no conception of false money, and very little of the true, knowing better how to make a Roman As than one of our threepenny pieces.

My master's tyranny rendered insupportable that labor I should otherwise have loved, and drove me to vices I naturally despised, such as falsehood, idleness, and theft. Nothing ever gave me a clearer demonstration of the difference between filial dependence and abject slavery, than the remembrance of the change produced in me at that period. Hitherto I had enjoyed a reasonable liberty; this I had suddenly lost. I was enterprising at my father's, free at M. Lambercier's, discreet at my uncle's; but, with my master, I became fearful, and from that moment my mind was vitiated. Accustomed to live on terms of perfect equality, to be witness of no pleasures I could not command, to see no dish I was not to partake of, or be sensible of a desire I might not express; to be able to bring every wish of my heart to my lips—what a transition!—at my master's I was scarce allowed to speak, was forced to quit the table without tasting what I most longed for, and the room when I had nothing particular to do there; was incessantly confined to my work, while the liberty my master and his journeymen enjoyed, served only to increase the weight of my subjection. When disputes happened to arise, though conscious that I understood the subject better than any of them, I dared not offer my opinion; in a word, everything I saw became an object of desire, for no other reason than because I was not permitted to enjoy anything. Farewell gayety, ease, those happy turns of expression, which formerly even made my faults escape correction. I recollect, with pleasure, a circumstance that happened at my father's, which even now makes me smile. Being for some fault ordered to bed without my supper, as I was passing through the kitchen, with my poor morsel of bread in my hand, I saw the meat turning on the spit; my father and the rest were round the fire; I must bow to every one as I passed. When I had gone through this ceremony, leering with a wishful eye at the roast meat, which looked so inviting, and smelt so savory, I could not abstain from making that a bow likewise, adding in a pitiful tone, *good-by, roast meat!* This unpremeditated pleasantry put them in such good humor, that I was permitted to stay, and partake of it. Perhaps the same thing might have produced a similar effect at my master's, but such a thought could never have occurred to me, or, if it had, I should not have had courage to express it.

Thus I learned to covet, dissemble, lie, and, at length, to steal, a propensity I never felt the least idea of before, though since that time I have never been able entirely to divest myself of it. Desire and inability united naturally led to this vice, which is the reason pilfering is so common among footmen and apprentices, though the latter, as they grow up, and find themselves in a situation where everything is at their command, lose this shameful propensity. As I never experienced the advantage, I never enjoyed the benefit.

Good sentiments, ill directed, frequently lead children into vice. Notwithstanding my continual wants and temptations, it was more than a year before I could resolve to take even eatables. My first theft was occasioned by complaisance, but it was productive of others which had not so plausible an excuse.

My master had a journeyman named Verrat, whose mother lived in the neighborhood, and had a garden at a considerable distance from the house, which produced excellent asparagus. This Verrat, who had no great plenty of money, took it in his head to rob her of the most early production of her garden, and by the sale of it procure those indulgences he could not otherwise afford himself; not being very nimble, he did not care to run the hazard of a surprise. After some preliminary flattery, which I did not comprehend the meaning of, he proposed this expedition to me, as an idea which had that moment struck him. At first I would not listen to the proposal; but he persisted in his solicitation, and as I could never resist the attacks of flattery, at length prevailed. In pursuance of this virtuous resolution, I every morning repaired to the garden, gathered the best of the asparagus, and took it to the *Molard* where some good old women, who guessed how I came by it, wishing to diminish the price, made no secret of their suspicions; this produced the desired effect, for, being alarmed, I took whatever they offered, which being taken to Mr. Verrat, was presently metamorphosed into a breakfast, and divided with a companion of his; for, though I procured it, I never partook of their good cheer, being fully satisfied with an inconsiderable bribe.

I executed my roguery with the greatest fidelity, seeking only to please my employer; and several days passed before it came into my head to rob the robber, and tithe Mr. Verrat's harvest. I never considered the hazard I run in these expeditions, not only of a torrent of abuse, but what I should have been still more sensible of, a hearty beating; for the miscreant, who received the whole benefit, would certainly have denied all knowledge of the fact, and I should only have received a double portion of punishment for daring to accuse him, since being only an apprentice, I stood no chance of being believed in opposition to a journeyman. Thus in every situation, powerful rogues know how to save themselves at the expense of the feeble.

This practice taught me it was not so terrible to thieve as I had imagined; I took care to make this discovery turn to some account, helping myself to everything within my reach, that I conceived an inclination for. I was not absolutely ill-fed at my master's, and temperance was only painful to me by comparing it with the luxury he enjoyed. The custom of sending young people from table precisely when those things are served up which seem most tempting, is calculated to increase their longing, and induces them to steal what they conceive to be so delicious. It may be supposed I was not backward in this particular: in general my knavery succeeded pretty well, though quite the reverse when I happened to be detected.

I recollect an attempt to procure some apples, which was attended with circumstances that make me smile and shudder even at this instant. The fruit was standing in a pantry, which by a lattice at a considerable height received light from the kitchen. One day, being alone in the house, I climbed up to see these precious apples, which, being out of my reach, made this pantry appear the garden of Hesperides. I fetched the spit —tried if it would reach them—it was too short—I lengthened it with a small one which was used for game,—my master being very fond of hunting, darted at them several times without success; at length was more fortunate; being transported to find I was bringing up an apple, I drew it gently to the lattice— was going to seize it, when (who can express my grief and astonishment!) I found it would not pass through—it was too large. I tried every expedient to accomplish my design, sought supporters to keep the spits in the same position, a knife to divide the apple, and a lath to hold it with; at length, I so far succeeded as to effect the division, and made no doubt of drawing the pieces through; but it was scarcely separated (compassionate reader, sympathize with my affliction) when both pieces fell into the pantry.

Though I lost time by this experiment, I did not lose courage, but, dreading a surprise, I put off the attempt till next day, when I hoped to be more successful, and returned to my work as if nothing had happened, without once thinking of what the two obvious witnesses I had left in the pantry deposed against me.

The next day (a fine opportunity offering) I renew the trial. I fasten the spits together: get on the stool; take aim; am just going to dart at my prey— unfortunately the dragon did not sleep; the pantry door opens, my master makes his appearance, and, looking up, exclaims, "Bravo!"—The horror of that moment returns—the pen drops from my hand.

A continual repetition of ill treatment rendered me callous; it seemed a kind of composition for my crimes, which authorized me to continue them, and, instead of looking back at the punishment, I looked forward to revenge. Being beat like a slave, I judged I had a right to all the vices of one. I was convinced that to rob and be punished were inseparable, and constituted, if I may so express myself, a kind of traffic, in which, if I perform my part of the bargain, my master would take care not to be deficient in his; that preliminary settled, I applied myself to thieving with great tranquillity, and whenever this interrogatory occurred to my mind, "What will be the consequence?" the reply was ready, "I know the worst, I shall be beat; no matter, I was made for it."

I love good eating; am sensual, but not greedy; I have such a variety of inclinations to gratify, that this can never predominate; and unless my heart is unoccupied, which very rarely happens, I pay but little attention to my appetite: to purloining eatables, but extended this propensity to everything I wished to possess, and if I did not become a robber in form, it was only because money never tempted me.

My master had a closet in the workshop, which he kept locked; this I contrived to open and shut as often as I pleased, and laid his best tools, fine drawings, impressions, in a word, everything he wished to keep from me, under contribution. These thefts were so far innocent, that they were always employed in his service, but I was transported at having the trifles in my possession, and imagined I stole the art with its productions. Besides what I have mentioned, his boxes contained threads of gold and silver, a number of small jewels, valuable medals, and money; yet, though I seldom had five sous in my pocket, I do not recollect ever having cast a wishful look at them; on the contrary, I beheld these valuables rather with terror than delight.

I am convinced the dread of taking money was, in a great measure, the effect of education. There was mingled with the idea of it the fear of infamy, a prison, punishment, and death: had I even felt the temptation, these objects would have made me tremble; whereas my failings appeared a species of waggery, and, in truth, they were little else; they could but occasion a good trimming, and this I was already prepared for. A sheet of fine drawing-paper was a greater temptation than money sufficient to have purchased a ream. This unreasonable caprice is connected with one of the most striking singularities of my character, and has so far influenced my conduct, that it requires a particular explanation.

My passions are extremely violent; while under their influence, nothing can equal my impetuosity; I am an absolute stranger to discretion, respect, fear, or decorum; rude, saucy, violent, and intrepid: no shame can stop, no danger intimidate me. My mind is frequently so engrossed by a single object, that beyond it the whole world is not worth a thought; this is the enthusiasm of a moment, the next, perhaps, I am plunged in a state of annihilation. Take me in my moments of tranquillity, I am indolence and timidity itself; a word to speak, the least trifle to perform, appear an intolerable labor; everything alarms and terrifies me; the very buzzing of a fly will make me shudder: I am so subdued by fear and shame, that I would gladly shield myself from mortal view.

When obliged to exert myself, I am ignorant what to do! when forced to speak, I am at a loss for words; and if any one looks at me, I am instantly out of countenance. If animated with my subject, I express my thoughts with ease, but, in ordinary conversations, I can say nothing—absolutely nothing; and, being obliged to speak, renders them insupportable.

I may add, that none of my predominant inclinations center in those pleasures which are to be purchased: money empoisons my delights; I must have them unadulterated; I love those of the table, for instance, but cannot endure the restraints of good company, or the intemperance of taverns; I can enjoy them only with a friend, for alone it is equally impossible; my imagination is then so occupied with other things, that I find no pleasure in eating. Women who are to be purchased have no charms for me; my beating heart cannot be satisfied without affection; it is the same with every other enjoyment, if not truly disinterested, they are absolutely insipid; in a word,

I am fond of those things which are only estimable to minds formed for the peculiar enjoyment of them.

I never thought money so desirable as it is usually imagined; if you would enjoy, you must transform it; and this transformation is frequently attended with inconvenience: you must bargain, purchase, pay dear, be badly served, and often duped. I buy an egg, am assured it is new-laid—I find it stale; fruit in its utmost perfection—'tis absolutely green; a girl, and she is tainted. I love good wine, but where shall I get it? Not at my wine merchant's—he will certainly poison me. I wish to be universally respected; how shall I compass my design? I must make friends, send messages, come, go, wait, and be frequently deceived. Money is the perpetual source of uneasiness; I fear it more than I love good wine.

A thousand times, both during and since my apprenticeship, have I gone out to purchase some nicety, I approach the pastry-cook's, perceive some women at the counter, and imagine they are laughing at me. I pass a fruit shop, see some fine pears, their appearance tempts me; but then two or three young people are near, or a man I am acquainted with is standing at the door; I take all that pass for persons I have some knowledge of, and my near sight contributes to deceive me; I am everywhere intimidated, restrained by some obstacle, and with money in my pocket return as I went, for want of resolution to purchase what I long for.

I should enter into the most insipid details was I

to relate the trouble, shame, repugnance, and inconvenience of all kinds which I have experienced in parting with my money, whether in my own person, or by the agency of others; as I proceed, the reader will get acquainted with my disposition, and perceive all this without my troubling him with the recital.

This once comprehended, one of my apparent contradictions will be easily accounted for, and the most sordid avarice reconciled with the greatest contempt of money. It is a movable which I consider of so little value, that, when destitute of it, I never wish to acquire any; and when I have a sum I keep it by me, for want of knowing how to dispose of it to my satisfaction; but let an agreeable and convenient opportunity present itself, and I empty my purse with the utmost freedom; not that I would have the reader imagine I am extravagant from a motive of ostentation, quite the reverse: it was ever in subservience to my pleasures, and, instead of glorying in expense, I endeavor to conceal it. I so well perceive that money is not made to answer my purposes, that I am almost ashamed to have any, and, still more, to make use of it.

Had I ever possessed a moderate independence, I am convinced I should have had no propensity to become avaricious. I should have required no more, and cheerfully lived up to my income; but my precarious situation has constantly and necessarily kept me in fear. I love liberty, and I loathe constraint, dependence, and all their kindred annoyances. As long as my purse contains money it secures my independence, and exempts me from the trouble of seeking other money, a trouble of which I have always had a perfect horror; and the dread of seeing the end of my independence, makes me proportionately unwilling to part with my money. The money that we possess is the instrument of liberty, that which we lack and strive to obtain is the instrument of slavery. Thence it is that I hold fast to aught that I have, and yet covet nothing more.

My disinterestedness, then, is in reality only idleness, the pleasure of possessing is not in my estimation worth the trouble of acquiring: and my dissipation is only another form of idleness; when we have an opportunity of disbursing pleasantly we should make the best possible use of it.

I am less tempted by money than by other objects, because between the moment of possessing the money and that of using it to obtain the desired object there is always an interval, however short; whereas to possess the thing is to enjoy it. I see a thing, and it tempts me; but if I see not the thing itself but only the means of acquiring it, I am not tempted. Therefore it is that I have been a pilferer, and am so even now, in the way of mere trifles to which I take a fancy, and which I find it easier to take than to ask for; but I never in my life recollect having taken a farthing from any one, except about fifteen years ago, when I stole seven francs and ten sous. The story is worth recounting, as it exhibits a concurrence of ignorance and stupidity

I should scarcely credit, did it relate to any but myself.

It was in Paris: I was walking with M. de Franceul at the Palais Royal: he pulled out his watch, he looked at it, and said to me, "Suppose we go to the opera?" —"With all my heart." We go; he takes two box tickets, gives me one, and enters himself with the other; I follow, find the door crowded; and, looking in, see every one standing; judging, therefore, that M. de Franceul might suppose me concealed by the company, I go out, ask for my ticket, and, getting the money returned, leave the house, without considering, that by then I had reached the door every one would be seated, and M. de Franceul might readily perceive I was not there.

As nothing could be more opposite to my natural inclination than this abominable meanness, I note it, to show there are moments of delirium when men ought not to be judged by their actions: this was not stealing the money, it was only stealing the use of it, and was the more infamous for wanting the excuse of a temptation.

I should never end these accounts, was I to describe all the gradations through which I passed, during my apprenticeship, from the sublimity of a hero to the baseness of a villain. Though I entered into most of the vices of my situation, I had no relish for its pleasures: the amusements of my companions were displeasing, and when too much restraint had made my business wearisome, I had nothing to amuse me. This renewed my taste for reading which had long been neglected. I thus committed a fresh offense, books made me neglect my work, and brought on additional punishment, while inclination, strengthened by constraint, became an unconquerable passion. La Tribu, a well-known librarian, furnished me with all kinds: good or bad, I perused them with avidity, and without discrimination.

It will be said, "at length, then, money became necessary"—true; but this happened at a time when a taste for study had deprived me both of resolution and activity: totally occupied by this new inclination, I only wished to read, I robbed no longer. This is another of my peculiarities; a mere nothing frequently calls me off from what I appear the most attached to; I give in to the new idea; it becomes a passion, and immediately every former desire is forgotten.

Reading was my new hobby; my heart beat with impatience to run over the new book I carried in my pocket; the first moment I was alone, I seized the opportunity to draw it out, and thought no longer of rummaging my master's closet. I was even ashamed to think I had been guilty of such meanness; and had my amusements been more expensive, I no longer felt an inclination to continue it. La Tribu gave me credit, and when once I had the book in my possession, I thought no more of the trifle I was to pay for it; as money came it naturally passed to this woman; and when she chanced to be pressing, nothing was so conveniently at hand as my own effects; to steal in advance required foresight, and robbing to pay was no temptation.

The frequent blows I received from my master, with my private and ill-chosen studies, rendered me reserved, unsociable, and almost deranged my reason. Though my taste had not preserved me from silly unmeaning books, by good fortune I was a stranger to licentious or obscene ones: not that La Tribu (who was very accommodating) made any scruple of lending these, on the contrary, to enhance their worth, she spoke of them with an air of mystery; this produced an effect she had not foreseen, for both shame and disgust made me constantly refuse them. Chance so well seconded my bashful disposition, that I was past the age of thirty before I saw any of those dangerous compositions.

In less than a year I had exhausted La Tribu's scanty library, and was unhappy for want of further amusement. My reading, though frequently bad, had worn off my childish follies, and brought back my heart to nobler sentiments than my condition had inspired; meantime, disgusted with all within my reach, and thinking everything charming that was out of it, my present situation appeared extremely miserable. My passions began to acquire strength, I felt their influence, without knowing whither they would conduct me. I was as far removed from actual enjoyment as if sexless. Sometimes I thought of former follies, but sought no further.

At this time my imagination took a turn which

helped to calm my increasing emotions; it was, to contemplate those situations in the books I had read, which produced the most striking effect on my mind; to recall, combine, and apply them to myself in such a manner, as to become one of the personages my recollection presented, and be continually in those fancied circumstances which were most agreeable to my inclinations; in a word, by contriving to place myself in these fictitious situations, the idea of my real one was in a great measure obliterated.

This fondness for imaginary objects, and the facility with which I could gain possession of them, completed my disgust for everything around me, and fixed that inclination for solitude which has ever since been predominant. We shall have more than once occasion to remark the effects of a disposition, misanthropic and melancholy in appearance, but which proceed, in fact, from a heart too affectionate, too ardent, which, for want of similar dispositions, is constrained to content itself with nonentities, and be satisfied with fiction. It is sufficient, at present, to have traced the origin of a propensity which has modified my passions, set bounds to each, and by giving too much ardor to my wishes, has ever rendered me too indolent to obtain them.

Thus I attained my sixteenth year, uneasy, discontented with myself and everything that surrounded me; displeased with my occupation, without enjoying the pleasures common to my age, weeping without a

cause, sighing I knew not why, and fond of my chimerical ideas for want of more valuable realities.

Every Sunday, after sermon-time, my companions
came to fetch me out, wishing me to partake of their
diversions. I would willingly have been excused, but
when once engaged in amusement, I was more animated and enterprising than any of them; it was
equally difficult to engage or restrain me: indeed, this
was ever a leading trait in my character. In our country walks I was ever foremost, and never thought of
returning till reminded by some of my companions.
I was twice obliged to be from my master's the whole
night, the city gates having been shut before I could
reach them. The reader may imagine what treatment
this procured me the following mornings; but I was
promised such a reception for the third, that I made
a firm resolution never to expose myself to the danger of it. Notwithstanding my determination, I repeated this dreaded transgression, my vigilance having been rendered useless by a cursed captain, named
M. Minutoli, who, when on guard, always shut the
gate he had charge of an hour before the usual time.
I was returning home with my two companions, and
had got within half a league of the city, when I heard
them beat the tattoo; I redouble my pace, I run with
my utmost speed, I approach the bridge, see the soldiers already at their posts, I call out to them in a
suffocated voice—it is too late; I am twenty paces
from the guard, the first bridge is already drawn up,
and I tremble to see those terrible horns advanced in

the air which announce the fatal and inevitable destiny, which from this moment began to pursue me.

I threw myself on the glacis in a transport of despair, while my companions, who only laughed at the accident, immediately determined what to do. My resolution, though different from theirs, was equally sudden: on the spot, I swore never to return to my master's, and the next morning, when my companions entered the city, I bade them an eternal adieu, conjuring them at the same time to inform my cousin Bernard of my resolution, and the place where he might see me for the last time.

From the commencement of my apprenticeship I had seldom seen him; at first, indeed, we saw each other on Sundays, but each acquiring different habits, our meetings were less frequent. I am persuaded his mother contributed greatly towards this change; he was to consider himself as a person of consequence, I was a pitiful apprentice; notwithstanding our relationship, equality no longer subsisted between us, and it was degrading himself to frequent my company. As he had a natural good heart his mother's lessons did not take an immediate effect, and for some time he continued to visit me.

Having learned my resolution, he hastened to the spot I had appointed, not, however, to dissuade me from it, but to render my flight agreeable, by some trifling presents, as my own resources would not have carried me far. He gave me, among other things, a small sword, which I was very proud of, and took with me as far as Turin, where absolute want constrained me to dispose of it. The more I reflect on his behavior at this critical moment, the more I am persuaded he followed the instructions of his mother, and perhaps his father likewise; for, had he been left to his own feelings, he would have endeavored to retain, or have been tempted to accompany me; on the contrary, he encouraged the design, and when he saw me resolutely determined to pursue it, without seeming much affected, left me to my fate. We never saw or wrote to each other from that time: I cannot but regret this loss, for his heart was essentially good, and we seemed formed for a more lasting friendship.

Before I abandon myself to the fatality of my destiny, let me contemplate for a moment the prospect that awaited me had I fallen into the hands of a better master. Nothing could have been more agreeable to my disposition, or more likely to confer happiness, than the peaceful condition of a good artificer, in so respectable a line as engravers are considered at Geneva. I could have obtained an easy subsistence, if not a fortune; this would have bounded my ambition; I should have had means to indulge in moderate pleasures, and should have continued in my natural sphere, without meeting with any temptation to go beyond it. Having an imagination sufficiently fertile to embellish with its chimeras every situation, and powerful enough to transport me from one to another, it was immaterial in which I was fixed; that was best adapted to me, which, requiring the least care or exertion, left the mind most at liberty; and this happiness I should have enjoyed. In my native country, in the bosom of my religion, family, and friends, I should have passed a calm and peaceful life in the uniformity of a pleasing occupation, and among connections dear to my heart. I should have been a good Christian, a good citizen, a good friend, a good man. I should have relished my condition, perhaps have been an honor to it, and after having passed a life of happy obscurity, surrounded by my family, I should have died at peace. Soon it may be forgotten, but while remembered it would have been with tenderness and regret.

Instead of this—what a picture am I about to draw!—Alas! why should I anticipate the miseries I have endured? The reader will have but too much of the melancholy subject.

BOOK II

BOOK II

[1728–1731]

HOWEVER mournful the moment which suggested flight, it did not seem more terrible than that wherein I put my design in execution appeared delightful. To leave my relations, my resources, while yet a child, in the midst of my apprenticeship, before I had learned enough of my business to obtain a subsistence; to run on inevitable misery and danger: to expose myself in that age of weakness and innocence to all the temptations of vice and despair; to set out in search of errors, misfortunes, snares, slavery, and death; to endure more intolerable evils than those I meant to shun, was the picture I should have drawn, the natural consequence of my hazardous enterprise. How different was the idea I entertained of it!—The independence I seemed to possess was the sole object of my contemplation; having obtained my liberty, I thought everything attainable: I entered with confidence on the vast theater of the world, which my merit was to captivate: at every step I expected to find amusements, treasures, and adventures: friends ready to serve, and mistresses eager to please me; I had but to show myself, and the whole universe would be interested in my concerns; not but I could have been content with something less; a charming society, with sufficient means, might have satisfied me. My moderation was such, that the sphere in which I proposed to shine was rather circumscribed, but then it was to possess the very quintessence of enjoyment, and myself the principal object. A single castle, for instance, might have bounded my ambition; could I have been the favorite of the lord and lady, the daughter's lover, the son's friend, and protector of the neighbors, I might have been tolerably content, and sought no further.

In expectation of this modest fortune, I passed a few days in the environs of the city, with some country people of my acquaintance, who received me with more kindness than I should have met with in town; they welcomed, lodged, and fed me cheerfully; I could not be said to live on charity, these favors were not conferred with a sufficient appearance of superiority to furnish out the idea.

I rambled about in this manner till I got to Confignon, in Savoy, at about two leagues distance from Geneva. The vicar was called M. de Pontverre: this name, so famous in the history of the Republic, caught my attention; I was curious to see what appearance the descendants of the gentlemen of the spoon exhibited: I went, therefore, to visit this M. de Pontverre, and was received with great civility.

He spoke of the heresy of Geneva, declaimed on

the authority of holy mother church, and then invited me to dinner. I had little to object to arguments which had so desirable a conclusion, and was inclined to believe that priests, who gave such excellent dinners, might be as good as our ministers. Notwithstanding M. de Pontverre's pedigree, I certainly possessed most learning; but I rather sought to be a good companion than an expert theologian; and his Frangi wine, which I thought delicious, argued so powerfully on his side, that I should have blushed at silencing so kind a host; I, therefore, yielded him the victory, or rather declined the contest. Any one who had observed my precaution, would certainly have pronounced me a dissembler, though, in fact, I was only courteous.

Flattery, or rather condescension, is not always a vice in young people; 'tis oftener a virtue. When treated with kindness, it is natural to feel an attachment for the person who confers the obligation: we do not acquiesce because we wish to deceive, but from dread of giving uneasiness, or because we wish to avoid the ingratitude of rendering evil for good. What interest had M. de Pontverre in entertaining, treating with respect, and endeavoring to convince me? None but mine; my young heart told me this, and I was penetrated with gratitude and respect for the generous priest; I was sensible of my superiority, but scorned to repay his hospitality by taking advantage of it. I had no conception of hypocrisy in this forbearance, or thought of changing my religion, nay, so far was the idea from being familiar to me, that I looked on it with a degree of horror which seemed to exclude the possibility of such an event; I only wished to avoid giving offense to those I was sensible caressed me from that motive; I wished to cultivate their good opinion, and meantime leave them the hope of success by seeming less on my guard than I really was. My conduct in this particular resembled the coquetry of some very honest women, who, to obtain their wishes, without permitting or promising anything, sometimes encourage hopes they never mean to realize.

Reason, piety, and love of order, certainly demanded that instead of being encouraged in my folly, I should have been dissuaded from the ruin I was courting, and sent back to my family; and this conduct any one that was actuated by genuine virtue would have pursued; but it should be observed that though M. de Pontverre was a religious man, he was not a virtuous one, but a bigot, who knew no virtue except worshiping images and telling his beads; in a word, a kind of missionary, who thought the height of merit consisted in writing libels against the ministers of Geneva. Far from wishing to send me back, he endeavored to favor my escape, and put it out of my power to return even had I been so disposed. It was a thousand to one but he was sending me to perish with hunger, or become a villain; but all this was foreign to his purpose; he saw a soul snatched from heresy, and restored to the bosom of the church: whether I was an honest man or a knave was very immaterial, provided I went to mass.

This ridiculous mode of thinking is not peculiar to Catholics, it is the voice of every dogmatical persuasion where merit consists in belief, and not in virtue.

"You are called by the Almighty," said M. de Pontverre; "go to Annecy, where you will find a good and charitable lady, whom the bounty of the king enables to turn souls from those errors she has happily renounced." He spoke of a Madam de Warrens, a new convert, to whom the priests contrived to send those wretches who were disposed to sell their faith, and with these she was in a manner constrained to share a pension of two thousand francs bestowed on her by the King of Sardinia. I felt myself extremely humiliated at being supposed to want the assistance of a good and *charitable* lady. I had no objection to be accommodated with everything I stood in need of, but did not wish to receive it on the footing of charity, and to owe this obligation to a devotee was still worse: notwithstanding my scruples the persuasions of M. de Pontverre, the dread of perishing with hunger, the pleasures I promised myself from the journey, and hope of obtaining some desirable situation, determined me; and I set out, though reluctantly, for Annecy. I could easily have reached it in a day, but being in no great haste to arrive there, it took me three. My head was filled with the idea of adventures, and I approached every country-seat I

saw in my way, in expectation of having them realized. I had too much timidity to knock at the doors,
or even enter if I saw them open, but I did what I
dared—which was to sing under those windows that
I thought had the most favorable appearance; and
was very much disconcerted to find I wasted my
breath to no purpose, and that neither young nor old
ladies were attracted by the melody of my voice, or
the wit of my poetry, though some songs my companions had taught me I thought excellent, and that
I sung them incomparably. At length I arrived at
Annecy, and saw Madam de Warrens.

As this period of my life, in a great measure, determined my character, I could not resolve to pass it
lightly over. I was in the middle of my sixteenth year,
and though I could not be called handsome, was well
made for my height; I had a good foot, a well turned
leg, and animated countenance; a well proportioned
mouth, black hair and eyebrows, and my eyes, though
small and rather too far in my head, sparkling with
vivacity, darted that innate fire which inflamed my
blood; unfortunately for me, I knew nothing of all
this, never having bestowed a single thought on my
person till it was too late to be of any service to me.
The timidity common to my age was heightened by
a natural benevolence, which made me dread the idea
of giving pain. Though my mind had received some
cultivation, having seen nothing of the world, I was
an absolute stranger to polite address, and my mental
acquisitions, so far from supplying this defect, only

served to increase my embarrassment, by making me sensible of every deficiency.

Depending little, therefore, on external appearances, I had recourse to other expedients: I wrote a most elaborate letter, where, mingling all the flowers of rhetoric which I had borrowed from books with the phrases of an apprentice, I endeavored to strike the attention, and insure the good will of Madam de Warrens. I enclosed M. de Pontverre's letter in my own, and waited on the lady with a heart palpitating with fear and expectation. It was Palm Sunday, of the year 1728; I was informed she was that moment gone to church: I hasten after her, overtake, and speak to her.—The place is yet fresh in my memory —how can it be otherwise? often have I moistened it with my tears and covered it with kisses.—Why cannot I enclose with gold the happy spot, and render it the object of universal veneration? Whoever wishes to honor monuments of human salvation would only approach it on their knees.

It was a passage at the back of the house, bordered on the right hand by a little rivulet, which separated it from the garden, and, on the right, by the court-yard wall; at the end was a private door, which opened into the church of the Cordeliers. Madam de Warrens was just passing this door; but, on hearing my voice, instantly turned about. What an effect did the sight of her produce! I expected to see a devout, forbidding old woman; M. de Pontverre's pious and worthy lady could be no other in my conception:

instead of which, I see a face beaming with charms, fine blue eyes full of sweetness, a complexion whose whiteness dazzled the sight, the form of an enchanting neck, nothing escaped the eager eye of the young proselyte; for that instant I was hers!—a religion preached by such missionaries must lead to paradise!

My letter was presented with a trembling hand; she took it with a smile—opened it, glanced an eye over M. de Pontverre's and again returned to mine, which she read through, and would have read again, had not her footman that instant informed her that service was beginning—"Child," said she, in a tone of voice which made every nerve vibrate, "you are wandering about at an early age—it is really a pity!" —and, without waiting for an answer, added—"Go to my house, bid them give you something for breakfast, after mass I will speak to you."

Louisa-Eleanora de Warrens was of the noble and ancient family of La Tour de Pit, of Vevay, a city in the country of the Vaudois. She was married very young to a M. de Warrens, of the house of Loys, eldest son of M. de Villardin, of Lausanne: there were no children by this marriage, which was far from being a happy one. Some domestic uneasiness made Madam de Warrens take the resolution of crossing the Lake, and throwing herself at the feet of Victor Amadeus, who was then at Evian; thus abandoning her husband, family, and country by a giddiness similar to mine, which precipitation she, too, has found sufficient time and reason to lament.

The king, who was fond of appearing a zealous promoter of the Catholic faith, took her under his protection, and complimented her with a pension of fifteen hundred livres of Piedmont, which was a considerable appointment for a prince who never had the character of being generous; but finding his liberality made some conjecture he had an affection for the lady, he sent her to Annecy, escorted by a detachment of his guards, where, under the direction of Michael Gabriel de Bernex, titular Bishop of Geneva, she abjured her former religion at the Convent of the Visitation.

I came to Annecy just six years after this event; Madam de Warrens was then eight-and-twenty, being born with the century. Her beauty, consisting more in the expressive animation of the countenance than a set of features, was in its meridian; her manner, soothing and tender; an angelic smile played about her mouth, which was small and delicate; she wore her hair (which was of an ash color, and uncommonly beautiful) with an air of negligence that made her appear still more interesting; she was short, and rather thick for her height, though by no means disagreeably so; but there could not be a more lovely face, a finer neck, or hands and arms more exquisitely formed.

Her education had been derived from such a variety of sources, that it formed an extraordinary assemblage. Like me, she had lost her mother at her birth, and had received instruction as it chanced to present itself: she had learned something of her governess, something of her father, a little of her masters, but copiously from her lovers; particularly a M. de Tavel, who, possessing both taste and information, endeavored to adorn with them the mind of her he loved. These various instructions, not being properly arranged, tended to impede each other, and she did not acquire that degree of improvement her natural good sense was capable of receiving; she knew something of philosophy and physic, but not enough to eradicate the fondness she had imbibed from her father for empiricism and alchemy; she made elixirs, tinctures, balsams, pretended to secrets, and prepared magestry; while quacks and pretenders, profiting by her weakness, destroyed her property among furnaces, drugs, and minerals, diminishing those charms and accomplishments which might have been the delight of the most elegant circles.

But though these interested wretches took advantage of her ill-applied education to obscure her natural good sense, her excellent heart retained its purity; her amiable mildness, sensibility for the unfortunate, inexhaustible bounty, and open, cheerful frankness, knew no variation; even at the approach of old age, when attacked by various calamities, rendered more cutting by indigence, the serenity of her disposition preserved to the end of her life the pleasing gayety of her happiest days.

Her errors proceeded from an inexhaustible fund of activity, which demanded perpetual employment.

She found no satisfaction in the customary intrigues of her sex, but, being formed for vast designs, sought the direction of important enterprises and discoveries. In her place Madam de Longueville would have been a mere trifler, in Madam de Longueville's situation she would have governed the state. Her talents did not accord with her fortune; what would have gained her distinction in a more elevated sphere, became her ruin. In enterprises which suited her disposition, she arranged the plan in her imagination, which was ever carried to its utmost extent, and the means she employed being proportioned rather to her ideas than abilities, she failed by the mismanagement of those on whom she depended, and was ruined where another would scarce have been a loser. This active disposition, which involved her in so many difficulties, was at least productive of one benefit as it prevented her from passing the remainder of her life in the monastic asylum she had chosen, which she had some thought of. The simple and uniform life of a nun, and the little cabals and gossipings of their parlor, were not adapted to a mind vigorous and active, which, every day forming new systems, had occasion for liberty to attempt their completion.

The good Bishop of Bernex, with less wit than *Francis of Sales,* resembled him in many particulars, and Madam de Warrens, whom he loved to call his daughter, and who was like Madam de Chantel in several respects, might have increased the resemblance by retiring like her from the world, had she not been disgusted with the idle trifling of a convent. It was not want of zeal prevented this amiable woman from giving those proofs of devotion which might have been expected from a new convert, under the immediate direction of a prelate. Whatever might have influenced her to change her religion, she was certainly sincere in that she had embraced; she might find sufficient occasion to repent having abjured her former faith, but no inclination to return to it. She not only died a good Catholic, but truly lived one; nay, I dare affirm (and I think I have had the opportunity to read the secrets of her heart) that it was only her aversion to singularity that prevented her acting the devotee in public; in a word, her piety was too sincere to give way to any affectation of it. But this is not the place to enlarge on her principles; I shall find other occasions to speak of them.

Let those who deny the existence of a sympathy of souls, explain, if they know how, why the first glance, the first word of Madam de Warrens inspired me, not only with a lively attachment, but with the most unbounded confidence, which has since known no abatement. Say this was love (which will at least appear doubtful to those who read the sequel of our attachment) how could this passion be attended with sentiments which scarce ever accompany its commencement, such as peace, serenity, security, and confidence. How, when making application to an amiable and polished woman, whose situation in life was so superior to mine, so far above any I had yet approached, on whom, in a great measure, depended my future fortune, by the degree of interest she might take in it; how, I say, with so many reasons to depress me, did I feel myself as free, as much at my ease, as if I had been perfectly secure of pleasing her! Why did I not experience a moment of embarrassment, timidity, or restraint? Naturally bashful, easily confused, having seen nothing of the world, could I, the first time, the first moment I beheld her, adopt caressing language, and a familiar tone, as readily as after ten years' intimacy had rendered these freedoms natural? Is it possible to possess love, I will not say without desires, for I certainly had them, but without inquietude, without jealousy? Can we avoid feeling an anxious wish at least, to know whether our affection is returned? Yet such a question never entered my imagination: I should as soon have inquired, do I love myself; nor did she ever express a greater degree of curiosity; there was, certainly, something extraordinary in my attachment to this charming woman, and it will be found in the sequel, that some extravagances, which cannot be foreseen, attended it.

What could be done for me, was the present question, and in order to discuss the point with greater freedom, she made me dine with her. This was the first meal in my life where I had experienced a want of appetite, and her woman, who waited, observed it was the first time she had seen a traveler of my age and appearance deficient in that particular: this remark, which did me no injury in the opinion of her mistress, fell hard on an overgrown clown, who was my fellow guest, and devoured sufficient to have served at least six moderate feeders. For me, I was too much charmed to think of eating; my heart began to imbibe a delicious sensation, which engrossed my whole being, and left no room for other objects.

Madam de Warrens wished to hear the particulars of my little history—all the vivacity I had lost during my servitude returned and assisted the recital. In proportion to the interest this excellent woman took in my story, did she lament the fate to which I had exposed myself; compassion was painted on her features, and expressed by every action. She could not exhort me to return to Geneva, being too well aware that her words and actions were strictly scrutinized, and that such advice would be thought high treason against Catholicism, but she spoke so feelingly of the affliction I must give my father, that it was easy to perceive she would have approved my returning to console him. Alas! she little thought how powerfully this pleaded against herself; the more eloquently persuasive she appeared, the less could I resolve to tear myself from her. I knew that returning to Geneva would be putting an insuperable barrier between us, unless I repeated the expedient which had brought me here, and it was certainly better to preserve than expose myself to the danger of a relapse; besides all this, my conduct was predetermined, I was resolved not to return. Madam de Warrens, seeing her endeavors would be fruitless, became less explicit, and only added, with an air of commiseration, "Poor child! thou must go where Providence directs thee, but one day thou wilt think of me."—I believe she had no conception at that time how fatally her prediction would be verified.

The difficulty still remained how I was to gain a subsistence? I have already observed that I knew too little of engraving for that to furnish my resource, and had I been more expert, Savoy was too poor a country to give much encouragement to the arts. The above-mentioned glutton, who ate for us as well as himself, being obliged to pause in order to gain some relaxation from the fatigue of it, imparted a piece of advice, which, according to him, came express from Heaven: though to judge by its effects it appeared to have been dictated from a direct contrary quarter: this was that I should go to Turin, where, in a hospital instituted for the instruction of catechumens, I should find food, both spiritual and temporal, be reconciled to the bosom of the church, and meet with some charitable Christians, who would make it a point to procure me a situation that would turn to my advantage. "In regard to the expenses of the journey," continued our adviser, "his grace, my lord bishop, will not be backward, when once madam has proposed this holy work, to offer his charitable donation, and madam the baroness, whose charity is so well known," once more addressing himself to the continuation of his meal, "will certainly contribute."

I was by no means pleased with all these charities;

I said nothing, but my heart was ready to burst with vexation. Madam de Warrens, who did not seem to think so highly of this expedient as the projector pretended to do, contented herself by saying, every one should endeavor to promote good actions, and that she would mention it to his lordship; but the meddling devil, who had some private interest in this affair, and questioned whether she would urge it to his satisfaction, took care to acquaint the almoners with my story, and so far influenced those good priests, that when Madam de Warrens, who disliked the journey on my account, mentioned it to the bishop, she found it so far concluded on, that he immediately put into her hands the money designed for my little viaticum. She dared not advance anything against it; I was approaching an age when a woman like her could not, with any propriety, appear anxious to retain me.

My departure being thus determined by those who undertook the management of my concerns, I had only to submit; and I did it without much repugnance. Though Turin was at a greater distance from Madam de Warrens' than Geneva, yet being the capital of the country I was now in, it seemed to have more connection with Annecy than a city under a different government and of a contrary religion; besides, as I undertook this journey in obedience to her, I considered myself as living under her direction, which was more flattering than barely to continue in the neighborhood; to sum up all, the idea of a long journey coincided with my insurmountable passion for rambling, which already began to demonstrate itself. To pass the mountains, to my eye appeared delightful; how charming the reflection of elevating myself above my companions by the whole height of the Alps! To see the world is an almost irresistible temptation to a Genevan, accordingly I gave my consent.

He who suggested the journey was to set off in two days with his wife. I was recommended to their care; they were likewise made my purse-bearers, which had been augmented by Madam de Warrens, who, not contented with these kindnesses, added secretly a pecuniary reinforcement, attended with the most ample instructions, and we departed on the Wednesday before Easter.

The day following, my father arrived at Annecy, accompanied by his friend, a Mr. Rival, who was likewise a watchmaker; he was a man of sense and letters, who wrote better verses than La Motte, and spoke almost as well; what is still more to his praise, he was a man of the strictest integrity, but whose taste for literature only served to make one of his sons a comedian. Having traced me to the house of Madam de Warrens, they contented themselves with lamenting, like her, my fate, instead of overtaking me, which (as they were on horseback and I on foot) they might have accomplished with the greatest ease.

My uncle Bernard did the same thing, he arrived at Consignon, received information that I was gone to Annecy, and immediately returned back to Geneva thus my nearest relations seemed to have conspired with my adverse stars to consign me to misery and ruin. By a similar negligence, my brother was so entirely lost, that it was never known what was become of him.

My father was not only a man of honor but of the strictest probity, and endued with that magnanimity which frequently produces the most shining virtues: I may add, he was a good father, particularly to me whom he tenderly loved; but he likewise loved his pleasures, and since we had been separated other connections had weakened his paternal affection. He had married again at Nion, and though his second wife was too old to expect children, she had relations; my father was united to another family, surrounded by other objects, and a variety of cares prevented my returning to his remembrance. He was in the decline of life and had nothing to support the inconveniences of old age; my mother's property devolved to me and my brother, but, during our absence, the interest of it was enjoyed by my father: I do not mean to infer that this consideration had an immediate effect on his conduct, but it had an imperceptible one, and prevented him making use of that exertion to regain me which he would otherwise have employed; and this, I think, was the reason that having traced me as far as Annecy, he stopped short, without proceeding to Chambery, where he was almost certain I should be found; and likewise accounts why, on visiting him several times since my flight, he always received me with great kindness, but never made any efforts to retain me.

This conduct in a father, whose affection and virtue I was so well convinced of, has given birth to reflections on the regulation of my own conduct, which have greatly contributed to preserve the integrity of my heart. It has taught me this great lesson of morality, perhaps the only one that can have any conspicuous influence on our actions, that we should ever carefully avoid putting our interest in competition with our duty, or promise ourselves felicity from the misfortunes of others; certain that in such circumstances, however sincere our love of virtue may be, sooner or later it will give way, and we shall imperceptibly become unjust and wicked, in fact, however upright in our intentions.

This maxim, strongly imprinted on my mind, and reduced, though rather too late, to practice, has given my conduct an appearance of folly and whimsicality, not only in public, but still more among my acquaintances: it has been said, I affected originality, and sought to act different from other people; the truth is, I neither endeavor to conform or be singular, I desired only to act virtuously and avoid situations, which, by setting my interest in opposition to that of another person's, might inspire me with a secret, though involuntary, wish to his disadvantage.

Two years ago, My Lord Marshal would have put my name in his will, which I took every method to prevent, assuring him I would not for the world know myself in the will of any one, much less in his; he gave up the idea; but insisted, in return, that I should accept an annuity on his life; this I consented to. It will be said, I find my account in the alteration; perhaps I may: but oh, my benefactor! my father, I am now sensible that, should I have the misfortune to survive thee, I should have everything to lose, nothing to gain.

This, in my idea, is true philosophy, the surest bulwark of human rectitude; every day do I receive fresh conviction of its profound solidity. I have endeavored to recommend it in all my latter writings, but the multitude read too superficially to have made the remark. If I survive my present undertaking, and am able to begin another, I mean, in a continuation of Emilius, to give such a lively and marking example of this maxim as cannot fail to strike attention. But I have made reflections enough for a traveler, it is time to continue my journey.

It turned out more agreeable than I expected: my clownish conductor was not so morose as he appeared to be. He was a middle-aged man, wore his black, grizzly hair, in a queue, had a martial air, a strong voice, was tolerably cheerful, and to make up for not having been taught any trade, could turn his hand to every one. Having proposed to establish some kind of manufactory at Annecy, he had consulted Madam de Warrens, who immediately gave in to the project, and he was now going to Turin to lay the plan before the minister and get his approbation, for which journey he took care to be well rewarded.

This drole had the art of ingratiating himself with the priests, whom he ever appeared eager to serve; he adopted a certain jargon which he had learned by frequenting their company, and thought himself a notable preacher; he could even repeat one passage from the Bible in Latin, and it answered his purpose as well as if he had known a thousand, for he repeated it a thousand times a day. He was seldom at a loss for money when he knew what purse contained it; yet, was rather artful than knavish, and when dealing out in an affected tone his unmeaning discourses, resembled Peter the Hermit, preaching up the crusade with a saber by his side.

Madam Sabran, his wife, was a tolerable good sort of woman; more peaceable by day than by night; as I slept in the same chamber I was frequently disturbed by her wakefulness, and should have been more so had I comprehended the cause of it, but in this matter I was so stupid that nature alone could further instruct me.

I went on gayly with my pious guide and his hopeful companion, no sinister accident impeding our journey. I was in the happiest circumstances both of mind and body that I ever recollect having experienced; young, full of health and security, placing unbounded confidence in myself and others; in that short but charming moment of human life, whose expansive energy carries, if I may so express myself, our being to the utmost extent of our sensations, embellishing all nature with an inexpressible charm, flowing from the conscious and rising enjoyment of our existence.

My pleasing inquietudes became less wandering: I had now an object on which imagination could fix. I looked on myself as the work, the pupil, the friend, almost the lover of Madam de Warrens; the obliging things she had said, the caresses she had bestowed on me; the tender interest she seemed to take in everything that concerned me; those charming looks, which seemed replete with love, because they so powerfully inspired it, every consideration flattered my ideas during this journey, and furnished the most delicious reveries, which, no doubt, no fear of my future condition arose to embitter. In sending me to Turin, I thought they engaged to find me an agreeable subsistence there; thus eased of every care I passed lightly on, while young desires, enchanting hopes, and brilliant prospects employed my mind; each object that presented itself seemed to insure my approaching felicity. I imagined that every house was filled with joyous festivity, the meadows resounded with sports and revelry, the rivers offered refreshing baths, delicious fish wantoned in their streams, and how delightful was it to ramble along the flowery banks! The trees were loaded with the choicest fruits, while their shade afforded the most charming and voluptuous retreats to happy lovers; the mountains abounded with milk and cream, peace and leisure, simplicity and joy, mingled with the charm of going I knew not whither, and everything I saw carried to my heart some new cause for rapture. The grandeur, variety, and real beauty of the scene, in some measure rendered the charm reasonable, in which vanity came in for its share; to go so young to Italy, view such an extent of country, and pursue the route of Hannibal over the Alps, appeared a glory beyond my age; add to all this our frequent and agreeable halts, with a good appetite and plenty to satisfy it; for in truth it was not worth while to be sparing; at M. Sabran's table what I eat could scarce be missed.

In the whole course of my life I cannot recollect an interval more perfectly exempt from care, than the seven or eight days I was passing from Annecy to Turin. As we were obliged to walk Madam Sabran's pace, it rather appeared an agreeable jaunt than a fatiguing journey; there still remains the most pleasing impressions of it on my mind, and the idea of a pedestrian excursion, particularly among the mountains, has from this time seemed delightful.

It was only in my happiest days that I traveled on foot, and ever with the most unbounded satisfaction; afterwards, occupied with business and encumbered with baggage, I was forced to act the gentleman and employ a carriage, where care, embarrassment, and restraint, were sure to be my companions, and instead of being delighted with the journey, I only wished to arrive at the place of destination.

I was a long time at Paris, wishing to meet with

two companions of similar dispositions, who would each agree to appropriate fifty guineas of his property and a year of his time to making the tour of Italy on foot, with no other attendance than a young fellow to carry our necessaries I have met with many who seemed enchanted with the project, but considered it only as a visionary scheme, which served well enough to talk of, without any design of putting it in execution. One day, speaking with enthusiasm of this project to *Diderot* and *Grimm,* they gave in to the proposal with such warmth that I thought the matter concluded on; but it only turned out a journey on paper, in which *Grimm* thought nothing so pleasing as making *Diderot* commit a number of impieties, and shutting me up in the Inquisition for them, instead of him.

My regret at arriving so soon at Turin was compensated by the pleasure of viewing a large city, and the hope of figuring there in a conspicuous character, for my brain already began to be intoxicated with the fumes of ambition; my present situation appeared infinitely above that of an apprentice, and I was far from foreseeing how soon I should be much below it.

Before I proceed, I ought to offer an excuse, or justification to the reader, for the great number of unentertaining particulars I am necessitated to repeat. In pursuance of the resolution I have formed to enter on this public exhibition of myself, it is necessary that nothing should bear the appearance of obscurity or concealment. I should be continually under the eye of the reader, he should be enabled to follow me in all the wanderings of my heart, through every intricacy of my adventures; he must find no void or chasm in my relation, nor lose sight of me an instant, lest he should find occasion to say, what was he doing at this time; and suspect me of not having dared to reveal the whole: I give sufficient scope to malignity in what I say; it is unnecessary I should furnish still more by my silence.

My money was all gone, even that I had secretly received from Madam de Warrens: I had been so indiscreet as to divulge this secret, and my conductors had taken care to profit by it. Madam Sabran found means to deprive me of everything I had, even to a ribbon embroidered with silver, with which Madam de Warrens had adorned the hilt of my sword; this I regretted more than all the rest; indeed the sword itself would have gone the same way, had I been less obstinately bent on retaining it. They had, it is true, supported me during the journey, but left me nothing at the end of it, and I arrived at Turin without money, clothes, or linen, being precisely in the situation to owe to my merit alone the whole honor of that fortune I was about to acquire.

I took care in the first place to deliver the letters I was charged with, and was presently conducted to the hospital of the catechumens, to be instructed in that religion, for which, in return, I was to receive subsistence. On entering, I passed an iron-barred gate, which was immediately double-locked on me; this beginning was by no means calculated to give me a favorable opinion of my situation. I was then conducted to a large apartment, whose furniture consisted of a wooden altar at the farther end, on which was a large crucifix, and round it several indifferent chairs, of the same materials. In this hall of audience were assembled four or five ill-looking banditti, my comrades in instruction, who would rather have been taken for trusty servants of the devil than candidates for the kingdom of heaven. Two of these fellows were Sclavonians, but gave out they were African Jews, and (as they assured me) had run through Spain and Italy, embracing the Christian faith, and being baptized wherever they thought it worth their labor.

Soon after they opened another iron gate, which divided a large balcony that overlooked a courtyard, and by this avenue entered our sister catechumens, who, like me, were going to be regenerated, not by baptism but a solemn abjuration. A viler set of idle, dirty, abandoned harlots, never disgraced any persuasion: one among them, however, appeared pretty and interesting; she might be about my own age, perhaps a year or two older, and had a pair of roguish eyes, which frequently encountered mine; this was enough to inspire me with the desire of becoming acquainted with her, but she had been so strongly recommended to the care of the old governess of this respectable sisterhood, and was so narrowly watched by the pious missionary, who labored for her conversion with more zeal than diligence, that during the two months we remained together in this house (where she had already been three) I found it absolutely impossible to exchange a word with her. She must have been extremely stupid, though she had not the appearance of it, for never was a longer course of instruction; the holy man could never bring her to a state of mind fit for abjuration; meantime, she became weary of her cloister, declaring that, Christian or not, she would stay there no longer; and they were obliged to take her at her word, lest she should grow refractory, and insist on departing as great a sinner as she came.

This hopeful community were assembled in honor of the new-comer; when our guides made us a short exhortation: I was conjured to be obedient to the grace that Heaven had bestowed on me; the rest were admonished to assist me with their prayers, and give me edification by their good example. Our virgins then retired to another apartment, and I was left to contemplate, at leisure, that wherein I found myself.

The next morning we were again assembled for instruction: I now began to reflect, for the first time, on the step I was about to take, and the circumstances which had led me to it.

I repeat, and shall perhaps repeat again, an assertion I have already advanced, and of whose truth I every day receive fresh conviction, which is, that if ever child received a reasonable and virtuous education, it was myself. Born in a family of unexceptionable morals, every lesson I received was replete with maxims of prudence and virtue. My father (though fond of gallantry) not only possessed distinguished probity, but much religion; in the world he appeared a man of pleasure, in his family he was a Christian, and implanted early in my mind those sentiments he felt the force of. My three aunts were women of virtue and piety; the two eldest were professed devotees, and the third, who united all the graces of wit and good sense, was, perhaps, more truly religious than either, though with less ostentation. From the bosom of this amiable family I was transplanted to M. Lambercier's, a man dedicated to the ministry, who believed the doctrine he taught, and acted up to its precepts. He and his sister matured by their instructions those principles of judicious piety I had already imbibed, and the means employed by these worthy people were so well adapted to the effect they meant to produce, that so far from being fatigued, I scarce ever listened to their admonitions without finding myself sensibly affected, and forming resolutions to live virtuously, from which, except in moments of forgetfulness, I seldom swerved. At my uncle's, religion was rather more tiresome, because they made it an employment; with my master I thought no more of it, though my sentiments continued the same: I had no companions to vitiate my morals: I became idle, careless, and obstinate, but my principles were not impaired.

I possessed as much religion, therefore, as a child could be supposed capable of acquiring. Why should I now disguise my thoughts? I am persuaded I had more. In my childhood, I was not a child; I felt, I thought as a man: as I advanced in years, I mingled with the ordinary class; in my infancy I was distinguished from it. I shall doubtless incur ridicule by thus modestly holding myself up for a prodigy— I am content. Let those who find themselves disposed to it, laugh their fill; afterward, let them find a child that at six years old is delighted, interested, affected with romances, even to the shedding floods of tears; I shall then feel my ridiculous vanity, and acknowledge myself in an error.

Thus when I said we should not converse with children on religion, if we wished them ever to possess any; when I asserted they were incapable of communion with the Supreme Being, even in our confined degree, I drew my conclusions from general observation; I knew they were not applicable to particular instances: find J. J. Rousseaus of six years old, converse with them on religious subjects at seven, and I will be answerable that the experiment will be attended with no danger.

It is understood, I believe, that a child, or even a man, is likely to be most sincere while persevering in that religion in whose belief he was born and educated; we frequently detract from, seldom make any additions to it: dogmatical faith is the effect of education. In addition to this general principle, which attached me to the religion of my forefathers, I had that particular aversion our city entertains for Catholicism, which is represented there as the most monstrous idolatry, and whose clergy are painted in the blackest colors. This sentiment was so firmly imprinted on my mind, that I never dared to look into their churches —I could not bear to meet a priest in his surplice, and never did I hear the bells of a procession sound without shuddering with horror; these sensations soon wore off in great cities, but frequently returned in country parishes, which bore more similarity to the spot where I first experienced them; meantime this dislike was singularly contrasted by the remembrance of those caresses which priests in the neighborhood of Geneva are fond of bestowing on the children of that city. If the bells of the viaticum alarmed me, the chiming for mass or vespers called me to a breakfast, a collation, to the pleasure of regaling on fresh butter, fruits, or milk; the good cheer of M. de Pontverre had produced a considerable effect on me; my former abhorrence began to diminish, and looking on popery through the medium of amusement and good living, I easily reconciled myself to the idea of enduring, though I never entertained but a very transient and distant idea of making a solemn profession of it.

At this moment such a transaction appeared in all its horrors; I shuddered at the engagement I had entered into, and its inevitable consequences. The future neophytes with which I was surrounded were not calculated to sustain my courage by their example, and I could not help considering the holy work I was about to perform as the action of a villain. Though young, I was sufficiently convinced, that whatever religion might be the true one, I was about to sell mine; and even should I chance to choose the best, I lied to the Holy Ghost, and merited the disdain of every good man. The more I considered, the more I despised myself, and trembled at the fate which had led me into such a predicament, as if my present situation had not been of my own seeking. There were moments when these compunctions were so strong, that had I found the door open but for an instant, I should certainly have made my escape; but this was impossible, nor was the resolution of any long duration, being combated by too many secret motives to stand any chance of gaining the victory.

My fixed determination not to return to Geneva, the shame that would attend it, the difficulty of repassing the mountains, at a distance from my country, without friends, and without resources, everything concurred to make me consider my remorse of conscience, as a too late repentance. I affected to reproach myself for what I had done, to seek excuses for that I intended to do, and by aggravating the errors of the past, looked on the future as an inevitable consequence. I did not say, nothing is yet done, and you may be innocent if you please; but I said, tremble at the crime thou hast committed, which hath reduced thee to the necessity of filling up the measure of thine iniquities.

It required more resolution than was natural to my age to revoke those expectations which I had given them reason to entertain, break those chains with which I was enthralled, and resolutely declare I would continue in the religion of my forefathers, whatever might be the consequence. The affair was already too far advanced, and spite of all my efforts they would have made a point of bringing it to a conclusion.

The sophism which ruined me has had a similar effect on the greater part of mankind, who lament the want of resolution when the opportunity for exercising it is over. The practice of virtue is only difficult from our own negligence; were we always discreet, we should seldom have occasion for any painful exertion of it; we are captivated by desires we might readily surmount, give in to temptations that might easily be resisted, and insensibly get into embarrassing, perilous situations, from which we cannot extricate ourselves but with the utmost difficulty; intimidated by the effort, we fall into the abyss, saying to the Almighty, why hast thou made us such weak creatures? But, notwithstanding our vain pretexts, He replies, by our consciences, I formed ye too weak to get out of the gulf, because I gave ye sufficient strength not to have fallen into it.

I was not absolutely resolved to become a Catholic, but, as it was not necessary to declare my intentions immediately, I gradually accustomed myself to the idea; hoping, meantime, that some unforeseen event would extricate me from my embarrassment. In order to gain time, I resolved to make the best defense I possibly could in favor of my own opinion; but my vanity soon rendered this resolution unnecessary, for on finding I frequently embarrassed those who had the care of my instruction, I wished to heighten my triumph by giving them a complete overthrow, I zealously pursued my plan, not without the ridiculous hope of being able to convert my convertors; for I was simple enough to believe, that could I convince them of their errors, they would become Protestants; they did not find, therefore, that facility in the work which they had expected, as I differed both in regard to will and knowledge from the opinion they had entertained of me.

Protestants, in general, are better instructed in the principles of their religion than Catholics; the reason is obvious, the doctrine of the former requires discussion, of the latter a blind submission; the Catholic must content himself with the decision of others, the Protestant must learn to decide for himself; they were not ignorant of this, but neither my age nor appearance promised much difficulty to men so accustomed to disputation. They knew, likewise, that I had not received my first communion, nor the instructions which accompany it; but, on the other hand, they had no idea of the information I received with M. Lambercier, or that I had learned the history of the church and empire almost by heart at my father's; and though, since that time, nearly forgot, when warmed by the dispute (very unfortunately for these gentlemen), it again returned to my memory.

A little old priest, but tolerably venerable, held the first conference; at which we were all convened. On the part of my comrades, it was rather a catechism than a controversy, and he found more pains in giving them instruction than answering their objections; but when it came to my turn, it was a different matter; I stopped him at every article, and did not spare a single remark that I thought would create a difficulty: this rendered the conference long and extremely tiresome to the assistants. My old priest talked a great deal, was very warm, frequently rambled from the subject, and extricated himself from difficulties by saying he was not sufficiently versed in the French language.

The next day, lest my indiscreet objections should injure the minds of those who were better disposed, I was led into a separate chamber, and put under the care of a younger priest, a fine speaker; that is, one who was fond of long perplexed sentences, and proud of his own abilities, if ever doctor was. I did not, however, suffer myself to be intimidated by his overbearing looks: and being sensible that I could maintain my ground, I combated his assertions, exposed his mistakes, and laid about me in the best manner I was able. He thought to silence me at once with St. Augustin, St. Gregory, and the rest of the fathers, but found, to his ineffable surprise, that I could handle these almost as dexterously as himself; not that I had ever read them, or he either, perhaps, but I retained a number of passages taken from my Le Sueur, and when he bore hard on me with one citation, without standing to dispute, I parried it with another, which method embarrassed him extremely. At length, however, he got the better of me for two very potent reasons; in the first place, he was of the strongest side; young as I was, I thought it might be dangerous to drive him to extremities, for I plainly saw the old priest was neither satisfied with me nor my erudition. In the next place, he had studied, I had not; this gave a degree of method to his arguments which I could not follow; and whenever he found himself pressed by an unforeseen objection, he put it off to the next conference, pretending I rambled from the question in dispute. Sometimes he even rejected all my quotations, maintaining they were false, and, offering to fetch the book, defied me to find them. He know he ran very little risk, and that, with all my borrowed learning, I was not sufficiently accustomed to books, and too poor a Latinist to find a passage in a large volume, had I been ever so well assured it was there. I even suspected him of having been guilty of a perfidy with which he accused our ministers, and that he fabricated passages sometimes in order to evade an objection that incommoded him.

Meanwhile the hospital became every day more disagreeable to me, and seeing but one way to get out of it, I endeavored to hasten my abjuration with as much eagerness as I had hitherto sought to retard it.

The two Africans had been baptized with great ceremony; they were habited in white from head to foot, to signify the purity of their regenerated souls. My turn came a month after; for all this time was thought necessary by my directors, that they might have the honor of a difficult conversion, and every dogma of their faith was recapitulated, in order to triumph the more completely over my new docility.

At length, sufficiently instructed and disposed to the will of my masters, I was led in procession to the metropolitan church of St. John, to make a solemn abjuration, and undergo a ceremony made use of on these occasions, which, though not baptism, is very similar, and serves to persuade the people that Protestants are not Christians. I was clothed in a kind of gray robe, decorated with white Brandenburgs. Two men, one behind, the other before me, carried copper basins which they kept striking with a key, and in which those who were charitably disposed put their alms, according as they found themselves influenced by religion or good will for the new convert; in a word, nothing of Catholic pageantry was omitted that could render the solemnity edifying to the populace, or humiliating to me. The white dress might have been serviceable, but as I had not the honor to be either Moor or Jew, they did not think fit to compliment me with it.

The affair did not end here; I must now go to the Inquisition to be absolved from the dreadful sin of heresy, and return to the bosom of the church with the same ceremony to which Henry the Fourth was subjected by his ambassador. The air and manner of the right reverend Father Inquisitor was by no means calculated to dissipate the secret horror that seized my spirits on entering this holy mansion. After several questions relative to my faith, situation, and family, he asked me bluntly if my mother was damned? Terror repressed the first gust of indignation; this gave me time to recollect myself, and I answered, I hoped not, for God might have enlightened her last moments. The monk made no reply, but his silence was attended with a look by no means expressive of approbation.

All these ceremonies ended, the very moment I flattered myself I should be plentifully provided for, they exhorted me to continue a good Christian, and live in obedience to the grace I had received; then wishing me good fortune, with rather more than twenty francs of small money in my pocket, the produce of the above-mentioned collection, turned me out, shut the door on me, and I saw no more of them!

Thus, in a moment, all my flattering expectations were at an end; and nothing remained from my interested conversion but the remembrance of having been made both a dupe and an apostate. It is easy to imagine what a sudden revolution was produced in my ideas, when every brilliant expectation of making a fortune terminated by seeing myself plunged in the completest misery. In the morning I was deliberating what palace I should inhabit, before night I was reduced to seek my lodging in the street. It may be supposed that I gave myself up to the most violent transports of despair, rendered more bitter by a consciousness that my own folly had reduced me to these extremities; but the truth is, I experienced none of these disagreeable sensations. I had passed two months in absolute confinement; this was new to me; I was now emancipated, and the sentiment I felt most forcibly, was joy at my recovered liberty. After a slavery which had appeared tedious, I was again master of my time and actions, in a great city, abundant in resources, crowded with people of fortune, to whom my merit and talents could not fail to recommend me. I had sufficient time before me to expect this good fortune, for my twenty livres seemed an inexhaustible treasure, which I might dispose of without rendering an account of to any one. It was the first time I had found myself so rich, and far from giving way to melancholy reflections, I only adopted other hopes, in which self-love was by no means a loser. Never did I feel so great a degree of confidence and security; I looked on my fortune as already made, and was pleased to think I should have no one but myself to thank for the acquisition of it.

The first thing I did, was to satisfy my curiosity by rambling all over the city, and I seemed to consider it as a confirmation of my liberty; I went to see the soldiers mount guard, and was delighted with their military accouterments; I followed processions, and was pleased with the solemn music of the priests; I next went to see the king's palace, which I approached with awe, but seeing others enter, I followed their example, and no one prevented me; perhaps I owed this favor to the small parcel I carried under my arm; be that as it may, I conceived a high opinion of my consequence from this circumstance, and already thought myself an inhabitant there. The weather was hot; I had walked about till I was both fatigued and hungry; wishing for some refreshment, I went into a milk-house; they brought me some cream-cheese, curds and whey, with two slices of that excellent Piedmont bread, which I prefer to any other; and for five or six sous I had one of the most delicious meals I ever recollect to have made.

It was time to seek a lodging: as I already knew enough of the Piedmontese language to make myself understood, this was a work of no great difficulty; and I had so much prudence, that I wished to adapt it rather to the state of my purse than the bent of my inclination. In the course of my inquiries, I was informed that a soldier's wife, in Po-street, furnished lodgings to servants out of place at only one sou a night, and finding one of her poor beds disengaged, I took possession of it. She was young and newly married, though she already had five or six children. Mother, children, and lodgers, all slept in the same chamber, and it continued thus while I remained there. She was good-natured, swore like a carman, and wore neither cap nor handkerchief; but she had a gentle heart, was officious, and to me both kind and serviceable.

For several days I gave myself up to the pleasures of independence and curiosity; I continued wandering about the city and its environs, examining every object that seemed curious or new; and, indeed, most things had that appearance to a young novice. I never omitted visiting the court, and assisted regularly every morning at the king's mass. I thought it a great honor to be in the same chapel with this prince and his retinue; but my passion for music, which now began to make its appearance, was a greater incentive than the splendor of the court, which, soon seen and always the same, presently lost its attraction. The King of Sardinia had at that time the best music in Europe; Somis, Desjardins, and the Bezuzzis shone there alternately: all these were not necessary to fascinate a youth whom the sound of the most simple instrument, provided it was just, transported with joy. Magnificence only produced a stupid admiration, without any violent desire to partake of it; my thoughts were principally employed in observing whether any young princess was present that merited my homage, and whom I could make the heroine of a romance.

Meantime, I was on the point of beginning one; in a less elevated sphere, it is true, but where, could I have brought it to a conclusion, I should have found pleasures a thousand times more delicious.

Though I lived with the strictest economy, my purse insensibly grew lighter. This economy was, however, less the effect of prudence than that love of simplicity, which, even to this day, the use of the most expensive tables has not been able to vitiate. Nothing in my idea, either at that time or since, could exceed a rustic repast; give me milk, vegetables, eggs, and brown bread, with tolerable wine, and I shall always think myself sumptuously regaled; a good appetite will furnish out the rest, if the *maitre d'hôtel,* with a number of unnecessary footmen, do not satiate me with their important attentions. Six or seven sous would then procure me a more agreeable meal than as many francs would have done since; I was abstemious, therefore, for want of a temptation to be otherwise; though I do not know but I am wrong to call this abstinence, for with my pears, new cheese, bread, and some glasses of Montferrat wine, which you might have cut with a knife, I was the greatest of epicures. Notwithstanding my expenses were very moderate, it was possible to see the end of twenty francs; I was every day more convinced of this, and, spite of the giddiness of youth, my apprehensions for the future amounted almost to terror. All my castles in the air were vanished, and I became sensible of the necessity of seeking some occupation that would procure me a subsistence.

Even this was a work of difficulty: I thought of my engraving, but knew too little of it to be employed as a journeyman, nor do masters abound at Turin; I resolved, therefore, till something better presented itself, to go from shop to shop, offering to engrave ciphers, or coats of arms, on pieces of plate, etc., and hoped to get employment by working at a low price, or taking what they chose to give me. Even this expedient did not answer my expectation; almost all my applications were ineffectual, the little I procured being hardly sufficient to produce a few scanty meals.

Walking one morning pretty early in the *Contranova,* I saw a young tradeswoman behind a counter, whose looks were so charmingly attractive, that, notwithstanding my timidity with the ladies, I entered the shop without hesitation, offered my service as usual, and had the happiness to have it accepted. She made me sit down and relate my little history; pitied my forlorn situation; bade me be cheerful, and endeavored to make me so by an assurance that every good Christian would give me assistance; then (while she sent to a goldsmith's in the neighborhood for some tools I had occasion for) she went up stairs and fetched me something for breakfast. This seemed a promising beginning, nor was what followed less flattering: she was satisfied with my work, and, when I had a little recovered myself, still more with my discourse. She was rather elegantly dressed, and notwithstanding her gentle looks this appearance of gayety had disconcerted me; but her good nature, the compassionate tone of her voice, with her gentle and caressing manner, soon set me at ease with myself: I saw my endeavors to please were crowned with success, and this assurance made me succeed the more. Though an Italian, and too pretty to be entirely devoid of coquetry, she had so much modesty, and I so great a share of timidity, that our adventure was not likely to be brought to a very speedy conclusion, nor did they give us time to make any good of it. I cannot recall the few short moments I passed with this lovely woman without being sensible of an inexpressible charm, and can yet say, it was there I tasted in their utmost perfection the most delightful, as well as the purest, pleasures of love.

She was a lively pleasing brunette, and the good nature that was painted on her lovely face rendered her vivacity more interesting. She was called Madam Basile; her husband, who was considerably older than herself, consigned her, during his absence, to the care of a clerk, too disagreeable to be thought dangerous; but who, notwithstanding, had pretensions that he seldom showed any signs of, except of ill-humors, a good share of which he bestowed on me; though I was pleased to hear him play the flute, on which he was a tolerable musician. This second Egistus was sure to grumble whenever he saw me go into his mistress' apartment, treating me with a degree of disdain which she took care to repay him with interest; seeming pleased to caress me in his presence, on purpose to torment him. This kind of revenge, though perfectly to my taste, would have been still more charming in a *tête-à-tête,* but she did not proceed so far; at least there was a difference in the expression of her kindness. Whether she thought me too young, that it was my place to make advances, or that she was seriously resolved to be virtuous, she had at such times a kind of reserve, which though not absolutely discouraging, kept my passion within bounds.

I did not feel the same real and tender respect for

her as I did for Madam de Warrens: I was embarrassed, agitated, feared to look, and hardly dared to breathe in her presence, yet to have left her would have been worse than death. How fondly did my eyes devour whatever they could gaze on without being perceived! the flowers on her gown, the point of her pretty foot, the interval of a round white arm that appeared between her glove and ruffle, the least part of her neck, each object increased the force of all the rest, and added to the infatuation. Gazing thus on what was to be seen, and even more than was to be seen, my sight became confused, my chest seemed contracted, respiration was every moment more painful. I had the utmost difficulty to hide my agitation, to prevent my sighs from being heard, and this difficulty was increased by the silence in which we were frequently plunged. Happily, Madam Basile, busy at her work, saw nothing of all this, or seemed not to see it; yet I sometimes observed a kind of sympathy, especially by the frequent rising of her handkerchief, and this dangerous sight almost mastered every effort; but when on the point of giving way to my transports, she spoke a few words to me with an air of tranquillity, and in an instant the agitation subsided.

I saw her several times in this manner without a word, a gesture, or even a look, too expressive, making the least intelligence between us. This situation was both my torment and delight, for hardly in the simplicity of my heart, could I imagine the cause of my uneasiness. I should suppose these *tête-à-têtes* could not be displeasing to her, at least, she sought frequent occasions to renew them; this was a very disinterested labor, certainly, as appeared by the use she made, or ever suffered me to make of them.

Being, one day, wearied with the clerk's discourse, she had retired to her chamber; I made haste to finish what I had to do in the back shop, and followed her: the door was half open, and I entered without being perceived. She was embroidering near a window on the opposite side of the room; she could not see me, and the carts in the streets made too much noise for me to be heard. She was always well dressed, but this day her attire bordered on coquetry. Her attitude was graceful, her head leaning gently forward, discovered a small circle of her neck; her hair, elegantly dressed, was ornamented with flowers; her figure was universally charming, and I had an uninterrupted opportunity to admire it. I was absolutely in a state of ecstasy, and, involuntarily, sinking on my knees, I passionately extended my arms towards her, certain she could not hear, and having no conception that she could see me; but there was a chimney glass at the end of the room that betrayed all my proceedings. I am ignorant what effect this transport produced on her; she did not speak, she did not look on me; but, partly turning her head, with the movement of her finger only, she pointed to the mat which was at her feet— To start up, with an articulate cry of joy, and occupy the place she had indicated, was the work of a moment; but it will hardly be believed I dared attempt no more, not even to speak, raise my eyes to hers, or rest an instant on her knees, though in an attitude which seemed to render such a support necessary. I was dumb, immovable, but far enough from a state of tranquillity; agitation, joy, gratitude, ardent indefinite wishes, restrained by the fear of giving displeasure, which my unpractised heart too much dreaded, were sufficiently discernible. She neither appeared more tranquil, nor less intimidated than myself —uneasy at my present situation, confounded at having brought me there, beginning to tremble for the effects of a sign which she had made without reflecting on the consequences, neither giving encouragement, nor expressing disapprobation, with her eyes fixed on her work, she endeavored to appear unconscious of everything that passed; but all my stupidity could not hinder me from concluding that she partook of my embarrassment, perhaps, my transports, and was only restrained by a bashfulness like mine, without even that supposition giving me power to surmount it. Five or six years older than myself, every advance, according to my idea, should have been made by her, and, since she did nothing to encourage mine, I concluded they would offend her. Even at this time, I am inclined to believe I thought right; she certainly had wit enough to perceive that a novice like me had occasion, not only for encouragement, but instruction.

I am ignorant how this animated, though dumb scene would have ended, or how long I should have continued immovable in this ridiculous, though delicious, situation, had we not been interrupted—in the height of my agitation, I heard the kitchen door open, which joined Madam Basile's chamber; who, being alarmed, said, with a quick voice and action, "Get up!—Here's Rosina!" Rising hastily I seized one of her hands, which she held out to me, and gave it two eager kisses; at the second I felt this charming hand press gently on my lips. Never in my life did I enjoy so sweet a moment; but the occasion I had lost returned no more, this being the conclusion of our amours.

This may be the reason that her image yet remains imprinted on my heart in such charming colors, which have even acquired fresh luster since I became acquainted with the world and women. Had she been mistress of the least degree of experience, she would have taken other measures to animate so youthful a lover; but if her heart was weak, it was virtuous, and only suffered itself to be borne away by a powerful though involuntary inclination. This was, apparently, her first infidelity, and I should, perhaps, have found more difficulty in vanquishing her scruples than my own: but, without proceeding so far, I experienced in her company the most inexpressible delights. Never did I taste with any other woman pleasures equal to those two minutes which I passed at the feet of Madam Basile without even daring to touch her gown. I am convinced no satisfaction can be compared to that we feel with a virtuous woman we esteem; all is transport!—A sign with the finger, a hand lightly pressed against my lips, were the only favors I ever received from Madam Basile, yet the bare remembrance of these trifling condescensions continues to transport me.

It was in vain I watched the two following days for another *tête-à-tête;* it was impossible to find an opportunity; nor could I perceive on her part any desire to forward it; her behavior was not colder, but more distant than usual, and I believe she avoided my looks for fear of not being able sufficiently to govern her own. The cursed clerk was more vexatious than ever; he even became a wit, telling me, with a satirical sneer, that I should unquestionably make my way among the ladies. I trembled lest I should have been guilty of some indiscretion, and looking on myself as already engaged in an intrigue, endeavored to cover with an air of mystery an inclination which hitherto certainly had no great need of it; this made me more circumspect in my choice of opportunities, and by resolving only to seize such as should be absolutely free from the danger of a surprise, I met with none.

Another romantic folly, which I could never overcome, and which, joined to my natural timidity, tended directly to contradict the clerk's predictions, is, I always loved too sincerely, too perfectly, I may say, to find happiness easily attainable. Never were passions at the same time more lively and pure than mine; never was love more tender, more true, or more disinterested; freely would I have sacrificed my own happiness to that of the object of my affection; her reputation was dearer than my life, and I could promise myself no happiness for which I would have exposed her peace of mind for a moment. This disposition has ever made me employ so much care, use so many precautions, such secrecy in my adventures, that all of them have failed; in a word, my want of success with the women has ever proceeded from having loved them too well.

To return to our Egistus, the fluter; it was remarkable that in becoming more insupportable, the traitor put on the appearance of complaisance. From the first day Madam Basile had taken me under her protection, she had endeavored to make me serviceable in the warehouse; and, finding I understood arithmetic tolerably well, she proposed his teaching me to keep the books; a proposition that was but indifferently received by this humorist, who might, perhaps, be fearful of being supplanted. As this failed, my whole employ, besides what engraving I had to do, was to transcribe some bills and accounts, to write several books over fair, and translate commercial letters from Italian into French. All at once he thought fit to accept the before rejected proposal, saying he would teach me bookkeeping by double-entry, and put me in a situation to offer my services to M. Basile on his return; but there was something so false, malicious, and ironical, in his air and manner, that it was by no means calculated to inspire me with confidence. Madam Basile, replied archly, that I was much obliged to him for his kind offer, but she hoped fortune would be more favorable to my merits, for it would be a great misfortune, with so much sense, that I should only be a pitiful clerk.

She often said, she would procure me some acquaintance that might be useful; she doubtless felt the necessity of parting with me, and had prudently resolved on it. Our mute declaration had been made on a Thursday, the Sunday following she gave a dinner. A Jacobin of good appearance was among the guests, to whom she did me the honor to present me. The monk treated me very affectionately, congratulated me on my late conversion, mentioned several particulars of my story, which plainly showed he had been made acquainted with it, then, tapping me familiarly on the cheek, bade me be good, to keep up my spirits, and come to see him at his convent where he should have more opportunity to talk with me. I judged him to be a person of some consequence by the deference that was paid him; and by the paternal tone he assumed with Madam Basile, to be her confessor. I likewise remember that his decent familiarity was attended with an appearance of esteem, and even respect for his fair penitent, which then made less impression on me than at present. Had I possessed more experience, how should I have congratulated myself on having touched the heart of a young woman respected by her confessor!

The table not being large enough to accommodate all the company, a small one was prepared, where I had the satisfaction of dining with our agreeable clerk; but I lost nothing with regard to attention and good cheer, for several plates were sent to the side-table which were certainly not intended for him. Thus far all went well; the ladies were in good spirits, and the gentlemen very gallant, while Madam Basile did the honors of the table with peculiar grace. In the midst of the dinner we heard a chaise stop at the door, and presently some one coming up stairs—it was M. Basile. Methinks I now see him entering, in his scarlet coat with gold buttons—from that day I have held the color in abhorrence. M. Basile was a tall handsome man, of good address: he entered with a consequential look and an air of taking his family unawares, though none but friends were present. His wife ran to meet him, threw her arms about his neck, and gave him a thousand caresses, which he received with the utmost indifference; and without making any return saluted the company and took his place at table. They were just beginning to speak of his journey, when casting his eye on the small table he asked in a sharp tone, what lad that was? Madam Basile answered ingenuously. He then inquired whether I lodged in the house; and was answered in the negative. "Why not?" replied he, rudely, "since he stays here all day, he might as well remain all night too." The monk now interfered, with a serious and true eulogium on Madam Basile: in a few words he made mine also, adding, that so far from blaming, he ought to further the pious charity of his wife, since it was evident she had not passed the bounds of discretion. The husband answered with an air of petulance, which (restrained by the presence of the monk) he endeavored to stifle; it was, however, sufficient to let me understand he had already received information of me, and that our worthy clerk had rendered me an ill office.

We had hardly risen from table, when the latter came in triumph from his employer, to inform me, I must leave the house that instant, and never more during my life dare to set foot there. He took care to aggravate this commission by everything that could render it cruel and insulting. I departed without a word, my heart overwhelmed with sorrow, less for being obliged to quit this amiable woman, than at the thought of leaving her to the brutality of such a husband. He was certainly right to wish her faithful; but though prudent and well-born, she was an Italian, that is to say, tender and vindictive; which made me think, he was extremely imprudent in using means the most likely in the world to draw on himself the very evil he so much dreaded.

Such was the success of my first adventure. I walked several times up and down the street, wishing to get a sight of what my heart incessantly regretted; but I could only discover her husband, or the vigilant clerk, who, perceiving me, made a sign with the ell they used in the shop, which was more expressive than alluring: finding, therefore, that I was so completely watched, my courage failed, and I went no more. I wished, at least, to find out the patron she had provided me, but, unfortunately, I did not know his name. I ranged several times round the convent, endeavoring in vain to meet with him. At length, other events banished the delightful remembrance of Madam Basile; and in a short time I so far forgot her, that I remained as simple, as much a novice as ever, nor did my penchant for pretty women even receive any sensible augmentation.

Her liberality had, however, increased my little wardrobe, though she had done this with precaution and prudence, regarding neatness more than decoration, and to make me comfortable rather than brilliant. The coat I had brought from Geneva was yet wearable, she only added a hat and some linen. I had no ruffles, nor would she give me any, not but I felt a great inclination for them. She was satisfied with having put it in my power to keep myself clean, though a charge to do this was unnecessary while I was to appear before her.

A few days after this catastrophe, my hostess, who, as I have already observed, was very friendly, with great satisfaction informed me she had heard of a situation, and that a lady of rank desired to see me. I immediately thought myself in the road to great adventures; that being the point to which all my ideas tended: this, however, did not prove so brilliant as I had conceived it. I waited on the lady with the servant who had mentioned me: she asked a number of questions, and my answers not displeasing her, I immediately entered into her service; not indeed in the quality of favorite, but as a footman. I was clothed like the rest of her people, the only difference being, they wore a shoulder-knot, which I had not, and, as there was no lace on her livery, it appeared merely a tradesman's suit. This was the unforeseen conclusion of all my great expectancies!

The Countess of Vercellis, with whom I now lived, was a widow without children; her husband was a Piedmontese, but I always believed her to be a Savoyard, as I could have no conception that a native of Piedmont could speak such good French, and with so pure an accent. She was a middle-aged woman, of a noble appearance and cultivated understanding, being fond of French literature, in which she was well versed. Her letters had the expression, and almost the elegance of Madam de Sévigné's; some of them might have been taken for hers. My principal employ, which was by no means displeasing to me, was to write from her dictating; a cancer in the breast, from which she suffered extremely, not permitting her to write herself.

Madam de Vercellis not only possessed a good understanding, but a strong and elevated soul. I was with her during her last illness, and saw her suffer and die, without showing an instant of weakness, or the least effort of constraint; still retaining her feminine manners, without entertaining an idea that such fortitude gave her any claim to philosophy; a word which was not yet in fashion, nor comprehended by her in the sense it is held at present. This strength of disposition sometimes extended almost to apathy, ever appearing to feel as little for others as herself; and when she relieved the unfortunate, it was rather for the sake of acting right, than from a principle of real commiseration. I have frequently experienced this insensibility, in some measure, during the three months I remained with her. It would have been natural to have had an esteem for a young man of some abilities, who was incessantly under her observation, and that she should think, as she felt her dissolution approaching, that after her death he would have occasion for assistance and support: but whether she judged me unworthy of particular attention, or that those who narrowly watched all her motions, gave her no opportunity to think of any but themselves, she did nothing for me.

I very well recollect that she showed some curiosity to know my story, frequently questioning me, and appearing pleased when I showed her the letters I wrote to Madam de Warrens, or explained my sentiments; but as she never discovered her own, she certainly did not take the right means to come at them. My heart, naturally communicative, loved to display its feelings, whenever I encountered a similiar disposition; but dry, cold interrogatories, without any sign of blame or approbation on my answers, gave me no confidence. Not being able to determine whether my discourse was agreeable or displeasing, I was ever in fear, and thought less of expressing my ideas, than of being careful not to say anything that might seem to my disadvantage. I have since remarked that this dry method of questioning themselves into people's characters is a common trick among women who pride themselves on superior understanding. These imagine, that by concealing their own sentiments, they shall the more easily penetrate into those of others; being ignorant that this method destroys the confidence so necessary to make us reveal them. A man, on being questioned, is immediately on his guard: and if once he supposes that, without any interest in his concerns, you only wish to set him a-talking, either he entertains you with lies, is silent, or, examining every word before he utters it, rather chooses to pass for a fool, than to be the dupe of your curiosity. In short, it is ever a bad method to attempt to read the hearts of others by endeavoring to conceal our own.

Madam de Vercellis never addressed a word to me which seemed to express affection, pity, or benevolence. She interrogated me coldly, and my answers were uttered with so much timidity, that she doubtless entertained but a mean opinion of my intellects, for latterly she never asked me any questions, nor said anything but what was absolutely necessary for her service. She drew her judgment less from what I really was, than from what she had made me, and by considering me as a footman prevented my appearing otherwise.

I am inclined to think I suffered at that time by the same interested game of concealed maneuver, which has counteracted me throughout my life, and given me a very natural aversion for everything that has the least appearance of it. Madam de Vercellis having no children, her nephew, the Count de la Roque, was her heir, and paid his court assiduously, as did her principal domestics, who, seeing her end approaching, endeavored to take care of themselves; in short, so many were busy about her, that she could hardly have found time to think of me. At the head of her household was a M. Lorenzy, an artful genius, with a still more artful wife; who had so far insinuated herself into the good graces of her mistress, that she was rather on the footing of a friend than a servant. She had introduced a niece of hers as lady's maid: her name was Mademoiselle Pontal; a cunning gypsy, that gave herself all the airs of a waiting-woman, and assisted her aunt so well in besetting the countess, that she only saw with their eyes, and acted through their hands. I had not the happiness to please this worthy triumvirate; I obeyed, but did not wait on them, not conceiving that my duty to our general mistress required me to be a servant to her servants. Besides this, I was a person that gave them some inquietude; they saw I was not in my proper situation, and feared the countess would discover it likewise, and by placing me in it, decrease their portions; for such sort of people, too greedy to be just, look on every legacy given to others as a diminution of their own wealth; they endeavored, therefore, to keep me as much out of her sight as possible. She loved to write letters, in her situation, but they contrived to give her a distaste to it; persuading her, by the aid of the doctor, that it was too fatiguing; and, under pretense that I did not understand how to wait on her, they employed two great lubberly chairmen for that purpose; in a word, they managed the affair so well, that for eight days before she made her will, I had not been permitted to enter the chamber. Afterwards I went in as usual, and was even more assiduous than any one, being afflicted at the sufferings of the unhappy lady, whom I truly respected and beloved for the calmness and fortitude with which she bore her illness, and often did I shed tears of real sorrow without being perceived by any one.

At length I saw her expire. She had lived like a woman of sense and virtue, her death was that of a philosopher. She was naturally serious, but towards the end of her illness she possessed a kind of gayety, too regular to be assumed, which served as a counterpoise to the melancholy of her situation. She only kept her bed two days, continuing to discourse cheerfully with those about her to the very last. At last, when she could hardly speak, and in her death agony, she let a big wind escape. "Well!" said she, turning around, "a woman that can f . . . is not yet dead!" These were her last words.

She had bequeathed a year's wages to all the under servants, but, not being on the household list, I had nothing: the Count de la Roque, however, ordered me thirty livres, and the new coat I had on, which M. Lorenzy would certainly have taken from me. He even promised to procure me a place; giving me permission to wait on him as often as I pleased. Accordingly, I went two or three times, without being able to speak to him, and as I was easily repulsed, returned no more; whether I did wrong will be seen hereafter.

Would I had finished what I have to say of my living at Madame de Vercellis's. Though my situation apparently remained the same, I did not leave her house as I had entered it: I carried with me the long and painful remembrance of a crime; an insupportable weight of remorse which yet hangs on my conscience, and whose bitter recollection, far from weakening, during a period of forty years, seems to gather strength as I grow old. Who would believe, that a childish fault should be productive of such melancholy consequences? But it is for the more than probable effects that my heart cannot be consoled. I have, perhaps, caused an amiable, honest, estimable girl, who surely merited a better fate than myself, to perish with shame and misery.

Though it is very difficult to break up housekeeping without confusion, and the loss of some property; yet such was the fidelity of the domestics, and the vigilance of M. and Madam Lorenzy, that no article of the inventory was found wanting; in short, nothing was missing but a pink and silver ribbon, which had been worn, and belonged to Mademoiselle Pontal. Though several things of more value were in my reach, this ribbon alone tempted me, and accordingly I stole it. As I took no great pains to conceal the bauble, it was soon discovered; they immediately insisted on knowing from whence I had taken it; this perplexed me—

I hesitated, and at length said, with confusion, that Marion gave it me.

Marion was a young Mauriennese, and had been cook to Madam de Vercellis ever since she left off giving entertainments, for being sensible she had more need of good broths than fine ragouts, she had discharged her former one. Marion was not only pretty, but had that freshness of color only to be found among the mountains, and above all, an air of modesty and sweetness, which made it impossible to see her without affection; she was besides a good girl, virtuous, and of such strict fidelity, that every one was surprised at hearing her named. They had not less confidence in me, and judged it necessary to certify which of us was the thief. Marion was sent for; a great number of people were present, among whom was the Count de la Roque: she arrives; they show her the ribbon; I accuse her boldly; she remains confused and speechless, casting a look on me that would have disarmed a demon, but which my barbarous heart resisted. At length, she denied it with firmness, but without anger, exhorting me to return to myself, and not injure an innocent girl who had never wronged me. With infernal impudence, I confirmed my accusation, and to her face maintained she had given me the ribbon: on which, the poor girl, bursting into tears, said these words—"Ah, Rousseau! I thought you a good disposition—you render me very unhappy, but I would not be in your situation." She continued to defend herself with as much innocence as firmness, but without uttering the least invective against me. Her moderation, compared to my positive tone, did her an injury; as it did not appear natural to suppose, on one side such diabolical assurance; on the other, such angelic mildness. The affair could not be absolutely decided, but the presumption was in my favor; and the Count de la Roque, in sending us both away, contented himself with saying, "The conscience of the guilty would revenge the innocent." His prediction was true, and is being daily verified.

I am ignorant what became of the victim of my calumny, but there is little probability of her having been able to place herself agreeably after this, as she labored under an imputation cruel to her character in every respect. The theft was a trifle, yet it was a theft, and, what was worse, employed to seduce a boy; while the lie and obstinacy left nothing to hope from a person in whom so many vices were united. I do not even look on the misery and disgrace in which I plunged her as the greatest evil: who knows, at her age, whither contempt and disregarded innocence might have led her?—Alas! if remorse for having made her unhappy is insupportable, what must I have suffered at the thought of rendering her even worse than myself. The cruel remembrance of this transaction, sometimes so troubles and disorders me, that, in my disturbed slumbers, I imagine I see this poor girl enter and reproach me with my crime, as though I had committed it but yesterday. While in easy tranquil circumstances, I was less miserable on this account, but, during a troubled agitated life, it has robbed me of the sweet consolation of persecuted innocence, and made me woefully experience, what, I think, I have re-marked in some of my works, that remorse sleeps in the calm sunshine of prosperity, but wakes amid the storms of adversity. I could never take on me to dis-charge my heart of this weight in the bosom of a friend; nor could the closest intimacy ever encourage me to it, even with Madam de Warrens; all I could do, was to own I had to accuse myself of an atrocious crime, but never said in what it consisted. The weight, therefore, has remained heavy on my conscience to this day; and I can truly own the desire of relieving my-self, in some measure, from it, contributed greatly to the resolution of writing my Confessions.

I have proceeded truly in that I have just made, and it will certainly be thought I have not sought to palli-ate the turpitude of my offense; but I should not fulfill the purpose of this undertaking, did I not, at the same time, divulge my interior disposition, and excuse my-self as far as is conformable with truth.

Never was wickedness further from my thoughts, than in that cruel moment; and when I accused the unhappy girl, it is strange, but strictly true, that my friendship for her was the immediate cause of it. She was present to my thoughts; I formed my excuse from the first object that presented itself; I accused her with doing what I meant to have done, and as I designed to have given her the ribbon, asserted she had given it to me. When she appeared, my heart was agonized, but the presence of so many people was more powerful than my compunction. I did not fear punishment, but I dreaded shame: I dreaded it more than death, more than the crime, more than all the world. I would have buried, hid myself in the center of the earth: invincible shame bore down every other sentiment; shame alone caused all my impudence, and in proportion as I became criminal, the fear of discovery rendered me intrepid. I felt no dread but that of being detected, of being publicly, and to my face, declared a thief, liar, and calumniator; an unconquerable fear of this overcame every other sensation. Had I been left to myself, I should infallibly have declared the truth. Or if M. de la Roque had taken me aside, and said—"Do not injure this poor girl; if you are guilty own it,"—I am convinced I should instantly have thrown myself at his feet; but they intimidated, instead of encouraging me. I was hardly out of my childhood, or rather, was yet in it. It is also just to make some allowance for my age. In youth, dark, premeditated villany is more criminal than in a riper age, but weaknesses are much less so; my fault was truly nothing more; and I am less afflicted at the deed itself than for its consequences. It had one good effect, however, in preserving me through the rest of my life from any criminal action, from the terrible impression that has remained from the only one I ever committed; and I think my aversion for lying proceeds in a great measure from regret at having been guilty of so black a one. If it is a crime that can be expiated, as I dare believe, forty years of uprightness and honor on various difficult occasions, with the many misfortunes that have overwhelmed my latter years, may have completed it. Poor Marion has found so many avengers in this world, that however great my offense towards her, I do not fear to bear the guilt with me. Thus have I disclosed what I had to say on this painful subject; may I be permitted never to mention it again.

BOOK III

BOOK III.

BOOK III

[1728–1731]

HAVING left the service of Madam de Vercellis nearly as I had entered it, I returned to my former hostess, and remained there five or six weeks; during which time health, youth, and laziness, frequently rendered my temperament importunate. I was restless, absent, and thoughtful: I wept and sighed for a happiness I had no idea of, though at the same time highly sensible of some deficiency. This situation is indescribable, few men can even form any conception of it, because, in general, they have prevented that plenitude of life, at once tormenting and delicious. My thoughts were incessantly occupied with girls and women, but in a manner peculiar to myself: these ideas kept my senses in a perpetual and disagreeable activity, though, fortunately, they did not point out the means of deliverance. I would have given my life to have met with a Miss Goton, if only for a quarter of an hour, but the time was past in which the play of infancy predominated; increase of years had introduced shame, the inseparable companion of a conscious deviation from rectitude, which so confirmed my natural timidity as to render it invincible; and never, either at that time or since, could I prevail on myself to offer a proposition favorable to my wishes (unless in a manner constrained to it by previous advances) even with those whose scruples I had no cause to dread, and that I felt assured were ready to take me at my word.

My stay at Madam de Vercellis's had procured me some acquaintance, which I wished to retain. Among others, I sometimes visited a Savoyard abbé, M. Gaime, who was tutor to the Count of Melarede's children. He was young, and not much known, but possessed an excellent cultivated understanding, with great probity, and was, altogether, one of the best men I ever knew. He was incapable of doing me the service I then stood most in need of, not having sufficient interest to procure me a situation, but from him I reaped advantages far more precious, which have been useful to me through life, lessons of pure morality, and maxims of sound judgment.

In the successive order of my inclinations and ideas, I had ever been too high or too low. Achilles or Thersites; sometimes a hero, at others a villain. M. Gaime took pains to make me properly acquainted with myself, without sparing or giving me too much discouragement. He spoke in advantageous terms of my disposition and talents, adding, that he foresaw obstacles which would prevent my profiting by them; thus, according to him, they were to serve less as steps by which I should mount to fortune, than as resources which might enable me to exist without one. He gave me a true picture of human life, of which, hitherto, I had formed but a very erroneous idea, teaching me, that a man of understanding, though destined to experience adverse fortune, might, by skillful management, arrive at happiness; that there was no true felicity without virtue, which was practicable in every situation. He greatly diminished my admiration of grandeur, by proving that those in a superior situation are neither better nor happier than those they command. One of his maxims has frequently returned to my memory: it was, that if we could truly read the hearts of others we should feel more inclination to descend than rise: this reflection, the truth of which is striking without extravagance, I have found of great utility, in the various exigences of my life, as it tended to make me satisfied with my condition. He gave me the first just conception of relative duties, which my high-flown imagination had ever pictured in extremes, making me sensible that the enthusiasm of sublime virtues is of little use in society; that while endeavoring to rise too high we are in danger of falling; and that a virtuous and uniform discharge of little duties requires as great a degree of fortitude as actions which are called heroic, and would at the same time procure more honor and happiness. That it was infinitely more desirable to possess the lasting esteem of those about us, than at intervals to attract admiration.

In properly arranging the various duties between man and man, it was necessary to ascend to principles;

the step I had recently taken, and of which my present situation was the consequence, naturally led us to speak of religion. It will easily be conceived that the honest M. Gaime was, in a great measure, the original of the *Savoyard Vicar:* prudence only obliging him to deliver his sentiments, on certain points, with more caution and reserve, and explain himself with less freedom; but his sentiments and councils were the same, not even excepting his advice to return to my country; all was precisely as I have since given it to the public. Dwelling no longer, therefore, on conversations which every one may see the substance of, I shall only add, that these wise instructions (though they did not produce an immediate effect) were as so many seeds of virtue and religion in my heart which were never rooted out, and only required the fostering cares of friendship to bring to maturity.

Though my conversion was not very sincere, I was affected by his discourses, and far from being weary, was pleased with them on account of their clearness and simplicity, but above all because his heart seemed interested in what he said. My disposition is naturally tender, I have ever been less attached to people for the good they have really done me than for that they designed to do, and my feelings in this particular have seldom misled me: thus I truly esteemed M. Gaime. I was in a manner his second disciple, which even at that time was of inestimable service in turning me from a propensity to vice into which my idleness was leading me.

One day, when I least expected it, I was sent for by the Count de la Roque. Having frequently called at his house, without being able to speak with him, I grew weary, and supposing he had either forgot me or retained some unfavorable impression of me, returned no more: but I was mistaken in both these conjectures. He had more than once witnessed the pleasure I took in fulfilling my duty to his aunt: he had even mentioned it to her, and afterwards spoke of it, when I no longer thought of it myself.

He received me graciously, saying that instead of amusing me with useless promises, he had sought to place me to advantage; that he had succeeded, and would put me in a way to better my situation, but the rest must depend on myself. That the family into which he should introduce me being both powerful and esteemed, I should need no other patrons; and though at first on the footing of a servant, I might be assured, that if my conduct and sentiments were found above that station, I should not long remain in it. The end of this discourse cruelly disappointed the brilliant hopes the beginning had inspired. "What! forever a footman?" said I to myself, with a bitterness which confidence presently effaced, for I felt myself too superior to that situation to fear long remaining there.

He took me to the Count de Gauvon, Master of the Horse to the Queen, and Chief of the illustrious House of Solar. The air of dignity conspicuous in this respectable old man, rendered the affability with which he received me yet more interesting. He questioned me with evident interest, and I replied with sincerity. He then told the Count de la Roque, that my features were agreeable, and promised intellect, which he believed I was not deficient in; but that was not enough, and time must show the rest; after which, turning to me, he said, "Child, almost all situations are attended with difficulties in the beginning; yours, however, shall not have too great a portion of them; be prudent, and endeavor to please every one, that will be almost your only employment; for the rest fear nothing, you shall be taken care of." Immediately after he went to the Marchioness de Breil, his daughter-in-law, to whom he presented me, and then to the Abbé de Gauvon, his son. I was elated with this beginning, as I knew enough of the world already to conclude, that so much ceremony is not generally used at the reception of a footman. In fact, I was not treated like one. I dined at the steward's table; did not wear a livery; and the Count de Favria (a giddy youth) having commanded me to get behind his coach, his grandfather ordered that I should get behind no coach, nor follow any one out of the house. Meantime, I waited at table, and did, within doors, the business of a footman; but I did it, as it were, of my own free will, without being appointed to any particular service; and except writing some letters, which were dictated to me, and cutting out some ornaments for the Count de Favria, I was almost the absolute master of my time. This trial of my discretion, which I did not then perceive, was certainly very dangerous, and not very humane; for in this state of idleness I might have contracted vices which I should not otherwise have given in to. Fortunately, it did not produce that effect; my memory retained the lessons of M. Gaime, they had made an impression on my heart, and I sometimes escaped from the house of my patron to obtain a repetition of them. I believe those who saw me going out, apparently by stealth, had no conception of my business. Nothing could be more prudent than the advice he gave me respecting my conduct. My beginning was admirable; so much attention, assiduity, and zeal, had charmed every one. The Abbé Gaime advised me to moderate this first ardor, lest I should relax, and that relaxation should be considered as neglect. "Your setting out," said he, "is the rule of what will be expected of you; endeavor gradually to increase your attentions, but be cautious how you diminish them."

As they paid but little attention to my trifling talents, and supposed I possessed no more than nature had given me, there was no appearance (notwithstanding the promises of Count de Gauvon) of my meeting with any particular consideration. Some objects of more consequence had intervened. The Marquis de Breil, son of the Count de Gauvon, was then ambassador at Vienna; some circumstances had occurred at that court which for some weeks kept the family in continual agitation, and left them no time to think of me. Meantime, I had relaxed but little in my attentions, though one object in the family did me both good and harm, making me more secure from exterior dissipation, but less attentive to my duty.

Mademoiselle de Breil was about my own age, tolerably handsome, and very fair complexioned, with black hair, which, notwithstanding, gave to her features that air of softness so natural to the flaxen, and which my heart could never resist. The court dress, so favorable to youth, showed her fine neck and shape to advantage, and the mourning, which was then worn, seemed to add to her beauty. It will be said, a domestic should not take notice of these things; I was certainly to blame, yet I perceived all this, nor was I the only one; the *maître d'hôtel* and *valet de chambre* spoke of her sometimes at table with a vulgarity that pained me extremely. My head, however, was not sufficiently turned to allow of my being entirely in love; I did not forget myself, or my situation. I loved to see Mademoiselle de Breil; to hear her utter anything that marked wit, sense, or good humor; my ambition, confined to a desire of waiting on her, never exceeded its just rights. At table I was ever attentive to make the most of them; if her footman quitted her chair, I instantly supplied his place; in default of this, I stood facing her, seeking in her eyes what she was about to ask for, and watching the moment to change her plate. What would I not have given to hear her command, to have her look at, or speak the smallest word to me! but no, I had the mortification to be beneath her regard; she did not even perceive I was there. Her brother, who frequently spoke to me while at table,

having one day said something which I did not consider obliging, I made him so arch and well-turned an
answer, that it drew her attention; she cast her eyes
upon me, and this glance was sufficient to fill me with
transport. The next day, a second occasion presented
itself, which I fortunately made use of. A great dinner was given; and I saw, with astonishment, for the
first time, the *maître d'hôtel* waiting at table, with a
sword by his side, and hat on his head. By chance, the
discourse turned on the motto of the house of Solar,
which was, with the arms, worked in the tapestry:
Tel fiert qui ne tue pas. As the Piedmontese are not in
general very perfect in the French language, they
found fault with the orthography, saying, that in the
word *fiert* there should be no *t*. The old Count de
Gauvon was going to reply, when happening to cast
his eyes on me, he perceived I smiled without daring
to say anything; he immediately ordered me to speak
my opinion. I then said, I did not think the *t* superfluous, *fiert* being an old French word, not derived
from the noun *ferus,* proud, threatening; but from
the verb *fierit,* he strikes, he wounds; the motto, therefore, did not appear to mean, some threat, but, *Some
strike who do not kill*. The whole company fixed their
eyes on me, then on each other, without speaking a
word; never was a greater degree of astonishment; but
what most flattered me, was an air of satisfaction
which I perceived on the countenance of Mademoiselle
de Breil. This scornful lady deigned to cast on me a
second look at least as valuable as the former, and

turning to her grandfather, appeared to wait with impatience for the praise that was due to me, and which he fully bestowed, with such apparent satisfaction, that it was eagerly chorused by the whole table. This interval was short, but delightful in many respects; it was one of those moments so rarely met with, which place things in their natural order, and revenge depressed merit for the injuries of fortune. Some minutes after Mademoiselle de Breil again raised her eyes, desiring me with a voice of timid affability to give her some drink. It will easily be supposed I did not let her wait, but advancing towards her, I was seized with such a trembling, that having filled the glass too full, I spilled some of the water on her plate, and even on herself. Her brother asked me, giddily, why I trembled thus? This question increased my confusion, while the face of Mademoiselle de Breil was suffused with a crimson blush.

Here ended the romance; where it may be remarked (as with Madam Basile, and others in the continuation of my life) that I was not fortunate in the conclusion of my amours. In vain I placed myself in the antechamber of Madam de Breil. I could not obtain one mark of attention from her daughter; she went in and out without looking at me, nor had I the confidence to raise my eyes to her; I was even so foolishly stupid, that one day, on dropping her gloves as she passed, instead of seizing and covering it with kisses, as I would gladly have done, I did not dare to quit my place, but suffered it to be taken up by a great booby of a footman, whom I could willingly have knocked down for his officiousness. To complete my timidity, I perceived I had not the good fortune to please Madam de Breil; she not only never ordered, but even rejected, my services; and having twice found me in her antechamber, asked me, dryly, "If I had nothing to do?" I was obliged, therefore, to renounce this dear antechamber; as first it caused me some uneasiness, but other things intervening, I presently thought no more of it.

The disdain of Madam de Breil was fully compensated by the kindness of her father-in-law, who at length began to think of me. The evening after the entertainment, I have already mentioned, he had a conversation with me that lasted half an hour, which appeared to satisfy him, and absolutely enchanted me. This good man had less sense than Madam de Vercellis, but possessed more feeling; I therefore succeeded much better with him. He bade me attach myself to his son, the Abbé Gauvon, who had an esteem for me, which, if I took care to cultivate, might be serviceable in furnishing me with what was necessary to complete their views for my future establishment. The next morning I flew to M. the abbé, who did not receive me as a servant, but made me sit by his fireside, and questioned me with great affability. He soon found that my education, which had attempted many things, had completed none; but observing that I understood something of Latin, he undertook to teach me more, and appointed me to attend him every morning. Thus, by one of the whimsicalities which have marked the whole course of my life, at once above and below my natural situation, I was pupil and footman in the same house; and though in servitude, had a preceptor whose birth entitled him to supply that place only to the children of kings.

The Abbé de Gauvon was a younger son, and designed by his family for a bishopric, for which reason his studies had been pursued further than is usual with people of quality. He had been sent to the university of Sienna, where he had resided some years, and from whence he had brought a good portion of cruscantism, designing to be that at Turin which the Abbé de Dangeau was formerly at Paris. Being disgusted with theology, he gave in to the belles-lettres, which is very frequent in Italy with those who have entered the career of prelacy. He had studied the poets, and wrote tolerable Latin and Italian verses; in a word, his taste was calculated to form mine, and give some order to that chaos of insignificant trash with which my brain was encumbered; but whether my prating had misled him, or that he could not support the trouble of teaching the elementary parts of Latin, he put me at first too high; and I had scarcely translated a few fables of Phœdrus before he put me into Virgil, where I could hardly understand anything. It will be seen hereafter that I was destined frequently to learn Latin, but never to attain it. I labored with assiduity, and the abbé bestowed his attention with a degree of kindness, the remembrance of which, even at this time, both interests and softens me. I passed the greater part of the morning with him as much for my own instruction as his service; not that he ever permitted me to perform any menial office, but to copy, or write from his dictating; and my employment of secretary was more useful than that of scholar, and by this means I not only learned the Italian in its utmost purity, but also acquired a taste for literature, and some discernment of composition, which could not have been at La Tribu's, and which was useful to me when I afterwards wrote alone.

At this period of my life, without being romantic, I might reasonably have indulged the hope of preferment. The abbé, thoroughly pleased with me, expressed his satisfaction to every one, while his father had such a singular affection for me, that I was assured by the Count de Favria, that he had spoken of me to the king; even Madam de Breil had laid aside her disdainful looks; in short I was a general favorite, which gave great jealousy to the other servants, who, seeing me honored by the instructions of their master's son, were persuaded I should not remain their equal.

As far as I could judge by some words dropped at random, and which I reflected on afterwards, it appeared to me, that the House of Solar, wishing to run the career of embassies, and hoping perhaps in time to arrive at the ministry, wished to provide themselves with a person of merit and talents, who depending entirely on them, might obtain their confidence, and be of essential service. This project of the Count de

Gauvon was judicious, magnanimous, and truly worthy of a powerful nobleman, equally provident and generous; but besides my not seeing, at that time, its full extent, it was far too rational for my brain, and required too much confinement. My ridiculous ambition sought for fortune in the midst of brilliant adventures, and not finding one woman in all this scheme, it appeared tedious, painful, and melancholy; though I should rather have thought it more honorable on this account, as the species of merit generally patronized by women is certainly less worthy than that which I was supposed to possess.

Everything succeeded to my wish: I had obtained, almost forced, the esteem of all; the trial was over, and I was universally considered as a young man with flattering prospects, who was not at present in his proper sphere, but was expected soon to reach it; but my place was not assigned me by man, and I was to reach it by very different paths. I now come to one of those characteristic traits, which are so natural to me, and which, indeed, the reader, might have observed without this reflection.

There were at Turin several new converts of my own stamp, whom I neither liked nor wished to see; but I had met with some Genevese who were not of this description, and among others, a M. Mussard, nicknamed Wryneck, a miniature painter, and a distant relation. This M. Mussard, having learned my situation at the Count de Gauvon's, came to see me, with another Genevese, named Bacle, who had been my comrade during my apprenticeship. This Bacle was a very sprightly, amusing young fellow, full of lively sallies, which at his time of life appeared extremely agreeable. At once, then, behold me delighted with M. Bacle; charmed to such a degree, that I found it impossible to quit him. He was shortly to depart for Geneva; what a loss had I to sustain! I felt the whole force of it, and resolving to make the best use of this precious interval, I determined not to leave him, or, rather, he never quitted me, for my head was not yet sufficiently turned to think of quitting the house without leave; but it was soon perceived that he engrossed my whole time, and he was accordingly forbid the house. This so incensed me, that forgetting everything but my friend Bacle, I went neither to the abbé nor the count, and was no longer to be found at home. I paid no attention to repeated reprimands, and at length was threatened with dismissal. This threat was my ruin, as it suggested the idea that it was not absolutely necessary that Bacle should depart alone. From that moment I could think of no other pleasure, no other situation or happiness than taking this journey. To render the felicity still more complete, at the end of it (though at an immense distance) I pictured to myself Madam de Warrens; for as to returning to Geneva, it never entered into my imagination. The hills, fields, brooks, and villages, incessantly succeeded each other with new charms, and this delightful jaunt seemed worthy to absorb my whole existence. Memory recalled, with inexpressible pleasure, how charming the country had appeared in coming to Turin; what then must it be, when, to the pleasure of independence, should be added the company of a good-humored comrade of my own age and disposition, without any constraint or obligation, but free to go or stay as we pleased? Would it not be madness to sacrifice the prospect of so much felicity to projects of ambition, slow and difficult in their execution, and uncertain in their event? But even supposing them realized, and in their utmost splendor, they were not worth one quarter of an hour of the sweet pleasure and liberty of youth.

Full of these wise conclusions, I conducted myself so improperly, that (not indeed without some trouble) I got myself dismissed; for on my return one night the *maître d'hôtel* gave me warning on the part of the count. This was exactly what I wanted; for feeling, in spite of myself, the extravagance of my conduct, I wished to excuse it by the addition of injustice and ingratitude, by throwing the blame on others, and sheltering myself under the idea of necessity.

I was told the Count de Favria wished to speak with me the next morning before my departure; but, being sensible that my head was so far turned as to render it possible for me to disobey the injunction, the *maître d'hôtel* declined paying the money designed me, and which certainly I had very ill earned, till after this visit; for my kind patrons being unwilling to place me in the situation of a footman, I had not any fixed wages.

The Count de Favria, though young and giddy, talked to me on this occasion in the most sensible and serious manner: I might add, if it would not be thought vain, with the utmost tenderness. He reminded me, in the most flattering terms, of the cares of his uncle, and intentions of his grandfather; after having drawn in lively colors what I was sacrificing to ruin, he offered to make my peace, without stipulating any conditions, but that I should no more see the worthless fellow who had seduced me.

It was so apparent that he did not say all this of himself, that notwithstanding my blind stupidity, I powerfully felt the kindness of my good old master; but the dear journey was too firmly printed on my imagination for any consideration to balance the charm. Bereft of understanding, firm to my purpose, I hardened myself against conviction, and arrogantly answered, that as they had thought fit to give me warning, I had resolved to take it, and conceived it was now too late to retract, since, whatever might happen to me, I was fully resolved not to be driven a second time from the same house. The count, justly irritated, bestowed on me some names which I deserved, and putting me out of his apartment by the shoulders, shut the door on me. I departed triumphant, as if I had gained the greatest victory, and fearful of sustaining a second combat even had the ingratitude to leave the house without thanking the abbé for his kindness.

To form a just conception of my delirium at that

moment, the excess to which my heart is subject to be heated by the most trifling incidents, and the ardor with which my imagination seizes on the most attractive objects should be conceived. At these times, plans the most ridiculous, childish, and void of sense, flatter my favorite idea, and persuade me that it is reasonable to sacrifice everything to the possession of it. Would it be believed, that when near nineteen, any one could be so stupid as to build his hopes of future subsistence on an empty phial? For example:

The Abbé de Gauvon had made me a present, some weeks before, of a very pretty heron fountain, with which I was highly delighted. Playing with this toy, and speaking of our departure, the sage Bacle and myself thought it might be of infinite advantage, and enable us to lengthen our journey. What in the world was so curious as a heron fountain? This idea was the foundation on which we built our future fortune: we were to assemble the country people in every village we might pass through, and delight them with the sight of it, when feasting and good cheer would be sure to pour on us abundantly; for we were both firmly persuaded, that provisions could cost nothing to those who grew and gathered them, and if they did not stuff travelers, it was downright ill-nature. We pictured in all parts entertainments and weddings, reckoning that without any expense but wind from our lungs, and the water of our fountain, we should be maintained through Piedmont, Savoy, France, and, indeed, all the world over. There was no end to our projected travels, and we immediately directed our course northward, rather for the pleasure of crossing the Alps, than from a supposed necessity of being obliged to stop at any place.

Such was the plan on which I set out, abandoning without regret, my preceptors, studies, and hopes, with the almost certain attainment of a fortune, to lead the life of a real vagabond. Farewell to the capital; adieu to the court, ambition, love, the fair, and all the great adventures into which hope had led me during the preceding year! I departed with my fountain and my friend Bacle, a purse lightly furnished, but a heart overflowing with pleasure, and only thinking how to enjoy the extensive felicity which I supposed my project encircled.

This extravagant journey was performed almost as agreeably as I had expected, though not exactly on the same plan; not but our fountain highly amused the hostess and servants for some minutes at all the ale-houses where we halted, yet we found it equally necessary to pay on our departure; but that gave us no concern, as we never thought of depending on it entirely until our money should be expended. An accident spared us that trouble, our fountain was broken near Bramant, and in good time, for we both felt (though without daring to own it to each other) that we began to be weary of it. This misfortune rendered us gayer than ever; we laughed heartily at our giddiness in having forgotten that our clothes and shoes would wear out, or trusting to renew them by the play of our fountain. We continued our journey as merrily as we had begun it, only drawing faster towards that termination where our drained purses made it necessary for us to arrive.

At Chambery I became pensive; not for the folly I had committed, for never did any one think less of the past, but on account of the reception I should meet with from Madam de Warrens; for I looked on her house as my paternal home. I had written her an account of my reception at the Count de Gauvon's; she knew my expectancies, and, in congratulating me on my good fortune, had added some wise lessons on the return I ought to make for the kindness with which they treated me. She looked on my fortune as already made, if not destroyed by my own negligence; what then would she say on my arrival? for it never entered my mind that she might shut the door against me, but I dreaded the uneasiness I might give her; I dreaded her reproaches, to me more wounding than want; I resolved to bear all in silence, and, if possible, to appease her. I now saw nothing but Madam de Warrens in the whole universe, and to live in disgrace with her was impossible.

I was most concerned about my companion, whom I did not wish to offend, and feared I should not easily get rid of. I prefaced this separation by an affected coldness during the last day's journey. The drole understood me perfectly; in fact, he was rather giddy than deficient in point of sense—I expected he would have been hurt at my inconstancy, but I was quite mistaken; nothing affected my friend Bacle, for hardly had we set foot in town, on our arrival in Annecy, before he said, "You are now at home"—embraced— bade me adieu—turned on his heel, and disappeared; nor have I ever heard of him since.

How did my heart beat as I approached the habitation of Madam de Warrens! my legs trembled under me, my eyes were clouded with a mist, I neither saw, heard, nor recollected any one, and was obliged frequently to stop that I might draw breath, and recall my bewildered senses. Was it fear of not obtaining that succor I stood in need of, which agitated me to this degree? At the age I then was, does the fear of perishing with hunger give such alarms? No: I declare with as much truth as pride, that it was not in the power of interest or indigence, at any period of my life, to expand or contract my heart. In the course of a painful life, memorable for its vicissitudes, frequently destitute of an asylum, and without bread, I have contemplated with equal indifference, both opulence and misery. In want I might have begged or stolen, as others have done, but never could feel distress at being reduced to such necessities. Few men have grieved more than myself, few have shed so many tears; yet never did poverty, or the fear of falling into it, make me heave a sigh or moisten my eyelids. My soul, in despite of fortune, has only been sensible of real good and evil, which did not depend on her; and frequently, when in possession of everything that could make life pleasing, I have been the most miserable of mortals.

The first glance of Madam de Warrens banished all my fears—my heart leaped at the sound of her voice; I threw myself at her feet, and in transports of the most lively joy, pressed my lips upon her hand. I am ignorant whether she had received any recent information of me. I discovered but little surprise on her countenance, and no sorrow. "Poor child!" said she, in an affectionate tone, "art thou here again? I knew you were too young for this journey; I am very glad, however, that it did not turn out so bad as I apprehended." She then made me recount my history; it was not long, and I did it faithfully: suppressing only some trifling circumstances, but on the whole neither sparing nor excusing myself.

The question was, where I could lodge: she consulted her maid on this point—I hardly dared to breathe during the deliberation; but when I heard I was to sleep in the house, I could scarce contain my joy; and saw the little bundle I brought with me carried into my destined apartment with much the same sensations as St. Preux saw his chaise put up at Madam de Wolmar's. To complete all, I had the satisfaction to find that this favor was not to be transitory; for at a moment when they thought me attentive to something else, I heard Madam de Warrens say, "They may talk as they please, but since Providence has sent him back, I am determined not to abandon him."

Behold me, then, established at her house; not,

however, that I date the happiest days of my life from this period, but this served to prepare me for them. Though that sensibility of heart, which enables us truly to enjoy our being, is the work of Nature, and perhaps a mere effect of organization, yet it requires situations to unfold itself, and without a certain concurrence of favorable circumstances, a man born with the most acute sensibility may go out of the world without ever having been acquainted with his own temperament. This was my case till that time, and such perhaps it might have remained had I never known Madam de Warrens, or even having known her, had I not remained with her long enough to contract that pleasing habit of affectionate sentiments with which she inspired me. I dare affirm, that those who only love, do not feel the most charming sensations we are capable of: I am acquainted with another sentiment, less impetuous, but a thousand times more delightful; sometimes joined with love, but frequently separated from it. This feeling is not simply friendship; it is more enchanting, more tender; nor do I imagine it can exist between persons of the same sex; at least I have been truly a friend, if ever a man was, and yet never experienced it in that kind. This distinction is not sufficiently clear, but will become so hereafter: sentiments are only distinguishable by their effects.

Madam de Warrens inhabited an old house, but large enough to have a handsome spare apartment, which she made her drawing-room. I now occupied this chamber, which was in the passage I have before mentioned as the place of our first meeting. Beyond the brook and gardens was a prospect of the country, which was by no means uninteresting to the young inhabitant, being the first time, since my residence at Bossey, that I had seen anything before my windows but walls, roofs, or the dirty street. How pleasing then was this novelty! it helped to increase the tenderness of my disposition, for I looked on this charming landscape as the gift of my dear patroness, who I could almost fancy had placed it there on purpose for me. Peaceably seated, my eyes pursued her amidst the flowers and the verdure; her charms seemed to me confounded with those of the spring; my heart, till now contracted, here found means to expand itself, and my sighs exhaled freely in this charming retreat.

The magnificence I had been accustomed to at Turin was not to be found at Madam de Warrens', but in lieu of it there was neatness, regularity, and a patriarchal abundance, which is seldom attached to pompous ostentation. She had very little plate, no china, no game in her kitchen, or foreign wines in her cellar, but both were well furnished, and at every one's service; and her coffee, though served in earthenware cups, was excellent. Whoever came to her house was invited to dine there, and never did laborer, messenger, or traveler, depart without refreshment. Her family consisted of a pretty chambermaid from Fribourg, named Merceret; a valet from her own country called Claude Anet (of whom I shall speak hereafter), a cook, and two hired chairmen when she visited, which seldom happened. This was a great deal to be done out of two thousand livres a year; yet, with good management, it might have been sufficient, in a country where land is extremely good, and money very scarce. Unfortunately, economy was never her favorite virtue; she contracted debts—paid them— thus her money passed from hand to hand like a weaver's shuttle, and quickly disappeared.

The arrangement of her housekeeping was exactly what I should have chosen, and I shared it with satisfaction. I was least pleased with the necessity of remaining too long at table. Madam de Warrens was so much incommoded with the first smell of soup or meat, as almost to occasion fainting; from this she slowly recovered, talking meantime, and never attempting to eat for the first half hour. I could have dined thrice in the time, and had ever finished my meal long before she began; I then ate again for company; and though by this means I usually dined twice, felt no inconvenience from it. In short, I was perfectly at my ease, and the happier as my situation required no care. Not being at this time instructed in the state of her finances, I supposed her means were adequate to her expense; and though I afterwards found the same abundance, yet when instructed in her real situation, finding her pension ever anticipated, prevented me from enjoying the same tranquillity. Foresight with me has always embittered enjoyment; in vain I saw the approach of misfortunes, I was never the more likely to avoid them.

From the first moment of our meeting, the softest familiarity was established between us, and in the same degree it continued during the rest of her life. Child was my name, Mamma was hers, and child and mamma we have ever continued, even after a number of years had almost effaced the apparent difference of age between us. I think those names convey an exact idea of our behavior, the simplicity of our manners, and, above all, the similarity of our dispositions. To me she was the tenderest of mothers, ever preferring my welfare to her own pleasure; and if my own satisfaction found some interest in my attachment to her, it was not to change its nature, but only to render it more exquisite, and infatuate me with the charm of having a mother young and handsome, whom I was delighted to caress: I say literally, to caress, for never did it enter into her imagination to deny me the tenderest maternal kisses and endearments, or into my heart to abuse them. It will be said, our connection was of a different kind: I confess it; but have patience, that will come in its turn.

The sudden sight of her, on our first interview, was the only truly passionate moment she ever inspired me with; and even that was principally the work of surprise. My indiscreet glances never went searching beneath her neckerchief, although the ill-concealed plumpness was quite attractive for them. With her I had neither transports nor desires, but remained in a ravishing calm, sensible of a happiness I could not define.

She was the only person with whom I never experienced that want of conversation, which to me is so painful to endure. Our *tête-à-têtes* were rather an inexhaustible chat than conversation, which could only conclude from interruption. So far from finding discourse difficult, I rather thought it a hardship to be silent; unless, when contemplating her projects, she sank into a reverie; when I silently let her meditate, and gazing on her, was the happiest of men. I had another singular fancy, which was that without pretending to the favor of a *tête-à-tête,* I was perpetually seeking occasion to form them, enjoying such opportunities with rapture; and when importunate visitors broke in upon us, no matter whether it was man or woman, I went out murmuring, not being able to remain a secondary object in her company; then, counting the minutes in her antechamber, I used to curse these eternal visitors, thinking it inconceivable how they could find so much to say, because I had still more.

If ever I felt the full force of my attachment, it was when I did not see her. When in her presence, I was only content; when absent, my uneasiness reached almost to melancholy, and a wish to live with her gave me emotions of tenderness even to tears. Never shall I forget one great holiday, while she was at vespers, when I took a walk out of the city, my heart full of her image, and the ardent wish to pass my life with her. I could easily enough see that at present this was impossible; that the happiness I enjoyed would be of short duration, and this idea gave to my contemplations a tincture of melancholy, which, however, was not gloomy, but tempered with a flattering hope. The ringing of bells, which ever particularly affects me, the singing of birds, the fineness of the day, the beauty of the landscape, the scattered country houses, among which in idea I placed our future dwelling, altogether struck me with an impression so lively, tender, melancholy, and powerful, that I saw myself in ecstasy transported into that happy time and abode, where my heart, possessing all the felicity it could desire, might taste it with raptures inexpressible. I never recollect to have enjoyed the future with such force of illusion as at that time; and what has particularly struck me in the recollection of this reverie is that, when realized, I found my situation exactly as I had imagined it. If ever waking dream had an appearance of a prophetic vision, it was assuredly this; I was only deceived in its imaginary duration, for days, years, and life itself, passed ideally in perfect tranquillity, while the reality lasted but a moment. Alas! my most durable happiness was but as a dream, which I had no sooner had a glimpse of, than I instantly awoke.

I know not when I should have done, if I was to enter into a detail of all the follies that affection for my dear Madam de Warrens made me commit. When absent from her, how often have I kissed the bed on a supposition that she had slept there; the curtains and all the furniture of my chamber, on recollecting they were hers, and that her charming hands had touched them; nay, the floor itself, when I considered she had walked there. Sometimes even in her presence extravagancies escaped me, which only the most violent passions seemed capable of inspiring; in a word, there was but one essential difference to distinguish me from an absolute lover, and that particular renders my situation almost inconceivable.

I had returned from Italy, not absolutely as I went there, but as no one of my age, perhaps, ever did before, being equally unacquainted with women. My ardent constitution had found resources in those means by which youth of my disposition sometimes preserve their purity at the expense of health, vigor, and frequently of life itself. My local situation should likewise be considered—living with a pretty woman, cherishing her image in the bottom of my heart, seeing her during the whole day, at night surrounded with objects that recalled her incessantly to my remembrance, and sleeping in the bed where I knew she had slept. What a situation! Who can read this without supposing me on the brink of the grave? But quite the contrary; that which might have ruined me, acted as a preservative, at least for a time. Intoxicated with the charm of living with her, with the ardent desire of passing my life there, absent or present I saw in her a tender mother, an amiable sister, a respected friend, but nothing more; meantime, her image filled my heart, and left room for no other object. The extreme tenderness with which she inspired me excluded every other woman from my consideration, and preserved me from the whole sex: in a word, I was virtuous, because I loved her. Let these particulars, which I recount but indifferently, be considered, and then let any one judge what kind of attachment I had for her: for my part, all I can say, is, that if it hitherto appears extraordinary, it will appear much more so in the sequel.

My time passed in the most agreeable manner, though occupied in a way which was by no means calculated to please me; such as having projects to digest, bills to write fair, receipts to transcribe, herbs to pick, drugs to pound, or distillations to attend; and in the midst of all this, came crowds of travelers, beggars, and visitors of all denominations. Sometimes it was necessary to converse at the same time with a soldier, an apothecary, a prebendary, a fine lady, and a lay brother. I grumbled, swore, and wished all this troublesome medley at the devil, while she seemed to enjoy it, laughing at my chagrin till the tears ran down her cheeks. What excited her mirth still more, was to see that my anger was increased by not being able myself to refrain from laughter. These little intervals, in which I enjoyed the pleasure of grumbling, were charming; and if, during the dispute, another importunate visitor arrived, she would add to her amusement by maliciously prolonging the visit, meantime casting glances at me for which I could almost have beat her; nor could she without difficulty refrain from laughter on seeing my constrained politeness, though every moment glancing at her the look of a fury, while, even in spite of myself, I thought the scene truly diverting.

All this, without being pleasing in itself, contributed to amuse, because it made up a part of a life which I thought delightful. Nothing that was performed around me, nothing that I was obliged to do, suited my taste, but everything suited my heart; and I believe, at length, I should have liked the study of medicine, had not my natural distaste to it perpetually engaged us in whimsical scenes, that prevented my thinking of it in a serious light. It was, perhaps, the first time that this art produced mirth. I pretended to distinguish a physical book by its smell, and what was more diverting, was seldom mistaken. Madam de Warrens made me taste the most nauseous drugs; in vain I ran, or endeavored to defend myself; spite of resistance or wry faces, spite of my struggles, or even of my teeth, when I saw her charming fingers approach my lips, I was obliged to give up the contest.

When shut up in an apartment with all her medical apparatus, any one to have heard us running and shouting amidst peals of laughter would rather have imagined we had been acting a farce than preparing opiates or elixirs.

My time, however, was not entirely passed in these fooleries; in the apartment which I occupied I found a few books: there was the Spectator, Puffendorf, St.

Evremond, and the Henriade. Though I had not my old passion for books, yet I amused myself with reading a part of them. The Spectator was particularly pleasing and serviceable to me. The Abbé de Gauvon had taught me to read less eagerly, and with a greater degree of attention, which rendered my studies more serviceable. I accustomed myself to reflect on elocution and the elegance of composition; exercising myself in discerning pure French from my provincial idiom. For example, I corrected an orthographical fault (which I had in common with all Genevese) by these two lines of the Henriade:

Soit qu'un ancient respect pour le sang de leurs maîtres,
Parlât encore pour lui dans le cœur de ces traîtres.

I was struck with the word *parlât,* and found a *t* was necessary to form the third person of the subjunctive, whereas I had always written and pronounced it *parla,* as in the present of the indicative.

Sometimes my studies were the subject of conversation with Madam de Warrens; sometimes I read to her, in which I found great satisfaction; and as I endeavored to read well, it was extremely serviceable to me. I have already observed that her mind was cultivated; her understanding was at this time in its meridian. Several people of learning having been assiduous to ingratiate themselves, had taught her to distinguish works of merit; but her taste (if I may so express myself) was rather Protestant; ever speaking warmly of Bayle, and highly esteeming St. Evremond, though long since almost forgotten in France: but this did not prevent her having a taste for literature, or expressing her thoughts with elegance. She had been brought up with polite company, and coming young to Savoy, by associating with people of the best fashion, had lost the affected manners of her own country, where the ladies mistake wit for sense, and only speak in epigram.

Though she had seen the court but superficially, that glance was sufficient to give her a competent idea of it; and notwithstanding secret jealousies and the murmurs excited by her conduct and running in debt, she ever preserved friends there, and never lost her pension. She knew the world, and was possessed of sense and reflection to make her experience useful. This was her favorite theme in our conversations, and was directly opposite to my chimerical ideas, though the kind of instruction I particularly had occasion for. We read Bruyere together; he pleased her more than Rochefoucault, who is a dull, melancholy author, particularly to youth, who are not fond of contemplating man as he really is. In moralizing she sometimes bewildered herself by the length of her discourse; but by kissing her lips or hand from time to time I was easily consoled, and never found them wearisome.

This life was too delightful to be lasting; I felt this, and the uneasiness that thought gave me was the only thing that disturbed my enjoyment. Even in playfulness she studied my disposition, observed and interrogated me, forming projects for my future fortune, which I could readily have dispensed with. Happily it was not sufficient to know my disposition, inclinations, and talents; it was likewise necessary to find a situation in which they would be useful, and this was not the work of a day. Even the prejudices this good woman had conceived in favor of my merit put off the time of calling it into action, by rendering her more difficult in the choice of means: thus (thanks to the good opinion she entertained of me), everything answered to my wish; but a change soon happened which put a period to my tranquillity.

A relation of Madam de Warrens, named M. d'Aubonne, came to see her: a man of great understanding and intrigue, being, like her, fond of projects, though careful not to ruin himself by them. He had offered Cardinal Fleury a very compact plan for a lottery, which, however, had not been approved of, and he was now going to propose it to the court of Turin, where it was accepted and put into execution. He remained some time at Annecy, where he fell in love with the Intendant's lady, who was very amiable, much to my taste, and the only person I saw with pleasure at the house of Madam de Warrens. M. d'Aubonne saw me, I was strongly recommended by his relation; he promised, therefore, to question and see what I was fit for, and, if he found me capable to seek me a situation. Madam de Warrens sent me to him two or three mornings, under pretense of messages, without acquainting me with her real intention. He spoke to me gayly, on various subjects, without any appearance of observation; his familiarity presently set me talking, which by his cheerful and jesting manner he encouraged without restraint—I was absolutely charmed with him. The result of his observations was, that notwithstanding the animation of my countenance, and promising exterior, if not absolutely silly, I was a lad of very little sense, and without ideas of learning; in fine, very ignorant in all respects, and if I could arrive at being curate of some village, it was the utmost honor I ought ever to aspire to. Such was the account he gave of me to Madam de Warrens. This was not the first time such an opinion had been formed of me, neither was it the last; the judgment of M. Masseron having been repeatedly confirmed.

The cause of these opinions is too much connected with my character not to need a particular explanation; for it will not be supposed that I can in conscience subscribe to them: and with all possible impartiality, whatever M. Masseron, M. d'Aubonne and many others may have said, I cannot help thinking them mistaken.

Two things, very opposite, unite in me, and in a manner which I cannot myself conceive. My disposition is extremely ardent, my passions lively and impetuous, yet my ideas are produced slowly, with great embarrassment and after much afterthought. It might be said my heart and understanding do not belong to the same individual. A sentiment takes possession of my soul with the rapidity of lightning, but instead of illuminating, it dazzles and confounds me; I feel all, but see nothing; I am warm, but stupid; to think I must be cool. What is astonishing, my conception is clear and penetrating, if not hurried: I can make excellent impromptus at leisure, but on the instant, could never say or do anything worth notice. I could hold a tolerable conversation by the post, as they say the Spaniards play at chess, and when I read that anecdote of a duke of Savoy, who turned himself round, while on a journey, to cry out *à votre gorge, marchand de Paris!* I said, "Here is a trait of my character!"

This slowness of thought, joined to vivacity of feeling, I am not only sensible of in conversation, but even alone. When I write, my ideas are arranged with the utmost difficulty. They glance on my imagination and ferment till they discompose, heat, and bring on a palpitation; during this state of agitation, I see nothing properly, cannot write a single word, and must wait till it is over. Insensibly the agitation subsides, the chaos acquires form, and each circumstance takes its proper place. Have you never seen an opera in Italy? where during the change of scene everything is in confusion, the decorations are intermingled, and any one would suppose that all would be overthrown; yet by little and little, everything is arranged, nothing appears wanting, and we feel surprised to see the tumult succeeded by the most delightful spectacle. This is a resemblance of what passes in my brain when I attempt to write; had I always waited till that confusion was past, and then pointed, in their natural beauties, the objects that had presented themselves, few authors would have surpassed me.

Thence arises the extreme difficulty I find in writing; my manuscripts, blotted scratched, and scarcely legible, attest the trouble they cost me; nor is there one of them but I have been obliged to transcribe four or five times before it went to press. Never could I do anything when placed at a table, pen in hand; it must be walking among the rocks, or in the woods; it is at night in my bed, during my wakeful hours, that I compose; it may be judged how slowly, particularly for a man who has not the advantage of verbal memory, and never in his life could retain by heart six verses. Some of my periods I have turned and returned in my head five or six nights before they were fit to be put to paper: thus it is that I succeed better in works that require laborious attention, than those that appear more trivial, such as letters, in which I could never succeed, and being obliged to write one is to me a serious punishment; nor can I express my thoughts on the most trivial subjects without it costing me hours of fatigue. If I write immediately what strikes me, my letter is a long, confused, unconnected string of expressions, which, when read, can hardly be understood.

It is not only painful to me to give language to my ideas, but even to receive them. I have studied mankind, and think myself a tolerable observer, yet I know nothing from what I see, but all from what I remember, nor have I understanding except in my recollections. From all that is said, from all that passes in my presence, I feel nothing, conceive nothing, the exterior sign being all that strikes me; afterwards it returns to my remembrance; I recollect the place, the time, the manner, the look, and gesture, not a circumstance escapes me; it is, then, from what has been done or said, that I imagine what has been thought, and I have rarely found myself mistaken.

So little master of my understanding when alone, let any one judge what I must be in conversation, where to speak with any degree of ease you must think of a thousand things at the same time: the bare idea that I should forget something material would be sufficient to intimidate me. Nor can I comprehend how people can have the confidence to converse in large companies, where each word must pass in review before so many, and where it would be requisite to know their several characters and histories to avoid saying what might give offense. In this particular, those who frequent the world would have a great advantage, as they know better where to be silent, and can speak with greater confidence; yet even they sometimes let fall absurdities; in what predicament then must he be who drops as it were from the clouds? It is almost impossible he should speak ten minutes with impunity.

In a *tête-à-tête* there is a still worse inconvenience; that is, the necessity of talking perpetually, at least, the necessity of answering when spoken to, and keeping up the conversation when the other is silent. This insupportable constraint is alone sufficient to disgust me with society, for I cannot form an idea of a greater torment than being obliged to speak continually without time for recollection. I know not whether it proceeds from my mortal hatred to all constraint; but if I am obliged to speak, I infallibly talk nonsense. What is still worse, instead of learning how to be silent when I have absolutely nothing to say, it is generally at such times that I have a violent inclination; and, endeavoring to pay my debt of conversation as speedily as possible, I hastily gabble a number of words without ideas, happy when they only chance to mean nothing: thus endeavoring to conquer or hide my incapacity, I rarely fail to show it.

I think I have said enough to show that, though not a fool, I have frequently passed for one, even among people capable of judging; this was the more vexatious, as my physiognomy and eyes promised otherwise, and expectation being frustrated, my stupidity appeared the more shocking. This detail, which a particular occasion gave birth to, will not be useless in the sequel, being a key to many of my actions which might otherwise appear unaccountable; and have been attributed to a savage humor I do not possess. I love society as much as any man, was I not certain to exhibit myself in it, not only disadvantageously, but totally different from what I really am. The plan I have adopted of writing and retirement, is what exactly suits me. Had I been present, my worth would never have been known, no one would even have suspected it; thus it was with Madam Dupin, a woman of sense, in whose house I lived for several years; indeed, she has often since owned it to me: though on the whole this rule may be subject to some exceptions. I shall now return to my history.

The estimate of my talents thus fixed, the situation I was capable of premised, the question only remained how to render me capable of fulfilling my destined vocation. The principal difficulty was, I did not know Latin enough for a priest. Madam de Warrens determined to have me taught for some time at the seminary, and accordingly spoke of it to the superior, who was a Lazarist, called M. Gros, a good-natured little fellow, half blind, meager, gray-haired, insensible, and the least pedantic of any Lazarist I ever knew; which, in fact, is saying no great matter.

He frequently visited Madam de Warrens, who entertained, caressed, and made much of him, letting him sometimes lace her stays, an office he was willing enough to perform. While thus employed, she would run about the room, this way or that, as occasion happened to call her. Drawn by the lace, Monsieur the Superior followed, grumbling, repeating at every moment, "Pray, madam, do stand still;" the whole forming a scene truly diverting.

M. Gros willingly assented to the project of Madam de Warrens, and, for a very moderate pension, charged himself with the care of instructing me. The consent of the bishop was all that remained necessary, who not only granted it, but offered to pay the pension, permitting me to retain the secular habit till they could judge by a trial what success they might have in my improvement.

What a change! but I was obliged to submit; though I went to the seminary with about the same spirits as if they had been taking me to execution. What a melancholy abode! especially for one who left the house of a pretty woman. I carried one book with me, that I had borrowed of Madam de Warrens, and found it a capital resource! It will not be easily conjectured what kind of book this was—it was a music book. Among the talents she had cultivated, music was not forgotten; she had a tolerably good voice, sang agreeably, and played on the harpsichord. She had taken the pains to give me some lessons in singing, though before I was very uninformed in that respect, hardly knowing the music of our psalms. Eight or ten interrupted lessons, far from putting me in a condition to improve myself, did not teach me half the notes; notwithstanding, I had such a passion for the art, that I determined to exercise myself alone. The book I took was not of the most easy kind; it was the cantatas of Clerambault. It may be conceived with what attention and perseverance I studied, when I inform my reader, that without knowing anything of transposition or quantity, I contrived to sing, with tolerable correctness, the first recitative and air in the cantata of Alpheus and Arethusa: it is true this air is so justly set, that it is only necessary to recite the verses in their just measure to catch the music.

There was at the seminary a curst Lazarist, who by undertaking to teach me Latin made me detest it. His hair was coarse, black, and greasy, his face like those formed in gingerbread; he had the voice of a buffalo, the countenance of an owl, and the bristles of a boar in lieu of a beard; his smile was sardonic, and his limbs played like those of a puppet moved by wires. I have forgotten his odious name, but the re-membrance of his frightful precise countenance re-mains with me, though hardly can I recollect it with-out trembling; especially when I call to mind our meeting in the gallery, when he graciously advanced his filthy square cap as a sign for me to enter his apart-ment, which appeared more dismal in my apprehen-sion than a dungeon. Let any one judge the contrast between my present master and the elegant Abbé de Gauvon.

Had I remained two months at the mercy of this monster, I am certain my head could not have sus-tained it; but the good M. Gros, perceiving I was melancholy, grew thin, and did not eat my victuals, guessed the cause of my uneasiness (which indeed was not very difficult) and taking me from the claws of this beast, by another yet more striking contrast, placed me with the gentlest of men, a young Faucig-neran abbé, named M. Gatier, who studied at the seminary, and out of complaisance for M. Gros, and humanity to myself, spared some time from the prosecution of his own studies in order to direct mine. Never did I see a more pleasing countenance than that of M. Gatier. He was fair complexioned, his beard rather inclined to red; his behavior, like that of the generality of his countrymen (who under a coarseness of countenance conceal much understanding), marked in him a truly sensible and affectionate soul. In his large blue eyes there was a mixture of softness, tenderness, and melancholy, which made it impossible to see him without feeling one's self interested. From the looks and manner of this young abbé he might have been supposed to have foreseen his destiny, and that he was born to be unhappy.

His disposition did not belie his physiognomy: full of patience and complaisance, he rather appeared to study with than instruct me. So much was not necessary to make me love him, his predecessor having rendered that very easy; yet, notwithstanding all the time he bestowed on me, notwithstanding our mutual good inclinations, and that his plan of teaching was excellent, with much labor, I made little progress. It is very singular, that with a clear conception I could never learn much from masters except my father and M. Lambercier; the little I know besides I have learned alone, as will be seen hereafter. My spirit, impatient of every species of constraint, cannot submit to the law of the moment; even the fear of not learning prevents my being attentive, and a dread of wearying those who teach, makes me feign to understand them; thus they proceed faster than I can comprehend, and the conclusion is I learn nothing. My understanding must take its own time and cannot submit to that of another.

The time of ordination being arrived, M. Gatier returned to his province as deacon, leaving me with gratitude, attachment, and sorrow for his loss. The vows I made for him were no more answered than those I offered for myself. Some years after, I learned, that being vicar of a parish, a young girl was with child by him, being the only one (though he possessed a very tender heart) with whom he was ever in love. This was a dreadful scandal in a diocese severely governed, where the priests (being under good regulation) ought never to have children—except by married women. Having infringed this politic law, he was put in prison, defamed, and driven from his benefice. I know not whether it was ever after in his power to reëstablish his affairs; but the remembrance of his misfortunes, which were deeply engraven on my heart, struck me when I wrote Emilius, and uniting M. Gatier with M. Gaime, I formed from these two worthy priests the character of the Savoyard Vicar, and flatter myself the imitation has not dishonored the originals.

While I was at the seminary, M. d'Aubonne was obliged to quit Annecy, Moultou being displeased that he made love to his wife, which was acting like a dog in the manger, for though Madam Moultou was extremely amiable, he lived very ill with her, treating her with such brutality that a separation was talked of. Moultou, by repeated oppressions, at length procured a dismissal from his employment: he was a disagreeable man; a mole could not be blacker, nor an owl more knavish. It is said the provincials revenge themselves on their enemies by songs; M. d'Aubonne revenged himself on his by a comedy, which he sent to Madam de Warrens, who showed it to me. I was pleased with it, and immediately conceived the idea of writing one, to try whether I was so silly as the author had pronounced me. This project was not executed till I went to Chambery, where I wrote *The Lover of Himself.* Thus when I said in the preface to that piece, "it was written at eighteen," I cut off a few years.

Nearly about this time an event happened, not very important in itself, but whose consequence affected me, and made a noise in the world when I had forgotten it. Once a week I was permitted to go out; it is not necessary to say what use I made of this liberty. Being one Sunday at Madam de Warrens', a building belonging to the Cordeliers, which joined her house, took fire; this building which contained their oven, being full of dry fagots, blazed violently and greatly endangered the house; for the wind happening to drive the flames that way, it was covered with them. The furniture, therefore, was hastily got out and carried into the garden which fronted the windows, on the other side the before-mentioned brook. I was so alarmed that I threw indiscriminately everything that came to hand out of the window, even to a large stone mortar, which at another time I should have found it difficult to remove, and should have thrown a handsome looking-glass after it had not some one prevented me. The good bishop, who that day was visiting Madam de Warrens, did not remain idle; he took her into the garden, where they went to prayers with the rest that were assembled there, and where, some time afterwards, I found them on their knees, and presently joined them. While the good man was at his devotions the wind changed, so suddenly and critically that the flames, which had covered the house and began to enter the windows, were carried to the other side of the court, and the house received no damage. Two years after, Monsieur de Berner being dead, the Antoines, his former brethren, began to collect anecdotes which might serve as arguments of his beatification; at the desire of Father Baudet, I joined to these an attestation of what I had just related, in doing which, though I attested no more than the truth, I certainly acted ill, as it tended to make an indifferent occurrence pass for a miracle. I had seen the bishop in prayer, and had likewise seen the wind change during that prayer, and even much to the purpose, all this I could certify truly; but that one of these facts was the cause of the other, I ought not to have attested, because it is what I could not possibly be assured of. Thus much I may say, that as far as I can recollect what my ideas were at that time, I was sincerely, and in good earnest, a Catholic. Love of the marvelous is natural to the human heart; my veneration for the virtuous prelate, and secret pride in having, perhaps, contributed to the event in question, all helped to seduce me; and certainly, if this miracle was the effect of ardent prayer, I had a right to claim a share of the merit.

More than thirty years after, when I published the *Lettres de la Montagne,* M. Freron (I know not by what means) discovered this attestation, and made use of it in his paper. I must confess the discovery was very critically timed, and appeared very diverting, even to me.

I was destined to be the outcast of every condition; for notwithstanding M. Gatier gave the most favorable account he possibly could of my studies, they plainly saw the improvement I received bore no proportion to the pains taken to instruct me, which was no encouragement to continue them: the bishop and superior, therefore, were disheartened, and I was sent back to Madam de Warrens, as a subject not even fit to make a priest of; but as they allowed, at the same time, that I was a tolerably good lad, and far from being vicious, this account counterbalanced the former, and determined her not to abandon me.

I carried back in triumph the dear music book, which had been so useful to me, the air of Alpheus and Arethusa being almost all I had learned at the seminary. My predilection for this art started the idea of making a musician of me. A convenient opportunity offered: once a week, at least, she had a concert at her house, and the music-master from the cathedral, who directed this little band, came frequently to see her. This was a Parisian, named M. le Maitre, a good composer, very lively, gay, young, well made, of little understanding, but, upon the whole, a good sort of man. Madam de Warrens made us acquainted; I attached myself to him, and he seemed not displeased with me. A pension was talked of, and agreed on; in short, I went home with him, and passed the winter the more agreeably at his chambers, as they were not above twenty paces distance from Madam de Warrens', where we frequently supped together. It may easily be supposed that this situation, ever gay, and singing with the musicians and children of the choir, was more pleasing to me than the seminary and fathers of St. Lazarus. This life, though free, was regular; here I learned to prize independence, but never to abuse it. For six whole months I never once went out except to see Madam de Warrens, or to church, nor had I any inclination to it. This interval is one of those in which I enjoyed the greatest satisfaction, and which I have ever recollected with pleasure. Among the various situations I have been placed in, some were marked with such an idea of virtuous satisfaction, that the bare remembrance affects me as if they were yet present. I vividly recollect the time, the place, the persons, and even the temperature of the air, while the lively idea of a certain local impression peculiar to those times, transports me back again to the very spot; for example, all that was repeated at our meetings, all that was sung in the choir, everything that passed there; the beautiful and noble habits of the canons, the chasubles of the priests, the miters of the singers, the persons of the musicians; an old lame carpenter who played the counter-bass, a little fair abbé who performed on the violin, the ragged cassock which M. le Maitre, after taking off his sword, used to put over his secular habit, and the fine surplice with which he covered the rags of the former, when he went to the choir; the pride with which I held my little flute to my lips, and seated myself in the orchestra, to assist in a recitative which M. le Maitre had composed on purpose for me; the good dinner that afterwards awaited us, and the good appetites we carried to it. This concourse of objects, strongly retraced in my memory, has charmed me a hundred times as much, or perhaps more, than ever the reality had done. I have always preserved an effection for a certain air of the *Conditor alme Syderum,* because one Sunday in Advent I heard that hymn sung on the steps of the cathedral (according to the custom of that place) as I lay in bed before daybreak. Mademoiselle Merceret, Madam de Warrens' chambermaid, knew something of music; I shall never forget a little piece that M. le Maitre made me sing with her, and which her mistress listened to with great satisfaction. In a word, every particular, even down to the servant Perrine, whom the boys of the choir took such delight in teasing. The remembrance of these times of happiness and innocence frequently returning to my mind, both ravish and affect me.

I lived at Annecy during a year without the least reproach, giving universal satisfaction. Since my departure from Turin, I had been guilty of no folly, committed none while under the eye of Madam de Warrens. She was my conductor, and ever led me right; my attachment for her became my only passion, and what proves it was not a giddy one, my heart and understanding were in unison. It is true that a single sentiment, absorbing all my faculties, put me out of a capacity of learning even music: but this was not my fault, since to the strongest inclination, I added the utmost assiduity. I was inattentive and thoughtful; what could I do? Nothing was wanting towards my progress that depended on me; meantime, it only required a subject that might inspire me to occasion the commission of new follies: that subject presented itself, chance arranged it, and (as will be seen hereafter) my inconsiderate head gave in to it.

One evening, in the month of February, when it was very cold, being all sat round the fire, we heard some one knock at the street door. Perrine took a light, went down and opened it: a young man entering, came upstairs, presented himself with an easy air, and making M. le Maitre a short but well-turned compliment, announced himself as a French musician, constrained by the state of his finances to take this liberty. The heart of the good Le Maitre leaped at the name of a French musician, for he passionately loved both his country and profession; he therefore offered the young traveler his service and use of his apartment, which he appeared to stand much in need of, and which he accepted without much ceremony. I observed him while he was chatting and warming himself before supper; he was short and thick, having some fault in his shape, though without any particular deformity; he had (if I may so express myself) an appearance of being hunchbacked, with flat shoulders, and I think he limped. He wore a black coat, rather worn than old, which hung in tatters, a very fine but dirty shirt, frayed ruffles; a pair of splatter-dashes so large that he could have put both legs into either of them, and, to secure himself from the snow, a little hat, only fit to be carried under the arm. With this whimsical equipage he had, however, something elegant in his manners and conversation; his countenance was expressive and agreeable, and he spoke with facility if not with modesty; in short, everything about him bore the marks of a young debauchée, who did not crave assistance like a beggar, but as a thoughtless madcap. He told us his name was Venture de Villeneuve, that he came from Paris, had lost his way, and seeming to forget that he had announced himself for a musician, added that he was going to Grenoble to see a relation that was a member of parliament.

During supper we talked of music, on which subject he spoke well: he knew all the great virtuosi, all the celebrated works, all the actors, actresses, pretty women, and powerful lords; in short nothing was mentioned but what he seemed thoroughly acquainted with. Though no sooner was any topic started, than by some drollery, which set every one a-laughing, he made them forget what had been said. This was on a Saturday; the next day there was to be music at the cathedral: M. le Maitre asked if he would sing there—"Very willingly."—"What part would he choose?"—"The counter-tenor:" and immediately began speaking of other things. Before he went to church they offered him his part to peruse, but he did not even look at it. This Gasconade surprised Le Maitre—"You'll see," said he, whispering to me, "that he does not know a single note."—I replied, "I am very much afraid of him." I followed them into the church; but was extremely uneasy, and when they began, my heart beat violently, so much was I interested in his behalf.

I was presently out of pain: he sung his two recitatives with all imaginable taste and judgment; and what was yet more, with a very agreeable voice. I never enjoyed a more pleasing surprise. After mass, M. Venture received the highest compliments from the canons and musicians, which he answered jokingly, though with great grace. M. le Maitre embraced him heartily; I did the same; he saw I was rejoiced at his success, and appeared pleased at my satisfaction.

The reader will assuredly agree with me, that after having been delighted with M. Bacle, who had little to attract my admiration, I should be infatuated with M. Venture, who had education, wit, talents, and a knowledge of the world, and might be called an agreeable rake. It is true, he boasted of many things he did not understand, but of those he knew (which were very numerous) he said nothing, patiently waiting some occasion to display them, which he then did with ease, though without forwardness, and thus gave them more effect. Playful, giddy, inexhaustible, seducing in conversation, ever smiling, but never laughing, and repeating the rudest things in the most elegant manner. Even the most modest women were astonished at what they endured from him: it was in vain for them to determine to be angry; they could not assume the appearance of it. He only wished abandoned women, and I do not believe he was capable of having good luck with women, but could only add an infinite charm to the society of people who had his luck. It was extraordinary that with so many agreeable talents, in a country where they are so well understood, and so much admired, he so long remained only a musician.

My attachment to M. Venture, more reasonable in its cause, was also less extravagant in its effects, though more lively and durable than that I had conceived for M. Bacle. I loved to see him, to hear him, all his actions appeared charming, everything he said was an oracle to me, but the enchantment did not extend far enough to disable me from quitting him. I had a preservative against this excess near me. I found besides, that his maxims were very good for him, but felt that I had no use for them; I needed another kind of voluptuousness, of which he had no idea, and of which I not even dared speak, as I was sure, he would only make fun of me. Still I would unite this attachment to the one that governed me. I spoke of him with transport to Madam de Warrens, Le Maitre likewise spoke in his praise, and she consented we should bring him to her house. This interview did not succeed; he thought her affected, she found him a libertine, and, alarmed that I had formed such an ill acquaintance, not only forbade me bringing him there again, but likewise painted so strongly the danger I ran with this young man, that I became a little more circumspect in giving in to the attachment; and very happily, both for my manners and wits, we were soon separated.

M. le Maitre, like most of his profession, loved good wine; at table he was moderate, but when busy in his closet he must drink. His maid was so well acquainted with this humor that no sooner had he prepared his paper to compose, and taken his violoncello, than the bottle and glass arrived, and was replenished from time to time: thus, without being ever absolutely intoxicated, he was usually in a state of elevation. This was really unfortunate, for he had a good heart, and was so playful that Madam de Warrens used to call him *the kitten*. Unhappily, he loved his profession, labored much and drank proportionally, which injured his health, and at length soured his temper. Sometimes he was gloomy and easily offended, though incapable of rudeness, or giving offense to any one, for never did he utter a harsh word, even to the boys of the choir: on the other hand, he would not suffer another to offend him, which was but just: the misfortune was, having little understanding, he did not properly discriminate, and was often angry without cause.

The Chapter of Geneva, where so many princes and bishops formerly thought it an honor to be seated, though in exile it lost its ancient splendor, retained (without any diminution) its pride. To be admitted, you must either be a gentleman or Doctor of Sorbonne. If there is a pardonable pride, after that derived from personal merit, it is doubtless that arising from birth, though, in general, priests having laymen in their service treat them with sufficient haughtiness, and thus the canons behaved to poor Le Maitre. The chanter, in particular, who was called the Abbé de Vidonne, in other respects a well-behaved man, but too full of his nobility, did not always show him the attention his talents merited. M. le Maitre could not bear these indignities patiently; and this year, during passion week, they had a more serious dispute than ordinary. At an institution dinner that the bishop gave the canons, and to which Le Maitre was always invited, the abbé failed in some formality, adding, at the same time, some harsh words, which the other could not digest; he instantly formed the resolution to quit them the following night; nor could any consideration make him give up his design, though Madam de Warrens (whom he went to take leave of) spared no pains to appease him. He could not relinquish the pleasure of leaving his tyrants embarrassed for the Easter feast, at which time he knew they stood in greatest need of him. He was most concerned about his music, which he wished to take with him; but this could not easily be accomplished, as it filled a large case, and was very heavy, and could not be carried under the arms.

Madam de Warrens did what I should have done in her situation; and indeed, what I should yet do: after many useless efforts to retain him, seeing he was resolved to depart, whatever might be the event, she formed the resolution to give him every possible assistance. I must confess Le Maitre deserved it of her, for he was (if I may use the expression) dedicated to her service, in whatever appertained to either his art or knowledge, and the readiness with which he obliged gave a double value to his complaisance: thus she only paid back, on an essential occasion, the many favors he had been long conferring on her; though I should observe, she possessed a soul that, to fulfill such duties, had no occasion to be reminded of previous obligation. Accordingly she ordered me to follow Le Maitre to Lyons, and continue with him as long as he might have occasion for my services. She has since avowed, that a desire of detaching me from Venture had a great hand in this arrangement. She consulted Claude Anet about the conveyance of the above-mentioned case. He advised, that instead of hiring a beast of Annecy, which would infallibly discover us, it would be better, at night, to take it to some neighboring village, and there hire an ass to carry it to Seyssel, which being in the French dominions, we should have nothing to fear. This plan was adopted; we departed the same night at seven, and Madam de Warrens, under pretense of paying my expenses, increased the purse of poor Le Maitre by an addition that was very acceptable. Claude Anet, the gardener, and myself, carried the case to the first village, then hired an ass, and the same night reached Seyssel.

I think I have already remarked that there are times in which I am so unlike myself that I might be taken for a man of a direct opposite disposition; I shall now give an example of this. M. Reydelet, curate of Seyssel, was canon of St. Peter's, consequently known to M. le Maitre, and one of the people from whom he should have taken most pains to conceal himself; my advice, on the contrary, was to present ourselves to him, and, under some pretext, entreat entertainment as if we visited him by consent of the chapter. Le Maitre adopted this idea, which seemed to give his revenge an appearance of satire and waggery; in short, we went boldly to Reydelet, who received us very kindly. Le Maitre told him he was going to Bellay by desire of the bishop, that he might superintend the music during the Easter holidays, and that he proposed returning that way in a few days. To support this tale, I told a hundred others, so naturally that M. Reydelet thought me a very agreeable youth, and treated me with great friendship and civility. We were well regaled and well lodged: M.

Reydelet scarcely knew how to make enough of us; and we parted the best friends in the world, with a promise to stop longer on our return. We found it difficult to refrain from laughter, or wait till we were alone to give free vent to our mirth: indeed, even now, the bare recollection of it forces a smile, for never was waggery better or more fortunately maintained. This would have made us merry during the remainder of our journey, if M. le Maitre (who did not cease drinking) had not been two or three times attacked with a complaint that he afterwards became very subject to, and which resembled an epilepsy. These fits threw me into the most fearful embarrassments, from which I resolved to extricate myself with the first opportunity.

According to the information given to M. Reydelet, we passed our Easter holidays at Bellay, and though not expected there, were received by the music-master, and welcomed by every one with great pleasure. M. le Maitre was of considerable note in his profession, and, indeed, merited that distinction. The music-master of Bellay (who was fond of his own works) endeavored to obtain the approbation of so good a judge; for besides being a connoisseur, M. le Maitre was equitable, neither a jealous, ill-natured critic, nor a servile flatterer. He was so superior to the generality of country music-masters, and they were so sensible of it, that they treated him rather as their chief than a brother musician.

Having passed four or five days very agreeably at

Bellay, we departed, and continuing our journey without meeting with any accidents, except those I have just spoken of, arrived at Lyons, and were lodged at *Notre Dame de Pitie*. While we waited for the arrival of the before-mentioned case (which by the assistance of another lie, and the care of our good patron, M. Reydelet, we had embarked on the Rhone) M. le Maitre went to visit his acquaintance, and among others Father Caton, a Cordelier, who will be spoken of hereafter, and the Abbé Dortan, Count of Lyons, both of whom received him well, but afterwards betrayed him, as will be seen presently; indeed, his good fortune terminated with M. Reydelet.

Two days after our arrival at Lyons, as we passed a little street not far from our inn, Le Maitre was attacked by one of his fits; but it was now so violent as to give me the utmost alarm. I screamed with terror, called for help, and naming our inn, entreated some one to bear him to it; then (while the people were assembled, and busy round a man that had fallen senseless in the street) he was abandoned by the only friend on whom he could have any reasonable dependence; I seized the instant when no one heeded me, turned the corner of the street and disappeared. Thanks to Heaven, I have made my third painful confession; if many such remained, I should certainly abandon the work I have undertaken.

Of all the incidents I have yet related, a few traces are remaining in the places where I then lived; but what I have to relate in the following book is almost

entirely unknown; these are the greatest extravagancies of my life, and it is happy they had not a worse
conclusion. My head (if I may use the simile) screwed
up to the pitch of an instrument it did not naturally
accord with, had lost its diapason; in time it returned
to it again, when I discontinued my follies, or at least
gave in to those more consonant to my disposition.
This epoch of my youth I am least able to recollect,
nothing having passed sufficiently interesting to influence my heart, or make me clearly retrace the remembrance. In so many successive changes, it is difficult
not to make some transpositions of time or place. I
write absolutely from memory, without notes or materials to help my recollection. Some events are as
fresh in my idea as if they had recently happened, but
there are certain chasms which I cannot fill up but by
the aid of recital, as confused as the remaining traces
of those to which they refer. It is impossible, therefore,
that I may have erred in trifles, and perhaps shall
again, but in every matter of importance I can answer
that the account is faithfully exact, and with the same
veracity the reader may depend I shall be careful to
continue it.

My resolution was soon taken after quitting Le
Maitre; I set out immediately for Annecy. The cause
and mystery of our departure had interested me for
the security of our retreat: this interest, which entirely
employed my thoughts for some days, had banished
every other idea; but no sooner was I secure and in
tranquillity, than my predominant sentiment regained

its place. Nothing flattered, nothing tempted me, I had no wish but to return to Madam de Warrens; the tenderness and truth of my attachment to her had rooted from my heart every imaginable project, and all the follies of ambition; I conceived no happiness but living near her, nor could I take a step without feeling that the distance between us was increased. I returned, therefore, as soon as possible, with such speed, and with my spirits in such a state of agitation, that though I recall with pleasure all my other travels, I have not the least recollection of this, only remembering my leaving Lyons and reaching Annecy. Let any one judge whether this last event can have slipped my memory, when informed that on my arrival I found Madam de Warrens was not there, having set out for Paris.

I was never well informed of the motives of this journey. I am certain she would have told me had I asked her, but never was man less curious to learn the secrets of his friend. My heart is ever so entirely filled with the present, or with past pleasures, which become a principal part of my enjoyment, that there is not a chink or corner for curiosity to enter. All that I conceive from what I heard of it, is, that in the revolution caused at Turin by the abdication of the King of Sardinia, she feared being forgotten, and was willing by favor of the intrigues of M. d'Aubonne to seek the same advantage in the court of France, where she has often told me she should have preferred it, as the multiplicity of business there prevents your conduct from being so closely inspected. If this was her business, it is astonishing that on her return she was not ill received; be that as it will, she continued to enjoy her allowance without any interruption. Many people imagined she was charged with some secret commission, either by the bishop, who then had business at the court of France, where he himself was soon after obliged to go, or some one yet more powerful, who knew how to insure her a gracious reception at her return. If this was the case, it is certain the ambassadress was not ill chosen, since being young and handsome, she had all the necessary qualifications to succeed in a negotiation.

BOOK IV

BOOK IV

[*1731–1732*]

LET any one judge my surprise and grief at not finding her on my arrival. I now felt regret at having abandoned M. le Maitre, and my uneasiness increased when I learned the misfortunes that had befallen him. His box of music, containing all his fortune, that precious box, preserved with so much care and fatigue, had been seized on at Lyons by means of Count Dortan, who had received information from the Chapter of our having absconded with it. In vain did Le Maitre reclaim his property, his means of existence, the labor of his life; his right to the music in question was at least subject to litigation, but even that liberty was not allowed him, the affair being instantly decided on the principle of superior strength. Thus poor Le Maitre lost the fruit of his talents, the labor of his youth, and principal dependence for the support of old age.

Nothing was wanting to render the news I had received truly afflicting, but I was at an age when even the greatest calamities are to be sustained; accordingly I soon found consolation. I expected shortly to hear news of Madam de Warrens, though I was ignorant of the address, and she knew nothing of my return. As to my desertion of Le Maitre (all things considered) I did not find it so very culpable. I had been serviceable to him in his retreat; it was not in my power to give him any further assistance. Had I remained with him in France it would not have cured his complaint. I could not have saved his music, and should only have doubled his expense: in this point of view I then saw my conduct; I see it otherwise now. It frequently happens that a villainous action does not torment us at the instant we commit it, but on recollection, and sometimes even after a number of years have elapsed, for the remembrance of crimes is not to be extinguished.

The only means I had to obtain news of Madam de Warrens was to remain at Annecy. Where should I seek her at Paris? or how bear the expense of such a journey? Sooner or later, there was no place where I could be so certain to hear of her as that I was now at; this consideration determined me to remain there, though my conduct was but indifferent. I did not go to the bishop, who had already befriended me, and might continue to do so: my patroness was not present, and I feared his reprimands on the subject of our flight; neither did I go to the seminary; M. Gros was no longer there; in short, I went to none of my acquaintance. I would gladly have visited the intendant's lady, but did not dare; I did worse, I sought out M. Venture, whom (notwithstanding my enthusiasm) I had never thought of since my departure. I found him quite gay, in high spirits, and the universal favorite of the ladies of Annecy.

This success completed my infatuation; I saw nothing but M. Venture; he almost made me forget even Madam de Warrens. That I might profit more at ease by his instructions and example, I proposed to share his lodging, to which he readily consented. It was at a shoemaker's; a pleasant, jovial fellow, who, in his country dialect, called his wife nothing but trollop; an appellation which she certainly merited. Venture took care to augment their differences, though under an appearance of doing the direct contrary, throwing out in a distant manner, and provincial accent, hints that produced the utmost effect, and furnished such scenes as were sufficient to make any one die with laughter. Thus the mornings passed without our thinking of them; at two or three o'clock we took some refreshment. Venture then went to his various engagements, where he supped, while I walked alone, meditating on his great merit, coveting and admiring his rare talents, and cursing my own unlucky stars, that did not call me to so happy a life. How little did I then know of myself! mine had been a hundred times more delightful, had I not been such a fool, or known better how to enjoy it.

Madam de Warrens had taken no one with her but Anet: Merceret, her chambermaid, whom I have before mentioned, still remained in the house. Merceret was something older than myself, not pretty, but tolerably agreeable; good-natured, free from malice, having no fault to my knowledge but being a little refractory with her mistress. I often went to see her; she was an old acquaintance, who recalled to my remembrance one more beloved, and this made her dear to me. She had several friends, and among others one Mademoiselle Giraud, a Genevese, who, for the punishment of my sins, took it in her head to have an inclination for me, always pressing Merceret, when she returned her visits, to bring me with her. As I liked Merceret, I felt no disinclination to accompany her; besides, I met there with other young people whose company pleased me. For Mademoiselle Giraud, who offered every kind of enticement, nothing could increase the aversion I had for her. When she drew near me, with her dried black snout, smeared with Spanish snuff, it was with the utmost difficulty that I could refrain from expressing my distaste; but, being pleased with her visitors, I took patience. Among these were two girls who (either to pay their court to Mademoiselle Giraud or myself) paid me every possible attention. I conceived this to be only friendship; but have since thought it depended only on myself to have discovered something more, though I did not even think of it at the time.

There was another reason for my stupidity. Seamstresses, chambermaids, or milliners, never tempted me; I sighed for ladies! Every one has his peculiar taste, this has ever been mine; being in this particular of a different opinion from Horace. Yet it is not vanity of riches or rank that attracts me; it is a well-preserved complexion, fine hands, elegance of ornaments, an air of delicacy and neatness throughout the whole person; more in taste, in the manner of expressing themselves, a finer or better made gown, a well-turned ankle, small foot, ribbons, lace, and well-dressed hair: I even prefer those who have less natural beauty, provided they are elegantly decorated. I freely confess this preference is very ridiculous; yet my heart gives in to it spite of my understanding: Well, even this advantage presented itself, and it only depended on my own resolution to have seized the opportunity.

How do I love, from time to time, to return to those moments of my youth, which were so charmingly delightful; so short, so scarce, and enjoyed at so cheap a rate!—how fondly do I wish to dwell on them! Even yet the remembrance of these scenes warms my heart with a chaste rapture, which appears necessary to reanimate my drooping courage, and enable me to sustain the weariness of my latter days.

The appearance of Aurora seemed so delightful one morning that, putting on my clothes, I hastened into the country, to see the rising of the sun. I enjoyed that pleasure in its utmost extent; it was one week after midsummer; the earth was covered with verdure and flowers, the nightingales, whose soft warblings were almost concluded, seemed to vie with each other, and in concert with birds of various kinds to bid adieu to spring, and hail the approach of a beautiful summer's day: one of those lovely days that are no longer to be enjoyed at my age, and which have never been seen on the melancholy soil I now inhabit.

I had rambled insensibly, to a considerable distance from the town—the heat augmented—I was walking in the shade along a valley, by the side of a brook, I heard behind me the step of horses, and the voice of some females who, though they seemed embarrassed, did not laugh the less heartily on that account. I turn round, hear myself called by name, and approaching, find two young people of my acquaintance, Mademoiselle de G—— and Mademoiselle Galley, who, not being very excellent horsewomen, could not make their horses cross the rivulet.

Mademoiselle de G—— was a young lady of Berne, very amiable: who, having been sent from that country for some youthful folly, had imitated Madam de Warrens, at whose house I had sometimes seen her; but not having, like her, a pension, she had been fortunate in this attachment to Mademoiselle Galley, who had prevailed on her mother to engage her young friend as a companion, till she could be otherwise provided for. Mademoiselle Galley was one year younger than her friend, handsomer, more delicate, more ingenious, and, to complete all, extremely well made. They loved each other tenderly, and the good disposition of both could not fail to render their union durable, if some lover did not derange it. They informed me they were going to Toune, an old castle belonging to Madam Galley, and implored my assistance to make their horses cross the stream, not being able to compass it themselves. I would have given each a cut or two with the whip, but they feared I might be kicked, and themselves thrown; I therefore had recourse to another expedient, I took hold of Mademoiselle Galley's horse and led him through the brook, the water reaching half-way up my legs. The other followed without any difficulty. This done, I would have paid my compliments to the ladies, and walked off like a great booby as I was, but after whispering each other, Mademoiselle de G—— said, "No, no, you must not think to escape thus; you have got wet in our service, and we ought in conscience to take care and dry you. If you please you must go with us, you are now our prisoner." My heart began to beat— I looked at Mademoiselle Galley—"Yes, yes," added she, laughing at my fearful look, "our prisoner of war; come, get up behind her, we shall give a good account of you." "But, mademoiselle," continued I, "I have not the honor to be acquainted with your mother; what will she say on my arrival?" "Her mother," replied Mademoiselle de G——, "is not at Toune, we are alone, we shall return at night, and you shall come back with us."

The stroke of electricity has not a more instantaneous effect than these words produced on me. Leaping behind Mademoiselle de G——, I trembled with joy, and when it became necessary to clasp her in order to hold myself on, my heart beat so violently that she perceived it, and told me hers beat also from a fear of falling. In my present posture, I might naturally have considered this an invitation to satisfy myself of the truth of her assertion, yet I did not dare, and during the whole way my arms served as a girdle (a very close one, I must confess), without being a moment displaced. Some women that may read this would be for giving me a box on the ear, and, truly, I deserved it.

The gayety of the journey, and the chat of these girls, so enlivened me, that during the whole time we passed together we never ceased talking a moment. They had set me so thoroughly at ease, that my tongue spoke as fast as my eyes, though not exactly the same things. Some minutes, indeed, when I was left alone with either, the conversation became a little embarrassed, but neither of them was absent long enough to allow time for explaining the cause.

Arrived at Toune, and myself well dried, we breakfasted together; after which it was necessary to settle the important business of preparing dinner. The young ladies cooked, kissing from time to time the farmer's children, while the poor scullion looked on grumbling. Provisions had been sent for from town, and there was everything necessary for a good dinner, but unhappily they had forgotten wine; this forgetfulness was by no means astonishing in girls who seldom drank any, but I was sorry for the omission, as I had reckoned on its help, thinking it might add to my confidence. They were sorry likewise, and perhaps from the same motive; though I had no reason to say this, for their lively and charming gayety was innocence itself; besides, there were two of them, what could they expect from me? They went everywhere about the neighborhood to seek for wine, but none could be procured, so pure and sober are the peasants in those parts. As they were expressing their concern, I begged them not to give themselves any uneasiness on my account, for while with them I had no occasion for wine to intoxicate me. This was the only gallantry I ventured at during the whole of the day, and I believe the sly rogues saw well enough that I said nothing but the truth.

We dined in the kitchen: the two friends were seated on the benches, one on each side the long table, and their guest at the end, between them, on a three-legged stool. What a dinner! how charming the remembrance! While we can enjoy, at so small an expense, such pure, such true delights, why should we be solicitous for others? Never did those *petite soupers,* so celebrated in Paris, equal this; I do not only say for real pleasure and gayety, but even for sensuality.

After dinner, we were economical; instead of drinking the coffee we had reserved at breakfast, we kept it for an afternoon collation, with cream, and some cakes they had brought with them. To keep our appetites in play, we went into the orchard, meaning to finish our dessert with cherries. I got into a tree, throwing them down bunches, from which they returned the stones through the branches. One time, Mademoiselle Galley, holding out her apron, and drawing back her head, stood so fair, and I took such good aim, that I dropped a bunch into her bosom. On her laughing, I said to myself, "Why are not my lips cherries? how gladly would I throw them there likewise!"

Thus the day passed with the greatest freedom, yet with the utmost decency; not a single equivocal word, not one attempt at double-meaning pleasantry; yet this delicacy was not affected, we only performed the parts our hearts dictated; in short, my modesty, some will say my folly, was such that the greatest familiarity that escaped me was once kissing the hand of Mademoiselle Galley; it is true, the attending circumstances helped to stamp a value on this trifling favor; we were alone, I was embarrassed, her eyes were fixed on the ground, and my lips, instead of uttering words, were pressed on her hand, which she drew gently back after the salute, without any appearance of displeasure. I know not what I should have said to her, but her friend entered, and at that moment I thought her ugly.

At length, they bethought themselves, that they must return to town before night; even now we had but just time to reach it by daylight; and we hastened our departure in the same order we came. Had I pleased myself, I should certainly have reversed this order, for the glance of Mademoiselle Galley had reached my heart, but I dared not mention it, and the proposal could not reasonably come from her. On the way, we expressed our sorrow that the day was over, but far from complaining of the shortness of its duration, we were conscious of having prolonged it by every possible amusement.

I quitted them in nearly the same spot where I had taken them up. With what regret did we part! With what pleasure did we form projects to renew our meeting! Delightful hours, which we passed innocently together, ye were worth ages of familiarity! The sweet remembrance of this day cost those amiable girls nothing; the tender union which reigned among us equaled more lively pleasure, with which it could not have existed. We loved each other without shame or mystery, and wished to continue our reciprocal affection. There is a species of enjoyment connected with innocence of manners which is superior to any other, because it has no interval; for myself, the remembrance of such a day touches me nearer, delights me more, and returns with greater rapture to my heart, than any other pleasures I ever tasted. I hardly knew what I wished with those charming girls. I do not say, that had the arrangement been in my power, I should have divided my heart between them; I certainly felt some degree of preference: though I should have been happy to have had Mademoiselle de G—— for a mistress, I think, by choice, I should have liked her better as a confidante; be that as it may, I felt on leaving them as though I could not live without either. Who would have thought that I should never see them more; and that here our ephemeral amours must end?

Those who read this will not fail to laugh at my gallantries, and remark, that after very promising preliminaries, my most forward adventures concluded by a kiss of the hand: yet be not mistaken, reader, in your estimate of my enjoyments; I have, perhaps, tasted more real pleasure in my amours, which concluded by a kiss of the hand, than you will ever have in yours, which, at least, begin there.

Venture, who had gone to bed late the night before, came in soon after me. I did not now see him with my usual satisfaction, and took care not to inform him how I had passed the day. The ladies had spoken of him slightingly, and appeared discontented at finding me in such bad hands; this hurt him in my esteem; besides, whatever diverted my ideas from them was at this time disagreeable. However, he soon brought me back to him and myself, by speaking of the situation of my affairs, which was too critical to last; for, though I spent very little, my slender finances were almost exhausted. I was without resource; no news of Madam de Warrens; not knowing what would become of me, and feeling a cruel pang at heart to see the friend of Mademoiselle Galley reduced to beggary.

I now learned from Venture that he had spoken of me to the Judge Major, and would take me next day to dine with him; that he was a man who by means of his friends might render me essential service. In other respects he was a desirable acquaintance, being a man of wit and letters, of agreeable conversation, one who possessed talents and loved them in others. After this discourse (mingling the most serious concerns with the most trifling frivolity) he showed me a pretty couplet, which came from Paris, on an air in one of Mouret's operas, which was then playing. Monsieur Simon (the judge major) was so pleased with this couplet, that he determined to make another in answer to it, on the same air. He had desired Venture to write one, and he wished me to make a third, that, as he expressed it, they might see couplets start up next day like incidents in a comic romance.

In the night (not being able to sleep) I composed a couplet, as my first essay in poetry. It was passable; better, or at least composed with more taste, than it would have been the preceding night, the subject being tenderness, to which my heart was now entirely disposed. In the morning I showed my performance to Venture, who, being pleased with the couplet, put it in his pocket, without informing me whether he had made his. We dined with M. Simon, who treated us very politely. The conversation was agreeable; indeed it could not be otherwise between two men of natural good sense, improved by reading. For me, I acted my proper part, which was to listen without attempting to join in the conversation. Neither of them mentioned the couplet, nor do I know that it ever passed for mine.

M. Simon appeared satisfied with my behavior; indeed, it was almost all he saw of me in this interview. We had often met at Madam de Warrens', but he had never paid much attention to me; it is from this dinner, therefore, that I date our acquaintance, which, though of no use in regard to the object I then had in view, was afterwards productive of advantages which make me recollect it with pleasure.

I should be wrong not to give some account of his person, since from his office of magistrate, and the reputation of wit on which he piqued himself, no idea could be formed of it. The judge major, Simon, certainly was not two feet high; his legs spare, ſtraight, and tolerably long, would have added something to his stature had they been vertical, but they stood in the direction of an open pair of compasses. His body was not only short, but thin, being in every respect of most inconceivable smallness—when naked he must have appeared like a grasshopper. His head was of the common size, to which appertained a well-formed face, a noble look, and tolerably fine eyes; in short, it appeared a borrowed head, stuck on a miserable stump. He might very well have dispensed with dress, for his large wig alone covered him from head to foot.

He had two voices, perfectly different, which intermingled perpetually in his conversation, forming at first a diverting, but afterwards a very disagreeable contrast. One grave and sonorous, was, if I may hazard the expression, the voice of his head: the other, clear, sharp, and piercing, the voice of his body. When he paid particular attention, and spoke leisurely, so as to preserve his breath, he could continue his deep tone; but if he was the least animated, or attempted a lively accent, his voice sounded like the whistling of a key, and it was with the utmost difficulty that he could return to the bass.

With the figure I have just described, and which is by no means overcharged, M. Simon was gallant, ever entertaining the ladies with soft tales, and carrying the decoration of his person even to foppery. Willing to make use of every advantage he, during the morning, gave audience in bed, for when a handsome head was discovered on the pillow no one could have imagined what belonged to it. This circumstance gave birth to scenes, which I am certain are yet remembered by all Annecy.

One morning, when he expected to give audience in bed, or rather on the bed, having on a handsome night-cap ornamented with rose-colored ribbon, a countryman arriving knocked at the door; the maid happened to be out; the judge, therefore, hearing the knock repeated, cried "Come in," and, as he spoke rather loud, it was in his shrill tone. The man entered, looked about, endeavoring to discover whence the female voice proceeded, and at length seeing a handsome head-dress set off with ribbons, was about to leave the room, making the supposed lady a hundred apologies. M. Simon, in a rage, screamed the more; and the countryman, yet more confirmed in his opinion, conceiving himself to be insulted, began railing in his turn, saying that, "Apparently, she was nothing better than a common street-walker, and that the judge major should be ashamed of setting such ill examples." The enraged magistrate, having no other weapon than the *jorden* under his bed, was just going to throw it at the poor fellow's head as his servant returned.

This dwarf, ill-used by nature as to his person, was recompensed by possessing an understanding naturally agreeable, and which he had been careful to cultivate. Though he was esteemed a good lawyer, he did not like his profession, delighting more in the finer parts of literature, which he studied with success: above all, he possessed that superficial brilliancy, the art of pleasing in conversation, even with the ladies. He knew by heart a number of little stories, which he perfectly well knew how to make the most of; relating with an air of secrecy, and as an anecdote of yesterday, what happened sixty years before. He understood music, and could sing agreeably; in short, for a magistrate, he had many pleasing talents. By flattering the ladies of Annecy, he became fashionable among them, appearing continually in their train. He even pretended to favors, at which they were much amused. A Madam D'Epigny used to say "The greatest favor he could aspire to, was to kiss a lady on her knees."

As he was well read, and spoke fluently, his conversation was both amusing and instructive. When I afterwards took a taste for study, I cultivated his acquaintance, and found my account in it: when at Chambery, I frequently went from thence to see him. His praises increased my emulation, to which he added some good advice respecting the prosecution of my studies, which I found useful. Unhappily, this weakly body contained a very feeling soul. Some years after, he was chagrined by I know not what unlucky affair, but it cost him his life. This was really unfortunate, for he was a good little man, whom at a first acquaintance one laughed at, but afterwards loved. Though our situations in life were very little connected with each other, as I received some useful lessons from him, I thought gratitude demanded that I should dedicate a few sentences to his memory.

As soon as I found myself at liberty, I ran into the street where Mademoiselle Galley lived, flattering myself that I should see some one go in or out, or at least open a window, but I was mistaken, not even a cat appeared, the house remaining as close all the time as if it had been uninhabited. The street was small and lonely, any one loitering about was, consequently, more likely to be noticed; from time to time people passed in and out of the neighborhood; I was much embarrassed, thinking my person might be known, and the cause that brought me there conjectured; this idea tortured me, for I have ever preferred the honor and happiness of those I love to my own pleasures.

At length, weary of playing the Spanish lover, and having no guitar, I determined to write to Mademoiselle de Graffenried. I should have preferred writing to her friend, but did not dare take that liberty, as it appeared more proper to begin with her to whom I owed the acquaintance, and with whom I was most familiar. Having written my letter, I took it to Mademoiselle Giraud, as the young ladies had agreed at parting, they having furnished me with this expedient. Mademoiselle Giraud was a quilter, and sometimes worked at Madam Galley's, which procured her free admission to the house. I must confess, I was not thoroughly satisfied with this messenger, but was cautious of starting difficulties, fearing that if I objected to her no other might be named, and it was impossible to intimate that she had an inclination to me herself. I even felt humiliated that she should think I could imagine her of the same sex as those young ladies: in a word, I accepted her agency rather than none, and availed myself of it at all events.

At the very first word, Giraud discovered me. I must own this was not a difficult matter, for if sending a letter to young girls had not spoken sufficiently plain, my foolish embarrassed air would have betrayed me. It will easily be supposed that the employment gave her little satisfaction, she undertook it, however, and performed it faithfully. The next morning I ran to her house and found an answer ready for me. How did I hurry away that I might have an opportunity to read and kiss it alone! though this need not be told, but the plan adopted by Mademoiselle Giraud (and in which I found more delicacy and moderation than I had expected) should. She had sense enough to conclude, that her thirty-seven years, hare's eyes, daubed nose, shrill voice, and black skin, stood no chance against two elegant young girls, in all the height and bloom of beauty; she resolved, therefore, neither to betray nor assist them, choosing rather to lose me entirely than entertain me for them.

As Merceret had not heard from her mistress for some time, she thought of returning to Fribourg, and the persuasions of Giraud determined her; nay more, she intimated it was proper some one should conduct her to her father's, and proposed me. As I happened to be agreeable to little Merceret, she approved the idea, and the same day they mentioned it to me as a fixed point. Finding nothing displeasing in the manner they had disposed of me, I consented, thinking it could not be above a week's journey at most; but Giraud, who had arranged the whole affair, thought otherwise. It was necessary to avow the state of my finances, and the conclusion was, that Merceret should defray my expenses; but to retrench on one hand what was expended on the older, I advised that her little baggage should be sent on before, and that we should proceed by easy journeys on foot.

I am sorry to have so many girls in love with me, but as there is nothing to be very vain of in the success of these amours, I think I may tell the truth without scruple. Merceret, younger and less artful than Giraud, never made me so many advances, but she imitated my manners, my actions, repeated my words, and showed me all those little attentions I ought to have had for her. Being very timorous, she took great care that we should both sleep in the same chamber; a circumstance that usually produces some consequences between a lad of twenty and a girl of twenty-five.

For once, however, it went no further; my simplicity being such, that though Merceret was by no means a disagreeable girl, an idea of gallantry never entered my head, and even if it had, I was too great a novice to have profited by it. I could not imagine how two young persons could bring themselves to sleep together, thinking that such familiarity must require an age of preparation. If poor Merceret paid my expenses in hopes of any return, she was terribly cheated, for we arrived at Fribourg exactly as we had quitted Annecy.

I passed through Geneva without visiting any one. While going over the bridges, I found myself so affected that I could scarcely proceed. Never could I see the walls of that city, never could I enter it, without feeling my heart sink from excess of tenderness, at the same time that the image of liberty elevated my soul. The ideas of equality, union, and gentleness of manners, touched me even to tears, and inspired me with a lively regret at having forfeited all these advantages. What an error was I in! but yet how natural! I imagined I saw all this in my native country, because I bore it in my heart.

It was necessary to pass through Nion: could I do this without seeing my good father? Had I resolved on doing so, I must afterwards have died with regret. I left Merceret at the inn, and ventured to his house. How wrong was I to fear him! On seeing me, his soul gave way to the parental tenderness with which it was filled. What tears were mingled with our embraces! He thought I was returned to him: I related my history, and informed him of my resolution. He opposed it feebly, mentioning the dangers to which I exposed myself, and telling me the shortest follies were best.

but did not attempt to keep me by force, in which particular I think he acted right; but it is certain he did not do everything in his power to retain me, even by fair means. Whether after the step I had taken, he thought I ought not to return, or was puzzled at my age to know what to do with me—I have since found that he conceived a very unjust opinion of my traveling companion. My step-mother, a good woman, a little coaxingly put on an appearance of wishing me to stay and sup; I did not, however, comply, but told them I proposed remaining longer with them on my return; leaving as a deposit my little packet, that had come by water, and would have been an incumbrance, had I taken it with me. I continued my journey the next morning, well satisfied that I had seen my father, and had taken courage to do my duty.

We arrived without any accident at Fribourg. Towards the conclusion of the journey, the politeness of Mademoiselle Merceret rather diminished, and, after our arrival, she treated me even with coldness. Her father, who was not in the best circumstances, did not show me much attention, and I was obliged to lodge at an ale-house. I went to see them the next morning, and received an invitation to dine there, which I accepted. We separated without tears at night; I returned to my paltry lodging, and departed the second day after my arrival, almost without knowing whither to go to.

This was a circumstance of my life in which Providence offered me precisely what was necessary to make my days pass happily. Merceret was a good girl, neither witty, handsome, nor ugly; not very lively, but tolerably rational, except while under the influence of some little humors, which usually evaporated in tears, without any violent outbreak of temper. She had a real inclination for me; I might have married her without difficulty, and followed her father's business. My taste for music would have made me love her; I should have settled at Fribourg, a small town, not pretty, but inhabited by very worthy people—I should certainly have missed great pleasures, but should have lived in peace to my last hour, and I must know best what I should have gained by such a step.

I did not return to Nion, but to Lausanne, wishing to gratify myself with a view of that beautiful lake which is seen there in its utmost extent. The greater part of my secret motives have not been so reasonable. Distant expectation has rarely strength enough to influence my actions; the uncertainty of the future ever making me regard projects whose execution requires a length of time as deceitful lures. I give in to visionary scenes of hope as well as others, provided they cost nothing, but if attended with any trouble, I have done with them. The smallest, the most trifling pleasure that is conveniently within my reach, tempts me more than all the joys of paradise. I must except, however, those pleasures which are necessarily followed by pain; I only love those enjoyments which are unadulterated, which can never be the case where we are conscious they must be followed by repentance.

It was necessary I should arrive at some place, and the nearest was best; for having lost my way on the road, I found myself in the evening at Moudon, where I spent all that remained of my little stock except ten creuzers, which served to purchase my next day's dinner. Arriving in the evening at Lausanne, I went into an ale-house, without a penny in my pocket to pay for my lodging, or knowing what would become of me. I found myself extremely hungry—setting, therefore, a good face on the matter, I ordered supper, made my meal, went to bed without thought and slept with great composure. In the morning, having breakfasted and reckoned with my host, I offered to leave my waistcoat in pledge for seven batz, which was the amount of my expenses. The honest man refused this, saying, thank Heaven, he had never stripped any one, and would not now begin for seven batz; adding I should keep my waistcoat and pay him when I could. I was affected with this unexpected kindness, but felt it less than I ought to have done, or have since experienced on the remembrance of it. I did not fail sending him his money, with thanks, by one I could depend on. Fifteen years after, passing Lausanne, on my return from Italy, I felt a sensible regret at having forgotten the name of the landlord and house. I wished to see him, and should have felt real pleasure in recalling to his memory that worthy action. Services, which doubtless have been much more important, but rendered with ostentation, have not appeared to me so worthy of gratitude as the simple unaffected humanity of this honest man.

As I approached Lausanne, I thought of my distress, and the means of extricating myself, without appearing in want to my step-mother. I compared myself, in this walking pilgrimage, to my friend Venture, on his arrival at Annecy, and was so warmed with the idea, that without recollecting that I had neither his gentility nor his talents, I determined to act the part of little Venture at Lausanne, to teach music, which I did not understand, and say I came from Paris, where I had never been.

In consequence of this noble project (as there was no company where I could introduce myself without expense, and not choosing to venture among professional people), I inquired for some little inn, where I could lodge cheap, and was directed to one named Perrotet, who took in boarders. This Perrotet, who was one of the best men in the world, received me very kindly, and after having heard my feigned story and profession, promised to speak of me, and endeavored to procure me scholars, saying he could not expect any money till I had earned it. His price for board, though moderate in itself, was a great deal to me; he advised me, therefore, to begin with half board, which consisted of good soup only for dinner, but a plentiful supper at night. I closed with this proposition, and the poor Perrotet trusted me with great cheerfulness, sparing, meantime, no trouble to be useful to me.

Having found so many good people in my youth, why do I find so few in my age? Is their race extinct? No; but I do not seek them in the same situation I did formerly, among the commonalty, where violent passions predominate only at intervals, and where nature speaks her genuine sentiments. In more elevated stations they are entirely smothered, and under the mask of sentiment, only interest or vanity is heard.

Having written to my father from Lausanne, he sent my packet and some excellent advice, of which I should have profited better. I have already observed that I have moments of inconceivable delirium, in which I am entirely out of myself. The adventure I am about to relate is an instance of this: to comprehend how completely my brain was turned, and to what degree I had *Venturised* (if I may be allowed the expression), the many extravagancies I ran into at the same time should be considered. Behold me, then, a singing master, without knowing how to note a common song; for if the five or six months passed with Le Maitre had improved me, they could not be supposed sufficient to qualify me for such an undertaking; besides, being taught by a master was enough (as I have before observed) to make me learn ill. Being a Parisian from Geneva, and a Catholic in a Protestant country, I thought I should change my name with my religion and country. He called himself Venture de Villeneuve. I changed, by anagram, the name Rousseau into that of Vaussore, calling myself Monsieur Vaussore de Villeneuve. Venture was a good composer, though he had not said so; without knowing anything of the art, I boasted of my skill to every one. This was not all: being presented to Monsieur de Freytorens, professor of law, who loved music, and who gave concerts at his house, nothing would do but I must give him a proof of my talents, and accordingly I set about composing a piece for his concerts, as boldly as if I had really understood the science. I tacked a pretty minuet to the end of it, that was played about the streets, and which many may remember from these words, so well known at that time:

> *Quelle caprice!*
> *Quelle injustice!*
> *Quoi! ta Clarice*
> *Trahiriait tes feux! etc.*

Venture had taught me this air with the bass, set to other words, by the help of which I had retained it: thus at the end of my composition, I put this minuet and his bass, suppressing the words, and uttering it for my own as confidently as if I had been speaking to the inhabitants of the moon. They assemble to perform my piece; I explain to each the movement, taste of execution, and references to his part—I was fully occupied. They were five or six minutes preparing, which were for me so many ages: at length, everything is adjusted, myself in a conspicuous situation, a fine roll of paper in my hand, gravely preparing to beat time. I gave four or five strokes with my paper, attending with "Attention!" they begin—No, never since French operas existed was there such a confused discord! The musicians could not keep from laughing; the audience opened their eyes wide and would like to shut their ears, but that was impossible. The musicians made merry and scraped their violins enough to burst your eardrums. I had the constancy to go through the performance, but large drops of perspiration were standing on my forehead, and it was only shame that prevented me from running away. I heard the assistants whisper to each other or rather to me: "It is pretty hard to stand!" Poor Jean-Jacques, in this cruel moment you little thought, that one day, in the presence of the King of France and his whole court, your sounds should produce murmurs of surprise and applaud, and that lovely women in the boxes should tell each other in a whisper: "What charming music! What beautiful sounds!"

Next day, one of the musicians, named Lutold, came to see me and was kind enough to congratulate me on my success. The profound conviction of my folly, shame, regret, and the state of despair to which I was reduced, with the impossibility of concealing the cruel agitation of my heart, made me open it to him; giving, therefore, a loose to my tears, not content with owning my ignorance, I told all, conjuring him to secrecy; he kept his word, as every one will suppose. The same evening, all Lausanne knew who I was, but what is remarkable, no one seemed to know, not even the good Perrotet, who (notwithstanding what had happened) continued to lodge and board me.

I led a melancholy life here; the consequences of such an essay had not rendered Lausanne a very agreeable residence. Scholars did not present themselves in crowds, not a single female, and no person of the city. I had only two or three great dunces, as stupid as I was ignorant, who fatigued me to death, and in my hands were not likely to edify much.

At length, I was sent for to a house, where a little serpent of a girl amused herself by showing me a parcel of music that I could not read a note of, and which she had the malice to sing before her master, to teach him how it should be executed; for I was so unable to read an air at first sight, that in the charming concert I have just described, I could not possibly follow the execution a moment, or know whether they played truly what lay before them, and I myself had composed.

In the midst of so many humiliating circumstances, I had the pleasing consolation, from time to time, of receiving letters from my two charming friends. I have ever found the utmost consolatory virtue in the fair; when in disgrace, nothing softens my affliction more than to be sensible that an amiable woman is interested for me. This correspondence ceased soon after, and was never renewed: indeed it was my own fault, for in changing situations I neglected sending my address, and forced by necessity to think perpetually of myself, I soon forgot them.

It is a long time since I mentioned Madam de Warrens, but it should not be supposed I had forgotten her; never was she a moment absent from my thoughts. I anxiously wished to find her, not merely because she was necessary to my subsistence, but because she was infinitely more necessary to my heart. My attachment to her (though lively and tender, as it really was) did not prevent my loving others, but then it was not in the same manner. All equally claimed my tenderness for their charms, but it was those charms alone I loved, my passion would not have survived them, while Madam de Warrens might have become old or ugly without my loving her the less tenderly. My heart had entirely transmitted to herself the homage it first paid to her beauty, and whatever change she might experience, while she remained herself, my sentiments could not change. I was sensible how much gratitude I owed to her, but in truth, I never thought of it, and whether she served me or not, it would ever have been the same thing. I loved her neither from duty, interest, nor convenience; I loved her because I was born to love her. During my attachment to another, I own this affection was in some measure deranged; I did not think so frequently of her, but still with the same pleasure, and never, in love or otherwise, did I think of her without feeling that I could expect no true happiness in life while in a state of separation.

Though in so long a time I had received no news from Madam de Warrens, I never imagined I had entirely lost her, or that she could have forgotten me. I said to myself, she will know sooner or later that I am wandering about, and will find some means to inform me of her situation: I am certain I shall find her. In the meantime, it was a pleasure to live in her native country, to walk in the streets where she had walked, and before the houses that she had lived in; yet all this was the work of conjecture, for one of my foolish peculiarities was, not daring to inquire after her, or even pronounce her name without the most absolute necessity. It seemed in speaking of her that I declared all I felt, that my lips revealed the secrets of my heart, and in some degree injured the object of my affection. I believe fear was likewise mingled with this idea; I dreaded to hear ill of her. Her management had been much spoken of, and some little of her conduct in other respects; fearing, therefore, that something might be said which I did not wish to hear, I preferred being silent on the subject.

As my scholars did not take up much of my time, and the town where she was born was not above four leagues from Lausanne, I made it a walk of three or four days; during which time a most pleasant emotion never left me. A view of the Lake of Geneva and its admirable banks, had ever, in my idea, a particular attraction which I cannot describe; not arising merely from the beauty of the prospect, but something else, I know not why, more interesting, which affects and softens me. Every time I have approached the Vaudois country I have experienced an impression composed of the remembrance of Madam de Warrens, who was born there; of my father, who lived there; of Miss Vulson, who had been my first love, and of several pleasant journeys I had made there in my childhood, mingled with some nameless charm, more powerfully attractive than all the rest. When that ardent desire for a life of happiness and tranquillity (which ever follows me, and for which I was born) inflames my mind, 'tis ever to the country of Vaud, near the lake, in those charming plains, that imagination leads me. An orchard on the banks of that lake, and no other, is absolutely necessary; a firm friend, an amiable woman, a cow, and a little boat; nor could I enjoy perfect happiness on earth without these concomitants. I laugh at the simplicity with which I have several times gone into that country for the sole purpose of seeking this imaginary happiness when I was ever surprised to find the inhabitants, particularly the women, of a quite different disposition to what I sought. How strange did this appear to me! The country and people who inhabit it, were never, in my idea, formed for each other.

Walking along these beautiful banks, on my way to Vevay, I gave myself up to the soft melancholy; my heart rushed with ardor into a thousand innocent felicities; melting to tenderness, I sighed and wept like a child. How often, stopping to weep more at my ease, and seated on a large stone, did I amuse myself with seeing my tears drop into the water.

On my arrival at Vevay, I lodged at the Key, and during the two days I remained there, without any acquaintance, conceived a love for that city, which has followed me through all my travels, and was finally

the cause that I fixed on this spot, in the novel I afterwards wrote, for the residence of my hero and
heroines. I would say to any one who has taste and
feeling, go to Vevay, visit the surrounding country,
examine the prospects, go on the lake and then say,
whether nature has not designed this country for a
Julia, a Clara, and a St. Preux; but do not seek them
there. I now return to my story.

Giving myself out for a Catholic, I followed without mystery or scruple the religion I had embraced.
On a Sunday, if the weather was fine, I went to hear
mass at Assans, a place two leagues distant from
Lausanne, and generally in company with other Catholics, particularly a Parisian embroiderer, whose name
I have forgotten. Not such a Parisian as myself, but a
real native of Paris, an arch-Parisian from his maker,
yet honest as a peasant. He loved his country so well,
that he would not doubt my being his countrymen, for
fear he should not have so much occasion to speak of
it. The lieutenant-governor, M. de Crouzas, had a
gardener, who was likewise from Paris, but not so
complaisant; he thought the glory of his country concerned, when any one claimed that honor who was
not really entitled to it; he put questions to me, therefore, with an air and tone, as if certain to detect me in
a falsehood, and once, smiling malignantly, asked
what was remarkable in the *Marcheneuf?* It may be
supposed I asked the question; but I have since passed
twenty years at Paris, and certainly know that city, yet
was the same question repeated at this day, I should be

equally embarrassed to answer it, and from this embarrassment it might be concluded I had never been there: thus, even when we meet with truths, we are subject to build our opinions on circumstances, which may easily deceive us.

I formed no ideas, while at Lausanne, that were worth recollecting, nor can I say exactly how long I remained there; I only know that not finding sufficient to subsist on, I went from thence to Neufchatel, where I passed the winter. Here I succeeded better, I got some scholars, and saved enough to pay my good friend Perrotet, who had faithfully sent my baggage, though at that time I was considerably in his debt.

By continuing to teach music, I insensibly gained some knowledge of it. The life I led was sufficiently agreeable, and any reasonable man might have been satisfied, but my unsettled heart demanded something more. On Sundays, or whenever I had leisure, I wandered, sighing and thoughtful, about the adjoining woods, and when once out of the city never returned before night. One day, being at Boudry, I went to dine at a public-house, where I saw a man with a long beard, dressed in a violet-colored Grecian habit, with a fur cap, and whose air and manner were rather noble. This person found some difficulty in making himself understood, speaking only an unintelligible jargon, which bore more resemblance to Italian than any other language. I understood almost all he said, and I was the only person present who could do so, for he was obliged to make his request known to the landlord and others about him by signs. On my speaking a few words in Italian, which he perfectly understood, he got up and embraced me with rapture; a connection was soon formed, and from that moment, I became his interpreter. His dinner was excellent, mine rather worse than indifferent; he gave me an invitation to dine with him, which I accepted without much ceremony. Drinking and chatting soon rendered us familiar, and by the end of the repast we had all the disposition in the world to become inseparable companions. He informed me he was a Greek prelate, and *Archimandrite* of Jerusalem; that he had undertaken to make a gathering in Europe for the reëstablishment of the Holy Sepulcher, and showed me some very fine patents from the czarina, the emperor, and several other sovereigns. He was tolerably content with what he had collected hitherto, though he had experienced inconceivable difficulties in Germany; for not understanding a word of German, Latin, or French, he had been obliged to have recourse to his Greek, Turkish, and the *Lingua Franca,* which did not procure him much in the country he was traveling through; his proposal, therefore, to me was, that I should accompany him in the quality of secretary and interpreter. In spite of my violet-colored coat, which accorded well enough with the proposed employment, he guessed from my meager appearance, that I should easily be gained; and he was not mistaken. The bargain was soon made, I demanded nothing, and he promised liberally; thus, without any security or knowledge of the person I was about to serve, I gave myself up entirely to his conduct, and the next day behold me on an expedition to Jerusalem.

We began our expedition unsuccessfully by the canton of Fribourg. Episcopal dignity would not suffer him to play the beggar, or solicit help from private individuals; but we presented his commission to the Senate, who gave him a trifling sum. From thence we went to Berne, where we lodged at the Falcon, then a good inn, and frequented by respectable company; the public table being well supplied and numerously attended. I had fared indifferently so long, that I was glad to make myself amends, therefore took care to profit by the present occasion. My lord, the Archimandrite, was himself an excellent companion, loved good cheer, was gay, spoke well for those who understood him, and knew perfectly well how to make the most of his Grecian erudition. One day, at dessert, while cracking nuts, he cut his finger pretty deeply, and as it bled freely showed it to the company, saying with a laugh, *"Mirate, signori; questo e sangue Pelasgo."*

At Berne, I was not useless to him, nor was my performance so bad as I had feared: I certainly spoke better and with more confidence than I could have done for myself. Matters were not conducted here with the same simplicity as at Fribourg; long and frequent conferences were necessary with the Premiers of the State, and the examination of his titles was not the work of a day; at length, everything being adjusted, he was admitted to an audience by the Senate; I entered with him as interpreter, and was ordered to speak. I expected nothing less, for it never entered my mind, that after such long and frequent conferences with the members, it was necessary to address the assembly collectively, as if nothing had been said. Judge my embarrassment!—a man so bashful to speak, not only in public, but before the whole of the Senate of Berne! to speak impromptu, without a single moment for recollection; it was enough to annihilate me—I was not even intimidated. I described distinctly and clearly the commission of the Archimandrite; extolled the piety of those princes who had contributed, and to heighten that of their excellencies by emulation, added that less could not be expected from their well-known munificence; then, endeavored to prove that this good work was equally interesting to all Christians, without distinction of sect; and concluded by promising the benediction of Heaven to all those who took part in it. I will not say that my discourse was the cause of our success, but it was certainly well received; and on our quitting the Archimandrite was gratified by a very genteel present, to which some very handsome compliments were added on the understanding of his secretary; these I had the agreeable office of interpreting, but could not take courage to render them literally.

This was the only time in my life that I spoke in public, and before a sovereign; and the only time, perhaps, that I spoke boldly and well. What difference in the disposition of the same person. Three years ago, having been to see my old friend, M. Roguin, at Yverdon, I received a deputation to thank me for some books I had presented to the library of that city; the Swiss are great speakers; these gentlemen, accordingly, made me a long harangue, which I thought myself obliged in honor to answer, but so embarrassed myself in the attempt, that my head became confused, I stopped short, and was laughed at. Though naturally timid, I have sometimes acted with confidence in my youth, but never in my advanced age: the more I have seen of the world the less I have been able to adopt its manners.

On leaving Berne, we went to Soleure; the Archimandrite designing to reënter Germany, and return through Hungary or Poland to his own country. This would have been a prodigious tour; but as the contents of his purse rather increased than diminished during his journey, he was in no haste to return. For me, who was almost as much pleased on horseback as on foot, I would have desired no better than to have traveled thus during my whole life; but it was preordained that my journey should soon end.

The first thing we did after our arrival at Soleure, was to pay our respects to the French ambassador there. Unfortunately for my bishop, this chanced to be the Marquis de Bonac, who had been ambassador at the Porte, and consequently was acquainted with every particular relative to the Holy Sepulcher. The Archimandrite had an audience that lasted about a quarter of an hour, to which I was not admitted, as the ambassador spoke the *Lingua Franca* and Italian at least as well as myself. On my Grecian's retiring, I was prepared to follow him, but was detained; it was now my turn. Having called myself a Parisian, as such, I was under the jurisdiction of his excellency: he therefore asked me who I was? exhorting me to tell the truth; this I promised to do, but entreated a private audience, which was immediately granted. The ambassador took me to his closet, and shut the door; there, throwing myself at his feet, I kept my word, nor should I have said less, had I promised nothing, for a continual wish to unbosom myself, puts my heart perpetually upon my lips. After having disclosed myself without reserve to the musician Lutold, there was no occasion to attempt acting the mysterious with the Marquis de Bonac, who was so well pleased with my little history, and the ingenuousness with which I had related it, that he led me to the ambassadress, and presented me, with an abridgment of my recital. Madam de Bonac received me kindly, saying, I must not be suffered to follow that Greek monk. It was accordingly resolved that I should remain at their hotel till something better could be done for me. I wished to bid adieu to my poor Archimandrite, for whom I had conceived an attachment, but was not permitted: they sent him word that I was to be detained there, and in quarter of an hour after, I saw my little bundle arrive. M. de la Martiniere, secretary to the embassy, had in a manner the care of me; while following him to the chamber appropriated to my use, he said, "This apartment was occupied under the Count de Luc, by a celebrated man of the same name as yourself; it is in your power to succeed him in every respect, and cause it to be said hereafter, Rousseau the First, Rousseau the Second." This similarity, which I did not then expect, would have been less flattering to my wishes could I have foreseen at what price I should one day purchase the distinction.

What M. de la Martiniere had said excited my curiosity; I read the works of the person whose chamber I occupied, and on the strength of the compliment that had been paid me (imagining I had a taste for poetry) made my first essay in a cantata in praise of Madam de Bonac. This inclination was not permanent, though from time to time I have composed tolerable verses. I think it is a good exercise to teach elegant turns of expression, and to write well in prose, but could never find attractions enough in French poetry to give entirely into it.

M. de la Martiniere wished to see my style, and asked me to write the detail I had before made the ambassador; accordingly I wrote him a long letter, which I have since been informed was preserved by M. de Marianne, who had been long attached to the Marquis de Bonac, and has since succeeded M. de la Martiniere as secretary to the embassy of M. de Courteillies.

The experience I began to acquire tended to moderate my romantic projects: for example, I did not fall in love with Madam de Bonac, but also felt I did not stand much chance of succeeding in the service of her husband. M. de la Martiniere was already in the only place that could have satisfied my ambition, and M. de Marianne in expectancy: thus my utmost hopes could only aspire to the office of under secretary, which did not infinitely tempt me; this was the reason that when consulted on the situation I should like to be placed in, I expressed a great desire to go to Paris. The ambassador readily gave in to the idea, which at least tended to disembarrass him of me. M. de Merveilleux interpreting secretary to the embassy, said, that his friend, M. Godard, a Swiss colonel, in the service of France, wanted a person to be with his nephew, who had entered very young into the service, and made no doubt that I should suit him. On this idea, so lightly formed, my departure was determined; and I, who saw a long journey to perform, with Paris at the end of it, was enraptured with the project. They gave me several letters, a hundred livres to defray the expenses of my journey, accompanied with some good advice, and thus equipped I departed.

I was a fortnight making this journey, which I may reckon among the happiest days of my life. I was young, in perfect health, with plenty of money, and the most brilliant hopes: add to this, I was on foot, and alone. It may appear strange I should mention the latter circumstance as advantageous, if my peculiarity of temper is not already familiar to the reader. I was continually occupied with a variety of pleasing chimeras, and never did the warmth of my imagination produce more magnificent ones. When offered an empty place in a carriage, or any person accosted me on the road, how vexed was I to see that fortune overthrown, whose edifice, while walking, I had taken such pains to rear.

For once, my ideas were all martial: I was going to live with a military man; nay, to become one, for it was concluded I should begin with being a cadet. I already fancied myself in regimentals, with a fine white feather nodding on my hat, and my heart was inflamed by the noble idea. I had some smattering of geometry and fortification; my uncle was an engineer; I was in a manner a soldier by inheritance. My short sight, indeed, presented some little obstacle, but did not by any means discourage me, as I reckoned to supply that defect by coolness and intrepidity. I had read, too, that Marshal Schomberg was remarkably short-sighted, and why might not Marshal Rousseau be the same? My imagination was so warm by these follies, that it presented nothing but troops, ramparts, gabions, batteries, and myself in the midst of fire and smoke, an eye-glass in hand, commanding with the utmost tranquillity. Notwithstanding, when the country presented a delightful prospect, when I saw charming groves and rivulets, the pleasing sight made me sigh with regret, and feel, in the midst of all this glory, that my heart was not formed for such havoc; and soon without knowing how, I found my thoughts wandering among my dear sheepfolds, renouncing forever the labors of Mars.

How much did Paris disappoint the idea I had formed of it! The exterior decorations I had seen at Turin, the beauty of the streets, the symmetry and regularity of the houses, contributed to this disappointment, since I concluded that Paris must be infinitely superior. I had figured to myself a splendid city, beautiful as large, of the most commanding aspect, whose streets were ranges of magnificent palaces, composed of marble and gold. On entering the faubourg St. Marceau, I saw nothing but dirty stinking streets, filthy black houses, an air of slovenliness and poverty, beggars, carters, butchers, cries of diet-drink and old hats. This struck me so forcibly, that all I have since seen of real magnificence in Paris could never erase this first impression, which has ever given me a particular disgust to residing in that capital; and I may say, the whole time I remained there afterwards was employed in seeking resources which might enable me to live at a distance from it. This is the consequence of too lively imagination, which exaggerates even beyond the voice of fame, and ever expects more than is told. I had heard Paris so flatteringly described, that I pictured it like the ancient Babylon, which, perhaps, had I seen, I might have found equally faulty, and unlike that idea the account had conveyed. The same thing happened at the Opera-house, to which I hastened the day after my arrival! I was sensible of the same deficiency at Versailles! and some time after on viewing the sea. I am convinced this would ever be the consequence of a too flattering description of any object; for it is impossible for man, and difficult even for nature herself, to surpass the riches of my imagination.

By the reception I met with from all those to whom my letters were addressed, I thought my fortune was certainly made. The person who received me the least kindly was M. de Surbeck, to whom I had the warmest recommendation. He had retired from the service, and lived philosophically at Bagneux, where I waited on him several times without his offering me even a glass of water. I was better received by Madam de Merveilleux, sister-in-law to the interpreter, and by his nephew, who was an officer in the guards. The mother and son not only received me kindly, but offered me the use of their table, which favor I frequently accepted during my stay at Paris.

Madam de Merveilleux appeared to have been handsome; her hair was of a fine black, which, according to the old mode, she wore curled on the temples. She still retained (what do not perish with a set of features) the beauties of an amiable mind. She appeared satisfied with mine, and did all she could to render me service; but no one seconded her endeavors, and I was presently undeceived in the great interest they had seemed to take in my affairs. I must, however, do the French nation the justice to say, they do not so exhaust themselves with protestations, as some have represented, and that those they make are usually sincere; but they have a manner of appearing interested in your affairs, which is more deceiving than words. The gross compliments of the Swiss can only impose

upon fools; the manners of the French are more seducing, and at the same time so simple, that you are
persuaded they do not express all they mean to do for
you, in order that you may be the more agreeably surprised. I will say more; they are not false in their
protestations, being naturally zealous to oblige, humane, benevolent, and even (whatever may be said
to the country) more sincere than any other nation;
but they are too flighty: in effect they feel the sentiments they profess for you, but that sentiment flies off
as instantaneously as it was formed. In speaking to
you, their whole attention is employed on you alone,
when absent you are forgotten. Nothing is permanent
in their hearts, all is the work of the moment.

Thus I was greatly flattered, but received little service. Colonel Godard, for whose nephew I was recommended, proved to be an avaricious old wretch,
who, on seeing my distress (though he was immensely
rich), wished to have my services for nothing, meaning to place me with his nephew, rather as a valet
without wages than a tutor. He represented that as
I was to be continually engaged with him, I should
be excused from duty, and might live on my cadet's
allowance; that is to say, on the pay of a soldier:
hardly would he consent to give me a uniform, thinking the clothing of the army might serve. Madam de
Merveilleux, provoked at his proposals, persuaded me
not to accept them; her son was of the same opinion;
something else was to be thought on, but no situation
was procured. Meantime, I began to be necessitated;

for the hundred livres with which I had commenced my journey could not last much longer; happily, I received a small remittance from the ambassador, which was very serviceable, nor do I think he would have abandoned me had I possessed more patience; but languishing, waiting, soliciting, are to me impossible: I was disheartened, displeased, and thus all my brilliant expectations came once more to nothing. I had not all this time forgotten my dear Madam de Warrens, but how was I to find her? Where should I seek her?—Madam de Merveilleux, who knew my story, assisted me in the search, but for a long time unavailingly; at length, she informed me that Madam de Warrens had set out from Paris about two months before, but it was not known whether for Savoy or Turin, and that some conjectured she had gone to Switzerland. Nothing further was necessary to fix my determination to follow her, certain that wherever she might be, I stood more chance of finding her at those places than I could possibly do at Paris.

Before my departure, I exercised my new poetical talent in an epistle to Colonel Godard, whom I ridiculed to the utmost of my abilities. I showed this scribble to Madam de Merveilleux, who, instead of discouraging me, as she ought to have done, laughed heartily at my sarcasms, as well as her son, who, I believe, did not like M. Godard; indeed, it must be confessed, he was a man not calculated to obtain affection. I was tempted to send him my verses, and they encouraged me in it; accordingly I made them up in a parcel directed to him, and there being no post then at Paris by which I could conveniently send this, I put it in my pocket, and sent it to him from Auxerre, as I passed through that place. I laugh, even yet, sometimes, at the grimaces I fancy he made on reading this panegyric, where he was certainly drawn to the life; it began thus:

Tu croyois, vieux pénard, qu'une folle manie
D'élever ton neveu m'inspirerait l'envie.

This little piece, which, it is true, was but indifferently written, did not want for salt, and announced a turn for satire; it is, notwithstanding, the only satirical writing that ever came from my pen. I have too little hatred in my heart to take advantage of such a talent; but I believe it may be judged from those controversies, in which from time to time I have been engaged in my own defense, that had I been of a vindictive disposition, my adversaries would rarely have had the laughter on their side.

What I most regret, is not having kept a journal of my travels, being conscious that a number of interesting details have slipped my memory; for never did I exist so completely, never live so thoroughly, never was so much myself, if I dare use the expression, as in those journeys made on foot. Walking animates and enlivens my spirits; I can hardly think when in a state of inactivity; my body must be exercised to make my judgment active. The view of a fine country, a succession of agreeable prospects, a free air, a good appetite, and the health I gain by walking; the freedom of inns, and the distance from everything that can make me recollect the dependence of my situation, conspire to free my soul, and give boldness to my thoughts, throwing me, in a manner, into the immensity of beings, where I combine, choose, and appropriate them to my fancy, without constraint or fear. I dispose of all nature as I please; my heart wandering from object to object, approximates and unites with those that please it, is surrounded by charming images, and becomes intoxicated with delicious sensations. If, attempting to render these permanent, I am amused in describing to myself, what glow of coloring, what energy of expression, do I give them!—It has been said, that all these are to be found in my works, though written in the decline of life. Oh! had those of my early youth been seen, those made during my travels, composed, but never written!—Why did I not write them? will be asked; and why should I have written them? I may answer. Why deprive myself of the actual charm of my enjoyments to inform others what I enjoyed? What to me were readers, the public, or all the world, while I was mounting the empyrean. Besides, did I carry pens, paper, and ink with me? Had I recollected all these, not a thought would have occurred worth preserving. I do not foresee when I shall have ideas; they come when they please, and not when I call for them; either they avoid me altogether, or rushing in crowds, overwhelm me with their force and number. Ten volumes a day would not suffice barely to enumerate my thoughts; how then should I find time to write them? In stopping, I thought of nothing but a hearty dinner; on departing, of nothing but a charming walk; I felt that a new paradise awaited me at the door, and eagerly leaped forward to enjoy it.

Never did I experience this so feelingly as in the perambulation I am now describing. On coming to Paris, I had confined myself to ideas which related to the situation I expected to occupy there. I had rushed into the career I was about to run, and should have completed it with tolerable éclat, but it was not that my heart adhered to. Some real beings obscured my imagined ones—Colonel Godard and his nephew could not keep pace with a hero of my disposition. Thank Heaven, I was soon delivered from all these obstacles, and could enter at pleasure into the wilderness of chimeras, for that alone remained before me, and I wandered in it so completely that I several times lost my way; but this was no misfortune, I would not have shortened it, for, feeling with regret, as I approached Lyons, that I must again return to the material world, I should have been glad never to have arrived there.

One day, among others, having purposely gone out of my way to take a nearer view of a spot that appeared delightful, I was so charmed with it, and wandered round it so often, that at length I completely lost myself, and after several hours' useless walking, weary, fainting with hunger and thirst, I entered a peasant's hut, which had not indeed a very promising appearance, but was the only one I could discover near me. I thought it was here, as at Geneva, or in Switzerland, where the inhabitants, living at ease, have it in their power to exercise hospitality. I entreated the countryman to give me some dinner, offering to pay for it: on which he presented me with some skimmed milk and coarse barley-bread, saying it was all he had. I drank the milk with pleasure, and ate the bread, chaff and all; but it was not very restorative to a man sinking with fatigue. The countryman judged the truth of my story by my appetite, and presently after (having said that he plainly saw I was an honest, good-natured young man,* and did not come to betray him) opened a trap door by the side of his kitchen, went down, and returned with a good brown loaf of pure wheat, the remains of a ham, and a bottle of wine: he then prepared a good thick omelet, and I made such a dinner as none but a walking traveler ever enjoyed.

When I again offered to pay, his inquietude and fears returned; he not only would have no money, but refused it with the most evident emotion; and what made this scene more amusing, I could not imagine the motive of his fear. At length, he pronounced tremblingly those terrible words, "Commissioners," and "Cellar-rats," which he explained by giving me to understand that he concealed his wine because of the excise, and his bread on account of the

---

* At that time my features did not resemble later portraits.

tax imposed on it; adding, he should be an undone man, if it was suspected he was not almost perishing with want. What he said to me on this subject (of which I had not the smallest idea) made an impression on my mind that can never be effaced, sowing seeds of that inextinguishable hatred which has since grown up in my heart against the vexations these unhappy people suffer, and against their oppressors. This man, though in easy circumstances, dare not eat the bread gained by the sweat of his brow, and could only escape destruction by exhibiting an outward appearance of misery!—I left his cottage with as much indignation as concern, deploring the fate of those beautiful countries, where nature has been prodigal of her gifts, only that they may become the prey of barbarous exactors.

The incident which I have just related, is the only one I have a distinct remembrance of during this journey: I recollect, indeed, that on approaching Lyons, I wished to prolong it by going to see the banks of the Lignon; for among the romances I had read with my father, Astrea was not forgotten, and returned more frequently to my thoughts than any other. Stopping for some refreshment (while chatting with my hostess), I inquired the way to Forez, and was informed that country was an excellent place for mechanics, as there were many forges, and much iron work done there. This eulogium instantly calmed my romantic curiosity, for I felt no inclination to seek Dianas and Sylvanders among a generation of blacksmiths. The good woman who encouraged me with this piece of information certainly thought I was a journeyman locksmith.

I had some view in going to Lyons: on my arrival, I went to the Chasattes, to see Mademoiselle du Chatelet, a friend of Madam de Warrens, for whom I had brought a letter when I came there with M. le Maitre, so that it was an acquaintance already formed. Mademoiselle du Chatelet informed me her friend had passed through Lyons, but could not tell whether she had gone on to Piedmont, being uncertain at her departure whether it would not be necessary to stop in Savoy; but if I choose, she would immediately write for information, and thought my best plan would be to remain at Lyons till she received it. I accepted this offer, but did not tell Mademoiselle du Chatelet how much I was pressed for an answer and that my exhausted purse would not permit me to wait long. It was not an appearance of coolness that withheld me, on the contrary, I was very kindly received, treated on the footing of equality, and this took from me the resolution of explaining my circumstances, for I could not bear to descend from a companion to a miserable beggar.

I seem to have retained a very connecting remembrance of that part of my life contained in this book; yet I think I remember, about the same period, another journey to Lyons (the particulars of which I cannot recollect) where I found myself much straitened, and a confused remembrance of the extremities to which I was reduced does not contribute to recall the idea agreeably. Had I been like many others, had I possessed the talent of borrowing and running in debt at every ale-house I came to, I might have fared better; but in that my incapacity equaled my repugnance, and to demonstrate the prevalence of both, it will be sufficient to say, that though I have passed almost my whole life in different circumstances, and frequently have been near wanting bread, I was never once asked for money by a creditor without having it in my power to pay it instantly; I could never bear to contract clamorous debts, and have ever preferred suffering to owing.

Being reduced to pass my nights in the streets, may certainly be called suffering, and this was several times the case at Lyons, having preferred buying bread with the few pence I had remaining, to bestowing them on a lodging; as I was convinced there was less danger of dying for want of sleep than of hunger. What is astonishing, while in this unhappy situation, I took no care for the future, was neither uneasy nor melancholy, but patiently waited an answer to Mademoiselle du Chatelet's letter, and lying in the open air, stretched on the earth, or on a bench, slept as soundly as if reposing on a bed of roses. I remember, particularly, to have passed a most delightful night at some distance from the city, in a road which had the Rhone, or Soane, I cannot recollect which, on the one side, and a range of raised gardens, with terraces, on the other. It had been a very hot day, the evening was delightful, the dew moistened the fading grass, no wind was stirring, the air was fresh without chillness, the setting sun had tinged the clouds with a beautiful crimson, which was again reflected by the water, and the trees that bordered the terrace were filled with nightingales who were continually answering each other's songs. I walked along in a kind of ecstasy, giving up my heart and senses to the enjoyment of so many delights, and sighing only from a regret of enjoying them alone. Absorbed in this pleasing reverie, I lengthened my walk till it grew very late, without perceiving I was tired; at length, however, I discovered it, and threw myself on the step of a kind of niche, or false door, in the terrace wall. How charming was the couch! the trees formed a stately canopy, a nightingale sat directly over me, and with his soft notes lulled me to rest: how pleasing my repose; my awaking more so. It was broad day; on opening my eyes I saw the water, the verdure, and the admirable landscape before me. I arose, shook off the remains of drowsiness, and finding I was hungry, retook the way to the city, resolving, with inexpressible gayety, to spend the two pieces of *six blancs* I had yet remaining in a good breakfast. I found myself so cheerful that I went all the way singing; I even remember I sang a cantata of Batistin's called the *Baths of Thomery*, which I knew by heart. May a blessing light on the good Batistin and his good cantata, which procured me a better breakfast than I had expected, and a still better dinner, which I did not expect at all! In the midst of my singing, I heard some one behind me, and turning round perceived an Antonine, who followed after and seemed to listen with pleasure to my song. At length accosting me, he asked, if I understood music. I answered, *"A little,"* but in a manner to have it understood I knew a great deal, and as he continued questioning of me, related a part of my story. He asked me, if I had ever copied music? I replied, "Often," which was true: I had learned most by copying. "Well," continued he, "come with me, I can employ you for a few days, during which time you shall want for nothing; provided you consent not to quit my room." I acquiesced very willingly, and followed him.

This Antonine was called M. Rolichon; he loved music, understood it, and sang in some little concerts with his friends; thus far all was innocent and right, but apparently this taste had become a furor, part of which he was obliged to conceal. He conducted me into a chamber, where I found a great quantity of music: he gave me some to copy, particularly the cantata he had heard me singing, and which he was shortly to sing himself.

I remained here three or four days, copying all the time I did not eat, for never in my life was I so hungry, or better fed. M. Rolichon brought my provisions himself from the kitchen, and it appeared that these good priests lived well, at least if every one fared as I did. In my life, I never took such pleasure in eating, and it must be owned this good cheer came very opportunely, for I was almost exhausted. I worked as heartily as I ate, which is saying a great deal; 'tis true I was not as correct as diligent, for some days after, meeting M. Rolichon in the street, he informed me there were so many omissions, repetitions, and transpositions, in the parts I had copied, that they could not be performed. It must be owned, that in choosing the profession of music, I hit on that I was least calculated for; yet my voice was good and I copied neatly; but the fatigue of long works bewilders me so much, that I spend more time in altering and scratching out than in pricking down, and if I do not employ the strictest attention in comparing the several parts, they are sure to fail in the execution. Thus, through endeavoring to do well, my performance was very faulty; for aiming at expedition, I did all amiss. This did not prevent M. Rolichon from treating me well to the last, and giving me half-a-crown at my departure, which I certainly did not deserve, and which completely set me up, for a few days after I received news from Madam de Warrens, who was at Chambery, with money to defray the expenses of my journey to her, which I performed with rapture. Since then my finances have frequently been very low, but never at such an ebb as to reduce me to fasting, and I mark this period with a heart fully alive to the bounty of Providence, as the last of my life in which I sustained poverty and hunger.

I remained at Lyons seven or eight days to wait for some little commissions with which Madam de Warrens had charged Mademoiselle du Chatelet, whom during this interval I visited more assiduously than before, having the pleasure of talking with her of her friend, and being no longer disturbed by the cruel remembrance of my situation, or painful endeavors to conceal it. Mademoiselle du Chatelet was neither young nor handsome, but did not want for elegance; she was easy and obliging, while her understanding gave price to her familiarity. She had a taste for that kind of moral observation which leads to the knowledge of mankind, and from her originated that study in myself. She was fond of the works of Le Sage, particularly Gil Blas, which she lent me, and recommended to my perusal. I read this performance with pleasure, but my judgment was not yet ripe enough to relish that sort of reading. I liked romances which abounded with high-flown sentiments.

Thus did I pass my time at the grate of Mademoiselle du Chatelet, with as much profit as pleasure. It is certain that the interesting and sensible conversation of a deserving woman is more proper to form the understanding of a young man than all the pedantic philosophy of books. I got acquainted at the Chasattes with some other boarders and their friends, and among the rest, with a young person of fourteen, called Mademoiselle Serre, whom I did not much notice at that time, though I was in love with her eight or nine years afterwards, and with great reason, for she was a most charming girl.

I was fully occupied with the idea of seeing Madam

de Warrens, and this gave some respite to my chimeras, for finding happiness in real objects I was the less inclined to seek it in nonentities. I had not only found her, but also by her means, and near her, an agreeable situation, having received word that she had procured one that would suit me, and by which I should not be obliged to quit her. I exhausted all my conjectures in guessing what this occupation could be, but I must have possessed the art of divination to have hit it on the right. I had money sufficient to make my journey agreeable: Mademoiselle du Chatelet persuaded me to hire a horse, but this I could not consent to, and I was certainly right, for by so doing I should have lost the pleasure of the last pedestrian expedition I ever made; for I cannot give that name to those excursions I have frequently taken about my own neighborhood, while I lived at Motiers.

It is very singular that my imagination never rises so high as when my situation, is least agreeable or cheerful. When everything smiles around me, I am least amused; my heart cannot confine itself to realities, cannot embellish, but must create. Real objects strike me as they really are, my imagination can only decorate ideal ones. If I would paint the spring, it must be in winter; if describe a beautiful landscape, it must be while surrounded with walls; and I have said a hundred times, that were I confined in the Bastile, I could draw the most enchanting picture of liberty. On my departure from Lyons, I saw nothing but an agreeable future, the content I now with reason enjoyed was as great as my discontent had been at leaving Paris, notwithstanding, I had not during this journey any of those delightful reveries I then enjoyed. My mind was serene, and that was all; I drew near the excellent friend I was going to see, my heart overflowing with tenderness, enjoying in advance, but without intoxication, the pleasure of living near her; I had always expected this, and it was as if nothing new had happened. Meantime, I was anxious about the employment Madam de Warrens had procured me, as if that alone had been material. My ideas were calm and peaceable, not ravishing and celestial; every object struck my sight in its natural form; I observed the surrounding landscape, remarked the trees, the houses, the springs, deliberated on the cross-roads, was fearful of losing myself, yet did not do so; in a word, I was no longer in the empyrean, but precisely where I found myself, or sometimes perhaps at the end of my journey, never farther.

I am in recounting my travels, as I was in making them, loath to arrive at the conclusion. My heart beat with joy as I approached my dear Madam de Warrens, but I went no faster on that account. I love to walk at my ease, and stop at leisure; a strolling life is necessary to me: traveling on foot, in a fine country, with fine weather, and having an agreeable object to terminate my journey, is the manner of living of all others most suited to my taste.

It is already understood what I mean by a fine country; never can a flat one, though ever so beautiful, appear such in my eyes: I must have torrents, fir trees, black woods, mountains to climb or descend, and rugged roads with precipices on either side to alarm me. I experienced this pleasure in its utmost extent as I approached Chambery, not far from a mountain which is called *Pas de l'Echelle*. Above the main road, which is hewn through the rock, a small river runs and rushes into fearful chasms, which it appears to have been millions of ages in forming. The road has been hedged by a parapet to prevent accidents, which enabled me to contemplate the whole descent, and gain vertigoes at pleasure; for a great part of my amusement in these steep rocks, is, they cause a giddiness and swimming in my head, which I am particularly fond of, provided I am in safety; leaning, therefore, over the parapet, I remained whole hours, catching, from time to time, a glance of the froth and blue water, whose rushing caught my ear, mingled with the cries of ravens, and other birds of prey that flew from rock to rock, and bush to bush, at six hundred feet below me. In places where the slope was tolerably regular, and clear enough from bushes to let stones roll freely, I went a considerable way to gather them, bringing those I could but just carry, which I piled on the parapet, and then threw down one after the other, being transported at seeing them roll, rebound, and fly into a thousand pieces, before they reached the bottom of the precipice.

Near Chambery I enjoyed an equal pleasing spectacle, though of a different kind; the road passing near the foot of the most charming cascade I ever saw. The water, which is very rapid, shoots from the top of an excessively steep mountain, falling at such a distance from its base that you may walk between the cascade and the rock without any inconvenience; but if not particularly careful it is easy to be deceived as I was, for the water, falling from such an immense height, separates, and descends in a rain as fine as dust, and on approaching too near this cloud, without perceiving it, you may be wet through in an instant.

At length I arrived at Madam de Warrens'; she was not alone, the intendant-general was with her. Without speaking a word to me, she caught my hand, and presenting me to him with that natural grace which charmed all hearts, said: "This, sir, is the poor young man I mentioned; deign to protect him as long as he deserves it, and I shall feel no concern for the remainder of his life." Then added, addressing herself to me, "Child, you now belong to the king, thank Monsieur the Intendant, who furnishes you with the means of existence." I stared without answering, without knowing what to think of all this; rising ambition almost turned my head; I was already prepared to act the intendant myself. My fortune, however, was not so brilliant as I had imagined, but it was sufficient to maintain me, which, as I was situated, was a capital acquisition. I shall now explain the nature of my employment.

King Victor Amadeus, judging by the event of

preceding wars, and the situation of the ancient patrimony of his fathers, that he should not long be able
to maintain it, wished to drain it beforehand. Resolving, therefore, to tax the nobility, he ordered a general survey of the whole country, in order that it
might be rendered more equal and productive. This
scheme, which was begun under the father, was completed by the son: two or three hundred men, part
surveyors, who were called geometricians, and part
writers, who were called secretaries, were employed
in this work: among those of the latter description
Madam de Warrens had got me appointed. This post,
without being very lucrative, furnished the means of
living eligibly in that country; the misfortune was,
this employment could not be of any great duration,
but it put me in train to procure something better, as
by this means she hoped to insure the particular protection of the intendant, who might find me some
more settled occupation before this was concluded.

I entered on my new employment a few days after
my arrival, and as there was no great difficulty in the
business, soon understood it; thus, after four or five
years of unsettled life, folly, and suffering, since my
departure from Geneva, I began, for the first time,
to gain my bread with credit.

These long details of my early youth must have
appeared trifling, and I am sorry for it: though born
a man, in a variety of instances, I was long a child,
and am so yet in many particulars. I did not promise
the public a great personage: I promised to describe

myself as I am, and to know me in my advanced age
it was necessary to have known me in my youth. As,
in general, objects that are present make less impression on me than the bare remembrance of them (my
ideas being all from recollection), the first traits which
were engraven on my mind have distinctly remained:
those which have since been imprinted there have
rather combined with the former than effaced them.
There is a certain, yet varied succession of affections
and ideas, which continue to regulate those that follow
them, and this progression must be known in order
to judge rightly of those they have influenced. I have
studied to develop the first causes, the better to show
the concatenation of effects. I would be able by some
means to render my soul transparent to the eyes of the
reader, and for this purpose endeavor to show it in
every possible point of view, to give him every insight,
and act in such a manner, that not a motion should
escape him, as by this means he may form a judgment
of the principles that produce them.

Did I take upon myself to decide, and say to the
reader, "Such is my character," he might think that
if I did not endeavor to deceive him, I at least deceived
myself; but in recounting simply all that has happened to me, all my actions, thoughts, and feelings,
I cannot lead him into an error, unless I do it willfully,
which by this means I could not easily effect, since
it is his province to compare the elements, and judge
of the being they compose: thus the result must be his
work, and if he is then deceived the error will be his

own. It is not sufficient for this purpose that my recitals should be merely faithful, they must also be minute; it is not for me to judge of the importance of facts, I ought to declare them simply as they are, and leave the estimate that is to be formed of them to him. I have adhered to this principle hitherto, with the most scrupulous exactitude, and shall not depart from it in the continuation; but the impressions of age are less lively than those of youth; I began by delineating the latter: should I recollect the rest with the same precision, the reader may, perhaps, become weary and impatient, but I shall not be dissatisfied with my labor. I have but one thing to apprehend in this undertaking: I do not dread saying too much, or advancing falsities, but I am fearful of not saying enough, or concealing truths.

BOOK V

BOOK V

[1732–1736]

I THINK it was in 1732, that I arrived at Chambery, as already related, and began my employment of registering land for the king. I was almost twenty-one, my mind well enough formed for my age, with respect to sense, but very deficient in point of judgment, and needing every instruction from those into whose hands I fell, to make me conduct myself with propriety; for a few years' experience had not been able to cure me radically of my romantic ideas; and notwithstanding the ills I had sustained, I knew as little of the world, of mankind, as if I had never purchased instruction. I slept at home, that is, at the house of Madam de Warrens; but it was not as at Annecy: here were no gardens, no brook, no landscape; the house was dark and dismal, and my apartment the most gloomy of the whole. The prospect a dead wall, an alley instead of a street, confined air, bad light, small rooms, iron bars, rats, and a rotten floor; an assemblage of circumstances that do not constitute a very agreeable habitation; but I was in the same house with my best friend, incessantly near her, at my desk or in her chamber, so that I could not perceive the gloominess of my own, or have time to think of it. It may appear whimsical that she should reside at Chambery on purpose to live in this disagreeable house; but it was a trait of contrivance which I ought not to pass over in silence. She had no great inclination for a journey to Turin, fearing that after the recent revolutions, and the agitation in which the court yet was, she should not be very favorably received there; but her affairs seemed to demand her presence, as she feared being forgotten or ill-treated, particularly as the Count de Saint-Laurent, Intendant-general of the Finances, was not in her interest. He had an old house at Chambery, ill-built, and standing in so disagreeable a situation that it was always untenanted; she hired, and settled in this house; a plan that succeeded much better than a journey to Turin would have done, for her pension was not suppressed, and the Count de Saint-Laurent was ever after one of her best friends.

Her household was much on the old footing; the faithful Claude Anet still remained with her. He was, as I have before mentioned, a peasant of Moutru, who in his childhood had gathered herbs in Jura for the purpose of making Swiss tea; she had taken him into her service for his knowledge of drugs, finding it convenient to have a herbalist among her domestics. Passionately fond of the study of plants, he became a real botanist, and had he not died young, might have acquired as much fame in that science as he deserved for being an honest man. Serious even to gravity, and older than myself, he was to me a kind of tutor, commanding respect, and preserving me from a number of follies, for I dared not forget myself before him. He commanded it likewise from his mistress, who knew his understanding, uprightness, and inviolable attachment to herself, and returned it. Claude Anet was of an uncommon temper. I never encountered a similar disposition: he was slow, deliberate, and circumspect in his conduct; cold in his manner; laconic and sententious in discourse; yet of an impetuosity in his passions, which (though careful to conceal) preyed upon him inwardly, and urged him to the only folly he ever committed; that folly, indeed was terrible, it was poisoning himself. This tragic scene passed soon after my arrival, and opened my eyes to the intimacy that subsisted between Claude Anet and his mistress, for had not the information come from her, I should never have suspected it; yet, surely, if attachment, fidelity, and zeal, could merit such a recompense, it was due to him, and what further proves him worthy such a distinction, he never once abused her confidence. They seldom disputed, and their disagreements ever ended amicably; one, indeed, was not so fortunate; his mistress, in a passion, said something affronting, which not being able to digest, he consulted only with despair, and finding a bottle of laudanum at hand, drank it off; then went peaceably to bed, expecting to awake no more. Madam de Warrens herself was uneasy, agitated. wandering about the house, and happily, finding the phial empty, guessed the rest. Her screams while flying to his assistance, alarmed me; she confessed all, implored my help, and was fortunate enough, after repeated efforts, to make him throw up the laudanum. Witness of this scene, I could not but wonder at my stupidity in never having suspected the connection; but Claude Anet was so discreet, that a more penetrating observer might have been deceived. Their reconciliation affected me, and added respect to the esteem I before felt for him. From this time I became, in some measure, his pupil, nor did I find myself the worse for his instruction.

I could not learn, without pain, that she lived in greater intimacy with another than with myself: it was a situation I had not even thought of, but (which was very natural) it hurt me to see another in possession of it. Nevertheless, instead of feeling any aversion to the person who had this advantage over me, I found the attachment I felt for her, actually extend to him. I desired her happiness above all things, and since he was concerned in her plan of felicity, I was content he should be happy likewise. Meantime he perfectly entered into the views of his mistress; conceived a sincere friendship for me, and without affecting the authority his situation might have entitled him to, he naturally possessed that which his superior judgment gave him over mine. I dared do nothing he disapproved of, but he was sure to disapprove only what merited disapprobation: thus we lived in an union which rendered us mutually happy, and which death alone could dissolve.

One proof of the excellence of this amiable woman's character, is, that all those who loved her, loved each other; even jealousy and rivalship submitting to the more powerful sentiment with which she inspired them, and I never saw any of those who surrounded her entertain the least ill will among themselves. Let the reader pause a moment on this encomium, and if he can recollect any other woman who deserves it, let him attach himself to her, if he would obtain happiness.

From my arrival at Chambery to my departure for Paris, 1741, included an interval of eight or nine years, during which time I have few adventures to relate; my life being as simple as it was agreeable. This uniformity was precisely what was most wanting to complete the formation of my character, which continual troubles had prevented from acquiring any degree of stability. It was during this pleasing interval, that my unconnected, unfinished education, gained consistence, and made me what I have unalterably remained amid the storms with which I have since been surrounded. The progress was slow, almost imperceptible, and attended by few memorable circumstances; yet it deserves to be followed and investigated.

At first, I was wholly occupied with my business, the constraint of a desk left little opportunity for other thoughts, the small portion of time I was at liberty was passed with my dear Madam de Warrens, and not having leisure to read, I felt no inclination for it; but when my business (by daily repetition) became familiar, and my mind was less occupied, study again became necessary, and (as my desires were ever irritated by any difficulty that opposed the indulgence of them) might once more have become a passion, as at my master's, had not other inclinations interposed and diverted it.

Though our occupation did not demand a very profound skill in arithmetic, it sometimes required enough to puzzle me. To conquer this difficulty, I purchased books which treated on that science, and learned well, for I now studied alone. Practical arithmetic extends further than is usually supposed, if you would attain exact precision. There are operations of extreme length in which I have sometimes seen good geometricians lose themselves. Reflection, assisted by practice, gives clear ideas, and enables you to devise shorter methods, these inventions flatter our self-complacency, while their exactitude satisfies our understanding, and renders a study pleasant, which is, of itself, heavy and unentertaining. At length I became so expert as not to be puzzled by any question that was solvable by arithmetical calculation; and even now, while everything I formerly knew fades daily on my memory, this acquirement, in a great measure remains, through an interval of thirty years. A few days ago, in a journey I made to Davenport, being with my host at an arithmetical lesson given his children, I did (with pleasure, and without errors) a most complicated work. While setting down my figures, methought I was still at Chambery, still in my days of happiness—how far I had to look back for them!

The colored plans of our geometricians had given me a taste for drawing: accordingly I bought colors, and began by attempting flowers and landscapes. It was unfortunate that I had not talents for this art, for my inclination was much disposed to it, and while surrounded with crayons, pencils, and colors, I could have passed whole months without wishing to leave them. This amusement engaged me so much, that they were obliged to force me from it; and thus it is with every inclination I give in to, it continues to augment, till at length it becomes so powerful, that I lose sight of everything except the favorite amusement. Years have not been able to cure me of that fault, nay, have not even diminished it; for while I am writing this, behold me, like an old dotard, infatuated with another, to me useless study, which I do not understand, and which even those who have devoted their youthful days to the acquisition of, are constrained to abandon, at the age I am beginning with it.

At that time, the study I am now speaking of would have been well placed, the opportunity was good, and I had some temptation to profit by it; for the satisfaction I saw in the eyes of Anet, when he came home loaded with new discovered plants, set me two or three times on the point of going to herbalize with him, and I am almost certain that had I gone once,

I should have been caught, and perhaps at this day might have been an excellent botanist, for I know no study more congenial to my natural inclination, than that of plants; the life I have led for these ten years past, in the country, being little more than a continual herbalizing, though I must confess, without object, and without improvement; but at the time I am now speaking of I had no inclination for botany, nay, I even despised, and was disgusted at the idea, considering it only as a fit study for an apothecary. Madam de Warrens was fond of it merely for this purpose, seeking none but common plants to use in her medical preparations; thus botany, chemistry, and anatomy were confounded in my idea under the general denomination of medicine, and served to furnish me with pleasant sarcasms the whole day, which procured me, from time to time, a box on the ear, applied by Madam de Warrens. Besides this, a very contrary taste grew up with me, and by degrees absorbed all others; this was music. I was certainly born for that science, I loved it from my infancy, and it was the only inclination I have constantly adhered to; but it is astonishing that what nature seemed to have designed me for should have cost me so much pains to learn, and that I should acquire it so slowly, that after a whole life spent in the practice of this art, I could never attain to sing with any certainty at sight. What rendered the study of music more agreeable to me at that time, was, being able to practice it with Madam de Warrens. In other respects our tastes were widely different: this was a point of coincidence, which I loved to avail myself of. She had no more objection to this than myself: I knew at that time almost as much of it as she did, and after two or three efforts, we could make shift to decipher an air. Sometimes, when I saw her busy at her furnace, I have said, "Here now is a charming duet, which seems made for the very purpose of spoiling your drugs;" her answer would be, "If you make me burn them, I'll make you eat them:" thus disputing, I drew her to the harpsichord; the furnace was presently forgotten, the extract of juniper or wormwood calcined (which I cannot recollect without transport), and these scenes usually ended by her smearing my face with the remains of them.

It may easily be conjectured that I had plenty of employment to fill up my leisure hours; one amusement, however, found room, that was well worth all the rest.

We lived in such a confined dungeon, that it was necessary sometimes to breathe the open air; Anet, therefore, engaged Madam de Warrens to hire a garden in the suburbs, both for this purpose and the convenience of rearing plants, etc.; to this garden was added a summer-house, which was furnished in the customary manner; we sometimes dined, and I frequently slept, there. Insensibly I became attached to this little retreat, decorated it with books and prints, spending part of my time in ornamenting it during the absence of Madam de Warrens, that I might surprise her the more agreeably on her return. Sometimes I quitted this dear friend, that I might enjoy the uninterrupted pleasure of thinking on her; this was a caprice I can neither excuse nor fully explain, I only know this really was the case, and therefore I avow it. I remember Madam de Luxembourg told me one day in raillery, of a man who used to leave his mistress that he might enjoy the satisfaction of writing to her; I answered, I could have been this man; I might have added, that I had done the very same.

I did not, however, find it necessary to leave Madam de Warrens that I might love her the more ardently, for I was ever as perfectly free with her as when alone; an advantage I never enjoyed with any other person, man or woman, however I might be attached to them; but she was so often surrounded by company who were far from pleasing me, that spite and weariness drove me to this asylum, where I could indulge her idea, without danger of being interrupted by impertinence.

Thus, my time being divided between business, pleasure, and instruction, my life passed in the most absolute serenity. Europe was not equally tranquil: France and the emperor had mutually declared war, the King of Sardinia had entered into the quarrel, and a French army had filed off into Piedmont to awe the Milanese. Our division passed through Chambery, and, among others, the regiment of Champaigne, whose colonel was the Duke de la Trimouille, to whom I was presented. He promised many things, but doubtless never more thought of me. Our little garden was exactly at the end of the suburb by which the troops entered, so that I could fully satisfy my curiosity in seeing them pass, and I became as anxious for the success of the war as if it had nearly concerned me. Till now I had never troubled myself about politics, for the first time I began reading the gazettes, but with so much partiality on the side of France, that my heart beat with rapture on its most trifling advantages, and I was as much afflicted on a reverse of fortune, as if I had been particularly concerned.

Had this folly been transient, I should not, perhaps, have mentioned it, but it took such root in my heart (without any reasonable cause) that when I afterwards acted the anti-despot and proud republican at Paris, in spite of myself, I felt a secret predilection for the nation I declared servile, and for that government I affected to oppose. The pleasantest of all was that, ashamed of an inclination so contrary to my professed maxims, I dared not own it to any one, but rallied the French on their defeats, while my heart was more wounded than their own. I am certainly the first man, that, living with a people who treated him well, and whom he almost adored, put on, even in their own country, a borrowed air of despising them; yet my original inclination is so powerful, constant, disinterested, and invincible, that even since my quitting that kingdom, since its government, magistrates, and authors, have outvied each other in rancor against me, since it has become fashionable to load me with injustice and abuse, I have not been able to get rid of this folly, but notwithstanding their ill-treatment, love them in spite of myself.

I long sought the cause of this partiality, but was never able to find any, except in the occasion that gave it birth. A rising taste for literature attached me to French books, to their authors, and their country: at the very moment the French troops were passing Chambery, I was reading *Brantôme's Celebrated Captains;* my head was full of the *Clissons, Bayards, Lautrecs, Colignys, Montmorencys,* and *Trimouilles,* and I loved their descendants as the heirs of their merit and courage. In each regiment that passed by methought I saw those famous black bands who had formerly done so many noble exploits in Piedmont; in fine, I applied to these all the ideas I had gathered from books; my reading continued, which, still drawn from the same nation, nourished my affection for that country, till, at length, it became a blind passion, which nothing could overcome. I have had occasion to remark several times in the course of my travels, that this impression was not peculiar to me for France, but was more or less active in every country, for that part of the nation who were fond of literature, and cultivated learning, and it was this consideration that balanced in my mind the general hatred which the conceited air of the French is so apt to inspire. Their romances, more than their men, attract the women of all countries, and the celebrated dramatic pieces of

France create a fondness in youth for their theaters; the reputation which that of Paris in particular has acquired, draws to it crowds of strangers, who return enthusiasts to their own country: in short, the excellence of their literature captivates the senses, and in the unfortunate war just ended, I have seen their authors and philosophers maintain the glory of France, so tarnished by its warriors.

I was, therefore, an ardent Frenchman; this rendered me a politician, and I attended in the public square, amid a throng of news-mongers, the arrival of the post, and, sillier than the ass in the fable, was very uneasy to know whose packsaddle I should next have the honor to carry, for it was then supposed we should belong to France, and that Savoy would be exchanged for Milan. I must confess, however, that I experienced some uneasiness, for had this war terminated unfortunately for the allies, the pension of Madam de Warrens would have been in a dangerous situation; nevertheless, I had great confidence in my good friends, the French, and for once (in spite of the surprise of M. de Broglio) my confidence was not ill-founded—thanks to the King of Sardinia, whom I had never thought of.

While we were fighting in Italy, they were singing in France: the operas of *Rameau* began to make a noise there, and once more raise the credit of his theoretic works, which, from their obscurity, were within the compass of very few understandings. By chance I heard of his Treatise on Harmony, and had no rest till I purchased it. By another chance I fell sick; my illness was inflammatory, short and violent, but my convalescence was tedious, for I was unable to go abroad for a whole month. During this time I eagerly ran over my Treatise on Harmony, but it was so long, so diffuse, and so badly disposed, that I found it would require a considerable time to unravel it: accordingly I suspended my inclination, and recreated my sight with music.

The cantatas of *Bernier* were what I principally exercised myself with. These were never out of my mind; I learned four or five by heart, and among the rest, *The Sleeping Cupids,* which I have never seen since that time, though I still retain it almost entirely; as well as *Cupid Stung by a Bee,* a very pretty cantata by *Clerambault,* which I learned about the same time.

To complete me, there arrived a young organist from *Valdost,* called the Abbé Palais, a good musician and an agreeable companion, who performed very well on the harpsichord; I got acquainted with him, and we soon became inseparable. He had been brought up by an Italian monk, who was a capital organist. He explained to me his principles of music, which I compared with *Rameau;* my head was filled with accompaniments, concords and harmony, but as it was necessary to accustom the ear to all this, I proposed to Madam de Warrens having a little concert once a month, to which she consented.

Behold me then so full of this concert, that night or day I could think of nothing else, and it actually employed a great part of my time to select the music; assemble the musicians, look to the instruments, and write out the several parts. Madam de Warrens sang; Father Cato (whom I have before mentioned, and shall have occasion to speak of again) sang likewise; a dancing-master named *Roche,* and his son, played on the violin; *Canavas,* a Piedmontese musician (who was employed like myself in the survey, and has since married at Paris), played on the violoncello; the Abbé *Palais* performed on the harpsichord, and I had the honor to conduct the whole. It may be supposed all this was charming: I cannot say it equaled my concert at Monsieur de *Tretoren's,* but certainly it was not far behind it.

This little concert, given by Madam de Warrens, the new convert, who lived (it was expressed) on the king's charity, made the whole tribe of devotees murmur, but was a very agreeable amusement to several worthy people, at the head of whom it would not be easily surmised that I should place a monk; yet, though a monk, a man of considerable merit, and even of a very amiable disposition, whose subsequent misfortunes gave me the most lively concern, and whose idea, attached to that of my happy days, is yet dear to my memory. I speak of Father Cato, a Cordelier, who, in conjunction with the Count d'Ortan, had caused the music of poor Le Maitre to be seized at Lyons; which action was far from being the brightest trait in his history. He was a Bachelor of Sorbonne; had lived long in Paris among the great world, and was particularly caressed by the Marquis d'Antremont, then Ambassador from Sardinia. He was tall and well made; full faced, with very fine eyes, and black hair, which formed natural curls on each side of his forehead. His manner was at once noble, open, and modest; he presented himself with ease and good manners, having neither the hypocritical nor impudent behavior of a monk, or the forward assurance of a fashionable coxcomb, but the manners of a well-bred man, who, without blushing for his habit, set a value on himself, and ever felt in his proper situation when in good company. Though Father Cato was not deeply studied for a doctor, he was much so for a man of the world, and not being compelled to show his talents, he brought them forward so advantageously that they appeared greater than they really were. Having lived much in the world, he had rather attached himself to agreeable acquirements than to solid learning; had sense, made verses, spoke well, sang better, and aided his good voice by playing on the organ and harpsichord. So many pleasing qualities were not necessary to make his company sought after, and, accordingly, it was very much so, but this did not make him neglect the duties of his function: he was chosen (in spite of his jealous competitors) Definitor of his Province, or, according to them, one of the greatest pillars of their order.

Father Cato became acquainted with Madam de Warrens at the Marquis of Antremont's; he had heard of her concerts, wished to assist at them, and by his company rendered our meetings truly agreeable. We were soon attached to each other by our mutual taste for music, which in both was a most lively passion, with this difference, that he was really a musician, and myself a bungler. Sometimes assisted by Canavas and the Abbé Palais, we had music in his apartment, or on holidays at his organ, and frequently dined with him; for, what was very astonishing in a monk, he was generous, profuse, and loved good cheer, without the least tincture of greediness. After our concerts, he always used to stay to supper, and these evenings passed with the greatest gayety and good-humor; we conversed with the utmost freedom, and sang duets; I was perfectly at my ease, had sallies of wit and merriment; Father Cato was charming, Madam de Warrens adorable, and the Abbé Palais, with his rough voice, was the butt of the company. Pleasing moments of sportive youth, how long since have ye fled!

As I shall have no more occasion to speak of poor Father Cato, I will here conclude in a few words his melancholy history. His brother monks, jealous, or rather exasperated to discover in him a merit and elegance of manners which favored nothing of monastic stupidity, conceived the most violent hatred to him, because he was not as despicable as themselves; the chiefs, therefore, combined against this worthy man, and set on the envious rabble of monks, who otherwise, would not have dared to hazard the attack. He received a thousand indignities; they degraded him from his office, took away the apartment which he had furnished with elegant simplicity, and, at length, banished him, I know not whither: in short, these wretches overwhelmed him with so many evils, that his honest and proud soul sank under the pressure, and, after having been the delight of the most amiable societies, he died of grief, on a wretched bed, hid in some cell or dungeon, lamented by all worthy people of his acquaintance, who could find no fault in him, except his being a monk.

Accustomed to this manner of life for some time, I became so entirely attached to music that I could think of nothing else. I went to my business with disgust, the necessary confinement and assiduity appeared an insupportable punishment, which I at length wished to relinquish, that I might give myself up without reserve to my favorite amusement. It will be readily believed that this folly met with some opposition, to give up a creditable employment and fixed salary to run after uncertain scholars was too giddy a plan to be approved of by Madam de Warrens, and even supposing my future success should prove as great as I flattered myself, it was fixing very humble limits to my ambition to think of reducing myself for life to the condition of a music-master. She, who formed for me the brightest projects, and no longer trusted implicitly to the judgment of M. d'Aubonne, seeing with concern that I was so seriously occupied by a talent which she thought frivolous, frequently repeated to me that provincial proverb, which does not hold quite so good in Paris, *Qui bien chante et bien danse, fait un métier qui peu avance.** On the other hand, she saw me hurried away by this irresistible passion, my taste for music having become a furor, and it was much to be feared that my employment, suffering by my distraction, might draw on me a discharge, which would be worse than a voluntary resignation. I represented to her, that this employment could not last long, that it was necessary I should have some permanent means of subsistence, and that it would be much better to complete by practice the acquisition of that art to which my inclination led me than to make fresh essays, which possibly might not succeed, since by this means, having passed the age most proper for improvement, I might be left without a single resource for gaining a livelihood: in short, I extorted her consent more by importunity and caresses than by any satisfactory reasons. Proud of my success, I immediately ran to thank M. Coccelli, Director-General of the Survey, as though I had performed the most heroic action, and quitted my employment without cause, reason, or pretext, with as much pleasure as I had accepted it two years before.

This step, ridiculous as it may appear, procured me a kind of consideration, which I found extremely useful. Some supposed I had resources which I did not possess; others, seeing me totally given up to music, judged of my abilities by the sacrifice I had made, and

* *He who can sweetly sing and featly dance,*
  His interests right little shall advance.

concluded that with such a passion for the art, I must possess it in a superior degree. In a nation of blind men, those with one eye are kings. I passed here for an excellent master, because all the rest were very bad ones. Possessing taste in singing, and being favored by my age and figure, I soon procured more scholars than were sufficient to compensate for the loss of my secretary's pay.

It is certain, that had it been reasonable to consider the pleasure of my situation only, it was impossible to pass more speedily from one extreme to the other. At our measuring, I was confined eight hours in the day to the most unentertaining employment, with yet more disagreeable company. Shut up in a melancholy counting-house, empoisoned by the smell and respiration of a number of clowns, the major part of whom were ill-combed and very dirty, what with attention, bad air, constraint, and weariness, I was sometimes so far overcome as to occasion a vertigo. Instead of this, behold me admitted into the fashionable world, sought after in the first houses, and everywhere received with an air of satisfaction; amiable and gay young ladies awaiting my arrival, and welcoming me with pleasure; I see nothing but charming objects, smell nothing but roses and orange flowers; singing, chatting, laughter, and amusements, perpetually succeed each other. It must be allowed, that reckoning all these advantages, no hesitation was necessary in the choice; in fact, I was so content with mine, that I never once repented it; nor do I even now, when, free from the irrational motives that influenced me at that time, I weigh in the scale of reason every action of my life.

This is, perhaps, the only time that, listening to inclination, I was not deceived in my expectations. The easy access, obliging temper, and free humor of this country, rendered a commerce with the world agreeable, and the inclination I then felt for it, proves to me, that if I have a dislike for society, it is more their fault than mine. It is a pity the Savoyards are not rich: though, perhaps, it would be a still greater pity if they were so, for altogether they are the best, the most sociable people that I know, and if there is a little city in the world where the pleasures of life are experienced in an agreeable and friendly commerce, it is at Chambery. The gentry of the province who assemble there have only sufficient wealth to live and not enough to spoil them; they cannot give way to ambition, but follow, through necessity, the counsel of *Cyneas,* devoting their youth to a military employment, and returning home to grow old in peace; an arrangement over which honor and reason equally preside. The women are handsome, yet do not stand in need of beauty, since they possess all those qualifications which enhance its value and even supply the want of it. It is remarkable, that being obliged by my profession to see a number of young girls, I do not recollect one at Chambery but what was charming: it will be said I was disposed to find them so, and perhaps there may be some truth in the surmise. I cannot remember my young scholars without pleasure. Why, in naming the most amiable, cannot I recall them and myself also to that happy age in which our moments, pleasing as innocent, were passed with such happiness together? The first was Mademoiselle de Mallarede, my neighbor, and sister to a pupil of Monsieur Gaime. She was a fine clear brunette, lively and graceful, without giddiness; thin as girls of that age usually are; but her bright eyes, fine shape, and easy air, rendered her sufficiently pleasing with that degree of plumpness which would have given a heightening to her charms. I went there of mornings, when she was usually in her dishabille, her hair carelessly turned up, and, on my arrival, ornamented with a flower, which was taken off at my departure for her hair to be dressed. There is nothing I fear so much as a pretty woman in an elegant dishabille; I should dread them a hundred times less in full dress. Mademoiselle de Menthon, whom I attended in the afternoon, was ever so. She made an equally pleasing, but quite different impression on me. Her hair was flaxen, her person delicate, she was very timid and extremely fair, had a clear voice, capable of just modulation, but which she had not courage to employ to its full extent. She had the mark of a scald on her bosom, which a scanty piece of blue chenille did not entirely cover, this scar sometimes drew my attention, though not absolutely on its own account. Mademoiselle des Challes, another of my neighbors, was a woman grown, tall, well-formed, jolly, very pleasing though not a beauty, and might be quoted for her gracefulness, equal temper, and good humor. Her sister, Madam de Charley, the handsomest woman of Chambery, did not learn music, but I taught her daughter, who was yet young, but whose growing beauty promised to equal her mother's, if she had not unfortunately been a little red-haired. I had likewise among my scholars a little French lady, whose name I have forgotten, but who merits a place in my list of preferences. She had adopted the slow drawling tone of the nuns, in which voice she would utter some very keen things, which did not in the least appear to correspond with her manner; but she was indolent, and could not generally take pains to show her wit, that being a favor she did not grant to every one. When with my scholars, I was fond enough of teaching, but could not bear the idea of being obliged to attend at a particular hour; constraint and subjection in every shape are to me insupportable, and alone sufficient to make me hate even pleasure itself. I am told that it is custom among the Mohammedans to have a man pass through the streets at daybreak, and cry out: "Husbands, do your duty to your wives." I should only make a poor Turk at this particular hour.

Among other scholars which I had, there was one who was the indirect cause of a change of relationship, which I must relate in its place. She was the daughter of a grocer, and was called Mademoiselle de Larnage, a perfect model for a Grecian statue, and whom I should quote for the handsomest girl I have ever seen, if true beauty could exist without life or soul. Her indolence, reserve, and insensibility were inconceivable; it was equally impossible to please or make her angry, and I am convinced that had any one formed a design upon her virtue, he might have succeeded, not through her inclination, but from her ftupidity. Her mother, who would run no risk of this, did not leave her a single moment. In having her taught to sing and providing a young master, she had hoped to enliven her, but it all proved ineffectual. While the master was admiring the daughter, the mother was admiring the master, but this was equally lost labor. Madam de Larnage added to her natural vivacity that portion of sprightliness which should have belonged to the daughter. She was a little, ugly, lively trollop, with small twinkling ferret eyes, and marked with smallpox. On my arrival in the morning, I always found my coffee and cream ready, and the mother never failed to welcome me with a kiss on the lips, which I would willingly have returned the daughter, to see how she would have received it. All this was done with such an air of carelessness and simplicity, that even when M. de Larnage was present, her kisses and caresses were not omitted. He was a good quiet fellow, the true original of his daughter; nor did his wife endeavor to deceive him, because there was absolutely no occasion for it.

I received all these caresses with my usual ftupidity, taking them only for marks of pure friendship, though they were sometimes troublesome; for the lively Madam Lard was displeased, if, during the day, I passed the shop without calling; it became necessary, therefore (when I had no time to spare), to go out of my way through another street, well knowing it was not so easy to quit her house as to enter it.

Madam Lard thought so much of me, that I could not avoid thinking something of her. Her attentions affected me greatly, and I spoke of them to Madam de Warrens, without supposing any mystery in the matter, but had there been one I should equally have divulged it, for to have kept a secret of any kind from her would have been impossible. My heart lay as open to Madam de Warrens as to Heaven. She did not understand the matter quite so simply as I had done, but saw advances where I only discovered friendship. She concluded that Madam Lard would make a point of not leaving me as great a fool as she found me, and, some way or other, contrive to make herself understood; but exclusive of the consideration that it was not just that another should undertake the instruction of her pupil, she had motives more worthy of her, wishing to guard me against the snares to which my youth and inexperience exposed me. Meantime, a more dangerous temptation offered which I likewise escaped, but which proved to her that such a succession of dangers required every preservative she could possibly apply.

The Countess of Menthon, mother to one of my scholars, was a woman of great wit, and reckoned to possess, at least, an equal share of mischief, having (as was reported) caused a number of quarrels, and, among others, one that terminated fatally for the house of D'Antremont. Madam de Warrens had seen enough of her to know her character: for having (very innocently) pleased some person to whom Madam de Menthon had pretensions, she found her guilty of the crime of this preference, though Madam de Warrens had neither sought after nor accepted it, and from that moment endeavored to play her rival a number of ill turns, none of which succeeded. I shall relate one of the most whimsical, by way of specimen.

They were together in the country, with several gentlemen of the neighborhood, and among the rest the lover in question. Madam de Menthon took an opportunity to say to one of these gentlemen, that Madam de Warrens was a prude, that she dressed ill, and particularly, that she covered her neck like a tradeswoman. "O, for that matter," replied the person she was speaking to (who was fond of a joke), "she has good reason, for I know she is marked with a great ugly rat on the bosom, so naturally, that it even appears to be running." Hatred, as well as love, renders its votaries credulous. Madam de Menthon resolved to make use of this discovery, and one day, while Madam de Warrens was at cards with this lady's ungrateful favorite, she contrived, in passing behind her rival, almost to overset the chair she sat on, and at the same instant, very dexterously displaced her handkerchief; but instead of this hideous rat, the gentleman beheld a far different object, which it was not more easy to forget than to obtain a sight of, and which by no means answered the intentions of the lady.

I was not calculated to engross the attention of Madam de Menthon, who loved to be surrounded by brilliant company; notwithstanding she bestowed some attention on me, not for the sake of my person, which she certainly did not regard, but for the reputation of wit which I had acquired, and which might have rendered me convenient to her predominant inclination. She had a very lively passion for ridicule, and loved to write songs and lampoons on those who displeased her: had she found me possessed of sufficient talents to aid the fabrication of her verses, and complaisance enough to do so, we should presently have turned Chambery upside down; these libels would have been traced to their source, Madam de Menthon would have saved herself by sacrificing me, and I should have been cooped up in prison, perhaps, for the rest of my life, as a recompense for having figured away as the Apollo of the ladies. Fortunately, nothing of this kind happened; Madam de Menthon made me stay for dinner two or three days, to chat with me, and soon found I was too dull for her purpose. I felt this myself, and was humiliated at the discovery, envying the talents of my friend Venture; though I should rather have been obliged to my stupidity for keeping me out of the reach of danger. I remained, therefore, Madam de Menthon's daughter's singing-master, and nothing more! but I lived happily, and was ever well received at Chambery, which was a thousand times more desirable than passing for a wit with her, and for a serpent with everybody else.

However this might be, Madam de Warrens conceived it necessary to guard me from the perils of youth by treating me as a man: this she immediately set about, but in the most extraordinary manner that any woman, in similar circumstances, ever devised. I all at once observed that her manner was graver, and her discourse more moral than usual. To the playful gayety with which she used to intermingle her instructions suddenly succeeded an uniformity of manner, neither familiar nor severe, but which seemed to prepare me for some explanation. After having vainly racked my brain for the reason of this change, I mentioned it to her; this she had expected and immediately proposed a walk to our garden the next day. Accordingly we went there the next morning; she had contrived that we should remain alone the whole day, which she employed in preparing me for those favors she meant to bestow; not as another woman would have done, by toying and folly, but by discourses full of sentiment and reason, rather tending to instruct than seduce, and which spoke more to my heart than to my senses. Meantime, however excellent and to the purpose these discourses might be, and though far enough from coldness or melancholy, I did not listen to them with all the attention they merited, nor fix them in my memory as I should have done at any other time. That air of preparation which she had adopted gave me a degree of inquietude; while she spoke (in spite of myself) I was thoughtful and absent, attending less to what she said than curious to know what she aimed at; and no sooner had I comprehended her design (which I could not easily do) than the novelty of the idea, which, during all the years I had passed with her, had never once entered my imagination, took such entire possession of me that I was no longer capable of minding what she said! I only thought of her; I heard her no longer.

Thinking to render young minds attentive to reason by proposing some highly interesting object as the result of it, is an error instructors frequently run into, and one which I have not avoided in my Emilius. The young pupil, struck with the object presented to him, is occupied only with that, and leaping lightly over your preliminary discourses, lights at once on the point, to which, in his idea, you lead him too tediously. To render him attentive, he must be prevented from seeing the whole of your design; and, in this particular, Madam de Warrens did not act with sufficient precaution.

By a singularity of her systematic disposition, she took the vain precaution of proposing conditions; but the moment I knew the price, I no longer even heard them, but consented to everything; and I doubt whether there is a man on the whole earth who would have been sincere or courageous enough to dispute terms, or one single woman who would have pardoned such a dispute. By the same whimsicality, she attached a number of the gravest formalities to the acquisition of her favors, and gave me eight days to think of them, which I assured her I had no need of, though far from a truth; I was very glad to have this intermission; so much had the novelty of these ideas struck me, and such disorder did I feel in mine, that it required time to arrange them.

It will be supposed, that these eight days appeared to me as many ages; on the contrary, I should have been very glad had the time been lengthened. I found myself in a strange state; it was a strange chaos of fear and impatience, dreading what I desired, and studying some pretext to evade my happiness.

Let the warmth of my constitution be remembered, my age, and my heart intoxicated with love; think of my strength, my health, my blood on fire; that in this state, burning with thirst for women, I had never yet approached one; that imagination, necessity, vanity and curiosity combined to excite in me the most ardent desire to be a man and to prove myself to be one, let my tender attachment to her be supposed, which far from having diminished, had daily gained additional strength; I was only happy when with her, that my heart was full, not only of her bounty, of her amiable disposition, but of her shape, of her sex, of her person, of her self; in a word, conceive me united to her by every affinity that could possibly render her dear; nor let it be supposed, that, being ten or twelve years older than myself, she began to grow an old woman, or was so in my opinion. The first sight of her had made such an impression on me, she had really altered very little. To me she was ever charming. She had got something jollier, but had the same fine eyes, the same complexion, the same bosom, the same gayety, and even the same voice. Naturally, what I most should have feared in waiting for the possession of a woman I loved so dearly, was to anticipate it, and not being strong enough to control my desires and my imagination sufficiently not to forget myself. It will be seen, that in a more advanced age, the bare idea of some trifling favors I had to expect from the person I loved, inflamed me so far that I could not support, with any degree of patience, the time necessary to traverse the short space that separated us; how then, by what miracle, when in the flower of my youth, had I so little impatience for a happiness I had never tasted but in idea? Why, instead of transports that should have intoxicated me with their deliciousness, did I experience only fears and repugnance? I have no doubt that if I could have avoided this happiness with any degree of decency, I should have relinquished it with all my heart. I have promised a number of extravagancies in the history of my attachment to her; this certainly is one that no idea could be formed of.

The reader supposes, that being in the situation I have before described with Claude Anet, she was already degraded in my opinion by this participation of her favors, and that a sentiment of disesteem weakened those she had before inspired me with; but he is mistaken. I never loved her more tenderly than when I felt so little propensity to avail myself of her condescension. The gratification of the senses had no influence over her; I was well convinced that her only motive was to guard me from dangers, which appeared otherwise inevitable, by this extraordinary favor, which she did not consider in the same light that women usually do; as will presently be explained. I pitied her, and I pitied myself. I would like to tell her: No, Mama, it is not necessary; you can rely upon me without this. But I dared not; in the first place it was a thing I hardly could tell her, and next, because I felt innermost, that it was not the truth, and that in reality there was only one woman who could shield me from other women and strengthen me against temptations. Without desiring to possess her, I knew well enough that she deprived me of the desire to possess others; to such a degree I considered anything a misfortune that might separate me from her.

The habit of living a long time innocently together far from weakening the first sentiments I felt for her, had contributed to strengthen them, giving a more lively, a more tender, but at the same time a less sensual, turn to my affection. Having ever accustomed myself to call her *Mama* and enjoying the familiarity of a son, it became natural to consider myself as such, and I am inclined to think this was the true reason of that insensibility with a person I so tenderly loved; for I can perfectly recollect that my emotions on first seeing her, though not more lively, were more voluptuous: at Annecy I was intoxicated, at Chambery I possessed my reason. I always loved her as passionately as possible, but I now loved her more for herself and less on my own account; or, at least, I rather sought for happiness than pleasure in her company. She was more to me than a sister, a mother, a friend, or even than a mistress, and for this very reason she was not a mistress; in a word, I loved her too much to desire her.

The day, more dreaded than hoped for, at length arrived. I have before observed, that I promised everything that was required of me, and I kept my word: my heart confirmed my engagements without desiring the fruits, though at length I obtained them. For the first time I found myself in the arms of a woman, and a woman whom I adored. Was I happy? No: I felt I know not what invincible sadness which empoisoned my happiness: it seemed that I had committed an incest, and two or three times, pressing her eagerly in my arms, I deluged her bosom with my tears. As to her, she was neither sad nor glad, she was caressing and calm. As she was not of a sensual nature and had not sought voluptuousness, she did not feel the delight of it, nor the stings of remorse.

I repeat it, all her failings were the effect of her errors, never of her passions. She was well born, her heart was pure, her manners noble, her desires regular and virtuous, her taste delicate: she seemed formed for that elegant purity of manners which she ever loved, but never practiced, because instead of listening to the dictates of her heart, she followed those of her reason, which led her astray: for when once corrupted by false principles it will ever run counter to its natural sentiments. Unhappily, she piqued herself on philosophy, and the morals she drew thence clouded the purity of her heart.

M. de Tavel, her first lover, was also her instructor in this philosophy, and the principles he instilled into her mind were such as tended to seduce her. Finding her firmly attached to her husband and her duty, he attacked her by sophisms, endeavoring to prove that the list of duties she thought so sacred, was but a sort of catechism, fit only for children. That the connection of the sexes which she thought so terrible, was, in itself, absolutely indifferent; that all the morality of conjugal faith consisted in opinion, the contentment of husbands being the only reasonable rule of duty in wives; consequently that concealed infidelities, doing no injury, could be no crimes; in a word, he persuaded her that the sin consisted only in the scandal, that woman being really virtuous who took care to appear so. Thus the deceiver obtained his end in subverting the reason of a girl, whose heart he found it impossible to corrupt, and received his punishment in a devouring jealousy, being persuaded she would treat him as she had treated her husband.

I don't know whether he was mistaken in this respect: the Minister Perret passed for his successor; all I know, is, that the coldness of temperament which it might have been supposed would have kept her from embracing this system, in the end prevented her from renouncing it. She could not conceive how so much importance should be given to what seemed to have none for her; nor could she honor with the name of virtue, an abstinence which would have cost her little.

She did not, therefore, give in to this false principle on her own account, but for the sake of others; and that from another maxim almost as false as the former, but more consonant to the generosity of her disposition.

She was persuaded that nothing could attach a man so truly to any woman as an unbounded freedom, and though she was only susceptible of friendship, this friendship was so tender, that she made use of every means which depended on her to secure the objects of it, and, which is very extraordinary, almost always succeeded: for she was so truly amiable, that an increase of intimacy was sure to discover additional reasons to love and respect her. Another thing worthy of remark is, that after her first folly, she only favored the unfortunate. Lovers in a more brilliant station lost their labor with her, but the man who at first attracted her pity, must have possessed very few good qualities if in the end he did not obtain her affection. Even when she made an unworthy choice, far from proceeding from base inclinations (which were strangers to her noble heart) it was the effect of a disposition too generous, humane, compassionate, and sensible, which she did not always govern with sufficient discernment.

If some false principles misled her, how many admirable ones did she not possess, which never forsook her! By how many virtues did she atone for her failings! if we can call by that name errors in which the senses had so little share. The man who in one particular deceived her so completely, had given her excellent instructions in a thousand others; and her passions, being far from turbulent, permitted her to follow the dictates. She ever acted wisely when her sophisms did not intervene, and her designs were laudable even in her failings. False principles might lead her to do ill, but she never did anything which she conceived to be wrong. She abhorred lying and duplicity, was just, equitable, humane, disinterested, true to her word, her friends, and those duties which she conceived to be such; incapable of hatred or revenge, and not even conceiving that there was a merit in pardoning; in fine (to return to those qualities which were less excusable), though she did not properly value, she never made a vile commerce of her favors; she lavished, but never sold them, though continually reduced to expedients for a subsistence: and I dare assert, that if Socrates could esteem Aspasia, he would have respected Madam de Warrens.

I am well aware that ascribing sensibility of heart with coldness of temperament to the same person, I shall generally, and with great appearance of reason, be accused of a contradiction. Perhaps Nature sported or blundered, and this combination ought not to have existed; I only know it did exist. All those who know Madam de Warrens (a great number of whom are yet living) have had opportunities of knowing this was a fact; I dare even aver she had but one pleasure in the world, which was serving those she loved. Let every one argue on the point as he pleases, and gravely prove that this cannot be; my business is to declare the truth, and not to enforce a belief of it.

I became acquainted with the particulars I have just related, in those conversations which succeeded our union, and alone rendered it delicious. She was right when she concluded her complaisance would be useful to me; I derived great advantages from it in point of useful instruction. Hitherto she had used me as a child, she now began to treat me as a man, and entertain me with accounts of herself. Everything she said was so interesting, and I was so sensibly touched with it, that, reasoning with myself, I applied these confidential relations to my own improvement and received more instruction from them than from her teaching. When we truly feel that the heart speaks, our own opens to receive its instructions, nor can all the pompous morality of a pedagogue have half the effect that is produced by the tender, affectionate, and artless conversation of a sensible woman, on him who loves her.

The intimacy in which I lived with Madam de

Warrens, having placed me more advantageously in her opinion than formerly, she began to think (notwithstanding my awkward manner) that I deserved cultivation for the polite world, and that if I could one day show myself there in an eligible situation, I should soon be able to make my way. In consequence of this idea, she set about forming not only my judgment, but my address, endeavoring to render me amiable, as well as estimable; and if it is true that success in this world is consistent with strict virtue (which, for my part, I do not believe), I am certain there is no other road than that she had taken, and wished to point out to me. For Madam de Warrens knew mankind, and understood exquisitely well the art of treating all ranks, without falsehood, and without imprudence, neither deceiving nor provoking them; but this art was rather in her disposition than her precepts, she knew better how to practice than explain it, and I was of all the world the least calculated to become master of such an attainment; accordingly, the means employed for this purpose were nearly lost labor, as well as the pains she took to procure me a fencing and a dancing master.

Though very well made, I could never learn to dance a minuet; for being plagued with corns, I had acquired a habit of walking on my heels, which *Roche,* the dancing master, could never break me of. It was still worse at the fencing-school, where, after three months' practice, I made but very little progress, and could never attempt fencing with any but my master. My wrist was not supple enough, nor my arm sufficiently firm to retain the foil, whenever he chose to make it fly out of my hand. Add to this, I had a mortal aversion both to the art itself and to the person who undertook to teach it to me, nor should I ever have imagined, that any one could have been so proud of the science of sending men out of the world. To bring his vast genius within the compass of my comprehension, he explained himself by comparisons drawn from music, which he understood nothing of. He found striking analogies between a hit in *quarte* or *tierce* with the intervals of music which bear those names: when he made a feint, he cried out, "Take care of this *diesis*," because anciently they called the diesis a *feint:* and when he had made the foil fly from my hand, he would add, with a sneer, that this was a *pause:* in a word, I never in my life saw a more insupportable pedant.

I made, therefore, but little progress in my exercises, which I presently quitted from pure disgust; but I succeeded better in an art of a thousand times more value, namely, that of being content with my situation, and not desiring one more brilliant, for which I began to be persuaded that Nature had not designed me. Given up to the endeavor of rendering Madam de Warrens happy, I was ever best pleased when in her company, and, notwithstanding my fondness for music, began to grudge the time I employed in giving lessons to my scholars.

I am ignorant whether Anet perceived the full ex-

tent of our union; but I am inclined to think he was
no stranger to it. He was a young man of great penetration, and still greater discretion; who never belied
his sentiments, but did not always speak them: without giving me the least hint that he was acquainted
with our intimacy, he appeared by his conduct to be
so; nor did this moderation proceed from baseness
of soul, but, having entered entirely into the principles
of his mistress, he could not reasonably disapprove of
the natural consequences of them. Though as young
as herself, he was so grave and thoughtful, that he
looked on us as two children who required indulgence,
and we regarded him as a respectable man, whose
esteem we had to preserve. It was not until after she
was unfaithful to Anet, that I learned the strength of
her attachment to him. She was fully sensible that I
only thought, felt, or lived for her; she let me see,
therefore, how much she loved Anet, that I might
love him likewise, and dwelt less on her friendship,
than on her esteem, for him, because this was the sentiment that I could most fully partake of. How often
has she affected our hearts and made us embrace with
tears, by assuring us that we were both necessary to
her happiness! Let not women read this with an ill-
natured smile; with the temperament she possessed,
this necessity was not equivocal, it was only that of
the heart.

Thus there was established, among us three, a
union without example, perhaps, on the face of the
earth. All our wishes, our cares, our very hearts, were

for each other, and absolutely confined to this little circle. The habit of living together, and living exclusively from the rest of the world, became so strong, that if at our repasts one of the three was wanting, or a fourth person came in, everything seemed deranged; and, notwithstanding our particular attachments, even our *tête-à-têtes* were less agreeable than our reunion. What banished every species of constraint from our little community, was a lively reciprocal confidence, and dullness or insipidity could find no place among us, because we were always fully employed. Madam de Warrens, always projecting, always busy, left us no time for idleness, though, indeed, we had each sufficient employment on our own account. It is my maxim, that idleness is as much the pest of society as of solitude. Nothing more contracts the mind, or engenders more tales, mischief, gossiping, and lies, than for people to be eternally shut up in the same apartment together, and reduced, from the want of employment, to the necessity of an incessant chat. When every one is busy (unless you have really something to say), you may continue silent; but if you have nothing to do, you must absolutely speak continually, and this, in my mind, is the most burdensome and the most dangerous constraint. I will go further, and maintain, that to render company harmless, as well as agreeable, it is necessary, not only that they should have something to do, but something that requires a degree of attention.

Knitting, for instance, is absolutely as bad as doing

nothing; you must take as much pains to amuse a woman whose fingers are thus employed, as if she sat with her arms across; but let her embroider, and it is a different matter; she is then so far busied, that a few intervals of silence may be borne with. What is most disgusting and ridiculous, during these intermissions of conversation, is to see, perhaps, a dozen overgrown fellows, get up, sit down again, walk backwards and forwards, turn on their heels, play with the chimney ornaments, and rack their brains to maintain an inexhaustible chain of words: what a charming occupation! Such people, wherever they go, must be troublesome both to others and themselves. When I was at Motiers, I used to employ myself in making laces with my neighbors, and were I again to mix with the world, I would always carry a cup-and-ball in my pocket; I would sometimes play with it the whole day, that I might not be constrained to speak when I had nothing to discourse about; and I am persuaded, that if every one would do the same, mankind would be less mischievous, their company would become more rational, and, in my opinion, a vast deal more agreeable: in a word, let wits laugh if they please, but I maintain, that the only practical lesson of morality within the reach of the present age, is that of the cup-and-ball.

At Chambery they did not give us the trouble of studying expedients to avoid weariness when by ourselves, for a troop of importunate visitors gave us too much by their company, to feel any when alone. The annoyance they formerly gave me had not diminished; all the difference was, that I now found less opportunity to abandon myself to my dissatisfaction. Poor Madam de Warrens had not lost her old predilection for schemes and systems; on the contrary, the more she felt the pressure of her domestic necessities, the more she endeavored to extricate herself from them by visionary projects; and, in proportion to the decrease of her present resources, she contrived to enlarge, in idea, those of the future. Increase of years only strengthened this folly: as she lost her relish for the pleasures of the world and youth, she replaced it by an additional fondness for secrets and projects: her house was never clear of quacks, contrivers of new manufactures, alchemists, projects of all kinds and of all descriptions, whose discourses began by a distribution of millions and concluded by giving you to understand that they were in want of a crown-piece. No one went from her empty-handed; and what astonished me most was, how she could so long support such profusion, without exhausting the source or wearying her creditors.

Her principal project at the time I am now speaking of, was that of establishing a Royal Physical Garden at Chambery, with a Demonstrator attached to it; it will be unnecessary to add for whom this office was designed. The situation of this city, in the midst of the Alps, was extremely favorable to botany, and as Madam de Warrens was always for helping out one project with another, a College of Pharmacy was to be added, which really would have been a very useful foundation in so poor a country, where apothecaries are almost the only medical practitioners. The retreat of the chief physician, Grossi, to Chambery, on the demise of King Victor, seemed to favor this idea, or perhaps, first suggested it; however this may be, by flattery and attention she set about managing Grossi, who, in fact, was not very manageable, being the most caustic and brutal, for a man who had any pretensions to the quality of a gentleman, that ever I knew. The reader may judge for himself by two or three traits of character, which I shall add by way of specimen.

He assisted one day at a consultation with some other doctors, and among the rest, a young gentleman from Annecy, who was physician in ordinary to the sick person. This young man, being but indifferently taught for a doctor, was bold enough to differ in opinion from M. Grossi, who only answered him by asking him when he should return, which way he meant to take, and what conveyance he should make use of? The other, having satisfied Grossi in these particulars, asked him if there was anything he could serve him in? "Nothing, nothing," answered he, "only I shall place myself at a window in your way, that I may have the pleasure of seeing an ass ride on horseback." His avarice equaled his riches and want of feeling. One of his friends wanted to borrow some money of him, on good security. "My friend," answered he, shaking him by the arm, and grinding his teeth, "should St. Peter descend from heaven to borrow ten pistoles of me, and offer the Trinity as sureties, I would not lend them." One day, being invited to dinner with Count Picon, Governor of Savoy, who was very religious, he arrived before it was ready, and found his excellency busy at his devotions, who proposed to him the same employment: not knowing how to refuse, he knelt down with a frightful grimace, but had hardly recited two *Ave-Marias,* when, not able to contain himself any longer, he rose hastily, snatched his hat and cane, and, without speaking a word, was making towards the door; Count Picon ran after him, crying, "Monsieur Grossi! Monsieur Grossi! stop, there's a most excellent ortolan on the spit for you." "Monsieur le Count," replied the other, turning his head, "though you should give me a roasted angel, I would not stay." Such was M. Grossi, whom Madam de Warrens undertook and succeeded in civilizing. Though his time was very much occupied, he accustomed himself to come frequently to her house, conceived a friendship for Anet, seemed to think him intelligent, spoke of him with esteem, and, what would not have been expected from such a brute, affected to treat him with respect, wishing to efface the impressions of the past; for though Anet was no longer on the footing of a domestic, it was known that he had been one, and nothing less than the countenance and example of the chief physician was necessary to set an example of respect which would not otherwise have been paid him. Thus Claude Anet, with a black coat, a well-dressed wig, a grave, decent behavior, a circumspect conduct, and a tolerable knowledge in medical and botanical matters, might reasonably have hoped to fill, with universal satisfaction, the place of public demonstrator, had the proposed establishment taken place. Grossi highly approved the plan, and only waited an opportunity to propose it to the administration, whenever a return of peace should permit them to think of useful institutions, and enable them to spare the necessary pecuniary supplies.

But this project, whose execution would probably have plunged me into botanical studies, for which I am inclined to think Nature designed me, failed through one of those unexpected strokes which frequently overthrow the best concerted plans. I was destined to become an example of human misery; and it might be said that Providence, who called me by degrees to these extraordinary trials, disconcerted every opportunity that could prevent my encountering them.

In an excursion which Anet made to the top of the mountain to seek for genipi, a scarce plant that grows only on the Alps, and which Monsieur Grossi had occasion for, unfortunately he heated himself so much, that he was seized with a pleurisy, which the genipi could not relieve, though said to be specific in that disorder; and, notwithstanding all the art of Grossi (who certainly was very skillful), and all the care of his good mistress and myself, he died the fifth day of his disorder, in the most cruel agonies. During his illness he had no exhortations but mine, bestowed with such transports of grief and zeal that, had he been in a state to understand them, they must have been some consolation to him. Thus I lost the firmest friend I ever had; a man estimable and extraordinary; in whom Nature supplied the defects of education, and who (though in a state of servitude) possessed all the virtues necessary to form a great man, which, perhaps, he would have shown himself, and been acknowledged, had he lived to fill the situation he seemed so perfectly adapted to.

The next day I spoke of him to Madam de Warrens with the most sincere and lively affection; when, suddenly, in the midst of our conversation, the vile, ungrateful thought occurred, that I should inherit his wardrobe, and particularly a handsome black coat, which I thought very becoming. As I thought this, I consequently uttered it; for when with her, to think and to speak was the same thing. Nothing could have made her feel more forcibly the loss she had sustained, than this unworthy and odious observation; disinterestedness and greatness of soul being qualities which poor Anet had eminently possessed. The generous Madam de Warrens turned from me, and (without any reply) burst into tears. Dear and precious tears! your reprehension was fully felt; ye ran into my very heart, washing from thence even the smallest traces of such despicable and unworthy sentiments, never to return.

This loss caused Madam de Warrens as much in-convenience as sorrow, since from this moment her affairs were still more deranged. Anet was extremely exact, and kept everything in order: his vigilance was universally feared, and this set some bounds to that profusion they were too apt to run into; even Madam de Warrens, to avoid his censure, kept her dissipation within bounds; his attachment was not sufficient, she wished to preserve his esteem, and avoid the just re-monstrances he sometimes took the liberty to make her, by representing that she squandered the property of others as well as her own. I thought as he did, nay, I even sometimes expressed myself to the same effect, but had not an equal ascendancy over her, and my advice did not make the same impression. On his de-cease, I was obliged to occupy his place, for which I had as little inclination as abilities, and therefore filled it ill. I was not sufficiently careful, and so very timid, that though I frequently found fault to myself, I saw ill-management without taking courage to oppose it; besides, though I acquired an equal share of respect, I had not the same authority. I saw the disorder that prevailed, trembled at it, sometimes complained, but was never attended to. I was too young and lively to have any pretension to the exercise of reason, and when I would have acted the reformer, Madam de Warrens, calling me her little Mentor, with two or three playful slaps on the cheek, reduced me to my natural thoughtlessness. Notwithstanding, an idea of the certain distress in which her ill-regulated expenses, sooner or later, must necessarily plunge her, made a stronger impression on me since I had become the inspector of her household, and had a better opportunity of calculating the inequality that subsisted between her income and her expenses. I even date from this period the beginning of that inclination to avarice which I have ever since been sensible of. I was never foolishly prodigal, except by intervals; but till then I was never concerned whether I had much or little money. I now began to pay more attention to this circumstance, taking care of my purse, and becoming mean from a laudable motive; for I only sought to insure Madam de Warrens some resource against that catastrophe which I dreaded the approach of. I feared her creditors would seize her pension, or that it might be discontinued and she reduced to want, when I foolishly imagined that the trifle I could save might be of essential service to her; but to accomplish this, it was necessary I should conceal what I meant to make a reserve of; for it would have been an awkward circumstance, while she was perpetually driven to expedients, to have her know that I hoarded money. Accordingly, I sought out some hiding places, where I laid up a few *louis,* resolving to augment this stock from time to time, till a convenient opportunity to lay it at her feet; but I was so incautious in the choice of my repositories, that she always discovered them, and, to convince me that she did so, changed the *louis* I had concealed for a larger sum in different pieces of coin. Ashamed of these discoveries, I brought back to the common purse my little treasure, which she never failed to lay out in clothes, or other things for my use, such as a silver hilted sword, watch, etc. Being convinced that I should never succeed in accumulating money, and that what I could save would furnish but a very slender resource against the misfortune I dreaded, made me wish to place myself in such a situation that I might be enabled to provide for her, whenever she might chance to be reduced to want. Unhappily, seeking these resources on the side of my inclinations, I foolishly determined to consider music as my principal dependence; and ideas of harmony rising in my brain, I imagined, that if placed in a proper situation to profit by them, I should acquire celebrity, and presently become a modern Orpheus, whose mystic sounds would attract all the riches of Peru.

As I began to read music tolerably well, the question was, how I should learn composition? The difficulty lay in meeting with a good master, for, with the assistance of my *Rameau* alone, I despaired of ever being able to accomplish it; and, since the departure of M. le Maitre, there was nobody in Savoy that understood anything of the principles of harmony.

I am now about to relate another of those inconsequences, which my life is full of, and which have so frequently carried me directly from my designs, even when I thought myself immediately within reach of them. Venture had spoken to me in very high terms of the Abbé Blanchard, who had taught him composition; a deserving man, possessed of great talents, who was music-master to the cathedral at Besançon, and is now in that capacity at the Chapel of Versailles. I therefore determined to go to Besançon, and take some lessons from the Abbé Blanchard, and the idea appeared so rational to me, that I soon made Madam de Warrens of the same opinion, who immediately set about the preparations for my journey, in the same style of profusion with which all her plans were executed. Thus this project for preventing a bankruptcy, and repairing in future the waste of dissipation, began by causing her to expend eight hundred livres; her ruin being accelerated that I might be put in a condition to prevent it. Foolish as this conduct may appear, the illusion was complete on my part, and even on hers, for I was persuaded I should labor for her emolument, and she thought she was highly promoting mine.

I expected to find Venture still at Annecy, and promised myself to obtain a recommendatory letter from him to the Abbé Blanchard; but he had left that place, and I was obliged to content myself, in the room of it, with a mass in four parts, of his composition, which he had left with me. With this slender recommendation I set out for Besançon by the way of Geneva, where I saw my relations; and through Nion, where I saw my father, who received me in his usual manner, and promised to forward my portmanteau, which, as I traveled on horseback, came after me. I arrived at Besançon, and was kindly received by the

Abbé Blanchard, who promised me his instruction, and offered his services in any other particular. We had just set about our music, when I received a letter from my father, informing me that my portmanteau had been seized and confiscated at *Rousses,* a French barrier on the side of Switzerland. Alarmed at the news, I employed the acquaintance I had formed at Besançon, to learn the motive of this confiscation. Being certain there was nothing contraband among my baggage, I could not conceive on what pretext it could have been seized on; at length, however, I learned the rights of the story, which (as it is a very curious one) must not be omitted.

I became acquainted at Chambery with a very worthy old man, from Lyons, named Monsieur Duvivier, who had been employed at the *Visa,* under the regency, and for want of other business, now assisted at the survey. He had lived in the polite world, possessed talents, was good-humored, and understood music. As we both wrote in the same chamber, we preferred each other's acquaintance to that of the unlicked cubs that surrounded us. He had some correspondents at Paris, who furnished him with those little nothings, those daily novelties, which circulate one knows not why, and die one cares not when, without any one thinking of them longer than they are heard. As I sometimes took him to dine with Madam de Warrens, he in some measure treated me with respect, and (wishing to render himself agreeable) endeavored to make me fond of these trifles, for which

I naturally had such a distaste, that I never in my life read any of them. Unhappily one of these cursed papers happened to be in the waistcoat pocket of a new suit, which I had only worn two or three times to prevent its being seized by the commissioners of the customs. This paper contained an insipid Jansenist parody on that beautiful scene in Racine's Mithridates: I had not read ten lines of it, but by forgetfulness left it in my pocket, and this caused all my necessaries to be confiscated. The commissioners at the head of the inventory of my portmanteau, set a most pompous verbal process, in which it was taken for granted that this most terrible writing came from Geneva for the sole purpose of being printed and distributed in France, and then ran into holy invectives against the enemies of God and the Church, and praised the pious vigilance of those who had prevented the execution of these most infernal machinations. They doubtless found also that my shirts smelt of heresy, for on the strength of this dreadful paper, they were all seized, and from that time I never received any account of my unfortunate portmanteau. The revenue officers whom I applied to for this purpose required so many instructions, informations, certificates, memorials, etc., etc., that, lost a thousand times in the perplexing labyrinth, I was glad to abandon them entirely. I feel a real regret for not having preserved this verbal process from the office of *Rousses,* for it was a piece calculated to hold a distinguished rank in the collection which is to accompany this Work.

The loss of my necessaries immediately brought me back to Chambery, without having learned anything of the Abbé Blanchard. Reasoning with myself on the events of this journey, and seeing that misfortunes attended all my enterprises, I resolved to attach myself entirely to Madam de Warrens, to share her fortune, and distress myself no longer about future events, which I could not regulate. She received me as if I had brought back treasures, replaced by degrees my little wardrobe, and though this misfortune fell heavy enough on us both, it was forgotten almost as suddenly as it arrived.

Though this mischance had rather damped my musical ardor, I did not leave off studying my *Rameau,* and, by repeated efforts, was at length able to understand it, and to make some little attempts at composition, the success of which encouraged me to proceed. The Count de Bellegarde, son to the Marquis of Antremont, had returned from Dresden after the death of King Augustus. Having long resided at Paris, he was fond of music, and particularly that of Rameau. His brother, the Count of Nangis, played on the violin; the Countess de la Tour, their sister, sung tolerably; this rendered music the fashion at Chambery, and a kind of public concert was established there, the direction of which was at first designed for me, but they soon discovered I was not competent to the undertaking, and it was otherwise arranged. Notwithstanding this, I continued writing a number of little pieces, in my own way, and, among others, a cantata, which gained great approbation; it could not, indeed, be called a finished piece, but the airs were written in a style of novelty, and produced a good effect, which was not expected from me. These gentlemen could not believe that, reading music so indifferently, it was possible I should compose any that was passable, and made no doubt that I had taken to myself the credit of some other person's labors. Monsieur de Nangis, wishing to be assured of this, called on me one morning with a cantata of Clerambault's which he had transposed, as he said, to suit his voice, and to which another bass was necessary, the transposition having rendered that of Clerambault impracticable. I answered, it required considerable labor, and could not be done on the spot. Being convinced I only sought an excuse, he pressed me to write at least the bass to a recitative: I did so, not well, doubtless, because to attempt anything with success I must have both time and freedom, but I did it at least according to rule, and he being present, could not doubt but I understood the elements of composition. I did not, therefore, lose my scholars, though it hurt my pride that there should be a concert at Chambery in which I was not necessary.

About this time, peace being concluded, the French army repassed the Alps. Several officers came to visit Madam de Warrens, and among others the Count de Lautrec, Colonel of the regiment of Orleans, since Plenipotentiary of Geneva, and afterwards Marshal of France, to whom she presented me. On her recommendation, he appeared to interest himself greatly in my behalf, promising a great deal, which he never remembered till the last year of his life, when I no longer stood in need of his assistance. The young Marquis of Sennecterre, whose father was then ambassador at Turin, passed through Chambery at the same time, and dined one day at Madam de Menthon's, when I happened to be among the guests. After dinner, the discourse turned on music, which the marquis understood extremely well. The opera of Jephtha was then new; he mentioned this piece, it was brought him, and he made me tremble by proposing to execute it between us. He opened the book at that celebrated double chorus,

La Terre, l' Enfèr, le Ciel même
*Tout tremble devant le Seigneur.**

He said, "How many parts will you take? I will do these six." I had not yet been accustomed to this trait of French vivacity, and though acquainted with divisions, could not comprehend how one man could undertake to perform six, or even two parts at the same time. Nothing has cost me more trouble in music than to skip lightly from one part to another, and have the eye at once on a whole division. By the manner in which I evaded this trial, he must have been inclined to believe I did not understand music, and perhaps it was to satisfy himself in this particular that he proposed my noting a song for Mademoiselle de

* *The Earth, and Hell, and Heaven itself, tremble before the Lord.*

Menthon, in such a manner that I could not avoid it. He sang this song, and I wrote from his voice, without giving him much trouble to repeat it. When finished he read my performance, and said (which was very true) that it was very correctly noted. He had observed my embarrassment, and now seemed to enhance the merit of this little success. In reality, I then understood music very well, and only wanted that quickness at first sight which I possess in no one particular, and which is only to be acquired in this art by long and constant practice. Be that as it may, I was fully sensible of his kindness in endeavoring to efface from the minds of others, and even from my own, the embarrassment I had experienced on this occasion. Twelve or fifteen years afterwards, meeting this gentleman at several houses in Paris, I was tempted to make him recollect this anecdote, and show him I still remembered it; but he had lost his sight since that time; I feared to give him pain by recalling to his memory how useful it formerly had been to him, and was therefore silent on that subject.

I now touch on the moment that binds my past existence to the present, some friendships of that period, prolonged to the present time, being very dear to me, have frequently made me regret that happy obscurity, when those who called themselves my friends were really so; loved me for myself, through pure good will, and not from the vanity of being acquainted with a conspicuous character, perhaps for the secret purpose of finding more occasions to injure him.

From this time I date my first acquaintance with my old friend Gauffecourt, who, notwithstanding every effort to disunite us, has still remained so.—Still remained so!—No, alas! I have just lost him!—but his affection terminated only with his life—death alone could put a period to our friendship. Monsieur de Gauffecourt was one of the most amiable men that ever existed; it was impossible to see him without affection, or to live with him without feeling a sincere attachment. In my life I never saw features more expressive of goodness and serenity, or that marked more feeling, more understanding, or inspired greater confidence. However reserved one might be, it was impossible even at first sight to avoid being as free with him as if he had been an acquaintance of twenty years; for myself, who find so much difficulty to be at ease among new faces, I was familiar with him in a moment. His manner, accent, and conversation, perfectly suited his features: the sound of his voice was clear, full and musical; it was an agreeable and expressive bass, which satisfied the ear, and sounded full upon the heart. It was impossible to possess a more equal and pleasing vivacity, or more real and unaffected gracefulness, more natural talents, or cultivated with greater taste; join to all these good qualities an affectionate heart, but loving rather too diffusively, and bestowing his favors with too little caution; serving his friends with zeal, or rather making himself the friend of every one he could serve, yet contriving very dexterously to manage his own affairs, while warmly pursuing the interest of others.

Gauffecourt was the son of a clock-maker, and would have been a clock-maker himself had not his person and desert called him to a superior situation. He became acquainted with M. de la Closure, the French Resident at Geneva, who conceived a friendship for him, and procured him some connections at Paris, which were useful, and through whose influence he obtained the privilege of furnishing the salts of Valais, which was worth twenty thousand livres a year. This very amply satisfied his wishes with respect to fortune, but with regard to women he was more difficult; he had to provide for his own happiness, and did what he supposed most conducive to it. What renders his character most remarkable, and does him the greatest honor, is, that though connected with all conditions, he was universally esteemed and sought after without being envied or hated by any one, and I really believe he passed through life without a single enemy.—Happy man!

He went every year to the baths of Aix, where the best company from the neighboring countries resorted, and being on terms of friendship with all the nobility of Savoy, came from Aix to Chambery to see the young Count de Bellegarde and his father the Marquis of Antremont. It was here Madam de Warrens introduced me to him, and this acquaintance, which appeared at that time to end in nothing, after many years had elapsed, was renewed on an occasion which I should relate, when it became a real friendship. I apprehend I am sufficiently authorized in speaking of a man to whom I was so firmly attached, but I had no personal interest in what concerned him; he was so truly amiable, and born with so many natural good qualities, that, for the honor of human nature, I should think it necessary to preserve his memory. This man, estimable as he certainly was, had, like other mortals, some failings, as will be seen hereafter; perhaps had it not been so, he would have been less amiable, since, to render him as interesting as possible, it was necessary he should sometimes act in such a manner as to require a small portion of indulgence.

Another connection of the same time, that is not yet extinguished, and continues to flatter me with the idea of temporal happiness, which is so difficult to obliterate from the human heart, is Monsieur de Conzié, a Savoyard gentleman, then young and amiable, who had a fancy to learn music, or rather to be acquainted with the person who taught it. With great understanding and taste for polite acquirements, M. de Conzié possessed a mildness of disposition which rendered him extremely attractive, and my temper being somewhat similar, when it found a counterpart, our friendship was soon formed. The seeds of literature and philosophy, which began to ferment in my brain, and only waited for culture and emulation to spring up, found in him exactly what was wanting to render them prolific. M. de Conzié had no great inclination to music, and even this was useful to me, for the hours destined for lessons were passed anyhow rather than musically; we breakfasted, chatted, and read new publications, but not a word of music.

The correspondence between Voltaire and the Prince Royal of Prussia then made a noise in the world, and these celebrated men were frequently the subject of our conversation, one of whom recently seated on a throne, already indicated what he would prove himself hereafter, while the other, as much disgraced as he is now admired, made us sincerely lament the misfortunes that seemed to pursue him, and which are so frequently the appendage of superior talents. The Prince of Prussia had not been happy in his youth, and it appeared that Voltaire was formed never to be so. The interest we took in both parties extended to all that concerned them, and nothing that Voltaire wrote escaped us. The inclination I felt for these performances inspired me with a desire to write elegantly, and caused me to endeavor to imitate the coloring of that author, with whom I was so much enchanted. Some time after, his philosophical letters (though certainly not his best work) greatly augmented my fondness for study; it was a rising inclination, which, from that time, has never been extinguished.

But the moment was not yet arrived when I should give in to it entirely; my rambling disposition (rather contracted than eradicated) being kept alive by our manner of living at Madam de Warrens', which was too unsettled for one of my solitary temper. The crowd of strangers who daily swarmed about her from all parts, and the certainty I was in that these people sought only to dupe her, each in his particular mode, rendered home disagreeable. Since I had succeeded Anet in the confidence of his mistress, I had strictly examined her circumstances, and saw their evil tendency with horror. I had remonstrated a hundred times, prayed, argued, conjured, but all to no purpose. I had thrown myself at her feet, and strongly represented the catastrophe that threatened her, had earnestly entreated that she would reform her expenses, and begin with myself, representing that it was better to suffer something while she was yet young, than by multiplying her debts and creditors, expose her old age to vexation and misery.

Sensible of the sincerity of my zeal, she was frequently affected, and would then make the finest promises in the world: but only let an artful schemer arrive, and in an instant all her good resolutions were forgotten. After a thousand proofs of the inefficacy of my remonstrances, what remained but to turn away my eyes from the ruin I could not prevent; and fly myself from the door I could not guard! I made therefore little journeys to Nion, to Geneva and Lyons, which diverted my mind in some measure from this secret uneasiness, though it increased the cause by these additional expenses. I can truly aver that I should have acquiesced with pleasure in every retrenchment, had Madam de Warrens really profited by it, but being persuaded that what I might refuse myself would be distributed among a set of interested villains, I took advantage of her easiness to partake with them, and, like the dog returning from the shambles, carried off a portion of that morsel which I could not protect.

Pretenses were not wanting for all these journeys; even Madam de Warrens would alone have supplied me with more than were necessary, having plenty of connections, negotiations, affairs, and commissions, which she wished to have executed by some trusty hand. In these cases she usually applied to me; I was always willing to go, and consequently found occasions enough to furnish out a rambling kind of life. These excursions procured me some good connections, which have since been agreeable or useful to me. Among others, I met at Lyons, with M. Perrichon, whose friendship I accuse myself with not having sufficiently cultivated, considering the kindness he had for me; and that of the good Parisot, which I shall speak of in its place; at Grenoble, that of Madam Deybens and Madam la Presidente de Bardonanche, a woman of great understanding, and who would have entertained a friendship for me had it been in my power to have seen her oftener; at Geneva, that of M. de la Closure, the French Resident, who often spoke to me of my mother, the remembrance of whom neither death nor time had erased from his heart; likewise those of the two Barillots, the father, who was very amiable, a good companion, and one of the most worthy men I ever met, calling me his grandson. During the troubles of the republic, these two citizens took contrary sides, the son siding with the people, the father with the magistrates. When they took up arms in 1737, I was at Geneva, and saw the father and son quit the same house armed, the one going to the town-house, the other to his quarters, almost certain to meet face to face in the course of two hours, and prepared to give or receive death from each other. This unnatural sight made so lively an impression on me, that I solemnly vowed never to interfere in any civil war, nor assist in deciding our internal dispute by arms, either personally or by my influence, should I ever enter into my rights as a citizen. I can bring proofs of having kept this oath on a very delicate occasion, and it will be confessed (at least I should suppose so) that this moderation was of some worth.

But I had not yet arrived at that fermentation of patriotism which the first sight of Geneva in arms has since excited in my heart, as may be conjectured by a very grave fact that will not tell to my advantage, which I forgot to put in its proper place, but which ought not to be omitted.

My uncle Bernard died at Carolina, where he had been employed some years in the building of Charles Town, which he had formed the plan of. My poor cousin, too, died in the Prussian service; thus my aunt lost, nearly at the same period, her son and husband. These losses reanimated in some measure her affection for the nearest relative she had remaining, which was myself. When I went to Geneva, I reckoned her house my home, and amused myself with rummaging and turning over the books and papers my uncle had left. Among them I found some curious ones, and some letters which they certainly little thought of. My aunt, who set no store by these dusty papers, would willingly have given the whole to me, but I contented myself with two or three books, with notes written by the Minister Bernard, my grandfather, and among the rest, the posthumous works of Rohault in quarto, the margins of which were full of excellent commentaries, which gave me an inclination to the mathematics. This book remained among those of Madam de Warrens', and I have since lamented that I did not preserve it. To these I added five or six memorials in manuscript, and a printed one, composed by the famous Micheli Ducret, a man of considerable talents, being both learned and enlightened, but too much, perhaps, inclined to sedition, for which he was cruelly treated by the magistrates of Geneva, and lately died in the fortress of Arberg, where he had been confined many years, for being, as it was said, concerned in the conspiracy of Berne.

This memorial was a judicious critique on the extensive but ridiculous plan of fortification, which had been adopted at Geneva, though censured by every person of judgment in the art, who was unacquainted with the secret motives of the council, in the execution of this magnificent enterprise. Monsieur de Micheli, who had been excluded from the committee of fortification for having condemned this plan, thought that, as a citizen, and a member of the two hundred, he might give his advice at large, and therefore, did so in this memorial, which he was imprudent enough to have printed, though he never published it, having only those copies struck off which were meant for the two hundred, and which were all intercepted at the post-house by order of the senate.* I found this memorial among my uncle's papers, with the answer he had been ordered to make to it, and took both. This was soon after I had left my place at the survey, and I yet remained on good terms with the Counselor de Coccelli, who had the management of it. Some time after, the director of the custom-house entreated me to stand godfather to his child, with Madam Coccelli, who was to be godmother: proud of being placed on such terms of equality with the counselor, I wished to assume importance, and show myself worthy of that honor.

Full of this idea, I thought I could do nothing better than show him Micheli's memorial, which was really a scarce piece, and would prove I was connected with people of consequence in Geneva, who were intrusted with the secrets of the state, yet by a kind of reserve which I should find it difficult to account for, I did not show him my uncle's answer, perhaps, because it was manuscript, and nothing less than print was worthy to approach the counselor. He understood, however, so well the importance of this paper, which

* *The grand council of Geneva, in December, 1728, pronounced this paper highly disrespectful to the councils, and injurious to the committee of fortification.*

I had the folly to put into his hands, that I could never after get it into my possession, and being convinced that every effort for that purpose would be ineffectual, I made a merit of my forbearance, transforming the theft into a present. I made no doubt that this writing (more curious, however, than useful) answered his purpose at the court of Turin, where probably he took care to be reimbursed in some way or other for the expense which the acquisition of it might be supposed to have cost him. Happily, of all future contingencies, the least probable, is, that the King of Sardinia ever should besiege Geneva, but as that event is not absolutely impossible, I shall ever reproach my foolish vanity with having been the means of pointing out the greatest defects of that city to its most ancient enemy.

I passed two or three years in this manner, between music, magistery, projects, and journeys, floating incessantly from one object to another, and wishing to fix though I knew not on what, but insensibly inclining towards study. I was acquainted with men of letters, I heard them speak of literature, and sometimes mingled in the conversation, yet rather adopted the jargon of books, than the knowledge contained. In my excursions, I frequently called on my good old friend Monsieur Simon, who greatly promoted my rising emulation by fresh news from the republic of letters, extracted from *Baillet* or Colomies. I frequently saw too, at Chambery, a Jacobin professor of physic, a good kind of friar, who often made little chemical experiments which greatly amused me. In imitation of him, I attempted to make some sympathetic ink, and having for that purpose more than half filled a bottle with quicklime, orpiment, and water, the effervescence immediately became extremely violent; I ran to unstop the bottle, but had not time to effect it, for, during the attempt, it burst in my face like a bomb, and I swallowed so much of the orpiment and lime, that it nearly cost me my life. I remained blind for six weeks, and by the event of this experiment learned to meddle no more with experimental chemistry while the elements were unkown to me.

This adventure happened very unluckily for my health, which, for some time past, had been visibly on the decline. This was rather extraordinary, as I was guilty of no kind of excess; nor could it have been expected from my make, for my chest, being well formed and rather capacious, seemed to give my lungs full liberty to play; yet I was short breathed, felt a very sensible oppression, sighed involuntarily, had palpitations of the heart, and spitting of blood, accompanied with a lingering fever, which I have never since entirely overcome. How is it possible to fall into such a state in the flower of one's age, without any inward decay, or without having done anything to destroy health?

It is sometimes said, "the sword wears out the scabbard," this was truly the case with me: the violence of my passions both kept me alive and hastened my dissolution. What passions? will be asked: mere nothings: the most trivial objects in nature, but which affected me as forcibly as if the acquisition of a Helen, or the throne of the universe were at stake. In the first place—women, when I possessed one my senses, for instance, were at ease with one woman, but my heart never was, and the necessities of love consumed me in the very bosom of happiness. I had a tender, respected and lovely friend, but I sighed for a mistress; my prolific fancy painted her as such, and gave her a thousand forms, for had I conceived that my endearments had been lavished on Madam de Warrens, they would not have been less tender, though infinitely more tranquil. If I had believed that I held Madam de Warrens in my arms, when I held her there, my embraces would not have been less spirited, but all my desires would have been extinguished; I should have sobbed from love, but I should not have enjoyed it. Enjoyment! Can ever man be so happy? Ah! If only once in my life I had tasted all the delights of love in their fullness, I imagine that my frail body would be inadequate, and I should have died on the spot. But is it possible for man to taste, in their utmost extent, the delights of love? I cannot tell, but I am persuaded my frail existence would have sunk under the weight of them.

I was, therefore, dying for love without an object, and this state, is of all others, the most dangerous. I was tormented at the bad state of poor Madam de Warrens' circumstances, and the imprudence of her conduct, which could not fail to bring to her total ruin.

Music was a passion less turbulent, but not less consuming, from the ardor with which I attached myself to it, by the obstinate study of the obscure books of Rameau; by an invincible resolution to charge my memory with rules it could not contain; by continual application, and by long and immense compilations which I frequently passed whole nights in copying: but why dwell on these particularly, while every folly that took possession of my wandering brain, the most transient ideas of a single day, a journey, a concert, a supper, a walk, a novel to read, a play to see, things in the world the least premeditated in my pleasures or occupation became for me the most violent passions, which by their ridiculous impetuosity conveyed the most serious torments; even the imaginary misfortunes of Cleveland, read with avidity and frequent interruption, have, I am persuaded, disordered me more than my own.

There was a Genevese, named Bagueret, who had been employed under Peter the Great, of the court of Russia, one of the most worthless, senseless fellows I ever met with, full of projects as foolish as himself, which were to rain down millions on those who took part in them. This man, having come to Chambery on account of some suit depending before the senate, immediately got acquainted with Madam de Warrens, and with great reason on his side, since for those imaginary treasures that cost him nothing, and which he bestowed with the utmost prodigality, he gained, in exchange, the unfortunate crown pieces one by one out of her pocket. I did not like him, and he plainly perceived this, for with me it is not a very difficult discovery, nor did he spare any sort of meanness to gain my good will, and among other things proposed teaching me to play at chess, which game he understood something of. I made an attempt, though almost against my inclination, and after several efforts, having learned the moves, my progress was so rapid, that before the end of the first sitting I gave him the rook, which in the beginning he had given me. Nothing more was necessary; behold me fascinated with chess! I buy a chess-board and a "Calabrois," and shutting myself up in my chamber pass whole days and nights in studying all the varieties of the game, being determined by playing alone, without end or relaxation, to drive them into my head, right or wrong. After incredible efforts, during two or three months passed in this curious employment, I go to the coffee-house, thin, sallow, and almost stupid; I seat myself, and again attack M. Bagueret: he beats me, once, twice, twenty times; so many combinations were fermenting in my head, and my imagination was so stupefied, that all appeared confusion. I tried to exercise myself with *Philidor's* or *Stamma's* book of instructions, but I was still equally perplexed, and, after having exhausted myself with fatigue, was further to seek than ever, and whether I abandoned my chess for a time, or resolved to surmount every difficulty by unremitted practice, it was the same thing. I could never advance one step beyond the improvement of the first sitting, nay, I am convinced that had I studied it a thousand ages, I should have ended by being able to give Bagueret the rook and nothing more.

It will be said my time was well employed, and not a little of it passed in this occupation, nor did I quit my first essay till unable to persist in it, for on leaving my apartment I had the appearance of a corpse, and had I continued this course much longer I should certainly have been one.

Any one will allow that it would have been extraordinary, especially in the ardor of youth, that such a head should suffer the body to enjoy continued health; the alteration of mine had an effect on my temper, moderating the ardor of my chimerical fancies, for as I grew weaker they became more tranquil, and I even lost, in some measure, my rage for traveling. I was not seized with heaviness, but melancholy; vapors succeeded passions, languor became sorrow: I wept and sighed without cause, and felt my life ebbing away before I had enjoyed it. I only trembled to think of the situation in which I should leave my dear Madam de Warrens; and I can truly say, that quitting her, and leaving her in these melancholy circumstances, was my only concern. At length I fell quite ill, and was nursed by her as never mother nursed a child. The care she took of me was of real utility to her affairs, since it diverted her mind from schemes, and kept projectors at a distance. How pleasing would death have been at that time, when, if I had not tasted many of the pleasures of life, I had felt but few of its misfortunes. My tranquil soul would have taken her flight, without having experienced those cruel ideas of the injustice of mankind which embitters both life and death. I should have enjoyed the sweet consolation that I still survived in the dearer part of myself: in the situation I then was, it could hardly be called death; and had I been divested of my uneasiness on her account, it would have appeared but a gentle sleep; yet even these disquietudes had such an affectionate and tender turn, that their bitterness was tempered by a pleasing sensibility. I said to her, "You are the depository of my whole being, act so that I may be happy." Two or three times, when my disorder was most violent, I crept to her apartment to give her my advice respecting her future conduct and I dare affirm these admonitions were both wise and equitable, in which the interest I took in her future concerns were strongly marked. As if tears had been both nourishment and medicine, I found myself the better for those I shed with her, while seated on her bed-side, and holding her hands between mine. The hours crept insensibly away in these nocturnal discourses; I returned to my chamber better than I had quitted it, being content and calmed by the promises she made, and the hopes with which she had inspired me: I slept on them with my heart at peace, and fully resigned to the dispensations of Providence. God grant, that after having had so many reasons to hate life, after being agitated with so many storms, after it has even become a burden, that death, which must terminate all, may be no more terrible than it would have been at that moment!

By inconceivable care and vigilance, she saved my life; and I am convinced she alone could have done this. I have little faith in the skill of physicians, but depend greatly on the assistance of real friends, and am persuaded that being easy in those particulars on which our happiness depends, is more salutary than any other application. If there is a sensation in life peculiarly delightful, we experienced it in being restored to each other; our mutual attachment did not increase, for that was impossible, but it became, I know not how, more exquisitely tender, fresh softness being added to its former simplicity. I became in a manner her work; we got into the habit, though without design, of being continually with each other, and enjoying, in some measure, our whole existence together, feeling reciprocally that we were not only necessary, but entirely sufficient for each other's happiness. Accustomed to think of no subject foreign to ourselves, our happiness and all our desires were confined to that pleasing and singular union, which, perhaps, had no equal, which is not, as I have before observed, love, but a sentiment inexpressibly more intimate, neither depending on the senses, sex, age, nor figure, but an assemblage of every endearing sensation that composes our rational existence and which can cease only with our being.

How was it that this delightful crisis did not secure our mutual felicity for the remainder of her life and mine? I have the consoling conviction that it was not my fault; nay, I am persuaded, she did not willfully destroy it; the invincible peculiarity of my disposition was doomed soon to regain its empire; but this fatal return was not suddenly accomplished, there was, thank Heaven, a short but precious interval, that did not conclude by my fault, and which I cannot reproach myself with having employed amiss.

Though recovered from my dangerous illness, I did not regain my strength; my chest was weak, some remains of the fever kept me in a languishing condition, and the only inclination I was sensible of, was to end my days near one so truly dear to me; to confirm her in those good resolutions she had formed; to convince her in what consisted the real charms of a happy life, and, as far as depended on me, to render hers so; but I foresaw that in a gloomy, melancholy house, the continual solitude of our *tête-à-têtes* would at length become too dull and monotonous: a remedy presented itself: Madam de Warrens had prescribed milk for me, and insisted that I should take it in the country; I consented, provided she would accompany me; nothing more was necessary to gain her compliance, and whither we should go was all that remained to be determined on. Our garden (which I have before mentioned) was not properly in the country, being surrounded by houses and other gardens, and possessing none of those attractions so desirable in a rural retreat; besides, after the death of Anet, we had given up this place from economical principles, feeling no longer a desire to rear plants, and other views making us not regret the loss of that little retreat. Improving the distaste I found she began to imbibe for the town, I proposed to abandon it entirely, and settle ourselves in an agreeable solitude, in some small house, distant enough from the city to avoid the perpetual intrusion of her hangers-on. She followed my advice, and this plan, which her good angel and mine suggested, might fully have secured our happiness and tranquillity till death had divided us—but this was not the state we were appointed to; Madam de Warrens was destined to endure all the sorrows of indigence and poverty, after having passed the former part of her life in abundance, that she might learn to quit it with the less regret; and myself, by an assemblage of misfortunes of all kinds, was to become a striking example to those, who, inspired with a love of justice and the public good, and trusting too implicitly to their own innocence, shall openly dare to assert truth to mankind, unsupported by cabals, or without having previously formed parties to protect them.

An unhappy fear furnished some objections to our plan: she did not dare to quit her ill-contrived house, for fear of displeasing the proprietor. "Your proposed retirement is charming," said she, "and much to my taste, but we are necessitated to remain here, for, on quitting this dungeon, I hazard losing the very means of life, and when these fail us in the woods, we must again return to seek them in the city. That we may have the least possible cause for being reduced to this necessity, let us not leave this house entirely, but pay a small pension to the Count of Saint-Laurent, that he may continue mine. Let us seek some little habitation, far enough from the town to be at peace, yet near enough to return when it may appear convenient."

This mode was finally adopted; and after some small search, we fixed at Charmettes, on an estate belonging to M. de Conzié, at a very small distance from Chambery; but as retired and solitary as if it had been a hundred leagues off. The spot we had concluded on was a valley between two tolerably high hills, which ran north and south; at the bottom, among the trees and pebbles, ran a rivulet, and above the declivity, on either side, were scattered a number of houses, forming altogether a beautiful retreat for those who love a peaceful romantic asylum. After having examined two or three of these houses, we chose that which we thought the most pleasing, which was the property of a gentleman of the army, called M. Noiret. This house was in good condition, before it a garden, forming a terrace; below that on the declivity an orchard, and on the ascent, behind the house, a vineyard: a little wood of chestnut trees opposite; a fountain just by, and higher up the hill, meadows for the cattle; in short, all that could be thought necessary for the country retirement we proposed to establish. To the best of my remembrance, we took possession of it towards the latter end of the summer of 1736. I was delighted on going to sleep there—"Oh!" said I, to this dear friend, embracing her with tears of tenderness and delight, "this is the abode of happiness and innocence; if we do not find them here together it will be in vain to seek them elsewhere."

BOOK VI

BOOK VI

[1736]

Hoc erat in votis: Modus agri non ita magnus
Hortus ubi, et tecto vicinus jugis aquæ fons;
Et paulum sylvæ super his foret.

ICANNOT add: *auctius atque di melius fecere.*
But no matter, the former is enough for my purpose; I had no occasion to have any property there, it was sufficient that I enjoyed it; for I have long since both said and felt, that the proprietor and possessor are two very different people, even leaving husbands and lovers out of the question.

At this moment began the short happiness of my life, those peaceful and rapid moments, which have given me a right to say, *I have lived.* Precious and ever-regretted moments! Ah! recommence your delightful course; pass more slowly through my memory, if possible, than you actually did in your fugitive succession. How shall I prolong, according to my inclination, this recital at once so pleasing and simple? How shall I continue to relate the same occurrences, without wearying my readers with the repetition, any more than I was satiated with the enjoyment? Again, if all this consisted of facts, actions, or words, I could somehow or other convey an idea of it; but how shall I describe what was neither said nor done, nor even thought, but enjoyed, felt, without being able to particularize any other object of my happiness than the bare idea? I rose with the sun, and was happy; I walked, and was happy; I saw Madam de Warrens, and was happy; I quitted her, and still was happy!— Whether I rambled through the woods, over the hills, or strolled along the valley; read, was idle, worked in the garden, or gathered fruits, happiness continually accompanied me; it was fixed on no particular object, it was within me, nor could I depart from it a single moment.

Nothing that passed during that charming epocha, nothing that I did, said, or thought, has escaped my memory. The time that preceded or followed it, I only recollect by intervals, unequally and confused; but here I remember all as distinctly as if it existed at this moment. Imagination, which in my youth was perpetually anticipating the future, but now takes a retrograde course, makes some amends by these charming recollections for the deprivation of hope, which I have lost forever. I no longer see anything in the future that can tempt my wishes, it is a recollection of the past alone that can flatter me, and the remembrance of the period I am now describing is so true and lively, that it sometimes makes me happy, even in spite of my misfortunes.

Of these recollections I shall relate one example,

which may give some idea of their force and precision. The first day we went to sleep at Charmettes, the way being up-hill, and Madam de Warrens rather heavy, she was carried in a chair, while I followed on foot. Fearing the chairmen would be fatigued, she got out about half-way, designing to walk the rest of it. As we passed along, she saw something blue in the hedge, and said, "There's some periwinkle in flower yet!" I had never seen any before, nor did I stop to examine this: my sight is too short to distinguish plants on the ground, and I only cast a look at this as I passed: an interval of near thirty years had elapsed before I saw any more periwinkle, at least before I observed it, when being at Cressier, in 1764, with my friend, M. du Peyrou, we went up a small mountain, on the summit of which there is a level spot, called with reason, *Belle-vue;* I was then beginning to herbalize; —walking and looking among the bushes, I exclaimed with rapture, "Ah, there's some periwinkle!" Du Peyrou, who perceived my transport, was ignorant of the cause, but will some day be informed, I hope, on reading this. The reader may judge by this impression, made by so small an incident, what an effect must have been produced by every occurrence of that time.

Meantime, the air of the country did not restore my health; I was languishing and became more so; I could not endure milk, and was obliged to discontinue the use of it. Water was at this time the fashionable remedy for every complaint; accordingly I entered on a course of it, and so indiscreetly, that it almost released me, not only from my illness but also from my life. Every morning I went to the fountain and drank about two bottles, while I walked. I stopped drinking wine at meals. The water was rather hard and difficult to pass, as water from mountains generally is; in two months I ruined my stomach, which had been very good, and no longer digested anything properly. At this time an accident happened, as singular in itself as in its subsequent consequences, which can only terminate with my existence.

One morning, being no worse than usual, while putting up the leaf of a small table, I felt a sudden and almost inconceivable revolution throughout my whole frame. I know not how to describe it better than as a kind of tempest, which suddenly rose in my blood, and spread in a moment over every part of my body. My arteries began beating so violently that I not only felt their motion, but even heard it, particularly that of the carotids, attended by a loud noise in my ears, which was of three, or rather four, distinct kinds. For instance, first a grave hollow buzzing; then a more distinct murmur, like the running of water; then an extremely sharp hissing, attended by the beating I before mentioned, and whose throbs I could easily count, without feeling my pulse, or putting a hand to any part of my body. This internal tumult was so violent that it has injured my auricular organs, and rendered me, from that time, not entirely deaf, but hard of hearing.

My surprise and fear may easily be conceived; imagining it was the stroke of death, I went to bed, and the physician being sent for, trembling with apprehension, I related my case, judging it past all cure. I believe the doctor was of the same opinion; however he performed his office, running over a long string of causes and effects beyond my comprehension, after which, in consequence of this sublime theory, he set about, *in anima vili,* the experimental part of his art, but the means he was pleased to adopt in order to effect a cure were so troublesome, disgusting, and followed by so little effect, that I soon discontinued it, and after some weeks, finding I was neither better nor worse, left my bed, and returned to my usual method of living but the beating of my arteries and the buzzing in my ears, has never quitted me a moment during the thirty years which has elapsed since that time.

Till now, I had been a great sleeper, but a total privation of repose, with other alarming symptoms which have accompanied it, even to this time, persuaded me I had but a short time to live. This idea tranquillized me for a time: I became less anxious about a cure, and being persuaded I could not prolong life, determined to employ the remainder of it as usefully as possible. This was practicable by a particular indulgence of Nature, which, in this melancholy state, exempted me from sufferings which it might have been supposed I should have experienced. I was incommoded by the noise, but felt no pain, nor was it accompanied by any habitual inconvenience, except noctural wakefulness, and at all times a shortness of breath, which is not violent enough to be called an asthma, but was troublesome when I attempted to run, or use any degree of exertion.

This accident, which seemed to threaten the dissolution of my body, only killed my passions, and I have reason to thank Heaven for the happy effect produced by it on my soul. I can truly say, I only began to live when I considered myself as entering the grave; for, estimating at their real value those things I was quitting, I began to employ myself on nobler objects, namely by anticipating those I hoped shortly to have the contemplation of, and which I had hitherto too much neglected. I had often made light of religion, but was never totally devoid of it; consequently, it cost me less pain to employ my thoughts on that subject, which is generally thought melancholy, though highly pleasing to those who make it an object of hope and consolation; Madam de Warrens, therefore, was more useful to me on this occasion than all the theologians in the world would have been.

She, who brought everything into a system, had not failed to do as much by religion; and this system was composed of ideas that bore no affinity to each other. Some were extremely good, and others very ridiculous, being made up of sentiments proceeding from her disposition, and prejudices derived from education. Men, in general, make God like themselves; the virtuous make Him good, and the profligate make Him wicked; ill-tempered and bilious devotees see nothing but hell, because they would willingly damn all mankind; while loving and gentle souls disbelieve it altogether; and one of the astonishments I could never overcome, is to see the good Fenelon speak of it in his Telemachus as if he really gave credit to it; but I hope he lied in that particular for however strict he might be in regard to truth, a bishop absolutely must lie sometimes. Madam de Warrens spoke truth with me, and that soul, made up without gall, who could not imagine a revengeful and ever angry God, saw only clemency and forgiveness, where devotees bestowed inflexible justice, and eternal punishment.

She frequently said there would be no justice in the Supreme Being should He be strictly just to us; because, not having bestowed what was necessary to render us essentially good, it would be requiring more than He had given. The most whimsical idea was, that not believing in hell, she was firmly persuaded of the reality of purgatory. This arose from her not knowing what to do with the wicked, being loath to damn them utterly, nor yet caring to place them with the good till they had become so; and we must really allow, that both in this world and the next, the wicked are very troublesome company.

It is clearly seen that the doctrine of original sin and the redemption of mankind is destroyed by this system; consequently that the basis of the Christian dispensation, as generally received, is shaken, and that the Catholic faith cannot subsist with these principles; Madam de Warrens, notwithstanding, was a good

Catholic, or at least pretended to be one, and certainly desired to become such, but it appeared to her that the scriptures were too literally and harshly explained, supposing that all we read of everlasting torments were figurative threatenings, and the death of Jesus Christ an example of charity, truly divine, which should teach mankind to love God and each other; in a word, faithful to the religion she had embraced, she acquiesced in all its professions of faith, but on a discussion of each particular article, it was plain she thought diametrically opposite to that church whose doctrines she professed to believe. In these cases, she exhibited simplicity of art, a frankness more eloquent than sophistry, which frequently embarrassed her confessor; for she disguised nothing from him. "I am a good Catholic," she would say, "and will ever remain so; I adopt with all the powers of my soul the decisions of our holy Mother Church; I am not mistress of my faith, but I am of my will, which I submit to you without reserve; I will endeavor to believe all,—what can you require more?"

Had there been no Christian morality established, I am persuaded she would have lived as if regulated by its principles, so perfectly did they seem to accord with her disposition. She did everything that was required; and she would have done the same had there been no such requisition: but all this morality was subordinate to the principles of M. Tavel, or rather she pretended to see nothing in religion that contradicted them; thus she would have favored twenty lovers in a day, without any idea of a crime, her conscience being no more moved in that particular than her passions. I know that a number of devotees are not more scrupulous, but the difference is, they are seduced by constitution, she was blinded by her sophisms. In the midst of conversations the most affecting, I might say the most edifying, she would touch on this subject, without any change of air or manner, and without being sensible of any contradiction in her opinions; so much was she persuaded that our restrictions on that head are merely political, and that any person of sense might interpret, apply, or make exceptions to them, without any danger of offending the Almighty.

Though I was far enough from being of the same opinion in this particular, I confess I dared not combat hers; indeed, as I was situated, it would have been putting myself in rather awkward circumstances, since I could only have sought to establish my opinion for others, myself being an exception. Besides, I entertained but little hopes of making her alter hers, which never had any great influence on her conduct, and at the time I am speaking of none; but I have promised faithfully to describe her principles, and I will perform my engagement——I now return to myself.

Finding in her all those ideas I had occasion for, to secure me from the fears of death and its future consequences, I drew confidence and security from this source; my attachment became warmer than ever, and I would willingly have transmitted to her my whole existence, which seemed ready to abandon me.

From this redoubled attachment, a persuasion that I had but a short time to live, and profound security on my future state, arose an habitual and even pleasing serenity, which, calming every passion that extends our hopes and fears, made me enjoy without inquietude or concern the few days which I imagined remained for me. What contributed to render them still more agreeable was an endeavor to encourage her rising taste for the country, by every amusement I could possibly devise, wishing to attach her to her garden, poultry, pigeons, and cows: I amused myself with them and these little occupations, which employed my time without injuring my tranquillity, were more serviceable than a milk diet, or all the remedies bestowed on my poor shattered machine, even to effecting the utmost possible reëstablishment of it.

The vintage and gathering in our fruit employed the remainder of the year; we became more and more attached to a rustic life, and the society of our honest neighbors. We saw the approach of winter with regret, and returned to the city as if going into exile. To me this return was particularly gloomy, who never expected to see the return of spring, and thought I took an everlasting leave of Charmettes. I did not quit it without kissing the very earth and trees, casting back many a wishful look as I went towards Chambery.

Having left my scholars for so long a time, and lost my relish for the amusements of the town, I seldom went out, conversing only with Madam de Warrens and a Monsieur Salomon, who had lately become our physician. He was an honest man, of good understanding, a great Cartesian, spoke tolerably well on the system of the world, and his agreeable and instructive conversations were more serviceable than his prescriptions. I could never bear that foolish trivial mode of conversation which is so generally adopted; but useful instructive discourse has always given me great pleasure, nor was I ever backward to join in it. I was much pleased with that of M. Salomon; it appeared to me, that when in his company, I anticipated the acquisition of that sublime knowledge which my soul would enjoy when freed from its mortal fetters. The inclination I had for him extended to the subjects which he treated on, and I began to look after books which might better enable me to understand his discourse. Those which mingled devotion with science were most agreeable to me, particularly the Oratory and Port-Royal, and I began to read or rather to devour them. One fell into my hands written by Father Lami, called *Entretiens sur les Sciences,* which was a kind of introduction to the knowledge of those books it treated of. I read it over a hundred times, and resolved to make this my guide; in short, I found (notwithstanding my ill state of health) that I was irresistibly drawn towards study, and though looking on each day as the last of my life, read with as much avidity as if certain I was to live forever.

I was assured that reading would injure me; but on the contrary, I am rather inclined to think it was serviceable, not only to my soul, but also to my body; for this application, which soon became delightful, diverted my thoughts from my disorders, and I soon found myself much less affected by them. It is certain, however, that nothing gave me absolute ease, but having no longer any acute pain, I became accustomed to languishment and wakefulness; to thinking instead of acting; in short, I looked on the gradual and slow decay of my body as inevitably progressive and only to be terminated by death.

This opinion not only detached me from all the vain cares of life, but delivered me from the importunity of medicine, to which hitherto, I had been forced to submit, though contrary to my inclination. Salomon, convinced that his drugs were unavailing, spared me the disagreeable task of taking them, and contented himself with amusing the grief of my poor Madam de Warrens by some of those harmless preparations, which serve to flatter the hopes of the patient and keep up the credit of the doctor. I discontinued the strict regimen I had latterly observed, resumed the use of wine, and lived in every respect like a man in perfect health, as far as my strength would permit, only being careful to run into no excess; I even began to go out and visit my acquaintance, particularly M. de Conzié, whose conversation was extremely pleasing to me. Whether it struck me as heroic to study to my last hour, or that some hopes of life yet lingered in the bottom of my heart, I cannot tell, but the apparent certainty of death, far from relaxing my inclination for improvement, seemed to animate it, and I hastened to acquire knowledge for the other world, as if convinced I should only possess that portion I could carry with me. I took a liking to the shop of a bookseller, whose name was Bouchard, which was frequented by some men of letters, and as the spring (whose return I had never expected to see again) was approaching, furnished myself with some books for Charmettes, in case I should have the happiness to return there.

I had that happiness, and enjoyed it to the utmost extent. The rapture with which I saw the trees put out their first bud, is inexpressible! The return of spring seemed to me like rising from the grave into paradise. The snow was hardly off the ground when we left our dungeon and returned to Charmettes, to enjoy the first warblings of the nightingale. I now thought no more of dying, and it is really singular, that from this time I never experienced any dangerous illness in the country. I have suffered greatly, but never kept my bed, and have often said to those about me, on finding myself worse than ordinary, "Should you see me at the point of death, carry me under the shade of an oak, and I promise you I shall recover."

Though weak, I resumed my country occupations, as far as my strength would permit, and conceived a real grief at not being able to manage our garden without help; for I could not take five or six strokes with the spade without being out of breath and overcome with perspiration: when I stooped the beating redoubled, and the blood flew with such violence to my head, that I was instantly obliged to stand upright. Being therefore confined to less fatiguing employments, I busied myself about the dove-house, and was so pleased with it, that I sometimes passed several hours there without feeling a moment's weariness. The pigeon is very timid and difficult to tame, yet I inspired mine with so much confidence that they followed me everywhere, letting me catch them at pleasure, nor could I appear in the garden without having two or three on my arms or head in an instant, and notwithstanding the pleasure I took in them, their company became so troublesome that I was obliged to lessen the familiarity. I have ever taken great pleasure in taming animals, particularly those that are wild and fearful. It appeared delightful to me, to inspire them with a confidence which I took care never to abuse, wishing them to love me freely.

I have already mentioned that I purchased some books: I did not forget to read them, but in a manner more proper to fatigue than instruct me. I imagined that to read a book profitably, it was necessary to be acquainted with every branch of knowledge it even mentioned; far from thinking that the author did not do this himself, but drew assistance from other books, as he might see occasion. Full of this silly idea, I was stopped every moment, obliged to run from one book to another, and sometimes, before I could reach the tenth page of that I was studying, found it necessary to turn over a whole library. I was so attached to this ridiculous method, that I lost a prodigious deal of time, and had bewildered my head to such a degree, that I was hardly capable of doing, seeing, or comprehending anything. I fortunately perceived, at length, that I was in the wrong road, which would entangle me in an inextricable labyrinth, and quitted it before I was irrevocably lost.

When a person has any real taste for the sciences, the first thing he perceives in the pursuit of them is that connection by which they mutually attract, assist, and enlighten each other, and that it is impossible to attain one without the assistance of the rest. Though the human understanding cannot grasp all, and one must ever be regarded as the principal object, yet if the rest are totally neglected, the favorite study is generally obscure. I was convinced that my resolution to improve was good and useful in itself, but that it was necessary I should change my method; I, therefore, had recourse to the encyclopædia. I began by a distribution of the general mass of human knowledge into its various branches, but soon discovered that I must pursue a contrary course, that I must take each separately, and trace it to that point where it united with the rest; thus I returned to the general synthetical method, but returned thither with a conviction that I was going right. Meditation supplied the want of knowledge, and a very natural reflection gave strength to my resolutions, which was, that whether I lived or died, I had no time to lose; for having learned but little before the age of five-and-twenty, and then resolving to learn everything, was engaging to employ the future time profitably. I was ignorant at what point accident or death might put a period to my endeavors, and resolved at all events to acquire with the utmost expedition some idea of every species of knowledge, as well to try my natural disposition as to judge for myself what most deserved cultivation.

In the execution of my plan, I experienced another advantage which I had never thought of; this was, spending a great deal of time profitably. Nature certainly never meant me for study, since attentive application fatigues me so much that I find it impossible to employ myself half an hour together intently on any one subject; particularly while following another person's ideas, for it has frequently happened that I have pursued my own for a much longer period with success. After reading a few pages of an author with close application, my understanding is bewildered, and should I obstinately continue, I tire myself to no purpose, a stupefaction seizes me, and I am no longer conscious of what I read; but in a succession of various subjects, one relieves me from the fatigue of the other, and without finding respite necessary, I can follow then with pleasure.

I took advantage of this observation in the plan of my studies, taking care to intermingle them in such a manner that I was never weary: it is true that domestic and rural concerns furnished many pleasing relaxations; but as my eagerness for improvement increased, I contrived to find opportunities for my studies, frequently employing myself about two things at the same time, without reflecting that both were consequently neglected.

In relating so many trifling details, which delight me, but frequently tire my reader, I make use of the caution to suppress a great number, though, perhaps, he would have no idea of this, if I did not take care to inform him of it: for example, I recollect with pleasure all the different methods I adopted for the distribution of my time, in such a manner as to produce the utmost profit and pleasure. I may say, that the portion of my life which I passed in this retirement, though in continual ill-health, was that in which I was least idle and least wearied. Two or three months were thus employed in discovering the bent of my genius; meantime, I enjoyed, in the finest season of the year, and in a spot it rendered delightful, the charms of a life whose worth I was so highly sensible of, in such a society, as free as it was charming; if a union so perfect, and the extensive knowledge I purposed to acquire, can be called society. It seemed to me as if I already possessed the improvements I was only in pursuit of: or rather better, since the pleasure of learning constituted a great part of my happiness.

I must pass over these particulars, which were to me the height of enjoyment, but are too trivial to bear repeating: indeed, true happiness is indescribable, it is only to be felt, and this consciousness of felicity is proportionably more, the less able we are to describe it; because it does not absolutely result from a concurse of favorable incidents, but is an affection of the mind itself. I am frequently guilty of repetitions, but should be infinitely more so, did I repeat the same thing as often as it recurs with pleasure to my mind. When, at length, my variable mode of life was reduced to a more uniform course, the, following was nearly the distribution of time which I adopted: I rose every morning before the sun, and passed through a neighboring orchard into a pleasant path, which, running by a vineyard, led towards Chambery. While walking, I offered up my prayers, not by a vain motion of the lips, but a sincere elevation of my heart, to the Great Author of delightful nature, whose beauties were so charmingly spread out before me! I never love to pray in a chamber; it seems to me that the walls and all the little workmanship of man interposed between God and myself: I love to contemplate Him in his works, which elevate my soul, and raise my thoughts to Him. My prayers were pure, I can affirm it, and therefore worthy to be heard:—I asked for myself and her from whom my thoughts were never divided, only an innocent and quiet life, exempt from vice, sorrow, and want; I prayed that we might die the death of the just, and partake their lot hereafter: for the rest, it was rather admiration and contemplation than request, being satisfied that the best means to obtain what is necessary from the Giver of every perfect good, is rather to deserve than to solicit. Returning from my walk, I lengthened the way by taking a roundabout path, still contemplating with earnestness and delight the beautiful scenes with which I was surrounded, those objects only that never fatigue either the eye or the heart. As I approached our habitation, I looked forward to see if Madam de Warrens was stirring, and when I perceived her shutters open, I even ran with joy towards the house: if they were yet shut I went into the garden to wait their opening, amusing myself, meantime, by a retrospection of what I had read the preceding evening, or in gardening. The moment the shutter drew back I hastened to embrace her, frequently half asleep, in her bed; and this salute, pure as it was affectionate, even from its innocence, possessed a charm which the senses can never bestow. We usually breakfasted on milk-coffee; this was the time of day when we had most leisure, and when we chatted with the greatest freedom. These sittings, which were usually pretty long, have given me a fondness for breakfasts, and I infinitely prefer those of England, or Switzerland, which are considered as a meal, at which all the family assemble, than those of France, where they breakfast alone in their several apartments, or more frequently have none at all. After an hour or two passed in discourse, I went to my study till dinner; beginning with some philosophical work, such as the logic of Port-Royal, Locke's Essays, Mallebranche, Leibnitz, Descartes, etc. I soon found that these authors perpetually contradict each other, and formed the chimerical project of reconciling them which cost me much labor and loss of time, bewildering my head without any profit. At length (renouncing this idea) I adopted one infinitely more profitable, to which I attribute all the progress I have since made, notwithstanding the defects of my capacity; for 'tis certain I had very little for study. On reading each author, I acquired a habit of following all his ideas, without suffering my own or those of any other writer to interfere with them, or entering into any dispute on their utility. I said to myself, "I will begin by laying up a stock of ideas, true or false, but clearly conceived, till my understanding shall be sufficiently furnished to enable me to compare and make choice of those that are most estimable." I am sensible this method is not without its inconveniences, but it succeeded in furnishing me with a fund of instruction. Having passed some years in thinking after others, without reflection, and almost without reasoning, I found myself possessed of sufficient materials to set about thinking on my own account, and when journeys or business deprived me of the opportunities of consulting books, I amused myself with recollecting and comparing what I had read, weighing every opinion on the balance of reason, and frequently judging my masters. Though it was late before I began to exercise my judicial faculties, I have not discovered that they had lost their vigor, and on publishing my own ideas, have never been accused of being a servile disciple or of swearing *in verba magistri.*

From these studies I passed to the elements of geometry, for I never went further, forcing my weak memory to retain them by going the same ground a hundred and a hundred times over. I did not admire

Euclid, who rather seeks a chain of demonstration than a connection of ideas: I preferred the geometry of Father Lama, who from that time became one of my favorite authors, and whose works I yet read with pleasure. Algebra followed, and Father Lama was still my guide: when I made some progress, I perused Father Reynaud's Science of Calculation, and then his Analysis Demonstrated; but I never went far enough thoroughly to understand the application of algebra to geometry. I was not pleased with this method of performing operations by rule without knowing what I was about: resolving geometrical problems by the help of equations seemed like playing a tune by turning round a handle. The first time I found by calculation that the square of a binocular figure was composed of the square of each of its parts, and double the product of one by the other; though convinced that my multiplication was right, I could not be satisfied till I had made and examined the figure: not but I admire algebra when applied to abstract quantities, but when used to demonstrate dimensions, I wished to see the operation, and unless explained by lines, could not rightly comprehend it.

After this came Latin, in which I never made great progress. I began by Port-Royal's Rudiments, but without success. These barbarous verses gave a pain to my heart and could not find a place in my ears. I lost myself in a crowd of rules; and in studying the last forgot all that preceded it. A study of words is not calculated for a man without memory, and it was principally an endeavor to make my memory more retentive, that urged me obstinately to persist in this study, which at length I was obliged to relinquish. As I understood enough to read an easy author by the aid of a dictionary, I followed that method, and found it succeeded tolerably well. I likewise applied myself to translation, not by writing, but mentally, and by exercise and perseverance attained to read Latin authors easily, but have never been able to speak or write that language, which has frequently embarrassed me when I have found myself (I know not by what means) enrolled among men of letters.

Another inconvenience that arose from this manner of learning is, that I never understood prosody, much less the rules of versification; yet, anxious to understand the harmony of the language, both in prose and verse, I have made many efforts to obtain it, but am convinced, that without a master it is almost impossible. Having learned the composition of the hexameter, which is the easiest of all verses, I had the patience to measure out the greater part of Virgil into feet and quantity, and whenever I was dubious whether a syllable was long or short, immediately consulted my Virgil. It may easily be conceived that I ran into many errors in consequence of those licenses permitted by the rules of versification; and it is certain, that if there is an advantage in studying alone, there are also great inconveniences and inconceivable labor, as I have experienced more than any one.

At twelve, I quitted my books, and if dinner was not ready, paid my friends, the pigeons, a visit, or worked in the garden till it was, and when I heard myself called, ran very willingly, and with a good appetite to partake of it, for it is very remarkable, that let me be ever so indisposed my appetite never fails. We dined very agreeably, chatting till Madam de Warrens could eat. Two or three times a week, when it was fine, we drank our coffee in a cool shady arbor behind the house, that I had decorated with hops, and which was very refreshing during the heat; we usually passed an hour in viewing our flowers and vegetables, or in conversation relative to our manner of life, which greatly increased the pleasure of it. I had another little family at the end of the garden; these were several hives of bees, which I never failed to visit once a day, and was frequently accompanied by Madam de Warrens. I was greatly interested in their labor, and amused myself seeing them return to the hives, their little thighs so loaded with the precious store than they could hardly walk. At first, curiosity made me indiscreet, and they stung me several times, but afterwards, we were so well acquainted, that let me approach as near as I would, they never molested me, though the hives were full and the bees ready to swarm. At these times I have been surrounded, having them on my hands and face without apprehending any danger. All animals are distrustful of man, and with reason, but when once assured he does not mean to injure them, their confidence becomes so great that he must be worse than a barbarian who abuses it.

After this I returned to my books; but my afternoon employment ought rather to bear the name of recreation and amusement, than labor or study. I have never been able to bear application after dinner, and in general any kind of attention is painful to me during the heat of the day. I employed myself, 'tis true, but without restraint or rule, and read without studying. What I most attended to at these times, was history and geography, and as these did not require intense application, made as much progress in them as my weak memory would permit. I had an inclination to study Father Petau, and launched into the gloom of chronology, but was disgusted at the critical part, which I found had neither bottom nor banks; this made me prefer the more exact measurement of time by the course of the celestial bodies. I should even have contracted a fondness for astronomy, had I been in possession of instruments, but was obliged to content myself with some of the elements of that art, learned from books, and a few rude observations made with a telescope, sufficient only to give me a general idea of the situation of the heavenly bodies; for my short sight is insufficient to distinguish the stars without the help of a glass.

I recollect an adventure on this subject, the remembrance of which has often diverted me. I had bought a celestial planisphere to study the constellations by, and, having fixed it on a frame, when the nights were fine and the sky clear, I went into the garden; and fixing the frame on four sticks, something higher than myself, which I drove into the ground, turned the planisphere downwards, and contrived to light it by means of a candle (which I put in a pail to prevent the wind from blowing it out) and then placed in the center of the above-mentioned four supporters; this done, I examined the stars with my glass, and, from time to time referring to my planisphere, endeavored to distinguish the various constellations. I think I have before observed that M. Noiret's garden was on a terrace, and lay open to the road. One night, some country people passing very late, saw me in a most grotesque habit, busily employed in these observations: the light, which struck directly on the planisphere, proceeding from a cause they could not divine —the candle being concealed by the sides of the pail), the four stakes supporting a large paper, marked over with various uncouth figures, with the motion of the telescope, which they saw turning backwards and forwards, gave the whole an air of conjuration that struck them with horror and amazement. My figure was by no means calculated to dispel their fears; a flapped hat put on over my night-cap, and a short cloak about my shoulder (which Madam de Warrens had obliged me to put on presented in their idea the image of a real sorcerer. Being near midnight, they made no doubt but this was the beginning of some diabolical assembly, and having no curiosity to pry further into these mysteries, they fled with all possible speed, awakened their neighbors, and described this most dreadful vision. The story spread so fast that the next day the whole neighborhood was informed that a nocturnal assembly of witches was held in the garden that belonged to Monsieur Noiret, and I am ignorant what might have been the consequence of this rumor if one of the countrymen who had been witness to my conjurations had not the same day carried his complaint to two Jesuits, who frequently came to visit us, and who, without knowing the foundation of the story, undeceived and satisfied them. These Jesuits told us the whole affair, and I acquainted them with the cause of it, which altogether furnished us with a hearty laugh. However, I resolved for the future to make my observations without light, and consult my planisphere in the house. Those who have read Venetian magic, in the *Letters from the Mountain,* may find that I long since had the reputation of being a conjurer.

Such was the life I led at Charmettes when I had no rural employments, for they ever had the preference, and in those that did not exceed my strength, I worked like a peasant; but my extreme weakness left me little except the will; besides, as I have before observed, I wished to do two things at once, and therefore did neither well. I obstinately persisted in forcing my memory to retain a great deal by heart, and, for that purpose, I always carried some book with me, which, while at work, I studied with inconceivable labor. I was continually repeating something, and am really amazed that the fatigue of these vain and continual efforts did not render me entirely stupid. I must have learned and relearned the Eclogues of Virgil twenty times over, though at this time I cannot recollect a single line of them. I have lost or spoiled a great number of books by a custom I had of carrying them with me into the dove-house, the garden, orchard, or vineyard, when, being busy about something else, I laid my book at the foot of a tree, on the hedge, or the first place that came to hand, and frequently left them there, finding them a fortnight after, perhaps, rotted to pieces, or eaten by the ants or snails; and this ardor for learning became so far a madness that it rendered me almost stupid, and I was perpetually muttering some passage or other to myself.

The writings of Port-Royal, and those of the Oratory, being what I most read, had made me half a Jansenist, and, notwithstanding all my confidence, their harsh theology sometimes alarmed me. A dread of hell, which till then I had never much apprehended, by little and little disturbed my security, and had not Madam de Warrens tranquilized my soul, would at length have been too much for me. My confessor, who was hers likewise, contributed all in his power to keep up my hopes. This was a Jesuit, named Father Hemet; a good and wise old man, whose memory I shall ever hold in veneration. Though a Jesuit, he had the simplicity of a child, and his manners, less relaxed than gentle, were precisely what was necessary to balance the melancholy impressions made on me by Jansenism. This good man and his companion, Father Coppier, came frequently to visit us at Charmettes, though the road was very rough and tedious for men of their age. These visits were very comfortable to me, which may the Almighty return to their souls, for they were so old that I cannot suppose them yet living. I sometimes went to see them at Chambery, became acquainted at their convent, and had free access to the library. The remembrance of that happy time is so connected with the idea of those Jesuits, that I love one on account of the other, and though I have ever thought their doctrines dangerous, could never find myself in a disposition to hate them cordially.

I should like to know whether there ever passed such childish notions in the hearts of other men as sometimes do in mine. In the midst of my studies, and of a life as innocent as man could lead, notwithstanding every persuasion to the contrary, the dread of hell frequently tormented me. I asked myself, "What state am I in? Should I die at this instant, must I be damned?" According to my Jansenists the matter was indubitable, but according to my conscience it appeared quite the contrary: terrified and floating in this cruel uncertainty, I had recourse to the most laughable expedient to resolve my doubts, for which I would willingly shut up any man as a lunatic should I see him practice the same folly. One day, meditating on this melancholy subject, I exercised myself in throwing stones at the trunks of trees, with my usual dexterity, that is to say, without hitting any of them. In the height of this charming exercise, it entered my mind to make a kind of prognostic, that might calm my inquietude; I said, "I will throw this stone at the tree facing me; if I hit my mark, I will consider it as a sign of salvation; if I miss, as a token of damnation." While I said this, I threw the stone with a trembling hand and beating breast but so happily that it struck the body of the tree, which truly was not a difficult matter, for I had taken care to choose one that was very large and very near me. From that moment I never doubted my salvation: I know not on recollecting this trait, whether I ought to laugh or shudder at myself. Ye great geniuses, who surely laugh at my folly, congratulate yourselves on your superior wisdom, but insult not my unhappiness, for I swear to you that I feel it most sensibly.

These troubles, these alarms, inseparable, perhaps, from devotion, were only at intervals; in general I was tranquil, and the impression made on my soul by the idea of approaching death, was less that of melancholy than a peaceful languor, which even had its pleasures. I have found among my old papers a kind of congratulation and exhortation which I made to myself on dying at an age when I had the courage to meet death with serenity, without having experienced any great evils, either of body or mind. How much justice was there in the thought! A preconception of what I had to suffer made me fear to live, and it seemed that I dreaded the fate which must attend my future days. I have never been so near wisdom as during this period, when I felt no great remorse for the past, nor tormenting fear for the future; the reigning sentiment of my soul being the enjoyment of the present. Serious people usually possess a lively sensuality, which makes them highly enjoy those innocent pleasures that are allowed them. Worldlings (I know not why) impute this to them as a crime: or rather, I well know the cause of this imputation, it is because they envy others the enjoyment of those simple and pure delights which they have lost the relish of. I had these inclinations, and found it charming to gratify them in security of conscience. My yet inexperienced heart gave in to all with the calm happiness of a child, or rather (if I dare use the expression) with the raptures of an angel; for in reality these pure delights are as serene as those of paradise. Dinners on the grass at Montagnole, suppers in our arbor, gathering in the fruits, the vintage, a social meeting with our neighbors; all these were so many holidays, in which Madam de Warrens took as much pleasure as myself. Solitary walks afforded yet purer pleasure, because in them our hearts expanded with greater freedom. One particularly remains in my memory; it was on a St. Louis' day, whose name Madam de Warrens bore: we set out together early and unattended, after having heard a mass at break of day in a chapel adjoining our house, from a Carmelite, who attended for that purpose. As I proposed walking over the hills opposite our dwelling, which we had not yet visited, we sent our provisions on before; the excursion being to last the whole day. Madam de Warrens, though rather corpulent, did not walk ill, and we rambled from hill to hill and wood to wood, sometimes in the sun, but oftener in the shade, resting from time to time, and regardless how the hours stole away; speaking of ourselves, of our union, of the gentleness of our fate, and offering up prayers for its duration, which were never heard. Everything conspired to augment our happiness: it had rained for several days previous to this, there was no dust, the brooks were full and rapid, a gentle breeze agitated the leaves, the air was pure, the horizon free from clouds, serenity reigned in the sky as in our hearts. Our dinner was prepared at a peasant's house, and shared with him and his family, whose benedictions we received. These poor Savoyards are the worthiest of people! After dinner we regained the shade, and while I was picking up bits of dried sticks, to boil our coffee, Madam de Warrens amused herself with herbalizing among the bushes, and with the flowers I had gathered for her in my way. She made me remark in their construction a thousand natural beauties, which greatly amused me, and which ought to have given me a taste for botany; but the time was not yet come, and my attention was arrested by too many other studies. Besides this, an idea struck me, which diverted my thoughts from flowers and plants: the situation of my mind at that moment, all that we had said or done that day,

every object that had struck me, brought to my remembrance the kind of waking dream I had at
Annecy seven or eight years before, and which I have
given an account of in its place. The similarity was so
striking that it affected me even to tears: in a transport of tenderness I embraced Madam de Warrens.
"My dearest friend," said I, "this day has long since
been promised me: I can see nothing beyond it: my
happiness, by your means, is at its height; may it
never decrease; may it continue as long as I am sensible of its value—then it can only finish with my
life."

Thus happily passed my days, and the more happily as I perceived nothing that could disturb or bring
them to a conclusion; not that the cause of my former
uneasiness had absolutely ceased, but I saw it take another course which I directed with my utmost care
to useful objects, that the remedy might accompany
the evil. Madam de Warrens naturally loved the country, and this taste did not cool while with me. By
little and little she contracted a fondness for rustic
employments, wished to make the most of her land,
and had in that particular a knowledge which she
practiced with pleasure. Not satisfied with what belonged to the house, she hired first a field, then a
meadow, transferring her enterprising humor to the
objects of agriculture, and instead of remaining unemployed in the house, was in the way of becoming a
complete farmer. I was not greatly pleased to see this
passion increase, and endeavored all I could to oppose

it; for I was certain she would be deceived, and that her liberal extravagant disposition would infallibly carry her expenses beyond her profits; however, I consoled myself by thinking the produce could not be useless, and would at least help her to live. Of all the projects she could form, this appeared the least ruinous: without regarding it, therefore, in the light she did, as a profitable scheme, I considered it as a perpetual employment, which would keep her from more ruinous enterprises, and out of the reach of impostors. With this idea, I ardently wished to recover my health and strength, that I might superintend her affairs, overlook her laborers, or, rather, be the principal one myself. The exercise this naturally obliged me to take, with the relaxation it procured me from books and study, was serviceable to my health.

The winter following, Barillot returning from Italy, brought me some books; and among others, the *Bontempi* and *la Cartella per Musica,* of Father Banchieri; these gave me a taste for the history of music and for the theoretical researches of that pleasing art. Barillot remained some time with us, and, as I had been of age some months, I determined to go to Geneva the following spring, and demand my mother's inheritance, or, at least that part which belonged to me, till it could be ascertained what had become of my brother. This plan was executed as it had been resolved: I went to Geneva; my father met me there, for he had occasionally visited Geneva a long time since, without its being particularly noticed, though the decree that had been pronounced against him had never been reversed; but being esteemed for his courage, and respected for his probity, the situation of his affairs was pretended to be forgotten; or perhaps, the magistrates, employed with the great project that broke out some little time after, were not willing to alarm the citizens by recalling to their memory, at an improper time, this instance of their former partiality.

I apprehended that I should meet with difficulties, on account of having changed my religion, but none occurred; the laws of Geneva being less harsh in that particular than those of Berne, where, whoever changes his religion, not only loses his freedom, but his property. My rights, however, were not disputed, but I found my patrimony, I know not how, reduced to very little, and though it was known almost to a certainty that my brother was dead, yet, as there was no legal proof, I could not lay claim to his share, which I left without regret to my father, who enjoyed it as long as he lived. No sooner were the necessary formalities adjusted, and I had received my money, some of which I expended in books, than I flew with the remainder to Madam de Warrens. My heart beat with joy during the journey, and the moment in which I gave the money into her hands, was to me a thousand times more delightful than that which gave it into mine. She received this with a simplicity common to great souls, who, doing similar actions without effort, see them without admiration;

indeed it was almost all expended for my use, for it would have been employed in the same manner had it come from any other quarter.

My health was not yet reëstablished; I decayed visibly, was pale as death, and reduced to an absolute skeleton; the beating of my arteries was extreme, my palpitations were frequent: I was sensible of a continual oppression, and my weakness became at length so great, that I could scarcely move or step without danger of suffocation, stoop without vertigoes, or lift even the smallest weight, which reduced me to the most tormenting inaction for a man so naturally stirring as myself. It is certain my disorder was in a great measure hypochondriacal. The vapors is a malady common to people in fortunate situations: the tears I frequently shed, without reason; the lively alarms I felt on the falling of a leaf, or the fluttering of a bird; inequality of humor in the calm of a most pleasing life; lassitude which made me weary even of happiness, and carried sensibility to extravagance, were an instance of this. We are so little formed for felicity, that when the soul and body do not suffer together, they must necessarily endure separate inconveniences, the good state of the one being almost always injurious to the happiness of the other. Had all the pleasure of life courted me, my weakened frame would not have permitted the enjoyment of them, without my being able to particularize the real seat of my complaint; yet in the decline of life, after having encountered very serious and real evils, my body seemed to regain its strength, as if on purpose to encounter additional misfortunes; and, at the moment I write this, though infirm, near sixty, and overwhelmed with every kind of sorrow, I feel more ability to suffer than I ever possessed for enjoyment, when in the very flower of my age, and in the bosom of real happiness.

To complete me, I had mingled a little physiology among my other readings: I set about studying anatomy, and considering the multitude, movement, and wonderful construction of the various parts that compose the human machine; my apprehensions were instantly increased, I expected to feel mine deranged twenty times a day, and far from being surprised to find myself dying, was astonished that I yet existed! I could not read the description of any malady without thinking it mine, and, had I not been already indisposed, I am certain I should have become so from this study. Finding in every disease symptoms similar to mine, I fancied I had them all, and, at length, gained one more troublesome than any I yet suffered, which I had thought myself delivered from; this was, a violent inclination to seek a cure; which it is very difficult to suppress, when once a person begins reading physical books. By searching, reflecting, and comparing, I became persuaded that the foundation of my complaint was a polypus at the heart, and Doctor Salomon appeared to coincide with the idea. Reasonably this opinion should have confirmed my former resolution of considering myself past cure; this, however, was not the case; on the contrary, I exerted

every power of my understanding in search of a remedy for a polypus, resolving to undertake this marvelous cure.

In a journey which Anet had made to Montpellier,
to see the physical garden there, and visit Monsieur
Sauvages, the demonstrator, he had been informed
that Monsieur Fizes had cured a polypus similar to
that I fancied myself afflicted with. Madam de Warrens, recollecting this circumstance, mentioned it to
me, and nothing more was necessary to inspire me
with a desire to consult Monsieur Fizes. The hope of
recovery gave me courage and strength to undertake
the journey; the money from Geneva furnished the
means; Madam de Warrens, far from dissuading, entreated me to go: behold me, therefore, without further ceremony, set out for Montpellier!—but it was
not necessary to go so far to find the cure I was in
search of.

Finding the motion of the horse too fatiguing, I
had hired a chaise at Grenoble, and on entering Moi-
rans, five or six other chaises arrived in a rank after
mine. The greater part of these were in the train of a
new married lady called Madam du Colombier; with
her was a Madam de Larnage, not so young or handsome as the former, yet not less amiable. The bride
was to stop at Romans, but the other lady was to pursue her route as far as Saint-Andiol, near the bridge
du St. Esprit. With my natural timidity it will not
be conjectured that I was very ready at forming an
acquaintance with these fine ladies, and the company

that attended them; but traveling the same road, lodging at the same inns, and being obliged to eat at the same table, the acquaintance seemed unavoidable, as any backwardness on my part would have got me the character of a very unsociable being: it was formed then, and even sooner than I desired, for all this bustle was by no means convenient to a person in ill health, particularly to one of my humor. Curiosity renders these vixens extremely insinuating; they accomplish their design of becoming acquainted with a man by endeavoring to turn his brain, and this was precisely what happened to me. Madam du Colombier was too much surrounded by her young gallants to have any opportunity of paying much attention to me; beside, it was not worth while, as we were to separate in so short a time; but Madam de Larnage (less attended to than her young friend) had to provide herself for the remainder of the journey. Behold me, then, attacked by Madam de Larnage, and adieu to poor Jean Jacques, or rather farewell to fever, vapors, and polypus; all completely vanished when in her presence. The ill state of my health was the first subject of our conversation; they saw I was indisposed, knew I was going to Montpellier, but my air and manner certainly did not exhibit the appearance of a libertine, since it was clear by what followed they did not suspect I was going there for a trip to the *stewing-pan* (to be placed in a vapor-bath, a cure for a dangerous venereal disease). Though a man's sick condition is no great recommendation for him among women, still it made me an object of interest for them in this case.

Once (according to my praiseworthy custom of speaking without thought) I replied, "I did not know," which answer naturally made them conclude I was a fool; but on questioning me further, the examination turned out so far to my advantage, that I rather rose in their opinion, and I once heard Madam du Colombier say to her friend, "He is amiable, but not sufficiently acquainted with the world."

As we became more familiar, it was natural to give each other some little account of whence we came and who we were: this embarrassed me greatly, for I was sensible that in good company and among women of spirit, the very name of a new convert would utterly undo me. I know not by what whimsicality I resolved to pass for an Englishman; however, in consequence of that determination I gave myself out for a Jacobite, and was readily believed. They called me Monsieur Dudding, which was the name I assumed with my new character, and a cursed Marquis Torignan, who was one of the company, an invalid like myself, and both old and ill-tempered, took it in his head to begin a long conversation with me. He spoke of King James, of the Pretender, and the old court of St. Germain's; I sat on thorns the whole time, for I was totally unacquainted with all these except what little I had picked up in the account of Earl Hamilton, and from the gazettes; however, I made such fortunate use of the little I did know, as to extricate myself from this dilemma, happy in not being questioned on the

English language, which I did not know a single word of.

The company were all very agreeable; we looked forward to the moment of separation with regret, and therefore made snails' journeys. We arrived one Sunday at St. Marcellin's. Madam de Larnage would go to mass; I accompanied her, and had nearly ruined all my affairs, for by my modest reserved countenance during the service, she concluded me a bigot, and conceived a very indifferent opinion of me, as I learned from her own account two days after. It required a great deal of gallantry on my part to efface this ill impression, or rather Madam de Larnage (who was not easily disheartened) determined to risk the first advances, and see how I should behave. She made several, but far from being presuming on my figure, I thought she was making sport of me: full of this ridiculous idea there was no folly I was not guilty of. Madam de Larnage persisted in such caressing behavior, that a much wiser man than myself could hardly have taken it seriously. The more obvious her advances were, the more I was confirmed in my mistake, and what increased my torment, I found I was really in love with her. I frequently said to myself, and sometimes to her, sighing, "Ah! why is not all this real? then should I be the most fortunate of men." I am inclined to think my stupidity did but increase her resolution, and make her determine to get the better of it.

We left Madam du Colombier at Romans; after

which Madam de Larnage, the Marquis de Torignan, and myself continued our route slowly, and in the most agreeable manner. The marquis, though indisposed, and rather ill-humored, was an agreeable companion, but was not best pleased at seeing the lady bestow all her attentions on me, while he passed unregarded; for Madam de Larnage took so little care to conceal her inclination, that he perceived it sooner than I did, and his sarcasms must have given me that confidence I could not presume to take from the kindness of the lady, if by a surmise, which no one but myself could have blundered on, I had not imagined they perfectly understood each other, and were agreed to turn my passion into ridicule. This foolish idea completed my stupidity, making me act the most ridiculous part, while, had I listened to the feelings of my heart, I might have been performing one far more brilliant. I am astonished that Madam de Larnage was not disgusted, and did not discard me with disdain; but she plainly perceived there was more bashfulness than indifference in my composition.

She at last succeeded in making me understand her; but it was not easy for her. We arrived at Valence to dinner, and according to our usual custom passed the remainder of the day there. We lodged out of the city, at the St. James, an inn I shall never forget. After dinner, Madam de Larnage proposed a walk; she knew the marquis was no walker, consequently, this was an excellent plan for a *tête-à-tête,* which she was pre-determined to make the most of. While we were walking round the city by the side of the moats, I entered on a long history of my complaint, to which she answered in so tender an accent, frequently pressing my arm, which she held to her heart, that it required all my stupidity not to be convinced of the sincerity of her attachment. I have already observed that she was amiable, love rendered her charming, adding all the loveliness of youth; and she managed her advances with so much art, that they were sufficient to have seduced the most insensible: I was, therefore, in very uneasy circumstances, and frequently on the point of making a declaration; but the dread of offending her, and the still greater of being laughed at, ridiculed, made table-talk, and complimented on my enterprise by the satirical marquis, had such unconquerable power over me, that, though ashamed of my ridiculous bashfulness, I could not take courage to surmount it. I had ended the history of my complaints, which I felt the ridiculousness of at this time; and not knowing how to look, or what to say, continued silent, giving the finest opportunity in the world for that ridicule I so much dreaded. Happily, Madam de Larnage took a more favorable resolution, and suddenly interrupted this silence by throwing her arm round my neck, while, at the same instant, her lips spoke too plainly on mine to be any longer misunderstood. This was reposing that confidence in me the want of which has almost always prevented me from appearing myself: for once I was at ease, my heart, eyes, and tongue, spoke freely what I felt; never did

I make better reparation for my mistakes, and if this little conquest had cost Madam de Larnage some difficulties, I have reason to believe she did not regret them.

Was I to live a hundred years, I should never forget this charming woman. It was possible to see her without falling in love, but those she favored could not fail to adore her; which proves, in my opinion, that she was not generally so prodigal of her favors. It is true, her inclination for me was so sudden and lively, that it scarce appears excusable; though from the short, but charming interval I passed with her, I have reason to think her heart was more influenced than her passions, and during the short and delightful time I was with her, I undoubtedly believe that she showed me a consideration that was not natural to her, as she was sensual and voluptuous; but she preferred my health for her own pleasure.

Our good intelligence did not escape the penetration of the marquis; not that he discontinued his usual raillery; on the contrary, he treated me as a sighing, hopeless swain, languishing under the rigors of his mistress; not a word, smile, or look escaped him by which I could imagine he suspected my happiness; and I should have thought him completely deceived, had not Madam de Larnage, who was more clear-sighted than myself, assured me of the contrary; but he was a well-bred man, and it was impossible to behave with more attention, or greater civility, than he constantly paid me (notwithstanding his satirical sallies), especially after my success, which, as he was un-acquainted with my stupidity, he perhaps gave me the honor of achieving. It has already been seen that he was mistaken in this particular; but no matter, I prof-ited by his error, for being conscious that the laugh was on my side, I took all his sallies in good part, and sometimes parried them with tolerable success; for, proud of the reputation of wit which Madam de Lar-nage had thought fit to discover in me, I no longer appeared the same man.

We were both in a country and season of plenty, and had everywhere excellent cheer, thanks to the good cares of the marquis; though I would willingly have relinquished this advantage to have been more satisfied with the situation of our chambers; but he always sent his footman on to provide them; and whether of his own accord, or by the order of his mas-ter, the rogue always took care that the marquis' chamber should be close by Madam de Larnage's, while mine was at the further end of the house: but that made no great difference, or perhaps it rendered our rendezvous the more charming; this happiness lasted four or five days, during which time I was in-toxicated with delight, which I tasted pure and serene without any alloy; an advantage I could never boast before; and, I may add, it is owing to Madam de Larnage that I did not go out of the world without having tasted real pleasure.

If the sentiment I felt for her was not precisely love, it was at least a very tender return of that she testified for me; our meetings were so delightful, that they possessed all the sweets of love; without that kind of delirium which affects the brain, and even tends to diminish our happiness. I never experienced true love but once in my life, and that was not with Madam de Larnage, neither did I feel that affection for her which I had been sensible of, and yet continued to possess, for Madam de Warrens; but for this very reason, our *tête-à-têtes* were a hundred times more delightful. When with Madam de Warrens, my felicity was always disturbed by a secret sadness, a compunction of heart, which I found it impossible to surmount. Instead of being delighted at the acquisition of so much happiness, I could not help reproaching myself for contributing to render her I loved unworthy: on the contrary, with Madam de Larnage, I was proud to be a man and happy; I gave way to my sensual impulses confidently; I took part in the impressions I made on hers; I contemplated my triumph with as much vanity as voluptuousness, and was doubly proud.

I do not recollect exactly where we quitted the marquis, who resided in this country, but I know we were alone on our arrival at Montélimar, where Madam de Larnage made her chambermaid get into my chaise, and accommodate me with a seat in hers. It will easily be believed, that traveling in this manner was by no means displeasing to me, and that I should be very much puzzled to give any account of the country we passed through. She had some business at

Montélimar, which detained her there two or three days; during this time she quitted me but one-quarter of an hour, for a visit she could not avoid. We walked together every day, in the most charming country, and under the finest sky imaginable. Oh! these three days! what reason have I to regret them! Never did such happiness return again.

The amours of a journey cannot be very durable: it was necessary we should part, and I must confess it was almost time; not that I was weary of my happiness, or nearly so; I became every day more attached to her; but notwithstanding all the consideration the lady had shown me, there was nothing left me but the good will. We endeavored to comfort each other for the pain of parting, by forming plans for our reunion; and it was concluded, that after staying five or six weeks at Montpellier (which would give Madam de Larnage time to prepare for my reception in such a manner as to prevent scandal) I should return to Saint-Andiol, and spend the winter under her direction. She gave me ample instruction on what it was necessary I should know, on what it would be proper to say, and how I should conduct myself. She wished me to correspond with her, and spoke much and earnestly on the care of my health, conjured me to consult skillful physicians, and be attentive and exact in following their prescriptions whatever they might happen to be. I believe her concern was sincere, for she loved me, and gave a thousand proofs of her affection less equivocal than the prodigality of her favors; for judging by my mode of traveling, that I was not in very affluent circumstances (though not rich herself), on our paring, she would have had me share the contents of her purse, which she had brought pretty well furnished from Grenoble, and it was with great difficulty I could make her put up with a denial. In a word, we parted; my heart full of her idea, and leaving in hers (if I am not mistaken) a firm attachment to me.

While pursuing the remainder of my journey, remembrance ran over everything that had passed from the commencement of it, and I was well satisfied at finding myself alone in a comfortable chaise, where I could ruminate at ease on the pleasures I had enjoyed, and those which awaited my return. I only thought of Saint-Andiol; of the life I was to lead there; I saw nothing but Madam de Larnage, or what related to her; the whole universe besides was nothing to me—even Madam de Warrens was forgotten!—I set about combining all the details by which Madam de Larnage had endeavored to give me in advance an idea of her house, of the neighborhood, of her connections, and manner of life, finding everything charming.

She had a daughter, whom she had often described in the warmest terms of maternal affection: this daughter was fifteen, lively, charming, and of an amiable disposition. Madam de Larnage promised me her friendship; I had not forgotten that promise, and was curious to know how Mademoiselle de Larnage would treat her mother's *bon ami*. These were the subjects of my reveries from the bridge of St. Esprit to Remoulin: I had been advised to visit the Pont-du-Gard; I did not fail to do so. After a breakfast of excellent figs, I took a guide and went to the Pont-du-Gard. Hitherto I had seen none of the remaining monuments of Roman magnificence, and I expected to find this worthy the hands by which it was constructed; for once, the reality surpassed my expectation; this was the only time in my life it ever did so, and the Romans alone could have produced that effect. The view of this noble and sublime work struck me the more forcibly, from being in the midst of a desert, where silence and solitude render the majestic edifice more striking, and admiration more lively, for though called a bridge it is nothing more than an aqueduct. One cannot help exclaiming, what strength could have transported these enormous stones so far from any quarry? And what motive could have united the labors of so many millions of men, in a place that no one inhabited? I went through the three stories of this superb edifice. I hardly dared to put my feet on these old stones, I reverenced them so much. I remained here whole hours, in the most ravishing contemplation, and returned, pensive and thoughtful to my inn. This reverie was by no means favorable to Madam de Larnage; she had taken care to forewarn me against the girls of Montpellier, but not against the Pont-du-Gard—it is impossible to provide for every contingency.

On my arrival at Nimes, I went to see the amphitheater, which is a far more magnificent work than even the Pont-du-Gard, yet it made a much less impression on me, perhaps, because my admiration had been already exhausted on the former object; or that the situation of the latter, in the midst of a city, was less proper to excite it. The amphitheater at Verona is a vast deal smaller, and less beautiful than that at Nimes, but preserved with all possible care and neatness, by which means alone it made a much stronger and more agreeable impression on me. The French pay no regard to these things, respect no monument of antiquity; ever eager to undertake, they never finish, nor preserve anything that is already finished to their hands.

I was so much better, and had gained such an appetite by exercise, that I stopped a whole day at Pont-de-Lunel, for the sake of good entertainment and company, this being deservedly esteemed at that time the best inn in Europe; for those who kept it, knowing how to make its fortunate situation turn to advantage, took care to provide both abundance and variety. It was really curious to find in a lonely country-house, in the middle of the Campagna, a table every day furnished with sea and fresh-water fish, excellent game, and choice wines, served up with all the attention and care, which are only to be expected among the great or opulent, and all this for thirty-five sous each person: but the Pont-du-Lunel did not long remain on this footing, for the proprietor, presuming too much on its reputation, at length lost it entirely.

During this journey, I really forgot my complaints, but recollected them again on my arrival at Montpellier. My vapors were absolutely gone, but every other complaint remained, and though custom had rendered them less troublesome, they were still sufficient to make any one who had been suddenly seized with them, suppose himself attacked by some mortal disease. In effect, they were rather alarming than painful, and made the mind suffer more than the body, though it apparently threatened the latter with destruction. While my attention was called off by the vivacity of my passions, I paid no attention to my health; but as my complaints were not altogether imaginary, I thought of them seriously when the tumult had subsided. Recollecting the salutary advice of Madam de Larnage, and the cause of my journey, I consulted the most famous practitioners, particularly Monsieur Fizes; and through superabundance of precaution boarded at a doctor's, who was an Irishman, and named Fitz-Morris.

This person boarded a number of young gentlemen who were studying physic; and what rendered his house very commodious for an invalid, he contented himself with a moderate pension for provision, lodging, etc., and took nothing of his boarders for attendance as a physician. He even undertook to execute the orders of M. Fizes, and endeavor to reëstablish my health. He certainly acquitted himself very well in this employment; as to regimen, indigestions were not to be gained at his table; and though I am not

much hurt at privations of that kind, the objects of
comparison were so near, that I could not help thinking with myself sometimes, that M. de Torignan was
a much better provider than M. Fitz-Morris; notwithstanding, as there was no danger of dying with hunger, and all the youths were gay and good-humored,
I believe this manner of living was really serviceable,
and prevented my falling into those languors I had
latterly been so subject to. I passed the morning in
taking medicines, particularly, I know not what kind
of waters, but believe they were those of Vals, and in
writing to Madam de Larnage; for the correspondence was regularly kept up, and Rousseau kindly undertook to receive these letters for his good friend
Dudding. At noon I took a walk to the *Canourgue,*
with some of our young boarders, who were all very
good lads; after this we assembled for dinner; when
this was over, an affair of importance employed the
greater part of us till night; this was, going a little
way out of town to take our afternoon's collation, and
make up two or three parties at mall, or mallet. As
I had neither strength nor skill, I did not play myself,
but I betted on the game, and, interested for the success of my wager, followed the players and their balls
over the rough and stony roads, procuring by this
means both an agreeable and salutary exercise. We
took our afternoon's refreshment at an inn out of the
city. I need not observe that these meetings were
extremely merry, but should not omit that they were
equally innocent, though the girls of the house were

very pretty. M. Fitz-Morris (who was a great mall player himself) was our president; and I must observe, notwithstanding the imputation of wildness that is generally bestowed on students, that I found more virtuous dispositions among these youths than could easily be found among an equal number of men: they were rather noisy than fond of wine, and more merry than libertine.

I accustomed myself so much to this mode of life, and it accorded so entirely with my humor, that I should have been very well content with a continuance of it. Several of my fellow-boarders were Irish, from whom I endeavored to learn some English words, as a precaution for Saint-Andiol. The time now drew near for my departure; every letter Madam de Larnage wrote, she entreated me not to delay it, and at length I prepared to obey her.

I was convinced that the physicians (who understood nothing of my disorder) looked on my complaint as imaginary, and treated me accordingly, with their waters and whey. In this respect physicians and philosophers differ widely from theologians; admitting the truth only of what they can explain, and making their knowledge the measure of possibilities. These gentlemen understood nothing of my illness, therefore concluded I could not be ill; and who would presume to doubt the profound skill of a physician? I plainly saw they only meant to amuse, and make me swallow my money; and judging their substitute at Saint-Andiol would do me quite as much service, and be infinitely more agreeable, I resolved to give her the preference; full, therefore, of this wise resolution, I quitted Montpellier.

I set off towards the end of November, after a stay of six weeks or two months in that city, where I left a dozen louis, without either my health or understanding being the better for it, except from a short course of anatomy begun under M. Fitz-Morris, which I was soon obliged to abandon, from the horrible stench of the bodies he dissected, which I found it impossible to endure.

Not thoroughly satisfied in my own mind on the rectitude of this expedition, as I advanced towards the bridge of St. Esprit (which was equally the road to Saint-Andiol and to Chambery) I began to reflect on Madam de Warrens, the remembrance of whose letters, though less frequent than those from Madam de Larnage, awakened in my heart a remorse that passion had stifled in the first part of my journey, but which became so lively on my return, that, setting just estimate on the love of pleasure, I found myself in such a situation of mind that I could listen wholly to the voice of reason. Besides, in continuing to act the part of an adventurer, I might be less fortunate than I had been in the beginning; for it was only necessary that in all Saint-Andiol there should be one person who had been in England, or who knew the English, or anything of their language, to prove me an impostor. The family of Madam de Larnage might not be pleased with me, and would, perhaps, treat me unpolitely; her daughter too made me uneasy, for, spite of myself, I thought more of her than was necessary. I trembled lest I should fall in love with this girl, and that very fear had already half done the business. Was I going, in return for the mother's kindness, to seek the ruin of the daughter? To sow dissension, dishonor, scandal, and hell itself, in her family? The very idea struck me with horror, and I took the firmest resolution to combat and vanquish this unhappy attachment, should I be so unfortunate as to experience it. But why expose myself to this danger? How miserable must the situation be to live with the mother, whom I should be weary of, and sigh for the daughter, without daring to make known my affection! What necessity was there to seek this situation, and expose myself to misfortunes, affronts and remorse, for the sake of pleasures whose greatest charm was already exhausted? For I was sensible this attachment had lost its first vivacity. With these thoughts were mingled reflections relative to my situation and duty to that good and generous friend, who already loaded with debts, would become more so from the foolish expenses I was running into, and whom I was deceiving so unworthily. This reproach at length became so keen that it triumphed over every temptation, and on approaching the bridge of St. Esprit I formed the resolution to burn my whole magazine of letters from Saint-Andiol, and continue my journey right forward to Chambery.

I executed this resolution courageously, with some

sighs I confess, but with the heart-felt satisfaction, which I enjoyed for the first time in my life, of saying, "I merit my own esteem, and know how to prefer duty to pleasure." This was the first real obligation I owed my books, since these had taught me to reflect and compare. After the virtuous principles I had so lately adopted, after all the rules of wisdom and honor I had proposed to myself, and felt so proud to follow, the shame of possessing so little stability, and contradicting so egregiously my own maxims, triumphed over the allurements of pleasure. Perhaps, after all, pride had as much share in my resolution as virtue; but if this pride is not virtue itself, its effects are so similar that we are pardonable in deceiving ourselves.

One advantage resulting from good actions is that they elevate the soul to a disposition of attempting still better; for such is human weakness, that we must place among our good deeds an abstinence from those crimes we are tempted to commit. No sooner was my resolution confirmed than I became another man, or rather, I became what I was before I had erred, and saw in its true colors what the intoxication of the moment had either concealed or disguised. Full of worthy sentiments and wise resolutions, I continued my journey, intending to regulate my future conduct by the laws of virtue, and dedicate myself without reserve to that best of friends, to whom I vowed as much fidelity in future as I felt real attachment. The sincerity of this return to virtue appeared to promise a better destiny; but mine, alas! was fixed, and already begun: even at the very moment when my heart, full of good and virtuous sentiments, was contemplating only innocence and happiness through life, I touched on the fatal period that was to draw after it the long chain of my misfortunes!

My impatience to arrive at Chambery had made me use more diligence than I meant to do. I had sent a letter from Valence, mentioning the day and hour I should arrive, but I had gained half a day on this calculation, which time I passed at Chaparillan, that I might arrive exactly at the time I mentioned. I wished to enjoy to its full extent the pleasure of seeing her, and preferred deferring this happiness a little, that expectancy might increase the value of it. This precaution had always succeeded; hitherto my arrival had caused a little holiday; I expected no less this time, and these preparations, so dear to me, would have been well worth the trouble of contriving them.

I arrived then exactly at the hour, and while at a considerable distance, looked forward with an expectancy of seeing her on the road to meet me. The beating of my heart increased as I drew near the house; at length I arrived, quite out of breath; for I had left my chaise in the town. I see no one in the garden, at the door, or at the windows; I am seized with terror, fearful that some accident has happened. I enter; all is quiet; the laborers are eating their luncheon in the kitchen, and far from observing any preparation, the servant seems surprised to see me, not

knowing I was expected. I go up-stairs, at length I
see her!—that dear friend! so tenderly, truly, and
entirely beloved. I instantly ran towards her, and threw
myself at her feet. "Ah! child!" said she, "art thou
returned then!" embracing me at the same time.
"Have you had a good journey? How do you do?"
This reception amused me for some moments, I then
asked, whether she had received my letter? She answered, "Yes." "I should have thought not," replied
I; and the information concluded there. A young man
was with her at this time. I recollected having seen
him in the house before my departure, but at present
he seemed established there; in short, he was so; I
found my place already supplied!

This young man came from the country of Vaud;
his father, named Vintzenried, was keeper of the
prison, or, as he expressed himself, Captain of the
Castle of Chillon. This son of the captain was a journeyman peruke-maker, and gained his living in that
capacity when he first presented himself to Madam
de Warrens, who received him kindly, as she did all
comers, particularly those from her own country. He
was a tall, fair, silly youth; well enough made, with
an unmeaning face, and a mind of the same description, speaking always like the beau in a comedy, and
mingling the manners and customs of his former situation with a long history of his gallantry and success; naming, according to his account, not above half
the marchionesses he had slept with, and pretending
never to have dressed the head of a pretty woman,

without having likewise decorated her husband's; vain, foolish, ignorant and insolent; such was the worthy substitute taken in my absence, and the companion offered me on my return!

O! if souls disengaged from their terrestrial bonds, yet view from the bosom of eternal light what passes here below, pardon, dear and respectable shade, that I show no more favor to your failings than my own, but equally unveil both. I ought and will be just to you as to myself; but how much less will you lose by this resolution than I shall! How much do your amiable and gentle disposition, your inexhaustible goodness of heart, your frankness and other amiable virtues, compensate for your foibles, if a subversion of reason alone can be called such. You had errors, but not vices; your conduct was reprehensible, but your heart was ever pure.

The new-comer had shown himself zealous and exact in all her little commissions, which were ever numerous, and he diligently overlooked the laborers. As noisy and insolent as I was quiet and forbearing, he was seen or rather heard at the plow, in the hay-loft, wood-house, stable, farm-yard, at the same instant. He neglected the gardening, this labor being too peaceful and moderate; his chief pleasure was to load or drive the cart, to saw or cleave wood; he was never seen without a hatchet or pick-ax in his hand, running, knocking and hallooing with all his might. I know not how many men's labor he performed, but he certainly made noise enough for ten or a dozen at least. All this bustle imposed on poor Madam de War-rens; she thought this young man a treasure, and, willing to attach him to herself, employed the means she imagined necessary for that purpose, not forget-ting what she most depended on, the surrender of her person.

Those who have thus far read this work should be able to form some judgment of my heart; its senti-ments were the most constant and sincere, particu-larly those which had brought me back to Chambery; what a sudden and complete overthrow was this to my whole being! but to judge fully of this, the reader must place himself for a moment in my situation. I saw all the future felicity I had promised myself van-ish in a moment; all the charming ideas I had in-dulged so affectionately, disappear entirely; and I, who even from childhood had not been able to con-sider my existence for a moment as separate from hers, for the first time, saw myself utterly alone. This mo-ment was dreadful, and those that succeeded it were ever gloomy. I was yet young, but the pleasing senti-ments of enjoyment and hope, which enliven youth, were extinguished. From that hour my existence seemed half annihilated. I contemplated in advance the melancholy remains of an insipid life, and if at any time an image of happiness glanced through my mind, it was not that which appeared natural to me, and I felt that even should I obtain it I must still be wretched.

I was so dull of apprehension, and my confidence

in her was so great, that, notwithstanding the familiar tone of the new-comer, which I looked on as an effect of the easy disposition of Madam de Warrens, which rendered her free with every one, I never should have suspected his real situation had not she herself informed me of it; but she hastened to make this avowal with a freedom calculated to inflame me with resentment, could my heart have turned to that point. Speaking of this connection as quite immaterial with respect to herself, she reproached me with negligence in the care of the family, and mentioned my frequent absence, as though she had been in haste to supply my place. "Ah!" said I, my heart bursting with the most poignant grief, "what do you dare to inform me of? Is this the reward of an attachment like mine? Have you so many times preserved my life, for the sole purpose of taking from me all that could render it desirable? Your infidelity will bring me to the grave, but you will regret my loss!" She answered with a tranquillity sufficient to distract me, that I talked like a child; that people did not die from such slight causes; that our friendship need be no less sincere, nor we any less intimate, for that her tender attachment to me could neither diminish nor end but with herself; in a word she gave me to understand that my happiness need not suffer any decrease from the good fortune of this new favorite.

Never did the purity, truth and force of my attachment to her appear more evident; never did I feel the sincerity and honesty of my soul more forcibly, than at that moment. I threw myself at her feet, embracing her knees with torrents of tears. "No, madam," replied I, with the most violent agitation, "I love you too much to disgrace you thus far, and too truly to share you; the regret that accompanied the first acquisition of your favors has continued to increase with my affection. I cannot preserve them by so violent an augmentation of it. You shall ever have my adoration: be worthy of it; to me that is more necessary than all you can bestow. It is to you, O my dearest friend! that I resign my rights; it is to the union of our hearts that I sacrifice my pleasure; rather would I perish a thousand times than thus degrade her I love."

I preserved this resolution with a constancy worthy, I may say, of the sentiment that gave it birth. From this moment I saw this beloved woman but with the eyes of a real son. It should be remarked here, that this resolve did not meet her private approbation, as I too well perceived; yet she never employed the least art to make me renounce it either by insinuating proposals, caresses, or any of those means which women so well know how to employ without exposing themselves to violent censure, and which seldom fail to succeed. Reduced to seek a fate independent of hers, and not able to devise one, I passed to the other extreme, placing my happiness so absolutely in her, that I became almost regardless of myself. The ardent desire to see her happy, at any rate, absorbed all my affections; it was in vain she endeavored to separate her felicity from mine, I felt I had a part in it, spite of every impediment.

Thus those virtues whose seeds in my heart begun to spring up with my misfortunes: they had been cultivated by study, and only waited the fermentation of adversity to become prolific. The first-fruit of this disinterested disposition was to put from my heart every sentiment of hatred and envy against him who had supplanted me. I even sincerely wished to attach myself to this young man; to form and educate him; to make him sensible of his happiness, and, if possible, render him worthy of it; in a word, to do for him what Anet had formerly done for me. But the similarity of dispositions was wanting. More insinuating and enlightened than Anet, I possessed neither his coolness, fortitude, nor commanding strength of character, which I must have had in order to succeed. Neither did the young man possess those qualities which Anet found in me; such as gentleness, gratitude, and above all, the knowledge of a want of his instructions, and an ardent desire to render them useful. All these were wanting; the person I wished to improve, saw in me nothing but an importunate, chattering pedant: while on the contrary he admired his own importance in the house, measuring the services he thought he rendered by the noise he made, and looking on his saws, hatchets, and pick-axes, as infinitely more useful than all my old books: and, perhaps, in this particular, he might not be altogether blamable; but he gave himself a number of airs sufficient to make any one die with laughter. With the peasants he assumed the airs of a country gentleman; presently he did as much with me, and at length with Madam de Warrens herself. His name, Vintzenried, did not appear noble enough, he therefore changed it to that of Monsieur de Courtilles, and by the latter appellation he was known at Chambery, and in Maurienne, where he married.

At length this illustrious personage gave himself such airs of consequence, that he was everything in the house, and myself nothing. When I had the misfortune to displease him, he scolded Madam de Warrens, and a fear of exposing her to his brutality rendered me subservient to all his whims, so that every time he cleaved wood (an office which he performed with singular pride) it was necessary I should be an idle spectator and admirer of his prowess. This lad was not, however, of a bad disposition; he loved Madam de Warrens, indeed it was impossible to do otherwise; nor had he any aversion even to me, and when he happened to be out of his airs would listen to our admonitions, and frankly own he was a fool; yet notwithstanding these acknowledgments his follies continued in the same proportion. His knowledge was so contracted, and his inclinations so mean, that it was useless to reason, and almost impossible to be pleased with him. Not content with a most charming woman, he amused himself with an old red-haired, toothless waiting-maid, whose unwelcome service Madam de Warrens had the patience to endure, though it was absolutely disgusting. I soon perceived this new inclination, and was exasperated at it; but I saw something else, which affected me yet more, and made a deeper impression on me than anything had hitherto done; this was a visible coldness in the behavior of Madam de Warrens towards me.

The privation I had imposed on myself, and which she affected to approve, is one of those affronts which women scarcely ever forgive. Take the most sensible, the most philosophic female, one the least attached to pleasure, and slighting her favors, if within your reach, will be found the most unpardonable crime, even though she may care nothing for the man. This rule is certainly without exception; since a sympathy so natural and ardent was impaired in her, by an abstinence founded only on virtue, attachment, and esteem, I no longer found with her that union of hearts which constituted all the happiness of mine; she seldom sought me but when we had occasion to complain of this new-comer, for when they were agreed, I enjoyed but little of her confidence, and, at length, was scarcely ever consulted in her affairs. She seemed pleased, indeed, with my company, but had I passed whole days without seeing her she would hardly have missed me.

Insensibly, I found myself desolate and alone in that house where I had formerly been the very soul; where, if I may so express myself, I had enjoyed a double life, and, by degrees, I accustomed myself to disregard everything that passed, and even those who dwelt there. To avoid continual mortifications, I shut myself up with my books, or else wept and sighed unnoticed in the woods. This life soon became insupportable; I felt that the presence of a woman so dear to me, while estranged from her heart, increased my unhappiness, and was persuaded, that, ceasing to see her, I should feel myself less cruelly separated.

I resolved, therefore, to quit the house, mentioned it to her, and she, far from opposing my resolution, approved it. She had an acquaintance at Grenoble, called Madam de Deybens, whose husband was on terms of friendship with Monsieur Mably, chief Provost of Lyons. M. Deybens proposed my educating M. Mably's children; I accepted this offer, and departed for Lyons, without causing, and almost without feeling, the least regret at a separation, the bare idea of which, a few months before, would have given us both the most excruciating torments.

I had almost as much knowledge as was necessary for a tutor, and flattered myself that my method would be unexceptionable; but the year I passed at M. Mably's, was sufficient to undeceive me in that particular. The natural gentleness of my disposition seemed calculated for the employment, if hastiness had not been mingled with it. While things went favorably, and I saw the pains (which I did not spare) succeed, I was an angel; but a devil when they went contrary. If my pupils did not understand me, I was hasty, and when they showed any symptoms of an untoward disposition, I was so provoked that I could have killed them; which behavior was not likely to render them either good or wise. I had two under my care, and they were of very different tempers. *Ste.-Marie,* who was between eight and nine years old, had a good person and quick apprehension, was giddy, lively, playful and mischievous; but his mischief was ever good-humored. The younger one, named *Condillac,* appeared stupid and fretful, was headstrong as a mule, and seemed incapable of instruction. It may be supposed that between both I did not want employment, yet with patience and temper I might have succeeded; but wanting both, I did nothing worth mentioning, and my pupils profited very little. I could only make use of three means, which are very weak, and often pernicious with children; namely, sentiment, reasoning, passion. I sometimes exerted myself so much with *Ste.-Marie,* that I could not refrain from tears, and wished to excite similar sensations in him; as if it was reasonable to suppose a child could be susceptible of such emotions. Sometimes I exhausted myself in reasoning, as if persuaded he could comprehend me; and as he frequently formed very subtle arguments, concluded he must be reasonable, because he bade fair to be so good a logician.

The little *Condillac* was still more embarrassing; for he neither understood, answered, nor was concerned at anything; he was of an obstinacy beyond belief, and was never happier than when he had succeeded in putting me in a rage, then, indeed, he was the philosopher, and I the child. I was conscious of all my faults, studied the tempers of my pupils, and became acquainted with them; but where was the use of seeing the evil, without being able to apply a remedy? My penetration was unavailing, since it never prevented any mischief; and everything I undertook failed, because all I did to effect my designs was precisely what I ought not to have done.

I was not more fortunate in what had only reference to myself, than in what concerned my pupils. Madam Deybens, in recommending me to her friend Madam de Mably, had requested her to form my manners, and endeavor to give me an air of the world. She took some pains on this account, wishing to teach me how to do the honors of the house; but I was so awkward, bashful, and stupid, that she found it necessary to stop there. This, however, did not prevent me from falling in love with her, according to my usual custom; I even behaved in such a manner, that she could not avoid observing it; but I never durst declare my passion; and as the lady never seemed in a humor to make advances, I soon became weary of my sighs and ogling, being convinced they answered no manner of purpose.

I had quite lost my inclination for little thieveries while with Madam de Warrens; indeed, as everything belonged to me, there was nothing to steal; besides, the elevated notions I had imbibed ought to have rendered me in future above such meanness, and generally speaking they certainly did so; but this rather proceeded from my having learned to conquer temptations, than have succeeded in rooting out the propensity, and I should even now greatly dread stealing, as in my infancy, were I yet subject to the same inclinations. I had a proof of this at M. Mably's, where, though surrounded by a number of little things that I could easily have pilfered, and which appeared no temptation, I took it into my head to covet some white Arbois wine, some glasses of which I had drank at table, and thought delicious. It happened to be rather thick, and as I fancied myself an excellent finer of wine, I mentioned my skill, and this was accordingly trusted to my care, but in attempting to mend, I spoiled it, though to the sight only, for it remained equally agreeable to the taste. Profiting by this opportunity, I furnished myself from time to time with a few bottles to drink in my own apartment; but unluckily, I could never drink without eating; the difficulty lay therefore, in procuring bread. It was impossible to make a reserve of this article, and to have it brought by the footman was discovering myself, and insulting the master of the house; I could not bear to purchase it myself; how could a fine gentleman, with a sword by his side, enter a baker's shop to buy a small loaf of bread?—it was utterly impossible. At length I recollected the thoughtless saying of a great princess, who, on being informed that the country people had no bread, replied, "Then let them eat pastry!" Yet even this resource was attended with a difficulty. I sometimes went out alone for this very purpose, running over the whole city, and passing thirty pastry cook's shops without daring to enter any one of them. In the first place, it was necessary there should be only one person in the shop, and that person's physiognomy must be so encouraging as to give me confidence to pass the threshold; but when once the dear little cake was procured, and I shut up in my chamber with that and a bottle of wine, taken cautiously from the bottom of a cupboard, how much did I enjoy drinking my wine, and reading a few pages of a novel; for when I have no company I always wish to read while eating; it seems a substitute for society, and I dispatch alternately a page and a morsel; 'tis indeed as if my book dined with me.

I was neither dissolute nor sottish, never in my whole life having been intoxicated with liquor; my little thefts were not very indiscreet, yet they were discovered; the bottles betrayed me, and though no notice was taken of it, I had no longer the management of the cellar. In all this Monsieur Mably conducted himself with prudence and politeness, being really a very deserving man, who, under a manner as harsh as his employment, concealed a real gentleness of disposition and uncommon goodness of heart: he was judicious, equitable, and (what would not be expected from an officer of the *Marechausse*) very humane.

Sensible of his indulgence, I became greatly attached to him, which made my stay at Lyons longer than it would otherwise have been; but at length, disgusted with an employment which I was not calculated for, and a situation of great confinement, consequently disagreeable to me, after a year's trial, during which time I spared no pains to fulfill my engagement, I determined to quit my pupils; being convinced I should never succeed in educating them properly. Monsieur Mably saw this as clearly as myself, though I am inclined to think he would never have dismissed me had I not spared him the trouble, which was an excess of condescension in this particular, that I certainly cannot justify.

What rendered my situation yet more insupportable was the comparison I was continually drawing between the life I now led and that which I had quitted; the remembrance of my dear Charmettes, my garden, trees, fountain and orchard, but above all, the company of her who was born to give life and soul to every other enjoyment. On calling to mind our pleasures and innocent life, I was seized with such oppressions and heaviness of heart, as deprived me of the power of performing anything as it should be. A hundred times was I tempted instantly to set off on foot to my dear Madam de Warrens, being persuaded that could I once more see her, I should be content to die that moment: in fine, I could no longer resist the tender emotions which recalled me back to her, whatever it might cost me. I accused myself of not having been sufficiently patient, complaisant and kind; concluding I might yet live happily with her on the terms of tender friendship, and by showing more for her than I had hitherto done. I formed the finest projects in the world, burned to execute them, left all, renounced everything, departed, fled, and arriving in all the transports of my early youth, found myself once more at her feet. Alas! I should have died there with joy, and I found in her reception, in her embrace, or in her heart, one-quarter of what I had formerly found there, and which I yet felt the undiminished warmth of.

Fearful illusion of transitory things, how often dost thou torment us in vain! She received me with that excellence of heart which could only die with her; but I sought the influence there which could never be recalled, and had hardly been half an hour with her before I was once more convinced that my former happiness had vanished forever, and that I was in the same melancholy situation which I had been obliged to fly from; yet without being able to accuse any person with my unhappiness, for Courtilles really was not to blame, appearing to see my return with more pleasure than dissatisfaction. But how could I bear to be a secondary person with her to whom I had been everything, and who could never cease being such to me? How could I live an alien in that house where I had been the child? The sight of every object that had been witness to my former happiness, rendered the comparison yet more distressing; I should have suffered less in any other habitation, for this incessantly recalled such pleasing remembrances, that it was irritating the recollection of my loss.

Consumed with vain regrets, given up to the most

gloomy melancholy, I resumed the custom of remaining alone, except at meals: shut up with my books, I sought to give some useful diversion to my ideas, and feeling the imminent danger of want, which I had so long dreaded, I sought means to prepare for and receive it, when Madam de Warrens should have no other resource. I had placed her household on a footing not to become worse; but since my departure everything had been altered. He who now managed her affairs was a spendthrift, and wished to make a great appearance; such as keeping a good horse with elegant trappings; loved to appear gay in the eyes of the neighbors, and was perpetually undertaking something he did not understand. Her pension was taken up in advance, her rent was in arrears, debts of every kind continued to accumulate; I could plainly foresee that her pension would soon be seized, and perhaps suppressed; in short, I expected nothing but ruin and misfortune, and the moment appeared to approach so rapidly that I already felt all its horrors.

My closet was my only amusement, and after a tedious search for remedies for the sufferings of my mind, I determined to seek some against the evil of distressing circumstances, which I daily expected would fall upon us, and returning to my old chimeras, behold me once more building castles in the air to relieve this dear friend from the cruel extremities into which I saw her ready to fall. I did not believe myself wise enough to shine in the republic of letters, or to stand any chance of making a fortune by that means;

a new idea, therefore, inspired me with that confidence, which the mediocrity of my talents could not
impart.

In ceasing to teach music I had not abandoned the
thoughts of it; on the contrary, I had studied the
theory sufficiently to consider myself well informed
on the subject. When reflecting on the trouble it had
cost me to read music, and the great difficulty I yet
experienced in singing at sight, I began to think the
fault might as well arise from the manner of noting as
from my own dullness, being sensible it was an art
which most people find difficult to understand. By
examining the formation of the signs, I was convinced
they were frequently very ill devised. I had before
thought of marking the gamut by figures, to prevent
the trouble of having lines to draw, on noting the
plainest air; but had been stopped by the difficulty of
the octaves, and by the distinction of measure and
quantity: this idea returned again to my mind, and on
a careful revision of it, I found the difficulties were by
no means insurmountable. I pursued it successfully,
and was at length able to note any music whatever by
figures, with the greatest exactitude and simplicity.
From this moment I supposed my fortune made, and
in the ardor of sharing it with her to whom I owed
everything, thought only of going to Paris, not doubting that on presenting my project to the Academy, it
would be adopted with rapture. I had brought some
money from Lyons; I augmented this stock by the sale
of my books, and in the course of a fortnight my reso-

lution was both formed and executed: in short, full of the magnificent ideas it had inspired, and which were common to me on every occasion, I departed from Savoy with my new system of music, as I had formerly done from Turin with my heron-fountain.

Such have been the errors and faults of my youth: I have related the history of them with a fidelity which my heart approves; if my riper years were dignified with some virtues, I should have related them with the same frankness; it was my intention to have done this, but I must forego that pleasing task and stop here. Time, which renders justice to the characters of most men, may withdraw the veil; and should my memory reach posterity, they may one day discover what I had to say—they will then understand why I am now silent.

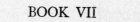

BOOK VII

BOOK VII

BOOK VII

[*1741*]

AFTER two years silence and patience, and notwithstanding my resolutions, I again take up my pen. Reader, suspend your judgment as to the reasons which force me to such a step: of these you can be no judge until you shall have read my book.

You have seen my youth pass away calmly without any great disappointments or remarkable prosperity. This was mostly owing to my ardent yet feeble nature, less prompt in undertaking than easy to discourage: quitting repose by violent agitations, but returning to it from lassitude and inclinations, and which, placing me in an idle and tranquil state for which alone I felt I was born, at a distance from the paths of great virtues and still further from those of great vices.

The first part of my confessions was written entirely from memory, and is consequently full of errors. As I am obliged to write the second part from memory also, the errors in it will probably be still more numerous. The remembrance of the finest portion of my years, passed with so much tranquillity and innocence, has left in my heart a thousand charming impressions which I love to call to my recollection. Far from increasing that of my situation by these sorrowful reflections, I repel them as much as possible, and in this endeavor often succeed so well as to be unable to find them at will. This facility of forgetting my misfortunes is a consolation which Heaven has reserved to me in the midst of those which fate has one day to accumulate upon my head. My memory, which presents to me no objects but such as are agreeable, is the happy counterpoise of my terrified imagination, by which I foresee nothing but a cruel futurity.

All the papers I had collected to aid my recollection, and guide me in this undertaking, are no longer in my possession, nor can I ever again hope to regain them.

I have but one faithful guide on which I can depend: this is the chain of the sentiments by which the succession of my existence has been marked, and by these the events which have been either the cause or the effect of the manner of it. I easily forget my misfortunes, but I cannot forget my faults, and still less my virtuous sentiments. The remembrance of these is too dear to me ever to suffer them to be effaced from my mind. I may omit facts, transpose events, and fall into some errors of dates; but I cannot be deceived in what I have felt, nor in that which from sentiment I have done; and to relate this is the chief end of my present work. The real object of my confessions is to communicate an exact knowledge of what I interiorly am and have been in every situation of my life. I have promised the history of my mind, and to write it faithfully I have no need of other memoirs: to enter into my own heart, as I have hitherto done, will alone be sufficient.

There is, however, and very happily, an interval of six or seven years, relative to which I have exact references, in a collection of letters copied from the originals, in the hands of M. du Peyrou. This collection, which concludes in 1760, comprehends the whole time of my residence at the hermitage, and my great quarrel with those who called themselves my friends; that memorable epocha of my life, and the source of all my other misfortunes. With respect to more recent original letters which may remain in my possession, and are but few in number, instead of transcribing them at the end of this collection, too voluminous to enable me to deceive the vigilance of my Arguses, I will copy them into the work whenever they appear to furnish any explanation, be this either for or against myself; for I am not under the least apprehension lest the reader should forget I make my confession, and be induced to believe I make my apology; but he cannot expect I shall conceal the truth when it testifies in my favor.

This second part, it is likewise to be remembered, contains nothing in common with the first, except truth; nor has any other advantage over it, but the importance of the facts; in everything else, it is inferior to the former. I wrote the first with pleasure, with satisfaction, and at my ease, at Wootton, or in the castle of Trye: everything I had to recollect was a new enjoyment. I returned to my closet with an increased pleasure, and, without constraint, gave that turn to my descriptions which most flatters my imagination.

At present my head and memory are become so weak as to render me almost incapable of every kind of application: my present undertaking is the result of constraint, and a heart full of sorrow. I have nothing to treat of but misfortunes, treacheries, perfidies, and circumstances equally afflicting. I would give the world, could I bury in the obscurity of time, everything I have to say, and which, in spite of myself, I am obliged to relate. I am, at the same time, under the necessity of being mysterious and subtle, of endeavoring to impose and of descending to things the most foreign to my nature. The ceiling under which I write has eyes; the walls of my chamber have ears. Surrounded by spies and by vigilant and malevolent inspectors, disturbed, and my attention diverted, I hastily commit to paper a few broken sentences, which I have scarcely time to read, and still less to correct. I know that, notwithstanding the barriers which are multiplied around me, my enemies are afraid truth should escape by some little opening. What means can I take to introduce it to the world? This, however, I attempt with but few hopes of success. The reader will judge whether or not such a situation furnishes the means of agreeable descriptions, or of giving them a seductive coloring! I therefore inform such as may undertake to read this work, that nothing can secure them from weariness in the prosecution of their task, unless it be the desire of becoming more fully acquainted with a man whom they already know, and a sincere love of justice and truth.

In my first part I brought down my narrative to my departure with infinite regret from Paris, leaving my heart at Charmettes, and, there building my last castle in the air, intending some day to return to the feet of Mama, restored to herself, with the treasures I should have acquired, and depending upon my system of music as upon a certain fortune.

I made some stay at Lyons to visit my acquaintance, procure letters of recommendation to Paris, and to sell my books of geometry which I had brought with me. I was well received by all whom I knew. M. and Madam de Mably seemed pleased to see me again, and several times invited me to dinner. At their house I became acquainted with the Abbé de Mably, as I had already done with the Abbé de Condillac, both of whom were on a visit to their brother. The Abbé de Mably gave me letters to Paris; among others, one to M. de Fontenelle, and another to the Comte de Caylus. These were very agreeable acquaintances, especially the first, to whose friendship for me his death only put a period, and from whom, in our private conversations, I received advice which I ought to have more exactly followed.

I likewise saw M. Bordes, with whom I had been long acquainted, and who had frequently obliged me with the greatest cordiality and the most real pleasure.

He it was who enabled me to sell my books; and he also gave me from himself good recommendations to Paris. I again saw the intendant for whose acquaintance I was indebted to M. Bordes, and who introduced me to the Duke de Richelieu, who was then passing through Lyons. M. Pallu presented me. The duke received me well, and invited me to come and see him at Paris; I did so several times; although this great acquaintance, of which I shall frequently have occasion to speak, was never of the most trifling utility to me.

I visited the musician David, who, in one of my former journeys, and in my distress, had rendered me service. He had either lent or given me a cap and a pair of stockings, which I have never returned, nor has he ever asked me for them, although we have since that time frequently seen each other. I, however, made him a present, something like an equivalent. I would say more upon this subject, were what I have owed in question; but I have to speak of what I have done, which, unfortunately, is far from being the same thing.

I also saw the noble and generous Perrichon, and not without feeling the effects of his accustomed munificence; for he made me the same present he had previously done to "Gentil-Bernard," by paying for my place in the diligence. I visited the surgeon Parisot, the best and most benevolent of men; as also his beloved Godefroi, who had lived with him ten years, and whose merit chiefly consisted in her gentle manners and goodness of heart. It was impossible to see this woman without pleasure, or to leave her without regret. Nothing better shows the inclinations of a man, than the nature of his attachments* Those who had once seen the gentle Godefroi, immediately knew the good and amiable Parisot.

I was much obliged to all these good people, but I afterwards neglected them all; not from ingratitude, but from that invincible indolence which so often assumes its appearance. The remembrance of their services, has never been effaced from my mind, nor the impression they made, from my heart; but I could more easily have proved my gratitude, than assiduously have shown them the exterior of that sentiment. Exactitude in correspondence is what I never could observe; the moment I begin to relax, the shame and embarrassment of repairing my fault make me aggravate it, and I entirely desist from writing; I have, therefore, been silent, and appeared to forget them. Parisot and Perrichon took not the least notice of my negligence, and I ever found them the same. But, twenty years afterwards it will be seen, in M. Bordes, to what a degree the self-love of a wit can make him

* *Unless he be deceived in his choice, or that she, to whom he attaches himself, changes her character by an extraordinary concurrence of causes, which is not absolutely impossible. Were this consequence to be admitted without modification, Socrates must be judged by his wife Xantippe, and Dion by his friend Calippus, which would be the most false and iniquitous judgment ever made. However, let no injurious application be here made to my wife. She is weak and more easily deceived than I at first imagined, but by her pure and excellent character she is worthy of all my esteem.*

carry his vengeance when he feels himself neglected.

Before I leave Lyons, I must not forget an amiable person, whom I again saw with more pleasure than ever, and who left in my heart the most tender remembrance. This was Mademoiselle Serre, of whom I have spoken in my first part; I renewed my acquaintance with her whilst I was at M. de Mably's.

Being this time more at leisure, I saw her more frequently, and she made the most sensible impressions on my heart. I had some reason to believe her own was not unfavorable to my pretensions; but she honored me with her confidence so far as to remove from me all temptation to allure her partiality. She had no fortune, and in this respect exactly resembled myself; our situations were too similar to permit us to become united; and with the views I then had, I was far from thinking of marriage. She gave me to understand that a young merchant, one M. Genève, seemed to wish to obtain her hand. I saw him once or twice at her lodgings; he appeared to me to be an honest man, and this was his general character. Persuaded she would be happy with him, I was desirous he should marry her, which he afterwards did; and that I might not disturb their innocent love, I hastened my departure; offering up, for the happiness of that charming woman, prayers, which, here below, were not long heard. Alas! her time was very short, for I afterwards heard she died in the second or third year after her marriage. My mind, during the journey, was wholly absorbed in tender regret. I felt, and since that time, when these circumstances have been present to my recollection, have frequently done the same; that although the sacrifices made to virtue and our duty may sometimes be painful, we are well rewarded by the agreeable remembrance they leave deeply engraven in our hearts.

I this time saw Paris in as favorable a point of views as it had appeared to me in an unfavorable one at my first journey; not that my ideas of its brilliancy arose from the splendor of my lodgings: for in consequence of an address given me by M. Bordes, I resided at the Hôtel St. Quentin, Rue des Cordiers, near the Sorbonne; a vile street, a miserable hotel, and a wretched apartment: but nevertheless a house in which several men of merit, such as Gresset, Bordes, Abbé Mably, Condillac, and several others, of whom unfortunately I found not one, had taken up their quarters: but I there met with M. Bonnefond, a man unacquainted with the world, lame, litigious, and who affected to be a purist. To him I owe the acquaintance of M. Roguin, at present the oldest friend I have, and by whose means I became acquainted with Diderot, of whom I shall soon have occasion to say a good deal.

I arrived at Paris in the autumn of 1741, with fifteen louis in my purse, and with my comedy of *Narcissus* and my musical project in my pocket. These composed my whole stock, consequently, I had not much time to lose before I attempted to turn the latter to some advantage. I therefore immediately thought of making use of my recommendations.

A young man who arrives at Paris, with a tolerable figure, and announces himself by his talents, is sure to be well received. This was my good fortune, which procured me some pleasures without leading to anything solid. Of all the persons to whom I was recommended, three only were useful to me. M. Damesin, a gentleman of Savoy, at that time equerry, and I believe favorite, of the Princess of Carignan; M. de Boze, secretary to the Academy of Inscriptions, and keeper of the medals of the king's cabinet; and Father Castle, a Jesuit, author of the *Clavecin oculaire.**

All these recommendations, except that to M. Damesin, were given me by the Abbé de Mably.

M. Damesin provided me with that which was most needful, by means of two persons with whom he brought me acquainted. One was M. Gasc, *president a mortier* of the parliament of Bordeaux, and who played very well upon the violin; the other, the Abbé de Léon, who then lodged in the Sorbonne, a young nobleman, extremely amiable, who died in the flower of his age, after having, for a few moments, made a figure in the world under the name of the Chevalier de Rohan. Both these gentlemen had an inclination to learn composition. In this I gave them lessons for a few months, by which means my decreasing purse received some little aid. The Abbé Léon conceived a friendship for me, and wished me to become his secretary; but he was far from being rich, and all the

* *An effort to produce sensations of melody by combinations of colors.*

salary he could offer me was eight hundred livres, which, with infinite regret, I refused; since it was insufficient to defray the expenses of my lodging, food and clothing.

I was well received by M. de Boze. He had a thirst for knowledge, of which he possessed not a little, but was somewhat pedantic. Madam de Boze much resembled him; she was lively and affected. I sometimes dined with them, and it is impossible to be more awkward than I was in her presence. Her easy manner intimidated me, and rendered mine more remarkable. When she presented me a plate, I modestly put forward my fork to take one of the least bits of what she offered me, which made her give the plate to her servant, turning her head aside that I might not see her laugh. She had not the least suspicion that in the head of the rustic with whom she was so diverted there was some small portion of wit. M. de Boze presented me to M. de Réaumur, his friend, who came to dine with him every Friday, the day on which the Academy of Sciences met. He mentioned to him my project, and the desire I had of having it examined by the academy. M. de Réaumur consented to make the proposal, and his offer was accepted. On the day appointed I was introduced and presented by M. de Réaumur, and on the same day, August 22d, 1742, I had the honor to read to the academy the memoir I had prepared for that purpose. Although this illustrious assembly might certainly well be expected to inspire me with awe, I was less intimidated on this occasion than I had been in the presence of Madam de Boze, and I got tolerably well through my reading and the answers I was obliged to give. The memoir was well received, and acquired me some compliments by which I was equally surprised and flattered, imagining that before such an assembly, whoever was not a member of it could not have common-sense. The persons appointed to examine my system were M. Mairan, M. Hellot, and M. de Fouchy, all three men of merit, but not one of them understood music, at least not enough of composition to enable them to judge of my project.

During my conference with these gentlemen, I was convinced with no less certainty than surprise, that if men of learning have sometimes fewer prejudices than others, they more tenaciously retain those they have. However weak or false most of their objections were, and although I answered them with great timidity, and I confess, in bad terms, yet with decisive reasons, I never once made myself understood, or gave them any explanation in the least satisfactory. I was constantly surprised at the facility with which, by the aid of a few sonorous phrases, they refuted, without having comprehended me. They had learned, I know not where, that a monk of the name of Souhaitti had formerly invented a mode of noting the gamut by ciphers: a sufficient proof that my system was not new. This might, perhaps, be the case; for although I had never heard of Father Souhaitti, and notwithstanding his manner of writing the seven notes without attending to the octaves was not, under any point of view, worthy of entering into competition with my simple and commodious invention for easily noting by ciphers every possible kind of music, keys, rests, octaves, measure, time, and length of note; things on which Souhaitti had never thought: it was nevertheless true, that with respect to the elementary expression of the seven notes, he was the first inventor.

But besides their giving to this primitive invention more importance than was due to it, they went still further, and, whenever they spoke of the fundamental principles of the system, talked nonsense. The greatest advantage of my scheme was to supersede transpositions and keys, so that the same piece of music was noted and transposed at will by means of the change of a single initial letter at the head of the air. These gentlemen had heard from the music-masters of Paris that the method of executing by transposition was a bad one; and on this authority converted the most evident advantage of my system into an invincible objection against it, and affirmed that my mode of notation was good for vocal music, but bad for instrumental; instead of concluding as they ought to have done, that it was good for vocal, and still better for instrumental. On their report the academy granted me a certificate full of fine compliments, amidst which it appeared that in reality it judged my system to be neither new nor useful. I did not think proper to ornament with such a paper the work entitled, *Dissertation* *sur la musique moderne,** by which I appealed to the public.

I had reason to remark on this occasion that, even with a narrow understanding, the sole but profound knowledge of a thing is preferable for the purpose of judging of it, to all the lights resulting from a cultivation of the sciences, when to these particular study of that in question has not been joined. The only solid objection to my system was made by Rameau. I had scarcely explained it to him before he discovered its weak part. "Your signs," said he, "are very good, inasmuch as they clearly and simply determine the length of notes, exactly represent intervals, and show the simple in the double note, which the common notation does not do; but they are objectionable on account of their requiring an operation of the mind, which cannot always accompany the rapidity of execution. The position of our notes," continued he, "is described to the eye without the concurrence of this operation. If two notes, one very high and the other very low, be joined by a series of intermediate ones, I see at the first glance the progress from one to the other by conjoined degrees; but in your system, to perceive this series, I must necessarily run over your ciphers one after the other; the glance of the eye is here useless." The objection appeared to me insurmountable, and I instantly assented to it. Although it be simple and striking, nothing can suggest it but great knowledge and practice of the art, and it is by no

* *Dissertation on modern music.*

[430]

means astonishing that not one of the academicians should have thought of it. But what creates much surprise is, that these men of great learning, and who are supposed to possess so much knowledge, should so little know that each ought to confine his judgment to that which relates to the study with which he has been conversant.

My frequent visits to the literati appointed to examine my system and the other academicians gave me an opportunity of becoming acquainted with the most distinguished men of letters in Paris, and by this means the acquaintance that would have been the consequence of my sudden admission amongst them which afterwards came to pass, was already established. With respect to the present moment, absorbed in my new system of music, I obstinately adhered to my intention of effecting a revolution in the art, and by that means of acquiring a celebrity which, in the fine arts, is in Paris mostly accompanied by fortune. I shut myself in my chamber and labored three or four months with inexpressible ardor, in forming into a work for the public eye, the memoir I had read before the academy. The difficulty was to find a bookseller to take my manuscript; and this on account of the necessary expenses for new characters, and because booksellers give not their money by handfuls to young authors; although to me it seemed but just my work should render me the bread I had eaten while employed in its composition.

Bonnefond introduced me to Quillau the father,

with whom I agreed to divide the profits, without reckoning the privilege, of which I paid the whole expense. Such were the future proceedings of this Quillau that I lost the expenses of my privilege, never having received a farthing from that edition; which, probably, had but very middling success, although the Abbé des Fontaines promised to give it celebrity, and, notwithstanding the other journalists, had spoken of it very favorably.

The greatest obstacle to making the experiment of my system was the fear, in case of its not being received, of losing the time necessary to learn it. To this I answered, that my notes rendered the ideas so clear, that to learn music by means of the ordinary characters, time would be gained by beginning with mine. To prove this by experience, I taught music gratis to a young American lady, Mademoiselle des Roulins, with whom M. Roguin had brought me acquainted. In three months she read every kind of music, by means of my notation, and sung at sight better than I did myself, any piece that was not too difficult. This success was convincing, but not known; any other person would have filled the journals with the detail, but with some talents for discovering useful things, I never have possessed that of setting them off to advantage.

Thus was my heron-fountain again broken; but this time I was thirty years of age, and in Paris, where it is impossible to live for a trifle. The resolution I took upon this occasion will astonish none, but those by whom the first part of these memoirs has not been read with attention. I had just made great and fruitless efforts, and was in need of relaxation. Instead of sinking with despair I gave myself up quietly to my indolence and to the care of providence; and the better to wait for its assistance with patience, I laid down a frugal plan for the slow expenditure of a few louis, which still remained in my possession, regulating the expense of my supine pleasures without retrenching it; going to the coffee-house but every other day, and to the theater but twice a week. With respect to the expenses of girls of easy virtue, I had no retrenchment to make; never having in the whole course of my life applied so much as a farthing to that use except once, of which I shall soon have occasion to speak. The security, voluptuousness, and confidence with which I gave myself up to this indolent and solitary life, which I had not the means of continuing for three months, is one of the singularities of my life, and the oddities of my disposition. The extreme desire I had the public should think of me was precisely what discouraged me from showing myself; and the necessity of paying visits rendered them to such a degree insupportable, that I ceased visiting the academicians and other men of letters, with whom I had cultivated an acquaintance. Marivaux, the Abbé Mably, and Fontenelle, were almost the only persons whom I sometimes went to see. To the first I showed my comedy of *Narcissus*. He was pleased with it, and had the goodness to make in it some improvements. Diderot, younger than these, was much about my own age. He was fond of music, and knew it theoretically; we conversed together, and he communicated to me some of his literary projects. This soon formed betwixt us a more intimate connection, which lasted fifteen years, and which probably would still exist were not I, unfortunately, and by his own fault, of the same profession with himself.

It would be impossible to imagine in what manner I employed this short and precious interval which still remained to me, before circumstances forced me to beg my bread:—in learning by memory passages from the poets which I had learned and forgotten a hundred times. Every morning, at ten o'clock, I went to walk in the Luxembourg with a Virgil and a Rousseau in my pocket, and there, until the hour of dinner, I passed away the time in restoring to my memory a sacred ode or a bucolic, without being discouraged by forgetting, by the study of the morning, what I had learned the evening before. I recollected that after the defeat of Nicias at Syracuse the captive Athenians obtained a livelihood by reciting the poems of Homer. The use I made of this erudition to ward off misery was to exercise my happy memory by learning all the poets by rote.

I had another expedient, not less solid, in the game of chess, to which I regularly dedicated, at Maugis's, the evenings on which I did not go to the theater. I became acquainted with M. de Légal, M. Husson, Philidor, and all the great chess players of the day, without making the least improvement in the game.

However, I had no doubt but, in the end, I should become superior to them all, and this, in my own opinion, was a sufficient resource. The same manner of reasoning served me in every folly to which I felt myself inclined. I said to myself: whoever excels in anything is sure to acquire a distinguished reception in society. Let us therefore excel, no matter in what, I shall certainly be sought after; opportunities will present themselves, and my own merit will do the rest. This childishness was not the sophism of my reason; it was that of my indolence. Dismayed at the great and rapid efforts which would have been necessary to call forth my endeavors, I strove to flatter my idleness, and by arguments suitable to the purpose, veiled from my own eyes the shame of such a state.

I thus calmly waited for the moment when I was to be without money; and had not Father Castel, whom I sometimes went to see in my way to the coffee-house, roused me from my lethargy, I believe I should have seen myself reduced to my last farthing without the least emotion. Father Castel was a mad-man, but a good man upon the whole; he was sorry to see me thus impoverish myself to no purpose. "Since musicians and the learned," said he, "do not sing by your scale, change the string, and apply to the women. You will perhaps succeed better with them. I have spoken of you to Madam de Beuzenval; go to her from me; she is a good woman who will be glad to see the countryman of her son and husband. You will find at her house Madam de Broglie, her daughter, who is a woman of wit. Madam Dupin is another to whom I also have mentioned you; carry her your work; she is desirous of seeing you, and will receive you well. Nothing is done in Paris without the women. They are the curves, of which the wise are the asymptotes; they incessantly approach each other, but never touch."

After having from day to day delayed these very disagreeable steps, I at length took courage, and called upon Madam de Beuzenval. She received me with kindness; and Madam de Broglie entering the chamber, she said to her: "Daughter, this is M. Rousseau, of whom Father Castel has spoken to us." Madam de Broglie complimented me upon my work, and going to her harpsichord proved to me she had already given it some attention. Perceiving it to be about one o'clock, I prepared to take my leave. Madam de Beuzenval said to me: "You are at a great distance from the quarter of the town in which you reside; stay and dine here." I did not want asking a second time. A quarter of an hour afterwards, I understood, by a word, that the dinner to which she had invited me was that of her servants' hall. Madam de Beuzenval was a very good kind of woman, but of a confined understanding, and too full of her illustrious Polish nobility: she had no idea of the respect due to talents. On this occasion, likewise, she judged me by my manner rather than by my dress, which, although very plain, was very neat, and by no means announced a man to dine with servants. I had too long forgotten the way to the place where they eat to be inclined to take it again. Without suffering my anger to appear, I told Madam de Beuzenval that I had an affair of a trifling nature which I had just recollected obliged me to return home, and I immediately prepared to depart. Madam de Broglie approached her mother, and whispered in her ear a few words which had their effect. Madam de Beuzenval rose to prevent me from going, and said "I expect that you will do us the honor to dine *with us.*" In this case I thought to show pride would be a mark of folly, and I determined to stay. The goodness of Madam de Broglie had besides made an impression upon me, and rendered her interesting in my eyes. I was very glad to dine with her, and hoped, that when she knew me better, she would not regret having procured me that honor. The President de Lamoignon, very intimate in the family, dined there also. He, as well as Madam de Broglie, was a master of all the modish and fashionable small talk jargon of Paris. Poor Jean-Jacques was unable to make a figure in this way. I had sense enough not to pretend to it, and was silent. Happy would it have been for me, had I always possessed the same wisdom; I should not be in the abyss into which I am now fallen.

I was vexed at my own stupidity, and at being unable to justify to Madam de Broglie what she had done in my favor. After dinner I thought of my ordinary resource. I had in my pocket an epistle in verse, written to Parisot during my residence at Lyons. This fragment was not without some fire, which I increased by my manner of reading, and made them all three shed tears. Whether it was vanity, or really the truth, I thought the eyes of Madam de Broglie seemed to say to her mother: "Well, mamma, was I wrong in telling you this man was fitter to dine with us than with your women?" Until then my heart had been rather burdened, but after this revenge I felt myself satisfied. Madam de Broglie, carrying her favorable opinion of me rather too far, thought I should immediately acquire fame in Paris, and become a favorite with fine ladies. To guide my inexperience she gave me the confessions of the Count de———. "This book," said she, "is a Mentor, of which you will stand in need in the great world. You will do well by sometimes consulting it." I kept the book upwards of twenty years with a sentiment of gratitude to her from whose hand I had received it, although I frequently laughed at the opinion the lady seemed to have of my merit in gallantry. From the moment I had read the work, I was desirous of acquiring the friendship of the author. My inclination led me right; he is the only real friend I ever possessed amongst men of letters.*

From this time I thought I might depend on the services of Madam the Baroness of Beuzenval, and the Marchioness of Broglie, and that they would not

---

* *I have so long been of the same opinion, and so perfectly convinced of its being well founded, that since my return to Paris I confided to him the manuscript of my confessions. The suspicious J. J. never suspected perfidy and falsehood until he had been their victim.*

long leave me without resource. In this I was not deceived. But I must now speak of my first visit to
Madam Dupin, which produced more lasting consequences.

Madam Dupin was, as every one in Paris knows, the
daughter of Samuel Bernard and Madam Fontaine.
There were three sisters, who might be called the
three graces. Madam de la Touche who played a little
prank, and went to England with the Duke of Kings-
ton. Madam d'Arty, the eldest of the three; the friend,
the only sincere friend of the Prince of Conti, an
adorable woman, as well by her sweetness and the
goodness of her charming character, as by her agreeable wit and incessant cheerfulness. Lastly, Madam
Dupin, more beautiful than either of her sisters, and
the only one who has not been reproached with some
levity of conduct.

She was the reward of the hospitality of Madam
Dupin, to whom her mother gave her in marriage
with the place of farmer-general and an immense fortune, in return for the good reception he had given
her in his province. When I saw her for the first time,
she was still one of the finest women in Paris. She received me at her toilette, her arms were uncovered,
her hair disheveled, and her combing-cloth ill-
arranged. This scene was new to me; it was too powerful for my poor head, I became confused, my senses
wandered; in short, I was violently smitten by Madam
Dupin.

My confusion was not prejudicial to me; she did

not perceive it. She kindly received the book and the author; spoke with information of my plan, sung, accompanied herself on the harpsichord, kept me to dinner, and placed me at table by her side. Less than this would have turned my brain; I became mad. She permitted me to visit her, and I abused the permission. I went to see her almost every day, and dined with her twice or thrice a week. I burned with inclination to speak, but never dared attempt it. Several circumstances increased my natural timidity. Permission to visit in an opulent family was a door open to fortune, and in my situation I was unwilling to run the risk of shutting it against myself. Madam Dupin, amiable as she was, was serious and unanimated; I found nothing in her manners sufficiently alluring to embolden me. Her house, at that time, as brilliant as any other in Paris, was frequented by societies the less numerous, as the persons by whom they were composed were chosen on account of some distinguished merit. She was fond of seeing every one who had claims to a marked superiority; the great men of letters, and fine women. No person was seen in her circle but dukes, ambassadors, and blue ribbons. The Princess of Rohan, the Countess of Forcalquier, Madam de Mirepoix, Madam de Brignolé, and Lady Hervey, passed for her intimate friends. The Abbés de Fontenelle, de Saint-Pierre, and Sallier, M. de Fourmont, M. de Bernis, M. de Buffon, and M. de Voltaire, were of her circle and her dinners. If her reserved manner did not attract many young people, her society inspired the greater awe, as it was composed of graver persons, and the poor Jean-Jacques had no reason to flatter himself he should be able to take a distinguished part in the midst of such superior talents. I therefore had not courage to speak; but no longer able to contain myself, I took a resolution to write. For the first two days she said not a word to me upon the subject. On the third day, she returned me my letter, accompanying it with a few exhortations which froze my blood. I attempted to speak, but my words expired upon my lips; my sudden passion was extinguished with my hopes, and after a declaration in form I continued to live with her upon the same terms as before, without so much as speaking to her even by the language of the eyes.

I thought my folly was forgotten, but I was deceived. M. de Francueil, son to M. Dupin, and son-in-law to Madam Dupin, was much the same with herself and me. He had wit, a good person, and might have pretensions. This was said to be the case, and probably proceeded from his mother-in-law's having given him an ugly wife of a mild disposition, with whom, as well as with her husband, she lived upon the best of terms. M. de Francueil was fond of talents in others, and cultivated those he possessed. Music, which he understood very well, was a means of producing a connection between us. I frequently saw him, and he soon gained my friendship. He, however, suddenly gave me to understand that Madam Dupin thought my visits too frequent, and begged me to discontinue them. Such a compliment would have been proper when she returned my letter; but eight or ten days afterwards, and without any new cause, it appeared to me ill-timed. This rendered my situation the more singular, as M. and Madam de Francueil still continued to give me the same good reception as before.

I however made the intervals between my visits longer, and I should entirely have ceased calling on them, had not Madam Dupin, by another unexpected caprice, sent to desire I would for a few days take care of her son, who, changing his preceptor, remained alone during that interval. I passed eight days in such torments as nothing but the pleasure of obeying Madam Dupin could render supportable: for poor Chenonceaux already displayed the evil disposition which nearly brought dishonor on his family, and caused his death in the Isle de Bourton. As long as I was with him I prevented him from doing harm to himself or others, and that was all; besides it was no easy task, and I would not have undertaken to pass eight other days like them had Madam Dupin given me herself for the recompense.

M. de Francueil conceived a friendship for me, and I studied with him. We began together a course of chemistry at Rouelles. That I might be nearer at hand, I left my Hôtel St. Quentin, and went to lodge at the Tennis Court, Rue Verdelet, which leads into the Rue Plâtière, where M. Dupin lived. There, in consequence of a cold neglected, I contracted an inflammation of the lungs that had like to have carried me off. In my younger days I frequently suffered from inflammatory disorders, pleurisies, and especially quinsies, to which I was very subject, and which frequently brought me near enough to death to familiarize me to its image. The evening preceding the day on which I was taken ill, I went to an opera by Royer; the name I have forgotten. Notwithstanding my prejudice in favor of the talents of others, which has ever made me distrustful of my own, I still thought the music feeble, and devoid of animation and invention. I sometimes had the vanity to flatter myself: I think I could do better than that. But the terrible idea I had formed of the composition of an opera, and the importance I heard men of the profession affix to such an undertaking, instantly discouraged me, and made me blush at having so much as thought of it. Besides, where was I to find a person to write the words, and one who would give himself the trouble of turning the poetry to my liking? These ideas of music and the opera had possession of my mind during my illness, and in the delirium of my fever I composed songs, duets, and choruses. I am certain I composed two or three little pieces, *di prima intenzione,** perhaps worthy of the admiration of masters, could they have heard them executed. Oh, could an account be taken of the dreams of a man in a fever, what great and sublime things would sometimes proceed from his delirium!

These subjects of music and opera still engaged my

* *Off-hand.*

attention during my convalescence, but my ideas were less energetic. Long and frequent meditations, and which were often involuntary, and made such an impression upon my mind that I resolved to attempt both words and music. This was not the first time I had undertaken so difficult a task. Whilst I was at Chambery I had composed an opera entitled *Iphis and Anaxarête,* which I had the good sense to throw into the fire. At Lyons I had composed another, entitled *La Decouverte du Nouveau Monde,** which, after having read it to M. Bordes, the Abbés Mably, Trublet, and others, had met the same fate, notwithstanding I had set the prologue and the first act to music, and although David, after examining the composition, had told me there were passages in it worthy of Buononcini.

Before I began the work I took time to consider of my plan. In a heroic ballet I proposed three different subjects, in three acts, detached from each other, set to music of a different character, taking for each subject the amours of a poet. I entitled this opera *Les Muses Galantes.* My first act, in music strongly characterized, was Tasso; the second in tender harmony, Ovid; and the third, entitled Anacreon, was to partake of the gayety of the dithyrambus. I tried my skill on the first act, and applied to it with an ardor which, for the first time, made me feel the delightful sensation produced by the creative power of composition. One evening, as I entered the opera, feeling myself strongly

* *The Discovery of the New World.*

incited and overpowered by my ideas, I put my money
again into my pocket, returned to my apartment,
locked the door, and, having close drawn all the curtains, that every ray of light might be excluded, I went
to bed, abandoning myself entirely to this musical and
poetical *æstrum,* and in seven or eight hours rapidly
composed the greatest part of an act. I can truly say
my love for the Princess of Ferrara (for I was Tasso
for the moment) and my noble and lofty sentiment
with respect to her unjust brother, procured me a night
a hundred times more delicious than one passed in the
arms of the princess would have been. In the morning but a very little of what I had done remained in my
head, but this little, almost effaced by sleep and lassitude, still sufficiently evinced the energy of the pieces
of which it was the scattered remains.

I this time did not proceed far with my undertaking, being interrupted by other affairs. Whilst I attached myself to the family of Dupin, Madam de
Beuzenval and Madam de Broglie, whom I continued
to visit, had not forgotten me. The Count de Montaigu, captain in the guards, had just been appointed
ambassador to Venice. He was an ambassador made
by Barjac, to whom he assiduously paid his court. His
brother, the Chevalier de Montaigu, *gentilhomme de
la manche* to the dauphin, was acquainted with these
ladies, and with the Abbé Alary of the French academy, whom I sometimes visited. Madam de Broglie,
having heard the ambassador was seeking a secretary,
proposed me to him. A conference was opened be-

tween us. I asked a salary of fifty guineas, a trifle for an employment which required me to make some appearance. The ambassador was unwilling to give more than a thousand livres, leaving me to make the journey at my own expense. The proposal was ridiculous. We could not agree, and M. de Francueil, who used all his efforts to prevent my departure, prevailed.

I stayed, and M. de Montaigu set out on his journey, taking with him another secretary, one M. Follau, who had been recommended to him by the office for foreign affairs. They no sooner arrived at Venice than they quarreled. Follau perceiving he had to do with a madman, left him there, and M. de Montaigu having nobody with him, except a young abbé of the name of Binis, who wrote under the secretary, and was unfit to succeed him, had recourse to me. The chevalier, his brother, a man of wit, by giving me to understand there were advantages annexed to the place of secretary, prevailed upon me to accept the thousand livres. I was paid twenty louis in advance for my journey, and immediately departed.

At Lyons I would most willing have taken the route by Mount Cenis, to see my poor mamma. But I went down the Rhône, and embarked at Toulon, as well on account of the war, and from a motive of economy, as to obtain a passport from M. de Mirepoix, who then commanded in Provence, and to whom I was recommended. M. de Montaigu not being able to do without me, wrote letter after letter, desiring I would hasten my journey; this, however, an accident considerably prolonged.

It was at the time of the plague at Messina, and the English fleet had anchored there, and visited the felucca, on board of which I was, and this circumstance subjected us, on our arrival at Genoa, after a long and difficult voyage, to a quarantine of one-and-twenty days.

The passengers had the choice of performing it on board or in the Lazaretto, which we were told was not yet furnished. They all chose the felucca. The insupportable heat, the closeness of the vessel, the impossibility of walking in it, and the vermin with which it swarmed, made me at all risks prefer the Lazaretto. I was therefore conducted to a large building of two stories, quite empty, in which I found neither window, bed, table, nor chair, not so much as even a joint-stool or bundle of straw. My night sack and my two trunks being brought me, I was shut in by great doors with huge locks, and remained at full liberty to walk at my ease from chamber to chamber and story to story, everywhere finding the same solitude and nakedness.

This, however, did not induce me to repent that I had preferred the Lazaretto to the felucca; and, like another Robinson Crusoe, I began to arrange myself for my one-and-twenty days, just as I should have done for my whole life. In the first place, I had the amusement of destroying the vermin I had caught in the felucca. As soon as I had got clear of these, by means of changing my clothes and linen, I proceeded to furnish the chamber I had chosen. I made a good mattress with my waistcoats and shirts; my napkins I converted, by sewing them together, into sheets; my robe de chamber into a counterpane; and my cloak into a pillow. I made myself a seat with one of my trunks laid flat, and a table with the other. I took out some writing paper and an inkstand, and distributed, in the manner of a library, a dozen books which I had with me. In a word, I so well arranged my few movables, that, except curtains and windows, I was almost as commodiously lodged in this Lazaretto, absolutely empty as it was, as I had been at the Tennis Court in the Rue Verdelet. My dinners were served with no small degree of pomp; they were escorted by two grenadiers with bayonets fixed; the staircase was my dining-room, the landing-place my table, and the step served me for a seat; and as soon as my dinner was served up a little bell was rung to inform me I might sit down to table.

Between my repasts, when I did not either read or write or work at the furnishing of my apartment, I went to walk in the burying-ground of the Protestants, which served me as a courtyard. From this place I ascended to a lanthorn which looked into the harbor, and from which I could see the ships come in and go out. In this manner I passed fourteen days, and should have thus passed the whole time of the quarantine without the least weariness had not M. Jonville, envoy from France, to whom I found means to send a letter, vinegared, perfumed and half burnt, procured eight days of the time to be taken off: these I went and spent at his house, where I confess I found myself better lodged than in the Lazaretto. He was extremely civil to me. Dupont, his secretary, was a good creature: he introduced me, as well at Genoa as in the country, to several families, the company of which I found very entertaining and agreeable; and I formed with him an acquaintance and a correspondence which we kept up for a considerable length of time. I continued my journey, very agreeably, through Lombardy. I saw Milan, Verona, Brescia, and Padua, and at length arrived at Venice, where I was impatiently expected by the ambassador.

I found there piles of despatches, from the court and from other ambassadors, the ciphered part of which he had not been able to read, although he had all the ciphers necessary for that purpose, never having been employed in any office, nor even seen the cipher of a minister. I was at first apprehensive of meeting with some embarrassment; but I found nothing could be more easy, and in less than a week I had deciphered the whole, which certainly was not worth the trouble; for not to mention the little activity required in the embassy of Venice, it was not to such a man as M. de Montaigu that government would confide a negotiation of even the most trifling importance. Until my arrival he had been much embarrassed, neither knowing how to dictate nor to write legibly. I was very useful to him, of which he was sensible;

and he treated me well. To this he was also induced by another motive. Since the time of M. de Froulay, his predecessor, whose head became deranged, the consul from France, M. le Blond, had been charged with the affairs of the embassy, and after the arrival of M. de Montaigu continued to manage them until he had put him into the track. M. de Montaigu, hurt at this discharge of his duty by another, although he himself was incapable of it, became disgusted with the consul, and as soon as I arrived deprived him of the functions of secretary to the embassy to give them to me. They were inseparable from the title, and he told me to take it. As long as I remained with him he never sent any person except myself under this title to the senate, or to conference, and upon the whole it was natural enough he should prefer having for secretary to the embassy a man attached to him, to a consul or a clerk of office named by the court.

This rendered my situation very agreeable, and prevented his gentlemen, who were Italians, as well as his pages, and most of his suite from disputing precedence with me in his house. I made an advantageous use of the authority annexed to the title he had conferred upon me, by maintaining his right of protection, that is, the freedom of his neighborhood, against the attempts several times made to infringe it; a privilege which his Venetian officers took no care to defend. But I never permitted banditti to take refuge there, although this would have produced me advantages of which his excellency would not have disdained to partake. He thought proper, however, to claim a part of those of the secretaryship, which is called the chancery. It was in time of war, and there were many passports issued. For each of these passports a sequin was paid to the secretary who made it out and countersigned it. All my predecessors had been paid this sequin by Frenchmen and others without distinction. I thought this unjust, and although I was not a Frenchman, I abolished it in favor of the French; but I so rigorously demanded my right from persons of every other nation, that the Marquis de Scotti, brother to the favorite of the Queen of Spain, having asked for a passport without taking notice of the sequin, I sent to demand it; a boldness which the vindictive Italian did not forget. As soon as the new regulation I had made, relative to passports, was known, none but pretended Frenchmen, who in a gibberish the most mispronounced, called themselves Provençals, Picards, or Burgundians, came to demand them. My ear being very fine, I was not thus made a dupe, and I am almost persuaded that not a single Italian ever cheated me of my sequin, and that not one Frenchmen ever paid it. I was foolish enough to tell M. de Montaigu, who was ignorant of everything that passed, what I had done. The word sequin made him open his ears, and without giving me his opinion of the abolition of that tax upon the French, he pretended I ought to account with him for the others, promising me at the same time equivalent advantages. More filled with indignation at this meanness, than concerned for my own interest, I rejected his proposal. He insisted, and I grew warm. "No, sir," said I, with some heat, "your excellency may keep what belongs to you, but do not take from me that which is mine; I will not suffer you to touch a penny of the perquisites arising from passports." Perceiving he could gain nothing by these means he had recourse to others, and blushed not to tell me that since I had appropriated to myself the profits of the chancery, it was but just I should pay the expenses. I was unwilling to dispute upon this subject, and from that time I furnished at my own expense, ink, paper, wax, wax-candle, tape, and even a new seal, for which he never reimbursed me to the amount of a farthing. This, however, did not prevent my giving a small part of the produce of the passports to the Abbé de Binis, a good creature, and who was far from pretending to have the least right to any such right. If he was obliging to me my politeness to him was an equivalent, and we always lived together on the best of terms.

On the first trial I made of his talents in my official functions, I found him less troublesome than I expected he would have been, considering he was a man without experience, in the service of an ambassador who possessed no more than himself, and whose ignorance and obstinacy constantly counteracted everything with which common-sense and some information inspired me for his service and that of the king. The next thing the ambassador did was to connect himself with the Marquis Mari, ambassador from Spain, an ingenious and artful man, who, had he wished so to do, might have led him by the nose, yet on account of the union of the interests of the two crowns he generally gave him good advice, which might have been of essential service, had not the other, by joining his own opinion, counteracted it in the execution. The only business they had to conduct in concert with each other was to engage the Venetians to maintain their neutrality. These did not neglect to give the strongest assurances of their fidelity to their engagement at the same time that they publicly furnished ammunition to the Austrian troops, and even recruits under pretense of desertion. M. de Montaigu, who I believed wished to render himself agreeable to the republic, failed not on his part, notwithstanding my representations, to make me assure the government in all my despatches, that the Venetians would never violate an article of the neutrality. The obstinacy and stupidity of this poor wretch made me write and act extravagantly: I was obliged to be the agent of his folly, because he would have it so, but he sometimes rendered my employment insupportable and the functions of it almost impracticable. For example, he insisted on the greatest part of his despatches to the king, and of those to the minister, being written in cipher, although neither of them contained anything that required that precaution. I represented to him that between the Friday, the day the despatches from the court arrived, and Saturday, on which ours were sent off, there was not sufficient time to write so much in cipher, and carry on the considerable correspondence with which I was charged for the same courier. He found an admirable expedient, which was to prepare on Thursday the answer to the despatches we were expected to receive on the next day. This appeared to him so happily imagined, that notwithstanding all I could say on the impossibility of the thing, and the absurdity of attempting its execution, I was obliged to comply during the whole time I afterwards remained with him, after having made notes of the few loose words he spoke to me in the course of the week, and of some trivial circumstances which I collected by hurrying from place to place. Provided with these materials I never once failed carrying to him on the Thursday morning a rough draft of the despatches which were to be sent off on Saturday, excepting the few additions and corrections I hastily made in answer to the letters which arrived on the Friday, and to which ours served for answer. He had another custom, diverting enough, and which made his correspondence ridiculous beyond imagination. He sent back all information to its respective source, instead of making it follow its course. To M. Amelot he transmitted the news of the court; to M. Maurepas, that of Paris; to M. d'Havrincourt, the news from Sweden; to M. de Chetardie, that from Petersbourg; and sometimes to each of those the news they had respectively sent to him, and which I was employed to dress up in terms different from those in which it was conveyed to us. As he read nothing of what I laid before him, except the despatches for the court, and signed those to other ambassadors without reading them, this left me more at liberty to give what turn I thought proper to the latter, and in these, there-fore, I made the articles of information cross each other. But it was impossible for me to do the same by despatches of importance; and I thought myself happy when M. de Montaigu did not take it into his head to cram into them an impromptu of a few lines after his manner. This obliged me to return, and hastily transcribe the whole despatch decorated with his new nonsense, and honor it with the cipher, without which he would have refused his signature. I was frequently almost tempted, for the sake of his reputation, to cipher something different from what he had written, but feeling that nothing could authorize such a de-ception, I left him to answer for his own folly, satisfy-ing myself with having spoken to him with freedom, and discharged at my own peril the duties of my station. This is what I always did with an uprightness, a zeal and courage, which merited on his part a very different recompense from that which in the end I received from him. It was time I should once be what Heaven, which had endowed me with a happy dis-position, what the education that had been given me by the best of women, and that I had given myself, had prepared me for, and I became so. Left to my own reflections, without a friend or advice, without expe-rience, and in a foreign country, in the service of a foreign nation, surrounded by a crowd of knaves, who, for their own interest, and to avoid the scandal of good example, endeavored to prevail upon me to imitate them; far from yielding to their solicitations, I served France well, to which I owed nothing, and the ambassador still better, as it was right and just I should do to the utmost of my power. Irreproachable in a post, sufficiently exposed to censure, I merited and obtained the esteem of the republic, that of all the ambassadors with whom we were in correspondence, and the affection of the French who resided at Venice, not even excepting the consul, whom with regret I supplanted in the functions which I knew belonged to him, and which occasioned me more embarrassment than they afforded me satisfaction.

M. de Montaigu, confiding without reserve to the Marquis Mari, who did not thoroughly understand his duty, neglected it to such a degree that without me the French who were at Venice would not have perceived that an ambassador from their nation resided there. Always put off without being heard when they stood in need of his protection, they became disgusted and no longer appeared in his company or at his table, to which indeed he never invited them. I frequently did from myself what it was his duty to have done; I rendered to the French, who applied to me, all the services in my power. In any other country I should have done more, but, on account of my employment, not being able to see persons in place, I was often obliged to apply to the consul, and the consul, who was settled in the country with his family, had many persons to oblige, which prevented him from acting as he otherwise would have done. However, perceiving him unwilling and afraid to speak, I ventured hazardous measures, which sometimes succeeded. I recollect one which still makes me laugh. No person would suspect it was to me the lovers of the theater at Paris owe Coralline and her sister Camille; nothing, however, can be more true. Veronese, their father, had engaged himself with his children in the Italian company, and after having received two thousand livres for the expenses of his journey, instead of setting out for France, quietly continued at Venice, and accepted an engagement in the theater of Saint Luke,* to which Coralline, a child as she still was, drew great numbers of people. The Duke de Gesvres, as first gentleman of the chamber, wrote to the ambassador to claim the father and the daughter. M. de Montaigu when he gave me the letter, confined his instructions to saying, *voyez cela,* without giving me further details. I went to M. Blond to beg he would speak to the patrician, to whom the theater belonged, and who, I believe, was named Zustinian, that he might discharge Veronese, who had engaged in the name of the king. Le Blond, to whom the commission was not very agreeable, executed it badly.

Zustinian answered vaguely, and Veronese was not discharged. I was piqued at this. It was during the carnival, and having taken the bahute and a mask, I

---

* *I doubt if it was St. Samuel; proper names absolutely escape my memory.*

set out for the palace Zustinian. Those who saw my gondola arrive with the livery of the ambassador, were lost in astonishment. Venice had never seen such a thing. I entered, and announced myself as *Una Siora Maschera* (a lady in a mask). As soon as I was introduced I took off my mask and told my name. The senator turned pale and appeared stupefied with surprise. "Sir," said I to him in Venetian, "it is with much regret I importune your excellency with this visit; but you have in your theater of Saint Luke, a man of the name of Veronese, who is engaged in the service of the king, and whom you have been requested, but in vain, to give up: I come to claim him in the name of his majesty." My short harangue was effectual. I had no sooner left the palace than Zustinian ran to communicate the adventure to the state inquisitors, by whom he was severely reprehended. Veronese was discharged the same day. I sent him word that if he did not set off within a week I would have him arrested. He did not wait for my giving him this intimation a second time.

On another occasion I relieved from difficulty solely by my own means, and almost without the assistance of any other person, the captain of a merchant-ship. This was one Captain Olivet, from Marseilles; the name of the vessel I have forgotten. His men had quarreled with the Sclavonians in the service of the republic, some violence had been committed, and the vessel was under so severe an embargo that nobody except the master was suffered to go on board or leave it without permission. He applied to the ambassador, who would hear nothing he had to say. He afterwards went to the consul, who told him it was not an affair of commerce, and that he could not interfere in it. Not knowing what further steps to take he applied to me. I told M. de Montaigu he ought to permit me to lay before the senate a memoir on the subject. I do not recollect whether or not he consented, or that I presented the memoir; but I perfectly remember that if I did it was ineffectual, and the embargo still continuing, I took another method, which succeeded. I inserted a relation of the affairs in one of our letters to M. de Maurepas, though I had difficulty in prevailing upon M. de Montaigu to suffer the article to pass.

I knew that our despatches, although their contents were insignificant, were opened at Venice. Of this I had a proof by finding the articles they contained verbatim in the gazette, a treachery of which I had in vain attempted to prevail upon the ambassador to complain. My object in speaking of the affair in the letter was to turn the curiosity of the ministers of the republic to advantage, to inspire them with some apprehensions, and to induce the state to release the vessel: for had it been necessary to this effect to wait for an answer from the court, the captain would have been ruined before it could have arrived. I did still more, I went alongside the vessel to make inquiries of the ship's company. I took with me the Abbé Patizel, chancellor of the consulship, who would rather have been excused, so much were these poor creatures afraid of displeasing the senate. As I could not go on board, on account of the order from the states, I remained in my gondola, and there took the depositions successively, interrogating each of the mariners, and directing my questions in such a manner as to produce answers which might be to their advantage. I wished to prevail upon Patizel to put the questions and take depositions himself, which in fact was more his business than mine; but to this he would not consent; he never once opened his mouth and refused to sign the depositions after me. This step, somewhat bold, was, however, successful, and the vessel was released long before an answer came from the minister. The captain wished to make me a present; but without being angry with him on that account, I tapped him on the shoulder, saying, "Captain Olivet, can you imagine that he who does not receive from the French his perquisite for passports, which he found his established right, is a man likely to sell them the king's protection?" He, however, insisted on giving me a dinner on board his vessel, which I accepted, and took with me the secretary to the Spanish embassy, M. Carrio, a man of wit and amiable manners, to partake of it: he has since been secretary to the Spanish embassy at Paris and chargé des affaires. I had formed an intimate connection with him after the example of our ambassadors.

Happy should I have been, if, when in the most disinterested manner I did all the service I could, I had known how to introduce sufficient order into all these little details, that I might not have served others at my own expense. But in employments similar to that I held, in which the most trifling faults are of consequence, my whole attention was engaged in avoiding all such mistakes as might be detrimental to my service. I conducted, till the last moment, everything relative to my immediate duty, with the greatest order and exactness. Excepting a few errors which a forced precipitation made me commit in ciphering, and of which the clerks of M. Amelot once complained, neither the ambassador nor any other person had ever the least reason to reproach me with negligence in any one of my functions. This is remarkable in a man so negligent as I am. But my memory sometimes failed me, and I was not sufficiently careful in the private affairs with which I was charged; however, a love of justice always made me take the loss on myself, and this voluntarily, before anybody thought of complaining. I will mention but one circumstance of this nature; it relates to my departure from Venice, and I afterwards felt the effects of it in Paris.

Our cook, whose name was Rousselot, had brought from France an old note for two hundred livres, which a hair-dresser, a friend of his, had received from a noble Venetian of the name of Zanetto Nani, who had had wigs of him to that amount. Rousselot brought me the note, begging I would endeavor to obtain payment of some part of it, by way of accommodation. I knew, and he knew it also, that the con-

stant custom of noble Venetians was, when once returned to their country, never to pay the debts they
had contracted abroad. When means are taken to
force them to payment, the wretched creditor finds
so many delays, and incurs such enormous expenses,
that he becomes disgusted and concludes by giving
up his debt or accepting the most trifling composition.
I begged M. le Blond to speak to Zanetto. The Vene-
tion acknowledged the note, but did not agree to payment. After a long dispute he at length promised
three sequins; but when Le Blond carried him the
note even these were not ready, and it was necessary
to wait. In this interval happened my quarrel with
the ambassador and I quitted his service. I had left
the papers of the embassy in the greatest order, but
the note of Rousselot was not to be found. M. le Blond
assured me he had given me it back. I knew him to be
too honest a man to have the least doubt of the matter;
but it was impossible for me to recollect what I had
done with it. As Zanetto had acknowledged the debt,
I desired M. le Blond to endeavor to obtain from him
the three sequins on giving him a receipt for the
amount, or to prevail upon him to renew the note
by way of duplicate. Zanetto, knowing the note to be
lost, would not agree to either. I offered Rousselot
the three sequins from my own purse, as a discharge
of the debt. He refused them, and said I might settle
the matter with the creditor at Paris, of whom he gave
me the address. The hair-dresser, having been informed of what had passed, would either have his

note or the whole sum for which it was given. What, in my indignation, would I have given to have found this vexatious paper! I paid the two hundred livres, and that in my greatest distress. In this manner the loss of the note produced to the creditor the payment of the whole sum, whereas had it, unfortunately for him, been found, he would have had some difficulty in recovering even the ten crowns, which his excellency, Zanetto Nani, had promised to pay.

The talents I thought I felt in myself for my employment made me discharge the functions of it with satisfaction, and except the society of my friend de Carrio, that of the virtuous Altuna, of whom I shall soon have an occasion to speak, the innocent recreations of the place Saint Mark, of the theater, and of a few visits which we, for the most part, made together, my only pleasure was in the duties of my station. Although these were not considerable, especially with the aid of the Abbé de Binis, yet as the correspondence was very extensive and there was a war, I was a good deal employed. I applied to business the greatest part of every morning, and on the days previous to the departure of the courier, in the evenings, and sometimes till midnight. The rest of my time I gave to the study of the political professions I had entered upon, and in which I hoped, from my successful beginning, to be advantageously employed. In fact I was in favor with every one; the ambassador himself spoke highly of my services, and never complained of anything I did for him; his dissatisfaction proceeded from my having insisted on quitting him, in consequence of the useless complaints I had frequently made on several occasions. The ambassadors and ministers of the king with whom we were in correspondence complimented him on the merit of his secretary, in a manner by which he ought to have been flattered, but which in his poor head produced quite a contrary effect. He received one in particular relative to an affair of importance, for which he never pardoned me.

He was so incapable of bearing the least constraint, that on the Saturday, the day of the despatches for most of the courts, he could not contain himself, and wait till the business was done before he went out, and incessantly pressing me to hasten the despatches to the king and ministers, he signed them with precipitation, and immediately went I know not where, leaving most of the other letters without signing; this obliged me, when these contained nothing but news, to convert them into journals; but when affairs which related to the king were in question it was necessary somebody should sign, and I did it. This once happened relative to some important advice we had just received from M. Vincent, chargé des affaires from the king, at Vienna. The Prince Lobkowitz was then marching to Naples, and Count Gages had just made the most memorable retreat, the finest military maneuver of the whole century, of which Europe has not sufficiently spoken. The despatch informed us that a man, whose person M. Vincent described, had set out from Vienna, and was to pass by Venice, on his way into Abruzzo, where he was secretly to stir up the people at the approach of the Austrians.

In the absence of M. le Comte de Montaigu, who did not give himself the least concern about anything, I forwarded this advice to the Marquis de l'Hôpital, so apropos, that it is perhaps to the poor Jean-Jacques, so abused and laughed at, that the house of Bourbon owes the preservation of the kingdom of Naples.

The Marquis de l'Hôpital, when he thanked his colleague, as it was proper he should do, spoke to him of his secretary, and mentioned the service he had just rendered to the common cause. The Comte de Montaigu, who in that affair had to reproach himself with negligence, thought he perceived in the compliment paid him by M. de l'Hôpital, something like a reproach, and spoke of it to me with signs of ill-humor. I found it necessary to act in the same manner with the Count de Castellane, ambassador at Constantinople, as I had done with the Marquis de l'Hôpital, although in things of less importance. As there was no other conveyance to Constantinople than by couriers, sent from time to time by the senate to its Bailli, advice of their departure was given to the ambassador of France, that he might write by them to his colleague, if he thought proper so to do. This advice was commonly sent a day or two beforehand; but M. de Montaigu was held in so little respect, that merely for the sake of form he was sent to a couple of hours before the couriers set off. This frequently obliged me to write the dispatch in his absence. M. de Castellane in his answer made honorable mention of me; M. de Jonville, at Genoa, did the same, and these instances of their regard and esteem became new grievances.

I acknowledge I did not neglect any opportunity of making myself known; but I never sought one improperly, and in serving well I thought I had a right to aspire to the natural return for essential services; the esteem of those capable of judging of, and rewarding them. I will not say whether or not my exactness in discharging the duties of my employment was a just subject of complaint from the ambassador; but I cannot refrain from declaring that it was the sole grievance he ever mentioned previous to our separation.

His house, which he had never put on a good footing, was constantly filled with rabble; the French were ill-treated in it, and the ascendancy was given to the Italians; of these even, the more honest part, they who had long been in the service of the embassy, were indecently discharged, his first gentleman in particular, whom he had taken from the Comte de Froulay, and who, if I remember right, was called Comte de Peati, or something very like that name. The second gentleman, chosen by M. de Montaigu, was an outlawed highwayman from Mantua, called Dominic Vitali, to whom the ambassador intrusted the care of his house, and who had by means of flattery and sordid economy, obtained his confidence, and became his favorite to the great prejudice of the few honest people he still had about him, and of the secretary who was at their head. The countenance of an upright man always gives inquietude to knaves. Nothing more was necessary to make Vitali conceive a hatred against me: but for this sentiment there was still another cause which rendered it more cruel. Of this I must give an account, that I may be condemned if I am found in the wrong.

The ambassador had, according to custom, a box at each of the theaters. Every day at dinner he named the theater to which it was his intention to go: I chose after him, and the gentlemen disposed of the other boxes. When I went out I took the key of the box I had chosen. One day, Vitali not being in the way, I ordered the footman who attended on me, to bring me the key to a house which I named to him. Vitali, instead of sending the key, said he had disposed of it. I was the more enraged at this as the footman delivered his message in public. In the evening Vitali wished to make me some apology, to which however I would not listen. "To-morrow," said I to him, "you will come at such an hour and apologize to me in the house where I received the affront, and in the presence of the persons who were witnesses to it; or after to-morrow, whatever may be the consequence, either you or I will leave the house." This firmness intimidated him. He came to the house at the hour appointed, and made me a public apology,

with a meanness worthy of himself. But he afterwards took his measures at leisure, and, at the same
time that he cringed to me in public, he secretly
acted in so vile a manner, that, although unable to
prevail on the ambassador to give me my dismission,
he laid me under the necessity of resolving to leave
him.

A wretch like him, certainly, could not know me,
but he knew enough of my character to make it serviceable to his purposes. He knew I was mild to an
excess, and patient in bearing involuntary wrongs;
but haughty and impatient when insulted with premeditated offenses; loving decency and dignity in
things in which these were requisite, and not more
exact in requiring the respect due to myself than
attentive in rendering that which I owed to others.
In this he undertook to disgust me, and in this he
succeeded. He turned the house upside down, and
destroyed the order and subordination I had endeavored to establish in it. A house without a woman
stands in need of rather a severe discipline to preserve
that modesty which is inseparable from dignity. He
soon converted ours into a place of filthy debauch and
scandalous licentiousness, the haunt of knaves and
debauchees. He procured for second gentlemen to his
excellency, in the place of him whom he got discharged, another pimp like himself, who kept a house
of ill-fame, at the Cross of Malta; and the indecency
of these two rascals was equaled by nothing but their
insolence. Except the bed-chamber of the ambassador,

which, however, was not in very good order, there was not a corner in the whole house supportable to a modest man.

As his excellency did not sup, the gentleman and myself had a private table, at which the Abbé de Binis and the pages also eat. In the most paltry ale-house people are served with more cleanliness and decency, have cleaner linen, and a table better supplied. We had but one little and very filthy candle, pewter plates, and iron forks.

I could have overlooked what passed in secret, but I was deprived of my gondola. I was the only secretary to an ambassador, who was obliged to hire one or go on foot, and the livery of his excellency no longer accompanied me, except when I went to the senate. Besides, everything which passed in the house was known in the city. All those who were in the service of the other ambassadors loudly exclaimed; Dominic, the only cause of all, exclaimed louder than anybody, well knowing the indecency with which we were treated was more affecting to me than to any other person. Though I was the only one in the house who said nothing of the matter abroad, I complained loudly of it to the ambassador, as well as of himself, who, secretly excited by the wretch, entirely devoted to his will, daily made me suffer some new affront. Obliged to expend a good deal to keep up a footing with those in the same situation with myself, and to make an appearance proper to my employment, I could not touch a farthing of my salary, and when I asked him for money, he spoke of his esteem for me, and his confidence, as if either of these could have filled my purse, and provided for everything.

These two banditti at length quite turned the head of their master, who naturally had not a good one, and ruined him by a continual traffic, and by bargains, of which he was the dupe, whilst they persuaded him they were greatly in his favor. They persuaded him to take, upon the Brenta, a Palazzo at twice the rent it was worth, and divided the surplus with the proprietor. The apartments were inlaid with mosaic, and ornamented with columns and pilasters, in the taste of the country. M. de Montaigu, had all these superbly masked by fir wainscoting, for no other reason than because at Paris apartments were thus fitted up. It was for a similar reason that he only, of all the ambassadors who were at Venice, took from his pages their swords, and from his footmen their canes. Such was the man, who, perhaps from the same motive, took a dislike to me on account of my serving him faithfully.

I patiently endured his disdain, his brutality, and ill-treatment, as long as, perceiving them accompanied by ill-humor, I thought they had in them no portion of hatred; but the moment I saw the design formed of depriving me of the honor I merited by my faithful services, I resolved to resign my employment. The first mark I received of his ill will was relative to a dinner he was to give to the Duke of Modena and his family, who were at Venice, and at

which he signified to me I should not be present. I
answered, piqued, but not angry, that having the
honor daily to dine at his table, if the Duke of Modena, when he came, required I should not appear
at it, my duty as well as the dignity of his excellency
would not suffer me to consent to such a request.
"How," said he, passionately, "my secretary, who is
not a gentleman, pretends to dine with a sovereign
when my gentlemen do not!" "Yes, sir," replied I,
"the post with which your excellency has honored
me, as long as I discharge the functions of it, so far
ennobles me that my rank is superior to that of your
gentlemen or of the persons calling themselves such;
and I am admitted where they cannot appear. You
cannot but know that on the day on which you shall
make your public entry, I am called to the ceremony
by etiquette; and by an immemorial custom, to follow
you in a dress of ceremony, and afterwards to dine
with you at the palace of Saint Mark; and I know
not why a man who has a right and is to eat in public
with the doge and the senate of Venice should not
eat in private with the Duke of Modena." Though
this argument was unanswerable, it did not convince
the ambassador; but we had no occasion to renew the
dispute, as the Duke of Modena did not come to dine
with him.

From that moment he did everything in his power
to make things disagreeable to me; and endeavored
unjustly to deprive me of my right, by taking from
me the pecuniary advantages annexed to my employ-

ment, to give them to his dear Vitali; and I am convinced that had he dared to send him to the senate, in my place, he would have done it. He commonly employed the Abbé Binis in his closet, to write his private letters: he made use of him to write to M. de Maurepas an account of the affair of Captain Olivet, in which, far from taking the least notice of me, the only person who gave himself any concern about the matter, he deprived me of the honor of the depositions, of which he sent him a duplicate, for the purpose of attributing them to Patizel, who had not opened his mouth. He wished to mortify me, and please his favorite; but had no desire to dismiss me his service. He perceived it would be more difficult to find me a successor, than M. Follau, who had already made him known to the world. An Italian secretary was absolutely necessary to him, on account of the answers from the senate; one who could write all his despatches, and conduct his affairs, without his giving himself the least trouble about anything; a person who, to the merit of serving him well, could join the baseness of being the toad-eater of his gentlemen, without honor, merit, or principles. He wished to retain, and humble me, by keeping me far from my country, and his own, without money to return to either, and in which he would, perhaps, have succeeded, had he begun with more moderation: but Vitali, who had other views, and wished to force me to extremities, carried his point. The moment I perceived, I lost all my trouble, that the ambassador imputed to me my services as so many crimes, instead of being satisfied with them; that with him I had nothing to expect, but things disagreeable at home, and injustice abroad; and that, in the general disesteem into which he was fallen, his ill offices might be prejudicial to me, without the possibility of my being served by his good ones; I took my resolution, and asked him for my dismission, leaving him sufficient time to provide himself with another secretary. Without answering yés or no, he continued to treat me in the same manner, as if nothing had been said. Perceiving things to remain in the same state, and that he took no measures to procure himself a new secretary, I wrote to his brother, and, explaining to him my motives, begged he would obtain my dismission from his excellency, adding that whether I received it or not, I could not possibly remain with him. I waited a long time without any answer, and began to be embarrassed: but at length the ambassador received a letter from his brother, which must have remonstrated with him in very plain terms; for although he was extremely subject to ferocious rage, I never saw him so violent as on this occasion. After torrents of unsufferable reproaches, not knowing what more to say, he accused me of having sold his ciphers. I burst into a loud laughter, and asking him, in a sneering manner, if he thought there was in Venice a man who would be fool enough to give half a crown for them all. He threatened to call his servants to throw me out of the window. Until then I had been very composed; but on this threat, anger and indignation seized me in my turn. I sprang to the door, and after having turned a button which fastened it within: "No, count," said I, returning to him with a grave step, "your servants shall have nothing to do with this affair; please to let it be settled between ourselves." My action and manner instantly made him calm; fear and surprise were marked in his countenance. The moment I saw his fury abated, I bid him adieu in a very few words, and without waiting for his answer, went to the door, opened it, and passed slowly across the antechamber, through the midst of his people, who rose according to custom, and who, I am of opinion, would rather have lent their assistance against him than me. Without going back to my apartment, I descended the stairs, and immediately went out of the palace never more to enter it.

I hastened immediately to M. le Blond and related to him what had happened. Knowing the man, he was but little surprised. He kept me to dinner. This dinner, although without preparation, was splendid. All the French of consequence, who were at Venice, partook of it. The ambassador had not a single person. The consul related my case to the company. The cry was general, and by no means in favor of his excellency. He had not settled my account, nor paid me a farthing, and being reduced to the few louis I had in my pocket, I was extremely embarrassed about my return to France. Every purse was opened to me. I took twenty sequins from that of M. le Blond, and as many from that of M. St. Cyr, with whom, next to M. le Blond, I was the most intimately connected. I returned thanks to the rest; and, till my departure, went to lodge at the house of the chancellor of the consulship, to prove to the public, the nation was not an accomplice in the injustice of the ambassador.

His excellency, furious at seeing me taken notice of in my misfortune, at the same time that, notwithstanding his being an ambassador, nobody went near his house, quite lost his senses and behaved like a madman. He forgot himself so far as to present a memoir to the senate to get me arrested. On being informed of this by the Abbé de Binis, I resolved to remain a fortnight longer, instead of setting off the next day as I had intended. My conduct had been known and approved of by everybody; I was universally esteemed. The senate did not deign to return an answer to the extravagant memoir of the ambassador, but sent me word I might remain in Venice as long as I thought proper, without making myself uneasy about the attempts of a madman. I continued to see my friends: I went to take leave of the ambassador from Spain, who received me well, and of the Comte de Finochietti, minister from Naples, whom I did not find at home. I wrote him a letter and received from his excellency the most polite and obliging answer. At length I took my departure, leaving behind me, notwithstanding my embarrassment, no other debts than the two sums I had borrowed, and of which I have just spoken; and an account of fifty crowns with a shopkeeper, of the name of Morandi, which Carrio promised to pay, and which I have never reimbursed him, although we have frequently met since that time; but with respect to the two sums of money, I returned them very exactly the moment I had it in my power.

I cannot take leave of Venice without saying something of the celebrated amusements of that city, or at least of the little part of them of which I partook during my residence there. It has been seen how little in my youth I ran after the pleasures of that age, or those that are so called. My inclinations did not change at Venice, but my occupations, which moreover would have prevented this, rendered more agreeable to me the simple recreations I permitted myself. The first and most pleasing of all was the society of men of merit. M. le Blond, de St. Cyr, Carrio Altuna, and a Porlinian gentleman, whose name I am very sorry to have forgotten, and whom I never call to my recollection without emotion: he was the man of all I ever knew whose heart most resembled my own. We were connected with two or three Englishmen of great wit and information, and, like ourselves, passionately fond of music. All these gentlemen had their wives, female friends, or mistresses: the latter were most of them women of talents, at whose apartments there were balls and concerts. There was but little play; a lively turn, talents, and the theaters rendered this amusement insipid. Play is the resource of none but men whose time hangs heavy on their hands. I had brought with me from Paris the prejudice of that city against Italian music; but I had also received from nature a sensibility and niceness of the distinction which prejudice cannot withstand. I soon contracted that passion for Italian music with which it inspires all those who are capable of feeling its excellence. In listening to *barcaroles,* I found I had not yet known what singing was, and I soon became so fond of the opera that, tired of babbling, eating, and playing in the boxes when I wished to listen, I frequently withdrew from the company to another part of the theater. There, quite alone, shut up in my box, I abandoned myself, notwithstanding the length of the representation, to the pleasure of enjoying it at ease unto the conclusion. One evening at the theater of Saint Chrysostom, I fell into a more profound sleep than I should have done in my bed. The loud and brilliant airs did not disturb my repose. But who can explain the delicious sensations given me by the soft harmony of the angelic music, by which I was charmed from sleep; what an awaking! what ravishment! what ecstasy, when at the same instant I opened my ears and eyes! My first idea was to believe I was in paradise. The ravishing air, which I still recollect and shall never forget, began with these words:

Conservami la bella,
Che si m'accende il cor.

I was desirous of having it; I had and kept it for a time; but it was not the same thing upon paper as in my head. The notes were the same but the thing was different. This divine composition can never be executed but in my mind, in the same manner as it was the evening on which it awoke me from sleep.

A kind of music far superior, in my opinion, to that of operas, and which in all Italy has not its equal, nor perhaps in the whole world, is that of the *scuole*. The *scuole* are houses of charity, established for the education of young girls without fortune, to whom the republic afterwards gives a portion either in marriage or for the cloister. Amongst talents cultivated in these young girls, music is in the first rank. Every Sunday at the church of each of the four *scuole*, during vespers, motettos or anthems with full choruses, accompanied by a great orchestra, and composed and directed by the best masters in Italy, are sung in the galleries by girls only; not one of whom is more than twenty years of age. I have not an idea of anything so voluptuous and affecting as this music; the richness of the art, the exquisite taste of the vocal part, the excellence of the voices, the justness of the execution, everything in these delightful concerts concurs to produce an impression which certainly is not the mode, but from which I am of opinion no heart is secure. Carrio and I never failed being present at these vespers of the *Mendicanti,* and we were not alone. The church was always full of the lovers of the art, and even the actors of the opera came there to form their tastes after these excellent models. What vexed me was the iron grate, which suffered nothing to escape but sounds, and concealed from me the angels of which they were worthy. I talked of nothing else. One day I spoke of it at Le Blond's: "If you are so desirous," said he, "to see those little girls, it will be an easy matter to satisfy your wishes. I am one of the administrators of the house, I will give you a collation with them." I did not let him rest until he had fulfilled his promise. I entering the saloon, which contained these beauties I so much sighed to see, I felt a trembling of love which I had never before experienced M. le Blond presented to me, one after the other, these celebrated female singers, of whom the names and voices were all with which I was acquainted. Come, Sophia,—she was horrid. Come, Cattina,—she had but one eye. Come, Bettina,—the small-pox had entirely disfigured her. Scarcely one of them was without some striking defect. Le Blond laughed at my surprise; however, two or three of them appeared tolerable; these never sung but in the choruses; I was almost in despair. During the collation we endeavored to excite them, and they soon became enlivened; ugliness does not exclude the graces, and I found they possessed them. I said to myself, they cannot sing in this manner without intelligence and sensibility, they must have both; in fine, my manner of seeing them changed to such a degree that I left the house almost in love with each of these ugly faces. I had scarcely courage enough to return to vespers. But after having seen the girls, the danger was lessened. I still found their singing delightful; and their voices so much embellished their persons that, in spite of my eyes, I obstinately continued to think them beautiful.

Music in Italy is accompanied with so trifling an expense, that it is not worth while for such as have a taste for it to deny themselves the pleasure it affords. I hired a harpsichord, and, for half a crown, I had at my apartment four or five symphonists, with whom I practiced once a week in executing such airs, etc., as had given me most pleasure at the opera. I also had some symphonies performed from my *Muses Galantes*. Whether these pleased the performers, or the ballet-master of St. John Chrysostom wished to flatter me, he desired to have two of them; and I had afterwards the pleasure of hearing these executed by that admirable orchestra. They were danced to by a little *Bettina,* pretty and amiable, and kept by a Spaniard, M. Fagoaga, a friend of ours with whom we often went to spend the evening. But apropos of girls of easy virtue: it is not in Venice that a man abstains from them. Have you nothing to confess, somebody will ask me, upon this subject? Yes: I have something to say upon it, and I will proceed to this confession with the same ingenuousness with which I have made all my former ones.

I always had a disinclination to common prostitutes, but at Venice those were all I had within my reach; most of the houses being shut against me on account of my place. The daughters of M. le Blond were very amiable, but difficult of access; and I had too much respect for the father and mother ever once to have the least desire for them.

I should have had a much stronger inclination to a young lady named Mademoiselle de Catanéo, daughter to the agent from the King of Prussia, but Carrio was in love with her: there was even between them some question of marriage. He was in easy circumstances, and I had no fortune: his salary was a hundred louis (guineas) a year, and mine amounted to no more than a thousand livres (about forty pounds sterling): and, besides, my being unwilling to oppose a friend, I knew that in all places, and especially at Venice, with a purse so ill furnished as mine was, gallantry was out of the question. I had not lost the pernicious custom of deceiving my wants. Too busily employed forcibly to feel those proceeding from the climate, I lived upwards of a year in that city as chastely as I had done in Paris, and at the end of eighteen months I quitted it without having approached the sex, except twice by means of the singular opportunities of which I am going to speak.

The first was procured me by that honest gentleman, Vitali, some time after the formal apology I obliged him to make me. The conversation at the table turned on the amusements of Venice. These gentlemen reproached me with my indifference with regard to the most delightful of them all; at the same time extolling the gracefulness and elegant manners of the women of easy virtue of Venice; and adding that they were superior to all others of the same description in any other part of the world. Dominic said I must make the acquaintance of the most amiable of them all; and he offered to take me to her apartments, assuring me I should be pleased with her. I laughed at this obliging offer: and Count Peati, a man in years and venerable, observed to me, with more candor than I should have expected from an Italian, that he thought me too prudent to suffer myself to be taken to such a place by my enemy. In fact I had no inclination to do it: but notwithstanding this, by an incoherence I cannot myself comprehend, I at length was prevailed upon to go, contrary to my inclination, the sentiment of my heart, my reason, and even my will; solely from weakness, and being ashamed to show an appearance to the least mistrust; and besides, as the expression of the country is, *per non parer troppo coglione.** The *Padoana* whom we went to visit was pretty, she was even handsome, but her beauty was not of that kind which pleased me. Dominic left me with her, I sent for *Sorbetti,* and asked her to sing. In about half an hour I wished to take my leave, after having put a ducat on the table, but this by a singular scruple she refused until she had deserved it, and I from as singular a folly consented to remove her doubts. I returned to the palace so fully persuaded that I should feel the consequences of this step, that the first thing I did was to send for the king's surgeon to ask him for ptisans. Nothing can equal the uneasiness of mind I suffered for three

---

* *Not to appear too great a blockhead.*

weeks, without its being justified by any real inconvenience or apparent sign. I could not believe it was
possible to withdraw with impunity from the arms of
the *padoana*. The surgeon himself had the greatest
difficulty in removing my apprehensions; nor could
he do this by any other means than by persuading
me I was formed in such a manner as not to be easily
infected: and although in the experiment I exposed
myself less than any other man would have done, my
health in that respect never having suffered the least
inconvenience, is in my opinion a proof the surgeon
was right. However, this has never made me imprudent, and if in fact I have received such an advantage
from nature I can safely assert I have never abused it.

My second adventure, although likewise with a
common girl, was of a nature very different, as well
in its origin as in its effects. I have already said that
Captain Olivet gave me a dinner on board his vessel,
and that I took with me the secretary of the Spanish
embassy. I expected a salute of cannon. The ship's
company was drawn up to receive us, but not so much
as a priming was burnt, at which I was mortified,
on account of Carrio, whom I perceived to be rather
piqued at the neglect. A salute of cannon was given
on board merchantships to people of less consequence
than we were; I besides thought I deserved some distinguished mark of respect from the captain. I could
not conceal my thoughts, because this at all times was
impossible to me, and although the dinner was a very
good one, and Olivet did the honors of it perfectly

well, I began it in an ill humor, eating but little, and speaking still less. At the first health, at least, I expected a volley;—nothing. Carrio, who read what passed within me, laughed at hearing me grumble like a child. Before dinner was half over I saw a gondola approach the vessel. "Bless me, sir," said the captain, "take care of yourself, the enemy approaches." I asked him what he meant, and he answered jocosely. The gondola made the ship's side, and I observed a gay young damsel come on board very lightly, and coquettishly dressed, and who at three steps was in the cabin, seated by my side, before I had time to perceive a cover was laid for her. She was equally charming and lively, a brunette, not more than twenty years of age. She spoke nothing but Italian, and her accent alone was sufficient to turn my head. As she ate and chattered she cast her eyes upon me; steadfastly looked at me for a moment, and then exclaimed, "Good Virgin! Ah, my dear Brémond, what an age it is since I saw thee!" Then she threw herself into my arms, sealed her lips to mine, and pressed me almost to strangling. Her large black eyes, like those of the beauties of the East, darted fiery shafts into my heart, and although the surprise at first stupefied my senses, voluptuousness made a rapid progress within, and this to such a degree that the beautiful seducer herself was, notwithstanding the spectators, obliged to restrain my ardor, for I was intoxicated, or rather become furious. When she perceived she had made the impression she desired, she became more moderate in her caresses, but not in her vivacity, and when she thought proper to explain to us the real or false cause of all her petulance, she said I resembled M. de Brémond, director of the customs of Tuscany, to such a degree as to be mistaken for him; that she had turned this M. de Brémond's head, and would do it again; that she had quitted him because he was a fool; that she took me in his place; that she would love me because it pleased her so to do, for which reason I must love her as long as it was agreeable to her, and when she thought proper to send me about my business, I must be patient as her dear Brémond had been. What was said was done. She took possession of me as of a man that belonged to her, gave me her gloves to keep, her fan, her *cinda,* and her coif, and ordered me to go here or there, to do this or that, and I instantly obeyed her. She told me to go and send away her gondola, because she chose to make use of mine, and I immediately sent it away; she bid me to move from my place, and prey Carrio to sit down in it, because she had something to say to him; and I did as she desired. They chatted a good while together, but spoke low, and I did not interrupt them. She called me, and I approached her. "Hark thee, Zanetto," said she to me, "I will not be loved in the French manner; this indeed will not be well. In the first moment of lassitude, get thee gone: but stay not by the way, I caution thee." After dinner we went to see the glass manufactory at Murano. She bought a great number of little curiosities; for which she left me to pay without the least ceremony. But she everywhere gave away little trinkets to a much greater amount than of the things we had purchased. By the indifference with which she threw away her money, I perceived she annexed to it but little value. When she insisted upon a payment, I am of opinion it was more from a motive of vanity than avarice. She was flattered by the price her admirers set upon her favors.

In the evening we conducted her to her apartments. As we conversed together, I perceived a couple of pistols upon her toilette. "Ah! ah!" said I, taking one of them up, "this is a patch-box of a new construction: may I ask what is its use? I know you have other arms which give more fire than those upon your table." After a few pleasantries of the same kind, she said to us, with an ingenuousness which rendered her still more charming, "When I am complaisant to persons whom I do not love, I make them pay for the weariness they cause me; nothing can be more just; but if I suffer their caresses, I will not bear their insults; nor miss the first who shall be wanting to me in respect."

At taking leave of her, I made another appointment for the next day. I did not make her wait. I found her *in vestito di confidenza,* in an undress more than wanton, unknown to northern countries, and which I will not amuse myself in describing, although I recollect it perfectly well. I shall only remark that her ruffles and collar were edged with silk network ornamented with rose-colored pompons. This, in my eyes, much enlivened a beautiful complexion. I afterwards found it to be the mode at Venice, and the effect is so charming that I am surprised it has never been introduced in France. I had no idea of the transports which awaited me. I have spoken of Madam de Larnage with the transport which the remembrance of her still sometimes gives me; but how old, ugly and cold she appeared, compared with my Zulietta! Do not attempt to form to yourself an idea of the charms and graces of this enchanting girl, you will be far too short of truth. Young virgins in cloisters are not so fresh: the beauties of the seraglio are less animated: the houris of paradise less engaging. Never was so sweet an enjoyment offered to the heart and senses of a mortal. Ah! had I at least been capable of fully tasting of it for a single moment!—I had tasted of it, but without a charm. I enfeebled all its delights: I destroyed them as at will. No; Nature has not made me capable of enjoyment. She has infused into my wretched head the poison of that ineffable happiness, the desire of which she first placed in my heart.

If there be a circumstance in my life, which describes my nature, it is that which I am going to relate. The forcible manner in which I at this moment recollect the object of my book, will here make me hold in contempt the false delicacy which would prevent me from fulfilling it. Whoever you may be who are desirous of knowing a man, have the courage to read the two or three following pages, and you will become fully acquainted with J. J. Rousseau.

I entered the room of a courtesan as if it had been the sanctuary of love and beauty: and in her person, I thought I saw the divinity. I should have been inclined to think that without respect and esteem it was impossible to feel anything like that which she made me experience. Scarcely had I, in her first familiarities, discovered the force of her charms and caresses, before I wished, for fear of losing the fruit of them, to gather it beforehand. Suddenly, instead of the flame which consumed me, I felt a mortal cold run through all my veins; my legs failed me; and ready to faint away, I sat down and wept like a child.

Who would guess the cause of my tears, and what, at this moment, passed within me? I said to myself: the object in my power is the masterpiece of love; her wit and person equally approach perfection; she is as good and generous as she is amiable and beautiful. Yet she is a miserable prostitute, abandoned to the public. The captain of a merchantship disposed of her at will; she has thrown herself into my arms, although she knows I have nothing; and my merit with which she cannot be acquainted, can be to her no inducement. In this there is something inconceivable. Either my heart deceives me, fascinates my senses, and makes me the dupe of an unworthy slut, or some secret defect, of which I am ignorant, destroys the effect of her charms, and renders her odious in the eyes of those by whom her charms would otherwise be disputed. I endeavored, by an extraordinary effort of mind, to discover this defect, but it did not so much as strike me that even the consequences to be apprehended, might possibly have some influence. The clearness of her skin, the brilliancy of her complexion, her white teeth, sweet breath, and the appearance of neatness about her person, so far removed from me this idea, that still in doubt relative to my situation after the affair of the *padoana,* I rather apprehended I was not sufficiently in health for her: and I am firmly persuaded I was not deceived in my opinion. These reflections, so apropos, agitated me to such a degree as to make me shed tears. Zulietta, to whom the scene was quite novel, was struck speechless for a moment. But having made a turn in her chamber, and passing before her glass, she comprehended, and my eyes confirmed her opinion, that disgust had no part in what had happened. It was not difficult for her to recover me and dispel this shamefacedness.

But, at the moment in which I was ready to faint upon a bosom, which for the first time seemed to suffer the impression of the hand and lips of a man, I perceived she had a withered *teton*. I struck my forehead: I examined, and thought I perceived this *teton* was not formed like the other. I immediately began to consider how it was possible to have such a defect, and persuaded of its proceeding from some great natural vice, I was clearly convinced, that, instead of the most charming person of whom I could form to myself an idea, I had in my arms a species of a monster, the refuse of nature, of men and of love. I carried my stupidity so far as to speak to her of the discovery I had made. She, at first, took what I said jocosely; and in her frolicsome humor, did and said things which made me die of love. But perceiving an inquietude I could not conceal, she at length reddened, adjusted her dress, raised herself up, and, without saying a word, went and placed herself at a window. I attempted to place myself by her side: she withdrew to a sofa, rose from it the next moment, and fanning herself as she walked about the chamber, said to me in a reserved and disdainful tone of voice, "Zanetto, *lascia le donne, e studia la matematica.*" *

Before I took leave I requested her to appoint another rendezvous for the next day, which she postponed for three days, adding, with a satirical smile, that I must needs be in want of repose. I was very ill at ease during the interval; my heart was full of her charms and graces; I felt my extravagance, and reproached myself with it, regretting the loss of the moments I had so ill employed, and which, had I chosen, I might have rendered more agreeable than any in my whole life; waiting with the most burning impatience for the moment in which I might repair the loss, and yet, notwithstanding all my reasoning upon what I had discovered, anxious to reconcile the perfections of this adorable girl with the indignity of her situation. I ran, I flew to her apartment at the

* *Leave women, and study the mathematics.*

hour appointed. I know not whether or not her ardor would have been more satisfied with this visit, her pride at least would have been flattered by it, and I already rejoiced at the idea of my convincing her, in every respect, that I knew how to repair the wrongs I had done. She spared me this justification. The gondolier whom I had sent to her apartment brought me for answer that she had set off, the evening before, for Florence. If I had not felt all the love I had for her person when this was in my possession, I felt it in the most cruel manner on losing her. Amiable and charming as she was in my eyes, I could have consoled myself for the loss of her; but this I have never been able to do relative to the contemptuous idea which at her departure she must have had of me.

These are my two adventures. The eighteen months I passed at Venice furnished me with no other of the same kind, except a simple prospect at most. Carrio was a gallant. Tired of visiting girls engaged to others, he took a fancy to have one to himself, and, as we were inseparable, he proposed to me an arrangement common enough at Venice, which was to keep one girl for us both. To this I consented. The question was, to find one who was safe. He was so industrious in his researches that he found out a little girl of from eleven to twelve years of age, whom her infamous mother was endeavoring to sell, and I went with Carrio to see her. The sight of the child moved me to the most lively compassion. She was fair and as gentle as a lamb. Nobody would have taken her for an Italian.

Living is very cheap at Venice; we gave a little money to the mother, and provided for the subsistence of her daughter. She had a voice, and to procure her some resource we gave her a spinnet, and a singing-master. All these expenses did not cost each of us more than two sequins a month, and we contrived to save a much greater sum in other matters; but as we were obliged to wait until she became of a riper age, this was sowing a long time before we could possibly reap. However, satisfied with passing our evenings, chatting and innocently playing with the child, we perhaps enjoyed greater pleasure than if we had received the last favors. So true is it that men are more attached to women by a certain pleasure they have in living with them, than by any kind of libertinism. My heart became insensibly attached to the little Anzoletta, but my attachment was paternal, in which the senses had so little share, that in proportion as the former increased, to have connected it with the latter would have been less possible; and I felt I should have experienced, at approaching this little creature when become nubile, the same horror with which the abominable crime of incest would have inspired me. I perceived the sentiments of Carrio take, unobserved by himself, exactly the same turn. We thus prepared for ourselves, without intending it, pleasure not less delicious, but very different from that of which we first had an idea; and I am fully persuaded that however beautiful the poor child might have become, far from being the corrupters of her innocence we should have been the protectors of it. The circumstance which shortly afterwards befell me deprived me of the happiness of taking part in this good work, and my only merit in the affair was the inclination of my heart.

I will now return to my journey.

My first intention after leaving M. de Montaigu, was to retire to Geneva, until time and more favorable circumstances should have removed the obstacles which prevented my union with my poor mamma; but the quarrel between me and M. de Montaigu being become public, and he having had the folly to write about it to the court, I resolved to go there to give an account of my conduct and complain of that of a madman. I communicated my intention, from Venice, to M. du Theil, charged *per interim* with foreign affairs after the death of M. Amelot. I set off as soon as my letter, and took my route through Bergamo, Como, and Duomo d'Ossola, and crossing the Simplon. At Sion, M. de Chaignon, *charge des affaires* from France, showed me great civility; at Geneva M. de la Closure treated me with the same polite attention. I there renewed my acquaintance with M. de Gauffecourt from whom I had some money to receive. I had passed through Nyon without going to see my father; not that this was a matter of indifference to me, but because I was unwilling to appear before my mother-in-law, after the disaster which had befallen me, certain of being condemned by her without being heard. The bookseller, Du Villard, an old friend of my father's, reproached me severely with this neglect. I gave him my reasons for it, and to repair my fault, without exposing myself to meet my mother-in-law, I took a chaise and we went together to Nyon and stopped at a public house. Du Villard went to fetch my father, who came running to embrace me. We supped together, and, after passing an evening very agreeable to the wishes of my heart, I returned the next morning to Geneva with Du Villard, for whom I have ever since retained a sentiment of gratitude in return for the service he did me on this occasion.

Lyons was a little out of my direct road, but I was determined to pass through that city in order to convince myself of a knavish trick played me by M. de Montaigu. I had sent me from Paris a little box containing a waistcoat, embroidered with gold, a few pairs of ruffles, and six pairs of white silk stockings; nothing more. Upon a proposition made me by M. de Montaigu, I ordered this box to be added to his baggage. In the apothecary's bill he offered me in payment of my salary, and which he wrote out himself, he stated the weight of this box, which he called a bale, at eleven hundred pounds, and charged me with the carriage of it at an enormous rate. By the cares of M. Boy de la Tour, to whom I was recommended by M. Roguin, his uncle, it was proved from the registers of the customs of Lyons and Marseilles, that the said bale weighed no more than forty-five pounds, and had paid carriage according to that weight. I joined this authentic extract to the memoir of M. de Montaigu, and provided with these papers and others containing stronger facts, I returned to Paris, very impatient to make use of them. During the whole of this long journey I had little adventures: at Como, in Valais, and elsewhere. I there saw many curious things, amongst others the Borromean Islands, which are worthy of being described. But I am pressed by time, and surrounded by spies. I am obliged to write in haste, and very imperfectly, a work which requires the leisure and tranquillity I do not enjoy. If ever providence in its goodness grants me days more calm, I shall destine them to new modeling this work, should I be able to do it, or at least to give a supplement, of which I perceive it stands in the greatest need.*

The news of my quarrel had reached Paris before me, and on my arrival I found the people in all the offices, and the public in general, scandalized at the follies of the ambassador. Notwithstanding this, the public talk of Venice, and the unanswerable proof I exhibited, I could not obtain even the shadow of justice. Far from obtaining satisfaction or reparation, I was left at the discretion of the ambassador for my salary, and this for no other reason than because, not being a Frenchman, I had no right to national protection, and that it was a private affair between him and myself. Everybody agreed I was insulted, injured, and unfortunate; that the ambassador was mad, cruel, and iniquitous, and that the whole of the affair dishonored

* *I have given up this project.*

him forever. But what of this! He was the ambassador, and I was nothing more than the secretary.

Order, or that which is so called, was in opposition to my obtaining justice, and of this the least shadow was not granted me. I supposed that, by loudly complaining, and by publicly treating this madman in the manner he deserved, I should at length be told to hold my tongue; this was what I wished for, and I was fully determined not to obey until I had obtained redress. But at that time there was no minister for foreign affairs. I was suffered to exclaim, nay, even encouraged to do it, and joined with; but the affair still remained in the same state, until, tired of being in the right without obtaining justice, my courage at length failed me, and let the whole drop.

The only person by whom I was ill received, and from whom I should have least expected such an injustice, was Madam de Beuzenval. Full of the prerogatives of rank and nobility, she could not conceive it was possible an ambassador could ever be in the wrong with respect to his secretary. The reception she gave me was conformable to this prejudice. I was so piqued at it that, immediately after leaving her, I wrote her perhaps one of the strongest and most violent letters that ever came from my pen, and since that time I never once returned to her house. I was better received by Father Castel; but, in the midst of his jesuitical wheedling I perceived him faithfully to follow one of the great maxims of his society, which is to sacrifice the weak to the powerful. The strong conviction I felt of the justice of my cause, and my natural greatness of mind did not suffer me patiently to endure this partiality. I ceased visiting Father Castel, and on that account, going to the college of the Jesuits, where I knew nobody but himself. Besides the intriguing and tyrannical spirit of his brethren, so different from the cordiality of the good Father Hemet, gave me such a disgust to their conversation that I have never since been acquainted with, nor seen any one of them except Father Berthier, whom I saw twice or thrice at M. Dupin's, in conjunction with whom he labored with all his might at the refutation of Montesquieu.

That I may not return to the subject, I will conclude what I have to say of M. de Montaigu. I had told him in our quarrels that a secretary was not what he wanted, but an attorney's clerk. He took the hint, and the person whom he procured to succeed me was a real attorney, who in less than a year robbed him of twenty or thirty thousand livres. He discharged him, and sent him to prison, dismissed his gentleman with disgrace, and, in wretchedness, got himself everywhere into quarrels, received affronts which a footman would not have put up with, and, after numerous follies, was recalled, and sent from the capital. It is very probable that among the reprimands he received at court, his affair with me was not forgotten. At least, a little time after his return he sent his maitre d'hotel, to settle my account, and give me some money. I was in want of it at that moment; my debts at Venice, debts of honor, if ever there were any, lay heavy upon my mind. I made use of the means which offered to discharge them, as well as the note of Zanetto Nani. I received what was offered me, paid all my debts, and remained as before, without a farthing in my pocket, but relieved from a weight which had become insupportable. From that time I never heard speak of M. de Montaigu until his death, with which I became acquainted by means of the Gazette. The peace of God be with that poor man! He was as fit for the functions of an ambassador as in my infancy I had been for those of *Grapignan.** However, it was in his power to have honorably supported himself by my services, and at the same time to have rapidly advanced me in a career to which the Comte de Gauvon had destined me in my youth, and of the functions of which I had in a more advanced age rendered myself capable.

The justice and inutility of my complaints left in my mind seeds of indignation against our foolish civil institutions, by which the welfare of the public and real justice are always sacrificed to I know not what appearance of order, and which does nothing more than add the sanction of public authority to the oppression of the weak, and the iniquity of the powerful. Two things prevented these seeds from putting forth at that time as they afterwards did: one was, myself being in question in the affair, and private interest, whence nothing great or noble ever proceeded,

---

* Term of disparagement for an attorney.—La Rousse.

could not draw from my heart the divine soarings, which the most pure love, only of that which is just and sublime, can produce. The other was the charm of friendship which tempered and calmed my wrath by the ascendancy of a more pleasing sentiment. I had become acquainted at Venice with a Biscayan, a friend of my friend Carrio's, and worthy of being that of every honest man. This amiable young man, born with every talent and virtue, had just made the tour of Italy to gain a taste for the fine arts, and, imagining he had nothing more to acquire, intended to return by the most direct road to his own country. I told him the arts were nothing more than a relaxation to a genius like his, fit to cultivate the sciences; and to give him a taste for these, I advised him to make a journey to Paris and reside there for six months. He took my advice, and went to Paris. He was there and expected me when I arrived. His lodging was too considerable for him, and he offered me the half of it, which I instantly accepted. I found him absorbed in the study of the sublimest sciences. Nothing was above his reach. He digested everything with a prodigious rapidity. How cordially did he thank me for having procured him this food for his mind, which was tormented by a thirst after knowledge, without his being aware of it! What a treasure of light and virtue I found in the vigorous mind of this young man! I felt he was the friend I wanted. We soon became intimate. Our tastes were not the same, and we constantly disputed. Both opinionated, we never could agree about anything. Nevertheless we could not separate; and, notwithstanding our reciprocal and incessant contradiction, we neither of us wished the other to be different from what he was.

Ignacio Emmanuel de Altuna was one of those rare beings whom only Spain produces, and of whom she produces too few for her glory. He had not the violent national passions common in his own country. The idea of vengeance could no more enter his head, than the desire of it could proceed from his heart. His mind was too great to be vindictive, and I have frequently heard him say, with the greatest coolness, that no mortal could offend him. He was gallant, without being tender. He played with women as with so many pretty children. He amused himself with the mistresses of his friends, but I never knew him to have one of his own, nor the least desire for it. The emanations from the virtue with which his heart was stored never permitted the fire of the passions to excite sensual desires.

After his travels he married, died young, and left children; and, I am as convinced as of my existence, that his wife was the first and only woman with whom he ever tasted of the pleasures of love.

Externally he was devout, like a Spaniard, but in his heart he had the piety of an angel. Except myself, he is the only man I ever saw whose principles were not intolerant. He never in his life asked any person his opinion in matters of religion. It was not of the least consequence to him whether his friend was a

Jew, a Protestant, a Turk, a Bigot, or an Atheist, provided he was an honest man. Obstinate and headstrong in matters of indifference, but the moment religion was in question, even the moral part, he collected himself, was silent, or simply said: *"I am charged with the care of myself only."* It is astonishing so much elevation of mind should be compatible with a spirit of detail carried to minuteness. He previously divided the employment of the day by hours, quarters and minutes; and so scrupulously adhered to this distribution, that had the clock struck while he was reading a phrase, he would have shut his book without finishing it. His portions of time thus laid out, were some of them set apart to studies of one kind, and others to those of another: he had some for reflection, conversation, divine service, the reading of Locke, for his rosary, for visits, music and painting; and neither pleasure, temptation, nor complaisance, could interrupt this order: a duty he might have had to discharge was the only thing that could have done it. When he gave me a list of his distribution, that I might conform myself thereto, I first laughed, and then shed tears of admiration. He never constrained anybody nor suffered constraint: he was rather rough with people, who from politeness attempted to put it upon it. He was passionate without being sullen. I have often seen him warm, but never saw him really angry with any person. Nothing could be more cheerful than his temper: he knew how to pass and receive a joke; raillery was one of his distinguished talents, and with which he possessed that of pointed wit and repartee. When he was animated, he was noisy and heard at a great distance; but whilst he loudly inveighed, a smile was spread over his countenance, and in the midst of his warmth he used some diverting expression which made all his hearers break out into a loud laugh. He had no more of the Spanish complexion than of the phlegm of that country. His skin was white, his cheeks finely colored, and his hair of a light chestnut. He was tall and well made: his body was well formed for the residence of his mind.

This wise-hearted, as well as wise-headed man, knew mankind, and was my friend; this is my only answer to such as are not so. We were so intimately united, that our intention was to pass our days together. In a few years I was to go to Ascoytia to live with him at his estate; every part of the project was arranged the eve of his departure; nothing was left undetermined, except that which depends not upon men in the best concerted plans, posterior events. My disasters, his marriage, and finally, his death, separated us forever. Some men would be tempted to say, that nothing succeeds except the dark conspiracies of the wicked, and that the innocent intentions of the good are seldom or never accomplished. I had felt the inconvenience of dependence, and took a resolution never again to expose myself to it; having seen the projects of ambition, which circumstances had induced me to form, overturned in their birth. Discouraged in the career I had so well begun, from which, however, I had just been expelled, I resolved never more to attach myself to any person, but to remain in an independent state, turning my talents to the best advantage: of these I at length began to feel the extent, and that I had hitherto had too modest an opinion of them. I again took up my opera, which I had laid aside to go to Venice; and, that I might be less interrupted after the departure of Altuna, I returned to my old hotel St. Quentin; which, in a solitary part of the town, and not far from the Luxembourg, was more proper for my purpose than noisy Rue St. Honoré.

There the only consolation which Heaven suffered me to taste in my misery, and the only one which rendered it supportable, awaited me. This was not a transient acquaintance; I must enter into some detail relative to the manner in which it was made.

We had a new landlady from Orleans; to help her with the linen, she had a young girl from her own country, of between twenty-two and twenty-three years of age, and who, as well as the hostess, ate at our table. This girl, named Thérèsa le Vasseur, was of a good family; her father was an officer in the mint of Orleans, and her mother a shopkeeper; they had many children. The function of the mint of Orleans being suppressed, the father found himself without employment; and the mother having suffered losses, was reduced to narrow circumstances. She quitted her business and came to Paris with her husband and daughter, who, by her industry, maintained all the three.

The first time I saw this girl at table, I was struck with her modesty; and still more so with her lively, yet charming look; which, with respect to the impression it made upon me, was never equaled. Beside M. de Bonnefond, the company was composed of several Irish priests, Gascons, and others of much the same description. Our hostess herself had not made the best possible use of her time, and I was the only person at the table who spoke and behaved with decency. Allurements were thrown out to the young girl. I took her part, and the joke was then turned against me. Had I had no natural inclination to the poor girl, compassion and contradiction would have produced it in me: I was always a great friend to decency in manners and conversation, especially in the fair sex. I openly declared myself her champion, and perceived she was not insensible of my attention; her looks, animated by the gratitude she dared not express by words, were for this reason still more penetrating.

She was very timid, and I was as much so as herself. The connection which this disposition common to both seemed to remove to a distance, was however rapidly formed. Our landlady perceiving its progress, became furious, and her brutality forwarded my affair with the young girl, who, having no person in the house except myself to give her the least support, was sorry to see me go from home, and sighed for the return of her protector. The affinity our hearts bore to each other, and the similarity of our dispositions, had soon their ordinary effect. She thought she saw in me an honest man, and in this she was not deceived. I thought I perceived in her a woman of great sensibility, simple in her manners, and devoid of all coquetry:—I was no more deceived in her than she in me. I began by declaring to her that I would never either abandon or marry her. Love, esteem, artless sincerity were the ministers of my triumph, and it was because her heart was tender and virtuous, that I was happy without being presuming.

The apprehensions she was under of my not finding in her that for which I sought, retarded my happiness more than every other circumstance. I perceived her disconcerted and confused before she yielded her consent, wishing to be understood and not daring to explain herself. Far from suspecting the real cause of her embarrassment, I falsely imagined it to proceed from another motive, a supposition highly insulting to her morals, and thinking she gave me to understand my health might be exposed to danger, I fell into so perplexed a state that, although it was no restraint upon me, it poisoned my happiness during several days. As we did not understand each other, our conversations upon this subject were so many enigmas more than ridiculous. She was upon the point of believing I was absolutely mad; and I on my part was as near not knowing what else to think of her. At last we came to an explanation; she confessed to me with tears the only fault of the kind of her whole life, immediately after she became nubile; the fruit of her ignorance and the address of her seducer. The moment I comprehended what she meant, I gave a shout of joy. "Virginity!" exclaimed I; "sought for at Paris, and at twenty years of age! Ah, my Thérèsa! I am happy in possessing thee, virtuous and healthy as thou art, and in not finding that for which I never sought."

At first, amusement was my only object; I perceived I had gone further, and had given myself a companion. A little intimate connection with this excellent girl, and a few reflections upon my situation, made me discover that, while thinking of nothing more than my pleasures, I had done a great deal towards my happiness. In the place of extinguished ambition, a lively sentiment, which had entire possession of my heart, was necessary to me. In a word, I wanted a successor to mamma: since I was never again to live with her, it was necessary some person should live with her pupil, and a person, too, in whom I might find that simplicity and docility of mind and heart which she had found in me. It was, moreover, necessary that the happiness of domestic life should indemnify me for the splendid career I had just renounced. When I was quite alone there was a void in my heart, which wanted nothing more than another heart to fill it up. Fate had deprived me of this, or at least in part alienated me from that for which by nature I was formed. From that moment I was alone, for there never was for me the least thing intermediate between everything and nothing. I found in Thérèsa the supplement of which I stood in need; by means of her I lived as happily as I possibly could do, according to the course of events.

I first attempted to improve her mind. In this my pains were useless. Her mind is as nature formed it; it was not susceptible of cultivation. I do not blush in acknowledging she never knew how to read well, although she writes tolerably. When I went to lodge in the Rue Neuve-des-Petits-Champs, opposite to my windows at the Hôtel de Pontchartrain, there was a sun-dial, on which for a whole month I used all my efforts to teach her to know the hours; yet, she scarcely knows them at present. She never could enumerate the twelve months of the year in order, and cannot distinguish one numeral from another, notwithstanding all the trouble I took endeavoring to teach them to her. She neither knows how to count money, nor to reckon the price of anything. The word which when she speaks, presents itself to her mind, is frequently opposite to that of which she means to make use. I formerly made a dictionary of her phrases, to amuse M. de Luxembourg, and her *qui pro quos* often became celebrated among those with whom I was most intimate. But this person, so confined in her intellects, and, if the world pleases, so stupid, can give excellent advice in cases of difficulty. In Switzerland, in England, and in France, she frequently saw what I had not myself perceived; she has often given me the best advice I could possibly follow; she has rescued me from dangers into which I had blindly precipitated myself, and in the presence of princes and the great, her sentiments, good sense, answers, and conduct have acquired her universal esteem, and myself the most sincere congratulations on her merit. With persons whom we love, sentiment fortifies the mind as well as the heart; and they who are thus attached, have little need of searching for ideas elsewhere.

I lived with my Thérèsa as agreeably as with the finest genius in the world. Her mother, proud of having been brought up under the Marchioness of Monpipeau, attempted to be witty, wished to direct the judgment of her daughter, and by her knavish cunning destroyed the simplicity of our intercourse.

The fatigue of this importunity made me in some degree surmount the foolish shame which prevented me from appearing with Thérèsa in public; and we took short country walks, *tête-à-tête,* and partook of little collations, which, to me, were delicious. I perceived she loved me sincerely, and this increased my tenderness. This charming intimacy left me nothing to wish; futurity no longer gave me the least concern, or at most appeared only as the present moment prolonged: I had no other desire than that of insuring its duration.

This attachment rendered all other dissipation superfluous and insipid to me. I never went but for the purpose of going to the apartment of Thérèsa, her place of residence almost became my own. My retirement was so favorable to the work I had undertaken, that, in less than three months, my opera was entirely finished, both words and music, except a few accompaniments, and fillings up which still remained to be added. This maneuvring business was very fatiguing to me. I proposed it to Philidor, offering him at the same time a part of the profits. He came twice, and did something to the middle parts in the act of Ovid; but he could not confine himself to an assiduous application by the allurement of advantages which were distant and uncertain. He did not come a third time, and I finished the work myself.

My opera completed, the next thing was to make something of it: this was by much the more difficult task of the two. A man living in solitude in Paris will never succeed in anything. I was on the point of making my way by means of M. de la Poplinière, to whom Gauffecourt, at my return to Geneva, had introduced me. M. de la Poplinière was the Mecænas of Rameau. Madam de la Poplinière his very humble scholar. Rameau was said to govern in that house. Judging that he would with pleasure protect the work of one of his disciples, I wished to show him what I had done. He refused to examine it; saying he could not read score, it was too fatiguing to him. M. de la Poplinière, to obviate this difficulty, said he might hear it; and offered me to send for musicians to execute certain detached pieces. I wished for nothing better. Rameau consented with an ill grace, incessantly repeating that the composition of a man not regularly bred to the science, and who had learned music without a master, must certainly be very fine! I hastened to copy into parts five or six select passages. Ten symphonies were procured, and Albert, Bérard, and Mademoiselle Bourdonnais undertook the vocal part. Rameau, the moment he heard the overture, was purposely extravagant in his eulogium, by which he intended it should be understood it could not be my composition. He showed signs of impatience at every passage: but after a counter tenor song, the air of which was noble and harmonious, with a brilliant accompaniment, he could no longer contain himself; he apostrophized me with a brutality at which everybody was shocked, maintaining that a part of what he had heard was by a man experienced in the art, and the rest by some ignorant person who did not so much as understand music. It is true my composition, unequal and without rule, was sometimes sublime, and at others insipid, as that of a person who forms himself in an art by the soarings of his own genius, unsupported by science, must necessarily be. Rameau pretended to see nothing in me but a contemptible pilferer, without talents or taste. The rest of the company, among whom I must distinguish the master of the house, were of a different opinion. M. de Richelieu, who at that time frequently visited M. and Madam de la Poplinière, heard them speak of my work, and wished to hear the whole of it, with an intention, if it pleased him, to have it performed at court. The opera was executed with full choruses, and by a great orchestra, at the expense of the king, at M. de Bonneval's, Intendant of the Menus; Francœur directed the band. The effect was surprising: the duke never ceased to exclaim and applaud; and, at the end of one of the choruses, in the act of Tasso, he arose and came to me, and pressing my hand, said: "M. Rousseau, this is transporting harmony. I never heard anything finer. I will get this performed at Versailles."

Madam de la Poplinière, who was present, said not a word. Rameau, although invited, refused to come. The next day, Madam de la Poplinière received me at her toilette very ungraciously, affected to undervalue my piece, and told me, that although a little false glitter had at first dazzled M. de Richelieu, he had recovered from his error, and she advised me not to place the least dependence upon my opera. The duke arrived soon after, and spoke to me in quite a different language. He said very flattering things of my talents, and seemed as much disposed as ever to have my composition performed before the king. "There is nothing," said he, "but the act of Tasso which cannot pass at court: you must write another." Upon this single word I shut myself up in my apartment; and in three weeks produced, in the place of Tasso, another act, the subject of which was Hesiod inspired by the muses. In this I found the secret of introducing a part of the history of my talents, and of the jealousy with which Rameau had been pleased to honor me. There was in the new act an elevation less gigantic and better supported than in the act of Tasso. The music was as noble and the composition better; and had the other two acts been equal to this, the whole piece would have supported a representation to advantage. But whilst I was endeavoring to give it the last finishing, another undertaking suspended the completion of that I had in my hand. In the winter which succeeded the battle of Fontenoi, there were many galas at Versailles, and several operas performed at the theater of the little stables. Among the number of the latter was the dramatic piece of Voltaire, entitled *La Princess de Navarre,* the music by Rameau, the name of which had just been changed to that of the *Fêtes de Ramire.* This new subject required several changes to be made in the *divertissements,* as well in the poetry as in the music.

A person capable of both was now sought after. Voltaire was in Lorraine, and Rameau also; both of whom were employed on the opera of *The Temple of Glory,* and could not give their attention to this. M. de Richelieu thought of me, and sent to desire I would undertake the alterations; and, that I might the better examine what there was to do, he gave me separately the poem and the music. In the first place, I would not touch the words without the consent of the author, to whom I wrote upon the subject a very polite and respectful letter, such a one as was proper; and received from him the following answer:

"December 15th, 1745.

"Sir: In you two talents, which hitherto have always been separate, are united. These are two good reasons for me to esteem and to endeavor to love you. I am sorry, on your account, you should employ these talents in a work which is so little worthy of them. A few months ago the Duke de Richelieu commanded me to make, absolutely in the twinkling of an eye, a little and bad sketch of a few insipid and imperfect scenes to be adapted to *divertissements* which are not of a nature to be joined with them. I obeyed with the greatest exactness. I wrote very fast, and very ill. I sent this wretched production to M. de Richelieu, imagining he would make no use of it, or that I should have it again to make the necessary corrections. Happily it is in your hands, and you are at full liberty to do with it whatever you please: I have entirely lost sight of the thing. I doubt not but you will have corrected all the faults which cannot but abound in so hasty a composition of such a very simple sketch, and am persuaded you will have supplied whatever was wanting.

"I remember that, among other stupid inattentions, no account is given in the scenes which connect the *divertissements* of the manner in which the Princess Grenadine immediately passes from a prison to a garden or palace. As it is not a magician but a Spanish nobleman who gives her the gala, I am of opinion nothing should be effected by enchantment.

"I beg, sir, you will examine this part, of which I have but a confused idea.

"You will likewise consider, whether or not it be necessary the prison should be opened, and the princess conveyed from it to a fine palace, gilt and varnished, and prepared for her. I know all this is wretched, and that it is beneath a thinking being to make a serious affair of such trifles; but, since we must displease as little as possible, it is necessary we should conform to reason, even in a bad *divertissement* of an opera.

"I depend wholly upon you and M. Ballod, and soon expect to have the honor of returning you my thanks, and assuring you how much I am, etc."

There is nothing surprising in the great politeness of this letter, compared with the almost rude ones which he has since written to me. He thought I was in great favor with Madam Richelieu; and the courtly suppleness, which every one knows to be the character of this author, obliged him to be extremely polite to a new-comer, until he became better acquainted with the measure of the favor and patronage he enjoyed.

Authorized by M. de Voltaire, and not under the necessity of giving myself the least concern about M. Rameau, who endeavored to injure me, I set to work, and in two months my undertaking was finished. With respect to the poetry, it was confined to a mere trifle; I aimed at nothing more than to prevent the difference of style from being perceived, and had the vanity to think I had succeeded. The musical part was longer and more laborious. Besides my having to compose several preparatory pieces, and, amongst others, the overture, all the recitative, with which I was charged, was extremely difficult on account of the necessity there was of connecting, in a few verses, and by very rapid modulations, symphonies and choruses, in keys very different from each other; for I was determined neither to change nor transpose any of the airs, that Rameau might not accuse me of having disfigured them. I succeeded in the recitative; it was well accented, full of energy and excellent modulation. The idea of two men of superior talents, with whom I was associated, had elevated my genius, and I can assert, that in this barren and inglorious task, of which the public could have no knowledge, I was for the most part equal to my models.

The piece, in the state to which I had brought it, was rehearsed in the great theater of the opera. Of the three authors who had contributed to the production, I was the only one present. Voltaire was not in Paris, and Rameau either did not come, or concealed himself. The words of the first monologue were very mournful; they began with:

O Mort! viens terminer les malheurs de ma vie. *

To these, suitable music was necessary. It was, however, upon this that Madam de la Poplinière founded her censure; accusing me, with much bitterness, of having composed a funeral anthem. M. de Richelieu very judiciously began by informing himself who was the author of the poetry of this monologue; I presented him the manuscript he had sent me, which proved it was by Voltaire. "In that case," said the duke, "Voltaire alone is to blame." During the re-

* *O Death! hasten to terminate the misfortunes of my life.*

hearsal, everything I had done was disapproved by Madam de la Poplinière, and approved of by M. de Richelieu; but I had afterwards to do with too powerful an adversary. It was signified to me that several parts of my composition wanted revising, and that on this it was necessary I should consult M. Rameau; my heart was wounded by such a conclusion, instead of the eulogium I expected, and which certainly I merited, and I returned to my apartment overwhelmed with grief, exhausted with fatigue, and consumed by chagrin. I was immediately taken ill, and confined to my chamber for upwards of six weeks.

Rameau, who was charged with the alterations indicated by Madam de la Poplinière, sent to ask me for the overture of my great opera, to substitute it for that I had just composed. Happily I perceived the trick he intended to play me, and refused him the overture. As the performance was to be in five or six days, he had not time to make one, and was obliged to leave that I had prepared. It was in the Italian taste, and in a style at that time quite new in France. It gave satisfaction, and I learned from M. de Valmalette, maitre d'hotel to the king, and son-in-law to M. Mussard, my relation and friend, that the connoisseurs were highly satisfied with my work, and that the public had not distinguished it from that of Rameau. However, he and Madam de la Poplinière took measures to prevent any person from knowing I had any concern in the matter. In the books distributed to the audience, and in which the authors are always named, Voltaire was the only person mentioned, and Rameau preferred the suppression of his own name to seeing it associated with mine.

As soon as I was in a situation to leave my room, I wished to wait upon M. de Richelieu, but it was too late; he had just set off from Dunkirk, where he was to command the expedition destined to Scotland. At his return, said I to myself, to authorize my idleness, it will be too late for my purpose, not having seen him since that time. I lost the honor of my work and the emoluments it should have produced me, besides considering my time, trouble, grief, and vexation, my illness, and the money this cost me, without ever receiving the least benefit, or, rather, recompense. However, I always thought M. de Richelieu was disposed to serve me, and that he had a favorable opinion of my talents; but my misfortune, and Madam de la Poplinière, prevented the effect of his good wishes.

I could not divine the reason of the aversion this lady had to me. I had always endeavored to make myself agreeable to her, and regularly paid her my court. Gauffecourt explained to me the causes of her dislike: "The first," said he, "is her friendship for Rameau, of whom she is the declared panegyrist, and who will not suffer a competitor; the next is an original sin, which ruins you in her estimation, and which she will never forgive; you are a Genevese." Upon this he told me the Abbé Hubert, who was from the same city, and the sincere friend of M. de la Poplinière, had used all his efforts to prevent him from marrying this lady, with whose character and temper he was very well acquainted; and that after the marriage she had vowed him an implacable hatred, as well as all the Genevese. "Although La Poplinière has a friendship for you, do not," said he, "depend upon his protection: he is still in love with his wife: she hates you, and is vindictive and artful; you will never do anything in that house." All this I took for granted.

The same Gauffecourt rendered me much about this time a service of which I stood in the greatest need. I had just lost my virtuous father, who was about sixty years of age. I felt this loss less severely than I should have done at any other time, when the embarrassments of my situation had less engaged my attention. During his life-time I had never claimed what remained of the property of my mother, and of which he received the little interest. His death removed all my scruples upon this subject. But the want of a legal proof of the death of my brother created a difficulty which Gauffecourt undertook to remove, and this he effected by means of the good offices of the advocate De Lolme. As I stood in need of the little resource, and the event being doubtful, I waited for a definitive account with the greatest anxiety.

One evening on entering my apartment I found a letter, which I knew to contain the information I wanted, and I took it up with an impatient trembling, of which I was inwardly ashamed. What? said I to myself, with disdain, shall Jean-Jacques thus suffer himself to be subdued by interest and curiosity? I immediately laid the letter again upon the chimney-piece. I undressed myself, went to bed with great composure, slept better than ordinary, and rose in the morning at a late hour, without thinking more of my letter. As I dressed myself, it caught my eye; I broke the seal very leisurely, and found under the envelope a bill of exchange. I felt a variety of pleasing sensations at the same time: but I can assert, upon my honor, that the most lively of them all was that proceeding from having known how to be master of myself.

I could mention twenty such circumstances in my life, but I am too much pressed for time to say everything. I sent a small part of this money to my poor mamma; regretting, with my eyes suffused with tears, the happy time when I should have laid it all at her feet. All her letters contained evident marks of her distress. She sent me piles of recipes, and numerous secrets, with which she pretended I might make my fortune and her own. The idea of her wretchedness already affected her heart and contracted her mind. The little I sent her fell a prey to the knaves by whom she was surrounded; she received not the least advantage from anything. The idea of dividing what was necessary to my own subsistence with these wretches disgusted me, especially after the vain attempt I had made to deliver her from them, and of which I shall have occasion to speak. Time slipped away, and with it the little money I had; we were two, or indeed, four persons; or, to speak still more correctly, seven or eight. Although Thérèsa was disinterested to a degree of which there are but few examples, her mother was not so. She was no sooner a little relieved from her necessities by my care, than she sent for her whole family to partake of the fruits of them. Her sisters, sons, daughters, all, except her eldest daughter, married to the director of the coaches of Angers, came to Paris. Everything I did for Thérèsa her mother diverted from its original destination in favor of these people who were starving. I had not to do with an avaricious person; and, not being under the influence of an unruly passion, I was not guilty of follies. Satisfied with genteelly supporting Thérèsa without luxury, and unexposed to pressing wants, I readily consented to let all the earnings of her industry go to the profit of her mother; and to this even I did not confine myself; but, by a fatality by which I was pursued, whilst mamma was a prey to the rascals about her, Thérèsa was the same to her family; and I could not do anything on either side for the benefit of her to whom the succor I gave was destined. It was odd enough the youngest child of M. de la Vasseur, the only one who had not received a marriage portion from her parents, should provide for their subsistence; and that, after having a long time been beaten by her brothers, sisters, and even her nieces, the poor girl should be plundered by them all, without being more able to defend herself from their thefts than from their blows. One of her nieces, named Goton le Duc, was of a mild and amiable character; although spoiled by the lessons and examples of the others. As I frequently saw them together, I gave them names, which they afterwards gave to each other; I called the niece *my niece,* and the aunt *my aunt;* they both called me uncle. Hence the name of *aunt,* by which I continued to call Thérèsa, and which my friends sometimes jocosely repeated. It will be judged that in such a situation I had not a moment to lose, before I attempted to extricate myself. Imagining M. de Richelieu had forgotten me, and, having no more hopes from the court, I made some attempts to get my opera brought out at Paris; but I met with difficulties which could not immediately be removed, and my situation became daily more painful. I presented my little comedy of *Narcisse* to the Italians; it was received, and I had the freedom of the theater, which gave much pleasure. But this was all; I could never get my piece performed, and, tired of paying my court to players, I gave myself no more trouble about them. At length I had recourse to the last expedient which remained to me, and the only one of which I ought to have made use. While frequenting the house of M. de la Poplinière, I had neglected the family of Dupin. The two ladies, although related, were not upon good terms, and never saw each other. There was not the least intercourse between the two families, and Thiériot was the only person who visited both. He was desired to endeavor to bring me again to M. Dupin's. M. de Francueil was then studying natural history and chemistry, and collecting a cabinet. I believe he aspired to become a member of the Academy of Sciences; to this effect he intended to write a book, and judged I might be of use to him in the undertaking. Madam de Dupin, who, on her part, had another work in contemplation, had much the same views with respect to me. They wished to have me in common as a kind of secretary, and this was the reason of the invitations of Thiériot.

I required that M. de Francueil should previously employ his interest with that of Jelyote to get my work rehearsed at the opera-house; to this he consented. The *Muses Galantes* were several times rehearsed, first at the *Magazin,* and afterwards in the *Grand Théâtre.* The audience was very numerous at the great rehearsal, and several parts of the composition were highly applauded. However, during this rehearsal, very ill-conducted by Rebel, I felt the piece would not be received; and that, before it could appear, great alterations were necessary. I therefore withdrew it without saving a word, or exposing myself to a refusal; but I plainly perceived, by several indications, that the work, had it been perfect, could not have succeeded. M. de Francueil had promised me to get it rehearsed, but not that it should be received. He exactly kept his word. I thought I perceived on this occasion, as well as many others, that neither Madam Dupin nor himself were willing I should acquire a certain reputation in the world, lest, after the publication of their books, it should be supposed they had grafted their talents upon mine. Yet as

Madam Dupin always supposed those I had to be very moderate, and never employed me except it was to write what she dictated, or in researches of pure erudition, the reproach, with respect to her, would have been unjust.

This last failure of success completed my discouragement, I abandoned every prospect of fame and advancement; and, without further troubling my head about real or imaginary talents, with which I had so little success, I dedicated my whole time and cares to procure myself and Thérèsa a subsistence in the manner most pleasing to those to whom it should be agreeable to provide for it. I therefore entirely attached myself to Madam Dupin and M. de Francueil. This did not place me in a very opulent situation; for with eight or nine hundred livres, which I had the first two years, I had scarcely enough to provide for my primary wants; being obliged to live in their neighborhood, a dear part of the town, in a furnished lodging, and having to pay for another lodging at the extremity of Paris, at the very top of the Rue Saint-Jacques, to which, let the weather be as it would, I went almost every evening to supper. I soon got into the track of my new occupations, and conceived a taste for them. I attached myself to the study of chemistry, and attended several courses of it with M. de Francueil at M. Rouelle's, and we began to scribble over paper upon that science, of which we scarcely possessed the elements. In 1747, we went to pass the autumn in Touraine, at the castle of Chenonceaux, a royal mansion upon the Cher, built by Henry the II., for Diana of Poitiers, of whom the ciphers are still seen, and which is now in the possession of M. Dupin, a farmer-general. We amused ourselves very agreeably in this beautiful place, and lived very well: I became as fat there as a monk. Music was a favorite relaxation. I composed several trios full of harmony, and of which I may perhaps speak in my supplement if ever I should write one. Theatrical performances were another resource. I wrote a comedy in fifteen days, entitled *l'Engagement téméraire,** which will be found amongst my papers; it has no other merit than that of being lively. I composed several other little things: amongst others a poem entitled, *l'Allée de Sylvie,†* from the name of an alley in the park upon the bank of the Cher; and this without discontinuing my chemical studies, or interrupting what I had to do for Madam Dupin.

Whilst I was increasing my corpulency at Chenonceaux, that of my poor Thérèsa was augmented at Paris in another manner, and at my return I found the work I had put upon the frame in greater forwardness than I had expected. This, on account of my situation, would have thrown me into the greatest embarrassment, had not one of my messmates furnished me with the only resource which could relieve me from it. This is one of those essential narratives which I cannot give with too much simplicity; because, in making an improper use of their names, I

* *The Rash Engagement.*   † *The Alley of Sylvia.*

should either excuse or inculpate myself, both of which in this place are entirely out of the question.

During the residence of Altuna at Paris, instead of going to eat at a *Troiteurs,* he and I commonly ate in the neighborhood, almost opposite the cul-de-sac of the opera, at the house of a Madam la Selle, the wife of a tailor, who gave but very ordinary dinners, but whose table was much frequented on account of the safe company which generally resorted to it; no person was received without being introduced by one of those who used the house. The commander, de Graville, an old debauchee, with much wit and politeness, but obscene in conversation, lodged at the house, and brought to it a set of riotous and extravagant young men; officers in the guards and mousquetaires. The Commander de Nonant, chevalier to all the girls of the opera, was the daily oracle, who conveyed to us the news of this motley crew. M. du Plessis, a lieutenant-colonel, retired from the service, an old man of great goodness and wisdom; and M. Ancelet,* an

---

* It was to this M. Ancelet I gave a little comedy, after my own manner entitled "Les Prisonniers de Guerre," † which I wrote after the disasters of the French in Bavaria and Bohemia: I dared not either avow this comedy or show it, and this for the singular reason that neither the King of France nor the French were ever better spoken of nor praised with more sincerity of heart than in my piece; though written by a professed republican, I dared not declare myself the panegyrist of a nation, whose maxims were exactly the reverse of my own. More grieved at the misfortunes of France than the French themselves, I was afraid the public would construe into flattery and mean complaisance the marks of a sincere attachment, of which in

† The Prisoners of War.

officer in the mousquetaires kept the young people in a certain kind of order. This table was also frequented by commercial people, financiers and contractors, but extremely polite, and such as were distinguished amongst those of the same profession. M. de Besse, M. de Forcade, and others whose names I have forgotten, in short, well-dressed people of every description were seen there; except abbés and men of the long robe, not one of whom I ever met in the house, and it was agreed not to introduce men of either of these professions. This table, sufficiently resorted to, was very cheerful without being noisy, and many of the guests were waggish, without descending to vulgarity. The old commander with all his smutty stories, with respect to the substance, never lost sight of the politeness of the old court; nor did any indecent expression, which even women would not have pardoned him, escape his lips. His manner served as a rule to every person at table; all the young men related their adventures of gallantry with equal grace and freedom, and these narratives were the more complete, as the seraglio was at the door; the entry which led to it was the same; for there was a communication between this and the shop of La Duchapt, a celebrated milliner, who at that time had several very pretty girls, with whom our young people went to chat before or after dinner. I should thus have amused myself as well as the rest, had I been less modest; I

---

my first part I have mentioned the date and the cause, and which I was ashamed to show.

had only to go in as they did, but this I never had courage enough to do. With respect to Madam de Selle, I often went to eat at her house after the departure of Altuna. I learned a great number of amusing anecdotes and by degrees I adopted, thank God, not the morals, but the maxims I found to be established there. Honest men injured, husbands deceived, women seduced, secret accouchements, were the most ordinary topics, and he who had best filled the foundling hospital was always the most applauded. I caught the manners I daily had before my eyes: I formed my manner of thinking upon that I observed to be the reigning one amongst amiable, and upon the whole, very honest people. I said to myself, since it is the custom of the country, they who live here may adopt it; this is the expedient for which I sought. I cheerfully determined upon it without the least scruple, and the only one I had to overcome was that of Thérèsa, whom, with the greatest imaginable difficulty, I persuaded to adopt this only means of saving her honor. Her mother, who was moreover apprehensive of a new embarrassment by an increase of family, came to my aid, and she at length suffered herself to be prevailed upon. We made choice of a midwife, a safe and prudent woman, Mademoiselle Gouin, who lived at the *Pointe Saint-Eustache,* and when the time came, Thérèsa was conducted to her house by her mother.

I went thither several times to see her, and gave her a cipher which I had made double upon two cards;

one of them was put into the linen of the child, and by the midwife deposited with the infant in the office of the foundling hospital according to the customary form. The year following, a similar inconvenience was remedied by the same expedient, excepting the cipher, which was forgotten: no more reflection on my part, nor approbation on that of the mother; she obeyed with trembling. All the vicissitudes which this fatal conduct has produced in my manner of thinking, as well as in my destiny, will be successively seen. For the present, we will confine ourselves to this first period; its cruel and unforeseen consequences will but too frequently oblige me to refer to it.

I here mark that of my first acquaintance with Madam D'Epinay, whose name will frequently appear in these memoirs. She was a Mademoiselle D'Esclavelles, and had lately been married to M. D'Epinay, son to M. de Lalive de Bellegarde, a farmer general. She understood music, and a passion for the art produced between these three persons the greatest intimacy. Madam Francueil introduced me to Madam D'Epinay, and we sometimes supped together at her house. She was amiable, had wit and talent, and was certainly a desirable acquaintance; but she had a female friend, a Mademoiselle d'Ette, who was said to have much malignancy in her disposition; she lived with the Chevalier de Valory, whose temper was far from being one of the best. I am of opinion, an acquaintance with these two persons was prejudicial to Madam D'Epinay, to whom, with a disposition which required the greatest attention from those about her, nature had given very excellent qualities to regulate or counterbalance her extravagant pretensions. M. de Francueil inspired her with a part of the friendship he had conceived for me, and told me of the connection between them, of which, for that reason, I would not now speak, were it not become so public as not to be concealed from M. D'Epinay himself.

M. de Francueil confided to me secrets of a very singular nature relative to this lady, of which she herself never spoke to me, nor so much as suspected my having a knowledge; for I never opened my lips to her upon the subject, nor will I ever do it to any person. The confidence all parties had in my prudence rendered my situation very embarrassing, especially with Madam de Francueil, whose knowledge of me was sufficient to remove from her all suspicion on my account, although I was connected with her rival. I did everything I could to console this poor woman, whose husband certainly did not return the affection she had for him. I listened to these three persons separately; I kept all their secrets so faithfully that not one of the three ever drew from me those of the two others, and this, without concealing from either of the women my attachment to each of them. Madam de Francueil, who frequently wished to make me an agent, received refusals in form, and Madam D'Epinay, once desiring me to charge myself with a letter to M. de Francueil received the same mortification, accompanied by a very express declaration, that if ever she wished to drive me forever from the house, she had only a second time to make me a like proposition.

In justice to Madam D'Epinay, I must say, that far from being offended with me she spoke of my conduct to M. de Francueil in terms of the highest approbation, and continued to receive me as well, and as politely as ever. It was thus, amidst the heart-burnings of three persons to whom I was obliged to behave with the greatest circumspection, on whom I in some measure depended, and for whom I had conceived an attachment, that by conducting myself with mildness and complaisance, although accompanied with the greatest firmness, I preserved unto the last not only their friendship, but their esteem and confidence. Notwithstanding my absurdities and awkwardness, Madam D'Epinay would have me make one of the party to the Chevrette, a country-house, near Saint Denis, belonging to M. de Bellegarde. There was a theater, in which performances were not unfrequent. I had a part given me, which I studied for six months without intermission, and in which, on the evening of the representation, I was obliged to be prompted from the beginning to the end. After this experiment no second proposal of the kind was ever made to me.

My acquaintance with M. D'Epinay procured me that of her sister-in-law, Mademoiselle de Bellegarde, who soon afterwards became Countess of Houdetot. The first time I saw her she was upon the point of marriage; when she conversed with me a long time, with that charming familiarity which was natural to her. I thought her very amiable, but I was far from perceiving that this young person would lead me, although innocently, into the abyss in which I still remain.

Although I have not spoken of Diderot since my return from Venice, no more than of my friend M. Roguin, I did not neglect either of them, especially the former, with whom I daily became more intimate. He had a Nanette, as well as I a Thérèsa; this was between us another conformity of circumstances. But my Thérèsa, as fine a woman as his Nanette, was of a mild and amiable character, which might gain and fix the affections of a worthy man; whereas Nanette was a vixen, a troublesome prater, and had no qualities in the eyes of others which in any measure compensated for her want of education. However he married her, which was well done of him, if he had given a promise to that effect. I, for my part, not having entered into any such engagement, was not in the least haste to imitate him.

I was also connected with the Abbé de Condillac, who had acquired no more literary fame than myself, but in whom there was every appearance of his becoming what he now is. I was perhaps the first who discovered the extent of his abilities, and esteemed them as they deserved. He on his part seemed satisfied with me, and, whilst shut up in my chamber in the Rue Jean St. Denis, near the opera-house, I composed my act of Hesiod, he sometimes came to dine with me *tête-à-tête*. We sent for our dinner, and paid share and share alike. He was at that time employed on his Essay on the Origin of Human Knowledge, which was his first work. When this was finished, the difficulty was to find a bookseller who would take it. The booksellers of Paris are shy of every author at his beginning, and metaphysics, not much then in vogue, were no very inviting subject. I spoke to Diderot of Condillac and his work, and I afterwards brought them acquainted with each other. They were worthy of each other's esteem, and were presently on the most friendly terms. Diderot persuaded the bookseller, Durant, to take the manuscript from the abbé, and this great metaphysician received for his first work, and almost as a favor, a hundred crowns, which perhaps he would not have obtained without my assistance. As we lived in a quarter of the town very distant from each other, we all assembled once a week at the Palais-Royal, and went to dine at the Hôtel du Panier Fleuri. These little weekly dinners must have been extremely pleasing to Diderot; for he who failed in almost all his appointments never missed one of these. At our little meeting I formed the plan of a periodical paper, entitled *le Persifleur,** which Diderot and I were alternately to write. I sketched out the first sheet, and this brought me acquainted with D'Alembert, to whom Diderot had mentioned it. Unforeseen events frustrated our intention, and the project was carried no further.

* *The Jeerer.*

These two authors had just undertaken the *Dictionnaire Encyclopedique,* which at first was intended to be nothing more than a kind of translation of Chambers', something like that of the Medical Dictionary of James, which Diderot had just finished. Diderot was desirous I should do something in this second undertaking, and proposed to me the musical part, which I accepted. This I executed in great haste, and consequently very ill, in the three months he had given me, as well as all the authors who were engaged in the work. But I was the only person in readiness at the time prescribed. I gave him my manuscript, which I had copied by a lackey, belonging to M. de Francueil of the name of Dupont, who wrote very well. I paid him ten crowns out of my own pocket, and these have never been reimbursed me. Diderot had promised me a retribution on the part of the booksellers, of which he has never since spoken to me nor I to him.

This undertaking of the *Encyclopedie* was interrupted by his imprisonment. The *Penses Philosophiquies,** drew upon him some temporary inconvenience which had no disagreeable consequences. He did not come off so easily on account of the *Lettre sur les Aveugles,*† in which there was nothing reprehensible, but some personal attacks with which Madam du Pré St. Maur, and M. de Réaumur were displeased: for this he was confined in the dungeon of Vincennes.

* *Philosophical Thoughts.*
† *Letter concerning blind persons.*

Nothing can describe the anguish I felt on account of the misfortune of my friend. My wretched imagination, which always sees everything in the worst light, was terrified. I imagined him to be confined for the remainder of his life: I was almost distracted with the thought. I wrote to Madam de Pompadour, beseeching her to release him or obtain an order to shut me up in the same dungeon. I received no answer to my letter: this was too reasonable to be efficacious, and I do not flatter myself that it contributed to the alleviation which, some time afterwards, was granted to the severities of the confinement of poor Diderot. Had this continued for any length of time with the same rigor, I verily believe I should have died in despair at the foot of the hated dungeon. However, if my letter produced but little effect, I did not on account of it attribute to myself much merit, for I mentioned it but to very few people, and never to Diderot himself.

BOOK VIII

BOOK VIII

THE

CONFESSIONS

OF

JEAN-JACQUES

ROUSSEAU

BOOK VIII

[*1749*]

I HAVE been obliged to pause at the end of the preceding book. With this begins the long chain of my misfortunes deduced from their origin. Having lived in the two most splendid houses in Paris, I had, notwithstanding my candor and modesty, made some acquaintance. Amongst others at Dupin's, that of the young hereditary prince of Saxe-Gotha, and of the Baron de Thun, his governor; at the house of M. de le Popliniére, that of M. Seguy, friend to the Baron de Thun, and known in the literary world by his beautiful edition of Rousseau.* The baron invited M. Seguy and myself to go and pass a day or two at Fontenai-sous-Bois, where the prince had a house. As

* *Jean Baptiste Rousseau, the poet.*

I passed Vincennes, at the sight of the dungeon, my feelings were acute; the effect of which the baron perceived on my countenance. At supper the prince mentioned the confinement of Diderot. The baron, to hear what I had to say, accused the prisoner of imprudence; and I showed not a little of the same in the impetuous manner in which I defended him. There were present two Germans in the service of the prince. M. Klüpffel, a man of great wit, his chaplain, and who afterwards, having supplanted the baron, became his governor. The other was a young man named M. Grimm, who served him as a reader until he could obtain some place, and whose indifferent appearance sufficiently proved the pressing necessity he was under of immediately finding one. From this very evening Klüpffel and I began an acquaintance which soon led to friendship. That with the Sieur Grimm did not make quite so rapid a progress: he made but few advances, and was far from having that haughty presumption which prosperity afterwards gave him. The next day at dinner, the conversation turned upon music: he spoke well on the subject. I was transported with joy when I learned from him he could play an accompaniment on the harpsichord. After dinner was over music was introduced, and we amused ourselves the rest of the afternoon on the harpsichord of the prince. Thus began that friendship which, at first, was so agreeable to me, afterwards so fatal, and of which I shall hereafter have so much to say.

On my return to Paris, I learned the agreeable news

that Diderot was released from the dungeon, and that he had on his parole the castle and park of Vincennes for a prison, with permission to see his friends. How painful was it to me not to be able instantly to fly to him! But I was detained two or three days at Madam Dupin's by indispensable business. After ages of impatience, I flew to the arms of my friend. He was not alone: D'Alembert and the treasurer of the *Sainte Chapelle* were with him. As I entered I saw nobody but himself, I made but one step, one cry: I riveted my face to his: I pressed him in my arms, without speaking to him, except by tears and sighs: I stifled him with my affection and joy. The first thing he did, after quitting my arms, was to turn himself towards the ecclesiastic, and say: "You see, sir, how much I am beloved by my friends." My emotion was so great, that it was then impossible for me to reflect upon this manner of turning it to advantage; but I have since thought that, had I been in the place of Diderot, the idea he manifested would not have been the first that would have occurred to me.

I found him much affected by his imprisonment. The dungeon had made a terrible impression upon his mind, and, although he was very agreeably situated in the castle, and at liberty to walk where he pleased in the park, which was not inclosed even by a wall, he wanted the society of his friends to prevent him from yielding to melancholy. As I was the person most concerned for his sufferings, I imagined I should also be the friend, the sight of whom would give him consolation; on which account, notwithstanding very pressing occupations, I went every two days at farthest, either alone, or accompanied by his wife, to pass the afternoon with him.

The heat of the summer was this year (1749) excessive. Vincennes is two leagues from Paris. The state of my finances not permitting me to pay for hackney coaches, at two o'clock in the afternoon, I went on foot, when alone, and walked as fast as possible, that I might arrive the sooner. The trees by the side of the road, always lopped, according to the custom of the country, afforded but little shade, and, exhausted by fatigue, I frequently threw myself on the ground, being unable to proceed any further. I thought a book in my hand might make me moderate my pace. One day I took the *Mercure de France,* and as I walked and read, I came to the following question proposed by the academy of Dijon, for the premium of the ensuing year, *Has the progress of sciences and arts contributed to corrupt or purify morals?*

The moment I had read this, I seemed to behold another world, and became a different man. Although I have a lively remembrance of the impression it made upon me, the detail has escaped my mind, since I communicated it to M. de Malesherbes in one of my four letters to him. This is one of the singularities of my memory which merits to be remarked. It serves me in proportion to my dependence upon it; the moment I have committed to paper that with which it was charged, it forsakes me, and I have no sooner written a thing than I have forgotten it entirely. This singularity is the same with respect to music. Before I learned the use of notes I knew a great number of songs; the moment I had made a sufficient progress to sing an air set to music, I could not recollect any one of them; and, at present, I much doubt whether I should be able entirely to go through one of those of which I was the most fond. All I distinctly recollect upon this occasion is, that on my arrival at Vincennes, I was in an agitation which approached a delirium. Diderot perceived it; I told him the cause, and read to him the Prosopopœia of Fabricius, written with a pencil under a tree. He encouraged me to pursue my ideas, and to become a competitor for the premium. I did so, and from that moment I was ruined.

All the rest of my misfortunes during my life were the inevitable effect of this moment of error.

My sentiments became elevated with the most inconceivable rapidity to the level of my ideas. All my little passions were stifled by the enthusiasm of truth, liberty, and virtue; and, what is most astonishing, this effervescence continued in my mind upwards of five years, to as great a degree perhaps as it has ever done in that of any other man. I composed the discourse in a very singular manner, and in that which I have always followed in all my other works. I dedicated to it the hours of the night in which sleep deserted me, I meditated in my bed with my eyes closed, and in my mind turned over and over again my periods with incredible labor and care; the moment they were finished to my satisfaction, I deposited them in my memory, until I had an opportunity of committing them to paper; but the time of rising and putting on my clothes made me lose everything, and when I took up my pen I recollected but little of what I had composed. I made Madam le Vasseur my secretary; I had lodged her with her daughter, and husband, nearer to myself; and she, to save me the expense of a servant, came every morning to make my fire, and to do such other little things as were necessary. As soon as she arrived I dictated to her while in bed what I had composed in the night, and this method, which for a long time I observed, preserved me many things I should otherwise have forgotten.

As soon as the discourse was finished, I showed it to Diderot. He was satisfied with the production, and pointed out some corrections he thought necessary to be made. However, this composition, full of force and fire, absolutely wants logic and order; of all the works I ever wrote, this is the weakest in reasoning, and the most devoid of number and harmony. With whatever talent a man may be born, the art of writing is not easily learned.

I sent off this piece without mentioning it to anybody, except, I think, to Grimm, with whom, after his going to live with the Comte de Frièse, I began to be upon the most intimate footing. His harpsichord served as a rendezvous, and I passed with him at it all the moments I had to spare, in singing Italian airs, and *barcarolles;* sometimes without intermission, from morning till night, or rather from night until morning; and when I was not to be found at Madam Dupin's, everybody concluded I was with Grimm at his apartment, the public walk, or the theater. I left off going to the *Comédie Italienne,* of which I was free, to go with him, and pay, to the *Comédie Française,* of which he was passionately fond. In short, so powerful an attraction connected me with this young man, and I became so inseparable from him, that the poor aunt herself was rather neglected, that is, I saw her less frequently; for in no moment of my life has my attachment to her been diminished.

This impossibility of dividing, in favor of my inclinations, the little time I had to myself, renewed more strongly than ever the desire I had long entertained of having but one home for Thérèsa and myself; but the embarrassment of her numerous family, and especially the want of money to purchase furniture, had hitherto withheld me from accomplishing it. An opportunity to endeavor at it presented itself, and of this I took advantage. M. de Francueil and Madam Dupin, clearly perceiving that eight or nine hundred livres a year were unequal to my wants, increased of their own accord, my salary to fifty guineas; and Madam Dupin, having heard I wished to furnish myself lodgings, assisted me with some articles for that purpose. With this furniture and that Thérèsa already had, we made one common stock, and, having an apartment in the Hôtel de Languedoc, Rue de

Grenelle St.-Honoré, kept by very honest people, we arranged ourselves in the best manner we could, and lived there peaceably and agreeably during seven years, at the end of which I removed to go and live at the Hermitage.

Thérèsa's father was a good old man, very mild in his disposition, and much afraid of his wife; for this reason he had given her the surname of Criminal-Lieutenant, which Grimm, jocosely, afterwards transferred to the daughter. Madam le Vasseur did not want sense, that is address; and pretended to the politeness and airs of the first circles; but she had a mysterious wheedling, which to me was insupportable, gave bad advice to her daughter, endeavored to make her dissemble with me, and separately, cajoled my friends at my expense, and that of each other; excepting these circumstances, she was a tolerably good mother, because she found her account in being so, and concealed the faults of her daughter to turn them to her own advantage. This woman, who had so much of my care and attention, to whom I made so many little presents, and by whom I had it extremely at heart to make myself beloved, was, from the impossibility of my succeeding in this wish, the only cause of the uneasiness I suffered in my little establishment. Except the effects of this cause I enjoyed, during these six or seven years, the most perfect domestic happiness of which human weakness is capable. The heart of my Thérèsa was that of an angel; our attachment increased with our intimacy, and we were more and more daily convinced how much we were made for each other. Could our pleasures be described, their simplicity would cause laughter. Our walks, *tête-à-tête,* on the outside of the city, where I magnificently spent eight or ten sols in each *guinguette.** Our little suppers at my window, seated opposite to each other upon two little chairs, placed upon a trunk, which filled up the space of the embrasure. In this situation the window served us as a table, we breathed the fresh air, enjoyed the prospect of the environs and the people who passed; and, although upon the fourth story, looked down into the street as we ate.

Who can describe, and how few can feel, the charms of these repasts, consisting of a quartern loaf, a few cherries, a morsel of cheese, and half-a-pint of wine which we drank between us? Friendship, confidence, intimacy, sweetness of disposition, how delicious are your reasonings! We sometimes remained in this situation until midnight, and never thought of the hour, unless informed of it by the old lady. But let us quit these details, which are either insipid or laughable; I have always said and felt that real enjoyment was not to be described.

Much about the same time I indulged in one not so delicate, and the last of the kind with which I have to reproach myself. I have observed that the minister Klüpffel was an amiable man; my connections with him were almost as intimate as those I had with Grimm, and in the end became as familiar; Grimm

* *Ale-house.*

and he sometimes ate at my apartment. These repasts, a little more than simple, were enlivened by the witty and extravagant wantonness of expression of Klüpffel, and the diverting Germanicisms of Grimm, who was not yet become a purist.

Sensuality did not preside at our little orgies, but joy, which was preferable, reigned in them all, and we enjoyed ourselves so well together that we knew not how to separate. Klüpffel had furnished a lodging for a little girl, who, notwithstanding this, was at the service of anybody, because he could not support her entirely himself. One evening as we were going into the coffee-house, we met him coming out to go and sup with her. We rallied him; he revenged himself gallantly, by inviting us to the same supper, and there rallying us in our turn. The poor young creature appeared to be of a good disposition, mild and little fitted to the way of life to which an old hag she had with her, prepared her in the best manner she could. Wine and conversation enlivened us to such a degree that we forgot ourselves. The amiable Klüpffel was unwilling to do the honors of his table by halves, and we all three successively took a view of the next chamber, in company with his little friend, who knew not whether she should laugh or cry. Grimm has always maintained that he never touched her; it was therefore to amuse himself with our impatience, that he remained so long in the other chamber, and if he abstained, there is not much probability of his having done so from scruple, because previous of his going to live with the Comte de Frièse, he lodged with girls of the town in the same quarter of St. Roch.

I left the Rue des Moineaux, where this girl lodged, as much ashamed as Saint-Preux left the house in which he had become intoxicated, and when I wrote his story I well remembered my own. Thérèsa perceived by some sign, and especially by my confusion, I had something with which I reproached myself; I relieved my mind by my free and immediate confession. I did well, for the next day Grimm came in triumph to relate to her my crime with aggravation, and since that time he has never failed maliciously to recall it to her recollection; in this he was the more culpable, since I had freely and voluntarily given him my confidence, and had a right to expect he would not make me repent of it. I never had a more convincing proof than on this occasion, of the goodness of my Thérèsa's heart; she was more shocked at the behavior of Grimm than at my infidelity, and I received nothing from her but tender reproaches, in which there was not the least appearance of anger.

The simplicity of mind of this excellent girl was equal to her goodness of heart; and this is saying everything: but one instance of it, which is present to my recollection, is worthy of being related. I had told her Klüpffel was a minister, and chaplain to the prince of Saxe-Gotha. A minister was to her so singular a man, that oddly confounding the most dissimilar ideas, she took it into her head to take Klüpffel for the pope. I thought her mad the first time she told me when I came in, that the pope had called to see me. I made her explain herself and lost not a moment in going to relate the story to Grimm and Klüpffel, who amongst ourselves never lost the name of pope. We gave to the girl in the Rue des Moineaux the name of Pope Joan. Our laughter was incessant; it almost stifled us. They, who in a letter which it hath pleased them to attribute to me, have made me say I never laughed but twice in my life, did not know me at this period, nor in my younger days; for if they had, the idea could never have entered into their heads.

The year following (1750), I learned that my discourse, of which I had not thought any more, gained the premium at Dijon. This news awakened all the ideas which had dictated it to me, gave them new animation, and completed the fermentation of my heart of that first leaven of heroism and virtue which my father, my country, and Plutarch had inspired in my infancy. Nothing now appeared great in my eyes but to be free and virtuous, superior to fortune and opinion, and independent of all exterior circumstance. Although a false shame, and the fear of disapprobation at first prevented me from conducting myself according to these principles, and from suddenly quarreling with the maxims of the age in which I lived, I from that moment took a decided resolution to do it.*

* *And of this I purposely delayed the execution, that irritated by contradiction, it might be rendered triumphant.*

[548]

While I was philosophizing upon the duties of man, an event happened which made me better reflect upon my own. Thérèsa became pregnant for the third time. Too sincere with myself, too haughty in my mind to contradict my principles by my actions, I began to examine the destination of my children, and my connections with the mother, according to the laws of nature, justice, and reason, and those of that religion, pure, holy, and eternal, like its author, which men have polluted while they pretended to purify it, and which by their formularies they have reduced to a religion of words, since the difficulty of prescribing impossibilities is but trifling to those by whom they are not practiced.

If I deceived myself in my conclusions, nothing can be more astonishing than the security with which I depended upon them. Were I one of those men unfortunately born deaf to the voice of nature, in whom no sentiment of justice or humanity ever took the least root, this obduracy would be natural. But that warmth of heart, strong sensibility, and facility of forming attachments; the force with which they subdue me; my cruel sufferings when obliged to break them; the innate benevolence I cherish towards my fellow-creatures; the ardent love I bear to great virtues, to truth and justice, the horror in which I hold evil of every kind; the impossibility of hating, of injuring or wishing to injure any one; the soft and lively emotion I feel at the sight of whatever is virtuous, generous and amiable; can these meet in the same mind with the depravity which without scruple treads under foot the most pleasing of all our duties? No, I feel, and openly declare this to be impossible. Never in his whole life could J. J. be a man without sentiment or an unnatural father. I may have been deceived, but it is impossible I should have lost the least of my feelings. Were I to give my reasons, I should say too much; since they have seduced me, they would seduce many others. I will not therefore expose those young persons by whom I may be read to the same danger. I will satisfy myself by observing that my error was such, that in abandoning my children to public education for want of the means of bringing them up myself; in destining them to become workmen and peasants, rather than adventurers and fortune-hunters, I thought I acted like an honest citizen, and a good father, and considered myself as a member of the republic of Plato. Since that time the regrets of my heart have more than once told me I was deceived; but my reason was so far from giving me the same intimation, that I have frequently returned thanks to Heaven for having by this means preserved them from the fate of their father, and that by which they were threatened the moment I should have been under the necessity of leaving them. Had I left them to Madam d'Epinay, or Madam de Luxembourg, who, from friendship, generosity, or some other motive, offered to take care of them in due time, would they have been more happy, better brought up, or honester men? To this I cannot answer; but I am certain they would have been taught to hate and perhaps betray their parents: it is much better that they have never known them.

My third child was therefore carried to the Foundling Hospital as well as the two former, and the next two were disposed of in the same manner; for I have had five children in all. This arrangement seemed to me to be so good, reasonable and lawful, that if I did not publicly boast of it, the motive by which I was withheld was merely my regard for their mother: but I mentioned it to all those to whom I had declared our connection, to Diderot, to Grimm, afterwards to M. d'Epinay, and after another interval, to Madam de Luxembourg; and this freely and voluntarily, without being under the least necessity of doing it, having it in my power to conceal the step from all the world: for La Gouin was an honest woman, very discreet, and a person on whom I had the greatest reliance. The only one of my friends to whom it was in some measure my interest to open myself, was Thierry the physician, who had the care of my poor aunt in one of her lyings in, in which she was very ill. In a word, there was no mystery in my conduct, not only on account of my never having concealed anything from my friends, but because I never found any harm in it. Everything considered, I chose the best destination for my children, or that which I thought to be such. I could have wished, and still should be glad, had I been brought up as they have been.

Whilst I was thus communicating what I had done,

Madam le Vasseur did the same thing amongst her acquaintance, but with less disinterested views. I introduced her and her daughter to Madam Dupin, who, from friendship to me, showed them the greatest kindness. The mother confided to her the secret of the daughter. Madam Dupin, who is generous and kind, and to whom she never told how attentive I was to her, notwithstanding my moderate resources, in providing for everything, provided on her part for what was necessary, with a liberality which, by order of her mother, the daughter concealed from me during my residence at Paris, nor ever mentioned it until we were at the Hermitage, when she informed me of it, after having disclosed to me several other secrets of her heart. I did not know Madam Dupin, who never took the least notice to me of the matter, was so well informed: I know not yet whether Madam de Chenonceaux, her daughter-in-law, was as much in the secret: but Madam de Francueil knew the whole and could not refrain from prattling. She spoke of it to me the following year, after I had left her house. This induced me to write her a letter upon the subject, which will be found in my collections, and wherein I gave such of my reasons as I could make public, without exposing Madam le Vasseur and her family; the most determinative of them came from that quarter, and these I kept profoundly secret.

I can rely upon the discretion of Madam Dupin, and the friendship of Madam de Chenonceaux; I had the same dependence upon that of Madam de Francueil, who, however, was long dead before my secret made its way into the world. This it could never have done except by means of the persons to whom I intrusted it, nor did it until after my rupture with them. By this single fact they are judged: without exculpating myself from the blame I deserve, I prefer it to that resulting from their malignity. My fault is great, but it was an error. I have neglected my duty, but the desire of doing an injury never entered my heart; and the feelings of a father were never more eloquent in favor of children whom he never saw. But betraying the confidence of friendship, violating the most sacred of all engagements, publishing secrets confided to us, and wantonly dishonoring the friend we have deceived, and who in detaching himself from our society still respects us, are not faults, but baseness of mind, and the last degree of heinousness.

I have promised my confession and not my justification; on which account I shall stop here. It is my duty faithfully to relate the truth, that of the reader to be just; more than this I never shall require of him.

The marriage of M. de Chenonceaux rendered his mother's house still more agreeable to me, by the wit and merit of the new bride, a very amiable young person, who seemed to distinguish me amongst the scribes of M. Dupin. She was the only daughter of the Viscomtesse de Rochechouart, a great friend of the Comte de Frièse, and consequently of Grimm's, who was very attentive to her. However, it was I who introduced him to her daughter; but their characters not suiting each other, this connection was not of long duration; and Grimm, who from that time aimed at what was solid, preferred the mother, a woman of the world, to the daughter who wished for steady friends, such as were agreeable to her, without troubling her head about the least intrigue, or making any interest amongst the great. Madam Dupin no longer finding in Madam de Chenonceaux all the docility she expected, made her house very disagreeable to her, and Madam de Chenonceaux, having a great opinion of her own merit, and, perhaps, of her birth, chose rather to give up the pleasures of society, and remain almost alone in her apartment, than to submit to a yoke she was not disposed to bear. This species of exile increased my attachment to her, by that natural inclination which excites me to approach the wretched. I found her mind metaphysical and reflective, although at times a little sophistical; her conversation, which was by no means that of a young woman coming from a convent, had for me the greatest attractions; yet she was not twenty years of age. Her complexion was seducingly fair; her figure would have been majestic had she held herself more upright. Her hair, which was fair, bordering upon ash color, and uncommonly beautiful, called to my recollection that of my poor mamma in the flower of her age, and strongly agitated my heart. But the severe principles I had just laid down for myself, by which at all events I was determined to be guided, secured me from the danger of her and her charms. During a whole summer I passed three or four hours a day in a *tête-à-tête* conversation with her, teaching her arithmetic, and fatiguing her with my innumerable ciphers, without uttering a single word of gallantry, or even once glancing my eyes upon her. Five or six years later I should not have had so much wisdom or folly; but it was decreed I was never to love but once in my life, and that another person was to have the first and last sighs of my heart.

Since I had lived in the house of Madam Dupin, I had always been satisfied with my situation, without showing the least sign of a desire to improve it. The addition which, in conjunction with M. de Francueil, she had made to my salary, was entirely of their own accord. This year M. de Francueil, whose friendship for me daily increased, had it in his thoughts to place me more at ease, and in a less precarious situation. He was Receiver-General of finance. M. Dudoyer, his cashkeeper, was old and rich, and wished to retire. M. de Francueil offered me this place, and to prepare myself for it, I went, during a few weeks, to M. Dudoyer, to take the necessary instructions. But whether my talents were ill-suited to the employment, or that Dudoyer, who I thought wished to procure his place for another, was not in earnest in the instructions he gave me, I acquired by slow degrees, and very imperfectly, the knowledge I was in want of, and could never understand the nature of accounts, rendered intricate, perhaps designedly. However, without having possessed myself of the whole scope of the business, I learned enough of the method to pursue it without the least difficulty; I even entered on my new office; I kept the cash-book and the cash; I paid and received money, took and gave receipts; and although this business was so ill suited to my inclinations as to my abilities, maturity of years beginning to render me sedate, I was determined to conquer my disgust, and entirely devote myself to my new employment.

Unfortunately for me, I had no sooner begun to proceed without difficulty, than M. de Francueil took a little journey, during which I remained intrusted with the cash, which, at that time, did not amount to more than twenty-five to thirty thousand francs. The anxiety of mind this sum of money occasioned me, made me perceive I was very unfit to be a cash-keeper, and I have no doubt but my uneasy situation, during his absence, contributed to the illness with which I was seized after his return.

I have observed in my first part that I was born in a dying state. A defect in the bladder caused me, during my early years, to suffer an almost continual retention of urine; and my aunt Suson, to whose care I was intrusted, had inconceivable difficulty in preserving me. However, she succeeded, and my robust constitution at length got the better of all my weakness, and my health became so well established that except the illness from languor, of which I have given an account, and frequent heats in the bladder which the least heating of the blood rendered troublesome, I arrived at the age of thirty almost without feeling my original infirmity. The first time this happened was upon my arrival at Venice. The fatigue of the voyage, and the extreme heat I had suffered, renewed the burnings, and gave me a pain in the loins, which continued until the beginning of winter. After having seen *padoana,* I thought myself near the end of my career, but I suffered not the least inconvenience. After exhausting my imagination more than my body for my Zulietta, I enjoyed better health than ever. It was not until after the imprisonment of Diderot that the heat of blood, brought on by my journeys to Vincennes during the terrible heat of that summer, gave me a violent nephritic colic, since which I have never recovered my primitive good state of health.

At the time of which I speak, having perhaps fatigued myself too much in the filthy work of the cursed receiver-general's office, I fell into a worse state than ever, and remained five or six weeks in my bed in the most melancholy state imaginable. Madam Dupin sent me the celebrated Morand who, notwithstanding his address and the delicacy of his touch, made me suffer the greatest torments. He advised me to have recourse to Daran, who managed to introduce his *bougies:* but Morand, when he gave Madam Dupin an account of the state I was in, declared to her I should not be alive in six months. This afterwards came to my ear, and made me reflect seriously on my situation and the folly of sacrificing the repose of the

few days I had to live to the slavery of an employment for which I felt nothing but disgust. Besides,
how was it possible to reconcile the severe principles
I had just adopted to a situation with which they had
so little relation? Should not I, the cash-keeper of a
receiver-general of finances, have preached poverty
and disinterestedness with a very ill grace? These
ideas fermented so powerfully in my mind with the
fever, and were so strongly impressed, that from that
time nothing could remove them; and, during my
convalescence, I confirmed myself with the greatest
coolness in the resolutions I had taken during my
delirium. I forever abandoned all projects of fortune
and advancement, resolved to pass in independence
and poverty the little time I had to exist. I made every
effort of which my mind was capable to break the fetters of prejudice, and courageously to do everything
that was right without giving myself the least concern about the judgment of others. The obstacles I
had to combat, and the efforts I made to triumph
over them, are inconceivable. I succeeded as much as
it was possible I should, and to a greater degree than
I myself had hoped for. Had I at the same time
shaken off the yoke of friendship as well as that of
prejudice, my design would have been accomplished,
perhaps the greatest, at least the most useful one to
virtue, that mortal ever conceived; but whilst I despised the foolish judgments of the vulgar tribe called
great and wise, I suffered myself to be influenced and
led by persons who called themselves my friends.

These, hurt at seeing me walk alone in a new path, while I seemed to take measures for my happiness, used all their endeavors to render me ridiculous, and that they might afterwards defame me, first strove to make me contemptible. It was less my literary fame than my personal reformation, of which I here state the period, that drew upon me their jealousy; they perhaps might have pardoned me for having distinguished myself in the art of writing; but they could never forgive my setting them, by my conduct, an example, which, in their eyes, seemed to reflect on themselves. I was born for friendship; my mind and easy disposition nourished it without difficulty. As long as I lived unknown to the public I was beloved by all my private acquaintance, and I had not a single enemy. But the moment I acquired literary fame, I had no longer a friend. This was a great misfortune; but a still greater was that of being surrounded by people who called themselves my friends, and used the rights attached to that sacred name to lead me on to destruction. The succeeding part of these memoirs will explain this odious conspiracy. I here speak of its origin, and the manner of the first intrigue will shortly appear.

In the independence in which I lived, it was, however, necessary to subsist. To this effect I thought of very simple means: which were copying music at so much a page. If any employment more solid would have fulfilled the same end I would have taken it up; but this occupation being to my taste, and the only one which, without personal attendance, could procure me daily bread, I adopted it. Thinking I had no longer need of foresight, and, stifling the vanity of cash-keeper to a financier, I made myself a copyist of music. I thought I had made an advantageous choice, and of this I so little repented, that I never quitted my new profession until I was forced to do it, after taking a fixed resolution to return to it as soon as possible.

The success of my first discourse rendered the execution of this resolution more easy. As soon as it had gained the premium, Diderot undertook to get it printed. Whilst I was in my bed, he wrote me a note informing me of the publication and effect: *"It is praised,"* said he, *"beyond the clouds; never was there an instance of a like success."*

This favor of the public, by no means solicited, and to an unknown author, gave me the first real assurance of my talents, of which, notwithstanding an internal sentiment, I had always had my doubts. I conceived the great advantage to be drawn from it in favor of the way of life I had determined to pursue; and was of opinion, that a copyist of some celebrity in the republic of letters was not likely to want employment.

The moment my resolution was confirmed, I wrote a note to M. de Francueil, communicating to him my intentions, thanking him and Madam Dupin for all goodness, and offering them my services in the way of my new profession. Francueil did not understand my note, and, thinking I was still in the delirium of fever, hastened to my apartment; but he found me so determined, that all he could say to me was without the least effect. He went to Madam Dupin, and told her and everybody he met, that I was become insane. I let him say what he pleased, and pursued the plan I had conceived. I began the change in my dress; I quitted laced cloaths and white stockings; I put on a round wig, laid aside my sword, and sold my watch; saying to myself, with inexpressible pleasure: "Thank Heaven! I shall no longer want to know the hour!" M. de Francueil had the goodness to wait a considerable time before he disposed of my place. At length, perceiving me inflexibly resolved, he gave it to M. d'Alibard, formerly tutor to the young Chenonceaux, and known as a botanist by his *Flora Parisiensis.**

However austere my sumptuary reform might be, I did not at first extend it to my linen, which was fine and in great quantity, the remainder of my stock when at Venice, and to which I was particularly attached. I had made it so much an object of cleanliness, that it became one of luxury, which was rather expensive. Some person, however, did me the favor to deliver me from this servitude. On Christmas Eve, whilst the women-folk were at vespers, and I was at the spiritual concert, the door of a garret, in which

* *I doubt not but these circumstances are now differently related by M. Francueil and his consorts; but I appeal to what he said of them at the time, and long afterwards, to everybody he knew, until the forming of the conspiracy, and of which, men of common sense and honor, must have preserved a remembrance.*

all our linen was hung up after being washed, was broken open. Everything was stolen; and amongst other things, forty-two of my shirts, of very fine linen, and which were the principal part of my stock. By the manner in which the neighbors described a man whom they had seen come out of the hotel with several parcels whilst we were all absent, Thèrésa and myself suspected her brother, whom we knew to be a worthless man. The mother strongly endeavored to remove this suspicion, but so many circumstances concurred to prove it to be well founded, that, notwithstanding all she could say, our opinions remained still the same: I dared not make a strict search for fear of finding more than I wished to do. The brother never returned to the place where I lived, and, at length, was no more heard of by any of us. I was much grieved Thérèsa and myself should be connected with such a family, and I exhorted her more than ever to shake off so dangerous a yoke. This adventure cured me of my inclination for fine linen, and since that time all I have had has been very common, and more suitable to the rest of my dress.

Having thus completed the change of that which related to my person, all my cares tended to render it solid and lasting, by striving to root out from my heart everything susceptible of receiving an impression from the judgment of men, or which, from the fear of blame, might turn me aside from anything good and reasonable in itself. In consequence of the success of my work, my resolution made some noise in the world also, and procured me employment; so that I began my new profession with great appearance of success. However, several causes prevented me from succeeding in it to the same degree I should under any other circumstances have done. In the first place my ill state of health. The attack I had just had, brought on consequences which prevented my ever being so well as I was before; and I am of opinion, the physicians, to whose care I intrusted myself, did me as much harm as my illness. I was successively under the hands of Morand, Daran, Helvétius, Malouin, and Thierry: men able in their profession, and all of them my friends, who treated me each according to his own manner, without giving me the least relief, and weakened me considerably. The more I submitted to their direction, the yellower, thinner, and weaker I became. My imagination, which they terrified, judging of my situation by the effect of their drugs, presented to me, on this side of the tomb, nothing but continued sufferings from the gravel, stone, and retention of urine. Everything which gave relief to others, ptisans, baths, and bleeding, increased my tortures. Perceiving the *bougies* of Daran, the only ones that had any favorable effect, and without which I thought I could no longer exist, to give me a momentary relief, I procured a prodigious number of them, that, in case of Daran's death, I might never be at a loss. During the eight or ten years in which I made such frequent use of these, they must, with what I had left, cost me fifty louis.

It will easily be judged, that such expensive and painful means did not permit me to work without interruption; and that a dying man is not ardently industrious in the business by which he gains his daily bread.

Literary occupations caused another interruption not less prejudicial to my daily employment. My discourse had no sooner appeared, than the defenders of letters fell upon me as if they had agreed with each to do it. My indignation was so raised at seeing so many blockheads, who did not understand the question, attempt to decide upon it imperiously, that in my answer I gave some of them the worſt of it. One M. Gautier, of Nancy, the firſt who fell under the lash of my pen, was very roughly treated in a letter to M. Grimm. The second was King Stanislaus, himself, who did not disdain to enter the lists with me. The honor he did me, obliged me to change my manner in combating his opinions; I made use of a graver ſtyle, but not less nervous; and without failing in respeċt to the author, I completely refuted his work. I knew a Jesuit, Father de Menou, had been concerned in it. I depended on my judgment to distinguish what was written by the prince, from the production of the monk, and falling without mercy upon all the Jesuitical phrases, I remarked, as I went along, an anachronism which I thought could come from nobody but the prieſt. This composition, which, for what reason I knew not, has been less spoken of than any of my other writings, is the only one of its kind.

I seized the opportunity which offered of showing to the public in what manner an individual may defend the cause of truth even against a sovereign. It is difficult to adopt a more dignified and respectful manner than that in which I answered him. I had the happiness to have to do with an adversary to whom, without adulation, I could show every mark of the esteem of which my heart was full; and this I did with success and a proper dignity. My friends, concerned for my safety, imagined they already saw me in the Bastile. This apprehension never once entered my head, and I was right in not being afraid. The good prince, after reading my answer, said: *"I have enough of it; I will not return to the charge."* I have, since that time, received from him different marks of esteem and benevolence, some of which I shall have occasion to speak of; and what I had written was read in France, and throughout Europe, without meeting the least censure.

In a little time I had another adversary whom I had not expected; this was the same M. Bordes, of Lyons, who ten years before had shown me much friendship, and from whom I had received several services. I had not forgotten him, but had neglected him from idleness, and had not sent him my writings for want of an opportunity, without seeking for it, to get them conveyed to his hands. I was therefore in the wrong, and he attacked me; this, however, he did politely, and I answered in the same manner. He replied more decidedly. This produced my last answer; after which I heard no more from him upon the subject; but he became my most violent enemy, took the advantage of the time of my misfortunes, to publish against me the most indecent libels, and made a journey to London on purpose to do me an injury.

All this controversy employed me a good deal, and caused me a great loss of my time in my copying, without much contributing to the progress of truth, or the good of my purse. Pissot, at that time my bookseller, gave me but little for my pamphlets, frequently nothing at all, and I never received a farthing for my first discourse. Diderot gave it him. I was obliged to wait a long time for the little he gave me, and to take it from him in the most trifling sums. Notwithstanding this, my copying went on but slowly. I had two things together upon my hands, which was the most likely means of doing them both ill.

They were very opposite to each other in their effects by the different manners of living to which they rendered me subject. The success of my first writings had given me celebrity. My new situation excited curiosity. Everybody wished to know that whimsical man who sought not the acquaintance of any one, and whose only desire was to live free and happy in the manner he had chosen; this was sufficient to make the thing impossible to me. My apartment was continually full of people, who, under different pretenses, came to take up my time. The women employed a thousand artifices to engage me to dinner. The more unpolite I was with people, the more ob-

stinate they became. I could not refuse everybody.
While I made myself a thousand enemies by my refusals, I was incessantly a slave to my complaisance,
and, in whatever manner I made my engagements,
I had not an hour in a day to myself.

I then perceived it was not so easy to be poor and
independent, as I had imagined. I wished to live by
my profession: the public would not suffer me to do
it. A thousand means were thought of to indemnify
me for the time I lost. The next thing would have
been showing myself like Punch, at so much each person. I knew no dependence more cruel and degrading
than this. I saw no other method of putting an end
to it than refusing all kinds of presents, great and
small, let them come from whom they would. This
had no other effect than to increase the number of
givers, who wished to have the honor of overcoming
my resistance, and to force me, in spite of myself, to
be under an obligation to them. Many who would not
have given me half-a-crown had I asked it for them,
incessantly importuned me with their offers, and, in
revenge for my refusal, taxed me with arrogance and
ostentation.

It will naturally be conceived that the resolution
I had taken, and the system I wished to follow, were
not agreeable to Madam le Vasseur. All the disinterestedness of the daughter did not prevent her from
following the directions of her mother; and the *governesses,* as Gauffecourt called them, were not always
so steady in their refusals as I was. Although many

things were concealed from me, I perceived so many as were necessary to enable me to judge that I did not see all, and this tormented me less by the accusation of connivance, which it was so easy for me to foresee, than by the cruel idea of never being master in my own apartments, nor even of my own person. I prayed, conjured, and became angry, all to no purpose; the mother made me pass for an eternal grumbler, and a man who was peevish and ungovernable. She held perpetual whisperings with my friends; everything in my little family was mysterious and a secret to me; and, that I might not incessantly expose myself to noisy quarreling, I no longer dared to take notice of what passed in it. A firmness of which I was not capable, would have been necessary to withdraw me from this domestic strife. I knew how to complain, but not how to act: they suffered me to say what I pleased, and continued to act as they thought proper.

This constant teasing, and the daily importunities to which I was subject, rendered the house, and my residence at Paris, disagreeable to me. When my indisposition permitted me to go out, and I did not suffer myself to be led by my acquaintance first to one place and then to another, I took a walk, alone, and reflected on my grand system, something of which I committed to paper, bound up between two covers, which, with a pencil, I always had in my pocket. In this manner, the unforeseen disagreeableness of a situation I had chosen entirely led me back to literature, to which unsuspectedly I had recourse as a means of relieving my mind, and thus, in the first works I wrote, I introduced the peevishness and ill-humor which were the cause of my undertaking them. There was another circumstance which contributed not a little to this: thrown into the world in despite of myself, without having the manners of it, or being in a situation to adopt and conform myself to them, I took it into my head to adopt others of my own, to enable me to dispense with those of society. My foolish timidity, which I could not conquer, having for principle the fear of being wanting in the common forms, I took, by way of encouraging myself, a resolution to tread them under foot. I became sour and a cynic from shame, and affected to despise the politeness which I knew not how to practice. This austerity, conformable to my new principles, I must confess, seemed to ennoble itself in my mind; it assumed in my eyes the form of the intrepidity of virtue, and I dare assert it to be upon this noble basis, that it supported itself longer and better than could have been expected from anything so contrary to my nature. Yet, notwithstanding, I had the name of a misanthrope, which my exterior appearance and some happy expressions had given me in the world: it is certain I did not support the character well in private, that my friends and acquaintance led this untractable bear about like a lamb, and that, confining my sarcasms to severe but general truths, I was never capable of saying an uncivil thing to any person whatsoever.

The *Devin du Village* brought me completely into vogue, and presently after there was not a man in Paris whose company was more sought after than mine. The history of this piece, which is a kind of era in my life, is joined with that of the connections I had at that time. I must enter a little into particulars to make what is to follow the better understood.

I had a numerous acquaintance, yet no more than two friends: Diderot and Grimm. By an effect of the desire I have ever felt to unite everything that is dear to me, I was too much a friend to both not to make them shortly become so to each other. I connected them: they agreed well together, and shortly became more intimate with each other than with me. Diderot had a numerous acquaintance, but Grimm, a stranger and a new-comer, had his to procure, and with the greatest pleasure I procured him all I could. I had already given him Diderot. I afterwards brought him acquainted with Gauffecourt. I introduced him to Madam Chenonceaux, Madam D'Epinay, and the Baron d'Holbach; with whom I had become connected almost in spite of myself. All my friends became his: this was natural: but not one of his ever became mine; which was inclining to the contrary. Whilst he yet lodged at the house of the Comte de Frièse, he frequently gave us dinners in his apartment, but I never received the least mark of friendship from the Comte de Frièse, Comte de Schomberg, his relation, very familiar with Grimm, nor from any other person, man or woman, with whom Grimm, by their means, had any connection. I except the Abbé Raynal, who, although his friend, gave proofs of his being mine; and, in cases of need, offered me his purse with a generosity not very common. But I knew the Abbé Raynal long before Grimm had any acquaintance with him, and had entertained a great regard for him on account of his delicate and honorable behavior to me upon a slight occasion, which I shall never forget.

The Abbé Raynal is certainly a warm friend; of this I saw a proof, much about the time of which I speak, with respect to Grimm himself, with whom he was very intimate. Grimm, after having been some time on a footing of friendship with Mademoiselle Fel, fell violently in love with her, and wished to supplant Cahusac. The young lady, piquing herself on her constancy, refused her new admirer. He took this so much to heart, that the appearances of his affliction became tragical. He suddenly fell into the strangest state imaginable. He passed days and nights in a continued lethargy. He lay with his eyes open; and although his pulse continued to beat regularly, without speaking, eating, or stirring, yet sometimes seeming to hear what was said to him, but never answering, not even by a sign, and remaining almost as immovable as if he had been dead, yet without agitation, pain, or fever. The Abbé Raynal and myself watched over him; the abbé, more robust, and in better health than I was, by night, and I by day, without ever both being absent at one time. The Comte de Frièse was alarmed, and brought to him Senac, who, after having examined the state in which he was, said there was nothing to apprehend, and took his leave without giving a prescription. My fears for my friend made me carefully observe the countenance of the physician, and I perceived him smile as he went away. However, the patient remained several days almost motionless, without taking anything except a few preserved cherries, which from time to time I put upon his tongue, and which he swallowed without difficulty. At length he, one morning, rose, dressed himself, and returned to his usual way of life, without either at that time or afterwards speaking to me or the Abbé Raynal, at least that I know of, or to any other person, of this singular lethargy, or the care we had taken of him during the time it lasted.

The affair made a noise, and it would really have been a wonderful circumstance had the cruelty of an opera girl made a man die of despair. This strong passion brought Grimm into vogue; he was soon considered as a prodigy in love, friendship, and attachments of every kind. Such an opinion made his company sought after, and procured him a good reception in the first circles; by which means he separated from me, with whom he was never inclined to associate when he could do it with anybody else. I perceived him to be on the point of breaking with me entirely; for the lively and ardent sentiments, of which he made a parade, were those which, with less noise and pretension, I had really conceived for him. I was glad he succeeded in the world; but I did not wish him to do this by forgetting his friend. I one day said to him: "Grimm, you neglect me, and I forgive you for it. When the first intoxication of your success is over, and you begin to perceive a void in your enjoyments, I hope you will return to your friend, whom you will always find in the same sentiments: at present do not constrain yourself, I leave you at liberty to act as you please, and wait your leisure." He said I was right, made his arrangements in consequence, and shook off all restraint, so that I saw no more of him except in company with our common friends.

Our chief rendezvous, before he was connected with Madam d'Epinay as he afterwards became, was at the house of Baron d'Holbach. This said baron was the son of a man who had raised himself from obscurity. His fortune was considerable, and he used it nobly, receiving at his house men of letters and merit: and, by the knowledge he himself had acquired, was very worthy of holding a place amongst them. Having been long attached to Diderot, he endeavored to become acquainted with me by his means, even before my name was known to the world. A natural repugnancy prevented me a long time from answering his advances. One day, when he asked me the reason of my unwillingness, I told him he was too rich. He was, however, resolved to carry his point, and at length succeeded. My greatest misfortune proceeded from my being unable to resist the force of marked attention. I have ever had reason to repent of having yielded to it.

Another acquaintance which, as soon as I had any pretensions to it, was converted into friendship, was that of M. Duclos. I had several years before seen him, for the first time, at the Chevrette, at the house of Madam d'Epinay, with whom he was upon very good terms. On that day we only dined together, and he returned to town in the afternoon. But we had a conversation of a few moments after dinner. Madam d'Epinay had mentioned me to him, and my opera of the *Muses Gallantes*. Duclos, endowed with too great talents not to be a friend to those in whom the like were found, was prepossessed in my favor, and invited me to go and see him. Notwithstanding my former wish, increased by an acquaintance, I was withheld by my timidity and indolence, as long as I had no other passport to him than his complaisance. But encouraged by my first success, and by his eulogiums, which reached my ears, I went to see him; he returned my visit, and thus began the connection, between us, which will ever render him dear to me. By him, as well as from the testimony of my own heart, I learned that uprightness and probity may sometimes be connected with the cultivation of letters.

Many other connections less solid, and which I shall not here particularize, were the effects of my first success, and lasted until curiosity was satisfied. I was a man so easily known, that on the next day nothing new was to be discovered in me. However, a woman, who at that time was desirous of my acquaintance, became much more solidly attached to me than any of those whose curiosity I had excited: this was the Marchioness of Crequi, niece to M. le Bailli de Froulay, ambassador from Malta, whose brother had preceded M. de Montaigu in the embassay to Venice, and whom I had gone to see on my return from that city. Madam de Crequi wrote to me: I visited her: she received me into her friendship. I sometimes dined with her. I met at her table several men of letters, amongst others M. Saurin, the author of Spartacus, Barnevelt, etc., since become my implacable enemy; for no other reason, at least that I can imagine, than my bearing the name of a man whom his father has cruelly persecuted.

It will appear that for a copyist, who ought to be employed in his business from morning till night, I had many interruptions, which rendered my days not very lucrative, and prevented me from being sufficiently attentive to what I did to do it well; for which reason, half the time I had to myself was lost in erasing errors or beginning my sheet anew. This daily importunity rendered Paris more unsupportable, and made me ardently wish to be in the country. I several times went to pass a few days at Marcoussis, the vicar of which was known to Madam le Vasseur, and with whom we all arranged ourselves in such a manner as not to make things disagreeable to him. Grimm once went thither with us.* The vicar had a tolerable voice,

---

* Since I have neglected to relate here a trifling, but memorable adventure I had with the said Grimm one day, on which we were to dine at the fountain of St. Vandrille, I will let it pass: but when I thought of it afterwards, I concluded that he was brooding in his

sung well, and, although he did not read music, learned his part with great facility and precision. We passed our time in singing the trios I had composed at Chenonceaux. To these I added two or three new ones, to the words Grimm and the vicar wrote, well or ill. I cannot refrain from regretting these trios composed and sung in moments of pure joy, and which I left at Wootton, with all my music. Mademoiselle Davenport has perhaps curled her hair with them; but they are worthy of being preserved, and are, for the most part, of very good counterpoint. It was after one of these little excursions in which I had the pleasure of seeing the aunt at her ease and very cheerful, and in which my spirits were much enlivened, that I wrote to the vicar very rapidly and very ill, an epistle in verse which will be found amongst my papers.

I had nearer to Paris another station much to my liking with M. Mussard, my countryman, relation, and friend, who at Passy had made himself a charming retreat, where I have passed some very peaceful moments. M. Mussard was a jeweler, a man of good sense, who, after having acquired a genteel fortune, had given his only daughter in marriage to M. de Valmalette, the son of an exchange broker, and maître d'hotel to the king, took the wise resolution to quit business in his declining years, and to place an interval of repose and enjoyment between the hurry and the end of life. The good man Mussard, a real phi-

heart the conspiracy he has, with so much success, since carried into execution.

losopher in practice, lived without care, in a very pleasant house which he himself had built in a very pretty garden, laid out with his own hands. In digging the terraces of this garden he found fossil shells, and in such great quantities that his lively imagination saw nothing but shells in nature. He really thought the universe was composed of shells and the remains of shells, and that the whole earth was only the sand of these in different stratæ. His attention thus constantly engaged with his singular discoveries, his imagination became so heated with the ideas they gave him, that, in his head, they would soon have been converted into a system, that is into folly, if, happily for his reason, but unfortunately for his friends, to whom he was dear, and to whom his house was an agreeable asylum, a most cruel and extraordinary disease had not put an end to his existence. A constantly increasing tumor in his stomach prevented him from eating, long before the cause of it was discovered, and, after several years of suffering, absolutely occasioned him to die of hunger. I can never, without the greatest affliction of mind, call to my recollection the last moments of this worthy man, who still received with so much pleasure, Leneips and myself, the only friends whom the sight of his sufferings did not separate from him until his last hour, when he was reduced to devouring with his eyes the repasts he had placed before us, scarcely having the power of swallowing a few drops of weak tea, which came up again a moment afterwards. But before these days of sorrow, how many have I passed at his house, with the chosen friends he had made himself! At the head of the list I place the Abbé Prévot, a very amiable man, and very sincere, whose heart vivified his writings, worthy of immortality, and who, neither in his disposition nor in society, had the least of the melancholy coloring he gave to his works: Procope, the physician, a little Æsop, a favorite with the ladies; Boulanger, the celebrated posthumous author of *Despotisme Oriental*, and who, I am of opinion, extended the systems of Mussard on the duration of the world. The female part of his friends consisted of Madam Denis, niece to Voltaire, who, at that time, was nothing more than a good kind of woman, and pretended not to wit: Madam Vanloo, certainly not handsome, but charming, and who sang like an angel: Madam de Valmalette, herself, who sang also, and who, although very thin, would have been very amiable had she had fewer pretensions. Such, or very nearly such, was the society of M. Mussard, with which I should have been much pleased, had not his *conchyliomania* more engaged my attention; and I can say, with great truth, that, for upwards of six months, I worked with him in his cabinet with as much pleasure as he felt himself.

He had long insisted upon the virtue of the waters of Passy, that they were proper in my case, and recommended me to come to his house to drink them. To withdraw myself from the tumult of the city, I at length consented, and went to pass eight or ten days at Passy, which, on account of my being in the country, were of more service to me than the waters I drank during my stay there. Mussard played the violoncello, and was passionately fond of Italian music. This was the subject of a long conversation we had one evening after supper, particularly the *opere-buffe* we had both seen in Italy, and with which we were highly delighted. My sleep having forsaken me in the night, I considered in what manner it would be possible to give in France an idea of this kind of drama. The *Amours de Ragonde* did not in the least resemble it. In the morning, whilst I took my walk and drank the waters, I hastily threw together a few couplets to which I adapted such airs as occurred to me at the moments. I scribbled over what I had composed, in a kind of vaulted saloon at the end of the garden, and at tea. I could not refrain from showing the airs to Mussard and to Mademoiselle du Vernois, his *gouvernante,* who was a very good and amiable girl. Three pieces of composition I had sketched out were the first monologue: *J'ai perdu mon serviteur;* the air of the *Devin; L'amour croit s'il s'inquiète;* and the last duo: *A jamais, Colin, je t'engage,* etc. I was so far from thinking it worth while to continue what I had begun, that, had it not been for the applause and encouragement I received from both Mussard and Mademoiselle, I should have thrown my papers into the fire and thought no more of their contents, as I had frequently done by things of much the same merit; but I was so animated by the encomiums I received, that in six days, my drama, excepting a few couplets, was written. The music also was so far sketched out, that all I had further to do to it, after my return from Paris, was to compose a little of the recitative, and to add the middle parts, the whole of which I finished with so much rapidity, that in three weeks my work was ready for representation. The only thing now wanting, was the *divertissement,* which was not composed until a long time afterwards.

My imagination was so warmed by the composition of this work that I had the strongest desire to hear it performed, and would have given anything to have seen and heard the whole in the manner I should have chosen, which would have been that of Lully, who is said to have had *Armide* performed for himself only. As it was not possible I should hear the performance unaccompanied by the public, I could not see the effect of my piece without getting it received at the opera. Unfortunately it was quite a new species of composition, to which the ears of the public were not accustomed; and besides the ill success of the *Muses Gallantes* gave too much reason to fear for the *Devin,* if I presented it in my own name. Duclos relieved me from this difficulty, and engaged to get the piece rehearsed without mentioning the author. That I might not discover myself, I did not go to the rehearsal, and the *Petits violons,** by whom it was directed, knew not who the author was until after a general plaudit had borne the testimony of the work.

* *Rebel and Francœur, who, when they were very young, went together from house to house playing on the violin, were so called.*

Everybody present was so delighted with it, that, on the next day, nothing else was spoken of in the different companies. M. de Cury, *Intendant des Menus*, who was present at the rehearsal, demanded the piece to have it performed at court. Duclos, who knew my intentions, and thought I should be less master of my work at the court than at Paris, refused to give it. Cury claimed it authoritatively. Duclos persisted in his refusal, and the dispute between them was carried to such a length, that one day they would have left the opera-house together to fight a duel, had they not been separated. M. de Cury applied to me, and I referred him to Duclos. This made it necessary to return to the latter. The Duke d'Aumont interfered; and at length Duclos thought proper to yield to authority, and the piece was given to be played at Fontainebleau.

The part to which I had been most attentive, and in which I had kept at the greatest distance from the common track, was the recitative. Mine was accented in a manner entirely new, and accompanied the utterance of the word. The directors dared not suffer this horrid innovation to pass, lest it should shock the ears of persons who never judge for themselves. Another recitative was proposed by Francueil and Jelyotte, to which I consented; but refused at the same time to have anything to do with it myself.

When everything was ready and the day of performance fixed, a proposition was made me to go to Fontainebleau, that I might at least be at the last rehearsal. I went with Mademoiselle Fel, Grimm, and

I think the Abbé Raynal, in one of the stages to the court. The rehearsal was tolerable: I was more satisfied with it than I expected to have been. The orchestra was numerous, composed of the orchestras of the opera and the king's band. Jelyotte played *Colin,* Mademoiselle Fel, *Colette,* Cuvillier the *Devin:* the choruses were those of the opera. I said but little; Jelyotte had prepared everything; I was unwilling either to approve of or censure what he had done; and notwithstanding I had assumed the air of an old Roman, I was, in the midst of so many people, as bashful as a schoolboy.

The next morning, the day of performance, I went to breakfast at the coffee-house *du Grand Commun,* where I found a great number of people. The rehearsal of the preceding evening, and the difficulty of getting into the theater, were the subjects of conversation. An officer present said he entered with the greatest ease, gave a long account of what had passed, described the author, and related what he had said and done; but what astonished me most in this long narrative given with as much assurance as simplicity, was that it did not contain a syllable of truth. It was clear to me that he who spoke so positively of the rehearsal had not been at it, because, without knowing him, he had before his eyes that author whom he said he had seen and examined so minutely. However, what was more singular still in this scene, was its effect upon me. The officer was a man rather in years; he had nothing of the appearance of a coxcomb; his features appeared to announce a man of merit; and his cross of Saint Louis an officer of long standing. He interested me, notwithstanding his impudence. Whilst he uttered his lies, I blushed, looked down, and was upon thorns; I, for some time, endeavored within myself to find the means of believing him to be in an involuntary error. At length, trembling lest some person should know me, and by this means confound him, I hastily drank my chocolate, without saying a word, and, holding down my head, I passed before him, got out of the coffee-house as soon as possible, whilst the company were making their remarks upon the relation that had been given. I was no sooner in the street than I was in a perspiration, and had anybody known and named me before I left the room, I am certain all the shame and embarrassment of a guilty person would have appeared in my countenance, proceeding from what I felt the poor man would have had to have suffered had his lie been discovered.

I come to one of the critical moments of my life, in which it is difficult to do anything more than to relate, because it is almost impossible that even narrative should not carry with it the marks of censure or apology. I will, however, endeavor to relate how and upon what motives I acted, without adding either approbation or censure.

I was on that day in the same careless undress as usual; with a long beard and wig badly combed. Considering this want of decency as an act of courage, I entered the theater wherein the king, queen, the royal family, and the whole court were to enter immediately after. I was conducted to a box by M. de Cury, and which belonged to him. It was very spacious, upon the stage and opposite to a lesser, but more elevated one, in which the king sat with Madam de Pompadour. As I was surrounded by women, and the only man in front of the box, I had no doubt of my having been placed there purposely to be exposed to view. As soon as the theater was lighted up, finding I was in the midst of people all extremely well dressed, I began to be less at my ease, and asked myself if I was in my place? whether or not I was properly dressed? After a few minutes of inquietude: "Yes," replied I, with an intrepidity which perhaps proceeded more from the impossibility of retracting than the force of all my reasoning, "I am in my place, because I am going to see my own piece performed to which I have been invited, for which reason only I am come here; and after all, no person has a greater right than I have to reap the fruit of my labor and talents; I am dressed as usual, neither better nor worse; and if I once begin to subject myself to public opinion, I shall shortly become a slave to it in everything. To be always consistent with myself, I ought not to blush, in any place whatever, at being dressed in a manner suitable to the state I have chosen. My exterior appearance is simple, but neither dirty nor slovenly; nor is a beard either of these in itself, because it is given us by nature, and according to time, place and custom, is sometimes an ornament. People think I am ridiculous, nay, even absurd; but what signifies this to me? I ought to know how to bear censure and ridicule, provided I do not deserve them." After this little soliloquy I became so firm that, had it been necessary, I could have been intrepid. But whether it was the effect of the presence of his majesty, or the natural disposition of those about me, I perceived nothing but what was civil and obliging in the curiosity of which I was the object. This so much affected me that I began to be uneasy for myself, and the fate of my piece; fearing I should efface the favorable prejudices which seemed to lead to nothing but applause. I was armed against raillery; but, so far overcome by the flattering and obliging treatment I had not expected, that I trembled like a child when the performance was begun.

I had soon sufficient reason to be encouraged. The piece was very ill played with respect to the actors, but the musical part was well sung and executed. During the first scene, which was really of a delightful simplicity, I heard in the boxes a murmur of surprise and applause, which, relative to pieces of the same kind, had never yet happened. The fermentation was soon increased to such a degree as to be perceptible through the whole audience, and of which, to speak after the manner of Montesquieu, the effect was augmented by itself. In the scene between the two good little folks, this effect was complete. There is no clapping of hands before the king; therefore everything was heard, which was advantageous to the author and the piece. I heard about me a whispering of women, who appeared as beautiful as angels. They said to each other in a low voice: "This is charming: That is ravishing: There is not a sound which does not go to the heart." The pleasure of giving this emotion to so many amiable persons moved me to tears; and these I could not contain in the first duo, when I remarked that I was not the only person who wept. I collected myself for a moment, on recollecting the concert of M. de Treytorens. This reminiscence had the effect of the slave who held the crown over the head of the general who triumphed, but my reflection was short, and I soon abandoned myself without interruption to the pleasure of enjoying my success. However, I am certain the voluptuousness of the sex was more predominant than the vanity of the author, and had none but men been present, I certainly should not have had the incessant desire I felt of catching on my lips the delicious tears I had caused to flow. I have known pieces excite more lively admiration, but I never saw so complete, delightful, and affecting an intoxication of the senses reign, during a whole representation, especially at court, and at a first performance. They who saw this must recollect it, for it has never yet been equaled.

The same evening the Duke d'Aumont sent to desire me to be at the palace the next day at eleven o'clock, when he would present me to the king. M. de Cury, who delivered me the message, added that he thought a pension was intended, and that his majesty wished to announce it to me himself. Will it be believed that the night of so brilliant a day was for me a night of anguish and perplexity? My first idea, after that of being presented, was that of my frequently wanting to retire; this had made me suffer very considerably at the theater, and might torment me the next day when I should be in the gallery, or in the king's apartment, amongst all the great, waiting for the passing of his majesty. My infirmity was the principal cause which prevented me from mixing in polite companies, and enjoying the conversation of the fair. The idea alone of the situation in which this want might place me, was sufficient to produce it to such a degree as to make me faint away, or to recur to means to which, in my opinion, death was much preferable. None but persons who are acquainted with this situation can judge of the horror which being exposed to the risk of it inspires.

I then supposed myself before the king, presented to his majesty, who deigned to stop and speak to me. In this situation, justness of expression and presence of mind were peculiarly necessary in answering. Would my timidity, which disconcerts me in presence of any stranger whatever, have been shaken off in presence of the King of France; or would it have suffered me instantly to make choice of proper expressions? I wished, without laying aside the austere manner I had adopted, to show myself sensible of the honor done me by so great a monarch, and in a handsome and merited eulogium to convey some great and useful truth. I could not prepare a suitable answer without exactly knowing what his majesty was to say to me;

and had this been the case, I was certain that, in his presence, I should not recollect a word of what I had previously meditated. "What," said I, "will become of me in this moment, and before the whole court, if, in my confusion, any of my stupid expressions should escape me?" This danger alarmed and terrified me. I trembled to such a degree that at all events I was determined not to expose myself to it.

I lost, it is true, the pension which in some measure was offered me; but I at the same time exempted myself from the yoke it would have imposed. Adieu, truth, liberty, and courage! How should I afterwards have dared to speak of disinterestedness and independence? Had I received the pension I must either have become a flatterer or remained silent; and moreover, who would have insured to me the payment of it! What steps should I have been under the necessity of taking! How many people must I have solicited! I should have had more trouble and anxious cares in preserving than in doing without it. Therefore, I thought I acted according to my principles by refusing, and sacrificing appearances to reality. I communicated my resolution to Grimm, who said nothing against it. To others I alleged my ill state of health, and left the court in the morning.

My departure made some noise, and was generally condemned. My reasons could not be known to everybody, it was therefore easy to accuse me of foolish pride, and thus not irritate the jealousy of such as felt they would not have acted as I had done. The next day Jelyotte wrote me a note, in which he stated the success of my piece, and the pleasure it had afforded the king. "All day long," said he, "his majesty sings, with the worst voice in his kingdom: *J'ai perdu mon serviteur: j'ai perdu tout mon bonheur.*" He likewise added, that in a fortnight the *Devin* was to be performed a second time; which confirmed in the eyes of the public the complete success of the first.

Two days afterwards, about nine o'clock in the evening, as I was going to sup with Madam d'Epinay, I perceived a hackney-coach pass by the door. Somebody within made a sign to me to approach. I did so, and got into it, and found the person to be Diderot. He spoke of the pension with more warmth than, upon such a subject, I should have expected from a philosopher. He did not blame me for having been unwilling to be presented to the king, but severely reproached me with my indifference about the pension. He observed that although on my own account I might be disinterested, I ought not to be so on that of Madam Vasseur and her daughter; that it was my duty to seize every means of providing for their subsistence; and that as, after all, it could not be said I had refused the pension, he maintained I ought, since the king seemed disposed to grant it to me, to solicit and obtain it by one means or another. Although I was obliged to him for his good wishes, I could not relish his maxims, which produced a warm dispute, the first I ever had with him. All our disputes were of this kind, he prescribing to me what he pretended I ought to do, and I defending myself because I was of a different opinion.

It was late when we parted. I would have taken him to supper at Madam d'Epinay's, but he refused to go; and, notwithstanding all the efforts which at different times the desire of uniting those I love induced me to make, to prevail upon him to see her, even that of conducting her to his door which he kept shut against us, he constantly refused to do it, and never spoke of her but with the utmost contempt. It was not until after I had quarreled with both that they became acquainted and that he began to speak honorably of her.

From this time Diderot and Grimm seemed to have undertaken to alienate from me the governesses, by giving them to understand that if they were not in easy circumstances the fault was my own, and that they never would be so with me. They endeavored to prevail on them to leave me, promising them the privilege for retailing salt, a snuff shop, and I know not what other advantages by means of the influence of Madam d'Epinay. They likewise wished to gain over Duclos and d'Holbach, but the former constantly refused their proposals. I had at the time some intimation of what was going forward, but I was not fully acquainted with the whole until long afterwards; and I frequently had reason to lament the effects of the blind and indiscreet zeal of my friends, who, in my ill state of health, striving to reduce me to the most melancholy solitude, endeavored, as they imagined, to render me happy by the means which, of all others, were the most proper to make me miserable.

In the carnival following the conclusion of the year 1753, the *Devin* was performed at Paris, and in this interval I had sufficient time to compose the overture and *divertissement*. This *divertissement,* such as it stands engraved, was to be in action from the beginning to the end, and in a continued subject, which in my opinion, afforded very agreeable representations. But when I proposed this idea at the opera-house, nobody would so much as hearken to me, and I was obliged to tack together music and dances in the usual manner: on this account the *divertissement,* although full of charming ideas which do not diminish the beauty of scenes, succeeded but very middlingly. I suppressed the recitative of Jelyotte, and substituted my own, such as I had first composed it, and as it is now engraved; and this recitative a little after the French manner, I confess, drawled out, instead of pronounced by the actors, far from shocking the ears of any person, equally succeeded with the airs, and seemed in the judgment of the public to possess as much musical merit. I dedicated my piece to Duclos, who had given it his protection, and declared it should be my only dedication. I have, however, with his consent, written a second; but he must have thought himself more honored by the exception, than if I had not written a dedication to any person.

I could relate many anecdotes concerning this piece, but things of greater importance prevent me from entering into a detail of them at present. I shall perhaps resume the subject in a supplement. There is however one which I cannot omit, as it relates to the greater part of what is to follow. I one day examined the music of d'Holbach, in his closet. After having looked over many different kinds, he said, showing me a collection of pieces for the harpsichord: "These were composed for me; they are full of taste and harmony, and unknown to everybody but myself. You ought to make a selection from them for your *divertissement*." Having in my head more subjects of airs and symphonies than I could make use of, I was not the least anxious to have any of his. However, he pressed me so much, that, from a motive of complaisance, I chose a Pastoral, which I abridged and converted into a trio, for the entry of the companions of *Colette*. Some months afterwards, and whilst the *Devin* still continued to be performed, going into Grimm's I found several people about his harpsichord, whence he hastily rose on my arrival. As I accidentally looked towards his music stand, I there saw the same collection of the Baron d'Holbach, opened precisely at the piece he had prevailed upon me to take, assuring me at the same time that it should never go out of his hands. Some time afterwards, I again saw the collection open on the harpsichord of M. d'Epinay, one day when he gave a little concert. Neither Grimm, nor anybody else, ever spoke to me of the air, and my reason for mentioning it here is that some time afterwards, a rumor was spread that I was not the author of *Devin*. As I never made a great progress in the practical part, I am persuaded that had it not been for my dictionary of music, it would in the end have been said I did not understand composition.*

Sometime before the *Devin du Village* was performed, a company of Italian *Bouffons* had arrived at Paris, and were ordered to perform at the opera-house, without the effect they would produce there being foreseen. Although they were detestable, and the orchestra, at that time very ignorant, mutilated at will the pieces they gave, they did the French opera an injury that will never be repaired. The comparison of these two kinds of music, heard the same evening in the same theater, opened the ears of the French; nobody could endure their languid music after the marked and lively accents of Italian composition; and the moment the *Bouffons* had done, everybody went away. The managers were obliged to change the order of representation, and let the performance of the *Bouffons* be the last. *Egle, Pigmalion* and *le Sylphe* were successively given: nothing could bear the comparison. The *Devin du Village* was the only piece that did it, and this was still relished after *la Serva Padrona*. When I composed my interlude, my head was filled with these pieces, and they gave me the first idea of it: I was, however, far from imagining they would one day be passed in review by the side of my composition. Had I been a plagiarist, how many pilferings would

* *I little suspected this would be said of me, notwithstanding my dictionary.*

have been manifest, and what care would have been taken to point them out to the public! But I had done nothing of the kind. All attempts to discover any such thing were fruitless: nothing was found in my music which led to the recollection of that of any other person; and my whole composition compared with the pretended original, was found to be as new as the musical characters I had invented. Had Mondonville or Rameau undergone the same ordeal, they would have lost much of their substance.

The *Bouffons* acquired for Italian music very warm partisans. All Paris was divided into two parties, the violence of which was greater than if an affair of state or religion had been in question. One of them, the most powerful and numerous, composed of the great, of men of fortune, and the ladies, supported French music; the other, more lively and haughty, and fuller of enthusiasm, was composed of real connoisseurs, and men of talents and genius. This little group assembled at the opera-house, under the box belonging to the queen. The other party filled up the rest of the pit and the theater; but the heads were mostly assembled under the box of his majesty. Hence the party names of *Coin du Roi, Coin de la Reine*,* then in great celebrity. The dispute, as it became more animated, produced several pamphlets. The king's corner aimed at pleasantry; it was laughed at by the *Petit Prophète*. It attempted to reason; the *Lettre sur la Musique Française* refuted its reasoning. These two little pro-

* *King's corner,—Queen's corner.*

ductions, the former of which was by Grimm, the latter by myself, are the only ones which have outlived the quarrel; all the rest are long since forgotten.

But the *Petit Prophète,* which, notwithstanding all I could say, was for a long time attributed to me, was considered as a pleasantry, and did not produce the least inconvenience to the author: whereas the letter on music was taken seriously, and incensed against me the whole nation, which thought itself offended by this attack on its music. The description of the incredible effect of this pamphlet would be worthy of the pen of Tacitus. The great quarrel between the parliament and the clergy was then at its height. The parliament had just been exiled; the fermentation was general; everything announced an approaching insurrection. The pamphlet appeared: from that moment every other quarrel was forgotten; the perilous state of French music was the only thing by which the attention of the public was engaged, and the only insurrection was against myself. This was so general that it has never since been totally calmed. At court, the bastile or banishment was absolutely determined on, and a *lettre de cachet* would have been issued had not M. de Voyer set forth in the most forcible manner that such a step would be ridiculous. Were I to say this pamphlet probably prevented a revolution, the reader would imagine I was in a dream. It is, however, a fact, the truth of which all Paris can attest, it being no more than fifteen years since the date of this singular fact. Although no attempts were made on my liberty,

I suffered numerous insults; and even my life was in danger. The musicians of the opera orchestra humanely resolved to murder me as I went out of the theater. Of this I received information; but the only effect it produced on me was to make me more assiduously attend the opera; and I did not learn, until a considerable time afterwards, that M. Ancelot, officer in the mousquetaires, and who had a friendship for me, had prevented the effect of this conspiracy by giving me an escort, which, unknown to myself, accompanied me until I was out of danger. The direction of the opera-house had just been given to the Hotel de Ville. The first exploit performed by the Prévot des Marchands, was to take from me my freedom of the theater, and this in the most uncivil manner possible. Admission was publicly refused me on my presenting myself, so that I was obliged to take a ticket that I might not that evening have the mortification to return as I had come. This injustice was the more shameful, as the only price I had set on my piece when I gave it to the managers was a perpetual freedom of the house; for although this was a right common to every author, and which I enjoyed under a double title, I expressly stipulated for it in presence of M. Duclos. It is true, the treasurer brought me fifty louis, for which I had not asked; but, besides the smallness of the sum, compared with that which, according to the rules established in such cases, was due to me, this payment had nothing in common with the right of entry formally granted, and which was entirely independent of it. There was in this behavior such a complication of iniquity and brutality, that the public, notwithstanding its animosity against me, which was then at its highest, was universally shocked at it, and many persons who insulted me the preceding evening, the next day exclaimed in the open theater, that it was shameful thus to deprive an author of his right of entry; and particularly one who had so well deserved it, and was entitled to claim it for himself and another person. So true is the Italian proverb: *Ch'ognun un ama la giustizia in casa d'altrui.**

In this situation the only thing I had to do was to demand my work, since the price I had agreed to receive for it was refused me. For this purpose I wrote to M. d'Argenson, who had the department of the opera. I likewise inclosed to him a memoir which was unanswerable; but this, as well as my letter, was ineffectual, and I received no answer to either. The silence of that unjust man hurt me extremely, and did not contribute to increase the very moderate good opinion I always had of his character and abilities. It was in this manner the managers kept my piece while they deprived me of that for which I had given it them. From the weak to the strong, such an act would be a theft: from the strong to the weak, it is nothing more than an appropriation of property, without a right.

With respect to the pecuniary advantages of the work, although it did not produce me a fourth part

* *Every one loves justice in the affairs of another.*

of the sum it would have done to any other person, they were considerable enough to enable me to subsist several years, and to make amends for the ill success of copying, which went on but very slowly. I received a hundred louis from the king; fifty from Madam de Pompadour, for the performance at Bellevue, where she herself played the part of Colin; fifty from the opera; and five hundred livres from Pissot, for the engraving: so that this interlude, which cost me no more than five or six weeks' application, produced, notwithstanding the ill treatment I received from the managers and my stupidity at court, almost as much money as my *Emilius,* which had cost me twenty years' meditation, and three years' labor. But I paid dearly for the pecuniary ease I received from the piece, by the infinite vexations it brought upon me. It was the germ of the secret jealousies which did not appear until a long time afterwards. After its success I did not remark, either in Grimm, Diderot, or any of the men of letters, with whom I was acquainted, the same cordiality and frankness, nor that pleasure in seeing me, I had previously experienced. The moment I appeared at the baron's, the conversation was no longer general; the company divided into small parties; whispered into each other's ears; and I remained alone, without knowing to whom to address myself. I endured for a long time this mortifying neglect; and, perceiving that Madam d'Holbach, who was mild and amiable, still received me well, I bore with the vulgarity of her husband as long as it was possible. But he one day attacked me without reason or pretense, and with such brutality, in presence of Diderot, who said not a word, and Margency, who since that time has often told me how much he admired the moderation and mildness of my answers, that, at length driven from his house, by this unworthy treatment, I took leave with a resolution never to enter it again. This did not, however, prevent me from speaking honorably of him and his house, whilst he continually expressed himself relative to me in the most insulting terms, calling me that *petit cuistre:* the little college pedant, or servitor in a college; without, however, being able to charge me with having done either to himself or any person to whom he was attached the most trifling injury. In this manner he verified my fears and predictions. I am of opinion my pretended friends would have pardoned me for having written books, and even excellent ones, because this merit was not foreign to themselves; but that they could not forgive my writing an opera, nor the brilliant success it had; because there was not one amongst them capable of the same, nor in a situation to aspire to like honors. Duclos, the only person superior to jealousy, seemed to become more attached to me: he introduced me to Mademoiselle Quinault, in whose house I received polite attention, and civility to as great an extreme, as I had found a want of it in that of M. d'Holbach.

Whilst the performance of the *Devin du Village* was continued at the opera-house, the author of it had advantageous negotiation with the managers of the French comedy. Not having, during seven or eight years, been able to get my *Narcissus* performed at the Italian theater, I had, by the bad performance in French of the actors, become disgusted with it, and should rather have had my piece received at the French theater than by them. I mentioned this to La Noue, the comedian, with whom I had become acquainted, and who, as everybody knows, was a man of merit and an author. He was pleased with the piece, and promised to get it performed without suffering the name of the author to be known; and in the meantime procured me the freedom of the theater, which was extremely agreeable to me, for I always preferred it to the two others. The piece was favorably received, and without the author's name being mentioned; but I have reason to believe it was known to the actors and actresses, and many other persons. Mademoiselles Gaussin and Grandval played the amorous parts; and although the whole performance was, in my opinion, injudicious, the piece could not be said to be absolutely ill played. The indulgence of the public, for which I felt gratitude, surprised me; the audience had the patience to listen to it from the beginning to the end, and to permit a second representation without showing the least sign of disapprobation. For my part, I was so wearied with the first, that I could not hold out to the end; and the moment I left the theater, I went into the *Café de Procope,* where I found Boissi, and others of my acquaintance, who had probably been as much fatigued as myself. I there humbly or haughtily avowed myself the author of the piece, judging it as everybody else had done. This public avowal of an author of a piece which had not succeeded, was much admired, and was by no means painful to myself. My self-love was flattered by the courage with which I made it: and I am of opinion, that, on this occasion, there was more pride in speaking, than there would have been foolish shame in being silent. However, as it was certain the piece, although insipid in the performance, would bear to be read, I had it printed: and in the preface, which is one of the best things I ever wrote, I began to make my principles more public than I had before done.

I soon had an opportunity to explain them entirely in a work of the greatest importance: for it was, I think, this year, 1753, that the Programme of the Academy of Dijon upon the Origin of the Inequality of Mankind made its appearance. Struck with this great question, I was surprised the academy had dared to propose it: but since it had shown sufficient courage to do it, I thought I might venture to treat it, and immediately undertook the discussion.

That I might consider this grand subject more at my ease, I went to St. Germain for seven or eight days with Thérèsa, our hostess, who was a good kind of woman, and one of her friends. I consider this walk as one of the most agreeable ones I ever took. The weather was very fine. These good women took upon themselves all the care and expense. Thérèsa amused herself with them; and I, free from all domestic concerns, diverted myself, without restraint, at the hours of dinner and supper. All the rest of the day wandering in the forest, I sought for and found there the image of the primitive ages of which I boldly traced the history. I confounded the pitiful lies of men; I dared to unveil their nature; to follow the progress of time, and the things by which it has been disfigured; and comparing the man of art with the natural man, to show them, in their pretended improvement, the real source of all their misery. My mind, elevated by these contemplations, ascended to the Divinity, and thence, seeing my fellow creatures follow in the blind track of their prejudices that of their errors and misfortunes, I cried out to them, in a feeble voice, which they could not hear: "Madmen! know that all your evils proceed from yourselves!"

From these meditations resulted the discourse on Inequality, a work more to the taste of Diderot than any of my other writings, and in which his advice was of the greatest service to me.* It was, however, under-

* At the time I wrote this I had not the least suspicion of the grand conspiracy of Diderot and Grimm, otherwise I should easily have discovered how much the former abused my confidence, by giving to my writings that severity and melancholy which were not to be found in them from the moments he ceased to direct me. The passage of the philosopher, who argues with himself, and stops his ears against the complaints of a man in distress, is after his manner: and he gave me others still more extraordinary, which I could never resolve to make use of. But, attributing this melancholy to that he had acquired in the dungeon of Vincennes, and of which there is a very sufficient dose in his Clairval, I never once suspected the least unfriendly dealing.

stood but by few readers, and not one of these would ever speak of it. I had written it to become a competitor for the premium, and sent it away fully persuaded it would not obtain it; well convinced it was not for productions of this nature that academies were founded.

This excursion and this occupation enlivened my spirits and was of service to my health. Several years before, tormented by my disorder, I had entirely given myself up to the care of physicians, who, without alleviating my sufferings, exhausted my strength and destroyed my constitution. At my return from St. Germain, I found myself stronger and perceived my health to be improved. I followed this indication, and determined to cure myself or die without the aid of physicians and medicine. I bade them forever adieu, and lived from day to day, keeping close when I found myself indisposed, and going abroad the moment I had sufficient strength to do it. The manner of living in Paris amidst people of pretensions was so little to my liking; the cabals of men of letters, their little candor in their writings, and the air of importance they gave themselves in the world, were so odious to me; I found so little mildness, openness of heart and frankness in the intercourse even of my friends; that, disgusted with this life of tumult, I began ardently to wish to reside in the country, and not perceiving that my occupations permitted me to do it, I went to pass there all the time I had to spare. For several months I went after dinner to walk alone in the Bois de Boulogne, meditating on subjects for future works, and not returning until evening.

Gauffecourt, with whom I was at that time extremely intimate, being on account of his employment obliged to go to Geneva, proposed to me the journey, to which I consented. The state of my health was such as to require the cares of the governess; it was therefore decided she should accompany us, and that her mother should remain in the house. After thus having made our arrangements, we set off on the first of June, 1754.

This was the period when at the age of forty-two, I for the first time in my life felt a diminution of my natural confidence, to which I had abandoned myself without reserve or inconvenience. We had a private carriage, in which with the same horses we traveled very slowly. I frequently got out and walked. We had scarcely performed half our journey when Thérèsa showed the greatest uneasiness at being left in the carriage with Gauffecourt, and when, notwithstanding her remonstrances, I would get out as usual, she insisted upon doing the same, and walking with me. I chid her for this caprice, and so strongly opposed it, that at length she found herself obliged to declare to me the cause whence it proceeded. I thought I was in a dream; my astonishment was beyond expression, when I learned that my friend M. de Gauffecourt, upwards of sixty years of age, crippled by the gout, impotent and exhausted by pleasures, had, since our departure, incessantly endeavored to corrupt a person who belonged to his friend, and was no longer young nor handsome, by the most base and shameful means, such as presenting to her a purse, attempting to inflame her imagination by the reading of an abominable book, and by the sight of infamous figures, with which it was filled. Thérèsa, full of indignation, once threw his scandalous book out of the carriage; and I learned that on the first evening of our journey, a violent headache having obliged me to retire to bed before supper, he had employed the whole time of this *tête-à-tête* in actions more worthy of a satyr than a man of worth and honor, to whom I thought I had intrusted my companion and myself. What astonishment and grief of heart for me! I, who until then had believed friendship to be inseparable from every amiable and noble sentiment which constitutes all its charm, for the first time in my life found myself under the necessity of connecting it with disdain, and of withdrawing my confidence from a man for whom I had an affection, and by whom I imagined myself beloved! The wretch concealed from me his turpitude; and that I might not expose Thérèsa, I was obliged to conceal from him my contempt, and secretly to harbor in my heart such sentiments as were foreign to its nature. Sweet and sacred illusion of friendship! Gauffecourt first took the veil from before my eyes. What cruel hands have since that time prevented it from again being drawn over them!

At Lyons I quitted Gauffecourt to take the road to Savoy, being unable to be so near to mamma without seeing her. I saw her—Good God, in what a situation! How contemptible! What remained to her of primitive virtue? Was it the same Madam de Warrens, formerly so gay and lively, to whom the vicar of Pontverre had given me recommendations? How my heart was wounded! The only resource I saw for her was to quit the country. I earneſtly but vainly repeated the invitation I had several times given her in my letters to come and live peacefully with me, assuring her I would dedicate the reſt of my life, and that of Thérèsa, to render hers happy. Attached to her pension, from which, although it was regularly paid, she had not for a long time received the leaſt advantage, my offers were loſt upon her. I again gave her a trifling part of the contents of my purse, much less than I ought to have done, and considerably less than I should have offered her had not I been certain of its not being of the leaſt service to herself. During my residence at Geneva, she made a journey into Chablais, and came to see me at Grange-canal. She was in want of money to continue her journey: what I had in my pocket was insufficient to this purpose, but an hour afterwards I sent it her by Thérèsa. Poor mamma! I muſt relate this proof of the goodness of her heart. A little diamond ring was the laſt jewel she had left. She took it from her finger to put it upon that of Thérèsa, who inſtantly replaced it upon that whence it had been taken, kissing the generous hand which she bathed with her tears. Ah! this was the proper moment to discharge my debt! I should have abandoned everything to follow her, and share her fate, let it be what it would. I did nothing of the kind. My attention was engaged by another attachment, and I perceived the attachment I had to her was abated by the slender hopes there were of rendering it useful to either of us. I sighed after her, my heart was grieved at her situation, but I did not follow her. Of all the remorse I felt this was the strongest and most lasting. I merited the terrible chastisement with which I have since that time incessantly been overwhelmed: may this have expiated my ingratitude! Of this I appear guilty in my conduct, but my heart has been too much distressed by what I did ever to have been that of an ungrateful man.

Before my departure from Paris I had sketched out the dedication of my discourse on the Inequality of Mankind. I finished it at Chambery, and dated it from that place, thinking that, to avoid all chicane, it was better not to date it either from France or Geneva. The moment I arrived in that city I abandoned myself to the republican enthusiasm which had brought me to it. This was augmented by the reception I there met with. Kindly treated by persons of every description, I entirely gave myself up to a patriotic zeal, and mortified at being excluded from the rights of a citizen by the possession of a religion different from that of my forefathers, I resolved openly to return to the latter. I thought the gospel being the same for every Christian, and the only difference in religious opinions the result of the explanations given by men to that which they did not understand, it was the exclusive right of the sovereign power in every country to fix the mode of worship, and these unintelligible opinions; and that consequently it was the duty of a citizen to admit the one, and conform to the other in the manner prescribed by the law. The conversation of the encyclopædists, far from staggering my faith, gave it new strength by my natural aversion to disputes and party. The study of man and the universe had everywhere shown me the final causes and the wisdom by which they were directed. The reading of the Bible, and especially that of the New Testament, to which I had for several years past applied myself, had given me a sovereign contempt for the base and stupid interpretations given to the words of Jesus Christ by persons the least worthy of understanding his divine doctrine. In a word, philosophy, while it attached me to the essential part of religion, had detached me from the trash of the little formularies with which men had rendered it obscure. Judging that for a reasonable man there were not two ways of being a Christian, I was also of opinion that in each country everything relative to form and discipline was within the jurisdiction of the laws. From this principle, so social and pacific, and which has brought upon me such cruel persecutions, it followed that, if I wished to be a citizen of Geneva, I must become a Protestant, and conform to the mode of worship established in my country. This I resolved upon; I moreover put myself under the instructions of the pastor of the parish in which I lived, and which was without the city. All I desired was not to appear at the consistory. However, the ecclesiastical edict was expressly to that effect; but it was agreed upon to dispense with it in my favor, and a commission of five or six members was named to receive my profession of faith. Unfortunately, the minister Perdriau, a mild and an amiable man, took it into his head to tell me the members were rejoiced at the thoughts of hearing me speak in the little assembly. This expectation alarmed me to such a degree that having night and day during three weeks studied a little discourse I had prepared, I was so confused when I ought to have pronounced it that I could not utter a single word, and during the conference I had the appearance of the most stupid schoolboy. The persons deputed spoke for me, and I answered *yes* and *no,* like a block-head; I was afterwards admitted to the communion, and reinstated in my rights as a citizen. I was enrolled as such in the list of guards, paid by none but citizens and burgesses, and I attended at a council-general *extraordinary* to receive the oath from the syndic Mussard. I was so impressed with the kindness shown me on this occasion by the council and the consistory, and by the great civility and obliging behavior of the magistrates, ministers and citizens, that, pressed by the worthy De Luc, who was incessant in his persuasions, and still more so by my own inclination, I did not think of going back to Paris for any other purpose than to break up housekeeping, find a situation for M. and Madam le Vasseur, or provide for their subsistence, and then return with Thérèsa to Geneva, there to settle for the rest of my days.

After taking this resolution I suspended all serious affairs the better to enjoy the company of my friends until the time of my departure. Of all the amusements of which I partook, that with which I was most pleased, was sailing round the lake in a boat, with De Luc, the father, his daughter-in-law, his two sons, and my Thérèsa. We gave seven days to this excursion in the finest weather possible. I preserved a lively remembrance of the situation which struck me at the other extremity of the lake, and of which I, some years afterwards, gave a description in my *Nouvelle Héloïse*.

The principal connections I made at Geneva, besides the De Lucs, of which I have spoken, were the young Vernes, with whom I had already been acquainted at Paris, and of whom I then formed a better opinion than I afterwards had of him; M. Perdriau, then a country pastor, now professor of *Belles-Lettres,* whose mild and agreeable society will ever make me regret the loss of it, although he has since thought proper to detach himself from me; M. Jalabert, at that time professor of natural philosophy, since become counselor and syndic, to whom I read my discourse upon Inequality (but not the dedication), with which he seemed to be delighted; the Professor Lullin, with whom I maintained a correspondence until his death, and who gave me a commission to purchase books for the library; the Professor Vernet, who, like most other people, turned his back upon me after I had given him proofs of attachment and confidence of which he ought to have been sensible, if a theologian can be affected by anything; Chappins, clerk and successor to Gauffecourt, whom he wished to supplant, and who, soon afterwards, was himself supplanted; Marcet de Mézières, an old friend of my father's, and who had also shown himself to be mine: after having well deserved of his country, he became a dramatic author, and, pretending to be of the council of two hundred, changed his principles, and, before he died, became ridiculous. But he from whom I expected most was M. Moultout, a very promising young man by his talents and his brilliant imagination, whom I have always loved, although his conduct with respect to me was frequently equivocal, and, notwithstanding his being connected with my most cruel enemies, whom I cannot but look upon as destined to become the defender of my memory and the avenger of his friend.

In the midst of these dissipations, I neither lost the taste for my solitary excursions, nor the habit of them; I frequently made long ones upon the banks of the lake, during which my mind, accustomed to reflection, did not remain idle; I digested the plan already formed of my political institutions, of which I shall shortly have to speak; I meditated a history of the Valais; the plan of a tragedy in prose, the subject of which, nothing less than Lucretia, did not deprive me of the hope of succeeding, although I had dared again to exhibit that unfortunate heroine, when she could no longer be suffered upon any French stage. I at that time tried my abilities with Tacitus, and translated the first books of his history, which will be found amongst my papers.

After a residence of four months at Geneva, I returned in the month of October to Paris; and avoided passing through Lyons that I might not again have to travel with Gauffecourt. As the arrangement I had made did not require my being at Geneva until the spring following, I returned, during the winter, to my habits and occupations; the principal of the latter was examining the proof sheets of my discourse on the Inequality of Mankind, which I had procured to be printed in Holland, by the bookseller Rey, with whom I had just become acquainted at Geneva. This work was dedicated to the republic; but as the publication might be unpleasing to the council, I wished to wait until it had taken its effect at Geneva before I returned thither. This effect was not favorable to me; and the dedication, which the most pure patriotism had dictated, created me enemies in the council, and inspired even many of the burgesses with jealousy. M. Chouet, at that time first syndic, wrote me a polite but very cold letter, which will be found amongst my papers. I received from private persons, amongst others from De Luc and De Jalabert, a few compliments, and these were all. I did not perceive that a single Genevese was pleased with the hearty zeal found in the work. This indifference shocked all those by whom it was remarked. I remember that dining one day at Clichy, at Madam Dupin's, with Crommelin, resident from the republic, and M. de Mairan, the latter openly declared the council owed me a present and public honors for the work, and that it would dishonor itself if it failed in either. Crommelin, who was a black and mischievous little man, dared not reply in my presence, but he made a frightful grimace, which however forced a smile from Madam Dupin. The only advantage this work procured me, besides that resulting from the satisfaction of my own heart, was the title of citizen given me by my friends, afterwards by the public after their example, and which I afterwards lost by having too well merited.

This ill success would not, however, have prevented my retiring to Geneva, had not more powerful motives tended to the same effect. M. D'Epinay, wishing to add a wing which was wanting to the château of the Chevrette, was at an immense expense in completing it. Going one day with Madam D'Epinay to see the building, we continued our walk a quarter of a league further to the reservoir of the waters of the park which joined the forest of Montmorency, and where there was a handsome kitchen garden, with a little lodge, much out of repair, called the Hermitage. This solitary and very agreeable place had struck me when I saw it for the first time before my journey to Geneva. I had exclaimed in my transport: "Ah, madam, what a delightful habitation! This asylum was purposely prepared for me." Madam D'Epinay did not pay much attention to what I said; but at this second journey I was quite surprised to find, instead of the old decayed building, a little house almost entirely new, well laid out, and very habitable for a little family of three persons. Madam D'Epinay had caused this to be done in silence, and at a very small expense, by detaching a few materials and some of the workmen from the castle. She now said to me, on remarking my surprise: "My dear, here behold your asylum: it is you who have chosen it; friendship offers it to you. I hope this will remove from you the cruel idea of separating from me." I do not think I was ever in my life more strongly or more deliciously affected. I bathed with tears the beneficent hand of my friend; and if I were not conquered from that very instant even, I was extremely staggered. Madam D'Epinay, who would not be denied, became so pressing, employed so many means, so many people to circumvent me, proceeding even so far as to gain over Madam le Vasseur and her daughter, that at length she triumphed over all my resolutions. Renouncing the idea of residing in my own country, I resolved, I promised, to inhabit the Hermitage; and, whilst the building was drying, Madam D'Epinay took care to prepare furniture, so that everything was ready the following spring.

One thing which greatly aided me in determining, was the residence Voltaire had chosen near Geneva; I easily comprehended this man would cause a revolution there, and that I should find in my country the manners, which drove me from Paris; that I should be under the necessity of incessantly struggling hard, and have no other alternative than that of being an unsupportable pedant, a poltroon, or a bad citizen. The letter Voltaire wrote me on my last work, induced me to insinuate my fears in my answer; and the effect this produced confirmed them. From that moment I considered Geneva as lost, and I was not deceived. I perhaps ought to have met the storm, had I thought myself capable of resisting it. But what could I have done alone, timid, and speaking badly, against a man, arrogant, opulent, supported by the credit of the great, eloquent, and already the idol of the women and young men? I was afraid of uselessly exposing myself to danger to no purpose. I listened to nothing but my peaceful disposition, to my love of repose, which, if it then deceived me, still continues to deceive me on the same subject. By retiring to Geneva, I should have avoided great misfortunes; but I have my doubts whether, with all my ardent and patriotic zeal, I should have been able to effect anything great and useful for my country.

Tronchin, who about the same time went to reside at Geneva, came afterwards to Paris and brought with him treasures. At his arrival he came to see me, with the Chevalier Jaucourt. Madam D'Epinay had a strong desire to consult him in private, but this it was not easy to do. She addressed herself to me, and I engaged Tronchin to go and see her. Thus under my auspices they began a connection, which was afterwards increased at my expense. Such has ever been my destiny: the moment I had united two friends who were separately mine, they never failed to combine against me. Although, in the conspiracy then formed by the Tronchins, they must all have borne me a mortal hatred. The Doctor still continued friendly to me: he even wrote me a letter after his return to Geneva, to propose to me the place of honorary librarian. But I had taken my resolution, and the offer did not tempt me to depart from it.

About this time I again visited M. d'Holbach. My visit was occasioned by the death of his wife, which, as well as that of Madam Francueil, happened whilst I was at Geneva. Diderot, when he communicated to me these melancholy events, spoke of the deep affliction of the husband. His grief affected my heart. I myself was grieved for the loss of that excellent woman, and wrote to M. d'Holbach a letter of condolence. I forgot all the wrongs he had done me, and at my return from Geneva, and after he had made the tour of France with Grimm and other friends to alleviate his affliction, I went to see him, and continued my visits until my departure for the Hermitage. As soon as it was known in his circle that Madam D'Epinay was preparing me a habitation there, innumerable sarcasms, founded upon the want I must feel of the flattery and amusements of the city, and the supposition of my not being able to support the solitude for a fortnight, were uttered against me. Feeling within myself how I stood affected, I left him and his friends to say what they pleased, and pursued my intention. M. d'Holbach rendered me some services* in finding a place for the old Le Vasseur, who was eighty years of age, and a burden to his wife, from which she begged me to relieve her. He was put into a house of charity, where, almost as soon as he arrived there, age and the grief of finding himself removed from his family sent him to the grave. His wife and all his children, except Thérèsa, did not much regret his loss. But she, who loved him tenderly, has ever since been inconsolable, and never forgiven herself for having suffered him, at so advanced at age, to end his days in any other house than her own.

Much about the same time I received a visit I little expected, although it was from a very old acquaintance. My friend Venture, accompanied by another man, came upon me one morning by surprise. What a change did I discover in his person! Instead of his former gracefulness, he appeared sottish and vulgar, which made me extremely reserved with him. My eyes deceived me, or either debauchery had stupefied his mind, or all his first splendor was the effect of his youth which was past. I saw him almost with indifference, and we parted rather coolly. But when he was

---

* This is an instance of the treachery of my memory. A long time after I had written what I have stated above, I learned, in conversing with my wife, that it was not M. d'Holbach, but M. de Chenonceaux, then one of the administrators of the Hotel Dieu, who procured this place for her father. I had so totally forgotten the circumstance, and the idea of M. d'Holbach's having done it was so strong in my mind that I would have sworn it had been him.

gone, the remembrance of our former connection so strongly called to my recollection that of my younger days, so charmingly, so prudently dedicated to that angelic woman (Madam de Warrens) who was not much less changed than himself; the little anecdotes of that happy time, the romantic day at *Toune* passed with so much innocence and enjoyment between those two charming girls, from whom a kiss of the hand was the only favor, and which, notwithstanding its being so trifling, had left me such lively, affecting and lasting regrets; and the ravishing delirium of a young heart, which I had just felt in all its force, and of which I thought the season forever past for me. The tender remembrance of these delightful circumstances made me shed tears over my faded youth and its transports forever lost to me. Ah! how many tears should I have shed over their tardy and fatal return had I foreseen the evils I had yet to suffer from them.

Before I left Paris, I enjoyed during the winter which preceded my retreat, a pleasure after my own heart, and of which I tasted in all its purity. Palissot, academician of Nancy, known by a few dramatic compositions, had just had one of them performed at Lunéville before the King of Poland. He perhaps thought to make his court by representing in his piece a man who dared to enter into a literary dispute with the king. Stanislaus, who was generous, and did not like satire, was filled with indignation at the author's daring to be personal in his presence. The Comte de Tressan, by order of the prince, wrote to M. d'Alembert, as well as to myself, to inform me that it was the intention of his majesty to have Palissot expelled his academy. My answer was a strong solicitation in favor of Palissot, begging M. de Tressan to intercede with the king in his behalf. His pardon was granted, and M. de Tressan, when he communicated to me the information in the name of the monarch, added that the whole of what had passed should be inserted in the register of the academy. I replied that this was less granting a pardon than perpetuating a punishment. At length, after repeated solicitations, I obtained a promise, that nothing relative to the affair should be inserted in the register, and that no public trace should remain of it. The promise was accompanied, as well on the part of the king as on that of M. de Tressan, with assurance of esteem and respect, with which I was extremely flattered; and I felt on this occasion that the esteem of men who are themselves worthy of it, produced in the mind a sentiment infinitely more noble and pleasing than that of vanity. I have transcribed into my collection the letters of M. de Tressan, with my answers to them; and the original of the former will be found amongst my other papers.

I am perfectly aware that if ever these memoirs become public, I here perpetuate the remembrance of a fact which I would wish to efface every trace; but I transmit many others as much against my inclination. The grand object of my undertaking, constantly before my eyes, and the indispensable duty of fulfilling it to its utmost extent, will not permit me to be turned aside by trifling considerations, which would lead me from my purpose. In my strange and unparalleled situation I owe too much to truth to be further than this indebted to any person whatever. They who wish to know me well must be acquainted with me in every point of view, in every relative situation, both good and bad. My confessions are necessarily connected with those of many other people: I write both with the same frankness in everything that relates to that which has befallen me; and am not obliged to spare any person more than myself, although it is my wish to do it. I am determined always to be just and true, to say of others all the good I can, never speaking of evil except when it relates to my own conduct, and there is a necessity for my so doing. Who, in the situation in which the world has placed me, has a right to require more at my hands? My confessions are not intended to appear during my lifetime, nor that of those they may disagreeably affect. Were I master of my own destiny, and that of the book I am now writing, it should never be made public until after my death and theirs. But the efforts which the dread of truth obliges my powerful enemies to make to destroy every trace of it, render it necessary for me to do everything, which the strictest right, and the most severe justice, will permit, to preserve what I have written. Were the remembrance of me to be lost at my dissolution, rather than expose any person alive, I would without a murmur suffer an unjust and momentary reproach. But since my name is to live, it is my duty to endeavor to transmit with it to posterity the remembrance of the unfortunate man by whom it was borne, such as he really was, and not such as his unjust enemies incessantly endeavored to describe him.

BOOK IX

BOOK IX

[*1756*]

I WAS so impatient to take up my abode in Hermitage that I could not wait for the return of fine weather; the moment my lodging was prepared I hastened to take possession of it, to the great amusement of the *Coterie Holbachique,* which publicly predicted I should not be able to support solitude for three months, and that I should unsuccessfully return to Paris, and live there as they did. For my part, having for fifteen years been out of my element, finding myself upon the eve of returning to it, I paid no attention to their pleasantries. Since, contrary to my inclinations, I have again entered the world, I have incessantly regretted my dear Charmettes, and the agreeable life I led there. I felt a natural inclination to retirement and the country: it was impossible for me to live happily elsewhere. At Venice, in the train of public affairs, in the dignity of a kind of representation, in the pride of projects of advancement; at Paris, in the vortex of the great world, in the luxury of suppers, in the brilliancy of spectacles, in the rays of splendor; my groves, rivulets, and solitary

walks, constantly presented themselves to my recollection, interrupted my thought, rendered me melancholy and made me sigh with desire. All the labor
to which I had subjected myself, every project of
ambition which by fits had animated my ardor, all
had for object this happy country retirement, which
I now thought near at hand. Without having acquired a genteel independence, which I had judged
to be the only means of accomplishing my views, I
imagined myself, in my particular situation, to be
able to do without it, and that I could obtain the same
end by a means quite opposite. I had no regular income; but I possessed some talents, and had acquired
a name. My wants were few, and I had freed myself
from all those which were most expensive, and which
merely depended on prejudice and opinion. Besides
this, although naturally indolent, I was laborious
when I chose to be so, and my idleness was less that
of an indolent man, than that of an independent one
who applies to business when it pleases him. My profession of a copyist of music was neither splendid nor
lucrative, but it was certain. The world gave me credit
for the courage I had shown in making choice of it.
I might depend upon having sufficient employment
to enable me to live. Two thousand livres which remained of the produce of the *Devin du Village,* and
my other writings, were a sum which kept me from
being straitened, and several works I had upon the
stocks promised me, without extorting money from
the booksellers, supplies sufficient to enable me to

work at my ease without exhausting myself, even by turning to advantage the leisure of my walks. My little family, consisting of three persons, all of whom were usefully employed, was not expensive to support. Finally, from my resources, proportioned to my wants and desires, I might reasonably expect a happy and permanent existence, in that manner of life which my inclination had induced me to adopt.

I might have taken the interested side of the question, and, instead of subjecting my pen to copying, entirely devoted it to works which, from the elevation to which I had soared, and at which I found myself capable of continuing, might have enabled me to live in the midst of abundance, nay, even of opulence, had I been the least disposed to join the maneuvers of an author to the care of publishing a good book. But I felt that writing for bread would soon have extinguished my genius, and destroyed my talents, which were less in my pen than in my heart, and solely proceeded from an elevated and noble manner of thinking, by which alone they could be cherished and preserved. Nothing vigorous or great can come from a pen totally venal. Necessity, nay, even avarice, perhaps, would have made me write rather rapidly than well. If the desire of success had not led me into cabals, it might have made me endeavor to publish fewer true and useful works than those which might be pleasing to the multitude; and instead of a distinguished author, which I might possibly become, I should have been nothing more than a scribbler. No:

I have always felt that the profession of letters was illustrious in proportion as it was less a trade. It is too difficult to think nobly when we think for a livelihood. To be able to dare even to speak great truths, an author must be independent of success. I gave my books to the public with a certainty of having written for the general good of mankind, without giving myself the least concern about what was to follow. If the work was thrown aside, so much the worse for such as did not choose to profit by it. Their approbation was not necessary to enable me to live, my profession was sufficient to maintain me had not my works had a sale, for which reason alone they all sold.

. It was on the ninth of August, 1756, that I left cities, never to reside in them again: for I do not call a residence the few days I afterwards remained in Paris, London, or other cities, always on the wing, or contrary to my inclinations. Madam d'Epinay came and took us all three in her coach; her farmer carted away my little baggage, and I was put into possession the same day. I found my little retreat simply furnished, but neatly, and with some taste. The hand which had lent its aid in this furnishing rendered it inestimable in my eyes, and I thought it charming to be the guest of my female friend in a house I had made choice of, and which she had caused to be built purposely for me.

Although the weather was cold, and the ground lightly covered with snow, the earth began to vegetate: violets and primroses already made their appearance, the trees began to bud, and the evening of my arrival was distinguished by the song of the nightingale, which was heard almost under my window, in a wood adjoining the house. After a light sleep, forgetting when I awoke my change of abode, I still thought myself in the Rue Grenelle, when suddenly this warbling made me give a start, and I exclaimed in my transport: "At length, all my wishes are accomplished!" The first thing I did was abandon myself to the impression of the rural objects with which I was surrounded. Instead of beginning to set things in order in my new habitation, I began by doing it for my walks, and there was not a path, a copse, a grove, nor a corner in the environs of my place of residence that I did not visit the next day. The more I examined this charming retreat, the more I found it to my wishes. This solitary, rather than savage, spot transported me in idea to the end of the world. It had striking beauties which are but seldom found near cities, and never, if suddenly transported thither, could any person have imagined himself within four leagues of Paris.

After abandoning myself for a few days to this rural delirium, I began to arrange my papers, and regulate my occupations. I set apart, as I had always done, my mornings to copying, and my afternoons to walking, provided with my little paper book and a pencil, for never having been able to write and think at my ease except *sub dio,* I had no inclination to depart from this method, and I was persuaded the forest of Montmorency, which was almost at my door, would in future be my closet and study. I had several works begun; these I cast my eye over. My mind was indeed fertile in great projects, but in the noise of the city the execution of them had gone on but slowly. I proposed to myself to use more diligence when I should be less interrupted. I am of opinion I have sufficiently fulfilled this intention; and for a man frequently ill, often at La Chevrette, at Epinay, at Eaubonne, at the castle of Montmorency, at other times interrupted by the indolent and curious, and always employed half the day in copying, if what I produced during the six years I passed at the Hermitage and at Montmorency be considered, I am persuaded it will appear that if, in this interval, I lost my time, it was not in idleness.

Of the different works I had upon the stocks, that I had longest resolved in my mind, which was most to my taste, to which I destined a certain portion of my life, and which, in my opinion, was to confirm the reputation I had acquired, was my *Institutions Politiques*.* I had, fourteen years before, when at Venice, where I had an opportunity of remarking the defects of that government so much boasted of, conceived the first idea of them. Since that time my views had become much more extended by the historical study of morality. I had perceived everything to be radically connected with politics, and that, upon whatever principles these were founded, a people would

* *Political Institutions.*

never be more than that which the nature of the government made them; therefore the great question of the best government possible appeared to me to be reduced to this: What is the nature of a government the most proper to form the most virtuous and enlightened, the wisest and best people, taking the last epithet in its most extensive meaning? I thought this question was much if not quite of the same nature with that which follows: What government is that which, by its nature, always maintains itself nearest to the laws, or least deviates from the laws.* Hence, what is the law? and a series of questions of similar importance. I perceived these led to great truths, useful to the happiness of mankind, but more especially to that of my country, wherein, in the journey I had just made to it, I had not found notions of laws and liberty either sufficiently just or clear. I had thought this indirect manner of communicating these to my fellow-citizens would be least mortifying to their pride, and might obtain me forgiveness for having seen a little further than themselves.

Although I had already labored five or six years at the work, the progress I had made in it was not considerable. Writings of this kind require meditation, leisure, and tranquillity. I had besides written the *Institutions Politiques,* as the expression is, *en bonne fortune,* and had not communicated my project to any person, not even to Diderot. I was afraid it would be

---

* *Quel est le gouvernement qui par sa nature se tient toujours le plus pres de la loi?*

thought too daring for the age and country in which I wrote, and that the fears of my friends would restrain me from carrying it into execution.* I did not yet know that it would be finished in time, and in such a manner as to appear before my decease. I wished fearlessly to give to my subject everything it required; fully persuaded that not being of a satirical turn, and never wishing to be personal, I should in equity always be judged irreprehensible. I undoubtedly wished fully to enjoy the right of thinking which I had by birth; but still respecting the government under which I lived, without ever disobeying its laws, and very attentive not to violate the rights of persons, I would not from fear renounce its advantages.

I confess even that, as a stranger, and living in France, I found my situation very favorable in daring to speak the truth; well knowing that continuing, as I was determined to do, not to print anything in the kingdom without permission, I was not obliged to give to any person in it an account of my maxims nor of their publication elsewhere. I should have been less independent even at Geneva, where, in whatever

---

* It was more especially the wise severity of Duclos which inspired me with this fear; as for Diderot, I know not by what means all my conferences with him tended to make me more satirical than my natural disposition inclined me to be. This prevented me from consulting him upon an undertaking, in which I wished to introduce nothing but the force of reasoning, without the least appearance of ill humor or partiality. The manner of this work may be judged of by that of the Contrat Social† which is taken from it.

† Social Contract.

place my books might have been printed, the magistrate had a right to criticise their contents. This consideration had greatly contributed to make me yield to the solicitations of Madam d'Epinay, and abandon the project of fixing my residence at Geneva. I felt, as I have remarked in my Emilius, that unless an author be a man of intrigue, when he wishes to render his works really useful to any country whatsoever, he must compose them in some other.

What made me find my situation still more happy, was my being persuaded that the government of France would, perhaps, without looking upon me with a very favorable eye, make it a point to protect me, or at least not to disturb my tranquillity. It appeared to me a stroke of simple, yet dexterous policy, to make a merit of tolerating that which there was no means of preventing; since, had I been driven from France, which was all government had the right to do, my work would still have been written, and perhaps with less reserve; whereas if I were left undisturbed, the author remained to answer for what he wrote, and a prejudice, general throughout all Europe, would be destroyed by acquiring the reputation of observing a proper respect for the rights of persons.

They who, by the event, shall judge I was deceived, may perhaps be deceived in their turn. In the storm which has since broken over my head, my books served as a pretense, but it was against my person that every shaft was directed. My persecutors gave themselves but little concern about the author, but they

wished to ruin *Jean-Jacques;* and the greatest evil
they found in my writings was the honor they might
possibly do me. Let us not encroach upon the future.
I do not know that this mystery, which is still one to
me, will hereafter be cleared up to my readers; but
had my avowed principles been of a nature to bring
upon me the treatment I received, I should sooner
have become their victim, since the work in which
these principles are manifested with most courage,
not to call it audacity, seemed to have had its effect
previous to my retreat to the Hermitage, without I
will not only say my having received the least censure,
but without any steps having been taken to prevent
the publication of it in France, where it was sold as
publicly as in Holland. The New Eloisa afterwards
appeared with the same facility, I dare add, with the
same applause; and, what seems incredible, the profession of faith of this Eloisa at the point of death is
exactly similar to that of the Savoyard vicar. Every
strong idea in the Social Contract had been before published in the discourse on Inequality; and every bold
opinion in Emilius previously found in Eloisa. This
unrestrained freedom did not excite the least murmur
against the first two works; therefore it was not that
which gave cause to it against the latter.

Another undertaking much of the same kind, but
of which the project was more recent, then engaged
my attention: this was the extract of the works of the
Abbé de Saint Pierre, of which, having been led away
by the thread of my narrative, I have not hitherto been

able to speak. The idea was suggested to me, after my return from Geneva, by the Abbé Mably, not immediately from himself, but by the interposition of Madam Dupin, who had some interest in engaging me to adopt it. She was one of the three or four pretty women of Paris, of whom the Abbé de Saint Pierre had been the spoiled child, and although she had not decidedly had the preference, she had at least partaken of it with Madam d'Aiguillon. She preserved for the memory of the good man a respect and an affection which did honor to them both; and her self-love would have been flattered by seeing the still-born works of her friend brought to life by her secretary. These works contained excellent things, but so badly told that the reading of them was almost insupportable; and it is astonishing the Abbé de Saint Pierre, who looked upon his readers as schoolboys, should nevertheless have spoken to them as men, by the little care he took to induce them to give him a hearing. It was for this purpose that the work was proposed to me as useful in itself, and very proper for a man laborious in maneuver, but idle as an author, who finding the trouble of thinking very fatiguing, preferred, in things which pleased him, throwing a light upon and extending the ideas of others, to producing any himself. Besides, not being confined to the function of a translator, I was at liberty sometimes to think for myself; and I had it in my power to give such a form to my work, that many important truths would pass in it under the name of the Abbé de Saint

Pierre, much more safely than under mine. The undertaking also was not trifling; the business was nothing less than to read and meditate twenty-three volumes, diffuse, confused, full of long narrations and periods, repetitions, and false or little views, from amongst which it was necessary to select some few that were great and useful, and sufficiently encouraging to enable me to support the painful labor. I frequently wished to have given it up, and should have done so, could I have got it off my hands with a good grace; but when I received the manuscripts of the abbé, which were given me by his nephew, the Comte de Saint Pierre, I had, by the solicitation of St. Lambert, in some measure engaged to make use of them, which I must either have done, or have given them back. It was with the former intention I had taken the manuscripts to the Hermitage, and this was the first work to which I proposed to dedicate my leisure hours.

I had likewise in my own mind projected a third, the idea of which I owed to the observations I had made upon myself and I felt the more disposed to undertake this work, as I had reason to hope I could make it a truly useful one, and perhaps, the most so of any that could be offered to the world, were the execution equal to the plan I had laid down. It has been remarked that most men are in the course of their lives frequently unlike themselves, and seem to be transformed into others very different from what they were. It was not to establish a thing so generally known that I wished to write a book; I had a newer and more important object. This was to search for the causes of these variations, and, by confining my observations to those which depend on ourselves, to demonstrate in what manner it might be possible to direct them, in order to render us better and more certain of our dispositions. For it is undoubtedly more painful to an honest man to resist desires already formed, and which it is his duty to subdue, than to prevent, change, or modify the same desires in their source, were he capable of tracing them to it. A man under temptation resists once because he has strength of mind, he yields another time because this is overcome; had it been the same as before he would again have triumphed.

By examining within myself, and searching in others what could be the cause of these different manners of being, I discovered that, in a great measure they depended on the anterior impression of external objects; and that, continually modified by our senses and organs, we, without knowing it, bore in our ideas, sentiments, and even actions, the effect of these modifications. The striking and numerous observations I had collected were beyond all manner of dispute, and by their natural principle seemed proper to furnish and exterior regimen, which, varied according to circumstances, might place and support the mind in the state most favorable to virtue. From how many mistakes would reason be preserved, how many vices would be stifled in their birth, were it possible to force animal economy to favor moral order, which it so frequently disturbs! Climates, seasons, sounds, colors, light, darkness, the elements, aliments, noise, silence, motion, rest, all act on the animal machine, and consequently on the mind; all offer us a thousand means, almost certain of directing in their origin the sentiments by which we suffer ourselves to be governed. Such was the fundamental idea of which I had already made a sketch upon paper, and whence I hoped for an effect the more certain, in favor of persons well disposed, who, sincerely loving virtue, were afraid of their own weakness, as it appeared to me easy to make of it a book as agreeable to read as it was to compose. I have, however, applied myself but very little to this work, the title of which was to have been *Morale Sensitive ou le Materialisme du Sage.** Interruptions, the cause of which will soon appear, prevented me from continuing it, and the fate of the sketch, which is more connected with my own than it may appear to be, will hereafter be seen.

Besides this, I had for some time meditated a system of education, of which Madam de Chenonceaux, alarmed for her son by that of her husband, had desired me to consider. The authority of friendship placed this object, although less in itself to my taste, nearer to my heart than any other. On which account this subject, of all those of which I have just spoken, is the only one I carried to its utmost extent. The end I proposed to myself in treating of it should, I think, have procured the author a better fate. But I will not

* *Sensitive Morality, or the Materialism of the Sage.*

here anticipate this melancholy subject. I shall have too much reason to speak of it in the course of my work.

These different objects offered me subjects of meditation for my walks; for, as I believe I have already observed, I am unable to reflect when I am not walking: the moment I stop, I think no more, and as soon as I am again in motion my head resumes its workings. I had, however, provided myself with a work for the closet upon rainy days. This was my dictionary of music, which my scattered, mutilated, and unshapen materials made it necessary to rewrite almost entirely. I had with me some books necessary to this purpose; I had spent two months in making extracts from others, which I had borrowed from the king's library, whence I was permitted to take several to the Hermitage. I was thus provided with materials for composing in my apartment when the weather did not permit me to go out, and my copying fatigued me. This arrangement was so convenient that it made it turn to advantage as well at the Hermitage as at Montmorency, and afterwards even at Motiers, where I completed the work whilst I was engaged in others, and constantly found a change of occupation to be a real relaxation.

During a considerable time I exactly followed the distribution I had prescribed myself, and found it very agreeable; but as soon as the fine weather brought Madam d'Epinay more frequently to Epinay, or to the Chevrette, I found that attentions, in the first instance natural to me, but which I had not considered in my scheme, considerably deranged my projects. I have already observed that Madam d'Epinay had many amiable qualities; she sincerely loved her friends; served them with zeal; and, not sparing for them either time or pains, certainly deserved on their part every attention in return. I had hitherto discharged this duty without considering it as one; but at length I found that I had given myself a chain of which nothing but friendship prevented me from feeling the weight, and this was still aggravated by my dislike to numerous societies. Madam d'Epinay took advantage of these circumstances to make me a proposition seemingly agreeable to me, but which was more so to herself; this was to let me know when she was alone, or had but little company. I consented, without perceiving to what a degree I engaged myself. The consequence was that I no longer visited her at my own hour but at hers, and that I never was certain of being master of myself for a day together. This constraint considerably diminished the pleasure I had in going to see her. I found the liberty she had so frequently promised was given me upon no other condition than that of my never enjoying it; and once or twice when I wished to do this there were so many messages, notes, and alarms relative to my health, that I perceived I could have no excuse but being confined to my bed, for not immediately running to her upon the first intimation. It was necessary I should submit to this yoke, and I did it, even more voluntarily than could be expected from so great an enemy to dependence: the sincere attachment I had to Madam d'Epinay preventing me, in a great measure, from feeling the inconvenience with which it was accompanied. She, on her part, filled up, well or ill, the void which the absence of her usual circle left in her amusements. This for her was but a very slender supplement, although preferable to absolute solitude, which she could not support. She had the means of doing it much more at her ease after she began with literature, and at all events to write novels, letters, comedies, tales, and other trash of the same kind. But she was not so much amused in writing these as in reading them; and she never scribbled over two or three pages at one sitting, without being previously assured of having, at least, two or three benevolent auditors at the end of so much labor. I seldom had the honor of being the one of the chosen few except by means of another. When alone, I was, for the most part, considered as a cipher in everything; and this not only in the company of Madam d'Epinay, but in that of M. d'Holbach, and in every place where Grimm gave the *ton*. This nullity was very convenient to me, except in a *tête-à-tête,* when I knew not what countenance to put on, not daring to speak of literature, of which it was not for me to say a word; nor of gallantry, being too timid, and fearing, more than death, the ridiculousness of an old gallant; besides that, I never had such an idea when in the company of Madam d'Epinay, and that it perhaps would never have occurred to me, had I passed my whole life with her; not that her person was in the least disagreeable to me; on the contrary, I loved her perhaps too much as a friend to do it as a lover. I felt a pleasure in seeing and speaking to her. Her conversation, although agreeable enough in a mixed company, was uninteresting in private; mine, not more elegant or entertaining than her own, was no great amusement to her. Ashamed of being long silent, I endeavored to enliven our *tête-à-tête* and, although this frequently fatigued me, I was never disgusted with it. I was happy to show her little attentions, and gave her little fraternal kisses, which seemed not to be more sensual to herself; these were all. She was very thin, very pale, and had a bosom which resembled the back of her hand. This defect alone would have been sufficient to moderate my most ardent desires; my heart never could distinguish a woman in a person who had it; and, besides, other causes, useless to mention, always made me forget the sex of this lady.

Having resolved to conform to an assiduity which was necessary, I immediately and voluntarily entered upon it, and for the first year at least, found it less burthensome than I could have expected. Madam d'Epinay, who commonly passed the summer in the country, continued there but a part of this; whether she was more detained by her affairs at Paris, or that the absence of Grimm rendered the residence of the Chevrette less agreeable to her, I know not. I took the advantage of the intervals of her absence, or when the

company with her was numerous, to enjoy my solitude with my good Thérèsa and her mother, in such
a manner as to taste all its charms. Although I had
for several years past been frequently in the country,
I seldom had enjoyed much of its pleasures; and these
excursions, always made in company with people who
considered themselves as persons of consequence, and
rendered insipid by constraint, served to increase in
me the natural desire I had for rustic pleasures. The
want of these was the more sensible to me as I had
the image of them immediately before my eyes. I was
so tired of saloons, jets-d'eau, groves, parterres, and
of the more fatiguing persons by whom they were
shown; so exhausted with pamphlets, harpsichords,
trios, unravelings of plots, stupid *bon mots,* insipid
affectations, pitiful story-tellers, and great suppers;
that when I gave a side glance at a poor simple haw-
thorn bush, a hedge, a barn, or a meadow; when, in
passing through a hamlet, I scented a good chervil
omelette, and heard at a distance the burden of the
rustic song of the *Bisquières;* I wished all rouge, fur-
belows and ambergris at the devil, and envying the
dinner of the good housewife, and the wine of her
own vineyard, I heartily wished to give a slap on the
chaps to Monsieur le Chef and Monsieur le Maitre,
who made me dine at the hour of supper, and sup
when I should have been asleep, but especially to
Messieurs the lackeys, who devoured with their eyes
the morsel I put into my mouth, and, upon pain of
my dying with thirst, sold me the adulterated wine

of their master, ten times dearer than that of a better quality would have cost me at a public house.

At length I was settled in an agreeable and solitary asylum, at liberty to pass there the remainder of my days, in that peaceful, equal and independent life for which felt myself born. Before I relate the effects this situation, so new to me, had upon my heart, it is proper I should recapitulate its secret affections, that the reader may better follow in their causes the progress of these new modifications.

I have always considered the day on which I was united to Thérèsa as that which fixed my moral existence. An attachment was necessary for me, since that which should have been sufficient to my heart had been so cruelly broken. The thirst after happiness is never extinguished in the heart of man. Mamma was advancing into years, and dishonored herself! I had proofs that she could never more be happy here below; it therefore remained to me to seek my own happiness, having lost all hopes of partaking of hers. I was sometimes irresolute, and fluctuated from one idea to another, and from project to project. My journey to Venice would have thrown me into public life, had the man with whom, almost against my inclination, I was connected there had common sense. I was easily discouraged, especially in undertakings of length and difficulty. The ill success of this disgusted me with every other; and, according to my old maxims, considering distant objects as deceitful allurements I resolved in future to provide for immediate wants, seeing nothing in life which could tempt me to make extraordinary efforts.

It was precisely at this time we became acquainted. The mild character of the good Thérèsa seemed so fitted to my own, that I united myself to her with an attachment which neither time nor injuries have been able to impair, and which has constantly been increased by everything by which it might have been expected to be diminished. The force of this sentiment will hereafter appear when I come to speak of the wounds she has given my heart in the height of my misery, without my ever having, until this moment, once uttered a word of complaint to any person whatever.

When it shall be known, that after having done everything, braved everything, not to separate from her; that after passing with her twenty years in despite of fate and men; I have in my old age made her my wife, without the least expectation or solicitation on her part, or promise or engagement on mine, the world will think that love bordering upon madness, having from the first moment turned my head, led me by degrees to the last act of extravagance; and this will no longer appear doubtful when the strong and particular reasons which should forever have prevented me from taking such a step are made known. What, therefore, will the reader think when I shall have told him, with all the truth he has ever found in me, that, from the first moment in which I saw her, until that wherein I write, I have never felt the least love for her, that I never desired to possess her more than I did to possess Madam de Warrens, and that the physical wants which were satisfied with her person were, for me, solely those of the sex, and by no means proceeding from the individual? He will think that, being of a constitution different from that of other men, I was incapable of love, since this was not one of the sentiments which attached me to women the most dear to my heart. Patience, O my dear reader! the fatal moment approaches in which you will be but too much undeceived.

I fall into repetitions; I know it; and these are necessary. The first of my wants, the greatest, strongest, and most insatiable, was wholly in my heart; the want of an intimate connection, and as intimate as it could possibly be: for this reason especially, a woman was more necessary to me than a man, a female rather than a male friend. This singular want was such that the closest corporal union was not sufficient: two souls would have been necessary to me in the same body, without which I always felt a void. I thought I was upon the point of filling it up forever. This young person, amiable by a thousand excellent qualities, and at that time by her form, without the shadow of art or coquetry, would have confined within herself my whole existence, could hers, as I had hoped it would, have been totally confined to me. I had nothing to fear from men; I am certainly of being the only man she ever really loved, and her moderate passions seldom wanted another, not even after I ceased in this respect to be one to her. I had no family; she had one; and this family was composed of individuals whose dispositions were so different from mine, that I could never make it my own. This was the first cause of my unhappiness. What would I not have given to be the child of her mother? I did everything in my power to become so, but could never succeed. I in vain attempted to unite all our interests: this was impossible. She always created herself one different from mine, contrary to it, and to that even of her daughter, which already was no longer separated from it. She, her other children, and grand-children, became so many leeches, and the least evil these did to Thérèsa was robbing her. The poor girl, accustomed to submit, even to her nieces, suffered herself to be pilfered and governed without saying a word; and I perceived with grief that by exhausting my purse, and giving her advice, I did nothing that could be of any real advantage to her. I endeavored to detach her from her mother; but she constantly resisted such a proposal. I could not but respect her resistance, and esteemed her the more for it; but her refusal was not on this account less to the prejudice of us both. Abandoned to her mother and the rest of her family, she was more their companion than mine, and rather at their command than mistress of herself. Their avarice was less ruinous than their advice was pernicious to her; in fact, if, on account of the love she had for me, added to her good natural disposition, she was not quite their slave, she was enough so to prevent in a great measure the effect of the good maxims I endeavored to instill into her, and, notwithstanding all my efforts, to prevent our being united.

Thus was it, that notwithstanding a sincere and reciprocal attachment, in which I had lavished all the tenderness of my heart, the void in that heart was never completely filled. Children, by whom this effect should have been produced, were brought into the world, but these only made things worse. I trembled at the thought of intrusting them to a family ill brought up, to be still worse educated. The risk of the education of the foundling hospital was much less. This reason for the resolution I took, much stronger than all those I stated in my letter to Madam de Francueil, was, however, the only one with which I dared not make her acquainted; I chose rather to appear less excusable than expose to reproach the family of a person I loved. But by the conduct of her wretched brother, notwithstanding all that can be said in his defense, it will be judged whether or not I ought to have exposed my children to an education similar to his.

Not having it in my power to taste in all its plenitude the charms of that intimate connection of which I felt the want, I sought for substitutes which did not fill up the void, yet they made it less sensible. Not having a friend entirely devoted to me, I wanted others, whose impulse should overcome my indolence; for this reason I cultivated and strengthened my connections with Diderot and the Abbé de Condillac, formed with Grimm a new one still more intimate, till at length, by the unfortunate discourse, of which I have related some particulars, I unexpectedly found myself thrown back into a literary circle which I thought I had quitted forever.

My first steps conducted me by a new path to another intellectual world, the simple and noble economy of which I cannot contemplate without enthusiasm. I reflected so much on the subject that I soon saw nothing but error and folly in the doctrine of our sages, and oppression and misery in our social order. In the illusion of my foolish pride, I thought myself capable of destroying all imposture; and thinking that, to make myself listened to, it was necessary my conduct should agree with my principles, I adopted the singular manner of life which I have not been permitted to continue, the example of which my pretended friends have never forgiven me, which at first made me ridiculous, and would at length have rendered me respectable, had it been possible for me to persevere.

Until then I had been good; from that moment I became virtuous, or at least infatuated with virtue. This infatuation had begun in my head, but afterwards passed into my heart. The most noble pride there took root amongst the ruins of extirpated vanity. I affected nothing; I became what I appeared to be, and during four years at least, whilst this effervescence continued at its greatest height, there is nothing great and good that can enter the heart of man, of which I was not capable between heaven and myself. Hence flowed my sudden eloquence; hence, in my first writings, that fire really celestial, which consumed me, and whence during forty years not a single spark had escaped, because it was not yet lighted up.

I was really transformed; my friends and acquaintance scarcely knew me. I was no longer that timid, and rather bashful than modest man, who neither dared to present himself, nor utter a word; whom a single pleasantry disconcerted, and whose face was covered with a blush the moment his eyes met those of a woman. I became bold, haughty, intrepid, with a confidence the more firm, as it was simple, and resided in my soul rather than in my manner. The contempt with which my profound meditations had inspired me for the manners, maxims and prejudices of the age in which I lived, rendered me proof against the raillery of those by whom they were possessed, and I crushed their little pleasantries with a sentence, as I would have crushed an insect with my fingers. What a change! All Paris repeated the severe and acute sarcasms of the same man who, two years before, and ten years afterwards, knew not how to find what he had to say, nor the word he ought to employ. Let the situation in the world the most contrary to my natural disposition be sought after, and this will be found. Let one of the short moments of my life in which I became another man, and ceased to be myself, be recollected, this also will be found in the time of which I speak; but, instead of continuing only six days, or six weeks, it lasted almost six years, and would perhaps still continue, but for the particular circumstances which caused it to cease, and restored me to nature, above which I had wished to soar.

The beginning of this change took place as soon as I had quitted Paris, and the sight of the vices of that city no longer kept up the indignation with which it had inspired me. I no sooner had lost sight of men than I ceased to despise them, and once removed from those who designed me evil, my hatred against them no longer existed. My heart, little fitted for hatred, pitied their misery, and even their wickedness. This situation, more pleasing but less sublime, soon allayed the ardent enthusiasm by which I had so long been transported; and I insensibly, almost to myself even, again became fearful, complaisant and timid; in a word, the same Jean-Jacques I before had been.

Had this resolution gone no further than restoring me to myself, all would have been well; but unfortunately it rapidly carried me away to the other extreme. From that moment my mind in agitation passed the line of repose, and its oscillations, continually renewed, have never permitted it to remain here. I must enter into some detail of this second revolution; terrible and fatal era, of a fate unparalleled amongst mortals.

We were but three persons in our retirement; it

was therefore natural our intimacy should be increased by leisure and solitude. This was the case between Thérèsa and myself. We passed in conversations in the shade the most charming and delightful hours, more so than any I had hitherto enjoyed. She seemed to taste of this sweet intercourse more than I had until then observed her to do; she opened her heart, and communicated to me, relative to her mother and family, things she had had resolution enough to conceal for a great length of time. Both had received from Madam Dupin numerous presents, made them on my account, and mostly for me, but which the cunning old woman, to prevent my being angry, had appropriated to her own use and that of her other children, without suffering Thérèsa to have the least share, strongly forbidding her to say a word to me of the matter: an order the poor girl had obeyed with an incredible exactness.

But another thing which surprised me more than this had done, was the discovery that besides the private conversations Diderot and Grimm had frequently had with both to endeavor to detach them from me, in which, by means of the resistance of Thérèsa, they had not been able to succeed, they had afterwards had frequent conferences with the mother, the subject of which was a secret to the daughter. However, she knew little presents had been made, and that there were mysterious goings backward and forward, the motive of which was entirely unknown to her. When we left Paris, Madam le Vasseur had long been in the habit of going to see Grimm twice or thrice a month, and continuing with him for hours together, in conversation so secret that the servant was always sent out of the room.

I judged this motive to be of the same nature with the project into which they had attempted to make the daughter enter, by promising to procure her and her mother, by means of Madam d'Epinay, a salt huckster's license, or a snuff-shop; in a word, by tempting her with the allurements of gain. They had been told that, as I was not in a situation to do anything for them, I could not, on their account, do anything for myself. As in all this I saw nothing but good intentions, I was not absolutely displeased with them for it. The mystery was the only thing which gave me pain, especially on the part of the old woman, who moreover daily became more parasitical and flattering towards me. This, however, did not prevent her from reproaching her daughter in private with telling me everything, and loving me too much, observing to her she was a fool and would at length be made a dupe.

This woman possessed, to a supreme degree, the art of multiplying the presents made her, by concealing from one what she received from another, and from me what she received from all. I could have pardoned her avarice, but it was impossible I should forgive her dissimulation. What could she have to conceal from me whose happiness she knew principally consisted in that of herself and her daughter? What

I had done for the daughter I had done for myself, but the services I rendered the mother merited on her part some acknowledgment. She ought, at least, to have thought herself obliged for them to her daughter, and to have loved me for the sake of her by whom I was already beloved. I had raised her from the lowest state of wretchedness; she received from my hands the means of subsistence, and was indebted to me for her acquaintance with the persons from whom she found means to reap considerable benefit. Thérèsa had long supported her by her industry, and now maintained her with my bread. She owed everything to this daughter, for whom she had done nothing, and her other children, to whom she had given marriage portions, and on whose account she had ruined herself, far from giving her the least aid, devoured her substance and mine. I thought that in such a situation she ought to consider me as her only friend and most sure protector, and that, far from making of my own affairs a secret to me, and conspiring against me in my house, it was her duty faithfully to acquaint me with everything in which I was interested, when this came to her knowledge before it did to mine. In what light, therefore, could I consider her false and mysterious conduct? What could I think of the sentiments with which she endeavored to inspire her daughter? What monstrous ingratitude was hers, to endeavor to instill it into her from whom I expected my greatest consolation?

These reflections at length alienated my affections

from this woman, and to such a degree that I could no longer look upon her but with contempt. I nevertheless continued to treat with respect the mother of the friend of my bosom, and in everything to show her almost the reverence of a son; but I must confess I could not remain long with her without pain, and that I never knew how to bear constraint.

This is another short moment of my life, in which I approached near to happiness without being able to attain it, and this by no fault of my own. Had the mother been of a good disposition we all three should have been happy to the end of our days; the longest liver only would have been to be pitied. Instead of which, the reader will see the course things took, and judge whether or not it was in my power to change it.

Madam de Vasseur, who perceived I had got more full possession of the heart of Thérèsa, and that she had lost ground with her, endeavored to regain it; and, instead of striving to restore herself to my good opinion by the mediation of her daughter, attempted to alienate her affections from me. One of the means she employed was to call her family to her aid. I had begged Thérèsa not to invite any of her relations to the Hermitage, and she had promised me she would not. These were sent for in my absence, without consulting her, and she was afterwards prevailed upon to promise not to say anything of the matter. After the first step was taken all the rest were easy. When once we make a secret of anything to the person we love, we soon make little scruple of doing it in everything;

the moment I was at the Chevrette the Hermitage was full of people who sufficiently amused themselves. A mother has always great power over a daughter of a mild disposition; yet notwithstanding all the old woman could do, she was never able to prevail upon Thérèsa to enter into her views, nor to persuade her to join in the league against me. For her part, she resolved upon doing it forever, and seeing on one side her daughter and myself, who were in a situation to live, and that was all; on the other, Diderot, Grimm, D'Holbach and Madam d'Epinay, who promised great things, and gave some little ones, she could not conceive it was possible to be in the wrong with the wife of a farmer-general and a baron. Had I been more clear sighted, I should from this moment have perceived I nourished a serpent in my bosom. But my blind confidence, which nothing had yet diminished, was such that I could not imagine she wished to injure the person she ought to love. Though I saw numerous conspiracies formed on every side, all I complain of was the tyranny of persons who called themselves my friends, and who, as it seemed, would force me to be happy in the manner they should point out, and not in that I had chosen for myself.

Although Thérèsa refused to join in the confederacy with her mother, she afterwards kept her secret. For this her motive was commendable, although I will not determine whether she did it well or ill. Two women, who have secrets between them, love to prattle together; this attracted them towards each other, and Thérèsa, by dividing herself, sometimes let me feel I was alone; for I could no longer consider as a society that which we all three formed.

I now felt the neglect I had been guilty of during the first years of our connection, in not taking advantage of the docility with which her love inspired her, to improve her talents and give her knowledge, which, by more closely connecting us in our retirement would agreeably have filled up her time and my own, without once suffering us to perceive the length of a private conversation. Not that this was ever exhausted between us, or that she seemed disgusted with our walks; but we had not a sufficient number of ideas common to both to make ourselves a great store, and we could not incessantly talk of our future projects which were confined to those of enjoying the pleasure of life. The objects around us inspired me with reflections beyond the reach of her comprehension. An attachment of twelve years' standing had no longer need of words: we were too well acquainted with each other to have any new knowledge to acquire in that respect. The resource of puns, jests, gossiping and scandal, was all that remained. In solitude especially is it, that the advantage of living with a person who knows how to think is particularly felt. I wanted not this resource to amuse myself with her; but she would have stood in need of it to have always found amusement with me. The worst of all was our being obliged to hold our conversations when we could; her mother, who become importunate, obliged me to watch for opportunities to do it. I was under constraint in my own house: this is saying everything; the air of love was prejudicial to good friendship. We had an intimate intercourse without living in intimacy.

The moment I thought I perceived that Thérèsa sometimes sought for a pretext to elude the walks I proposed to her, I ceased to invite her to accompany me, without being displeased with her for not finding in them so much amusement as I did. Pleasure is not a thing which depends upon the will. I was sure of her heart, and the possession of this was all I desired. As long as my pleasures were hers, I tasted of them with her; when this ceased to be the case I preferred her contentment to my own.

In this manner it was that, half deceived in my expectation, leading a life after my own heart, in a residence I had chosen with a person who was dear to me, I at length found myself almost alone. What I still wanted prevented me from enjoying what I had. With respect to happiness and enjoyment, everything or nothing, was what was necessary to me. The reason of these observations will hereafter appear. At present I return to the thread of my narrative.

I imagined that I possessed treasures in the manuscripts given me by the Comte de Saint-Pierre. On examination I found they were a little more than the collection of the printed works of his uncle, with notes and corrections by his own hand, and a few other trifling fragments which had not yet been published. I confirmed myself by these moral writings in the idea I had conceived from some of his letters, shown me by Madam de Créqui, that he had more sense and ingenuity than at first I had imagined; but after a careful examination of his political works, I discerned nothing but superficial notions, and projects that were useful but impracticable, in consequence of the idea from which the author never could depart, that men conducted themselves by their sagacity rather than by their passions. The high opinion he had of the knowledge of the moderns had made him adopt this false principle of improved reason, the basis of all the institutions he proposed, and the source of his political sophisms. This extraordinary man, an honor to the age in which he lived, and to the human species, and perhaps the only person, since the creation of mankind, whose sole passion was that of reason, wandered in all his systems from error to error, by attempting to make men like himself, instead of taking them as they were, are, and will continue to be. He labored for imaginary beings, while he thought himself employed for the benefit of his contemporaries.

All these things considered, I was rather embarrassed as to the form I should give to my work. To suffer the author's visions to pass was doing nothing useful; fully to refute them would have been unpolite, as the care of revising and publishing his manuscripts, which I had accepted, and even requested, had been intrusted to me; this trust had imposed on me the obligation of treating the author honorably. I at length concluded upon that which to me appeared the most decent, judicious, and useful. This was to give separately my own ideas and those of the author, and, for this purpose, to enter into his views, to set them in a new light, to amplify, extend them, and spare nothing which might contribute to present them in all their excellence.

My work therefore was to be composed of two parts absolutely distinct: one, to explain, in the manner I have just mentioned, the different projects of the author; in the other, which was not to appear until the first had had its effect, I should have given my opinion upon these projects, which I confess might sometimes have exposed them to the fate of the sonnet of the misanthrope. At the head of the whole was to have been the life of the author. For this I had collected some good materials, and which I flattered myself I should not spoil in making use of them. I had been a little acquainted with the Abbé de Saint-Pierre, in his old age, and the veneration I had for his memory warranted to me, upon the whole, that the comte would not be dissatisfied with the manner in which I should have treated his relation.

I made my first essay on the Perpetual Peace, the greatest and most elaborate of all the works which composed the collection; and before I abandoned myself to my reflections I had the courage to read everything the abbé had written upon this fine subject, without once suffering myself to be disgusted either by his slowness or repetitions. The public has seen the extract, on which account I have nothing to say upon the subject. My opinion of it has not been printed, nor do I know that it ever will be; however, it was written at the same time the extract was made. From this I passed to the *Polysynodie,* or Plurality of Councils; a work written under the regent to favor the administration he had chosen, and which caused the Abbé de Saint Pierre to be expelled from the academy, on account of some remarks unfavorable to the preceding administration, and with which the Duchess of Maine and the Cardinal de Polignac were displeased. I completed this work as I did the former, with an extract and remarks; but I stopped here without intending to continue the undertaking which I ought never to have begun.

The reflection which induced me to give it up naturally presents itself, and it was astonishing I had not made it sooner. Most of the writings of the Abbé de Saint Pierre were either observations, or contained observations, on some parts of the government of France, and several of these were of so free a nature, that it was happy for him he had made them with impunity. But in the offices of all the ministers of state the Abbé de Saint Pierre had ever been considered as a kind of preacher rather than a real politician, and he was suffered to say what he pleased, because it appeared that nobody listened to him. Had I procured him readers the case would have been different. He was a Frenchman, and I was not one; and by repeating his censures, although in his own name. I exposed myself to be asked, rather rudely, but without injustice, what it was with which I meddled. Happily before I proceeded any further, I perceived the hold I was about to give the government against me, and I immediately withdrew. I knew that, living alone in the midst of men more powerful than myself, I never could by any means whatever be sheltered from the injury they chose to do me. There was but one thing which depended upon my own efforts: this was, to observe such a line of conduct that whenever they chose to make me feel the weight of authority they could not do it without being unjust. The maxim which induced me to decline proceeding with the works of the Abbé de Saint Pierre, has frequently made me give up projects I had much more at heart. People who are always ready to construe adversity into a crime, would be much surprised were they to know the pains I have taken, that during my misfortunes it might never with truth be said of me, *Thou hast well deserved them.*

After having given up the manuscript, I remained some time without determining upon the work which should succeed it, and this interval of inactivity was destructive, by permitting me to turn my reflections on myself, for want of another object to engage my attention. I had no project for the future which could amuse my imagination. It was not even possible to form any, as my situation was precisely that in which all my desires were united. I had not another to conceive, and yet there was a void in my heart. This state was the more cruel, as I saw no other that was to be preferred to it. I had fixed my most tender affections upon a person who made me a return of her own. I lived with her without constraint, and, so to speak, at discretion. Notwithstanding this, a secret grief of mind never quitted me for a moment, either when she was present or absent. In possessing Thérèsa, I still perceived she wanted something to her happiness; and the sole idea of my not being everything to her had such an effect upon my mind that she was next to nothing to me.

I had friends of both sexes, to whom I was attached by the purest friendship and most perfect esteem; I depended upon a real return on their part, and a doubt of their sincerity never entered my mind; yet this friendship was more tormenting than agreeable to me, by their obstinate perseverance, and even by their affectation, in opposing my taste, inclinations, and manner of living; and this to such a degree, that the moment I seemed to desire a thing which interested myself only, and depended not upon them, they immediately joined their efforts to oblige me to renounce it. This continued desire to control me in all my wishes, the more unjust, as I did not so much as make myself acquainted with theirs, became so cruelly oppressive, that I never received one of their letters without feeling a certain terror as I opened it, and which was but too well justified by the contents. I thought being treated like a child by persons younger than myself, and who, of themselves, stood in great need of the advice they so prodigally bestowed on me, was too much: "Love me," said I to them, "as I love you, but, in every other respect, let my affairs be as indifferent to you, as yours are to me: this is all I ask." If they granted me one of these two requests, it was not the latter.

I had a retired residence in a charming solitude, was master of my own house, and could live in it in the manner I thought proper, without being controlled by any person. This habitation imposed on me duties agreeable to discharge, but which were indispensable. My liberty was precarious. In a greater state of subjection than a person at the command of another, it was my duty to be so by inclination. When I arose in the morning, I never could say to myself, I will employ this day as I think proper. And, moreover, besides my being subject to obey the call of Madam d'Epinay, I was exposed to the still more disagreeable importunities of the public and chance comers. The distance I was at from Paris did not prevent crowds of idlers, not knowing how to spend their time, from daily breaking in upon me, and, without the least scruple, freely disposing of mine. When I least expected visitors I was unmercifully assailed by them, and I seldom made a plan for the agreeable employment of the day that was not counteracted by the arrival of some stranger.

In short, finding no real enjoyment in the midst of the pleasures I had been most desirous to obtain, I, by sudden mental transitions, returned in imagination to the serene days of my youth, and sometimes exclaimed with a sigh: "Ah! this is not *Les Charmettes!*"

The recollection of the different periods of my life led me to reflect upon that at which I was arrived, and I found I was already on the decline, a prey to painful disorders, and imagined I was approaching the end of my days without having tasted, in all its plenitude, scarcely any one of the pleasures after which my heart had so much thirsted, or having given scope to the lively sentiments I felt it had in reserve. I had not favored even that intoxicating voluptuousness with which my mind was richly stored, and which, for want of an object, was always compressed, and never exhaled but by signs.

How was it possible that, with a mind naturally expansive, I, with whom to live was to love, should not hitherto have found a friend entirely devoted to me; a real friend: I who felt myself so capable of being such a friend to another? How can it be accounted for that with such warm affections, such combustible senses, and a heart wholly made up of love, I had not once, at least, felt its flame for a determinate object? Tormented by the want of loving, without ever having been able to satisfy it, I perceived myself approaching the eve of old age, and hastening on to death without having lived.

These melancholy but affecting recollections led me to others which, although accompanied with regret, were not wholly unsatisfactory. I thought something I had not yet received was still due to me from destiny.

To what end was I born with exquisite faculties? To suffer them to remain unemployed? The sentiment of conscious merit, which made me consider myself as suffering injustice, was some kind of reparation, and caused me to shed tears which with pleasure I suffered to flow.

These were my meditations during the finest season of the year, in the month of June, in cool shades, to the songs of the nightingale, and the warbling of brooks. Everything concurred in plunging me into that too seducing state of indolence for which I was born, but from which my austere manner, proceeding from a long effervescence, should forever have delivered me. I unfortunately recollected the dinner of the Château de Toune, and my meeting with the two charming girls in the same season, in places much resembling that in which I then was. The remembrance of these circumstances, which the innocence that accompanied them rendered to me still more dear, brought several others of the nature to my recollection. I presently saw myself surrounded by all the objects which, in my youth, had given me emotion. Mademoiselle Galley, Mademoiselle de Graffenried, Mademoiselle de Breil, Madam Basile, Madam de Larnage, my pretty scholars, and even the bewitching Zulietta, whom my heart could not forget. I found myself in the midst of a seraglio of houris of my old acquaintance, for whom the most lively inclination was not new to me. My blood became inflamed, my head turned, notwithstanding my hair was almost gray, and the grave citizen of Geneva, the austere *Jean-Jacques,* at forty-five years of age, again became the fond shepherd. The intoxication, with which my mind was seized, although sudden and extravagant, was so strong and lasting, that, to enable me to recover from it, nothing less than the unforeseen and terrible crisis it brought on was necessary.

This intoxication, to whatever degree it was carried, went not so far as to make me forget my age and situation, to flatter me that I could still inspire love, nor to make me attempt to communicate the devouring flame by which ever since my youth I had felt my heart in vain consumed. For this I did not hope; I did not even desire it. I knew the season of love was past; I knew too well in what contempt the ridiculous pretensions of superannuated gallants were held, ever to add one to the number, and I was not a man to become an impudent coxcomb in the decline of life, after having been so little such during the flower of my age. Besides, as a friend to peace, I should have been apprehensive of domestic dissensions; and I too sincerely loved Thérèsa to expose her to the mortification of seeing me entertain for others more lively sentiments than those with which she inspired me for herself.

What step did I take upon this occasion? My reader will already have guessed it, if he has taken the trouble to pay the least attention to my narrative.

The impossibility of attaining real beings threw me into the regions of chimera, and seeing nothing in existence worthy of my delirium, I sought food for it in the ideal world, which my imagination quickly peopled with beings after my own heart. This resource never came more *àpropos,* nor was it ever so fertile. In my continual ecstasy I intoxicated my mind with the most delicious sentiments that ever entered the heart of man. Entirely forgetting the human species, I formed to myself societies of perfect beings, whose virtues were as celestial as their beauty, tender and faithful friends, such as I never found here below. I became so fond of soaring in the empyrean, in the midst of the charming objects with which I was surrounded, that I thus passed hours and days without perceiving it; and, losing the remembrance of all other things, I scarcely had eaten a morsel in haste before I was impatient to make my escape and run to regain my groves. When ready to depart for the enchanted world, I saw arrive wretched mortals who came to detain me upon earth, I could neither conceal nor moderate my vexation; and no longer master of myself, I gave them so uncivil a reception, that it might justly be termed brutal. This tended to confirm my reputation as a misanthrope, from the very cause which, could the world have read my heart, should have acquired me one of a nature directly opposite.

In the midst of my exaltation I was pulled down like a paper kite, and restored to my proper place by means of a smart attack of my disorder. I recurred to the only means that had before given me relief, and thus made a truce with my angelic amours; for besides that it seldom happens that a man is amorous when he suffers, my imagination, which is animated in the country and beneath the shade of trees, languishes and becomes extinguished in a chamber, and under the joists of a ceiling. I frequently regretted that there existed no dryads; it would certainly have been amongst these that I should have fixed my attachment.

Other domestic broils came at the same time to increase my chagrin. Madam le Vasseur, while making me the finest compliments in the world, alienated from me her daughter as much as she possibly could. I received letters from my late neighborhood, informing me that the good old lady had secretly contracted several debts in the name of Thérèsa, to whom these became known, but of which she had never mentioned to me a word. The debts to be paid hurt me much less than the secret that had been made of them. How could she, from whom I had never had a secret, have one from me? Is it possible to dissimulate with persons whom we love? The *Coterie Holbachique,* who found I never made a journey to Paris, began seriously to be afraid I was happy and satisfied in the country, and madman enough to reside there.

Hence the cabals by which attempts were made to recall me indirectly to the city. Diderot, who did not immediately wish to show himself, began by detaching from me De Leyre, whom I had brought acquainted with him, and who received and transmitted to me the impressions Diderot chose to give without suspecting to what end they were directed.

Everything seemed to concur in withdrawing me from my charming and mad reverie. I was not recovered from the late attack I had when I received the copy of the poem on the destruction of Lisbon, which I imagined to be sent by the author. This made it necessary I should write to him and speak of his composition. I did so, and my letter was a long time afterwards printed without my consent, as I shall hereafter have occasion to remark.

Struck by seeing this poor man overwhelmed, if I may so speak, with prosperity and honor, bitterly exclaiming against the miseries of this life, and finding everything to be wrong, I formed the mad project of making him turn his attention to himself, and of proving to him that everything was right. Voltaire, while he appeared to believe in God, never really believed in anything but the devil; since his pretended deity is a malicious being, who, according to him, had no pleasure but in evil. The glaring absurdity of this doctrine is particularly disgusting from a man enjoying the greatest prosperity; who, from the bosom of happiness, endeavors, by the frightful and cruel image of all the calamities from which he is exempt, to reduce his fellow creatures to despair. I, who had a better right than he to calculate and weigh all the evils of human life, impartially examined them, and proved to him that of all possible evils there was not one to be attributed to Providence, and which had not its source rather in the abusive use man made of his faculties than in nature. I treated him, in this letter, with the greatest respect and delicacy possible. Yet, knowing his self-love to be extremely irritable, I did not send the letter immediately to himself, but to Doctor Tronchin, his physician and friend, with full power either to give it him or destroy it. Voltaire informed me in a few lines that being ill, having likewise the care of a sick person, he postponed his answer until some future day, and said not a word upon the subject. Tronchin, when he sent me the letter, inclosed it in another, in which he expressed but very little esteem for the person from whom he received it.

I have never published, nor even shown, either of these two letters, not liking to make a parade of such little triumphs; but the originals are in my collections. Since that time Voltaire has published the answer he promised me, but which I never received. This is the novel of Candide, of which I cannot speak because I have not read it.

All these interruptions ought to have cured me of my fantastic amours, and they were perhaps the means offered me by Heaven to prevent their destructive consequences; but my evil genius prevailed, and I had scarcely begun to go out before my heart, my head, and my feet returned to the same paths. I say the same in certain respects; for my ideas, rather less exalted, remained this time upon earth, but yet were busied in making so exquisite a choice of all that was to be found there amiable of every kind, that it was not much less chimerical than the imaginary world I had abandoned.

I figured to myself love and friendship, the two idols of my heart, under the most ravishing images. I amused myself in adorning them with all the charms of the sex I had always adored. I imagined two female friends rather than two of my own sex, because, although the example be more rare, it is also more amiable. I endowed them with different characters, but analogous to their connection, with two faces, not perfectly beautiful, but according to my taste, and animated with benevolence and sensibility. I made one brown and the other fair, one lively and the other languishing, one wise and the other weak, but of so amiable a weakness that it seemed to add a charm to virtue. I gave to one of the two a lover, of whom the other was the tender friend, and even something more, but I did not admit either rivalry, quarrels, or jealousy: because every painful sentiment is painful to me to imagine, and I was unwilling to tarnish this delightful picture by anything which was degrading to nature. Smitten with my two charming models, I drew my own portrait in the lover and the friend, as much as it was possible to do it; but I made him young and amiable, giving him, at the same time, the virtues and the defects which I felt in myself.

That I might place my characters in a residence proper for them, I successively passed in review the most beautiful places I had seen in my travels. But I found no grove sufficiently delightful, no landscape that pleased me. The valleys of Thessaly would have satisfied me had I but once had a sight of them; but my imagination, fatigued with invention, wished for some real place which might serve it as a point to rest upon, and create in me an illusion with respect to the real existence of the inhabitants I intended to place there. I thought a good while upon the Borromean Islands, the delightful prospect of which had transported me, but I found in them too much art and ornament for my lovers. I however wanted a lake, and I concluded by making choice of that about which my heart has never ceased to wander. I fixed myself upon that part of the banks of this lake where my wishes have long since placed my residence in the imaginary happiness to which fate has confined me. The native place of my poor mamma had still for me a charm. The contrast of the situations, the richness and variety of the sites, the magnificence, the majesty of the whole, which ravishes the senses, affects the heart, and elevates the mind, determined me to give it the preference, and I placed my young pupils at Vervey. This is what I imagined at the first sketch; the rest was not added until afterwards.

I for a long time confined myself to this vague plan, because it was sufficient to fill my imagination with agreeable objects, and my heart with sentiments in which it delighted. These fictions, by frequently presenting themselves, at length gained a consistence, and took in my mind a determined form. I then had an inclination to express upon paper some of the situations fancy presented to me, and, recollecting everything I had felt during my youth, thus, in some measure, gave an object to that desire of loving, which I had never been able to satisfy, and by which I felt myself consumed.

I first wrote a few incoherent letters, and when I afterwards wished to give them connection, I frequently found a difficulty in doing it. What is scarcely credible, although most strictly true, is my having written the first two parts almost wholly in this manner, without having any plan formed, and not foreseeing I should one day be tempted to make it a regular work. For this reason the two parts afterwards formed of materials not prepared for the place in which they are disposed, are full of unmeaning expressions not found in the others.

In the midst of my reveries I had a visit from Madam d'Houdetot, the first she had ever made me, but which unfortunately was not the last, as will hereafter appear. The Comtesse d'Houdetot was the daughter of the late M. de Bellegarde, a farmer-general, sister to M. d'Epinay, and Messieurs de Lalive and De la Briche, both of whom have since been introductors to ambassadors. I have spoken of the acquaintance I made with her before she was married: since that event I had not seen her, except at the fêtes of La Chevrette, with Madam d'Epinay, her sister-in-law. Having frequently passed several days with her, both at La Chevrette and Epinay, I always thought her amiable, and that she seemed to be my well-wisher. She was fond of walking with me; we were both good walkers, and the conversation between us was inexhaustible. However, I never went to see her in Paris, although she had several times requested and solicited me to do it. Her connections with M. de St. Lambert, with whom I began to be intimate, rendered her more interesting to me, and it was to bring me some account of that friend who was, I believe, then at Mahon, that she came to see me at the Hermitage.

This visit had something of the appearance of the beginning of a romance. She lost her way. Her coachman, quitting the road, which turned to the right, attempted to cross straight over from the mill of Clairveaux to the Hermitage: her carriage stuck in a quagmire in the bottom of the valley, and she got out and walked the rest of the road. Her delicate shoes were soon worn through; she sank into the dirt, her servants had the greatest difficulty in extricating her, and she at length arrived at the Hermitage in boots, making the place resound with her laughter, in which I most heartily joined. She had to change everything. Thérèsa provided her with what was necessary, and I prevailed upon her to forget her dignity and partake of a rustic collation, with which she seemed highly satisfied. It was late, and her stay was short; but the interview was so mirthful that it pleased her, and she seemed disposed to return. She did not however put this project into execution until the next year: but, alas! the delay was not favorable to me in anything.

I passed the autumn in an employment no person would suspect me of undertaking: this was guarding the fruit of M. d'Epinay. The Hermitage was the reservoir of the waters of the park of the Chevrette; there was a garden walled round and planted with espaliers and other trees, which produced M. d'Epinay more fruit than his kitchen-garden at the Chevrette, although three-fourths of it were stolen from him. That I might not be a guest entirely useless, I took upon myself the direction of the garden and the inspection of the conduct of the gardener. Everything went on well until the fruit season, but as this became ripe, I observed that it disappeared without knowing in what manner it was disposed of. The gardener assured me it was the dormice which ate it all. I destroyed a great number of these animals, notwithstanding which the fruit still diminished. I watched the gardener's motions so narrowly, that I found he was the great dormouse. He lodged at Montmorency, whence he came in the night with his wife and children to take away the fruit he had concealed in the daytime, and which he sold in the market at Paris as publicly as if he had brought it from a garden of of his own. This wretch whom I loaded with kindness, whose children were clothed by Thérèsa, and whose father, who was a beggar, I almost supported, robbed us with as much ease as effrontery, not one of the three being sufficiently vigilant to prevent him: and one night he emptied my cellar.

Whilst he seemed to address himself to me only I suffered everything, but being desirous of giving an account of the fruit, I was obliged to declare by whom a great part of it had been stolen. Madam d'Epinay desired me to pay and discharge him, and look out for another; I did so. As this rascal rambled about the Hermitage in the night, armed with a thick club staff with an iron ferrule, and accompanied by other villains like himself, to relieve the governesses from their fears, I made his successor sleep in the house with us; and this not being sufficient to remove their apprehensions, I sent to ask M. d'Epinay for a musket, which I kept in the chamber of the gardener, with a charge not to make use of it except an attempt was made to break open the door or scale the walls of the garden, and to fire nothing but powder, meaning only to frighten the thieves. This was certainly the least precaution a man indisposed could take for the common safety of himself and family, having to pass the winter in the midst of a wood, with two timid women. I also procured a little dog to serve as a sentinel. De Leyre coming to see me about this time, I related to him my situation, and we laughed together at my military apparatus. At his return to Paris he wished to amuse Diderot with the story, and by this means the *Coterie d'Holbachique* learned that I was seriously resolved to pass the winter at the Hermitage. This perseverance, of which they had not imagined me to be capable, disconcerted them, and, until they could think of some other means of making my residence disagreeable to me, they sent back, by means of Diderot, the same De Leyre, who, though at first he had thought my precautions quite natural, now pretended to discover that they were inconsistent with my principles, and styled them more than ridiculous in his letters, in which he overwhelmed me with pleasantries sufficiently bitter and satirical to offend me had I been the least disposed to take offense. But at that time being full of tender and affectionate sentiments, and not susceptible of any other, I perceived in his biting sarcasms nothing more than a jest, and believed him only jocose when others would have thought him mad.

By my care and vigilance I guarded the garden so well, that, although there had been but little fruit that year the produce was triple that of the preceding years; it is true, I spared no pains to preserve it, and I went so far as to escort what I sent to the Chevrette and to Epinay, and to carry baskets of it myself. The "aunt" and I carried one of these, which was so heavy that we were obliged to rest at every dozen steps, and when we arrived with it we were quite wet with perspiration.

As soon as the bad season began to confine me to the house, I wished to return to my indolent amusements, but this I found impossible. I had everywhere two charming female friends before my eyes, their friend, everything by which they were surrounded, the country they inhabited, and the objects created or embellished for them by my imagination. I was no

longer myself for a moment, my delirium never left
me. After many useless efforts to banish all fictions
from my mind, they at length seduced me, and my
future endeavors were confined to giving them order
and coherence, for the purpose of converting them
into a species of novel.

What embarrassed me most was, that I had contradicted myself so openly and fully. After the severe
principles I had just so publicly asserted, after the
austere maxims I had so loudly preached, and my
violent invectives against books, which breathed
nothing but effeminacy and love, could anything be
less expected or more extraordinary, than to see me,
with my own hand, write my name in the list of
authors of those books, I had so severely censured? I
felt this incoherence in all its extent. I reproached
myself with it, I blushed at it and was vexed; but all
this could not bring me back to reason. Completely
overcome, I was at all risks obliged to submit, and to
resolve to brave the *What will the world say of it?*
Except only deliberating afterwards whether or not I
should show my work, for I did not yet suppose I
should ever determine to publish it.

This resolution taken, I entirely abandoned myself
to my reveries, and, by frequently resolving these in
my mind, formed with them the kind of plan of which
the execution has been seen. This was certainly the
greatest advantage that could be drawn from my
follies; the love of good which has never once been
effaced from my heart, turned them towards useful

objects, the moral of which might have produced its good effects. My voluptuous descriptions would have lost all their graces, had they been devoid of the coloring of innocence.

A weak girl is an object of pity, whom love may render interesting, and who frequently is not therefore the less amiable; but who can see without indignation the manners of the age; and what is more disgusting than the pride of an unchaste wife, who, openly treading under foot every duty, pretends that her husband ought to be grateful for her unwillingness to suffer herself to be taken in the fact? Perfect beings are not in nature, and their examples are not near enough to us. But whoever says that the description of a young person born with good dispositions, and a heart equally tender and virtuous, who suffers herself, when a girl, to be overcome by love, and when a woman, has resolution enough to conquer in her turn, is upon the whole scandalous and useless, is a liar and a hypocrite; hearken not to him.

Besides this object of morality and conjugal chastity which is radically connected with all social order, I had in view one more secret in behalf of concord and public peace, a greater, and perhaps more important object in itself, at least for the moment for which it was created. The storm brought on by the *Encyclopédie,* far from being appeased, was at this time at its height. Two parties exasperated against each other to the last degree of fury soon resembled enraged wolves, set on for their mutual destruction, rather than Christians and philosophers, who had a reciprocal wish to enlighten and convince each other, and lead their brethren to the way of truth. Perhaps nothing more was wanting to each party than a few turbulent chiefs, who possessed a little power, to make this quarrel terminate in a civil war; and God only knows what a civil war of religion founded on each side upon the most cruel intolerance would have produced. Naturally an enemy to all spirit of party, I had freely spoken severe truths to each, of which they had not listened. I thought of another expedient, which, in my simplicity, appeared to me admirable: this was to abate their reciprocal hatred by destroying their prejudices, and showing to each party the virtue and merit which in the other was worthy of public esteem and respect. This project, little remarkable for its wisdom, which supported sincerity in mankind, and whereby I fell into the error with which I reproached the Abbé de Saint-Pierre, had the success that was to be expected from it: it drew together and united the parties for no other purpose than that of crushing the author. Until experience made me discover my folly, I gave my attention to it with a zeal worthy of the motive by which I was inspired; and I imagined the two characters of Wolmar and Julia in an ecstasy, which made me hope to render them both amiable, and, what is still more, by means of each other.

Satisfied with having made a rough sketch of my plan, I returned to the situations in detail, which I had marked out; and from the arrangement I gave them resulted the first two parts of the Eloisa, which I finished during the winter with inexpressible pleasure, procuring gilt paper to receive a fair copy of them, azure and silver powder to dry the writing, and blue narrow ribbon to tack my sheets together; in a word, I thought nothing sufficiently elegant and delicate for my two charming girls, of whom, like another Pygmalion, I became madly enamoured. Every evening, by the fireside, I read the two parts to the governesses. The daughter, without saying a word, was like myself moved to tenderness, and we mingled our sighs; her mother, finding there were no compliments, understood nothing of the matter, remained unmoved, and at the intervals when I was silent always repeated: "*Sir, that is very fine.*"

Madam d'Epinay, uneasy at my being alone, in winter, in a solitary house, in the midst of woods, often sent to inquire after my health. I never had such real proofs of her friendship for me, to which mine never more fully answered. It would be wrong in me were not I, among these proofs, to make special mention of her portrait, which she sent me, at the same time requesting instructions from me in what manner she might have mine, painted by La Tour, and which had been shown at the exhibition. I ought equally to speak of another proof of her attention to me, which, although it be laughable, is a feature in the history of my character, on account of the impression received from it. One day when it froze to an extreme degree, in opening a packet she had sent me of several things

I had desired her to purchase for me, I found a little under-petticoat of English flannel, which she told me she had worn, and desired I would make of it an under-waistcoat.

This care, more than friendly, appeared to me so tender, and as if she had stripped herself to clothe me, that in my emotion I repeatedly kissed, shedding tears at the same time, both the note and the petticoat. Thérèsa thought me mad. It is singular that of all the marks of friendship Madam d'Epinay ever showed me this touched me the most, and that ever since our rupture I have never recollected it without being very sensibly affected. I for a long time preserved her little note, and it would still have been in my possession had not it shared the fate of my other notes received at the same period.

Although my disorder then gave me but little respite in winter, and a part of the interval was employed in seeking relief from pain, this was still upon the whole the season which since my residence in France I had passed with most pleasure and tranquillity. During four or five months, whilst the bad weather sheltered me from the interruptions of importunate visits, I tasted to a greater degree than I had ever yet or have since done, of that equally simple and independent life, the enjoyment of which still made it more desirable to me; without any other company than the two governesses in reality, and the two female cousins in idea. It was then especially that I daily congratulated myself upon the resolution I had had the good sense to take, unmindful of the clamors of my friends, who were vexed at seeing me delivered from their tyranny; and when I heard of the attempt of a madman, when De Leyre and Madam d'Epinay spoke to me in letters of the trouble and agitation which reigned in Paris, how thankful was I to Heaven for having placed me at a distance from all such spectacles of horror and guilt. These would have continued and increased the bilious humor which the sight of public disorders had given me; whilst seeing nothing around me in my retirement but gay and pleasing objects, my heart was wholly abandoned to sentiments which were amiable.

I remark here with pleasure the course of the last peaceful moments that were left me. The spring succeeding to this winter, which had been so calm, developed the germ of the misfortunes I have yet to describe; in the tissue of which, a like interval, wherein I had leisure to respite, will not be found.

I think however, I recollect, that during this interval of peace, and in the bosom of my solitude, I was not quite undisturbed by the Holbachiens. Diderot stirred me up some strife, and I am much deceived if it was not in the course of this winter that the *Fils Naturel,** of which I shall soon have occasion to speak, made its appearance. Independently of the causes which left me but few papers relative to that period, those even which I have been able to preserve are not very exact with respect to dates. Diderot never dated his letters. Madam d'Epinay and Madam d'Houdetot

---

* *Natural Son; a Comedy, by Diderot.*

seldom dated theirs, except the day of the week, and De Leyre mostly confined himself to the same rules. When I was desirous of putting these letters in order I was obliged to supply what was wanting by guessing at dates, so uncertain that I cannot depend upon them. Unable therefore to fix with certainty the beginning of these quarrels, I prefer relating in one subsequent article everything I can recollect concerning them.

The return of spring had increased my amorous delirium, and in my melancholy, occasioned by the excess of my transports, I had composed for the last parts of Eloisa several letters, wherein evident marks of the rapture in which I wrote them are found. Amongst others I may quote those from the Elysium, and the excursion upon the lake, which, if my memory does not deceive me, are at the end of the fourth part. Whoever, in reading these letters, does not feel his heart soften and melt into the tenderness by which they were dictated, ought to lay down the book: nature has refused him the means of judging of sentiment.

Precisely at the same time I received a second unforeseen visit from Madam d'Houdetot, in the absence of her husband, who was captain of the *Gendarmarie,* and of her lover, who was also in the service. She had come to Eaubonne, in the middle of the Valley of Montmorency, where she had taken a pretty house, from thence she made a new excursion to the Hermitage. She came on horseback, and dressed in men's clothes. Although I am not very fond of this kind of

masquerade, I was struck with the romantic appearance she made, and, for once, it was with love. As this
was the first and only time in all my life, the consequence of which will forever render it terrible to my
remembrance, I must take the permission to enter into
some particulars on the subject.

The Countess d'Houdetot was nearly thirty years
of age, and not handsome; her face was marked with
the smallpox, her complexion coarse, she was short-
sighted, and her eyes were rather round; but she had
fine long black hair, which hung down in natural
curls below her waist; her figure was agreeable, and
she was at once both awkward and graceful in her
motions; her wit was natural and pleasing; to this
gayety, heedlessness and ingenuousness were perfectly
suited: she abounded in charming sallies, after which
she so little sought, that they sometimes escaped her
lips in spite of herself. She possessed several agreeable
talents, played the harpsichord, danced well, and
wrote pleasing poetry. Her character was angelic—
this was founded upon a sweetness of mind, and except prudence and fortitude, contained in it every
virtue. She was besides so much to be depended upon
in all intercourse, so faithful in society, even her
enemies were not under the necessity of concealing
from her their secrets. I mean by her enemies the men,
or rather the women, by whom she was not beloved;
for as to herself she had not a heart capable of hatred,
and I am of opinion this conformity with mine greatly
contributed towards inspiring me with a passion for

her. In confidence of the most intimate friendship, I never heard her speak ill of persons who were absent, nor even of her sister-in-law. She could neither conceal her thoughts for any one, nor disguise any of her sentiments, and I am persuaded she spoke of her lover to her husband, as she spoke of him to her friends and acquaintance, and to everybody without distinction of persons. What proved, beyond all manner of doubt, the purity and sincerity of her nature was, that subject to very extraordinary absences of mind, and the most laughable inconsiderateness, she was often guilty of some very imprudent ones with respect to herself, but never in the least offensive to any person whatsoever.

She had been married very young and against her inclinations to the Comte d'Houdetot, a man of fashion, and a good officer; but a man who loved play and chicane, who was not very amiable, and whom she never loved. She found in M. de Saint Lambert all the merit of her husband, with more agreeable qualities of mind, joined with virtue and talents. If anything in the manners of the age can be pardoned, it is an attachment which duration renders more pure, to which its effects do honor, and which becomes cemented by reciprocal esteem. It was a little from inclination, as I am disposed to think, but much more to please Saint Lambert, that she came to see me. He had requested her to do it, and there was reason to believe the friendship which began to be established between us would render this society agreeable to all three. She knew I was acquainted with their con-

nection, and as she could speak to me without restraint, it was natural she should find my conversation
agreeable. She came; I saw her; I was intoxicated with
love without an object; this intoxication fascinated my
eyes; the object fixed itself upon her. I saw my Julia
in Madam d'Houdetot, and I soon saw nothing but
Madam d'Houdetot, but with all the perfections with
which I had just adorned the idol of my heart. To
complete my delirium she spoke to me of Saint Lambert with a fondness of a passionate lover. Contagious
force of love! while listening to her, and finding myself near her, I was seized with a delicious trembling
which I had never before experienced when near to
any person whatsoever. She spoke, and I felt myself
affected; I thought I was nothing more than interested by her sentiments, when I perceived I possessed
those which were similar; I drank freely of the
poisoned cup, of which I yet tasted nothing more than
the sweetness. Finally, imperceptibly to us both, she
inspired me for herself with all she expressed for her
lover. Alas! it was very late in life, and cruel was it to
consume with a passion not less violent than unfortunate for a woman whose heart was already in the
possession of another.

Notwithstanding the extraordinary emotions I had
felt when near to her, I did not at first perceive what
had happened to me; it was not until after her departure that, wishing to think of Julia, I was struck
with surprise at being unable to think of anything but
Madam d'Houdetot. Then was it my eyes were

opened: I felt my misfortune, and lamented what had happened, but I did not foresee the consequences.

I hesitated a long time on the manner in which I should conduct myself towards her, as if real love left behind it sufficient reason to deliberate and act accordingly. I had not yet determined upon this when she unexpectedly returned and found me unprovided. It was this time, perfectly acquainted with my situation, shame, the companion of evil, rendered me dumb, and made me tremble in her presence; I neither dared to open my mouth nor raise my eyes; I was in an inexpressible confusion which it was impossible she should not perceive. I resolved to confess to her my troubled state of mind, and left her to guess the cause whence it proceeded: this was telling her in terms sufficiently clear.

Had I been young and amiable, and Madam d'Houdetot, afterwards weak, I should here blame her conduct; but this was not the case, and I am obliged to applaud and admire it. The resolution she took was equally prudent and generous. She could not suddenly break with me without giving her reasons for it to Saint Lambert, who himself had desired her to come and see me; this would have exposed two friends to a rupture, and perhaps a public one, which she wished to avoid. She had for me esteem and good wishes; she pitied my folly without encouraging it, and endeavored to restore me to reason. She was glad to preserve to her lover and herself a friend for whom she had some respect; and she spoke of nothing with more pleasure than the intimate and agreeable society we might form between us three the moment I should become reasonable. She did not always confine herself to these friendly exhortations, and, in case of need, did not spare me more severe reproaches, which I had richly deserved.

I spared myself still less: the moment I was alone I began to recover; I was more calm after my declaration—love, known to the person by whom it is inspired, becomes more supportable.

The forcible manner in which I approached myself with mine ought to have cured me of it had the thing been possible. What powerful motives did I not call to my aid to stifle it? My morals, sentiments and principles; the shame, the treachery and crime, of abusing what was confided to friendship, and the ridiculousness of burning, at my age, with the most extravagant passion for an object whose heart was pre-engaged, and who could neither make me a return, nor least hope; moreover with a passion which, far from having anything to gain by constancy, daily became less sufferable.

We would imagine that the last consideration which ought to have added weight to all the others, was that whereby I eluded them! What scruple, thought I, ought I to make of a folly prejudicial to nobody but myself? Am I then a young man of whom Madam d'Houdetot ought to be afraid? Would not it be said by my presumptive remorse that, by my gallantry, manner and dress, I was going to seduce her? Poor

Jean-Jacques, love on at thy ease, in all safety of conscience, and be not afraid that thy sighs will be prejudicial to Saint Lambert.

It has been seen that I never was a coxcomb, not even in my youth. The manner of thinking, of which I have spoken, was according to my turn of mind, it flattered my passion; this was sufficient to induce me to abandon myself to it without reserve, and to laugh even at the impertinent scruple I thought I had made from vanity, rather than from reason. This is a great lesson for virtuous minds, which vice never attacks openly; it finds means to surprise them by masking itself with sophisms, and not unfrequently with a virtue.

Guilty without remorse, I soon became so without measure; and I entreat it may be observed in what manner my passion followed my nature, at length to plunge me into an abyss. In the first place, it assumed an air of humility to encourage me; and to render me intrepid it carried this humility even to mistrust. Madam d'Houdetot incessantly putting me in mind of my duty, without once for a single moment flattering my folly, treated me with the greatest mildness, and remained with me upon the footing of the most tender friendship. This friendship would, I protest, have satisfied my wishes, had I thought it sincere; but finding it too strong to be real, I took it into my head that love, so ill-suited to my age and appearance, had rendered me contemptible in the eyes of Madam d'Houdetot; that this young mad creature only wished to divert herself with me and my superannuated passion; that she had communicated this to Saint-Lambert; and that the indignation caused by my breach of friendship, having made her lover enter into her views, they were agreed to turn my head and then to laugh at me. This folly, which at twenty-six years of age, had made me guilty of some extravagant behavior to Madam de Larnage, whom I did not know, would have been pardonable in me at forty-five with Madam d'Houdetot had not I known that she and her lover were persons of too much uprightness to indulge themselves in such a barbarous amusement.

Madam d'Houdetot continued her visits, which I delayed not to return. She, as well as myself, was fond of walking, and we took long walks in an enchanting country. Satisfied with loving and daring to say I loved, I should have been in the most agreeable situation had not my extravagance spoiled all the charm of it. She, at first, could not comprehend the foolish pettishness with which I received her attentions; but my heart, incapable of concealing what passed in it, did not long leave her ignorant of my suspicions; she endeavored to laugh at them, but this expedient did not succeed; transports of rage would have been the consequence, and she changed her tone. Her compassionate gentleness was invincible; she made me reproaches, which penetrated my heart; she expressed an inquietude at my unjust fears, of which I took advantage. I required proofs of her being in earnest. She perceived there was no other means of relieving me from my apprehensions. I became pressing: the step was delicate. It is astonishing, and perhaps without example, that a woman having suffered herself to be brought to hesitate should have got herself off so well. She refused me nothing the most tender friendship could grant; yet she granted me nothing that rendered her unfaithful, and I had the mortification to see that the disorder into which her most trifling favors had thrown all my senses had not the least affect upon hers.

I have somewhere said, that nothing should be granted to the senses, when we wish to refuse them anything. To prove how false this maxim was relative to Madam d'Houdetot, and how far she was right to depend upon her own strength of mind, it would be necessary to enter into the detail of our long and frequent conversations, and follow them, in all their liveliness, during the four months we passed together in an intimacy almost without example between two friends of different sexes who contain themselves within the bounds which we never exceeded. Ah! if I had lived so long without feeling the power of real love, my heart and senses abundantly paid the arrears. What, therefore, are the transports we feel with the object of our affections by whom we are beloved, since the passions of which my idol did not partake inspired such as I felt?

But I am wrong in saying Madam d'Houdetot did not partake of the passion of love; that which I felt was in some measure confined to myself; yet love was equal on both sides, but not reciprocal. We were both intoxicated with the passion, she for her lover, and I for herself; our sighs and delicious tears were mingled together. Tender confidants of the secrets of each other, there was so great a similarity in our sentiments that it was impossible they should not find some common point of union. In the midst of this delicious intoxication, she never forgot herself for a moment, and I solemnly protest that, if ever, led away by my senses, I have attempted to render her unfaithful, I was never really desirous of succeeding. The vehemence itself of my passion restrained it within bounds. The duty of self-denial had elevated my mind. The luster of every virtue adorned in my eyes the idol of my heart; to have soiled their divine image would have been to destroy it. I might have committed the crime; it has been a hundred times committed in my heart; but to dishonor my Sophia! Ah! was this ever possible? No! I have told her a hundred times it was not. Had I had it in my power to satisfy my desires, had she consented to commit herself to my discretion, I should, except in a few moments of delirium, have refused to be happy at the price of her honor. I loved her too well to wish to possess her.

The distance from the Hermitage to Eaubonne is almost a league; in my frequent excursions to it I have sometimes slept there. One evening after having supped *tête-à-tête* we went to walk in the garden by a fine moonlight. At the bottom of the garden is a considerable copse, through which we passed on our way to a pretty grove ornamented with a cascade, of which I had given her the idea, and she had procured it to be executed accordingly.

Eternal remembrance of innocence and enjoyment! It was in this grove that, seated by her side upon a seat of turf under an acacia in full bloom, I found for the emotions of my heart a language worthy of them. It was the first and only time of my life; but I was sublime: if everything amiable and seducing with which the most tender and ardent love can inspire the heart of man can be so called. What intoxicating tears did I shed upon her knees! how many did I make her to shed involuntarily! At length in an involuntary transport she exclaimed: "No, never was man so amiable, nor ever was there one who loved like you! But your friend Saint Lambert hears us, and my heart is incapable of loving twice." I exhausted myself with sighs; I embraced her—what an embrace! But this was all. She had lived alone for the last six months, that is absent from her husband and lover; I had seen her almost every day during three months, and love seldom failed to make a third. We had supped *tête-à-tête,* we were alone, in the grove by moonlight, and after two hours of the most lively and tender conversation, she left this grove at midnight, and the arms of her lover, as morally and physically pure as she had entered it. Reader, weigh all these circumstances; I will add nothing more.

Do not, however, imagine that in this situation my passions left me as undisturbed as I was with Thérèsa and mamma. I have already observed I was this time inspired not only with love, but with love and all its energy and fury. I will not describe either the agitations, tremblings, palpitations, convulsionary emotions, nor faintings of the heart, I continually experienced; these may be judged of by the effect her image alone made upon me. I have observed the distance from the Hermitage to Eaubonne was considerable; I went by the hills of Andilly, which are delightful; I mused, as I walked, on her whom I was going to see, the charming reception she would give me, and upon the kiss which awaited me at my arrival. This single kiss, this pernicious embrace, even before I received it, inflamed my blood to such a degree as to affect my head, my eyes were dazzled, my knees trembled, and unable to support me; and I was obliged to stop and sit down; my whole frame was in inconceivable disorder, and I was upon the point of fainting. Knowing the danger, I endeavored at setting out to divert my attention from the object, and think of something else. I had not proceeded twenty steps before the same recollection, and all that was the consequence of it, assailed me in such a manner that it was impossible to avoid them, and in spite of all my efforts I do not believe I ever made this little excursion alone with impunity. I arrived at Eaubonne, weak, exhausted, and scarcely able to support myself. The moment I saw her everything was repaired; all I felt in her presence was the importunity of an inexhaustible and useless ardor. Upon the road to Eaubonne there was a pleasant terrace, called *Mont Olympe,* at which we sometimes met. I arrived first, it was proper I should wait for her; but how dear this waiting cost me! To divert my attention, I endeavored to write with my pencil billets, which I could have written with the purest drops of my blood; I never could finish one which was eligible. When she found a note in the niche upon which we had agreed, all she learned from the contents was the deplorable state in which I was when I wrote it. This state and its continuation, during three months of irritation and self-denial, so exhausted me, that I was several years before I recovered from it, and at the end of these it left me an ailment which I shall carry with me, or which will carry me to the grave. Such was the sole enjoyment of a man of the most combustible constitution, but who was, at the same time, perhaps, one of the most timid mortals nature ever produced. Such were the last happy days I can reckon upon earth; at the end of these began the long train of evils, in which there will be found but little interruption.

It has been seen that, during the whole course of my life, my heart, as transparent as crystal, has never been capable of concealing for the space of a moment any sentiment in the least lively which had taken refuge in it. It will therefore be judged whether or not it was possible for me long to conceal my affection for Madam d'Houdetot. Our intimacy struck the eyes of everybody, we did not make of it either a secret or a mystery. It was not of a nature to require any such precaution, and as Madam d'Houdetot had for me the most tender friendship with which she did not reproach herself, and I for her an esteem with the justice of which nobody was better acquainted than myself; she frank, absent, heedless; I true, awkward, haughty, impatient and choleric; we exposed ourselves more in deceitful security than we should have done had we been culpable. We both went to the Chevrette; we sometimes met there by appointment. We lived there according to our accustomed manner; walking together every day talking of our amours, our duties, our friend, and our innocent projects: all this in the park opposite the apartment of Madam d'Epinay, under her windows, whence incessantly examining us, and thinking herself braved, she by her eyes filled her heart with rage and indignation.

Women have the art of concealing their anger, especially when it is great. Madam d'Epinay, violent but deliberate, possessed this art to an eminent degree. She feigned not to see or suspect anything, and at the same time that she doubled towards me her cares, attention, and allurements, she affected to load her sister-in-law with incivilities and marks of disdain, which she seemingly wished to communicate to me. It will easily be imagined she did not succeed; but I was on the rack. Torn by opposite passions, at the same time that I was sensible of her caresses, I could scarcely contain my anger when I saw her wanting in good manners to Madam d'Houdetot. The angelic sweetness of this lady made her endure everything without a complaint, or even without being offended.

She was, in fact, so absent, and always so little attentive to these things, that half the time she did not perceive them.

I was so taken up with my passion, that, seeing nothing but Sophia (one of the names of Madam d'Houdetot), I did not perceive that I was become the laughing -stock of the whole house, and all those who came to it. The Baron d'Holbach, who never, as I heard of, had been at the Chevrette, was one of the latter. Had I at that time been as mistrustful as I am since become, I should strongly have suspected Madam d'Epinay to have contrived this journey to give the baron the amusing spectacle of the amorous citizen. But I was then so stupid that I saw not that even which was glaring to everybody. My stupidity did not, how-ever, prevent me from finding in the baron a more jovial and satisfied appearance than ordinary. Instead of looking upon me with his usual moroseness, he said to me a hundred jocose things without my knowing what he meant. Surprise was painted in my counte-nance, but I answered not a word: Madam d'Epinay shook her sides with laughing; I knew not what possessed them. As nothing yet passed the bounds of pleasantry, the best thing I could have done, had I been in the secret, would have been to have humored the joke. It is true, I perceived amid the rallying gayety of the baron, that his eyes sparkled with a malicious joy, which could have given me pain had

I then remarked it to the degree it has since occurred to my recollection.

One day when I went to see Madam d'Houdetot, at Eaubonne, after her return from one of her journeys to Paris, I found her melancholy, and observed that she had been weeping. I was obliged to put a restraint on myself, because Madam de Blainville, sister to her husband, was present; but the moment I found an opportunity, I expressed to her my uneasiness. "Ah," said she, with a sigh, "I am much afraid your follies will cost me the repose of the rest of my days. St. Lambert has been informed of what has passed, and ill informed of it. He does me justice, but he is vexed; and what is still worse, he conceals from me a part of his vexation. Fortunately I have not concealed from him anything relative to our connection which was formed under his auspices. My letters, like my heart, were full of yourself; I made him acquainted with everything, except your extravagant passion, of which I hoped to cure you, and which he imputes to me as a crime. Somebody has done us ill offices. I have been injured, but what does this signify? Either let us entirely break with each other, or do you be what you ought to be. I will not in future have anything to conceal from my lover."

This was the first moment in which I was sensible of the shame of feeling myself humbled by the sentiment of my fault, in presence of a young woman of whose just reproaches I approved, and to whom I ought to have been a mentor. The indignation I felt against myself would, perhaps, have been sufficient to overcome my weakness, had not the tender passion inspired me by the victim of it again softened my heart. Alas! was this a moment to harden it when it was overflowed by the tears which penetrated it in every part? This tenderness was soon changed into rage against the vile informers, who had seen nothing but the evil of a criminal but involuntary sentiment, without believing or even imagining the sincere uprightness of heart by which it was counteracted. We did not remain long in doubt about the hand by which the blow was directed.

We both knew that Madam d'Epinay corresponded with St. Lambert. This was not the first storm she had raised up against Madam d'Houdetot, from whom she had made a thousand efforts to detach her lover, the success of some of which made the consequences to be dreaded. Besides, Grimm, who, I think, had accompanied M. de Castries to the army, was in Westphalia, as well as Saint Lambert; they sometimes visited. Grimm had made some attempts on Madam d'Houdetot, which had not succeeded, and being extremely piqued, suddenly discontinued his visits to her. Let it be judged with what calmness, modest as he is known to be, he supposed she preferred to him a man older than himself, and of whom, since he had frequented the great, he had never spoken but as a person whom he patronized.

My suspicions of Madam d'Epinay were changed into a certainty the moment I heard what had passed in my own house. When I was at the Chevrette, Thérèsa frequently came there, either to bring me letters or to pay me that attention which my ill state of health rendered necessary. Madam d'Epinay had asked her if Madam d'Houdetot and I did not write to each other. Upon her answering in the affirmative, Madam d'Epinay pressed her to give her the letters of Madam d'Houdetot, assuring her she would reseal them in such a manner as it should never be known. Thérèsa, without showing how much she was shocked at the proposition, and without even putting me upon my guard, did nothing more than seal the letters she brought me more carefully; a lucky precaution, for Madam d'Epinay had her watched when she arrived, and, waiting for her in the passage, several times carried her audaciousness as far as to examine her tucker. She did more even than this: having one day invited herself with M. de Margency to dinner at the Hermitage, for the first time since I had resided there, she seized the moment I was walking with Margency to go into my closet with the mother and daughter, and to press them to show her the letters of Madam d'Houdetot. Had the mother known where the letters were, they would have been given to her; but, fortunately, the daughter was the only person who was in the secret, and denied my having preserved any one of them. A virtuous, faithful and generous falsehood; whilst truth would have been a perfidy. Madam d'Epinay, perceiving Thérèsa was not to be seduced, endeavored to irritate her by jealousy, reproaching her with her easy temper and blindness. "How is it possible," said she to her, "you cannot perceive there is a criminal intercourse between them? If besides what strikes your eyes you stand in need of other proofs, lend your assistance to obtain that which may furnish them; you say he tears the letters from Madam d'Houdetot as soon as he has read them. Well, carefully gather up the pieces and give them to me; I will take upon myself to put them together." Such were the lessons my friend gave to the partner of my bed.

Thérèsa had the discretion to conceal from me, for a considerable time, all these attempts; but perceiving how much I was perplexed, she thought herself obliged to inform me of everything, to the end that knowing with whom I had to do, I might take my measures accordingly. My rage and indignation are not to be described. Instead of dissembling with Madam d'Epinay, according to her own example, and making use of counterplots, I abandoned myself without reserve to the natural impetuosity of my temper; and with my accustomed inconsiderateness came to an open rupture. My imprudence will be judged of by the following letters, which sufficiently show the manner of proceeding of both parties on this occasion.

NOTE FROM MADAM D'EPINAY.

Packet A, No. 44.

"Why, my dear friend, do I not see you? You make me uneasy. You have so often promised me to do nothing but go and come between this place and the

Hermitage! In this I have left you at liberty; and you have suffered a week to pass without coming. Had not I been told you were well I should have imagined the contrary. I expected you either the day before yesterday, or yesterday, but found myself disappointed. My God, what is the matter with you? You have no business, nor can you have any uneasiness; for had this been the case, I flatter myself you would have come and communicated it to me. You are, therefore, ill! Relieve me, I beseech you, speedily from my fears. Adieu, my dear friend: let this adieu produce me a good-morning from you."

ANSWER.

Wednesday morning.

"I cannot yet say anything to you. I wait to be better informed, and this I shall be sooner or later. In the meantime be persuaded that innocence will find a defender sufficiently powerful to cause some repentance in the slanderers, be they who they may."

SECOND NOTE FROM THE SAME.

Packet A, No. 45.

"Do you know that your letter frightens me? What does it mean? I have read it twenty times. In truth I do not understand what it means. All I can perceive is, that you are uneasy and tormented, and that you wait until you are no longer so before you speak to me upon the subject. Is this, my dear friend, what we agreed upon? What then is become of that friendship and confidence, and by what means have I lost them? Is it with me or for me that you are angry? However this may be, come to me this evening I conjure you; remember you promised me no longer than a week ago to let nothing remain upon your mind, but immediately to communicate to me whatever might make it uneasy. My dear friend, I live in that confidence—There—I have just read your letter again; I do not understand the contents better, but they make me tremble. You seem to be cruelly agitated. I could wish to calm your mind, but as I am ignorant of the cause whence your uneasiness arises, I know not what to say, except that I am as wretched as yourself, and shall remain so until we meet. If you are not here this evening at six o'clock, I set off to-morrow for the Hermitage, let the weather be how it will, and in whatever state of health I may be; for I can no longer support the inquietude I now feel. Good day, my dear friend, at all risks I take the liberty to tell you, without knowing whether or not you are in need of such advice, to endeavor to stop the progress uneasiness makes in solitude. A fly becomes a monster. I have frequently experienced it."

ANSWER.

Wednesday evening.

"I can neither come to see you nor receive your visit so long as my present inquietude continues. The confidence of which you speak no longer exists, and it will be easy for you to recover it. I see nothing more in your present anxiety than the desire of drawing from the confessions of others some advantage agreeable to your views; and my heart, so ready to pour its overflowings into another which opens itself to receive them, is shut against trick and cunning. I distinguish your ordinary address in the difficulty you find in understanding my note. Do you think me dupe enough to believe you have not comprehended what it meant? No: but I shall know how to overcome your subtleties by my frankness. I will explain myself more clearly, that you may understand me still less.

"Two lovers closely united and worthy of each other's love are dear to me; I expect you will not know who I mean unless I name them. I presume attempts have been made to disunite them, and that I have been made use of to inspire one of the two with jealousy. The choice was not judicious, but it appeared convenient to the purposes of malice, and of this malice it is you whom I suspect to be guilty. I hope this becomes more clear.

"Thus the woman whom I most esteem would, with my knowledge, have been loaded with the infamy of dividing her heart and person between two lovers, and I with that of being one of these wretches. If I knew that, for a single moment in your life, you ever had thought this, either of her or myself, I should hate you until my last hour. But it is with having said, and not with having thought it, that I charge you. In this case, I cannot comprehend which of the three you wished to injure; but, if you love peace of mind, tremble lest you should have succeeded. I have not concealed either from you or her all the ill I think of certain connections, but I wish these to end by a means as virtuous as their cause, and that an illegitimate love may be changed into an eternal friendship. Should I, who never do ill to any person, be the innocent means of doing it to my friends? No, I should never forgive you; I should become your irreconcilable enemy. Your secrets are all I should respect; for I will never be a man without honor.

"I do not apprehend my present perplexity will continue a long time. I shall soon know whether or not I am deceived; I shall then perhaps have great injuries to repair, which I will do with as much cheerfulness as that with which the most agreeable act of my life has been accompanied. But do you know in what manner I will make amends for my faults during the short space of time I have to remain near to you? By doing what nobody but myself would do; by telling you freely what the world thinks of you, and the breaches you have to repair in your reputation. Notwithstanding all the pretended friends by whom you are surrounded, the moment you see me depart you may bid adieu to truth, you will no longer find any person who will tell it to you."

THIRD LETTER FROM THE SAME.

Packet A, No. 46.

"I did not understand your letter of this morning; this I told you because it was the case. I understand that of this evening; do not imagine I shall ever return an answer to it; I am too anxious to forget what it contains; and although you excite my pity, I am not proof against the bitterness with which it has filled my mind. I! descend to trick and cunning with you! I! accused of the blackest of all infamies! Adieu, I regret your having the—adieu. I know not what I say—adieu: I shall be very anxious to forgive you. You will come when you please; you will be better received than your suspicions deserve. All I have to desire of you is not to trouble yourself about my reputation. The opinion of the world concerning me is of but little importance in my esteem. My conduct is good, and this is sufficient for me. Besides, I am ignorant of what has happened to the two persons who are dear to me as they are to you."

This last letter extricated me from a terrible embarrassment, and threw me into another of almost the same magnitude. Although these letters and answers were sent and returned the same day with an extreme rapidity, the interval had been sufficient to place another between my rage and transport, and to give me time to reflect on the enormity of my imprudence. Madam d'Houdetot had not recommended to me anything so much as to remain quiet, to leave her the care of extricating herself, and to avoid, especially at that moment, all noise and rupture; and I, by the most open and atrocious insults, took the properest means of carrying rage to its greatest height in the heart of a woman who was already but too well disposed to it. I now could naturally expect nothing from her but an answer so haughty, disdainful, and expressive of contempt, that I could not, without the utmost meanness, do otherwise than immediately quit her house. Happily she, more adroit than I was furious, avoided, by the manner of her answer, reducing me to that extremity. But it was necesary either to quit or immediately go and see her; the alternative was inevitable; I resolved on the latter, though I foresaw how much I must be embarrassed in the explanation. For how was I to get through it without exposing either Madam d'Houdetot or Thérèsa? and woe to her whom I should have named! There was nothing that the vengeance of an implacable and an intriguing woman did not make me fear for the person who should be the object of it. It was to prevent this misfortune that in my letter I had spoken of nothing but suspicions, that I might not be under the necessity of producing my proofs. This, it is true, rendered my transports less excusable; no simple suspicions being sufficient to authorize me to treat a woman, and especially a friend, in the manner I had treated Madam d'Epinay. But here begins the noble task I worthily fulfilled of expiating my faults and secret weaknesses by charging myself with such of the former as I was incapable of committing, and which I never did commit.

I had not to bear the attack I had expected, and fear was the greatest evil I received from it. At my approach, Madam d'Epinay threw her arms about my neck, bursting into tears. This unexpected reception, and by an old friend, extremely affected me; I also shed many tears. I said to her a few words which had not much meaning; she uttered others with still less, and everything ended here. Supper was served; we sat down to table, where, in expectation of the explanation I imagined to be deferred until supper was over, I made a very poor figure; for I am so overpowered by the most trifling inquietude of mind that I cannot conceal it from persons the least clear-sighted. My embarrassed appearance must have given her courage, yet she did not risk anything upon that foundation. There was no more explanation after than before supper: none took place on the next day, and our little *tête-à-tête* conversations consisted of indifferent things, or some complimentary words on my part, by which, while I informed her I could not say more relative to my suspicions, I asserted, with the greatest truth, that, if they were ill-founded, my whole life should be employed in repairing the injustice. She did not show the least curiosity to know precisely what they were, nor for what reason I had formed them, and all our peace-making consisted, on her part as well as on mine, in the embrace at our first meeting. Since Madam d'Epinay was the only person offended, at least in form, I thought it was not for me to strive to bring about an *eclaircissement* for which she herself did not seem anxious, and I returned as I had come; continuing, besides, to live with her upon the same footing as before, I soon almost entirely forgot the quarrel, and foolishly believed she had done the same, because she seemed not to remember what had passed.

This, as it will soon appear, was not the only vexation caused me by weakness; but I had others not less disagreeable, which I had not brought upon myself. The only cause of these was a desire of forcing me from my solitude,* by means of tormenting me. These originated from Diderot and the d'Holbachiens. Since I had resided at the Hermitage, Diderot incessantly harassed me, either himself or by means of De Leyre, and I soon perceived from the pleasantries of the latter upon my ramblings in the groves, with what pleasure he had travestied the hermit into the gallant shepherd. But this was not the question in my quarrels with Diderot; the causes of these were more serious. After the publication of the *Fils Naturel* he had sent me a copy of it, which I had read with the interest and attention I ever bestowed on the works of a friend. In reading the kind of poem annexed to it, I was surprised and rather grieved to find in it, amongst several things, disobliging but supportable against men in solitude, this bitter and severe sentence without the least softening: *Il n'y a que le méchant qui foit seul.*† This sentence is equivocal, and seems to present a double meaning; the one true, the other false, since it is impossible that a man who is

* *That is to take from it the old woman who was wanted in the conspiracy. It is astonishing that, during this long quarrel, my stupid confidence prevented me from comprehending that it was not me but her whom they wanted at Paris.*

† *The wicked only are alone.*

determined to remain alone can do the least harm to anybody, and consequently he cannot be wicked. The sentence in itself therefore required an interpretation; the more so from an author who, when he sent it to the press, had a friend retired from the world. It appeared to me shocking and uncivil, either to have forgotten that solitary friend, or, in remembering him, not to have made from the general maxim the honorable and just exception which he owed, not only to his friend, but to so many respectable sages, who, in all ages, have sought for peace and tranquillity in retirement, and of whom, for the first time since the creation of the world, a writer took it into his head indiscriminately to make so many villains.

I had a great affection and the most sincere esteem for Diderot, and fully depended upon his having the same sentiments for me. But tired with his indefatigable obstinacy in continually opposing my inclinations, taste, and manner of living, and everything which related to no person but myself; shocked at seeing a man younger than I was wish, at all events, to govern me like a child; disgusted with his facility in promising, and his negligence in performing; weary of so many appointments given by himself, and capriciously broken, while new ones were again given only to be again broken; displeased at uselessly waiting for him three or four times a month on the days he had assigned, and in dining alone at night after having gone to Saint Denis to meet him, and waited the whole day for his coming; my heart was already full of these multiplied injuries. This last appeared to me still more serious, and gave me infinite pain. I wrote to complain of it, but in so mild and tender a manner that I moistened my paper with my tears, and my letter was sufficiently affecting to have drawn others from himself. It would be impossible to guess his answer on this subject: it was literally as follows: "I am glad my work has pleased and affected you. You are not of my opinion relative to hermits. Say as much good of them as you please, you will be the only one in the world of whom I shall think well: even on this there would be much to say were it possible to speak to you without giving you offense. A woman eighty years of age! etc. A phrase of a letter from the son of Madam d'Epinay which, if I know you well, must have given you much pain, has been mentioned to me."

The last two expressions of this letter want explanation.

Soon after I went to reside at the Hermitage, Madam le Vasseur seemed dissatisfied with her situation, and to think the habitation too retired. Having heard she had expressed her dislike to the place, I offered to send her back to Paris, if that were more agreeable to her; to pay her lodging, and to have the same care taken of her as if she remained with me. She rejected my offer, assured me she was very well satisfied with the Hermitage, and that the country air was of service to her. This was evident, for, if I may so speak, she seemed to become young again, and enjoyed better health than at Paris. Her daughter told me her mother would, on the whole, have been very sorry to quit the Hermitage, which was really a very delightful abode, being fond of the little amusements of the garden and the care of the fruit of which she had the handling, but that she had said, what she had been desired to say, to induce me to return to Paris.

Failing in this attempt they endeavored to obtain by a scruple the effect which complaisance had not produced, and construed into a crime my keeping the old woman at a distance from the succors of which, at her age, she might be in need. They did not recollect that she, and many other old people, whose lives were prolonged by the air of the country, might obtain these succors at Montmorency, near to which I lived; as if there were no old people, except in Paris, and that it was impossible for them to live in any other place. Madam le Vasseur, who ate a great deal, and with extreme voracity, was subject to overflowings of bile and to strong diarrhœas, which lasted several days, and served her instead of clysters. At Paris she neither did nor took anything for them, but left nature to itself. She observed the same rule at the Hermitage, knowing it was the best thing she could do. No matter, since there were not in the country either physicians or apothecaries, keeping her there must, no doubt, be with the desire of putting an end to her existence, although she was in perfect health. Diderot should have determined at what age, under pain of being punished for homicide, it is no longer permitted to let old people remain out of Paris.

This was one of the atrocious accusations from which he did not except me in his remark; that none but the wicked were alone: and the meaning of his pathetic exclamation with the *et cætera,* which he had benignantly added: *A woman of eighty years of age, etc.*

I thought the best answer that could be given to this reproach would be from Madam le Vasseur herself. I desired her to write freely and naturally her sentiments to Madam d'Epinay. To relieve her from all constraint I would not see her letter. I showed her that which I am going to transcribe. I wrote it to Madam d'Epinay upon the subject of an answer I wished to return to a letter still more severe from Diderot, and which she had prevented me from sending.

Thursday.

"My good friend. Madam le Vasseur is to write to you: I have desired her to tell you sincerely what she thinks. To remove from her all constraint, I have intimated to her that I will not see what she writes and I beg of you not to communicate to me any part of the contents of her letter.

"I will not send my letter because you do not choose I should; but, feeling myself grievously offended, it would be baseness and falsehood, of either of which it is impossible for me to be guilty, to acknowledge myself in the wrong. Holy writ commands him to whom a blow is given, to turn the other cheek, but not to ask pardon. Do you remember the man in comedy who exclaims, while he is giving another blows with his staff, 'This is the part of a philosopher!'

"Do not flatter yourself that he will be prevented from coming by the bad weather we now have. His rage will give him the time and strength which friendship refuses him, and it will be the first time in his life he ever came upon the day he had appointed.

"He will neglect nothing to come and repeat to me verbally the injuries with which he loads me in his letters; I will endure them all with patience. He will return to Paris to be ill again; and, according to custom, I shall be a very hateful man. What is to be done? Endure it all.

"But do not you admire the wisdom of the man who would absolutely come to Saint Denis in a hackney-coach to dine there, bring me home in a hackney-coach, and whose finances, eight days afterwards, obliges him to come to the Hermitage on foot? It is not possible, to speak his own language, that this should be the style of sincerity. But were this the case, strange changes of fortune must have happened in the course of a week.

"I join in your affliction for the illness of madam, your mother, but you will perceive your grief is not equal to mine. We suffer less by seeing the persons we love ill than when they are unjust and cruel.

"Adieu, my good friend, I shall never again mention to you this unhappy affair. You speak of going to Paris with an unconcern, which, at any other time, would give me pleasure."

I wrote to Diderot, telling him what I had done, relative to Madam le Vasseur, upon the proposal of Madam d'Epinay herself; and Madam le Vasseur having, as it may be imagined, chosen to remain at the Hermitage, where she enjoyed a good state of health, always had company, and lived very agreeably, Diderot, not knowing what else to attribute to me as a crime, construed my precaution into one, and discovered another in Madam le Vasseur continuing to reside at the Hermitage, although this was by her own choice; and though her going to Paris had depended, and still depended upon herself, where she would continue to receive the same succors from me as I gave to her in my house.

This is the explanation of the first reproach in the letter of Diderot. That of the second is in the letter which follows: "The learned man (a name given in a joke by Grimm to the son of Madam d'Epinay) must have informed you there were upon the rampart twenty poor persons who were dying with cold and hunger, and waiting for the farthing you customarily gave them. This is a specimen of our little babbling. . . . And if you understand the rest it would amuse you perhap."

My answer to this terrible argument, of which Diderot seemed so proud, was in the following words:

"I think I answered the *learned man;* that is, the farmer-general, that I did not pity the poor whom he had seen upon the rampart, waiting for my farthing; that he had probably amply made it up to them; that

I appointed him my substitute, that the poor of Paris would have no reason to complain of the change; and that I should not easily find so good a one for the poor of Montmorency, who were in much greater need of assistance. Here is a good and respectable old man, who, after having worked hard all his lifetime, no longer being able to continue his labors, is in his old days dying with hunger. My conscience is more satisfied with the two sols I give him every Monday, than with the hundred farthings I should have distributed amongst all the beggars on the rampart. You are pleasant men, you philosophers, while you consider the inhabitants of cities as the only persons whom you ought to befriend. It is in the country men learn how to love and serve humanity; all they learn in cities is to despise it."

Such were the singular scruples on which a man of sense had the folly to attribute to me as a crime my retiring from Paris, and pretended to prove to me by my own example, that it was not possible to live out of the capital without becoming a bad man. I cannot at present conceive how I could be guilty of the folly of answering him, and of suffering myself to be angry instead of laughing in his face. However, the decisions of Madam d'Epinay and the clamors of the *Coterie Holbachique* had so far operated in her favor, that I was generally thought to be in the wrong; and the D'Houdetot herself, very partial to Diderot, insisted upon my going to see him at Paris, and making all the advances towards an accommodation, which, full

and sincere as it was on my part, was not of long duration. The victorious argument by which she subdued
my heart was, that at that moment Diderot was in
distress. Besides the storm excited against the *Encyclopédie,* he had then another violent one to make head
against, relative to his piece, which, notwithstanding
the short history he had printed at the head of it, he
was accused of having entirely taken from Goldoni.
Diderot, more wounded by criticisms than Voltaire,
was overwhelmed by them. Madam de Grasigny had
been malicious enough to spread a report that I had
broken with him on this account. I thought it would
be just and generous publicly to prove the contrary,
and I went to pass two days, not only with him, but at
his lodgings. This, since I had taken up my abode at
the Hermitage, was my second journey to Paris. I had
made the first to run to poor Gauffecourt, who had
had a stroke of apoplexy, from which he has never
perfectly recovered: I did not quit the side of his pillow
until he was so far restored as to have no further need
of my assistance.

Diderot received me well. How many wrongs are
effaced by the embraces of a friend! after these, what
resentment can remain in the heart? We came to but
little explanation. This is needless for reciprocal invectives. The only thing necessary is to know how to
forget them. There had been no underhand proceedings, none at least that had come to my knowledge:
the case was not the same with Madam d'Epinay.

He showed me the plan of the *Pere de Famille*.*
"This," said I to him, "is the best defense of the *Fils
Naturel*. Be silent, give your attention to this piece,
and then throw it at the heads of your enemies as the
only answer you think proper to make them." He did
so, and was satisfied with what he had done. I had six
months before sent him the first two parts of my
Eloisa to have his opinion upon them. He had not yet
read the work over. We read a part of it together. He
found this *feuillet,* that was his term, by which he
meant loaded with words and redundancies. I myself
had already perceived it; but it was the babbling of
the fever: I have never been able to correct it. The last
parts are not the same. The fourth especially, and the
sixth, are masterpieces of diction.

The second day after my arrival, he would absolutely take me to sup with M. d'Holbach. We were
far from agreeing upon this point; for I wished even
to get rid of the bargain for the manuscript on chemistry, for which I was enraged to be obliged to that
man. Diderot carried all before him. He swore D'Holbach loved me with all his heart, said I must forgive
him his manner, which was the same to everybody,
and more disagreeable to his friends than to others.
He observed to me that, refusing the produce of this
manuscript, after having accepted it two years before,
was an affront to the donor which he had not deserved, and that my refusal might be interpreted into
a secret reproach, for having waited so long to con-

* *Father of the Family; a Comedy by Diderot.*

clude the bargain. "I see," added he, "D'Holbach every day, and know better than you do the nature of his disposition. Had you reason to be dissatisfied with him, do you think your friend capable of advising you to do a mean thing?" In short, with my accustomed weakness, I suffered myself to be prevailed upon, and we went to sup with the baron, who received me as he usually had done. But his wife received me coldly and almost uncivilly. I saw nothing in her which resembled the amiable Caroline, who, when a maid, expressed for me so many good wishes. I thought I had already perceived that since Grimm had frequented the house of D'Aine, I had not met there so friendly a reception.

Whilst I was at Paris, Saint Lambert arrived there from the army. As I was not acquainted with his arrival, I did not see him until after my return to the country, first at the Chevrette, and afterwards at the Hermitage; to which he came with Madam d'Houdetot, and invited himself to dinner with me. It may be judged whether or not I received him with pleasure! But I felt one still greater at seeing the good understanding between my guests. Satisfied with not having disturbed their happiness, I myself was happy in being a witness to it, and I can safely assert that, during the whole of my mad passion, and especially at the moment of which I speak, had it been in my power to take from him Madam d'Houdetot I would not have done it, nor should I have so much as been tempted to undertake it. I found her so amiable in her passion for Saint Lambert, that I could scarcely imagine she would have been as much so had she loved me instead of him; and without wishing to disturb their union, all I really desired of her was to permit herself to be loved. Finally, however violent my passion may have been for this lady, I found it as agreeable to be the confidant, as the object of her amours, and I never for a moment considered her lover as a rival, but always as my friend. It will be said this was not love: be it so, but it was something more.

As for Saint Lambert, he behaved like an honest and judicious man: as I was the only person culpable, so was I the only one who was punished; this, however, was with the greatest indulgence. He treated me severely, but in a friendly manner, and I perceived I had lost something in his esteem, but not the least part of his friendship. For this I consoled myself, knowing it would be much more easy to me to recover the one than the other, and that he had too much sense to confound an involuntary weakness and a passion with a vice of character. If even I were in fault in all that had passed, I was but very little so. Had I first sought after his mistress? Had not he himself sent her to me? Did not she come in search of me? Could I avoid receiving her? What could I do? They themselves had done the evil, and I was the person on whom it fell. In my situation they would have done as much as I did, and perhaps more: for, however estimable and faithful Madam d'Houdetot might be, she was still a woman; her lover was absent; opportunities were frequent; temptations strong; and it would have been very difficult for her always to have defended herself with the same success against a more enterprising man. We certainly had done a great deal in our situation, in placing boundaries beyond which we never permitted ourselves to pass.

Although at the bottom of my heart I found evidence sufficiently honorable in my favor, so many appearances were against me, that the invincible shame, always predominant in me, gave me in his presence the appearance of guilt, and of this he took advantage for the purpose of humbling me: a single circumstance will describe this reciprocal situation. I read to him, after dinner, the letter I had written the preceding year to Voltaire, and of which Saint Lambert had heard speak. Whilst I was reading he fell asleep, and I, lately so haughty, at present so foolish, dared not stop, and continued to read whilst he continued to snore. Such were my indignities and such his revenge; but his generosity never permitted him to exercise them, except between ourselves.

After his return to the army, I found Madam d'Houdetot greatly changed in her manner with me. At first I was as much surprised as if it had not been what I ought to have expected; it affected me more than it ought to have done, and did me considerable harm. It seemed that everything from which I expected a cure, still plunged deeper into my heart the dart, which I at length broke in rather than drew out.

I was quite determined to conquer myself, and

leave no means untried to change my foolish passion into a pure and lasting friendship. For this purpose I had formed the finest projects in the world; for the execution of which the concurrence of Madam d'Houdetot was necessary. When I wished to speak to her I found her absent and embarrassed; I perceived I was no longer agreeable to her, and that something had passed which she would not communicate to me, and which I have never yet known. This change, and the impossibility of knowing the reason of it, grieved me to the heart. She asked me for her letters; these I returned her with a fidelity of which she did me the insult to doubt for a moment.

This doubt was another wound given to my heart, with which she must have been so well acquainted. She did me justice, but not immediately: I understood that an examination of the packet I had sent her, made her perceive her error: I saw she reproached herself with it, by which I was a gainer of something. She could not take back her letters without returning me mine. She told me she had burnt them: of this I dared to doubt in my turn, and I confess I doubt of it at this moment. No, such letters as mine to her were, are never thrown into the fire. Those of Eloisa have been found ardent. Heavens! what would have been said of these? No, no, she who can inspire a like passion, will never have the courage to burn the proofs of it. But I am not afraid of her having made a bad use of them: of this I do not think her capable; and besides I had taken proper measures to prevent it.

The foolish, but strong apprehension of raillery, had made me begin this correspondence in a manner to secure my letters from all communication. I carried the familiarity I permitted myself with her in my intoxication so far as to speak to her in the singular number: but what *theeing* and *thouing!* she certainly could not be offended with it. Yet she several times complained, but this was always useless: her complaints had no other effect than that of awakening my fears, and I besides could not suffer myself to lose ground. If these letters be not yet destroyed, and should they ever be made public, the world will see in what manner I have loved.

The grief caused me by the coldness of Madam d'Houdetot, and the certainty of not having merited it, made me take the singular resolution to complain of it to Saint Lambert himself. While waiting the effect of the letter I wrote to him, I sought dissipations to which I ought sooner to have had recourse. Fêtes were given at the Chevrette for which I composed music. The pleasure of honoring myself in the eyes of Madam d'Houdetot by a talent she loved, warmed my imagination, and another object still contributed to give it animation, this was the desire the author of the *Devin du Village* had of showing he understood music; for I had perceived some persons had, for a considerable time past, endeavored to render this doubtful, at least with respect to composition. My beginning at Paris, the ordeal through which I had several times passed there, both at the house of

M. Dupin and that of M. de la Popliniere; the quantity of music I had composed during fourteen years in the midst of the most celebrated masters and before their eyes:——finally, the opera of the *Muses Gallantes,* and that even of the *Devin;* a motet I had composed for Mademoiselle Fel, and which she had sung at the spiritual concert; the frequent conferences I had had upon this fine art with the first composers, all seemed to prevent or dissipate a doubt of such a nature. This however existed even at the Chevrette, and in the mind of M. d'Epinay himself. Without appearing to observe it, I undertook to compose him a motet for the dedication of the chapel of the Chevrette, and I begged him to make choice of the words. He directed De Linant, the tutor to his son, to furnish me with these. De Linant gave me words proper to the subject, and in a week after I had received them the motet was finished. This time, spite was my Apollo, and never did better music come from my hand. The words began with: *Ecce sedes hic Tonantis.* (I have since learned these were by Santeuil, and that M. de Linant had without scruple appropriated them to himself.) The grandeur of the opening is suitable to the words, and the rest of the motet is so elegantly harmonious that every one was struck with it. I had composed it for a great orchestra. D'Epinay procured the best performers. Madam Bruna, an Italian singer, sung the motet, and was well accompanied. The composition succeeded so well that it was afterwards performed at the spiritual concert, where, in spite of secret cabals, and notwithstanding it was badly executed, it was twice generally applauded. I gave for the birthday of M. d'Epinay the idea of a kind of piece half dramatic and half pantomimical, of which I also composed the music. Grimm, on his arrival, heard speak of my musical success. An hour afterwards not a word more was said upon the subject; but there no longer remained a doubt, not at least that I know of, of my knowledge of composition.

Grimm was scarcely arrived at the Chevrette, where I already did not much amuse myself, before he made it insupportable to me by airs I never before saw in any person, and of which I had no idea. The evening before he came, I was dislodged from the chamber of favor, contiguous to that of Madam d'Epinay; it was prepared for Grimm, and instead of it, I was put into another further off. "In this manner," said I, laughingly, to Madam d'Epinay, "new-comers displace those which are established." She seemed embarrassed. I was better acquainted the same evening with the reason for the change, in learning that between her chamber and that I had quitted there was a private door which she had thought needless to show me. Her intercourse with Grimm was not a secret either in her own house or to the public, not even to her husband; yet, far from confessing it to me, the confidant of secrets more important to her, and which was sure would be faithfully kept, she constantly denied it in the strongest manner. I comprehended this reserve proceeded from Grimm, who, though intrusted with all my secrets, did not choose I should be with any of his.

However prejudiced I was in favor of this man by former sentiments, which were not extinguished, and by the real merit he had, all was not proof against the cares he took to destroy it. He received me like the *Comte de Tuffiére;* he scarcely deigned to return my salute; he never once spoke to me, and prevented my speaking to him by not making me any answer; he everywhere passed first, and took the first place without ever paying me the least attention. All this would have been supportable had he not accompanied it with a shocking affectation, which may be judged of by one example taken from a hundred. One evening Madam d'Epinay, finding herself a little indisposed, ordered something for her supper to be carried into her chamber, and went up stairs to sup by the side of the fire. She asked me to go with her, which I did. Grimm came afterwards. The little table was already placed, and there were but two covers. Supper was served: Madam d'Epinay took her place on one side of the fire, Grimm took an armed chair, seated himself at the other, drew the little table between them, opened his napkin, and prepared himself for eating without speaking to me a single word. Madam d'Epinay blushed at his behavior, and, to induce him to repair his rudeness, offered me her place. He said nothing, nor did he ever look at me. Not being able to approach the fire, I walked about the chamber until a cover was brought. Indisposed as

I was, older than himself, longer acquainted in the house than he had been, the person who had introduced him there, and to whom as favorite of the lady he ought to have done the honors of it, he suffered me to sup at the end of the table, at a distance from the fire, without showing me the least civility. His whole behavior to me corresponded with this example of it. He did not treat me precisely as his inferior, but he looked upon me as a cipher. I could scarcely recognize the same Grimm, who, to the house of the Prince de Saxe-Gotha, thought himself honored when I cast my eyes upon him. I had still more difficulty in reconciling this profound silence and insulting haughtiness with the tender friendship he possessed for me to those whom he knew to be real friends. It is true the only proofs he gave of it was pitying my wretched fortune, of which I did not complain; compassionating my sad fate, with which I was satisfied; and lamenting to see me obstinately refuse the benevolent services, he said, he wished to render me. Thus was it he artfully made the world admire his affectionate generosity, blame my ungrateful misanthropy, and insensibly accustomed people to imagine there was nothing more between a protector like him and a wretch like myself, than a connection founded upon benefactions on one part and obligations on the other, without once thinking of a friendship between equals. For my part, I have vainly sought to discover in what I was under an obligation to this new protector. I had lent him money, he had never lent me any; I had attended him in his illness, he scarcely came to see me in mine; I had given him all my friends, he never had given me any of his; I had said everything I could in his favor, and if ever he has spoken of me it has been less publicly and in another manner. He has never either rendered or offered me the least service of any kind. How, therefore, was he my Mecænas? In what manner was I protected by him? This was incomprehensible to me, and still remains so.

It is true he was more or less arrogant with everybody, but I was the only person with whom he was brutally so. I remember Saint Lambert once ready to throw a plate at his head, upon his, in some measure, giving him the lie at table by vulgarly saying, *"That is not true."* With his naturally imperious manner he had the self-sufficiency of an upstart, and became ridiculous by being extravagantly impertinent. An intercourse with the great had so far intoxicated him that he gave himself airs which none but the contemptible part of them ever assume. He never called his lackey but by *"Eh!"* as if amongst the number of his servants my lord had not known which was in waiting. When he sent him to buy anything, he threw the money upon the ground instead of putting it into his hand. In short, entirely forgetting he was a man, he treated him with such shocking contempt, and so cruel a disdain in everything, that the poor lad, a very good creature, whom Madam d'Epinay had recommended, quitted his service without any other complaint than that of the impossibility of enduring such treatment. This was the La Fleur of this new pre-suming upstart.

All these things were nothing more than ridiculous, but quite opposite to my character, they contributed to render him suspicious to me. I could easily imagine that a man whose head was so much deranged could not have a heart well placed. He piqued himself upon nothing so much as upon sentiments. How could this agree with defects which are peculiar to little minds? How can the continued overflowings of a susceptible heart suffer it to be incessantly employed in so many little cares relative to the person? He who feels his heart inflamed with this celestial fire strives to diffuse it, and wishes to show what he internally is. He would wish to place his heart in his countenance, and thinks not of other paint for his cheeks.

I remember the summary of his morality which Madam d'Epinay had mentioned to me and adopted. This consisted in one single article; that the sole duty of man is to follow all the inclinations of his heart. This morality, when I heard it mentioned, gave me great matter of reflection, although I at first consid-ered it solely as a play of wit. But I soon perceived it was a principle really the rule of his conduct, and of which I afterwards had, at my own expense, but too many convincing proofs. It is the interior doctrine Diderot has so frequently intimated to me, but which I never heard him explain.

I remember having several years before been fre-quently told that Grimm was false, that he had nothing more than the appearance of sentiment, and particularly that he did not love me. I recollected several little anecdotes which I had heard of him by M. de Francueil and Madam de Chenonceaux, neither of whom esteemed him, and to whom he must have been known, as Madam de Chenonceaux was daughter to Madam de Rochechouart, the intimate friend of the late Comte de Frièse, and that M. de Francueil, at that time very intimate with the Viscount de Polignac, had lived a good deal at the *Palaïs-Royal* precisely when Grimm began to introduce himself there. All Paris heard of his despair after the death of the Comte de Frièse. It was necessary to support the reputation he had acquired after the rigors of Mademoiselle Fel, and of which I, more than any other person, should have seen the imposture, had I been less blind. He was obliged to be dragged to the Hôtel de Castries where he worthily played his part, abandoned to the most mortal affliction. There, he every morning went into the garden to weep at his ease, holding before his eyes his handkerchief moistened with tears, as long as he was in sight of the hotel, but at the turning of a certain alley, people, of whom he little thought, saw him instantly put his handkerchief in his pocket and take out of it a book. This observation, which was repeatedly made, soon became public in Paris, and was almost as soon forgotten. I myself had forgotten it; a circumstance in which I was concerned brought it to my recollection. I was at the point of death in my bed, in the Rue de Grenelle, Grimm was in the country; he came one morning, quite out of breath, to see me, saying, he had arrived in town that very instant; and a moment afterwards I learned he had arrived the evening before, and had been seen at the theater.

I heard many things of the same kind; but an observation which I was surprised not to have made sooner, struck me more than everything else. I had given to Grimm all my friends without exception, they were become his. I was so inseparable from him, that I should have had some difficulty in continuing to visit at a house where he was not received. Madam de Créqui was the only person who refused to admit him into her company, and whom for that reason I have seldom since seen. Grimm on his part made himself other friends, as well by his own means, as by those of the Comte de Frièse. Of all these not one of them ever became my friend: he never said a word to induce me even to become acquainted with them, and not one of those I sometimes met at his apartments ever showed me the least good will; the Comte de Frièse, in whose house he lived, and with whom it consequently would have been agreeable to me to form some connection, not excepted, nor the Comte de Schomberg, his relation, with whom Grimm was still more intimate.

Add to this, my own friends, whom I made his, and who were all tenderly attached to me before this acquaintance, were no longer so the moment it was made. He never gave me one of his; I gave him all mine, and these he has taken from me. If these be the effects of friendship, what are those of enmity?

Diderot himself told me several times at the beginning that Grimm in whom I had so much confidence, was not my friend. He changed his language the moment he was no longer so himself.

The manner in which I had disposed of my children wanted not the concurrence of any person. Yet I informed some of my friends of it, solely to make it known to them, and that I might not in their eyes appear better than I was. These friends were three in number: Diderot, Grimm, and Madam d'Epinay. Duclos, the most worthy of my confidence, was the only real friend whom I did not inform of it. He nevertheless knew what I had done. By whom? This I know not. It is not very probable the perfidy came from Madam d'Epinay, who knew that by following her example, had I been capable of doing it, I had in my power the means of a cruel revenge. It remains therefore between Grimm and Diderot, then so much united, especially against me, and it is probable this crime was common to them both. I would lay a wager that Duclos, to whom I never told my secret, and who consequently was at liberty to make what use he pleased of his information, is the only person who has not spoken of it again.

Grimm and Diderot, in their project to take from me the governesses, had used the greatest efforts to make Duclos enter into their views; but this he refused to do with disdain. It was not until some time afterwards that I learned from him what had passed between them on the subject; but I learned at the time from Thérèsa enough to perceive there was some secret design, and that they wished to dispose of me, if not against my own consent, at least without my knowledge, or had an intention of making these two persons serve as instruments of some project they had in view. This was far from upright conduct. The opposition of Duclos is a convincing proof of it. They who think proper may believe it to be friendship.

This pretended friendship was as fatal to me at home as it was abroad. The long and frequent conversations with Madam le Vasseur, for several years past, had made a sensible change in this woman's behavior to me, and the change was far from being in my favor. What was the subject of these singular conversations? Why such a profound mystery? Was the conversation of that old woman agreeable enough to take her into favor, and of sufficient importance to make of it so great a secret? During the two or three years these colloquies had, from time to time, been continued, they had appeared to me ridiculous; but when I thought of them again, they began to astonish me. This astonishment would have been carried to inquietude had I then known what the old creature was preparing for me.

Notwithstanding the pretended zeal for my welfare of which Grimm made such a public boast, difficult to reconcile with the airs he gave himself when we were together, I heard nothing of him from any quarter the least to my advantage, and his feigned commiseration tended less to do me service than to render me contemptible. He deprived me as much as he possibly could of the resource I found in the employment I had chosen, by decrying me as a bad copyist. I confess he spoke the truth; but in this case it was not for him to do it. He proved himself in earnest by employing another copyist, and prevailing upon everybody he could, by whom I was engaged, to do the same. His intention might have been supposed to be that of reducing me to a dependence upon him and his credit for a subsistence, and to cut off the latter until I was brought to that degree of distress.

All things considered, my reason imposed silence upon my former prejudice, which still pleaded in his favor. I judged his character to be at least suspicious, and with respect to his friendship I positively decided it to be false. I then resolved to see him no more, and informed Madam d'Epinay of the resolution I had taken, supporting it with several unanswerable facts, but which I have now forgotten.

She strongly combated my resolution without knowing how to reply to the reasons on which it was founded. She had not concerted with him; but the next day, instead of explaining herself verbally, she, with great address, gave me a letter they had drawn up together, and by which, without entering into a detail of facts, she justified him by his concentrated character, attributed to me as a crime my having suspected him of perfidy towards his friend, and exhorted me to come to an accommodation with him. This letter staggered me. In a conversation we afterwards had together, and in which I found her better prepared than she had been the first time, I suffered myself to be quite prevailed upon, and was inclined to believe I might have judged erroneously. In this case I thought I really had done a friend a very serious injury, which it was my duty to repair. In short, as I had already done several times with Diderot, and the Baron d'Holbach, half from inclination, and half from weakness, I made all the advances I had a right to require; I went to M. Grimm, like another *George Dandin,* to make him my apologies for the offense he had given me; still in the false persuasion, which, in the course of my life has made me guilty of a thousand meannesses to my pretended friends, that there is no hatred which may not be disarmed by mildness and proper behavior; whereas, on the contrary, the hatred of the wicked becomes still more envenomed by the impossibility of finding anything to found it upon, and the sentiment of their own injustice is another cause of offense against the person who is the object of it. I have, without going further than my own history, a strong proof of this maxim in Grimm, and in Tronchin; both become my implacable enemies from inclination, pleasure and fancy, without having been able to charge me with having done either of them the most trifling injury,* and whose

* *I did not give the surname of Jongleur only to the latter until a long time after his enmity had been declared, and the persecutions*

rage, like that of tigers, becomes daily more fierce by the facility of satiating it.

I expected that Grimm, confused by my condescension and advances, would receive me with open arms, and the most tender friendship. He received me as a Roman Emperor would have done, and with a haughtiness I never saw in any person but himself. I was by no means prepared for such a reception. When, in the embarrassment of the part I had to act, and which was so unworthy of me, I had, in a few words and with a timid air, fulfilled the object which had brought me to him; before he received me into favor, he pronounced, with a deal of majesty, an harangue he had prepared, and which contained a long enumeration of his rare virtues, and especially those connected with friendship. He laid great stress upon a thing which at first struck me a good deal: this was his having always preserved the same friends. Whilst he was yet speaking, I said to myself, it would be cruel for me to be the only exception to this rule. He returned to the subject so frequently, and with such emphasis, that I thought, if in this he followed nothing but the sentiments of his heart, he would be less struck with the maxim, and that he made of it an art useful to his views by procuring the means of accomplishing them. Until then I had been in the

he brought upon me at Geneva and elsewhere. I soon suppressed the name the moment I perceived I was entirely his victim. Mean vengeance is unworthy of my heart, and hatred never takes the least root in it.

same situation; I had preserved all my first friends, those even from my tenderest infancy, without having lost one of them except by death, and yet I had never before made the reflection: it was not a maxim I had prescribed myself. Since, therefore, the advantage was common to both, why did he boast of it in preference, if he had not previously intended to deprive me of the merit? He afterwards endeavored to humble me by proofs of the preference our common friends gave to me. With this I was as well acquainted as himself; the question was, by what means he had obtained it? whether it was by merit or address? by exalting himself, or endeavoring to abase me? At last, when he had placed between us all the distance that he could add to the value of the favor he was about to confer, he granted me the kiss of peace, in a slight embrace which resembled the *accolade* which the king gives to new-made knights. I was stupefied with surprise: I knew not what to say; not a word could I utter. This whole scene had the appearance of the reprimand a preceptor gives to his pupil while he graciously spares inflicting the rod. I never think of it without perceiving to what degree judgments, founded upon appearances to which the vulgar give so much weight, are deceitful, and how frequently audaciousness and pride are found in the guilty, and shame and embarrassment in the innocent.

We were reconciled: this was a relief to my heart, which every kind of quarrel fills with anguish. It will naturally be supposed that a like reconciliation changed nothing in his manners; all it effected was to deprive me of the right of complaining of them. For this reason I took a resolution to endure every-thing, and for the future to say not a word.

So many successive vexations overwhelmed me to such a degree as to leave me but little power over my mind. Receiving no answer from Saint Lambert, neg-lected by Madam d'Houdetot, and no longer daring to open my heart to any person, I began to be afraid that by making friendship my idol, I should sacrifice my whole life to chimeras. After putting all those with whom I had been acquainted to the test, there remained but two who had preserved my esteem, and in whom my heart could confide: Duclos, of whom since my retreat to the Hermitage I had lost sight, and Saint Lambert. I thought the only means of re-pairing the wrongs I had done the latter, was to open myself to him without reserve, and I resolved to con-fess to him everything by which his mistress should not be exposed. I have no doubt but this was another snare of my passion to keep me nearer to her person; but I should certainly have had no reserve with her lover, entirely submitting to his direction, and carry-ing sincerity as far as it was possible to do it. I was upon the point of writing to him a second letter, to which I was certain he would have returned an an-swer, when I learned the melancholy cause of his silence relative to the first. He had been unable to support until the end the fatigues of the campaign. Madam d'Epinay informed me he had had an attack of the palsy, and Madam d'Houdetot, ill from affliction, wrote me two or three days afterwards from Paris, that he was going to Aix-la-Chapelle to take the benefit of the waters. I will not say this melancholy circumstance afflicted me as it did her; but I am of opinion my grief of heart was painful as her tears. The pain of knowing him to be in such a state, increased by the fear least inquietude should have contributed to occasion it, affected me more than anything that had yet happened, and I felt most cruelly a want of fortitude, which in my estimation was necessary to enable me to support so many misfortunes. Happily this generous friend did not long leave me so overwhelmed with affliction; he did not forget me, notwithstanding his attack; and I soon learned from himself that I had ill judged his sentiments, and been too much alarmed for his situation. It is now time I should come to the grand revolution of my destiny, to the catastrophe which has divided my life in two parts so different from each other, and, from a very trifling cause, produced such terrible effects.

One day, little thinking of what was to happen, Madam d'Epinay sent for me to the Chevrette. The moment I saw her I perceived in her eyes and whole countenance an appearance of uneasiness, which struck me the more, as this was not customary, nobody knowing better than she did how to govern her features and their movements. "My friend," said she to me, "I am immediately going to set off for Geneva; my chest is in a bad state, and my health so deranged that I must go and consult Tronchin." I was the more astonished at this resolution so suddenly taken, and at the beginning of the bad season of the year, as thirty-six hours before she had not, when I left her, so much as thought of it. I asked her who she would take with her. She said her son and M. de Linant; and afterwards carelessly added, "And you, bear, will not you go also?" As I did not think she spoke seriously, knowing that at the season of the year I was scarcely in a situation to go to my chamber, I joked upon the utility of the company, of one sick person to another. She herself had not seemed to make the proposition seriously, and here the matter dropped. The rest of our conversation ran upon the necessary preparations for her journey, about which she immediately gave orders, being determined to set off within a fortnight. She lost nothing by my refusal, having prevailed upon her husband to accompany her.

A few days afterwards I received from Diderot the note I am going to transcribe. This note, simply doubled up, so that the contents were easily read, was addressed to me at Madam d'Epinay's, and sent to M. de Linant, tutor to the son, and confidant to the mother.

NOTE FROM DIDEROT.

Packet A, No. 52.

"I am naturally disposed to love you, and am born to give you trouble. I am informed Madam d'Epinay is going to Geneva, and do not hear you are to accom-

pany her. My friend, you are satisfied with Madam
d'Epinay, you must go with her; if dissatisfied you
ought still less to hesitate. Do you find the weight of
the obligations you are under to her uneasy to you?
This is an opportunity of discharging a part of them,
and relieving your mind. Do you ever expect another
opportunity like the present one, of giving her proofs
of your gratitude? She is going to a country where
she will be quite a stranger. She is ill, and will stand
in need of amusement and dissipation. The winter
season too! Consider, my friend. Your ill state of
health may be a much greater objection than I think
it is; but are you now more indisposed than you were
a month ago, or than you will be at the beginning
of spring? Will you three months hence be in a situation to perform the journey more at your ease than
at present? For my part I cannot but observe to you
that were I unable to bear the shaking of the carriage
I would take my staff and follow her. Have you no
fears lest your conduct should be misinterpreted? You
will be suspected of ingratitude or of a secret motive.
I well know that let you do as you will you will have
in your favor the testimony of your conscience, but
will this alone be sufficient, and is it permitted to
neglect to a certain degree that which is necessary to
acquire the approbation of others? What I now write,
my good friend, is to acquit myself of what I think I
owe to us both. Should my letter displease you, throw
it into the fire and let it be forgotten. I salute, love,
and embrace you."

Although trembling, and almost blind with rage whilst I read this epistle, I remarked the address with which Diderot affected a milder and more polite language than he had done in his former ones, wherein he never went further than "My dear," without ever deigning to add the name of friend. I easily discovered the second-hand means by which the letter was conveyed to me; the superscription, manner and form awkwardly betrayed the maneuver; for we commonly wrote to each other by post, or the messenger of Montmorency, and this was the first and only time he sent me his letter by any other conveyance.

As soon as the first transports of my indignation permitted me to write, I, with great precipitation, wrote him the following answer, which I immediately carried from the Hermitage, where I then was, to the Chevrette, to show it to Madam d'Epinay, to whom, in my blind rage, I read the contents, as well as the letter from Diderot:

"You cannot, my dear friend, either know the magnitude of the obligations I am under to Madam d'Epinay, to what a degree I am bound by them, whether or not she is desirous of my accompanying her, that this is possible, or the reasons I may have for my non-compliance. I have no objection to discuss all these points with you; but you will in the meantime confess that prescribing to me so positively what I ought to do, without first enabling yourself to judge of the matter, is, my dear philosopher, acting very inconsiderately. What is still worse, I perceive the opinion you give comes not from yourself. Besides my being but little disposed to suffer myself to be led by the nose under your name by any third or fourth person, I observe in this secondary advice certain underhand dealing, which ill agrees with your candor, and from which you will on your account, as well as mine, do well in future to abstain.

"You are afraid my conduct should be misinterpreted; but I defy a heart like yours to think ill of mine. Others would perhaps speak better of me if I resembled them more. God preserve me from gaining their approbation! Let the vile and wicked watch over my conduct and misinterpret my actions, Rousseau is not a man to be afraid of them, nor is Diderot to be prevailed upon to hearken to what they say.

"If I am displeased with your letter, you wish me to throw it into the fire, and pay no attention to the contents. Do you imagine that anything coming from you can be forgotten in such a manner? You hold, my dear friend, my tears as cheap in the pain you give me, as you do my life and health, in the cares you exhort me to take. Could you but break yourself of this, your friendship would be more pleasing to me, and I should be less to be pitied."

On entering the chamber of Madam d'Epinay I found Grimm with her, with which I was highly delighted. I read to them, in a loud and clear voice, the two letters, with an intrepidity of which I should not have thought myself capable, and concluded with a few observations not in the least derogatory to it. At this unexpected audacity in a man generally timid, they were struck dumb with surprise; I perceived that arrogant man look down upon the ground, not daring to meet my eyes, which sparkled with indignation; but in the bottom of his heart he from that instant resolved upon my destruction, and, with Madam d'Epinay, I am certain concerted measures to that effect before they separated.

It was much about this time that I at length received, by Madam d'Houdetot, the answer from Saint Lambert, dated from Wolfenbuttle, a few days after the accident that happened to him, to my letter which had been long delayed upon the road. This answer gave me the consolation of which I then stood so much in need; it was full of assurance of esteem and friendship, and these gave me strength and courage to deserve them. From that moment I did my duty, but had Saint Lambert been less reasonable, generous, and honest, I was inevitably lost.

The season became bad, and people began to quit the country. Madam d'Houdetot informed me of the day on which she intended to come and bid adieu to the valley, and gave me a rendezvous at Eaubonne. This happened to be the same day on which Madam d'Epinay left the Chevrette to go to Paris for the purpose of completing the preparations for her journey. Fortunately she set off in the morning, and I had still time to go and dine with her sister-in-law. I had the letter from Saint Lambert in my pocket, and read it over several times as I walked along. This letter served me as a shield against my weakness. I made and kept to the resolution of seeing nothing in Madam d'Houdetot but my friend and the mistress of Saint Lambert; and I passed with her a tête-à-tête of four hours in a most delicious calm, infinitely preferable, even with respect to enjoyment, to the paroxysms of a burning fever, which, always, until that moment, I had had when in her presence. As she too well knew my heart not to be changed, she was sensible of the efforts I made to conquer myself, and esteemed me the more for them, and I had the pleasure of perceiving that her friendship for me was not extinguished. She announced to me the approaching return of Saint Lambert, who, although well enough recovered from his attack, was unable to bear the fatigues of war, and was quitting the service to come and live in peace with her. We formed the charming project of an intimate connection between us three, and had reason to hope it would be lasting, since it was founded upon every sentiment by which honest and susceptible hearts could be united; and we had moreover amongst us all the knowledge and talents necessary to be sufficient to ourselves, without the aid of any foreign supplement. Alas! in abandoning myself to the hope of so agreeable a life I little suspected that which awaited me.

We afterwards spoke of my situation with Madam d'Epinay. I showed her the letter from Diderot, with my answer to it; I related to her everything that had passed upon the subject, and declared to her my resolution of quitting the Hermitage. This she vehemently opposed, and by reasons all powerful over my heart. She expressed to me how much she could have wished I had been of the party to Geneva, foreseeing she should inevitably be considered as having caused the refusal, which the letter of Diderot seemed previously to announce. However, as she was acquainted with my reasons, she did not insist upon this point, but conjured me to avoid coming to an open rupture let it cost me what mortification it would, and to palliate my refusal by reasons sufficiently plausible to put away all unjust suspicions of her having been the cause of it. I told her the task she imposed on me was not easy; but that, resolved to expiate my faults at the expense of my reputation, I would give the preference to hers in everything that honor permitted me to suffer. It will soon be seen whether or not I fulfilled this engagement.

My passion was so far from having lost any part of its force that I never in my life loved my Sophia so ardently and tenderly as on that day, but such was the impression made upon me by the letter of Saint Lambert, the sentiment of my duty, and the horror in which I held perfidy, that during the whole time of the interview my senses left me in peace, and I was not so much as tempted to kiss her hand. At parting she embraced me before her servants. This embrace, so different from those I had sometimes stolen from her under the foliage, proved I was become master of myself; and I am certain that had my mind, undisturbed, had time to acquire more firmness, three months would have cured me radically.

Here ends my personal connections with Madam d'Houdetot; connections of which each has been able to judge by appearance according to the disposition of his own heart, but in which the passion inspired me by that amiable woman, the most lively passion, perhaps, man ever felt, will be honorable in our own eyes by the rare and painful sacrifice we both made to duty, honor, love, and friendship. We each had too high an opinion of the other easily to suffer ourselves to do anything derogatory to our dignity. We must have been unworthy of all esteem had we not set a proper value upon one like this, and the energy of my sentiments which have rendered us culpable, was that which prevented us from becoming so.

Thus after a long friendship for one of these women, and the strongest affection for the other, I bade them both adieu the same day, to one never to see her more, to the other to see her again twice, upon occasions of which I shall hereafter speak.

After their departure, I found myself much embarrassed to fulfill so many pressing and contradictory duties, the consequences of my imprudence; had I been in my natural situation, after the proposition and refusal of the journey to Geneva, I had only to remain quiet, and everything was as it should be. But I had foolishly made of it an affair which could not remain in the state it was, and an explanation was absolutely necessary, unless I quitted the Hermitage, which I had just promised Madam d'Houdetot not to do, at least for the present. Moreover she had required me to make known the reasons for my refusal to my pretended friends, that it might not be imputed to her. Yet I could not state the true reason without doing an outrage to Madam d'Epinay, who certainly had a right to my gratitude for what she had done for me. Everything well considered, I found myself reduced to the severe but indispensable necessity of failing in respect, either to Madam d'Epinay, Madam d'Houdetot or to myself; and it was the last I resolved to make my victim. This I did without hesitation, openly and fully, and with so much generosity as to make the act worthy of expiating the faults which had reduced me to such an extremity. This sacrifice, taken advantage of by my enemies, and which they, perhaps, did not expect, has ruined my reputation, and by their assiduity, deprived me of the esteem of the public; but it has restored to me my own, and given me consolation in my misfortune. This, as it will hereafter appear, is not the last time I made such a sacrifice, nor that advantages were taken of it to do me an injury.

Grimm was the only person who appeared to have taken no part in the affair, and it was to him I determined to address myself. I wrote him a long letter, in which I set forth the ridiculousness of considering it as my duty to accompany Madam d'Epinay to

Geneva, the inutility of the measure, and the embarrassment even it would have caused her, besides the inconvenience to myself. I could not resist the temptation of letting him perceive in this letter how fully I was informed in what manner things were arranged, and that to me it appeared singular I should be expected to undertake the journey whilst he himself dispensed with it, and that his name was never mentioned. This letter, wherein, on account of my not being able clearly to state my reasons, I was often obliged to wander from the text, would have rendered me culpable in the eyes of the public, but it was a model of reservedness and discretion for the people who, like Grimm, were fully acquainted with the things I forbore to mention, and which justified my conduct. I did not even hesitate to raise another prejudice against myself in attributing the advice of Diderot to my other friends. This I did to insinuate that Madam d'Houdetot had been in the same opinion as she really was, and in not mentioning that, upon the reasons I gave her, she thought differently, I could not better remove the suspicion of her having connived at my proceedings than by appearing dissatisfied with her behavior.

This letter was concluded by an act of confidence which would have had an effect upon any other man; for, in desiring Grimm to weigh my reasons and afterwards to give me his opinion, I informed him that, let this be what it would, I should act accordingly, and such was my intention had he even thought I ought to set off; for M. d'Epinay having appointed himself the conductor of his wife, my going with them would then have had a different appearance; whereas it was I who, in the first place, was asked to take upon me that employment, and he was out of the question until after my refusal.

The answer from Grimm was slow in coming: it was singular enough, on which account I will here transcribe it. (*See Packet A, No. 59.*)

"The departure of Madam d'Epinay is postponed: her son is ill, and it is necessary to wait until his health is reëstablished. I will consider the contents of your letter. Remain quiet at your Hermitage. I will send you my opinion as soon as this shall be necessary. As she will certainly not set off for some days, there is no immediate occasion for it. In the meantime you may, if you think proper, make her your offers, although this to me seems a matter of indifference. For, knowing your situation as well as you do yourself, I doubt not of her returning to your offers such an answer as she ought to do; and all the advantage which, in my opinion, can result from this, will be your having it in your power to say to those by whom you may be importuned, that your not being of the traveling party was not for want of having made your offers to that effect. Moreover, I do not see why you will absolutely have it that the philosopher is the speaking-trumpet of all the world, nor because he is of opinion you ought to go, why you should imagine all your friends think as he does? If you write to Madam d'Epinay, her answer will be yours to all your friends, since you have it so much at heart to give them all an answer. Adieu. I embrace Madam le Vasseur and the *Criminal*." *

Struck with astonishment at reading this letter I vainly endeavored to find out what it meant. How! instead of answering me with simplicity, he took time to consider of what I had written, as if the time he had already taken was not sufficient! He intimates even the state of suspense in which he wishes to keep me, as if a profound problem was to be resolved, or that it was of importance to his views to deprive me of every means of comprehending his intentions until the moment he should think proper to make them known. What therefore did he mean by these precautions, delays, and mysteries? Was this manner of acting consistent with honor and uprightness? I vainly sought for some favorable interpretation of his conduct; it was impossible to find one. Whatever his design might be, were this inimical to me, his situation facilitated the execution of it without its being possible for me in mine to oppose the least obstacle. In favor, in the house of a great prince, having an extensive acquaintance, and giving the tone to common circles of which he was the oracle, he had it in his power,

* M. le Vasseur, whose wife governed him rather rudely, called her the Lieutenant Criminal. Grimm in a joke gave the same name to the daughter, and by way of abridgment was pleased to retrench the first word.

with his usual address, to dispose everything in his favor; and I, alone in my Hermitage, far removed from all society, without the benefit of advice, and having no communication with the world, had nothing to do but to remain in peace. All I did was to write to Madam d'Epinay upon the illness of her son, as polite a letter as could be written, but in which I did not fall into the snare of offering to accompany her to Geneva.

After waiting for a long time in the most cruel uncertainty, into which that barbarous man had plunged me, I learned, at the expiration of eight or ten days, that Madam d'Epinay was set off, and received from him a second letter. It contained not more than seven or eight lines which I did not entirely read. It was a rupture, but in such terms as the most infernal hatred only can dictate, and these became unmeaning by the excessive degree of acrimony with which he wished to charge them. He forbade me his presence as he would have forbidden me his states. All that was wanting to his letter to make it laughable, was to be read over with coolness. Without taking a copy of it, or reading the whole of the contents, I returned it him immediately, accompanied by the following note:

"I refused to admit the force of the just reasons I had of suspicion: I now, when it is too late, am become sufficiently acquainted with your character.

"This then is the letter upon which you took time

to meditate: I return it to you, it is not for me. You may show mine to the whole world and hate me openly; this on your part will be a falsehood the less."

My telling he might show my preceding letter related to an article in his by which his profound address throughout the whole affair will be judged of.

I have observed that my letter might inculpate me in the eyes of persons unacquainted with the particulars of what had passed. This he was delighted to discover; but how was he to take advantage of it without exposing himself? By showing the letter he ran the risk of being reproached with abusing the confidence of his friend.

To relieve himself from this embarrassment he resolved to break with me in the most violent manner possible, and to set forth in his letter the favor he did me in not showing mine. He was certain that in my indignation and anger I should refuse his feigned discretion, and permit him to show my letter to everybody; this was what he wished for, and everything turned out as he had expected it would. He sent my letter all over Paris, with his own commentaries upon it, which, however, were not so successful as he had expected them to be. It was not judged that the permission he had extorted to make my letter public exempted him from the blame of having so lightly taken me at my word to do me an injury. People continually asked what personal complaints he had against me to authorize so violent a hatred. Finally, it was thought that if even my behavior had been such as to authorize him to break with me, friendship, although extinguished, had rights which he ought to have respected. But unfortunately the inhabitants of Paris are frivolous; remarks of the moment are soon forgotten; the absent and unfortunate are neglected; the man who prospers secures favor by his presence; the intriguing and malicious support each other, renew their vile efforts, and the effects of these, incessantly succeeding each other, efface everything by which they were preceded.

Thus, after having so long deceived me, this man threw aside his mask; convinced that, in the state to which he had brought things, he no longer stood in need of it. Relieved from the fear of being unjust towards the wretch, I left him to his reflections, and thought no more of him. A week afterwards I received an answer from Madam d'Epinay, dated from Geneva. I understood from the manner of her letter, in which, for the first time in her life, she put on airs of state with me, that both depending but little upon the success of their measures, and considering me as a man inevitably lost, their intentions were to give themselves the pleasure of completing my destruction.

In fact, my situation was deplorable. I perceived all my friends withdrew themselves from me without knowing how or for why. Diderot, who boasted of the continuation of his attachment, and who, for three months past, had promised me a visit, did not come. The winter began to make its appearance, and brought with it my habitual disorders. My constitution, although vigorous, had been unequal to the combat of so many opposite passions. I was so exhausted that I had neither strength nor courage sufficient to resist the most trifling indisposition. Had my engagements, and the continued remonstrances of Diderot and Madam d'Houdetot then permitted me to quit the Hermitage, I knew not where to go, nor in what manner to drag myself along. I remained stupid and immovable. The idea alone of a step to take, a letter to write, or a word to say, made me tremble. I could not however do otherwise than reply to the letter of Madam d'Epinay without acknowledging myself to be worthy of the treatment with which she and her friend overwhelmed me. I determined upon notifying to her my sentiments and resolutions, not doubting a moment that from humanity, generosity, propriety, and the good manner of thinking, I imagined I had observed in her, notwithstanding her bad one, she would immediately subscribe to them. My letter was as follows:

HERMITAGE, *23d Nov., 1757*.

"Were it possible to die of grief I should not now be alive. But I have at length determined to triumph over everything. Friendship, madam, is extinguished between us, but that which no longer exists still has its rights, and I respect them. I have not forgotten your goodness to me, and you may, on my part, expect as much gratitude as it is possible to have towards a person I no longer can love. All further explanation would be useless. I have in my favor my own conscience, and I return you your letter.

"I wished to quit the Hermitage, and I ought to have done it. My friends pretend I must stay there until spring; and since my friends desire it I will remain there until that season if you will consent to my stay."

After writing and despatching this letter all I thought of was remaining quiet at the Hermitage and taking care of my health; of endeavoring to recover my strength, and taking measures to remove in the spring without noise or making the rupture public. But these were not the intentions either of Grimm or Madam d'Epinay, as it will presently appear.

A few days afterwards, I had the pleasure of receiving from Diderot the visit he had so frequently promised, and in which he had as constantly failed. He could not have come more opportunely; he was my oldest friend; almost the only one who remained to me; the pleasure I felt in seeing him, as things were circumstanced, may easily be imagined. My heart was full, and I disclosed it to him. I explained to him several facts which either had not come to his knowledge, or had been disguised or supposed. I informed him, as far as I could do it with propriety, of all that had passed. I did not affect to conceal from him that with which he was but too well acquainted, that a passion, equally unreasonable and unfortunate, had been the cause of my destruction; but I never acknowledged that Madam d'Houdetot had been made acquainted with it, or at least that I had declared it to her. I mentioned to him the unworthy maneuvers of Madam d'Epinay to intercept the innocent letters her sister-in-law wrote to me. I was determined he should hear the particulars from the mouth of the persons whom she had attempted to seduce. Thérèsa related them with great precision; but what was my astonishment when the mother came to speak, and I heard her declare and maintain that nothing of this had come to her knowledge? These were her words from which she would never depart. Not four days before she herself had recited to me all the particulars Thérèsa had just stated, and in presence of my friend she contradicted me to my face. This, to me, was decisive, and I then clearly saw my imprudence in having so long a time kept such a woman near me. I made no use of invective; I scarcely deigned to speak to her a few words of contempt. I felt what I owed to the daughter, whose steadfast uprightness was a perfect contrast to the base maneuvers of the mother. But from that instant my resolution was taken relative to the old woman, and I waited for nothing but the moment to put it into execution.

This presented itself sooner than I expected. On the 10th of December I received from Madam d'Epinay the following answer to my preceding letter:

GENEVA, *1st December, 1757.*

"After having for several years given you every possible mark of friendship all I can now do is to pity you. You are very unhappy. I wish your conscience may be as calm as mine. This may be necessary to the repose of your whole life.

"Since you are determined to quit the Hermitage, and are persuaded that you ought to do it, I am astonished your friends have prevailed upon you to stay there. For my part I never consult mine upon my duty, and I have nothing further to say to you upon your own."

Such an unforeseen dismission, and so fully pronounced, left me not a moment to hesitate. It was necessary to quit immediately, let the weather and my health be in what state they might, although I were to sleep in the woods and upon the snow, with which the ground was then covered, and in defiance of everything Madam d'Houdetot might say; for I was willing to do everything to please her except render myself infamous.

I never had been so embarrassed in my whole life as I then was; but my resolution was taken. I swore, let what would happen, not to sleep at the Hermitage on the night of that day week. I began to prepare for sending away my effects, resolving to leave them in the open field rather than not give up the key in the course of the week: for I was determined everything should be done before a letter could be written to

Geneva, and an answer to it received. I never felt myself so inspired with courage: I had recovered all my strength. Honor and indignation, upon which Madam d'Epinay had not calculated, contributed to restore me to vigor. Fortune aided my audacity. M. Mathas, fiscal procuror, heard of my embarrassment. He sent to offer me a little house he had in his garden of Mont-Louis, at Montmorency. I accepted it with eagerness and gratitude. The bargain was soon concluded: I immediately sent to purchase a little furniture to add to that we already had. My effects I had carted away with a deal of trouble, and at a great expense: notwithstanding the ice and snow my removal was completed in a couple of days, and on the fifteenth of December, I gave up the keys of the Hermitage, after having paid the wages of the gardener, not being able to pay my rent.

With respect to Madam le Vasseur, I told her we must part; her daughter attempted to make me renounce my resolution, but I was inflexible. I sent her off to Paris in the carriage of the messenger with all the furniture and effects she and her daughter had in common. I gave her some money, and engaged to pay her lodging with her children, or elsewhere to provide for her subsistence as much as it should be possible for me to do it, and never to let her want bread as long as I should have it myself.

Finally the day after my arrival at Mont-Louis, I wrote to Madam d'Epinay the following letter:

MONTMORENCY, *17th December, 1757.*

"Nothing, madam, is so natural and necessary as to leave your house the moment you no longer approve of my remaining there. Upon your refusing your consent to my passing the rest of the winter at the Hermitage I quitted it on the fifteenth of December. My destiny was to enter it in spite of myself and to leave it the same. I thank you for the residence you prevailed upon me to make there, and I would thank you still more had I paid for it less dear. You are right in believing me unhappy; nobody upon earth knows better than yourself to what a degree I must be so. If being deceived in the choice of our friends be a misfortune, it is another not less cruel to recover from so pleasing an error."

Such is the faithful narration of my residence at the Hermitage, and of the reasons which obliged me to leave it. I could not break off the recital, it was necessary to continue it with the greatest exactness; this epoch of my life having had upon the rest of it an influence which will extend to my latest remembrance.

BOOK X

BOOK X

[1758]

THE extraordinary degree of strength a momentary effervescence had given me to quit the Hermitage, left me the moment I was out of it. I was scarcely established in my new habitation before I frequently suffered from retentions, which were accompanied by a new complaint; that of a rupture, from which I had for some time, without knowing what it was, felt great inconvenience. I soon was reduced to the most cruel state. The physician Thierry, my old friend, came to see me, and made me acquainted with my situation. The sight of all the apparatus of the infirmities of years, made me severely feel that when the body is no longer young, the heart is not so with impunity. The fine season did not restore me, and I passed the whole year, 1758, in a state of languor, which made me think I was almost at the end of my career. I saw, with impatience, the closing scene approach. Recovered from the chimeras of friendship, and detached from everything which had rendered life desirable to me, I saw nothing more in it that could make it agreeable; all I perceived was wretchedness and misery, which prevented me from enjoying myself. I sighed after the moment when I was to be free and escape from my enemies. But I must follow the order of events.

It appears my retreat to Montmorency disconcerted Madam d'Epinay; probably she did not expect it. My melancholy situation, the severity of the season, the general dereliction of me by my friends, all made her and Grimm believe, that by driving me to the last extremity, they should oblige me to implore mercy, and thus, by vile meanness, render myself contemptible, to be suffered to remain in an asylum which honor commanded me to leave. I left it so suddenly that they had not time to prevent the step from being taken, and they were reduced to the alternative of double or quit, to endeavor to ruin me entirely, or to prevail upon me to return. Grimm chose the former; but I am of opinion Madam d'Epinay would have preferred the latter, and this from her answer to my last letter, in which she seemed to have laid aside the airs she had given herself in the preceding ones, and to give an opening to an accommodation. The long delay of this answer, for which she made me wait a whole month, sufficiently indicates the difficulty she found in giving it a proper turn, and the deliberations by which it was preceded. She could not make any further advances without exposing herself; but after her former letters, and my sudden retreat from her house, it is impossible not to be struck with the care she takes in this letter not to suffer an offensive expression to escape her. I will copy it at length to enable my reader to judge of what she wrote (*Packet B, No. 23*):

GENEVA, *January 17, 1758.*

"SIR: I did not receive your letter of the 17th of December until yesterday. It was sent me in a box filled with different things, and which has been all this time upon the road. I shall answer only the post-script. You may recollect, sir, that we agreed the wages of the gardener of the Hermitage should pass through your hands, the better to make him feel that he depended upon you, and to avoid the ridiculous and indecent scenes which happened in the time of his predecessor. As a proof of this, the first quarter of his wages were given to you, and a few days before my departure we agreed I should reimburse you what you had advanced. I know that of this you, at first, made some difficulty; but I had desired you to make these advances; it was natural I should acquit myself towards you, and this we concluded upon. Cahouet informs me that you refused to receive the money. There is certainly some mistake in the matter. I have given orders that it may again be offered to you, and I see no reason for your wishing to pay my gardener, notwithstanding our conventions, and beyond the term even of your inhabiting the Hermitage. I therefore expect, sir, that recollecting everything I have the honor to state, you will not refuse to be reimbursed for the sums you have been pleased to advance for me."

After what had passed, not having the least confidence in Madam d'Epinay, I was unwilling to renew my connection with her; I returned no answer to this letter, and there our correspondence ended. Perceiving I had taken my resolution, she took hers; and, entering into all the views of Grimm and the *Coterie Holbachique,* she united her efforts with theirs to accomplish my destruction. Whilst they maneuvered at Paris, she did the same at Geneva. Grimm, who afterwards went to her there, completed what she had begun. Tronchin, whom they had no difficulty in gaining over, seconded them powerfully, and became the most violent of my persecutors, without having against me, any more than Grimm had, the least subject of complaint. They all three spread in silence that of which the effects were seen there four years afterwards.

They had more trouble at Paris, where I was better known to the citizens, whose hearts, less disposed to hatred, less easily received its impressions. The better to direct their blow, they began by giving out that it was I who had left them. Thence, still feigning to be my friends, they dexterously spread their malignant accusations by complaining of the injustice of their friend. Their auditors, thus thrown off their guard, listened more attentively to what was said of me, and were inclined to blame my conduct. The secret accusations of perfidy and ingratitude were made with greater precaution, and by that means with greater effect. I knew they imputed to me the most atrocious crimes without being able to learn in what these consisted. All I could infer from public rumor was that this was founded upon the four following capital offenses: my retiring to the country; my passion for Madam d'Houdetot; my refusing to accompany Madam d'Epinay to Geneva, and my leaving the Hermitage. If to these they added other griefs, they took their measures so well that it has hitherto been impossible for me to learn the subject of them.

It is therefore at this period that I think I may fix the establishment of a system, since adopted by those by whom my fate has been determined, and which has made such a progress as will seem miraculous to persons who know not with what facility everything which favors the malignity of man is established. I will endeavor to explain in a few words what to me appeared visible in this profound and obscure system.

With a name already distinguished and known throughout all Europe, I had still preserved my primitive simplicity. My mortal aversion to all party faction and cabal had kept me free and independent, without any other chain than the attachments of my heart. Alone, a stranger, without family or fortune, and unconnected with everything except my principles and duties, I intrepidly followed the paths of uprightness, never flattering or favoring any person at the expense of truth and justice. Besides, having lived for two years past in solitude, without observing the course of events, I was unconnected with the affairs of the world, and not informed of what passed, nor desirous of being acquainted with it. I lived four leagues from Paris as much separated from that capital by my negligence as I should have been in the Island of Tinian by the sea.

Grimm, Diderot and d'Holbach were, on the contrary, in the center of the vortex, lived in the great world, and divided amongst them almost all the spheres of it. The great wits, men of letters, men of long robe, and women, all listened to them when they chose to act in concert. The advantage three men in this situation united must have over a fourth in mine, cannot but already appear. It is true Diderot and d'Holbach were incapable, at least I think so, of forming black conspiracies; one of them was not base enough, nor the other sufficiently able; but it was for this reason that the party was more united. Grimm alone formed his plan in his own mind, and discovered more of it than was necessary to induce his associates to concur in the execution. The ascendency he had gained over them made this quite easy, and the effect of the whole answered to the superiority of his talents.

It was with these, which were of a superior kind, that, perceiving the advantage he might acquire from our respective situations, he conceived the project of overturning my reputation, and, without exposing himself, of giving me one of a nature quite opposite, by raising up about me an edifice of obscurity which it was impossible for me to penetrate, and by that means throw a light upon his maneuvers and unmask him.

This enterprise was difficult, because it was necessary to palliate the iniquity in the eyes of those of whose assistance he stood in need. He had honest men to deceive, to alienate from me the good opinion of everybody, and to deprive me of all my friends. What say I? He had to cut off all communication with me, that not a single word of truth might reach my ears. Had a single man of generosity come and said to me, "You assume the appearance of virtue, yet this is the manner in which you are treated, and these the circumstances by which you are judged; what have you to say?" truth would have triumphed and Grimm have been undone. Of this he was fully convinced; but he had examined his own heart and estimated men according to their merit. I am sorry, for the honor of humanity, that he judged with so much truth.

In these dark and crooked paths his steps to be the more sure were necessarily slow. He has for twelve years pursued his plan, and the most difficult part of the execution of it is still to come; this is to deceive the public entirely. He is afraid of this public, and dares not lay his conspiracy open.* But he has found the

---

* *Since this was written he has made the dangerous step with the fullest and most inconceivable success. I am of opinion it was Tronchin who inspired him with courage, and supplied him with the means.*

easy means of accompanying it with power, and this power has the disposal of me. Thus supported he advances with less danger. The agents of power piquing themselves but little on uprightness, and still less on candor, he has no longer the indiscretion of any honest man to fear. His safety is in my being enveloped in an impenetrable obscurity, and in concealing from me his conspiracy, well knowing that with whatever art he may have formed it, I could by a single glance of the eye discover the whole. His great address consists in appearing to favor whilst he defames me, and in giving to his perfidy an air of generosity.

I felt the first effects of this system by the secret accusations of the *Coterie Holbachique* without its being possible for me to know in what the accusations consisted, or to form a probable conjecture as to the nature of them. De Leyre informed me in his letters that heinous things were attributed to me. Diderot more mysteriously told me the same thing, and when I came to an explanation with both, the whole was reduced to the heads of accusation of which I have already spoken. I perceived a gradual increase of coolness in the letters from Madam d'Houdetot. This I could not attribute to Saint Lambert; he continued to write to me with the same friendship, and came to see me after his return. It was also impossible to think myself the cause of it, as we had separated well satisfied with each other, and nothing since that time had happened on my part, except my departure from the Hermitage, of which she felt the necessity. Therefore, not knowing whence this coolness, which she refused to acknowledge, although my heart was not to be deceived, could proceed, I was uneasy upon every account. I knew she greatly favored her sister-in-law and Grimm, in consequence of their connections with Saint Lambert; and I was afraid of their machinations. This agitation opened my wounds, and rendered my correspondence so disagreeable as quite to disgust her with it. I saw, as at a distance, a thousand cruel circumstances, without discovering anything distinctly. I was in a situation the most insupportable to a man whose imagination is easily heated. Had I been quite retired from the world, and known nothing of the matter, I should have become more calm; but my heart still clung to attachments, by means of which my enemies had great advantages over me; and the feeble rays which penetrated my asylum conveyed to me nothing more than a knowledge of the blackness of the mysteries which were concealed from my eyes.

I should have sunk, I have not a doubt of it, under these torments, too cruel and insupportable to my open disposition, which, by the impossibility of concealing my sentiments, makes me fear everything from those concealed from me, if fortunately objects sufficiently interesting to my heart to divert it from others with which, in spite of myself, my imagination was filled, had not presented themselves. In the last visit Diderot paid me, at the Hermitage, he had spoken of the article *Geneva,* which D'Alembert had inserted in the *Encyclopédie;* he had informed me that this article, concerted with people of the first consideration, had for object the establishment of a theater at Geneva, that measures had been taken accordingly, and that the establishment would soon take place. As Diderot seemed to think all this very proper, and did not doubt of the success of the measure, and as I had besides to speak to him upon too many other subjects to touch upon that article, I made him no answer; but scandalized at these preparatives to corruption and licentiousness in my country, I waited with impatience for the volume of the *Encyclopédie,* in which the article was inserted, to see whether or not it would be possible to give an answer which might ward off the blow. I received the volume soon after my establishment at Mont Louis, and found the articles to be written with much art and address, and worthy of the pen whence it proceeded. This, however, did not abate my desire to answer it, and notwithstanding the dejection of spirits I then labored under, my griefs and pains, the severity of the season, and the inconvenience of my new abode, in which I had not yet had time to arrange myself, I set to work with a zeal which surmounted every obstacle.

In a severe winter, in the month of February, and in the situation I have described, I went every day, morning and evening, to pass a couple of hours in an open alcove which was at the bottom of the garden in which my habitation stood. This alcove, which terminated an alley of a terrace, looked upon the valley and the pond of Montmorency, and presented to me, as the closing point of a prospect, the plain but respectable castle of St. Gratien, the retreat of the virtuous Catinat. It was in this place, then, exposed to freezing cold, that without being sheltered from the wind and snow, and having no other fire than that in my heart, I composed, in the space of three weeks, my letter to D'Alembert on theaters. It was in this, for my Eloisa was not then half written, that I found charms in philosophical labor. Until then virtuous indignation had been a substitute to Apollo, tenderness and a gentleness of mind now became so. The injustice I had been witness to had irritated me, that of which I became the object rendered me melancholy; and this melancholy without bitterness was that of a heart too tender and affectionate, and which, deceived by those in whom it had confided, was obliged to remain concentered. Full of that which had befallen me, and still affected by so many violent emotions, my heart added the sentiment of its sufferings to the ideas with which a meditation on my subject had inspired me: what I wrote bore evident marks of this mixture. Without perceiving it I described the situation I was then in, gave portraits of Grimm, Madam d'Epinay, Madam d'Houdetot, Saint Lambert and myself. What delicious tears did I shed as I wrote. Alas! in these descriptions there are proofs but too evident that love, the fatal love of which I made such efforts to cure myself, still remained in my heart. With all this there was a certain sentiment of tenderness relative to myself: I thought I was dying, and imagined I bid the public my last adieu. Far from fearing death, I joyfully saw it approach; but I felt some regret at leaving my fellow creatures without their having perceived my real merit, and being convinced how much I should have deserved their esteem had they known me better. These are the secret causes of the singular manner in which this work, opposite to that of the work by which it was preceded,* is written.

I corrected and copied the letter, and was preparing to print it when, after a long silence, I received one from Madam d'Houdetot, which brought upon me a new affliction more painful than any I had yet suffered. She informed me that my passion for her was known to all Paris, that I had spoken of it to persons who had made it public, that this rumor, having reached the ears of her lover, had nearly cost him his life; yet he did her justice, and peace was restored between them; but on his account, as well as on hers, and for the sake of her reputation, she thought it her duty to break off all correspondence with me, at the same time assuring me that she and her friend were both interested in my welfare, that they would defend me to the public, and that she herself would from time to time send to inquire after my health.

"And thou also, Diderot," exclaimed I, "unworthy friend!"—I could not, however, yet resolve to condemn him. My weakness was known to others who might have spoken of it. I wished to doubt—, but this

* *Discours sur l'inégalité.*—Discourse on the Inequality of Mankind.

was soon out of my power. Saint Lambert shortly after performed an action worthy of himself. Knowing my manner of thinking, he judged of the state in which I must be; betrayed by one part of my friends and forsaken by the other. He came to see me. The first time he had not many moments to spare. He came again. Unfortunately, not expecting him, I was not at home. Thérèsa had with him a conversation of upwards of two hours, in which they informed each other of facts of great importance to us all. The surprise with which I learned that nobody doubted of my having lived with Madam d'Epinay, as Grimm then did, cannot be equaled, except by that of Saint Lambert, when he was convinced that the rumor was false. He, to the great dissatisfaction of the lady, was in the same situation with myself, and the *eclaircissements* resulting from the conversation removed from me all regret, on account of my having broken with her forever. Relative to Madam d'Houdetot, he mentioned several circumstances with which neither Thérèsa nor Madam d'Houdetot herself were acquainted; these were known to me only in the first instance, and I had never mentioned them except to Diderot, under the seal of friendship; and it was to Saint Lambert himself to whom he had chosen to communicate them. This last step was sufficient to determine me. I resolved to break with Diderot forever, and this without further deliberation, except on the manner of doing it; for I had perceived secret ruptures turned to my prejudice, because they left the mask of friendship in possession of my most cruel enemies.

The rules of good breeding, established in the world on this head, seem to have been dictated by a spirit of treachery and falsehood. To appear the friend of a man when in reality we are no longer so, is to reserve to ourselves the means of doing him an injury by surprising honest men into an error. I recollected that when the illustrious Montesquieu broke with Father de Tournemine, he immediately said to everybody: "Listen neither to Father Tournemine nor myself, when we speak of each other, for we are no longer friends." This open and generous proceeding was universally applauded. I resolved to follow the example with Diderot; but what method was I to take to publish the rupture authentically from my retreat, and yet without scandal? I concluded on inserting in the form of a note, in my work, a passage from the book of Ecclesiasticus, which declared the rupture and even the subject of it, in terms sufficiently clear to such as were acquainted with the previous circumstances, but could signify nothing to the rest of the world. I determined not to speak, in my work of the friend whom I renounced, except with the honor always due to extinguished friendship. The whole may be seen in the work itself.

There is nothing in this world but time and misfortune, and every act of courage seems to be a crime in adversity. For that which had been admired in Montesquieu, I received only blame and reproach. As soon as my work was printed, and I had copies of it, I sent one to Saint Lambert, who, the evening before, had written to me in his own name and that of Madam d'Houdetot, a note expressive of the most tender friendship.

The following is the letter he wrote to me when he returned the copy I had sent him. (*Packet B, No. 38.*)

EAUBONNE, *10th October, 1758.*

"Indeed, sir, I cannot accept the present you have just made me. In that part of your preface where, relative to Diderot, you quote a passage from Ecclesiastes (he mistakes, it is from Ecclesiasticus) the book dropped from my hand. In the conversations we had together in the summer, you seemed to be persuaded Diderot was not guilty of the pretended indiscretions you had imputed to him. You may, for aught I know to the contrary, have reason to complain of him, but this does not give you a right to insult him publicly. You are not unacquainted with the nature of the persecutions he suffers, and you join the voice of an old friend to that of envy. I cannot refrain from telling you, sir, how much this heinous act of yours has shocked me. I am not acquainted with Diderot, but I honor him, and I have a lively sense of the pain you give to a man, whom, at least not in my hearing, you have never reproached with anything more than a trifling weakness. You and I, sir, differ too much in our principles ever to be agreeable to each other. Forget that I exist; this you will easily do. I have never done to men either good or evil of a nature to be long remembered. I promise you, sir, to forget your person and to remember nothing relative to you but your talents."

This letter filled me with indignation and affliction; and, in the excess of my pangs, feeling my pride wounded, I answered him by the following note:

MONTMORENCY, *11th October, 1758.*

"SIR: While reading your letter, I did you the honor to be surprised at it, and had the weakness to suffer it to affect me; but I find it unworthy of an answer.

"I will no longer continue the copies of Madam d'Houdetot. If it be not agreeable to her to keep that she has, she may send it me back and I will return her money. If she keeps it, she must still send for the rest of her paper and the money; and at the same time I beg she will return me the prospectus which she has in her possession. Adieu, sir."

Courage under misfortune irritates the hearts of cowards, but it is pleasing to generous minds. This note seemed to make Saint Lambert reflect with himself and to regret his having been so violent; but too haughty in his turn to make open advances, he seized and perhaps prepared, the opportunity of palliating what he had done.

A fortnight afterwards I received from Madam d'Epinay the following letter (*Packet B, No. 10*):

Thursday, 26th.

"SIR: I received the book you had the goodness to send me, and which I have read with much pleasure. I have always experienced the same sentiment in reading all the works which have come from your pen. Receive my thanks for the whole. I should have returned you these in person had my affairs permitted me to remain any time in your neighborhood; but I was not this year long at the Chevrette. M. and Madam Dupin came here on Sunday to dinner. I expect M. de Saint Lambert, M. de Francueil, and Madam d'Houdetot will be of the party; you will do me much pleasure by making one also. All the persons who are to dine with me, desire, and will, as well as myself, be delighted to pass with you a part of the day. I have the honor to be with the most perfect consideration," etc.

This letter made my heart beat violently: after having for a year past been the subject of conversation of all Paris, the idea of presenting myself as a spectacle before Madam d'Houdetot, made me tremble, and I had much difficulty to find sufficient courage to support that ceremony. Yet as she and Saint Lambert were desirous of it, and Madam d'Epinay spoke in the name of her guests without naming one whom I should not be glad to see, I did not think I should expose myself accepting a dinner to which I was in some degree invited by all the persons who with myself were to partake of it. I therefore promised to go: on Sunday the weather was bad, and Madam d'Epinay sent me her carriage.

My arrival caused a sensation. I never met a better reception. An observer would have thought the whole company felt how much I stood in need of encouragement. None but French hearts are susceptible of this kind of delicacy. However, I found more people than I expected to see. Amongst others the Comte d'Houdetot, whom I did not know, and his sister Madam de Blainville, without whose company I should have been as well pleased. She had the year before come several times to Eaubonne, and her sister-in-law had left her in our solitary walks to wait until she thought proper to suffer her to join us. She had harbored a resentment against me, which during this dinner she gratified at her ease. The presence of the Comte d'Houdetot and Saint Lambert did not give me the laugh on my side, and it may be judged that a man embarrassed in the most common conversations was not very brilliant in that which then took place. I never suffered so much, appeared so awkward, or received more unexpected mortifications. As soon as we had risen from table, I withdrew from that wicked woman; I had the pleasure of seeing Saint Lambert and Madam d'Houdetot approach me, and we conversed together a part of the afternoon, upon things very indifferent it is true, but with the same familiarity as before my involuntary error. This friendly attention was not lost upon my heart, and could Saint Lambert have read what passed there, he certainly would have been satisfied with it. I can safely assert that although on my arrival the presence of Madam d'Houdetot gave me the most violent palpitations, on returning from the house I scarcely thought of her; my mind was entirely taken up with Saint Lambert.

Notwithstanding the malignant sarcasms of Madam de Blainville, the dinner was of great service to me, and I congratulated myself upon not having refused the invitation. I not only discovered that the intrigues of Grimm and the Holbachiens had not deprived me of my old acquaintance,* but, what flattered me still more, that Madam d'Houdetot and Saint Lambert were less changed than I had imagined, and I at length understood that his keeping her at a distance from me proceeded more from jealousy than from disesteem. This was a consolation to me, and calmed my mind. Certain of not being an object of contempt in the eyes of persons whom I esteemed, I worked upon my own heart with greater courage and success. If I did not quite extinguish in it a guilty and an unhappy passion, I at least so well regulated the remains of it that they have never since that moment led me into the most trifling error. The copies of Madam d'Houdetot, which she prevailed upon me to take again, and my works, which I continued to send her as soon as they

* *Such in the simplicity of my heart was my opinion when I wrote these confessions.*

appeared, produced me from her a few notes and messages, indifferent but obliging. She did still more, as will hereafter appear, and the reciprocal conduct of her lover and myself, after our intercourse had ceased may serve as an example of the manner in which persons of honor separate when it is no longer agreeable to them to associate with each other.

Another advantage this dinner procured me was its being spoken of in Paris, where it served as a refutation of the rumor spread by my enemies, that I had quarreled with every person who partook of it, and especially with M. d'Epinay. When I left the Hermitage I had written him a very polite letter of thanks, to which he answered not less politely, and mutual civilities had continued, as well between us as between me and M. de la Lalive, his brother-in-law, who even came to see me at Montmorency, and sent me some of his engravings. Excepting the two sisters-in-law of Madam d'Houdetot, I have never been on bad terms with any person of the family.

My *Letter to D'Alembert* had great success. All my works had been very well received, but this was more favorable to me. It taught the public to guard against the insinuations of the *Coterie Holbachique*. When I went to the Hermitage, this *Coterie* predicted with its usual sufficiency, that I should not remain there three months. When I had stayed there twenty months, and was obliged to leave it, I still fixed my residence in the country. The *Coterie* insisted this was from a motive of pure obstinacy, and that I was weary even to death of my retirement; but that, eaten up with pride, I chose rather to become a victim to my stubbornness than to recover from it and return to Paris. The *Letter to D'Alembert* breathed a gentleness of mind which every one perceived not to be affected. Had I been dissatisfied with my retreat, my style and manner would have borne evident marks of my ill-humor. This reigned in all the works I had written at Paris; but in the first I wrote in the country not the least appearance of it was to be found. To persons who knew how to distinguish, this remark was decisive. They perceived I was returned to my element.

Yet the same work, notwithstanding all the mildness it breathed, made me by a mistake of my own and my usual ill-luck, another enemy amongst men of letters. I had become acquainted with Marmontel at the house of M. de la Poplinière, and this acquaintance had been continued at that of the baron. Marmontel at that time wrote the *Mercure de France.* As I had too much pride to send my works to the authors of periodical publications, and wishing to send him this without his imagining it was in consequence of that title, or being desirous he should speak of it in the *Mercure,* I wrote upon the book that it was not for the author of the *Mercure,* but for M. Marmontel. I thought I paid him a fine compliment; he mistook it for a cruel offense, and became my irreconcilable enemy. He wrote against the letter with politeness, it is true, but with a bitterness easily perceptible, and since that time has never lost an opportunity of injuring me in society, and of indirectly ill-treating me in his works. Such difficulty is there in managing the irritable self-love of men of letters, and so careful ought every person to be not to leave anything equivocal in the compliments they pay them.

Having nothing more to disturb me, I took advantage of my leisure and independence to continue my literary pursuits with more coherence. I this winter finished my Eloisa, and sent it to Rey, who had it printed the year following. I was, however, interrupted in my projects by a circumstance sufficiently disagreeable. I heard new preparations were making at the opera-house to give the *Devin du Village*. Enraged at seeing these people arrogantly dispose of my property, I again took up the memoir I had sent to M. D'Argenson, to which no answer had been returned, and having made some trifling alterations in it, I sent the manuscript by M. Sellon, resident from Geneva, and a letter with which he was pleased to charge himself, to the Comte de St. Florentin, who had succeeded M. D'Argenson in the opera department. Duclos, to whom I communicated what I had done, mentioned it to the *petits violons,* who offered to restore me, not my opera, but my freedom of the theater, which I was no longer in a situation to enjoy. Perceiving I had not from any quarter the least justice to expect, I gave up the affair; and the directors of the opera, without either answering or listening to my reasons, have continued to dispose as of their own property, and to turn to their profit, the *Devin du*

Village, which incontestably belongs to nobody but myself.*

Since I had shaken off the yoke of my tyrants, I led a life sufficiently agreeable and peaceful; deprived of the charm of too strong attachments I was delivered from the weight of their chains. Disgusted with the friends who pretended to be my protectors, and wished absolutely to dispose of me at will, and in spite of myself, to subject me to their pretended good services, I resolved in future to have no other connections than those of simple benevolence. These, without the least constraint upon liberty, constitute the pleasure of society, of which equality is the basis. I had of them as many as were necessary to enable me to taste of the charms of liberty without being subject to the dependence of it; and as soon as I had made an experiment of this manner of life, I felt it was the most proper to my age, to end my days in peace, far removed from the agitations, quarrels and cavillings, in which I had just been half submerged.

During my residence at the Hermitage, and after my settlement at Montmorency, I had made in the neighborhood some agreeable acquaintance, and which did not subject me to any inconvenience. The principal of these was young Loyseau de Mauléon, who, then beginning to plead at the bar, did not yet know what rank he would one day hold there. I for my part was not in the least doubt about the matter.

---

* *It now belongs to them by virtue of an agreement made to that effect.*

I soon pointed out to him the illustrious career in the midst of which he is now seen, and predicted that, if he laid down to himself rigid rules for the choice of causes, and never became the defender of anything but virtue and justice, his genius, elevated by this sublime sentiment, would be equal to that of the greatest orators. He followed my advice, and now feels the good effects of it. His defense of M. de Portes is worthy of Demosthenes. He came every year within a quarter of a league of the Hermitage to pass the vacation at St. Brice, in the fief of Mauléon, belonging to his mother, and where the great Bossuet had formerly lodged. This is a fief, of which a like succession of proprietors would render nobility difficult to support.

I had also for a neighbor in the same village of St. Brice, the bookseller Guerin, a man of wit, learning, of an amiable disposition, and one of the first in his profession. He brought me acquainted with Jean Néaulme, bookseller of Amsterdam, his friend and correspondent, who afterwards printed Emile.

I had another acquaintance still nearer than St. Brice, this was M. Maltor, vicar of Groslay, a man better adapted for the functions of a statesman and a minister, than for those of the vicar of a village, and to whom a diocese at least would have been given to govern if talents decided the disposal of places. He had been secretary to the Comte du Luc, and was formerly intimately acquainted with Jean-Baptiste Rousseau. Holding in as much esteem the memory of that illustrious exile, as he held the villain who ruined him in horror; he possessed curious anecdotes of both, which Seguy had not inserted in the life, still in manuscript, of the former, and he assured me that the Comte du Luc, far from ever having had reason to complain of his conduct, had until his last moment preserved for him the warmest friendship. M. Maltor, to whom M. de Vintimille gave this retreat after the death of his patron, had formerly been employed in many affairs of which, although far advanced in years, he still preserved a distinct remembrance, and reasoned upon them tolerably well. His conversation, equally amusing and instructive, had nothing in it resembling that of a village pastor: he joined the manners of a man of the world to the knowledge of one who passes his life in study. He, of all my permanent neighbors, was the person whose society was the most agreeable to me.

I was also acquainted at Montmorency with several fathers of the oratory, and amongst others Father Berthier, professor of natural philosophy; to whom, notwithstanding some little tincture of pedantry, I become attached on account of a certain air of cordial good nature which I observed in him. I had, however, some difficulty to reconcile this great simplicity with the desire and the art he had of everywhere thrusting himself into the company of the great, as well as that of the women, devotees, and philosophers. He knew how to accommodate himself to every one. I was greatly pleased with the man, and spoke of my satisfaction to all my other acquaintances. Apparently what I said of him came to his ear. He one day thanked me for having thought him a good-natured man. I observed something in his forced smile which, in my eyes, totally changed his physiognomy, and which has since frequently occurred to my mind. I cannot better compare this smile than to that of Panurge purchasing the Sheep of Dindenaut. Our acquaintance had begun a little time after my arrival at the Hermitage, to which place he frequently came to see me. I was already settled at Montmorency when he left it to go and reside at Paris. He often saw Madam le Vasseur there. One day, when I least expected anything of the kind, he wrote to me in behalf of that woman, informing me that Grimm offered to maintain her, and to ask my permission to accept the offer. This I understood consisted in a pension of three hundred livres, and that Madam le Vasseur was to come and live at Deuil, between the Chevrette and Montmorency. I will not say what impression the application made on me. It would have been less surprising had Grimm had ten thousand livres a year, or any relation more easy to comprehend with that woman, and had not such a crime been made of my taking her to the country, where, as if she had become younger, he was now pleased to think of placing her. I perceived the good old lady had no other reason for asking my permission, which she might easily have done without, but the fear of losing what I already gave her, should I think ill of the step she took. Although this charity appeared to be very extraordinary, it did not strike me so much then as afterwards. But had I known even everything I have since discovered, I would still as readily have given my consent as I did and was obliged to do, unless I had exceeded the offer of M. Grimm. Father Berthier afterwards cured me a little of my opinion of his good nature and cordiality with which I had so unthinkingly charged him.

This same Father Berthier was acquainted with two men, who, for what reason I know not, were to become so with me; there was but little similarity between their taste and mine. They were the children of Melchisédec, of whom neither the country nor the family was known, no more than, in all probability, the real name. They were Jansenists, and passed for priests in disguise, perhaps on account of their ridiculous manner of wearing long swords, to which they appeared to have been fastened. The prodigious mystery in all their proceedings gave them the appearance of the heads of a party, and I never had the least doubt of their being the authors of the *Gazette Ecclésiastique*. The one, tall, smooth-tongued, and sharping, was named Ferrand; the other, short, squat, a sneerer, and punctilious, was a M. Minard. They called each other cousin. They lodged at Paris with D'Alembert, in the house of his nurse named Madam Rousseau, and had taken at Montmorency a little apartment to pass the summers there. They did everything for themselves, and had neither a servant nor runner; each had his turn weekly to purchase provisions, do the business of the kitchen, and sweep the

house. They managed tolerably well, and we sometimes ate with each other. I know not for what reason
they gave themselves any concern about me: for my
part, my only motive for beginning an acquaintance
with them was their playing at chess, and to make a
poor little party I suffered four hours' fatigue. As they
thrust themselves into all companies, and wished to
intermeddle in everything, Thérèsa called them the
gossips, and by this name they were long known at
Montmorency.

Such, with my host M. Mathas, who was a good
man, were my principal country acquaintance. I still
had a sufficient number at Paris to live there agreeably whenever I chose it, out of the sphere of men of
letters, amongst whom Duclos was the only friend I
reckoned: for De Leyre was still too young, and although, after having been a witness to the maneuvers
of the philosophical tribe against me, he had withdrawn from it, at least I thought so, I could not yet
forget the facility with which he made himself the
mouthpiece of all the people of that description.

In the first place I had my old and respectable friend
Rougin. This was a good old-fashioned friend for
whom I was not indebted to my writings but to myself,
and whom for that reason I have always preserved. I
had the good Lenieps, my countryman, and his
daughter, then alive, Madam Lambert. I had a young
Genevese, named Coindet, a good creature, careful,
officious, zealous, who came to see me soon after I had
gone to reside at the Hermitage, and, without any

other introducer than himself, had made his way into my good graces. He had a taste for drawing, and was acquainted with artists. He was of service to me relative to the engravings of the New Eloisa; he undertook the direction of the drawings and the plates, and acquitted himself well of the commission.

I had free access to the house of M. Dupin which, less brilliant than in the young days of Madam Dupin, was still, by the merit of the heads of the family, and the choice of company which assembled there, one of the best houses in Paris. As I had not preferred anybody to them, and had separated myself from their society to live free and independent, they had always received me in a friendly manner, and I was always certain of being well received by Madam Dupin. I might even have counted her amongst my country neighbors after her establishment at Clichy, to which place I sometimes went to pass a day or two, and where I should have been more frequently had Madam Dupin and Madam de Chenonceaux been upon better terms. But the difficulty of dividing my time in the same house between two women whose manner of thinking was unfavorable to each other, made this disagreeable: however I had the pleasure of seeing her more at my ease at Deuil, where, at a trifling distance from me, she had taken a small house, and even at my own habitation, where she often came to see me.

I had likewise for a friend Madam de Crequi, who, having become devout, no longer received D'Alembert, Marmontel, nor a single man of letters, except, I believe, the Abbé Trublet, half a hypocrite, of whom she was weary. I, whose acquaintance she had sought, lost neither her good wishes nor intercourse. She sent me young fat pullets from Mans, and her intention was to come and see me the year following had not a journey, upon which Madam de Luxembourg determined, prevented her. I here owe her a place apart; she will always hold a distinguished one in my remembrance.

In this list I should also place a man whom, except Roguin, I ought to have mentioned as the first upon it: my old friend and brother politician, De Carrio, formerly titulary secretary to the embassy from Spain to Venice, afterwards in Sweden, where he was *chargé des affaires,* and at length really secretary to the embassy from Spain at Paris. He came and surprised me at Montmorency when I least expected him. He was decorated with the insignia of a Spanish order, the name of which I have forgotten, with a fine cross in jewelry. He had been obliged, in his proofs of nobility, to add a letter to his name, and to bear that of the Chevalier de Carrion. I found him still the same man, possessing the same excellent heart, and his mind daily improving, and becoming more and more amiable. We should have renewed our former intimacy had not Coindet interposed according to custom, taken advantage of the distance I was at from town to insinuate himself into my place, and, in my name, into his confidence, and supplant me by the excess of his zeal to render me services.

The remembrance of Carrion makes me recollect one of my country neighbors, of whom I should be inexcusable not to speak, as I have to make confession of an unpardonable neglect of which I was guilty towards him: this was the honest M. le Blond, who had done me a service at Venice, and, having made an excursion to France with his family, had taken a house in the country, at Briché, not far from Montmorency.* As soon as I heard he was my neighbor, I, in the joy of my heart, and making it more a pleasure than a duty, went to pay him a visit. I set off upon this errand the next day. I was met by people who were coming to see me, and with whom I was obliged to return. Two days afterwards I set off again for the same purpose: he had dined at Paris with all his family. A third time he was at home: I heard the voice of women, and saw, at the door, a coach which alarmed me. I wished to see him, at least for the first time, quite at my ease, that we might talk over what had passed during our former connection.

In fine, I so often postponed my visit from day to day, that the shame of discharging a like duty so late prevented me from doing it at all; after having dared to wait so long, I no longer dared to present myself. This negligence, at which M. le Blond could not but be justly offended, gave, relative to him, the appear-

---

* When I wrote this, full of my blind confidence, I was far from suspecting the real motive and the effect of this journey to Paris.

ance of ingratitude to my indolence, and yet I felt my heart so little culpable that, had it been in my power to do M. le Blond the least service, even unknown to himself, I am certain he would not have found me idle. But indolence, negligence and delay in little duties to be fulfilled have been more prejudicial to me than great vices. My greatest faults have been omissions: I have seldom done what I ought not to have done, and unfortunately it has still more rarely happened that I have done what I ought.

Since I am now upon the subject of my Venetian acquaintance, I must not forget one which I still preserved for a considerable time after my intercourse with the rest had ceased. This was M. de Joinville, who continued after his return from Genoa to show me much friendship. He was fond of seeing me and of conversing with me upon the affairs of Italy, and the follies of M. de Montaigu, of whom he of himself knew many anecdotes, by means of his acquaintance in the office for foreign affairs in which he was much connected. I had also the pleasure of seeing at my house my old comrade, Dupont, who had purchased a place in the province of which he was, and whose affairs had brought him to Paris. M. de Joinville became by degrees so desirous of seeing me, that he in some measure laid me under constraint; and, although our places of residence were at a great distance from each other, we had a friendly quarrel when I let a week pass without going to dine with him. When he went to Joinville he was always desirous of my accompanying him; but having once been there to pass a week I had not the least desire to return. M. de Joinville was certainly an honest man, and even amiable in certain respects, but his understanding was beneath mediocrity; he was handsome, rather fond of his person and tolerably fatiguing. He had one of the most singular collections perhaps in the world, to which he gave much of his attention, and endeavored to acquire it that of his friends, to whom it sometimes afforded less amusement than it did to himself. This was a complete collection of songs of the court and Paris for upwards of fifty years past, in which many anecdotes were to be found that would have been sought for in vain elsewhere. These are memoirs for the history of France, which would scarcely be thought of in any other country.

One day, whilst we were still upon the very best terms, he received me so coldly and in a manner so different from that which was customary to him, that after having given him an opportunity to explain, and even having begged him to do it, I left his house with a resolution, in which I have persevered, never to return to it again; for I am seldom seen where I have been once ill received, and in this case there was no Diderot who pleaded for M. de Joinville. I vainly endeavored to discover what I had done to offend him; I could not recollect a circumstance at which he could possibly have taken offense. I was certain of never having spoken of him or his in any other than in the most honorable manner; for he had acquired my friendship, and besides my having nothing but favorable things to say of him, my most inviolable maxim has been that of never speaking but in an honorable manner of the houses I frequented.

At length, by continually ruminating, I formed the following conjecture: the last time we had seen each other, I had supped with him at the apartment of some girls of his acquaintance, in company with two or three clerks in the office of foreign affairs, very amiable men, and who had neither the manner nor appearance of libertines; and on my part, I can assert that the whole evening passed in making melancholy reflections on the wretched fate of the creatures with whom we were. I did not pay anything, as M. de Joinville gave the supper, nor did I make the girls the least present, because I gave them not the opportunity I had done to the *padonana* of establishing a claim to the trifle I might have offered. We all came away together, cheerfully and upon very good terms. Without having made a second visit to the girls, I went three or four days afterwards to dine with M. de Joinville, whom I had not seen during that interval, and who gave me the reception of which I have spoken. Unable to suppose any other cause for it than some misunderstanding relative to the supper, and perceiving he had no inclination to explain, I resolved to visit him no longer, but I still continued to send him my works: he frequently sent me his compliments, and one evening, meeting him in the green-room of the French theater, he obligingly reproached me with not having called to see him, which, however, did not induce me to depart from my resolution. Therefore this affair had rather the appearance of a coolness than a rupture. However, not having heard of nor seen him since that time, it would have been too late after an absence of several years, to renew my acquaintance with him. It is for this reason M. de Joinville is not named in my list, although I had for a considerable time frequented his house.

I will not swell my catalogue with the names of many other persons with whom I was or had become less intimate, although I sometimes saw them in the country, either at my own house or that of some neighbor, such for instance as the Abbés De Condillac and De Mably, M. de Mairan, De la Lalive, De Boisgelou, Vatelet, Ancelet, and others. I will also pass lightly over that of M. de Margency, gentleman in ordinary of the king, an ancient member of the *Coterie Holbachique,* which he had quitted as well as myself, and the old friend of Madam d'Epinay from whom he had separated as I had done; I likewise consider that of M. Desmahis, his friend, the celebrated but short-lived author of the comedy of *L'Impertinent,* of much the same importance. The first was my neighbor in the country, his estate at Margency being near to Montmorency. We were old acquaintances, but the neighborhood and a certain conformity of experience connected us still more. The last died soon afterwards. He had merit and even wit, but he was in some degree the original of his comedy, and a little of a coxcomb with women, by whom he was not much regretted.

I cannot, however, omit taking notice of a new correspondence I entered into at this period, which has had too much influence over the rest of my life not to make it necessaary for me to mark its origin. The person in question is De Lamoignon de Malesherbes of the *Cour des aides,* then censor of books, which office he exercised with equal intelligence and mildness, to the great satisfaction of men of letters. I had not once been to see him at Paris; yet I had never received from him any other than the most obliging condescensions relative to the censorship, and I knew that he had more than once very severely reprimanded persons who had written against me. I had new proofs of his goodness upon the subject of the edition of Julie. The proofs of so great a work being very expensive from Amsterdam by post, he, to whom all letters were free, permitted these to be addressed to him, and sent them to me under the countersign of the chancellor his father. When the work was printed he did not permit the sale of it in the kingdom until, contrary to my wishes, an edition had been sold for my benefit. As the profit of this would on my part have been a theft committed upon Rey, to whom I had sold the manuscript, I not only refused to accept the present intended me, without his consent, which he very generously gave, but insisted upon dividing with him the hundred pistoles (a thousand livres—forty pounds), the amount of it, but of which he would not receive anything. For these hundred pistoles I had the mortification, against which M. de Malesherbes had not guarded me, of seeing my work horribly mutilated, and the sale of the good edition stopped until the bad one was entirely disposed of.

I have always considered M. de Malesherbes as a man whose uprightness was proof against every temptation. Nothing that has happened has even made me doubt for a moment of his probity; but, as weak as he is polite, he sometimes injures those he wishes to serve by the excess of his zeal to preserve them from evil. He not only retrenched a hundred pages in the edition of Paris, but he made another retrenchment, which no person but the author could permit himself to do, in the copy of the good edition he sent to Madam de Pompadour. It is somewhere said in that work that the wife of a coal-heaver is more respectable than the mistress of a prince. This phrase had occurred to me in the warmth of composition without any application. In reading over the work I perceived it would be applied, yet in consequence of the very imprudent maxim I had adopted of not suppressing anything, on account of the application which might be made, when my conscience bore witness to me that I had not made them at the time I wrote, I determined not to expunge the phrase, and contented myself with substituting the word Prince to *King,* which I had first written. This softening did not seem sufficient to M. de Malesherbes; he retrenched the whole expression in a new sheet which he had printed on purpose and stuck in between the other with as much exactness as possible in the copy of Madam de Pompadour. She was not ignorant of this maneuver. Some good-natured people took the trouble to inform her of it. For my part it was not until a long time afterwards, and when I began to feel the consequences of it, that the matter came to my knowledge.

Is not this the origin of the concealed but implacable hatred of another lady who was in a like situation, without my knowing it or even being acquainted with her person when I wrote the passage? When the book was published the acquaintance was made, and I was very uneasy. I mentioned this to the Chevalier de Lorenzi, who laughed at me, and said the lady was so little offended that she had not even taken notice of the matter. I believed him, perhaps rather too lightly, and made myself easy when there was much reason for my being otherwise.

At the beginning of the winter I received an additional mark of the goodness of M. de Malesherbes of which I was very sensible, although I did not think proper to take advantage of it. A place was vacant in the *Journal des Savants*. Margency wrote to me, proposing to me the place, as from himself. But I easily perceived from the manner of the letter that he was dictated to and authorized; he afterwards told me he had been desired to make me the offer. The occupations of this place were but trifling. All I should have had to do would have been to make two extracts a month, from the books brought to me for that purpose, without being under the necessity of going once to Paris, not even to pay the magistrate a visit of thanks. By this employment I should have entered a society of men of letters of the first merit; M. de Mairan, Clairaut, De Guignes and the Abbé Barthelemi, with the first two of whom I had already made an acquaintance, and that of the two others was very desirable. In fine, for this trifling employment, the duties of which I might so commodiously have discharged, there was a salary of eight hundred francs per annum. I was for a few hours undecided, and this from a fear of making Margency angry and displeasing M. de Malesherbes. But at length the insupportable constraint of not having it in my power to work when I thought proper, and to be commanded by time; and moreover the certainty of badly performing the functions with which I was to charge myself, prevailed over everything, and determined me to refuse a place for which I was unfit. I knew that my whole talent consisted in a certain warmth of mind with respect to the subjects of which I had to treat, and that nothing but the love of that which was great, beautiful and sublime, could animate my genius. What would the subjects of the extracts I should have had to make from books, or even the books themselves, have signified to me? My indifference about them would have frozen my pen, and stupefied my mind. People thought I could make a trade of writing, as most of the other men of letters did, instead of which I never could write but from the warmth of imagination. This certainly was not necessary for the *Journal des Savants*. I therefore wrote to Margency a letter of thanks in the politest terms possible, and so well explained to him my reasons, that it was not possible that either he or M. de Malesherbes could imagine there was pride or ill-humor in my refusal. They both approved of it without receiving me less politely, and the secret was so well kept that it was never known to the public.

The proposition did not come in a favorable moment. I had some time before this formed the project of quitting literature, and especially the trade of an author. I had been disgusted with men of letters by everything that had lately befallen me, and had learned from experience that it was impossible to proceed in the same track without having some connections with them. I was not much less dissatisfied with men of the world, and in general with the mixed life I had lately led, half to myself and half devoted to societies for which I was unfit. I felt more than ever, and by constant experience, that every unequal association is disadvantageous to the weaker person. Living with opulent people, and in a situation different from that I had chosen, without keeping a house as they did, I was obliged to imitate them in many things; and little expenses, which were nothing to their fortunes, were for me not less ruinous than indispensable. If another man goes to the country-house of a friend, he is served by his own servant, as well at table as in his chamber; he sends him to seek for everything he wants; having nothing directly to do with the servants of the house, not even seeing them, he gives them what he pleases, and when he thinks proper; but I, alone, and without a servant, was at the mercy of the servants of the house, of whom it was necessary to gain the good graces, that I might not have much to suffer; and being treated as the equal of their master, I was obliged to treat them accordingly, and better than another would have done, because, in fact, I stood in greater need of their services. This, where there are but few domestics, may be complied with; but in the houses I frequented there were a great number, and the knaves so well understood their interests that they knew how to make me want the services of them all successively. The women of Paris, who have so much wit, have no just idea of this inconvenience, and in their zeal to economize my purse they ruined me. If I supped in town, at any considerable distance from my lodgings, instead of permitting me to send for a hackney-coach, the mistress of the house ordered her horses to be put to and sent me home in her carriage; she was very glad to save me the twenty-four sous for the fiacre, but never thought of the écus I gave to her coachman and footman. If a lady wrote to me from Paris to the Hermitage or to Montmorency, she regretted the four sous the postage of the letter would have cost me, and sent it by one of her servants, who came sweating on foot, and to whom I gave a dinner and half an écu, which he certainly had well earned. If she proposed to me to pass with her a week or a fortnight at her country-house, she still said to herself,

"It will be a saving to the poor man; during that time his eating will cost him nothing." She never recollected that I was the whole time idle, that the expenses of my family, my rent, linen and clothes were still going on, that I paid my barber double, that it cost me more being in her house than in my own, and although I confined my little largesses to the house in which I customarily lived, that these were still ruinous to me. I am certain I have paid upwards of twenty-five écus in the house of Madam d'Houdetot, at Eaubonne, where I never slept more than four or five times, and upwards of a thousand pistoles as well at Epinay as at the Chevrette, during the five or six years I was most assiduous there. These expenses are inevitable to a man like me, who knows not how to provide anything for himself, and cannot support the sight of a lackey who grumbles and serves him with a sour look. With Madam Dupin, even where I was one of the family, and in whose house I rendered many services to the servants, I never received theirs but for my money. In course of time it was necessary to renounce these little liberalities, which my situation no longer permitted me to bestow, and I felt still more severely the inconvenience of associating with people in a situation different from my own.

Had this manner of life been to my taste, I should have been consoled for a heavy expense, which I dedicated to my pleasures; but to ruin myself at the same time that I fatigued my mind, was insupportable, and I had so felt the weight of this, that, profiting by the interval of liberty I then had, I was determined to perpetuate it, and entirely to renounce great companies, the composition of books, and all literary concerns, and for the remainder of my days to confine myself to the narrow and peaceful sphere in which I felt I was born to move.

The product of this *Letter to D'Alembert,* and of the *Nouvelle Héloïse,* had a little improved the state of my finances, which had been considerably exhausted at the Hermitage. *Emile,* to which, after I had finished *Héloïse,* I had given great application, was in forwardness, and the product of this could not be less than the sum of which I was already in possession. I intended to place this money in such a manner as to produce me a little annual income, which, with my copying, might be sufficient to my wants without writing any more. I had two other works upon the stocks. The first of these was my *Institutions Politiques.** I examined the state of this work, and found it required several years' labor. I had not courage enough to continue it, and to wait until it was finished before I carried my intentions into execution. Therefore, laying the book aside, I determined to take from it all I could, and to burn the rest; and continuing this with zeal without interrupting *Emile,* I finished the *Contrat Social.*†

The dictionary of music now remained. This was mechanical, and might be taken up at any time; the

* *Political Institutions.*   † *Social Contract.*

object of it was entirely pecuniary. I reserved to myself the liberty of laying it aside, or of finishing it at my ease, according as my other resources collected should render this necessary or superfluous. With respect to the *Morale Sensitive*,* of which I had made nothing more than a sketch, I entirely gave it up.

As my last project, if I found I could not entirely do without copying, was that of removing from Paris, where the affluence of my visitors rendered my house-keeping expensive, and deprived me of the time I should have turned to advantage to provide for it; to prevent in my retirement the state of lassitude into which an author is said to fall when he has laid down his pen, I reserved to myself an occupation which might fill up the void in my solitude without tempting me to print anything more. I know not for what reason they had long tormented me to write the memoirs of my life. Although these were not until that time interesting as to the facts, I felt they might become so by the candor with which I was capable of giving them, and I determined to make of these the only work of the kind, by an unexampled veracity, that, for once at least, the world might see a man such as he internally was. I had always laughed at the false ingenuousness of Montagne, who, feigning to confess his faults, takes great care not to give himself any, except such as are amiable; whilst I, who have ever thought, and still think myself, considering everything, the best of men, felt there is no human being,

Sensitive Morality.

however pure he may be, who does not internally conceal some odious vice. I knew I was described to the public very different from what I really was, and so opposite, that notwithstanding my faults, all of which I was determined to relate, I could not but be a gainer by showing myself in my proper colors. This, besides, not being to be done without setting forth others also in theirs, and the work for the same reason not being of a nature to appear during my lifetime, and that of several other persons, I was the more encouraged to make my confession, at which I should never have to blush before any person. I therefore resolved to dedicate my leisure to the execution of this undertaking, and immediately began to collect such letters and papers as might guide or assist my memory, greatly regretting the loss of all I had burned, mislaid and destroyed.

The project of absolute retirement, one of the most reasonable I had ever formed, was strongly impressed upon my mind, and for the execution of it I was already taking measures, when Heaven, which prepared me a different destiny, plunged me into another vortex.

Montmorency, the ancient and fine patrimony of the illustrious family of that name, was taken from it by confiscation. It passed by the sister of Duc Henri, to the house of Condé, which has changed the name of Montmorency to that of Enghien, and the duchy has no other castle than an old tower, where the archives are kept, and to which the vassals come to do homage. But at Montmorency, or Enghien, there is a private house, built by Crosat, called *le pauvre,* which having the magnificence of the most superb chateaux, deserves and bears the name of a castle. The majestic appearance of this noble edifice, the view from it, not equaled perhaps in any country; the spacious saloon, painted by the hand of a master; the garden, planted by the celebrated Le Nostre; all combined to form a whole strikingly majestic, in which there is still a simplicity that enforces admiration. The Maréchal Duc de Luxembourg, who then inhabited this house, came every year into the neighborhood where formerly his ancestors were the masters, to pass, at least, five or six weeks as a private inhabitant, but with a splendor which did not degenerate from the ancient luster of his family. On the first journey he made to it after my residing at Montmorency, he and his lady sent to me a valet de chamber, with their compliments, inviting me to sup with them as often as it should be agreeable to me; and at each time of their coming they never failed to reiterate the same compliments and invitation. This called to my recollection Madam Beuzenval sending me to dine in the servants' hall. Times were changed; but I was still the same man. I did not choose to be sent to dine in the servants' hall, and was but little desirous of appearing at the table of the great; I should have been much better pleased had they left me as I was, without caressing me and rendering me ridiculous. I answered politely and respectfully to Monsieur and Madam de Luxembourg, but

I did not accept their offers, and my indisposition and timidity, with my embarrassment in speaking, making me tremble at the idea alone of appearing in an assembly of people of the court. I did not even go to the castle to pay a visit of thanks, although I sufficiently comprehended this was all they desired, and that their eager politeness was rather a matter of curiosity than benevolence.

However, advances still were made, and even became more pressing. The Comtesse de Boufflers, who was very intimate with the lady of the maréchal, sent to inquire after my health, and to beg I would go and see her. I returned her a proper answer, but did not stir from my house. At the journey of Easter, the year following, 1759, the Chevalier de Lorenzy, who belonged to the court of the Prince of Conti, and was intimate with Madam de Luxembourg, came several times to see me, and we became acquainted; he pressed me to go to the castle, but I refused to comply. At length, one afternoon, when I least expected anything of the kind, I saw coming up to the house the Maréchal de Luxembourg, followed by five or six persons. There was now no longer any means of defense; and I could not, without being arrogant and unmannerly, do otherwise than return this visit, and make my court to *Madam la Maréchale,* from whom the marshal had been the bearer of the most obliging compliments to me. Thus, under unfortunate auspices, began the connections from which I could no longer preserve myself, although a too well-founded foresight made me afraid of them until they were made.

I was excessively afraid of Madam de Luxembourg. I knew she was amiable as to manner. I had seen her several times at the theater, and with the Duchess of Boufflers, and in the bloom of her beauty; but she was said to be malignant; and this in a woman of her rank made me tremble. I had scarcely seen her before I was subjugated. I thought her charming with that charm proof against time and which had the most powerful action upon my heart. I expected to find her conversation satirical and full of pleasantries and points. It was not so; it was much better. The conversation of Madam de Luxembourg is not remarkably full of wit; it has no sallies, nor even finesse; it is exquisitely delicate, never striking, but always pleasing. Her flattery is the more intoxicating as it is natural; it seems to escape her involuntarily, and her heart to overflow because it is too full. I thought I perceived, on my first visit, that notwithstanding my awkward manner and embarrassed expression, I was not displeasing to her. All the women of the court know how to persuade us of this when they please, whether it be true or not, but they do not all, like Madam de Luxembourg, possess the art of rendering that persuasion so agreeable that we are no longer disposed ever to have a doubt remaining. From the first day my confidence in her would have been as full as it soon afterwards became, had not the Duchess of Montmorency, her daughter-in-law, young, giddy, and malicious also, taken it into her head to attack me, and in the midst of the eulogiums of her mamma, and feigned allurements on her own account, made me suspect I was only considered by them as a subject of ridicule.

It would perhaps have been difficult to relieve me from this fear with these two ladies had not the extreme goodness of the maréchal confirmed me in the belief that theirs was not real. Nothing is more surprising, considering my timidity, than the promptitude with which I took him at his word on the footing of equality to which he would absolutely reduce himself with me, except it be that with which he took me at mine with respect to the absolute independence in which I was determined to live. Both persuaded I had reason to be content with my situation, and that I was unwilling to change it, neither he nor Madam de Luxembourg seemed to think a moment of my purse or fortune; although I can have no doubt of the tender concern they had for me, they never proposed to me a place nor offered me their interest, except it were once, when Madam de Luxembourg seemed to wish me to become a member of the French Academy. I alleged my religion; this she told me was no obstacle, or if it was one she engaged to remove it. I answered, that however great the honor of becoming a member of so illustrious a body might be, having refused M. de Tressan, and, in some measure, the King of Poland, to become a member of the Academy at Nancy, I could not with propriety enter into any other. Madam de Luxembourg did not insist, and nothing more

was said upon the subject. This simplicity of intercourse with persons of such rank, and who had the
power of doing anything in my favor, M. de Luxembourg being, and highly deserving to be, the particular friend of the king, affords a singular contrast
with the continual cares, equally importunate and
officious, of the friends and protectors from whom I
had just separated, and who endeavored less to serve
me than to render me contemptible.

When the marechal came to see me at Mont-Louis,
I was uneasy at receiving him and his retinue in my
only chamber; not because I was obliged to make
them all sit down in the midst of my dirty plates and
broken pots, but on account of the state of the floor,
which was rotten and falling to ruin, and I was afraid
the weight of his attendants would entirely sink it.
Less concerned on account of my own danger than
for that to which the affability of the maréchal exposed him, I hastened to remove him from it by conducting him, notwithstanding the coldness of the
weather, to my alcove, which was quite open to the
air, and had no chimney. When he was there I told
him my reason for having brought him to it; he told
it to his lady, and they both pressed me to accept, until the floor was repaired, a lodging at the castle; or,
if I preferred it, in a separate edifice called the Little
Castle, which was in the middle of the park. This
delightful abode deserves to be spoken of.

The park or garden of Montmorency is not a plain,
like that of the Chevrette. It is uneven, mountainous,

raised by little hills and valleys, of which the able artist has taken advantage, and thereby varied his groves, ornaments, waters, and points of view, and, if I may so speak, multiplied by art and genius a space in itself rather narrow. This park is terminated at the top by a terrace and the castle; at bottom it forms a narrow passage which opens and becomes wider towards the valley, the angle of which is filled up with a large piece of water. Between the orangery, which is in this widening, and the piece of water, the banks of which are agreeably decorated, stands the Little Castle, of which I have spoken. This edifice, and the ground about it, formerly belonged to the celebrated Le Brun, who amused himself in building and decorating it in the exquisite taste of architectural ornaments which that great painter had formed to himself. The castle has since been rebuilt, but still according to the plan and design of its first master. It is little and simple, but elegant. As it stands in a hollow between the orangery and the large piece of water, and consequently is liable to be damp, it is open in the middle by a peristyle between two rows of columns, by which means the air circulating throughout the whole edifice keeps it dry, notwithstanding its unfavorable situation. When the building is seen from the opposite elevation, which is a point of view, it appears absolutely surrounded with water, and we imagine we have before our eyes an enchanted island, or the most beautiful of the three Borromeans, called *Isola Bella,* in the greater lake.

In this solitary edifice I was offered the choice of four complete apartments it contains, besides the ground-floor, consisting of a dancing room, billiard room and a kitchen. I chose the smallest over the kitchen, which also I had with it. It was charmingly neat, with blue and white furniture. In this profound and delicious solitude, in the midst of woods, the singing of birds of every kind, and the perfume of orange flowers, I composed, in a continual ecstasy, the fifth book of *Emile,* the coloring of which I owed in a great measure to the lively impression I received from the place I inhabited.

With what eagerness did I run every morning at sunrise to respire the perfumed air in the peristyle! What excellent coffee I took there *tête-à-tête* with my Thérèsa. My cat and dog were our company. This retinue alone would have been sufficient for me during my whole life, in which I should not have had one weary moment. I was there in a terrestrial paradise; I lived in innocence and tasted of happiness.

At the journey of July, M. and Madam de Luxembourg showed me so much attention, and were so extremely kind, that, lodged in their house, and overwhelmed with their goodness, I could not do less than make them a proper return in assiduous respect near their persons; I scarcely quitted them; I went in the morning to pay my court to *Madam la Maréchale;* after dinner I walked with the maréchal; but did not sup at the castle on account of the numerous guests, and because they supped too late for me. Thus far everything was as it should be, and no harm would have been done could I have remained at this point. But I have never known how to preserve a medium in my attachments, and simply fulfill the duties of society. I have ever been everything or nothing. I was soon everything; and receiving the most polite attention from persons of the highest rank, I passed the proper bounds, and conceived for them a friendship not permitted except among equals. Of these I had all the familiarity in my manners, whilst they still preserved in theirs the same politeness to which they had accustomed me. Yet I was never quite at my ease with Madam de Luxembourg. Although I was not quite relieved from my fears relative to her character, I apprehended less danger from it than from her wit. It was by this especially that she impressed me with awe. I knew she was difficult as to conversation, and she had a right to be so. I knew women, especially those of her rank, would absolutely be amused, that it was better to offend than to weary them, and I judged by her commentaries upon what the people who went away had said what she must think of my blunders. I thought of an expedient to spare me with her the ambarrassment of speaking; this was reading. She had heard of my *Héloïse,* and knew it was in the press; she expressed a desire to see the work; I offered to read it to her, and she accepted my offer. I went to her every morning at ten o'clock; M. de Luxembourg was present, and the door was shut. I read by the side of her bed, and so well proportioned my readings that there would have been sufficient for the whole time she had to ſtay, had they even not been interrupted.* The success of this expedient surpassed my expectation. Madam de Luxembourg took a great liking to Julia and the author; she spoke of nothing but me, thought of nothing else, said civil things to me from morning till night, and embraced me ten times a day. She insisted on me always having my place by her side at table, and when any great lords wished to take it she told them it was mine, and made them sit down somewhere else. The impression these charming manners made upon me, who was subjugated by the least mark of affection, may easily be judged of. I became really attached to her in proportion to the attachment she showed me. All my fear in perceiving this infatuation, and feeling the want of agreeableness in myself to support it, was that it would be changed into disgust; and unfortunately this fear was but too well founded.

There must have been a natural opposition between her turn of mind and mine, since, independently of the numerous ſtupid things which at every inſtant escaped me in conversation, and even in my letters, and when I was upon the best terms with her, there were certain other things with which she was displeased without my being able to imagine the reason. I will quote one inſtance from among twenty. She knew I was writing for Madam d'Houdetot a copy of

* *The loss of a great battle, which much afflicted the king, obliged M. de Luxembourg precipitately to return to court.*

the *Nouvelle Héloïse*. She was desirous to have one on the same terms. I promised to do so; and entering her name as one of my customers, I wrote her a polite letter of thanks, at least such was my intention. Her answer, which was as follows, stupefied me with surprise. (*Packet C, No. 43.*)

VERSAILLES, *Tuesday*.

"I am ravished, I am satisfied: your letter has given me infinite pleasure, and I take the earliest moment to acquaint you with, and thank you for it.

"These are the exact words of your letter: *Although you are certainly a very good customer, I have some pain in receiving your money: according to regular order I ought to pay for the pleasure I should have in working for you.* I will not mention the subject again. I have to complain of your not speaking of your state of health: nothing interests me more. I love you with all my heart; and be assured that I write this to you in a very melancholy mood, for I should have much pleasure in telling it you myself. M. de Luxembourg loves and embraces you with all his heart."

On receiving the letter I hastened to answer it, reserving to myself more fully to examine the matter, protesting against all disobliging interpretation, and after having given several days to this examination with an inquietude which may easily be conceived, and still without being able to discover in what I could have erred, what follows was my final answer on the subject.

MONTMORENCY, 8th December, 1759.

"Since my last letter I have examined a hundred times the passage in question. I have considered it in its proper and natural meaning, as well as in every other which may be given to it, and I confess to you, madam, that I know not whether it be I who owe to you excuses, or you from whom they are due to me."

It is now ten years since these letters were written. I have since that time frequently thought of the subject of them; and such is still my stupidity that I have hitherto been unable to discover what in the passage, quoted from my letter, she could find offensive, or even displeasing.

I must here mention, relative to the manuscript copy of *Héloïse* Madam de Luxembourg wished to have, in what manner I thought to give it some marked advantage which should distinguish it from all others. I had written separately the adventures of Lord Edward, and had long been undetermined whether I should insert them wholly, or in extracts, in the work in which they seemed to be wanting. I at length determined to retrench them entirely, because, not being in the manner of the rest, they would have spoiled the interesting simplicity, which was its principal merit. I had still a stronger reason when I came to know Madam de Luxembourg. There was in these adventures a Roman marchioness, of a bad character, some parts of which, without being applicable, might have been applied to her by those to whom she was not particularly known. I was therefore, highly pleased with the determination to which I had come, and resolved to abide by it. But in the ardent desire to enrich her copy with something which was not in the other, what should I fall upon but these unfortunate adventures, and I concluded on making an extract from them to add to the work; a project dictated by madness, of which the extravagance is inexplicable, except by the blind fatality which led me on to destruction.

Quos vult perdere Jupiter dementat.

I was stupid enough to make this extract with the greatest care and pains, and to send it her as the finest thing in the world; it is true, I at the same time informed her the original was burned, which was really the case, that the extract was for her alone, and would never be seen, except by herself, unless she chose to show it; which, far from proving to her my prudence and discretion, as it was my intention to do, clearly intimated what I thought of the application by which she might be offended. My stupidity was such, that I had no doubt of her being delighted with what I had done. She did not make me the compliment upon it which I expected, and, to my great surprise, never once mentioned the paper I had sent her. I was so satisfied with myself, that it was not until a long time afterwards, I judged, from other indications, of the effect it had produced.

I had still, in favor of her manuscript, another idea more reasonable, but which, by more distant effects, has not been much less prejudicial to me; so much does everything concur with the work of destiny, when that hurries on a man to misfortune. I thought of ornamenting the manuscript with the engravings of the New Eloisa, which were of the same size. I asked Coindet for these engravings, which belonged to me by every kind of title, and the more so as I had given him the produce of the plates, which had a considerable sale. Coindet is as cunning as I am the contrary. By frequently asking him for the engravings he came to the knowledge of the use I intended to make of them. He then, under pretense of adding some new ornament, still kept them from me, and at length presented them himself.

Ego versiculos feci: tulit alter honores.

This gave him an introduction upon a certain footing to the Hotel de Luxembourg. After my establishment at the little castle he came rather frequently to see me, and always in the morning, especially when M. and Madam de Luxembourg were at Montmorency. Therefore that I might pass the day with him, I did not go to the castle. Reproaches were made me on account of my absence; I told the reason of them. I was desired to bring with me M. Coindet; I did so. This was what he had sought after. Therefore, thanks to the excessive goodness M. and Madam de Luxembourg had for me, a clerk to M. Trélusson, who was sometimes pleased to give him his table when he had nobody else to dine with him, was suddenly placed at that of a maréchal of France, with princes, duchesses, and persons of the highest rank at court. I shall never forget, that one day being obliged to return early to Paris, the maréchal said, after dinner, to the company, "Let us take a walk upon the road to St. Denis, and we will accompany M. Coindet." This was too much for the poor man; his head was quite turned. For my part my heart was so affected that I could not say a word. I followed the company, weeping like a child, and having the strongest desire to kiss the foot of the good maréchal; but the continuation of the history of the manuscript has made me anticipate. I will go a little back, and, as far as my memory will permit, mark each event in its proper order.

As soon as the little house of Mont-Louis was ready, I had it neatly furnished and again established myself there. I could not break through the resolution I had made on quitting the Hermitage of always having my apartment to myself; but I found a difficulty in resolving to quit the little castle. I kept the key of it, and being delighted with the charming breakfasts of the peristyle, frequently went to the castle to sleep, and stayed three or four days as at a country-house. I was at that time perhaps better and more agreeably lodged than any private individual in Europe. My host, M. Mathas, one of the best men in the world, had left me the absolute direction of the repairs at Mont-Louis, and insisted upon my disposing of his workmen without his interference. I found the means of making a single chamber upon the first story, into a complete set of apartments, consisting of a chamber, ante-chamber, and a water-closet. Upon the ground-floor was the kitchen and the chamber of Thérèsa. The alcove served me for a closet by means of a glazed partition and a chimney I had made there. After my return to this habitation, I amused myself in decorating the terrace, which was already shaded by two rows of linden trees; I added two others to make a cabinet of verdure, and placed in it a table and stone benches; I surrounded it with lilacs, seringa and honeysuckle, and had a beautiful border of flowers parallel with the two rows of trees. This terrace, more elevated than that of the castle, from which the view was at least as fine, and where I had tamed a great number of birds, was my drawing-room, in which I received M. and Madam de Luxembourg, the Duke of Villeroy, the Prince of Tingry, the Marquis of Armentières, the Duchess of Montmorency, the Duchess of Boufflers, the Countess of Valentinois, the Countess of Boufflers, and other persons of the first rank; who, from the castle, disdained not to make, over a very fatiguing mountain, the pilgrimage of Mont-Louis. I owed all these visits to the favor of M. and Madam de Luxembourg; this I felt, and my heart on that account did them all due homage. It was with the same sentiment that I once said to M. de Luxembourg, embracing him: "Ah! Monsieur le Maréchal, I hated the great before I knew you, and I have hated them still more since you have shown me with what ease they might acquire universal respect." Further than this, I defy any person with whom I was then acquainted, to say I was ever dazzled for an instant with splendor, or that the vapor of the incense I received ever affected my head; that I was less uniform in my manner, less plain in my dress, less easy of access to people of the lowest rank, less familiar with neighbors, or less ready to render service to every person when I had it in my power so to do, without ever once being discouraged by the numerous and frequently unreasonable importunities with which I was incessantly assailed.

Although my heart led me to the castle of Montmorency, by my sincere attachment to those by whom it was inhabited, it by the same means drew me back to the neighborhood of it, there to taste the sweets of the equal and simple life, in which my only happiness consisted. Thérèsa had contracted a friendship with the daughter of one of my neighbors, a mason of the name of Pilleu; I did the same with the father, and after having dined at the castle, not without some constraint, to please Madam de Luxembourg, with what eagerness did I return in the evening to sup with the good man Pilleu and his family, sometimes at his own house and at others at mine!

Besides my two lodgings in the country, I soon

had a third at the Hotel de Luxembourg, the proprietors of which pressed me so much to go and see them there that I consented, notwithstanding my aversion to Paris, where, since my retiring to the Hermitage, I had been but twice, upon the two occasions of which I have spoken. I did not now go there except on the days agreed upon, solely to supper, and the next morning I returned to the country. I entered and came out by the garden which faces the boulevard, so that I could with the greateſt truth, say I had not set my foot upon the ſtones of Paris.

In the midſt of this transient prosperity, a catastrophe, which was to be the conclusion of it, was preparing at a distance. A short time after my return to Mont-Louis, I made there, and as it was customary, againſt my inclination, a new acquaintance, which makes another era in my private hiſtory. Whether this be favorable or unfavorable, the reader will hereafter be able to judge. The person with whom I became acquainted was the Marchioness of Verdelin, my neighbor, whose husband had just bought a country-house at Soisy, near Montmorency. Mademoiselle d'Ars, daughter to the Comte d'Ars, a man of fashion, but poor, had married M. de Verdelin, old, ugly, deaf, uncouth, brutal, jealous, with gashes in his face, and blind of one eye, but, upon the whole, a good man when properly managed, and in possession of a fortune of from fifteen to twenty thousand a year. This charming objeƈt, swearing, roaring, scolding, storming, and making his wife cry all day long, ended by doing whatever she thought proper, and this to set her in a rage, because she knew how to persuade him that it was he who would, and she who would not have it so. M. de Margency, of whom I have spoken, was the friend of madam, and became that of monsieur. He had a few years before let them his castle of Margency, near Eaubonne and Andilly, and they resided there precisely at the time of my passion for Madam d'Houdetot. Madam d'Houdetot and Madam de Verdelin became acquainted with each other, by means of Madam d'Aubeterre their common friend; and as the garden of Margency was in the road by which Madam d'Houdetot went to Mont Olympe, her favorite walk, Madam de Verdelin gave her a key that she might pass through it. By means of this key I crossed it several times with her; but I did not like unexpected meetings, and when Madam de Verdelin was by chance upon our way I left them together without speaking to her, and went on before. This want of gallantry must have made on her an impression unfavorable to me. Yet when she was at Soisy she was anxious to have my company. She came several times to see me at Mont-Louis, without finding me at home, and perceiving I did not return her visit, took it into her head, as a means of forcing me to do it, to send me pots of flowers for my terrace. I was under the necessity of going to thank her; this was all she wanted, and we thus became acquainted.

This connection, like every other I formed, or was led into contrary to my inclination, began rather boisterously. There never reigned in it a real calm. The turn of mind of Madam de Verdelin was too opposite to me. Malignant expressions and pointed sarcasms came from her with so much simplicity, that a continual attention too fatiguing for me was necessary to perceive she was turning into ridicule the person to whom she spoke. One trivial circumstance which occurs to my recollection will be sufficient to give an idea of her manner. Her brother had just obtained the command of a frigate cruising against the English. I spoke of the manner of fitting out this frigate without diminishing its swiftness of sailing. "Yes," replied she, in the most natural tone of voice, "no more cannon are taken than are necessary for fighting." I seldom have heard her speak well of any of her absent friends without letting slip something to their prejudice. What she did not see with an evil eye she looked upon with one of ridicule, and her friend Margency was not excepted. What I found most insupportable in her was the perpetual constraint proceeding from her little messages, presents and billets, to which it was a labor for me to answer, and I had continual embarrassments either in thanking or refusing. However, by frequently seeing this lady I became attached to her. She had her troubles as well as I had mine. Reciprocal confidence rendered our conversations interesting. Nothing so cordially attaches two persons as the satisfaction of weeping together. We sought the company of each other for our reciprocal consolation, and the want of this has frequently made me pass over many things. I had been so severe in my frankness with her, that after having sometimes shown so little esteem for her character, a great deal was necessary to be able to believe she could sincerely forgive me.

The following letter is a specimen of the epistles I sometimes wrote to her, and it is to be remarked that she never once in any of her answers to them seemed to be in the least degree piqued.

MONTMORENCY, *5th November, 1760.*
"You tell me, madam, you have not well explained yourself, in order to make me understand I have explained myself ill. You speak of your pretended stupidity for the purpose of making me feel my own. You boast of being nothing more than a good kind of woman, as if you were afraid to be taken at your word, and you make me apologies to tell me I owe them to you. Yes, madam, I know it; it is I who am a fool, a good kind of man; and, if it be possible, worse than all this; it is I who make a bad choice of my expressions in the opinion of a fine French lady, who pays as much attention to words, and speaks as well as you do. But consider that I take them in the common meaning of the language without knowing or troubling my head about the polite acceptations in which they are taken in the virtuous societies of Paris. If my expressions are sometimes equivocal, I endeavored by my conduct to determine their meaning," etc. The rest of the letter is much the same.

Coindet, enterprising, bold, even to effrontery, and who was upon the watch after all my friends, soon introduced himself in my name to the house of Madam de Verdelin, and, unknown to me, shortly became there more familiar than myself. This Coindet was an extraordinary man. He presented himself in my name in the houses of all my acquaintance, gained a footing in them, and ate there without ceremony. Transported with zeal to do me service, he never mentioned my name without his eyes being suffused with tears; but, when he came to see me, he kept the most profound silence on the subject of all these connections, and especially on that in which he knew I must be interested. Instead of telling me what he had heard, said, or seen, relative to my affairs, he waited for my speaking to him, and even interrogated me. He never knew anything of what passed in Paris, except that which I told him: finally, although everybody spoke to me of him, he never once spoke to me of any person; he was secret and mysterious with his friend only; but I will for the present leave Coindet and Madam de Verdelin, and return to them at a proper time.

Sometime after my return to Mont-Louis, La Tour, the painter, came to see me, and brought with him my portrait in crayons, which a few years before he had exhibited at the saloon. He wished to give me this portrait, which I did not choose to accept. But Madam d'Epinay, who had given me hers, and would have had this, prevailed upon me to ask him for it.

He had taken some time to retouch the features. In the interval happened my rupture with Madam d'Epinay; I returned her her portrait; and giving her mine being no longer in question, I put it into my chamber, in the castle. M. de Luxembourg saw it there, and found it a good one; I offered it him, he accepted it, and I sent it to the castle. He and his lady comprehended I should be very glad to have theirs. They had them taken in miniature by a very skillful hand, set in a box of rock crystal, mounted with gold, and in a very handsome manner, with which I was delighted, made me a present of both. Madam de Luxembourg would never consent that her portrait should be on the upper part of the box. She had reproached me several times with loving M. de Luxembourg better than I did her; I had not denied it because it was true. By this manner of placing her portrait she showed very politely, but very clearly, she had not forgotten the preference.

Much about this time I was guilty of a folly which did not contribute to preserve to me her good graces. Although I had no knowledge of M. de Silhouette, and was not much disposed to like him, I had a great opinion of his administration. When he began to let his hand fall rather heavily upon financiers, I perceived he did not begin his operation in a favorable moment, but he had my warmest wishes for his success; and as soon as I heard he was displaced I wrote to him, in my intrepid, heedless manner, the following letter, which I certainly do not undertake to justify.

MONTMORENCY, *2d December, 1769.*

"Vouchsafe, sir, to receive the homage of a solitary man, who is not known to you, but who esteems you for your talents, respects you for your administration, and who did you the honor to believe you would not long remain in it. Unable to save the State, except at the expense of the capital by which it has been ruined, you have braved the clamors of the gainers of money. When I saw you crush these wretches, I envied you your place; and at seeing you quit it without departing from your system, I admire you. Be satisfied with yourself, sir; the step you have taken will leave you an honor you will long enjoy without a competitor. The malediction of knaves is the glory of an honest man."

Madam de Luxembourg, who knew I had written this letter, spoke to me of it when she came into the country at Easter. I showed it to her and she was desirous of a copy; this I gave her, but when I did it I did not know she was interested in under-farms, and the displacing of M. de Silhouette. By my numerous follies any person would have imagined I willfully endeavored to bring on myself the hatred of an amiable woman who had power, and to whom, in truth, I daily became more attached, and was far from wishing to occasion her displeasure, although by my awkward manner of proceeding, I did everything proper for that purpose. I think it superfluous to remark here, that it is to her the history of the opiate of M. Tronchin, of which I have spoken in the first part of my memoirs, relates; the other lady was Madam de Mirepoix. They have never mentioned to me the circumstance, nor has either of them, in the least, seemed to have preserved a remembrance of it; but to presume that Madam de Luxembourg can possibly have forgotten it appears to me very difficult, and would still remain so, even were the subsequent events entirely unknown. For my part, I fell into a deceitful security relative to the effects of my stupid mistakes, by an internal evidence of my not having taken any step with an intention to offend; as if a woman could ever forgive what I had done, although she might be certain the will had not the least part in the matter.

Although she seemed not to see or feel anything, and that I did not immediately find either her warmth of friendship diminished or the least change in her manner, the continuation and even increase of a too well founded foreboding made me incessantly tremble, lest disgust should succeed to infatuation. Was it possible for me to expect in a lady of such high rank, a constancy proof against my want of address to support it? I was unable to conceal from her this secret foreboding, which made me uneasy, and rendered me still more disagreeable. This will be judged of by the following letter, which contains a very singular prediction.

N. B. *This letter, without date in my rough copy, was written in October, 1760, at latest.*

"How cruel is your goodness! Why disturb the peace of a solitary mortal who had renounced the pleasures of life, that he might no longer suffer the fatigues of them? I have passed my days in vainly searching for solid attachments. I have not been able to form any in the ranks to which I was equal; is it in yours that I ought to seek for them? Neither ambition nor interest can tempt me; I am not vain, but little fearful; I can resist everything except caresses. Why do you both attack me by a weakness which I must overcome, because in the distance by which we are separated, the overflowings of susceptible hearts cannot bring mine near to you? Will gratitude be sufficient for a heart which knows not two manners of bestowing its affections, and feels itself incapable of everything except friendship? Of friendship, madam la maréchale! Ah! there is my misfortune! It is good in you and the maréchal to make use of this expression; but I am mad when I take you at your word. You amuse yourselves, and I become attached; and the end of this prepares for me new regrets. How do I hate all your titles, and pity you on account of your being obliged to bear them! You seem to me to be so worthy of tasting the charms of private life! Why do not you reside at Clarens? I would go there in search of happiness; but the castle of Montmorency, and the Hotel de Luxembourg! Is it in these places

Jean-Jacques ought to be seen? Is it there a friend to equality ought to carry the affections of a sensible heart, and who thus paying the esteem in which he is held, thinks he returns as much as he receives? You are good and susceptible also: this I know and have seen; I am sorry I was not sooner convinced of it; but in the rank you hold, in your manner of living, nothing can make a lasting impression; a succession of new objects efface each other so that not one of them remains. You will forget me, madam, after having made it impossible for me to imitate you. You have done a great deal to render me unhappy, to be inexcusable."

I joined with her the maréchal, to render the compliment less severe; for I was moreover so sure of him, that I never had a doubt in my mind of the continuation of his friendship. Nothing that intimidated me in madam la maréchale, ever for a moment extended to him. I never have had the least mistrust relative to his character, which I knew to be feeble, but constant. I no more feared a coldness on his part than I expected from him an heroic attachment. The simplicity and familiarity of our manners with each other proved how far dependence was reciprocal. We were both always right: I shall ever honor and hold dear the memory of this worthy man, and, notwithstanding everything that was done to detach him from me, I am as certain of his having died my friend as if I had been present in his last moments.

At the second journey to Montmorency, in the year

1760, the reading of Eloisa being finished, I had recourse to that of *Emile,* to support myself in the good graces of Madam de Luxembourg; but this, whether the subject was less to her taste, or that so much reading at length fatigued her, did not succeed so well. However, as she reproached me with suffering myself to be the dupe of booksellers, she wished me to leave to her care the printing the work, that I might reap from it a greater advantage. I consented to her doing it, on the express condition of its not being printed in France, on which we had a long dispute; I affirming that it was impossible to obtain, and even imprudent to solicit, a tacit permission; and being unwilling to permit the impression upon any other terms in the kingdom; she, that the censor could not make the least difficulty, according to the system government had adopted. She found means to make M. de Malesherbes enter into her views. He wrote to me on the subject a long letter with his own hand, to prove the profession of faith of the Savoyard vicar to be a composition which must everywhere gain the approbation of its readers and that of the court, as things were then circumstanced. I was surprised to see this magistrate, always so prudent, become so smooth in the business, as the printing of a book was by that alone legal, I had no longer any objection to make to that of the work. Yet, by an extraordinary scruple, I still required it should be printed in Holland, and by the bookseller Néaulme, whom, not satisfied with indicating him, I informed of my wishes, consenting the edition should be brought out for the profit of a French bookseller, and that as soon as it was ready it should be sold at Paris, or wherever else it might be thought proper, as with this I had no manner of concern. This is exactly what was agreed upon between Madam de Luxembourg and myself, after which I gave her my manuscript.

Madam de Luxembourg was this time accompanied by her granddaughter Mademoiselle de Boufflers, now Duchess of Lauzun. Her name was Amélie. She was a charming girl. She really had a maiden beauty, mildness and timidity. Nothing could be more lovely than her person, nothing more chaste and tender than the sentiments she inspired. She was, besides, still a child under eleven years of age. Madam de Luxembourg, who thought her too timid, used every endeavor to animate her. She permitted me several times to give her a kiss, which I did with my usual awkwardness. Instead of saying flattering things to her, as any other person would have done, I remained silent and disconcerted, and I know not which of the two, the little girl or myself, was most ashamed. I met her one day alone in the staircase of the little castle. She had been to see Thérèsa, with whom her governess still was. Not knowing what else to say, I proposed to her a kiss, which, in the innocence of her heart, she did not refuse; having in the morning received one from me by order of her grandmother, and in her presence. The next day, while reading *Emilie* by the side of the bed of Madam de Luxembourg, I came to a passage in which I justly censure that which I had done the preceding evening. She thought the reflection extremely just, and said some very sensible things upon the subject which made me blush. How was I enraged at my incredible stupidity, which has frequently given me the appearance of guilt when I was nothing more than a fool and embarrassed! a stupidity, which in a man known to be endowed with some wit, is considered as a false excuse. I can safely swear that in this kiss, as well as in the others, the heart and thoughts of Mademoiselle Amélie were not more pure than my own, and that if I could have avoided meeting her I should have done it; not that I had not great pleasure in seeing her, but from the embarrassment of not finding a word proper to say. Whence comes it that even a child can intimidate a man, whom the power of kings has never inspired with fear? What is to be done? How, without presence of mind, am I to act? If I strive to speak to the persons I meet, I certainly say some stupid thing to them: if I remain silent, I am a misanthrope, an unsociable animal, a bear. Total imbecility would have been more favorable to me; but the talents which I have failed to improve in the world have become the instruments of my destruction, and of that of the talents I possessed.

At the latter end of this journey, Madam de Luxembourg did a good action in which I had some share. Diderot having very imprudently offended the Princess of Robeck, daughter of M. de Luxembourg,

Palissot, whom she protected, took up the quarrel, and revenged her by the comedy of The Philosophers, in which I was ridiculed, and Diderot very roughly handled. The author treated me with more gentleness, less, I am of opinion, on account of the obligation he was under to me, than from the fear of displeasing the father of his protectress, by whom he knew I was beloved. The bookseller Duchesne, with whom I was not at that time acquainted, sent me the comedy when it was printed, and this I suspect was by the order of Palissot, who, perhaps, thought I should have a pleasure in seeing a man with whom I was no longer connected defamed. He was greatly deceived. When I broke with Diderot, whom I thought less ill-natured than weak and indiscreet, I still always preserved for his person an attachment, an esteem even, and a respect for our ancient friendship, which I know was for a long time as sincere on his part as on mine. The case was quite different with Grimm; a man false by nature, who never loved me, who is not even capable of friendship, and a person who, without the least subject of complaint, and solely to satisfy his gloomy jealousy, became, under the mask of friendship, my most cruel calumniator. This man is to me a cipher; the other will always be my old friend.

My very bowels yearned at the sight of this odious piece: the reading of it was insupportable to me, and, without going through the whole, I returned the copy to Duchesne with the following letter:

[839]

Montmorency, *21st May, 1760.*

"In casting my eye over the piece you sent me, I trembled at seeing myself well spoken of in it. I do not accept the horrid present. I am persuaded that in sending it me, you did not intend an insult; but you do not know, or have forgotten, that I have the honor to be the friend of a respectable man, who is shamefully defamed and calumniated in this libel."

Duchesne showed the letter. Diderot, upon whom it ought to have had an effect quite contrary, was vexed at it. His pride could not forgive me the superiority of a generous action, and I was informed his wife everywhere inveighed against me with a bitterness with which I was not in the least affected, as I knew she was known to everybody to be a noisy babbler.

Diderot in his turn found an avenger in the Abbé Morrellet, who wrote against Palissot a little work, imitated from the *Petit prophète,* and entitled the *Vision.* In this production he very imprudently offended Madam de Robeck, whose friends got him sent to the Bastile; though she, not naturally vindictive, and at that time in a dying state, I am certain had nothing to do in the affair.

D'Alembert, who was very intimately connected with Morrellet, wrote me a letter, desiring I would beg of Madam de Luxembourg to solicit his liberty, promising her in return encomiums in the *Encyclopédie;* my answer to his letter was as follows:

[840]

"I did not wait the receipt of your letter before I expressed to Madam de Luxembourg the pain the confinement of the Abbé Morrellet gave me. She knows my concern, and shall be made acquainted with yours, and her knowing that the abbé is a man of merit will be sufficient to make her interest herself in his behalf. However, although she and the maréchal honor me with a benevolence which is my greatest consolation, and that the name of your friend be to them a recommendation in favor of the Abbé Morrellet, I know not how far, on this occasion, it may be proper for them to employ the credit attached to the rank they hold, and the consideration due to their persons. I am not even convinced that the vengeance in question relates to the Princess of Robeck so much as you seem to imagine; and were this even the case, we must not suppose that the pleasure of vengeance belongs to philosophers exclusively, and that when they choose to become women, women will become philosophers.

"I will communicate to you whatever Madam de Luxembourg may say to me after having shown her your letter. In the meantime, I think I know her well enough to assure you that, should she have the pleasure of contributing to the enlargement of the Abbé Morrellet, she will not accept the tribute of acknowledgment you promise her in the *Encyclopédie,* although she might think herself honored by it, because she does not do good in the expectation of praise, but from the dictates of her heart."

I made every effort to excite the zeal and commiseration of Madame de Luxembourg in favor of the poor captive, and succeeded to my wishes. She went to Versailles on purpose to speak to M. de St. Florentin, and this journey shortened the residence at Montmorency, which the maréchal was obliged to quit at the same time to go to Rouen, whither the king sent him as governor of Normandy, on account of the motions of the parliament, which government wished to keep within bounds. Madame de Luxembourg wrote me the following letter the day after her departure (*Packet D, No. 23*):

VERSAILLES, *Wednesday.*

"M. de Luxembourg set off yesterday morning at six o'clock. I do not yet know that I shall follow him. I wait until he writes to me, as he is not yet certain of the stay it will be necessary for him to make. I have seen M. de St. Florentin, who is as favorably disposed as possible towards the Abbé Morrellet; but he finds some obstacles to his wishes, which, however, he is in hopes of removing the first time he has to do business with the king, which will be next week. I have also desired as a favor that he might not be exiled, because this was intended; he was to be sent to Nancy. This, sir, is what I have been able to obtain; but I promise you I will not let M. de St. Florentin rest until the affair is terminated in the manner you desire. Let me now express to you how sorry I am on account of my being obliged to leave you so soon, of which I flatter myself you have not the least doubt. I love you with all my heart, and shall do so for my whole life."

A few days afterwards I received the following note from D'Alembert, which gave me real joy. (*Packet D, No. 26.*)

August 1st.

"Thanks to your cares, my dear philosopher, the abbé has left the Bastile, and his imprisonment will have no other consequence. He is setting off for the country, and, as well as myself, returns you a thousand thanks and compliments. *Vale et me ama.*"

The abbé also wrote to me a few days afterwards a letter of thanks, which did not, in my opinion, seem to breathe a certain effusion of the heart, and in which he seemed in some measure to extenuate the service I had rendered him. Some time afterwards, I found that he and D'Alembert had, to a certain degree, I will not say supplanted, but succeeded me in the good graces of Madam de Luxembourg, and that I had lost in them all they had gained. However, I am far from suspecting the Abbé Morrellet of having contributed to my disgrace; I have too much esteem for him to harbor any such suspicion. With respect to D'Alembert, I shall at present leave him out of the question, and hereafter say of him what may seem necessary.

I had, at the same time, another affair which occasioned the last letter I wrote to Voltaire; a letter against which he vehemently exclaimed, as an abominable insult, although he never showed it to any person. I will here supply the want of that which he refused to do.

The Abbé Trublet, with whom I had a slight acquaintance, but whom I had but seldom seen, wrote to me on the 13th of June, 1760, informing me that M. Formey, his friend and correspondent, had printed in his *Journal* my letter to Voltaire upon the disaster at Lisbon. The abbé wished to know how the letter came to be printed, and, in his jesuitical manner, asked me my opinion, without giving me his own on the necessity of reprinting it. As I most sovereignly hate this kind of artifice and stratagem, I returned such thanks as were proper, but in a manner so reserved as to make him feel it, although this did not prevent him from wheedling me in two or three other letters until he had gathered all he wished to know.

I clearly understood that, notwithstanding all Trublet could say, Formey had not found the letter printed, and that the first impression of it came from himself. I knew him to be an impudent pilferer, who, without ceremony, made himself a revenue by the works of others. Although he had not yet had the incredible effrontery to take from a book already published the name of the author, to put his own in the place of it, and to sell the book for his own profit.* But by what means had this manuscript fallen into

* *In this manner he afterwards appropriated to himself Emile.*

his hands? That was a question not easy to resolve, but by which I had the weakness to be embarrassed. Although Voltaire was excessively honored by the letter, as in fact, notwithstanding his rude proceedings, he would have had a right to complain had I had it printed without his consent, I resolved to write to him upon the subject. The second letter was as follows, to which he returned no answer, and, giving greater scope to his brutality, he feigned to be irritated to fury.

MONTMORENCY, *17th June, 1760.*

SIR: I never thought I should ever have occasion to correspond with you. But learning the letter I wrote to you in 1756 has been printed at Berlin, I owe you an account of my conduct in that respect, and will fulfill this duty with truth and simplicity.

"The letter having really been addressed to you was not intended to be printed. I communicated the contents of it, on certain conditions, to three persons, to whom the rights of friendship did not permit me to refuse anything of the kind, and whom the same rights still less permitted to abuse my confidence by betraying their promise. These persons are Madam de Chenonceaux, daughter-in-law to Madam Dupin, the Comtesse d'Houdetot, and a German of the name of Grimm. Madam de Chenonceaux was desirous the letter should be printed, and asked my consent. I told her that depended upon yours. This was asked of you, which you refused, and the matter dropped.

"However, the Abbé Trublet, with whom I have

not the least connection, has just written to me from a motive of the most polite attention, that having received the papers of the *Journal* of M. Formey, he found in them this same letter with an advertisement, dated on the 23d of October, 1759, in which the editor states that he had a few weeks before found it in the shops of the booksellers of Berlin, and, as it is one of those loose sheets which shortly disappear, he thought proper to give it a place in his *Journal*.

"This, sir, is all I know of the matter. It is certain the letter had not until lately been heard of at Paris. It is also as certain that the copy, either in manuscript or print, fallen into the hands of M. de Formey, could never have reached them except by your means (which is not probable) or of those of one of the three persons I have mentioned. Finally, it is well known the two ladies are incapable of such a perfidy. I cannot, in my retirement, learn more relative to the affair. You have a correspondence by means of which you may, if you think it worth the trouble, go back to the source and verify the fact.

"In the same letter the Abbé Trublet informs me that he keeps the paper in reserve, and will not lend it without my consent, which most assuredly I will not give. But it is possible this copy may not be the only one in Paris. I wish, sir, the letter may not be printed there, and I will do all in my power to prevent this from happening; but if I cannot succeed, and that, timely perceiving it, I can have the preference, I will not then hesitate to have it immediately printed. This to me appears just and natural.

"With respect to your answer to the same letter, it has not been communicated to any one, and you may be assured it shall not be printed without your consent, which I certainly shall not be indiscreet enough to ask of you, well knowing that what one man writes to another is not written to the public. But should you choose to write one you wish to have published and address it to me, I promise you faithfully to add to it my letter and not to make to it a single word of reply.

"I love you not, sir; you have done me, your disciple and enthusiastic admirer, injuries that might have caused me the most exquisite pain. You have ruined Geneva, in return for the asylum it has afforded you; you have alienated from me my fellow-citizens, in return for the eulogiums I made of you amongst them; it is you who render to me the residence of my own country insupportable; it is you who will oblige me to die in a foreign land, deprived of all the consolations usually administered to a dying person; and cause me, instead of receiving funeral rites, to be thrown to the dogs, whilst all the honors a man can expect will accompany you in my country. Finally I hate you because you have been desirous I should; but I hate you as a man more worthy of loving you had you chosen it. Of all the sentiments with which my heart was penetrated for you, admiration, which cannot be refused your fine genius, and a partiality to your writings, are those you have not effaced. If I can honor nothing in you except your talents, the fault is not mine. I shall never be wanting in the respect due to them, nor in that which this respect requires."

In the midst of these little literary cavillings, which still fortified my resolution, I received the greatest honor letters ever acquired me, and of which I was the most sensible, in the two visits the Prince of Conti deigned to make to me, one at the Little Castle and the other at Mont-Louis. He chose the time for both these when M. de Luxembourg was not at Montmorency, in order to render it more manifest that he came there solely on my account. I have never had a doubt of my owing the first condescensions of this prince to Madam de Luxembourg and Madam de Boufflers; but I am of opinion I owe to his own sentiments and to myself those with which he has since that time continually honored me.*

My apartments at Mont-Louis being small, and the situation of the alcove charming, I conducted the prince to it, where, to complete the condescension he was pleased to show me, he chose I should have the honor of playing with him a game at chess. I knew he beat the Chevalier de Lorenzi, who played better than I did. However, notwithstanding the signs and grimace of the chevalier and the spectators, which I

---

* Remark the perseverance of this blind and stupid confidence in the midst of all the treatment which should soonest have undeceived me. It continued until my return to Paris in 1770.

feigned not to see, I won the two games we played. When they were ended, I said to him in a respectful but very grave manner: "My lord, I honor your serene highness too much not to beat you always at chess." This great prince, who had real wit, sense, and knowledge, and so was worthy not to be treated with mean adulation, felt in fact, at least I think so, that I was the only person present who treated him like a man, and I have every reason to believe he was not displeased with me for it.

Had this even been the case, I should not have reproached myself with having been unwilling to deceive him in anything, and I certainly cannot do it with having in my heart made an ill return for his goodness, but solely with having sometimes done it with an ill grace, whilst he himself accompanied with infinite gracefulness, the manner in which he showed me the marks of it. A few days afterwards he ordered a hamper of game to be sent me, which I received as I ought. This in a little time was succeeded by another, and one of his gamekeepers wrote me, by order of his highness, that the game it contained had been shot by the prince himself. I received this second hamper, but I wrote to Madam de Boufflers that I would not receive a third. This letter was generally blamed, and deservedly so. Refusing to accept presents of game from a prince of the blood, who moreover sends it in so polite a manner, is less the delicacy of a haughty man, who wishes to preserve his independence, than the rusticity of a clown, who does **not** know himself. I have never read this letter in my collection without blushing and reproaching myself for having written it. But I have not undertaken my Confession with an intention of concealing my faults, and that of which I have just spoken is too shocking in my own eyes to suffer me to pass it over in silence.

If I were not guilty of the offense of becoming his rival I was very near doing it; for Madam de Boufflers was still his mistress, and I knew nothing of the matter. She came rather frequently to see me with the Chevalier de Lorenzi. She was yet young and beautiful, affected to be whimsical, and my mind was always romantic, which was much of the same nature. I was near being laid hold of; I believe she perceived it; the chevalier saw it also, at least he spoke to me upon the subject, and in a manner not discouraging. But I was this time reasonable, and at the age of fifty it was time I should be so. Full of the doctrine I had just preached to graybeards in my letter to D'Alembert, I should have been ashamed of not profiting by it myself; besides, coming to the knowledge of that of which I had been ignorant, I must have been mad to have carried my pretensions so far as to expose myself to such an illustrious rivalry. Finally, ill cured perhaps of my passion for Madam d'Houdetot, I felt nothing could replace it in my heart, and I bade adieu to love for the rest of my life. I have this moment just withstood the dangerous allurements of a young woman who had her views; but if she feigned to forget my sixty years, I remembered them. After having thus withdrawn myself from danger, I am no longer afraid of a fall, and I answer for myself for the rest of my days.

Madam de Boufflers, perceiving the emotion she caused in me, might also observe I had triumphed over it. I am neither mad nor vain enough to believe I was at my age capable of inspiring her with the same feelings; but, from certain words which she let drop to Thérèsa, I thought I had inspired her with a curiosity; if this be the case, and that she has not forgiven me the disappointment she met with, it must be confessed I was born to be the victim of my weaknesses, since triumphant love was so prejudicial to me, and love triumphed over not less so.

Here finishes the collection of letters which has served me as a guide in the last two books. My steps will in future be directed by memory only; but this is of such a nature, relative to the period to which I am now come, and the strong impression of objects has remained so perfectly upon my mind, that lost in the immense sea of my misfortunes, I cannot forget the detail of my first shipwreck, although the consequences present to me but a confused remembrance. I therefore shall be able to proceed in the succeeding book with sufficient confidence. If I go further it will be groping in the dark.

BOOK XI

BOOK XI

[1761]

ALTHOUGH *Julie,* which for a long time had been in the press, was not yet published at the end of the year 1760, the work already began to make a great noise. Madam de Luxembourg had spoken of it at court, and Madam d'Houdetot at Paris. The latter had obtained from me permission for Saint Lambert to read the manuscript to the King of Poland, who had been delighted with it. Duclos, to whom I had also given the perusal of the work, had spoken of it at the academy. All Paris was impatient to see the novel; the booksellers of the Rue Saint-Jacques, and that of the Palais-Royal, were beset with people who came to inquire when it was to be published. It was at length brought out, and the success it had answered, contrary to custom, to the impatience with which it had been expected. The dauphiness, who was one of the first who read it, spoke of it to M. de Luxembourg as a ravishing performance. The opinions of men of letters differed from each other, but in those of every other class approbation was general, especially with the women, who became so intoxicated with the book and the author, that there was not one in high life with whom I might not have succeeded had I undertaken to do it. Of this I have such proofs as I will not commit to paper, and which without the aid of experience, authorized my opinion. It is singular that the book should have succeeded better in France than in the rest of Europe, although the French, both men and women, are severely treated in it. Contrary to my expectation it was least successful in Switzerland, and most so in Paris. Do friendship, love and virtue reign in this capital more than elsewhere? Certainly not; but there reigns in it an exquisite sensibility which transports the heart to their image, and makes us cherish in others the pure, tender and virtuous sentiments we no longer possess. Corruption is everywhere the same; virtue and morality no longer exist in Europe; but if the least love of them still remains, it is in Paris that this will be found.*

In the midst of so many prejudices and feigned passions, the real sentiments of nature are not to be distinguished from others, unless we well know to analyze the human heart. A very nice discrimination, not to be acquired except by the education of the world, is necessary to feel the finesses of the heart, if I dare use the expression, with which this work abounds. I do not hesitate to place the fourth part of it upon an equality with the *Princess of Clèves;* nor to assert that had these two works been read nowhere but in the provinces, their merit would never have

* *I wrote this in 1769.*

been discovered. It must not, therefore, be considered as a matter of astonishment, that the greatest success of my work was at court. It abounds with lively but veiled touches of the pencil; which could not but give pleasure there, because the persons who frequent it are more accustomed than others to discover them. A distinction must, however, be made. The work is by no means proper for the species of men of wit who have nothing but cunning, who possess no other kind of discernment than that which penetrates evil, and see nothing where good only is to be found. If, for instance, *Julie* had been published in a certain country which I have in my mind, I am convinced it would not have been read through by a single person, and the work would have been stifled in its birth.

I have collected most of the letters written to me on the subject of this publication, and deposited them, tied up together, in the hands of Madam de Nadillac. Should this collection ever be given to the world, very singular things will be seen, and an opposition of opinion, which shows what it is to have to do with the public. The thing least kept in view, and which will ever distinguish it from every other work, is the simplicity of the subject and the continuation of the interest, which, confined to three persons, is kept up throughout six volumes, without episode, romantic adventure, or anything malicious either in the persons or actions. Diderot complimented Richardson on the prodigious variety of his portraits and the multiplicity of his persons. In fact, Richardson has the merit of having well characterized them all; but with respect to their number, he has that in common with the most insipid writers of novels, who attempt to make up for the sterility of their ideas by multiplying persons and adventures. It is easy to awaken the attention by incessantly presenting unheard of adventures and new faces, which pass before the imagination as the figures in a magic lanthorn do before the eye; but to keep up that attention to the same objects, and without the aid of the wonderful, is certainly more difficult; and if, everything else being equal, the simplicity of the subject adds to the beauty of the work, the novels of Richardson, superior in so many other respects, cannot in this be compared to mine. I know it is already forgotten, and the cause of its being so; but it will be taken up again.

All my fear was that, by an extreme simplicity, the narrative would be fatiguing, and that it was not sufficiently interesting to engage the attention throughout the whole. I was relieved from this apprehension by a circumstance which alone was more flattering to my pride than all the compliments made me upon the work.

It appeared at the beginning of the carnival. A hawker carried it to the Princess of Talmont,* on the evening of a ball night at the opera. After supper the princess dressed herself for the ball, and until the

* *It was not the princess, but some other lady, whose name I do not know, but I have been assured of the fact.*

hour of going there, took up the new novel. At midnight she ordered the horses to be put into the carriage, and continued to read. The servant returned to tell her the horses were put to; she made no answer. Her people perceiving she forgot herself, came to tell her it was two o'clock. "There is yet no hurry," replied the princess, still reading on. Some time afterwards her watch having stopped, she rang to know the hour. She was told it was four o'clock. "That being the case," she said, "it is too late to go to the ball; let the horses be taken off." She undressed herself and passed the rest of the night in reading.

Ever since I came to the knowledge of this circumstance, I have had a constant desire to see the lady, not only to know from herself whether or not what I have related be exactly true, but because I have always thought it impossible to be interested in so lively a manner in the happiness of Julia, without having that sixth and moral sense with which so few hearts are endowed, and without which no person whatever can understand the sentiments of mine.

What rendered the women so favorable to me was, their being persuaded that I had written my own history, and was myself the hero of the romance. This opinion was so firmly established, that Madam de Polignac wrote to Madam de Verdelin, begging she would prevail upon me to show her the portrait of Julia. Everybody thought it was impossible so strongly to express sentiments without having felt them, or thus to describe the transports of love, unless immediately from the feelings of the heart. This was true, and I certainly wrote the novel during the time my imagination was inflamed to ecstasy; but they who thought real objects necessary to this effect were deceived, and far from conceiving to what a degree I can at will produce it for imaginary beings. Without Madam d'Houdetot, and the recollection of a few circumstances in my youth, the amours I have felt and described would have been with fairy nymphs. I was unwilling either to confirm or destroy an error which was advantageous to me. The reader may see in the preface a dialogue, which I had printed separately, in what manner I left the public in suspense. Rigorous people say, I ought to have explicitly declared the truth. For my part I see no reason for this, nor anything that could oblige me to it, and am of opinion there would have been more folly than candor in the declaration without necessity.

Much about the same time the *Paix Perpetuelle* * made its appearance, of this I had the year before given the manuscript to a certain M. de Bastide, the author of a journal called *Le Monde,*† into which he would at all events cram all my manuscripts. He was known to M. Duclos, and came in his name to beg I would help him to fill the *Monde.* He had heard speak of *Julie,* and would have me put this into his journal; he was also desirous of making the same use of *Emile;* he would have asked me for the *Contrat Social,* for the same purpose, had he suspected it to

* *Perpetual Peace.* † *The World.*

be written. At length, fatigued with his importunities, I resolved upon letting him have the *Paix Perpetuelle,* which I gave him for twelve louis. Our agreement was, that he should print it in his journal; but as soon as he became the proprietor of the manuscript, he thought proper to print it separately, with a few retrenchments, which the censor required him to make. What would have happened had I joined to the work my opinion of it, which fortunately I did not communicate to M. de Bastide, nor was it comprehended in our agreement? This remains still in manuscript amonst my papers. If ever it be made public, the world will see how much the pleasantries and self-sufficient manner of M. de Voltaire on the subject must have made me, who was so well acquainted with the short-sightedness of this poor man in political matters, of which he took it into his head to speak, shake my sides with laughter.

In the midst of my success with the women and the public, I felt I lost ground at the Hôtel de Luxembourg, not with the maréchal, whose goodness to me seemed daily to increase, but with his lady. Since I had had nothing more to read to her, the door of her apartment was not so frequently open to me, and during her stay at Montmorency, although I regularly presented myself, I seldom saw her except at table. My place even there was not distinctly marked out as usual. As she no longer offered me that by her side, and spoke to me but seldom, not having on my part much to say to her, I was as well satisfied with another, where I was more at my ease, especially in the evening; for I mechanically contracted the habit of placing myself nearer and nearer to the maréchal.

Apropos of the evening: I recollect having said I did not sup at the castle, and this was true, at the beginning of my acquaintance there; but as M. de Luxembourg did not dine, nor even sit down to table, it happened that I was for several months, and already very familiar in the family, without ever having eaten with him. This he had the goodness to remark upon, when I determined to sup there from time to time, when the company was not numerous; I did so, and found the suppers very agreeable, as the dinners were taken almost standing; whereas the former were long, everybody remaining seated with pleasure after a long walk; and very good and agreeable, because M. de Luxembourg loved good eating, and the honors of them were done in a charming manner by madam la maréchale. Without this explanation it would be difficult to understand the end of a letter from M. de Luxembourg, in which he says he recollects our walks with the greatest pleasure; especially, adds he, when in the evening we entered the court and did not find there the traces of carriages. The rake being every morning drawn over the gravel to efface the marks left by the coach wheels, I judged by the number of ruts of that of the persons who had arrived in the afternoon.

This year, 1761, completed the heavy losses this good man had suffered since I had had the honor of being known to him. As if it had been ordained that the evils prepared for me by destiny should begin by the man to whom I was most attached, and who was the most worthy of esteem. The first year he lost his sister, the Duchess of Villeroy; the second, his daughter, the Princess of Robeck; the third, he lost in the Duke of Montmorency his only son; and in the Comte de Luxembourg, his grandson, the last two supporters of the branch of which he was, and of his name. He supported all these losses with apparent courage, but his heart incessantly bled in secret during the rest of his life, and his health was ever after upon the decline. The unexpected and tragical death of his son must have afflicted him the more, as it happened immediately after the king had granted him for this child, and given him in promise for his grandson, the reversion of the commission he himself then held of the captain of the *Gardes du Corps*. He had the mortification to see the last, a most promising young man, perish by degrees, from the blind confidence of the mother in the physician, who giving the unhappy youth medicines for food, suffered him to die of inanition. Alas! had my advice been taken, the grandfather and the grandson would both still have been alive. What did not I say and write to the maréchal, what remonstrances did I make to Madam de Montmorency, upon the more than severe regimen, which, upon the faith of physicians, she made her son observe! Madam de Luxembourg, who thought as I did, would not usurp the authority of the mother; M. de

Luxembourg, a man of a mild and easy character, did not like to contradict her. Madam de Montmorency had in Bordeu a confidence to which her son at length became a victim. How delighted was the poor creature when he could obtain permission to come to Mont-Louis with Madam de Boufflers, to ask Thérèsa for some victuals for his famished stomach! How did I secretly deplore the miseries of greatness in seeing this only heir to an immense fortune, a great name, and so many dignified titles, devour with the greediness of a beggar a wretched morsel of bread! At length, notwithstanding all I could say and do, the physician triumphed, and the child died of hunger.

The same confidence in quacks, which destroyed the grandson, hastened the dissolution of the grandfather, and to this he added the pusillanimity of wishing to dissimulate the infirmities of age. M. de Luxembourg had at intervals a pain in the great toe; he was seized with it at Montmorency, which deprived him of sleep, and brought on slight fever. I had courage enough to pronounce the word "gout." Madam de Luxembourg gave me a reprimand. The surgeon, valet de chambre of the maréchal, maintained it was not the gout, and dressed the suffering part with *baume tranquille*. Unfortunately the pain subsided, and when it returned the same remedy was had recourse to. The constitution of the maréchal was weakened, and his disorder increased, as did his remedies in the same proportion. Madam de Luxembourg, who at length perceived the primary disorder to be the gout, objected to the dangerous manner of treating it. Things were afterwards concealed from her, and M. de Luxembourg in a few years lost his life in consequence of his obstinate adherence to what he imagined to be a method of cure. But let me not anticipate misfortune: how many others have I to relate before I come to this!

It is singular with what fatality everything I could say and do seemed of a nature to displease Madam de Luxembourg, even when I had it most at heart to preserve her friendship. The repeated afflictions which fell upon M. de Luxembourg still attached me to him the more, and consequently to Madam de Luxembourg; for they always seemed to me to be so sincerely united, that the sentiments in favor of the one necessarily extended to the other. The maréchal grew old. His assiduity at court, the cares this brought on, continually hunting, fatigue, and especially that of the service during the quarter he was in waiting, required the vigor of a young man, and I did not perceive anything that could support him in that course of life; since, besides after his death, his dignities were to be dispersed and his name extinct, it was by no means necessary for him to continue a laborious life of which the principal object had been to dispose the prince favorably to his children. One day when we three were together, and he complained of the fatigues of the court, as a man who had been discouraged by his losses, I took the liberty to speak of retirement, and to give him the advice Cyneas gave to Pyrrhus.

He sighed, and returned no positive answer. But the moment Madam de Luxembourg found me alone she reprimanded me severely for what I had said, at which she seemed to be alarmed. She made a remark of which I so strongly felt the justness that I determined never again to touch upon the subject: this was, that the long habit of living at court made that life necessary, that it was become a matter of amusement for M. de Luxembourg, and that the retirement I proposed to him would be less a relaxation from care than an exile, in which inactivity, weariness and melancholy would soon put an end to his existence. Although she must have perceived I was convinced, and ought to have relied upon the promise I made her, and which I faithfully kept, she still seemed to doubt of it; and I recollect that the conversations I afterwards had with the maréchal were less frequent and almost always interrupted.

Whilst my stupidity and awkwardness injured me in her opinion, persons whom she frequently saw and most loved, were far from being disposed to aid me in gaining what I had lost. The Abbé de Boufflers especially, a young man as lofty as it was possible for a man to be, never seemed well disposed towards me; and besides his being the only person of the society of Madam de Luxembourg who never showed me the least attention, I thought I perceived I lost something with her every time he came to the castle. It is true that without his wishing this to be the case, his presence alone was sufficient to produce the effect:

so much did his graceful and elegant manner render still more dull my stupid *spropositi*. During the first two years he seldom came to Montmorency, and by the indulgence of Madam de Luxembourg I had tolerably supported myself, but as soon as his visits began to be regular I was irretrievably lost. I wished to take refuge under his wing, and gain his friendship; but the same awkwardness which made it necessary I should please him prevented me from succeeding in the attempt I made to do it, and what I did with that intention entirely lost me with Madam de Luxembourg, without being of the least service to me with the abbé. With his understanding he might have succeeded in anything, but the impossibility of applying himself, and his turn for dissipation, prevented his acquiring a perfect knowledge of any subject. His talents are however various, and this is sufficient for the circles in which he wishes to distinguish himself. He writes light poetry and fashionable letters, strums on the cithern, and pretends to draw with crayons. He took it into his head to attempt the portrait of Madam de Luxembourg: the sketch he produced was horrid. She said it did not in the least resemble her, and this was true. The traitorous abbé consulted me, and I, like a fool and a liar, said there was a likeness. I wished to flatter the abbé, but I did not please the lady, who noted down what I had said, and the abbé, having obtained what he wanted, laughed at me in his turn. I perceived by the ill success of this my late beginning the necessity of never making another attempt to flatter *invita Minerva*.

My talent was that of telling men useful but severe truths with energy and courage; to this it was necessary to confine myself. Not only I was not born to flatter, but I knew not how to commend. The awkwardness of the manner in which I have sometimes bestowed eulogium has done me more harm than the severity of my censure. Of this I have to adduce one terrible instance, the consequences of which have not only fixed my fate for the rest of my life, but will perhaps decide on my reputation throughout all posterity.

During the residence of M. de Luxembourg at Montmorency, M. de Choiseul sometimes came to supper at the castle. He arrived there one day after I had left it. My name was mentioned, and M. de Luxembourg related to him what had happened at Venice between me and M. de Montaigu. M. de Choiseul said it was a pity I had quitted that track, and that if I chose to enter it again he would most willingly give me employment. M. de Luxembourg told me what had passed. Of this I was the more sensible as I was not accustomed to be spoiled by ministers, and had I been in a better state of health it is not certain that I should not have been guilty of a new folly. Ambition never had power over my mind except during the short intervals in which every other passion left me at liberty; but one of these intervals would have been sufficient to determine me. This good intention of M. de Choiseul gained him my attachment and increased the esteem which, in consequence of some operations in his administration, I had conceived for his talents; and the family compact in particular had appeared to me to evince a statesman of the first order. He moreover gained ground in my estimation by the little respect I entertained for his predecessors, not even excepting Madam de Pompadour, whom I considered as a species of prime minister, and when it was reported that one of these two would expel the other, I thought I offered up prayers for the honor of France when I wished that M. de Choiseul might triumph. I had always felt an antipathy to Madam de Pompadour, even before her preferment; I had seen her with Madam de la Poplinière when her name was still Madam d'Etioles. I was afterwards dissatisfied with her silence on the subject of Diderot, and with her proceedings relative to myself, as well on the subject of the *Fêtes de Raniere* and the *Muses Galantes,* as on that of the *Devin du Village,* which had not in any manner produced me advantages proportioned to its success; and on all occasions I had found her but little disposed to serve me. This however did not prevent the Chevalier de Lorenzi from proposing to me to write something in praise of that lady, insinuating that I might acquire some advantage by it. The proposition excited my indignation, the more as I perceived it did not come from himself, knowing that, passive as he was, he thought and acted according to the impulsion he received. I am so little accustomed to constraint that it was impossible for me to conceal from him my disdain, nor from anybody the moderate opinion I had of the favorite; this I am sure she knew, and thus my own interest was added to my natural inclination in the wishes I formed for M. de Choiseul. Having a great esteem for his talents, which was all I knew of him, full of gratitude for his kind intentions, and moreover unacquainted in my retirement with his taste and manner of living, I already considered him as the avenger of the public and myself; and being at that time writing the conclusion of my *Contrat Social,* I stated in it, in a single passage, what I thought of preceding ministers, and of him by whom they began to be eclipsed. On this occasion I acted contrary to my most constant maxim; and besides, I did not recollect that, in bestowing praise and strongly censuring in the same article, without naming the persons, the language must be so appropriated to those to whom it is applicable, that the most ticklish pride cannot find in it the least thing equivocal. I was in this respect in such an imprudent security, that I never once thought it was possible any one should make a false application.

One of my misfortunes was always to be connected with some female author. This I thought I might avoid amongst the great. I was deceived; it still pursued me. Madam de Luxembourg was not, however, at least that I know of, attacked with the mania of writing; but Madam de Boufflers was. She wrote a tragedy in prose, which, in the first place, was read, handed about, and highly spoken of in the society of the Prince of Conti, and upon which, not satisfied with the encomiums she received, she would absolutely consult me for the purpose of having mine. This she obtained, but with that moderation which the work deserved. She besides, had with it the information I thought it my duty to give her, that her piece, entitled *L'Esclave Généreux,* greatly resembled the English tragedy of *Oroonoko,* but little known in France, although translated into the French language. Madam de Boufflers thanked me for the remark, but, however, assured me there was not the least resemblance between her piece and the other. I never spoke of the plagiarism except to herself, and I did it to discharge a duty she had imposed on me; but this has not since prevented me from frequently recollecting the consequences of the sincerity of Gil Blas to the preaching archbishop.

Besides the Abbé de Boufflers, by whom I was not beloved, and Madam de Boufflers, in whose opinion I was guilty of that which neither women nor authors ever pardon, the other friends of Madam de Luxembourg never seemed much disposed to become mine, particularly the President Hénault, who, enrolled amongst authors, was not exempt from their weaknesses; also Madam du Deffand and Mademoiselle de Lespinasse, both intimate with Voltaire and the friends of D'Alembert, with whom the latter at length lived; however upon an honorable footing, for it cannot be understood I mean otherwise. I first began to interest myself for Madam du Deffand, whom the loss of her eyes made an object of commiseration in mine; but her manner of living, so contrary to my own, that her hour of going to bed was almost mine for rising; her unbounded passion for low wit, the importance she gave to every kind of printed trash, either complimentary or abusive, the despotism and transports of her oracles, her excessive admiration or dislike of everything, which did not permit her to speak upon any subject without convulsions, her inconceivable prejudices, invincible obstinacy, and the enthusiasm of folly to which this carried her in her passionate judgments; all disgusted me and diminished the attention I wished to pay her. I neglected her and she perceived it; this was enough to set her in a rage, and, although I was sufficiently aware how much a woman of her character was to be feared, I preferred exposing myself to the scourge of her hatred rather than to that of her friendship.

My having so few friends in the society of Madam de Luxembourg would not have been in the least dangerous had I had no enemies in her family. Of these I had but one, who, in my then situation, was as powerful as a hundred. It certainly was not M. de Villeroy, her brother; for he not only came to see me, but had several times invited me to Villeroy; and as I had answered to the invitation with all possible politeness and respect, he had taken my vague manner of doing it as a consent, and arranged with Madam de Luxembourg a journey of a fortnight, in which it was proposed to me to make one of the party. As the cares my health then required did not permit me to go from home without risk, I prayed Madam de Luxembourg to have the goodness to make my apologies. Her answer proves this was done with all possible ease, and M. de Villeroy still continued to show me his usual marks of goodness. His nephew and heir, the young Marquis of Villeroy, had not for me the same benevolence, nor had I for him the respect I had for his uncle. His hare-brained manner rendered him insupportable to me, and my coldness drew upon me his aversion. He insultingly attacked me one evening at table, and I had the worst of it because I am a fool, without presence of mind; and because anger, instead of rendering my wit more poignant, deprives me of the little I have. I had a dog which had been given me when he was quite young, soon after my arrival at the Hermitage, and which I had called *Duke*. This dog, not handsome, but rare of his kind, of which I had made my companion and friend, a title he certainly merited much more than most of the persons by whom it was taken, became in great request at the castle of Montmorency for his good nature and fondness, and the attachment we had to each other; but from a foolish pusillanimity I had changed his name to *Turk,* as if there were not many dogs called *Marquis,* without giving the least offense to any marquis whatsoever. The Marquis de Villeroy, who knew of this change of name, attacked me in such a manner that I was obliged openly at table to relate what I had done. Whatever there might be offensive in the name of duke, it was not in my having given, but in my having taken it away. The worst of it all was, there were many dukes present, amongst others M. de Luxembourg and his son; and the Marquis de Villeroy, who was one day to have, and now has that title, enjoyed in the most cruel manner the embarrassment into which he had thrown me. I was told the next day his aunt had severely reprimanded him, and it may be judged whether or not, supposing her to have been serious, this put me upon better terms with him.

To enable me to support his enmity I had no person, neither at the Hôtel de Luxembourg nor at the Temple, except the Chevalier de Lorenzi, who professed himself my friend; but he was more that of D'Alembert, under whose protection he passed with women for a great geometrician. He was moreover the cicisbeo, or rather the complaisant chevalier of the Countess of Boufflers, a great friend also to D'Alembert, and the Chevalier de Lorenzi was the most passive instrument in her hands. Thus, far from having in that circle any counterbalance to my inaptitude, to keep me in the good graces of Madam de Luxembourg, everybody who approached her seemed to concur in adjuring me in her opinion. Yet, besides *Emile,* with which she charged herself, she gave me at the same time another mark of her benevolence, which made me imagine that, although wearied with my conversation, she would still preserve for me the friendship she had so many times promised me for life.

As soon as I thought I could depend upon this, I began to ease my heart, by confessing to her all my faults, having made it an inviolable maxim to show myself to my friends such as I really was, neither better nor worse. I had declared to her my connection with Thérèsa, and everything that had resulted from it, without concealing the manner in which I had disposed of my children. She had received my confessions favorably, and even too much so, since she spared me the censures I so much merited; and what made the greatest impression upon me was her goodness to Thérèsa, making her presents, sending for her, and begging her to come and see her, receiving her with caresses, and often embracing her in public. This poor girl was in transports of joy and gratitude, of which I certainly partook; the friendship Madam de Luxembourg showed me in her condescensions to Thérèsa affected me much more than if they had been made immediately to myself.

Things remained in this state for a considerable time; but at length Madam de Luxembourg carried her goodness so far as to have a desire to take one of my children from the hospital. She knew I had put a cipher into the swaddling clothes of the eldest; she asked me for the counterpart of the cipher, and I gave it her. In this research she employed La Roche, her valet de chamber and confidential servant, who made vain inquiries, although after only about twelve or fourteen years, had the registers of the foundling hospital been in order, or the search properly made, the original cipher ought to have been found. However this may be, I was less sorry for his want of success than I should have been had I from time to time continued to see the child from his birth until that moment. If by the aid of the indications given, another child had been presented as my own, the doubt of its being so in fact, and the fear of having one thus substituted for it, would have contracted my affections, and I should not have tasted of the charm of the real sentiment of nature. This during infancy stands in need of being supported by habit. The long absence of a child whom the father has seen but for an instant, weakens, and at length annihilates paternal sentiment, and parents will never love a child sent to nurse, like that which is brought up under their eyes. This reflection may extenuate my faults in their effects, but it must aggravate them in their source.

It may not perhaps be useless to remark that by the means of Thérèsa, the same La Roche became acquainted with Madam de Vasseur, whom Grimm still kept at Deüil, near La Chevrette, and not far from Montmorency.

After my departure it was by means of La Roche that I continued to send this woman the money I had constantly sent her at stated times, and I am of opinion he often carried her presents from Madam de Luxembourg; therefore she certainly was not to be pitied, although she constantly complained. With respect to Grimm, as I am not fond of speaking of persons whom I ought to hate, I never mentioned his name to Madam de Luxembourg, except when I could not avoid it; but she frequently made him the subject of conversation, without telling me what she thought of the man, or letting me discover whether or not he was of her acquaintance. Reserve with people I love and who are open with me being contrary to my nature, especially in things relating to themselves, I have since that time frequently thought of that of Madam de Luxembourg; but never, except when other events rendered the recollection natural.

Having waited a long time without hearing speak of *Emile,* after I had given it to Madam de Luxembourg, I at last heard the agreement was made at Paris, with the bookseller Duchesne, and by him with Néaulme, of Amsterdam. Madam de Luxembourg sent me the original, and the duplicate of my agreement with Duchesne, that I might sign them. I discovered the writing to be by the same hand as that of the letters of M. de Malesherbes, which he himself did not write. The certainty that my agreement was made by the consent, and under the eye of that magistrate, made me sign without hesitation. Duchesne gave me for the manuscript six thousand livres, half down, and one or two hundred copies. After having signed the two documents, I sent them both to Madam de Luxembourg, according to her desire; she gave one to Duchesne, and instead of returning the other kept it herself, so that I never saw it afterwards.

My acquaintance with M. and Madam de Luxembourg, though it diverted me a little from my plan of retirement, did not make me entirely renounce it. Even at the time I was most in favor with Madam de Luxembourg, I always felt that nothing but my sincere attachment to the maréchal and herself could render to me supportable the people with whom they were connected, and all the difficulty I had was in conciliating this attachment with a manner of life more agreeable to my inclination, and less contrary to my health, which constraint and late suppers continually deranged, notwithstanding all the care taken to prevent it; for in this, as in everything else, attention was carried as far as possible; thus, for instance, every evening after supper the maréchal, who went early to bed, never failed, notwithstanding everything that could be said to the contrary, to make me withdraw at the same time. It was not until some little time before my catastrophe that, for what reason I know not, he ceased to pay me that attention. Before I perceived the coolness of Madam de Luxembourg, I was desirous, that I might not expose myself to it, to execute my old project; but not having the means to that effect, I was obliged to wait for the conclusion of the agreement for *Emile,* and in the time I finished the *Contrat Social,* and sent it to Rey, fixing the price of the manuscript at a thousand livres, which he paid me.

I ought not perhaps to omit a trifling circumstance relative to this manuscript. I gave it, well sealed up, to Du Voisin, a minister in the pays de Vaud and chaplain at the Hôtel de Hollande, who sometimes came to see me, and took upon himself to send the packet to Rey, with whom he was connected. The manuscript, written in a very small hand, was but very trifling, and did not fill his pocket. Yet, in passing the barrière, the packet fell, I know not by what means, into the hands of the *Commis,* who opened and examined it, and afterwards returned it to him, when he had reclaimed it in the name of the ambassador. This gave him an opportunity of reading it himself, which he ingenuously wrote me he had done, speaking highly of the work, without suffering a word of criticism or censure to escape him; undoubtedly reserving to himself to become the avenger of Christianity as soon as the work should appear. He sealed the packet and sent it to Rey. Such is the substance of his narrative in the letter in which he gave an account of the affair, and is all I ever knew of the matter.

Besides these two books and my dictionary of music, at which I still did something as opportunity offered, I had other works of less importance ready to make their appearance, and which I proposed to publish either separately or in my general collection, should I ever undertake it. The principal of these works, most of which are still in manuscript in the hands of De Peyrou, was an essay on the origin of Languages, which I had read to M. de Malesherbes and the Chevalier de Lorenzi, who spoke favorably of it. I expected all the productions together would produce me a net capital of from eight to ten thousand livres, which I intended to sink in annuities for my life and that of Thérèsa; after which, our design, as I have already mentioned, was to go and live together in the midst of some province, without further troubling the public about me, or myself with any other project than that of peacefully ending my days, and still continuing to do in my neighborhood all the good in my power, and to write at leisure the memoirs which I meditated.

Such was my intention, and the execution of it was facilitated by an act of generosity in Rey, upon which I cannot be silent. This bookseller, of whom so many unfavorable things were told me in Paris, is, notwithstanding, the only one with whom I have always had reason to be satisfied. It is true, we frequently disagreed as to the execution of my works; he was heedless and I was choleric; but in matters of interest which related to them, although I never made with him an agreement in form, I always found in him great exactness and probity. He is also the only person of his profession who frankly confessed to me he gained largely by my means; and he frequently, when he offered me a part of his fortune, told me I was the author of it all. Not finding the means of exercising his gratitude immediately upon myself, he wished at least to give me proofs of it in the person of my *governante,* upon whom he settled an annuity of three hundred livres, expressing in the deed that it was an acknowledgment for the advantages I had procured him. This he did between himself and me, without ostentation, pretension, or noise, and had not I spoken of it to everybody, not a single person would ever have known anything of the matter. I was so pleased with this action that I became attached to Rey, and conceived for him a real friendship. Sometime afterwards he desired I would become godfather to one of his children; I consented, and a part of my regret in the situation to which I am reduced, is my being deprived of the means of rendering in future my attachment to my goddaughter useful to her and her parents. Why am I, who am so sensible of the modest generosity of this bookseller, so little so of the noisy eagerness of many persons of the highest rank, who pompously fill the world with accounts of the services they say they wished to render me, but the good effects of which I never felt? Is it their fault or mine? Are they nothing more than vain; is my insensibility purely ingratitude? Intelligent reader, weigh and determine; for my part I say no more.

This pension was a great resource to Thérèsa and a considerable alleviation to me, although I was far from receiving from it a direct advantage, any more than from the presents that were made her.

She herself has always disposed of everything. When I kept her money I gave her a faithful account of it without ever applying any part of the deposit to our common expenses, not even when she was richer than myself. *"What is mine is ours,"* said I to her; *"and what is thine is thine."* I never departed from this maxim. They who have had the baseness to accuse me of receiving by her hands that which I refused to take with mine, undoubtedly judged of my heart by their own, and knew but little of me. I would willingly eat with her the bread she should have earned, but not that she should have had given her. For a proof of this I appeal to herself, both now and hereafter, when, according to the course of nature, she shall have survived me. Unfortunately, she understands but little of economy in any respect, and is, besides, careless and extravagant, not from vanity nor gluttony, but solely from negligence. No creature is perfect here below, and since her excellent qualities must be accompanied with some defects, I prefer these to vices; although her defects are more prejudicial to us both. The efforts I have made, as formerly I did for mamma, to accumulate something in advance which might some day be to her a never-failing resource, are not to be conceived; but my cares were always ineffectual.

Neither of these women ever called themselves to an account, and, notwithstanding all my efforts, everything I acquired was dissipated as fast as it came. Notwithstanding the great simplicity of Thérèsa's dress, the pension from Rey has never been sufficient to buy her clothes, and I have every year been under the necessity of adding something to it for that purpose. We are neither of us born to be rich, and this I certainly do not reckon amongst our misfortunes.

The *Contrat Social* was soon printed. This was not the case with *Emile,* for the publication of which I waited to go into the retirement I meditated. Duchesne, from time to time, sent me specimens of impression to choose from; when I had made my choice, instead of beginning he sent me others. When, at length, we were fully determined on the size and letter, and several sheets were already printed off, on some trifling alteration I made in a proof, he began the whole again, and at the end of six months we were in less forwardness than on the first day. During all these experiments I clearly perceived the work was printing in France as well as in Holland, and that two editions of it were preparing at the same time. What could I do? The manuscript was no longer mine. Far from having anything to do with the edition in France I was always against it; but since, at length, this was preparing in spite of all opposition, and was to serve as a model to the other, it was necessary I should cast my eyes over it and examine the proofs, that my work might not be mutilated. It was, besides, printed so much by the consent of the magistrate, that it was he who, in some measure, directed the undertaking; he likewise wrote to me frequently, and once came to see me and converse on the subject upon an occasion of which I am going to speak.

Whilst Duchesne crept like a snail, Néaulme, whom he withheld, scarcely moved at all. The sheets were not regularly sent him as they were printed. He thought there was some trick in the maneuver of Duchesne, that is, of Guy who acted for him; and perceiving the terms of the agreement to be departed from, he wrote me letter after letter full of complaints, and it was less possible for me to remove the subject of them than that of those I myself had to make. His

friend, Guerin, who at that time came frequently to
see my house, never ceased speaking to me about the
work, but always with the greatest reserve. He knew
and he did not know that it was printing in France,
and that the magistrate had a hand in it. In expressing his concern for my embarrassment, he seemed to
accuse me of imprudence without ever saying in what
this consisted; he incessantly equivocated, and seemed
to speak for no other purpose than to hear what I had
to say. I thought myself so secure that I laughed at his
mystery and circumspection as at a habit he had contracted with ministers and magistrates whose offices he
much frequented. Certain of having conformed to
every rule with the work, and strongly persuaded that
I had not only the consent and protection of the magistrate, but that the book merited and had obtained the
favor of the minister, I congratulated myself upon my
courage in doing good, and laughed at my pusillanimous friends who seemed uneasy on my account.
Duclos was one of these, and I confess my confidence
in his understanding and uprightness might have
alarmed me, had I had less in the utility of the work
and in the probity of those by whom it was patronized.
He came from the house of M. Baille to see me whilst
Emile was in the press; he spoke to me concerning it;
I read to him the Profession of Faith of the Savoyard
Vicar, to which he listened attentively and, as it
seemed to me, with pleasure. When I had finished he
said: "What! citizen, this is a part of a work now
printing at Paris?" "Yes," answered I, "and it ought

to be printed at the Louvre by order of the king." "I confess it," replied he; "but pray do not mention to anybody your having read to me this fragment."

This striking manner of expressing himself surprised without alarming me. I knew Duclos was intimate with M. de Malesherbes, and I could not conceive how it was possible he should think so differently from him upon the same subject.

I had lived at Montmorency for the last four years without ever having had there one day of good health. Although the air is excellent, the water is bad, and this may possibly be one of the causes which contributed to increase my habitual complaints. Towards the end of the autumn of 1761, I fell quite ill, and passed the whole winter in suffering almost without intermission. The physical ill, augmented by a thousand inquietudes, rendered these terrible. For some time past my mind had been disturbed by melancholy forebodings, without my knowing to what these directly tended. I received anonymous letters of an extraordinary nature, and others, that were signed, much of the same import. I received one from a counselor of the parliament of Paris, who, dissatisfied with the present constitution of things, and foreseeing nothing but disagreeable events, consulted me upon the choice of an asylum at Geneva or in Switzerland, to retire to with his family. Another was brought me from M. de ——, *president a mortier* of the parliament of ——, who proposed to me to draw up for this parliament, which was then at variance with the court, memoirs and remonstrances, and offering to furnish me with all the documents and materials necessary to that purpose.

When I suffer I am subject to ill humor. This was the case when I received these letters, and my answers to them, in which I flatly refused everything that was asked of me, bore strong marks of the effect they had had upon my mind. I do not however reproach myself with this refusal, as the letters might be so many snares laid by my enemies,* and what was required of me was contrary to the principles from which I was less willing than ever to swerve. But having it in my power to refuse with politeness I did it with rudeness, and in this consists my error.

The two letters of which I have just spoken will be found amongst my papers. The letter from the chancellor did not absolutely surprise me, because I agreed with him in opinion, and with many others, that the declining constitution of France threatened an approaching destruction. The disasters of an unsuccessful war, all of which proceeded from a fault in the government; the incredible confusion in the finances; the perpetual drawings upon the treasury by the administration, which was then divided between two or three ministers, amongst whom reigned nothing but discord, and who, to counteract the operations of each other, let the kingdom go to ruin; the discontent of the people, and of every other rank of subjects; the

---

*I knew, for instance, the President de —— to be connected with the Encyclopedists and the Holbachiens.

obstinacy of a woman who, constantly sacrificing her judgment, if she indeed possessed any, to her inclinations, kept from public employment persons capable of discharging the duties of them, to place in them such as pleased her best; everything concurred in justifying the foresight of the counselor, that of the public, and my own. This made me several times consider whether or not I myself should seek an asylum out of the kingdom before it was torn by the dissensions by which it seemed to be threatened; but relieved from my fears by my insignificance, and the peacefulness of my disposition, I thought, that in the state of solitude in which I was determined to live, no public commotion could reach me. I was sorry only that, in this state of things, M. de Luxembourg should accept commissions which tended to injure him in the opinion of the persons of the place of which he was governor. I could have wished he had prepared himself a retreat there, in case the great machine had fallen in pieces, which seemed much to be apprehended; and it still appears to me beyond a doubt, that if the reins of government had not fallen into a single hand, the French monarchy would now be at the last gasp.

Whilst my situation became worse the printing of *Emile* went on more slowly, and was at length suspended without my being able to learn the reason why; Guy did not deign to answer my letter of inquiry, and I could obtain no information from any person of what was going forward; M. de Malesherbes being then in the country. A misfortune never makes me uneasy provided I know in what it consists; but it is my nature to be afraid of darkness, I tremble at the appearance of it; mystery always gives me inquietude, it is too opposite to my natural disposition, in which there is an openness bordering on imprudence. The sight of the most hideous monster would, I am of opinion, alarm me but little; but if by night I were to see a figure in a white sheet I should be afraid of it. My imagination, wrought upon by this long silence, was now employed in creating phantoms. I tormented myself the more in endeavoring to discover the impediment to the printing of my last and best production, as I had the publication of it much at heart; and as I always carried everything to an extreme, I imagined that I perceived in the suspension the suppression of the work. Yet, being unable to discover either the cause or manner of it, I remained in the most cruel state of suspense. I wrote letter after letter to Guy, to M. de Malesherbes and to Madam de Luxembourg, and not receiving answers, at least when I expected them, my head became so affected that I was not far from a delirium. I unfortunately heard that Father Griffet, a Jesuit, had spoken of *Emile* and repeated from it some passages. My imagination instantly unveiled to me the mystery of iniquity; I saw the whole progress of it as clearly as if it had been revealed to me. I figured to myself that the Jesuits, furious on account of the contemptuous manner in which I had spoken of colleges, were in possession of my work; that it was they who had delayed the pub-

[888]

lication; that, informed by their friend Guerin of my situation, and foreseeing my approaching dissolution, of which I myself had no manner of doubt, they wished to delay the appearance of the work until after that event, with an intention to curtail and mutilate it, and in favor of their own views, to attribute to me sentiment not my own. The number of facts and circumstances which occurred to my mind, in confirmation of this silly proposition, and gave it an appearance of truth supported by evidence and demonstration, is astonishing. I knew Guerin to be entirely in the interest of the Jesuits. I attributed to them all the friendly advances he had made me; I was persuaded he had, by their entreaties, pressed me to engage with Néaulme, who had given them the first sheets of my work; that they had afterwards found means to stop the printing of it by Duchesne, and perhaps to get possession of the manuscript to make such alterations in it as they should think proper, that after my death they might publish it disguised in their own manner. I had always perceived, notwithstanding the wheedling of Father Berthier, that the Jesuits did not like me, not only as an Encyclopedist, but because all my principles were more in opposition to their maxims and influence than the incredulity of my colleagues, since atheistical and devout fanaticism, approaching each other by their common enmity to toleration, may become united; a proof of which is seen in China, and in the cabal against myself; whereas religion, both reasonable and moral, taking away all power over the conscience, deprives those who assume that power of every resource. I knew the chancelor was a great friend to the Jesuits, and I had my fears lest the son, intimidated by the father, should find himself under the necessity of abandoning the work he had protected. I besides imagined that I perceived this to be the case in the chicanery employed against me relative to the first two volumes, in which alterations were required for reasons of which I could not feel the force; whilst the other two volumes were known to contain things of such a nature as, had the censor objected to them in the manner he did to the passages he thought exceptionable in the others, would have required their being entirely written over again. I also understood, and M. de Malesherbes himself told me of it, that the Abbé de Grave, whom he had charged with the inspection of this edition, was another partisan of the Jesuits. I saw nothing but Jesuits, without considering that, upon the point of being suppressed, and wholly taken up in making their defense, they had something which interested them much more than the cavilings relative to a work in which they were not in question. I am wrong, however, in saying this did not occur to me; for I really thought of it, and M. de Malesherbes took care to make the observation to me the moment he heard of my extravagant suspicions. But by another of those absurdities of a man who, from the bosom of obscurity, will absolutely judge of the secret of great affairs, with which he is totally unacquainted, I never could bring myself to believe the Jesuits were in danger, and I considered the rumor of their suppression as an artful maneuver of their own to deceive their adversaries. Their past successes, which had been uninterrupted, gave me so terrible an idea of their power, that I already was grieved at the overthrow of the parliament. I knew M. de Choiseul had prosecuted his studies under the Jesuits, that Madam de Pompadour was not upon bad terms with them, and that their league with favorites and ministers had constantly appeared advantageous to their order against their common enemies. The court seemed to remain neuter, and persuaded as I was that should the society receive a severe check it would not come from the parliament, I saw in the inaction of government the ground of their confidence and the omen of their triumph.

In fine, perceiving in the rumors of the day nothing more than art and dissimulation on their part, and thinking they, in their state of security, had time to watch over all their interests, I had had not the least doubt of their shortly crushing Jansenism, the parliament and the Encyclopedists, with every other association which should not submit to their yoke; and that if they ever suffered my work to appear, this would not happen until it should be so transformed as to favor their pretensions, and thus make use of my name the better to deceive my readers.

I felt my health and strength decline; and such was the horror with which my mind was filled, at the idea of dishonor to my memory in the work most worthy of myself, that I am surprised so many extravagant ideas did not occasion a speedy end to my existence. I never was so much afraid of death as at this time, and had I died with the apprehensions I then had upon my mind, I should have died in despair. At present, although I perceived no obstacle to the execution of the blackest and most dreadful conspiracy ever formed against the memory of a man, I shall die much more in peace, certain of leaving in my writings a testimony in my favor, and one which, sooner or later, will triumph over the calumnies of mankind.

M. de Malesherbes, who discovered the agitation of my mind, and to whom I acknowledged it, used such endeavors to restore me to tranquillity as proved his excessive goodness of heart. Madam de Luxembourg aided him in this good work, and several times went to Duchesne to know in what state the edition was. At length the impression was again begun, and the progress of it became more rapid than ever, without my knowing for what reason it had been suspended. M. de Malesherbes took the trouble to come to Montmorency to calm my mind; in this he succeeded, and the full confidence I had in his uprightness having overcome the derangement of my poor head, gave efficacy to the endeavors he made to restore it. After what he had seen of my anguish and delirium, it was natural he should think I was to be pitied; and he really commiserated my situation. The expressions, incessantly repeated, of the philosophical cabal by which he was surrounded, occurred to his memory. When I went to live at the Hermitage, they, as I have already remarked, said I should not remain there long. When they saw I persevered, they charged me with obstinacy and pride, proceeding from a want of courage to retract, and insisted that my life was there a burden to me; in short, that I was very wretched. M. de Malesherbes believed this really to be the case, and wrote to me upon the subject. This error in a man for whom I had so much esteem gave me some pain, and I wrote to him four letters successively, in which I stated the real motives of my conduct, and made him fully acquainted with my taste, inclination and character, and with the most interior sentiments of my heart. These letters, written hastily, almost without taking pen from paper, and which I neither copied, corrected, nor even read, are perhaps, the only things I ever wrote with facility, which, in the midst of my sufferings, was, I think, astonishing. I sighed, as I felt myself declining, at the thought of leaving in the midst of honest men an opinion of me so far from truth; and by the sketch hastily given in my four letters, I endeavored, in some measure, to substitute them to the memoirs I had proposed to write. They are expressive of my grief to M. de Malesherbes, who showed them in Paris, and are, besides, a kind of summary of what I here give in detail, and, on this account, merit preservation. The copy I begged of them some years afterwards will be found amongst my papers.

The only thing which continued to give me pain, in the idea of my approaching dissolution, was my not having a man of letters for a friend, to whom I could confide my papers, that after my death he might take a proper choice of such as were worthy of publication.

After my journey to Geneva, I conceived a friendship for Moultou; this young man pleased me, and I could have wished him to receive my last breath. I expressed to him this desire, and am of opinion he would readily have complied with it, had not his affairs prevented him from so doing. Deprived of this consolation I still wished to give him a mark of my confidence by sending him the Profession of Faith of the Savoyard Vicar before it was published. He was pleased with the work, but did not in his answer seem so fully to expect from it the effect of which I had but little doubt. He wished to receive from me some fragment which I had not given to anybody else. I sent him the funeral oration of the late Duke of Orleans; this I had written for the Abbé Darty, who had not pronounced it, because, contrary to his expectation, another person was appointed to perform that ceremony.

The printing of *Emile,* after having been again taken in hand, was continued and completed without much difficulty; and I remarked this singularity, that after the curtailings so much insisted upon in the first two volumes, the last two were passed over without an objection, and their contents did not delay the publication for a moment. I had, however, some uneasiness which I must not pass over in silence. After having been afraid of the Jesuits, I began to fear the Jansenists and philosophers. An enemy to party, faction and cabal, I never heard the least good of persons concerned in them. The gossips had quitted their old abode, and taken up their residence by the side of me, so that in their chamber, everything said in mine, and upon the terrace, was distinctly heard; and from their garden it would have been easy to scale the low wall by which it was separated from my alcove. This was become my study; my table was covered with proof-sheets of *Emile* and the *Contrat Social,* and stitching these sheets as they were sent to me, I had all my volumes a long time before they were published. My negligence and the confidence I had in M. Mathas, in whose garden I was shut up, frequently made me forget to lock the door at night, and in the morning I several times found it wide open: this, however, would not have given me the least inquietude had I not thought my papers seemed to have been deranged. After having several times made the same remark, I became more careful, and locked the door. The lock was a bad one, and the key turned in it no more than half round. As I became more attentive, I found my papers in a much greater confusion than they were when I left everything open. At length I missed one of my volumes without knowing what was become of it until the morning of the third day, when I again found it upon the table. I never suspected either M. Mathas or his nephew M. du Moulin, knowing myself to be beloved by both, and my confidence in them was unbounded. That I had in the gossips began to diminish. Although they were Jansenists, I knew them to have some connection with D'Alembert, and moreover they all three lodged in the same house. This gave me some uneasiness, and put me more upon my guard. I removed my papers from the alcove to my chamber, and dropped my acquaintance with these people, having learned they had shown in several houses the first volume of Emilius, which I had been imprudent enough to lend them. Although they continued until my departure to be my neighbors, I never, after my first suspicions, had the least communication with them. The *Contrat Social* appeared a month or two before *Emile*. Rey, whom I had desired never secretly to introduced into France any of my books, applied to the magistrate for leave to send this book by Rouen, to which place he sent his package by sea. He received no answer, and his bales, after remaining at Rouen several months, were returned to him, but not until an attempt had been made to confiscate them; this, probably, would have been done had not he made a great clamor. Several persons, whose curiosity the work had excited, sent to Amsterdam for copies, which were circulated without being much noticed. Maulion, who had heard of this, and had, I believe, seen the work, spoke to me on the subject with an air of mystery which surprised me, and would likewise have made me uneasy if, certain of having conformed to every rule, I had not by virtue of my grand maxim, kept my mind calm. I moreover had no doubt but M. de

Choiseul, already well disposed towards me, and sensible of the eulogium of his administration, which my esteem for him had induced me to make in the work, would support me against the malevolence of Madam de Pompadour.

I certainly had then as much reason as ever to hope for the goodness of M. de Luxembourg, and even for his assistance in case of need; for he never at any time had given me more frequent or more pointed marks of his friendship. At the journey of Easter, my melancholy state no longer permitting me to go to the castle, he never suffered a day to pass without coming to see me, and at length, perceiving my sufferings to be incessant, he prevailed upon me to determine to see Friar Côme. He immediately sent for him, came with him, and had the courage, uncommon in a man of his rank, to remain with me during the operation which was cruel and tedious. Upon the first examination, Côme thought he found a great stone, and told me so; at the second, he could not find it again. After having made a third attempt with so much care and circumspection that I thought the time long, he declared there was no stone, but that the prostate gland was schirrous and considerably thickened. He besides added, that I had a great deal to suffer, and should live a long time. Should the second prediction be as fully accomplished as the first, my sufferings are far from being at an end.

It was thus I learned, after having been so many years treated for disorders which I never had, that my incurable disease, without being mortal, would last as long as myself. My imagination, repressed by this information, no longer presented to me in perspective a cruel death in the agonies of the stone.

Delivered from imaginary evils, more cruel to me than those which were real, I more patiently suffered the latter. It is certain I have since suffered less from my disorder than I had done before, and every time I recollect that I owe this alleviation to M. de Luxembourg, his memory becomes more dear to me.

Restored, as I may say, to life, and more than ever occupied with the plan according to which I was determined to pass the rest of my days, all the obstacle to the immediate execution of my design was the publication of *Emile*. I thought of Touraine where I had already been and which pleased me much, as well on account of the mildness of the climate, as on that of the character of the inhabitants.

> *La terra molle lieta e dilettosa*
> *Simile a se gli abitator produce.*

I had already spoken of my project to M. de Luxembourg, who endeavored to dissuade me from it; I mentioned it to him a second time as a thing resolved upon. He then offered me the castle of Merlou, fifteen leagues from Paris, as an asylum which might be agreeable to me, and where he and Madam de Luxembourg would have a real pleasure in seeing me settled. The proposition made a pleasing impression on my mind. But the first thing necessary was to see the place, and we agreed upon a day when the maréchal was to send his valet de chamber with a carriage to take me to it. On the day appointed, I was much indisposed; the journey was postponed, and different circumstances prevented me from ever making it. I have since learned the estate of Merlou did not belong to the maréchal but to his lady, on which account I was the less sorry I had not gone to live there.

Emile was at length given to the public, without my having heard further of retrenchments or difficulties. Previous to the publication, the maréchal asked me for all the letters M. de Malesherbes had written to me on the subject of the work. My great confidence in both, and the perfect security in which I felt myself, prevented me from reflecting upon this extraordinary and even alarming request. I returned all the letters, excepting one or two which, from inattention, were left between the leaves of a book. A little time before this, M. de Malesherbes told me he should withdraw the letters I had written to Duchesne during my alarm relative to the Jesuits, and, it must be confessed, these letters did no great honor to my reason. But in my answer I assured him I would not in anything pass for being better than I was, and that he might leave the letters where they were. I know not what he resolved upon.

The publication of this work was not succeeded by the applause which had followed that of all my other writings. No work was ever more highly spoken of in private, nor had any literary production ever had less public approbation. What was said and written to me upon the subject by persons most capable of judging, confirmed me in my opinion that it was the best, as well as the most important of all the works I had produced. But everything favorable was said with an air of the most extraordinary mystery, as if there had been a necessity of keeping it a secret. Madam de Boufflers, who wrote to me that the author of the work merited a statue, and the homage of mankind, at the end of her letter desired it might be returned to her. D'Alembert, who in his note said the work gave me a decided superiority, and ought to place me at the head of men of letters, did not sign what he wrote, although he had signed every note I had before received from him. Duclos, a sure friend, a man of veracity, but circumspect, although he had a good opinion of the work, avoided mentioning it in his letters to me. La Condomine fell upon the Profession of Faith, and wandered from the subject. Clairaut confined himself to the same part; but he was not afraid of expressing to me the emotion which the reading of it had caused in him, and in the most direct terms wrote to me that it had warmed his old imagination: of all those to whom I had sent my book, he was the only person who spoke freely what he thought of it.

Mathas, to whom also I had given a copy before the publication, lent it to M. de Blaire, counselor in the parliament of Strasbourg. M. de Blaire had a country-house at St. Gratien, and Mathas, his old acquaintance, sometimes went to see him there. He made him read

Emile before it was published. When he returned it to him, M. de Blaire expressed himself in the following terms, which were repeated to me the same day: "M. Mathas, this is a very fine work, but it will in a short time be spoken of more than, for the author, might be wished." I laughed at the prediction, and saw in it nothing more than the importance of a man of the robe, who treats everything with an air of mystery. All the alarming observations repeated to me made no impression upon my mind, and, far from foreseeing the catastrophe so near at hand, certain of the utility and excellence of my work, and that I had in every respect conformed to established rules; convinced, as I thought I was that I should be supported by all the credit of M. de Luxembourg and the favor of the ministry, I was satisfied with myself for the resolution I had taken to retire in the midst of my triumphs, and at my return to crush those by whom I was envied.

One thing in the publication of the work alarmed me, less on account of my safety than for the unburdening of my mind. At the Hermitage and at Montmorency I had seen with indignation the vexations which the jealous care of the pleasures of princes causes to be exercised upon wretched peasants, forced to suffer the havoc made by game in their fields, without daring to take any other measure to prevent this devastation than that of making a noise, passing the night amongst the beans and peas, with drums, kettles and bells, to keep off the wild boars. As I had been a witness to the barbarous cruelty with which the Comte de Charolois treated these poor people, I had towards the end of *Emile* exclaimed against it. This was another infraction of my maxims, which has not remained unpunished. I was informed that the people of the Prince of Conti were but little less severe upon his estates; I trembled lest that prince, for whom I was penetrated with respect and gratitude, should take to his own account what shocked humanity had made me say on that of others, and feel himself offended. Yet, as my conscience fully acquitted me upon this article, I made myself easy, and by so doing acted wisely: at least, I have not heard that this great prince took notice of the passage, which, besides, was written long before I had the honor of being known to him.

A few days either before or after the publication of my work, for I do not exactly recollect the time, there appeared another work upon the same subject, taken verbatim from my first volume, except a few stupid things which were joined to the extract. The book bore the name of a Genevese, one Balexsert, and, according to the title-page, had gained the premium in the Academy of Harlem. I easily imagined the academy and the premium to be newly founded, the better to conceal the plagiarism from the eyes of the public; but I further perceived there was some prior intrigue which I could not unravel; either by the lending of my manuscript, without which the theft could not have been committed, or for the purpose of forging the story of the pretended premium, to which it was necessary to give some foundation. It was not until several years afterwards, that by a word which escaped D'Ivernois, I penetrated the mystery, and discovered those by whom Balexsert had been brought forward.

The low murmurings which precede a storm began to be heard, and men of penetration clearly saw there was something gathering, relative to me and my book, which would shortly break over my head. For my part my stupidity was such, that, far from foreseeing my misfortune, I did not suspect even the cause of it after I had felt its effect. It was artfully given out that while the Jesuits were treated with severity, no indulgence could be shown to books nor the authors of them in which religion was attacked. I was reproached with having put my name to Emilius, as if I had not put it to all my other works of which nothing was said. Government seemed to fear it should be obliged to take some steps which circumstances rendered necessary on account of my imprudence. Rumors to this effect reached my ears, but gave me not much uneasiness: it never even came into my head, that there could be the least thing in the whole affair which related to me personally, so perfectly irreproachable and well supported did I think myself; having besides conformed to every ministerial regulation, I did not apprehend Madam de Luxembourg would leave me in difficulties for an error, which, if it existed, proceeded entirely from herself. But knowing the manner of proceeding in like cases, and that it was customary to punish booksellers while authors were favored, I had some uneasiness on the account of poor Duchesne, whom I saw exposed to danger, should M. de Malesherbes abandon him.

My tranquillity still continued. Rumors increased and soon changed their nature. The public and especially the parliament, seemed irritated by my composure. In a few days the fermentation became terrible, and the object of the menaces being changed, these were immediately addressed to me. The parliamentarians were heard to declare that burning books was of no effect, the authors also should be burned with them; not a word was said of the booksellers. The first time these expressions, more worthy of an inquisitor of Goa than a senator, were related to me, I had no doubt of their coming from the *Holbachiques* with an intention to alarm me and drive me from France. I laughed at their puerile maneuver, and said they would, had they known the real state of things, have thought of some other means of inspiring me with fear: but the rumor at length became such that I perceived the matter was serious. M. and Madam de Luxembourg had this year come to Montmorency in the month of June, which, for their second journey, was more early than common. I heard but little there of my new books, notwithstanding the noise they made at Paris; neither the maréchal nor his lady said a single word to me on the subject. However, one morning, when M. de Luxembourg and I were together, he asked me if, in the *Contrat Social,* I had spoken ill of M. de Choiseul. "I?" said I, retreating a few steps with surprise; "no, I swear to you I have not; but, on the contrary, I have made on him, and with a pen not given to praise, the finest eulogium a minister ever received." I then showed him the passage. "And in *Emile?*" replied he. "Not a word," said I; "there is not in it a single word which relates to him." "Ah!" said he, with more vivacity than was common to him, "you should have taken the same care in the other book, or have expressed yourself more clearly!" "I thought," replied I, "what I wrote could not be misconstrued; my esteem for him was such as to make me extremely cautious not to be equivocal."

He was again going to speak; I perceived him ready to open his mind: he stopped short and held his tongue. Wretched policy of a courtier, which, in the best of hearts, subjugates friendship itself!

This conversation, although short, explained to me my situation, at least in certain respects, and gave me to understand that it was against myself the anger of administration was raised. The unheard-of fatality, which turned to my prejudice all the good I did and wrote, afflicted my heart. Yet, feeling myself shielded in this affair by Madam de Luxembourg and M. de Malesherbes, I did not perceive in what my persecutors could deprive me of their protection. However, I, from that moment, was convinced equity and justice were no longer in question, and that no pains would be spared in examining whether or not I was culpable. The storm became still more menacing. Néaulme himself expressed to me, in the excess of his babbling, how much he repented having had anything to do in the business, and his certainty of the fate with which the book and the author were threatened. One thing, however, alleviated my fears: Madam de Luxembourg was so calm, satisfied and cheerful, that I concluded she must necessarily be certain of the sufficiency of her credit, especially if she did not seem to have the least apprehension on my account; moreover, she said not to me a word either of consolation or apology, and saw the turn the affair took with as much unconcern as if she had nothing to do with it or anything else that related to me. What surprised me most was her silence. I thought she should have said something on the subject. Madam de Boufflers seemed rather uneasy. She appeared agitated, strained herself a good deal, assured me the Prince of Conti was taking great pains to ward off the blow about to be directed against my person, and which she attributed to the nature of present circumstances, in which it was of importance to the parliament not to leave the Jesuits an opening whereby they might bring an accusation against it as being indifferent with respect to religion. She did not, however, seem to depend much either upon the success of her own efforts or even those of the prince. Her conversations, more alarming than consolatory, all tended to persuade me to leave the kingdom and go to England, where she offered me an introduction to many of her friends, amongst others one to the celebrated Hume, with whom she had long been upon a footing of intimate friendship. Seeing me still un-shaken, she had recourse to other arguments more capable of disturbing my tranquillity. She intimated that, in case I was arrested and interrogated, I should be under the necessity of naming Madam de Luxem-bourg, and that her friendship for me required, on my part, such precautions as were necessary to prevent her being exposed. My answer was, that should what she seemed to apprehend come to pass, she need not be alarmed; that I should do nothing by which the lady she mentioned might become a sufferer. She said such a resolution was more easily taken than adhered to, and in this she was right, especially with respect to me, determined as I always have been neither to prejudice myself nor lie before judges, whatever danger there might be in speaking the truth.

Perceiving this observation had made some impres-sion upon my mind, without however inducing me to resolve upon evasion, she spoke of the Bastile for a few weeks, as a means of placing me beyond the reach of the jurisdiction of the parliament, which has nothing to do with prisoners of state. I had no objection to this singular favor, provided it were not solicited in my name. As she never spoke of it a second time, I after-wards thought her proposition was made to sound me, and that the party did not think proper to have re-course to an expedient which would have put an end to everything.

A few days afterwards the maréchal received from the Curé of Deuil, the friend of Grimm and Madam d'Epinay, a letter informing him, as from good authority, that the parliament was to proceed against me with the greatest severity, and that, on a day which he mentioned, an order was to be given to arrest me. I imagined this was fabricated by the *Holbachiques;* I knew the parliament to be very attentive to forms, and that on this occasion, beginning by arresting me before it was juridically known I avowed myself the author of the book was violating them all. I observed to Madam de Boufflers that none but persons accused of crimes which tend to endanger the public safety were, on a simple information, ordered to be arrested lest they should escape punishment. But when government wish to punish a crime like mine, which merits honor and recompense, the proceedings are directed against the book, and the author is as much as possible left out of the question.

Upon this she made some subtle distinction, which I have forgotten, to prove that ordering me to be arrested instead of summoning me to be heard, was a matter of favor. The next day I received a letter from Guy, who informed me that having in the morning been with the attorney-general, he had seen in his office a rough draft of a requisition against *Emile* and the author. Guy, it is to be remembered, was the partner of Duchesne, who had printed the work, and without apprehensions on his own account, charitably gave this information to the author. The credit I gave to him may be judged of.

It was, no doubt, a very probable story, that a bookseller, admitted to an audience by the attorney-general, should read at ease scattered rough drafts in the office of that magistrate! Madam de Boufflers and others confirmed what he had said. By the absurdities which were incessantly rung in my ears, I was almost tempted to believe that everybody I heard speak had lost their senses.

Clearly perceiving that there was some mystery, which no one thought proper to explain to me, I patiently awaited the event, depending upon my integrity and innocence, and thinking myself happy, let the persecution which awaited me be what it would, to be called to the honor of suffering in the cause of truth. Far from being afraid and concealing myself, I went every day to the castle, and in the afternoon took my usual walk. On the eighth of June, the evening before the order was concluded on, I walked in company with two professors of the oratory, Father Alamanni and Father Mandard. We carried to Champeaux a little collation, which we ate with a keen appetite. We had forgotten to bring glasses, and supplied the want of them by stalks of rye, through which we sucked up the wine from the bottle, piquing ourselves upon the choice of large tubes to vie with each other in pumping up what we drank. I never was more cheerful in my life.

I have related in what manner I lost my sleep during my youth. I had since that time contracted a habit of reading every night in my bed, until I found my eyes begin to grow heavy. I then extinguished my wax taper, and endeavored to slumber for a few moments, which were in general very short. The book I commonly read at night was the Bible, which, in this manner, I read five or six times from the beginning to the end. This evening, finding myself less disposed to sleep than ordinary, I continued my reading beyond the usual hour, and read the whole book which finishes at the Levite of Ephraim, the Book of Judges, if I mistake not, for since that time I have never once seen it. This history affected me exceedingly, and, in a kind of dream, my imagination still ran on it, when suddenly I was roused from my stupor by a noise and light. Thérèsa, carrying a candle, lighted M. la Roche, who perceiving me hastily raise myself up, said: "Do not be alarmed; I come from Madam de Luxembourg, who, in her letter, incloses you another from the Prince of Conti." In fact, in the letter of Madam de Luxembourg I found another, which an express from the prince had brought her, stating that, notwithstanding all his efforts, it was determined to proceed against me with the utmost rigor. "The fermentation," said he, "is extreme; nothing can ward off the blow; the court requires it, and the parliament will absolutely proceed; at seven o'clock in the morning an order will be made to arrest him, and persons will immediately be sent to execute it. I have obtained a promise that he shall not be pursued if he makes his escape; but if he persists in exposing himself to be taken this will immediately happen." La Roche conjured me in behalf of Madam de Luxembourg to rise and go and speak to her. It was two o'clock, and she had just retired to bed. "She expects you," added he, "and will not go to sleep without speaking to you." I dressed myself in haste and ran to her.

She appeared to be agitated; this was for the first time. Her distress affected me. In this moment of surprise and in the night, I myself was not free from emotion; but on seeing her I forgot my own situation, and thought of nothing but the melancholy part she would have to act should I suffer myself to be arrested; for feeling I had sufficient courage strictly to adhere to truth, although I might be certain of its being prejudicial or even destructive to me, I was convinced I had not presence of mind, address, nor perhaps firmness enough, not to expose her should I be closely pressed. This determined me to sacrifice my reputation to her tranquillity, and to do for her that which nothing could have prevailed upon me to do for myself. The moment I had come to this resolution, I declared it, wishing not to diminish the magnitude of the sacrifice by giving her the least trouble to obtain it. I am sure she could not mistake my motive, although she said not a word, which proved to me she was sensible of it. I was so much shocked at her indifference that I, for a moment, thought of retracting; but the maréchal came in, and Madam de Boufflers arrived from Paris a few moments afterwards. They did what Madam de Luxembourg ought to have done. I suffered myself to be flattered; I was ashamed to retract; and the only thing that remained to be determined upon was the place of my retreat and the time of my departure. M. de Luxembourg proposed to me to remain incognito a few days at the castle, that we might deliberate at leisure, and take such measures as should seem most proper; to this I would not consent, no more than to go secretly to the temple. I was determined to set off the same day rather than remain concealed in any place whatever.

Knowing I had secret and powerful enemies in the kingdom, I thought, notwithstanding my attachment to France, I ought to quit it, the better to insure my future tranquillity. My first intention was to retire to Geneva, but a moment of reflection was sufficient to dissuade me from committing that act of folly; I knew the ministry of France, more powerful at Geneva than at Paris, would not leave me more at peace in one of these cities than in the other, were a resolution taken to torment me. I was also convinced the Discourse upon Inequality had excited against me in the council a hatred the more dangerous as the council dared not make it manifest. I had also learned, that when the *Nouvelle Héloïse* appeared, the same council had immediately forbidden the sale of that work, upon the solicitation of Doctor Tronchin; but, perceiving the example not to be imitated, even in Paris, the members were ashamed of what they had done, and withdrew the prohibition.

I had no doubt that, finding in the present case a more favorable opportunity, they would be very careful to take advantage of it. Notwithstanding exterior appearances, I knew there reigned against me in the heart of every Genevese a secret jealousy, which, in the first favorable moment, would publicly show itself. Nevertheless, the love of my country called me to it, and could I have flattered myself I should there have lived in peace, I should not have hesitated; but neither honor nor reason permitting me to take refuge as a fugitive in a place of which I was a citizen, I resolved to approach it only, and to wait in Switzerland until something relative to me should be determined upon in Geneva. This state of uncertainty did not, as it will soon appear, continue long.

Madam de Boufflers highly disapproved this resolution, and renewed her efforts to induce me to go to England, but all she could say was of no effect; I have never loved England nor the English, and the eloquence of Madam de Boufflers, far from conquering my repugnancy, seemed to increase it without my knowing why. Determined to set off the same day, I was from the morning inaccessible to everybody, and La Roche, whom I sent to fetch my papers, would not tell Thérèsa whether or not I was gone. Since I had determined to write my own memoirs, I had collected a great number of letters and other papers, so that he was obliged to return several times. A part of these papers, already selected, were laid aside, and I employed the morning in sorting the rest, that I might take with me such only as were necessary and destroy what remained. M. de Luxembourg was kind enough to assist me in this business, which we could not finish before it was necessary I should set off, and I had not time to burn a single paper. The maréchal offered to take upon himself to sort what I should leave behind me, and throw into the fire every sheet that he found useless, without trusting to any person whomsoever, and to send me those of which he should make choice. I accepted his offer, very glad to be delivered from that care, that I might pass the few hours I had to remain with persons so dear to me, from whom I was going to separate forever. He took the key of the chamber in which I had left these papers; and, at my earnest solicitation, sent for my poor "aunt," who, not knowing what was become of me, or what was to become of herself, and in momentary expectation of the arrival of the officers of justice, without knowing how to act or what to answer them, was miserable to an extreme. La Roche accompanied her to the castle in silence; she thought I was already far from Montmorency; on perceiving me, she made the place resound with her cries, and threw herself into my arms. Oh, friendship, affinity of sentiment, habit and intimacy.

In this pleasing yet cruel moment, the remembrance of so many days of happiness, tenderness, and peace passed together, augmented the grief of a first separation after an union of seventeen years, during which we had scarcely lost sight of each other for a single day.

The maréchal, who saw this embrace, could not suppress his tears. He withdrew. Thérèsa determined never more to leave me out of her sight. I made her feel the inconvenience of accompanying me at that moment, and the necessity of her remaining to take care of my effects and collect my money. When an order is made to arrest a man, it is customary to seize his papers and put a seal upon his effects, or to make an inventory of them and appoint a guardian to whose care they are intrusted. It was necessary Thérèsa should remain to observe what passed, and get everything settled in the most advantageous manner possible. I promised her she should shortly come to me; the maréchal confirmed my promise; but I did not choose to tell her to what place I was going, that, in case of being interrogated by the persons who came to take me into custody, she might with truth plead ignorance upon that head. In embracing her the moment before we separated I felt within me a most extraordinary emotion, and I said to her with an agitation which, alas! was but too prophetic: "My dear girl, you must arm yourself with courage. You have partaken of my prosperity; it now remains to you, since you have chosen it, to partake of my misery. Expect nothing in future but insult and calamity in following me. The destiny begun for me by this melancholy day will pursue me until my latest hour."

I had now nothing to think of but my departure. The officers were to arrive at ten o'clock. It was four in the afternoon when I set off, and they were not yet come. It was determined I should take post. I had no carriage. The maréchal made me a present of a cabriolet, and lent me horses and a postillion the first stage, where, in consequence of the measures he had taken, I had no difficulty in procuring others.

As I had not dined at table, nor made my appearance in the castle, the ladies came to bid me adieu in the entresol where I had passed the day. Madam de Luxembourg embraced me several times with a melancholy air; but I did not in these embraces feel the pressing I had done in those she had lavished upon me two or three years before. Madam de Boufflers also embraced me, and said to me many civil things. An embrace which surprised me more than all the rest had done was one from Madam de Mirepoix, for she also was at the castle. Madam la Maréchale de Mirepoix is a person extremely cold, decent, and reserved, and did not, at least as she appeared to me, seem quite exempt from the natural haughtiness of the house of Lorraine. She had never shown me much attention. Whether, flattered by an honor I had not expected, I endeavored to enhance the value of it; or that there really was in the embrace a little of that commiseration natural to generous hearts, I found in her manner and look something energetical which penetrated me. I have since that time frequently thought that, acquainted with my destiny, she could not refrain from a momentary concern for my fate.

The maréchal did not open his mouth; he was as pale as death. He would absolutely accompany me to the carriage which waited at the watering place. We crossed the garden without uttering a single word. I had a key of the park with which I opened the gate, and instead of putting it again into my pocket, I held it out to the maréchal without saying a word. He took it with a vivacity which surprised me, and which has since frequently intruded itself upon my thoughts. I have not in my whole life had a more bitter moment than that of this separation. Our embrace was long and silent: we both felt that this was our last adieu.

Between La Barre and Montmorency I met, in a hired carriage, four men in black, who saluted me smiling. According to what Thérèsa has since told me of the officers of justice, the hour of their arrival and their manner of behavior, I have no doubt, that they were the persons I met, especially as the order to arrest me, instead of being made out at seven o'clock, as I had been told it would, had not been given till noon. I had to go through Paris. A person in a cabriolet is not much concealed. I saw several persons in the streets who saluted me with an air of familiarity, but I did not know one of them. The same evening I changed my route to pass Villeroy. At Lyons the couriers were conducted to the commandant. This might have been embarrassing to a man unwilling either to lie or change his name. I went with a letter from Madam de Luxembourg to beg M. de Villeroy would spare me this disagreeable ceremony. M. de Villeroy gave me a letter of which I made no use, because I did not go through Lyons. This letter still remains sealed up amongst my papers. The duke pressed me to sleep at Villeroy, but I preferred returning to the great road, which I did, and traveled two more stages the same evening.

My carriage was inconvenient and uncomfortable, and I was too much indisposed to go far in a day. My appearance besides was not sufficiently distinguished for me to be well served, and in France post-horses feel the whip in proportion to the favorable opinion the postillion has of his temporary master. By paying the guides generously I thought I should make up for my shabby appearance: this was still worse. They took me for a worthless fellow who was carrying orders, and, for the first time in my life, traveling post. From that moment I had nothing but worn-out hacks, and I became the sport of the postillions. I ended as I should have begun by being patient, holding my tongue, and suffering myself to be driven as my conductors thought proper.

I had sufficient matter of reflection to prevent me from being weary on the road, employing myself in the recollection of that which had just happened; but this was neither my turn of mind nor the inclination of my heart. The facility with which I forget past evils, however recent they may be, is astonishing. The remembrance of them becomes feeble, and, sooner or later, effaced, in the inverse proportion to the greater degree of fear with which the approach of them inspires me. My cruel imagination, incessantly tormented by the apprehension of evils still at a distance, diverts my attention, and prevents me from recollecting those which are past. Caution is needless after the evil has happened, and it is time lost to give it a thought. I, in some measure, put a period to my misfortunes before they happen: the more I have suffered at their approach the greater is the facility with which I forget them; whilst, on the contrary, incessantly recollecting my past happiness, I, if I may so speak, enjoy it a second time at pleasure. It is to this happy disposition I am indebted for an exemption from that ill humor which ferments in a vindictive mind, by the continual remembrance of injuries received, and torments it with all the evil it wishes to do its enemy. Naturally choleric, I have felt all the force of anger, which in the first moments has sometimes been carried to fury, but a desire of vengeance never took root within me. I think too little of the offense to give myself much trouble about the offender. I think of the injury I have received from him on account of that he may do me a second time, but were I certain he would never do me another the first would be instantly forgotten. Pardon of offenses is continually preached to us. I knew not whether or not my heart would be capable of overcoming its hatred, for it never yet felt that passion, and I give myself too little concern about my enemies to have the merit of pardoning them. I will not say to what a degree, in order to torment me, they torment themselves. I am at their mercy, they have unbounded power, and make of it what use they please. There is but one thing in which I set them at defiance: which is in tormenting themselves about me, to force me to give myself the least trouble about them.

The day after my departure I had so perfectly forgotten what had passed, the parliament, Madam de Pompadour, M. de Choiseul, Grimm, and D'Alembert, with their conspiracies, that, had not it been for the necessary precautions during the journey I should have thought no more of them. The remembrance of one thing which supplied the place of all these was what I had read the evening before my departure. I recollect, also, the pastorals of Gessner, which his translator Hubert had sent me a little time before. These two ideas occurred to me so strongly, and were connected in such a manner in my mind, that I was determined to endeavor to unite them by treating after the manner of Gessner the subject of the Levite of Ephraim. His pastoral and simple style appeared to me but little fitted to so horrid a subject, and it was not to be presumed the situation I was then in would furnish me with such ideas as would enliven it. However, I attempted the thing, solely to amuse myself in my cabriolet, and without the least hope of success. I had no sooner begun than I was astonished at the liveliness of my ideas, and the facility with which I expressed them. In three days I composed the first three cantos of the little poem which I finished at Motiers, and I am certain of not having done anything in my life in which there is a more interesting mildness of manners, a greater brilliancy of coloring, more simple delineations, greater exactness of proportion, or more antique simplicity in general, notwithstanding the horror of the subject which in itself is abominable, so that besides every other merit I had still that of a difficulty conquered. If the Levite of Ephraim be not the best of my works, it will ever be that most esteemed. I have never read, nor shall I ever read it again without feeling interiorly the applause of a heart without acrimony, which, far from being embittered by misfortunes, is susceptible of consolation in the midst of them, and finds within itself a resource by which they are counterbalanced. Assemble the great philosophers, so superior in their books to adversity which, they do not suffer, place them in a situation similar to mine, and, in the first moments of the indignation of their injured honor, give them a like work to compose, and it will be seen in what manner they will acquit themselves of the task.

When I set off from Montmorency to go into Switzerland, I had resolved to stop at Yverdon, at the house of my old friend Roguin, who had several years before retired to that place, and had invited me to go and see him. I was told Lyons was not the direct road, for which reason I avoided going through it. But I was obliged to pass through Besançon, a fortified town, and consequently subject to the same inconvenience. I took it into my head to turn about and to go to Salins, under the pretense of going to see M. de Mairan, the nephew of M. Dupin, who had an employment at the salt-works, and formerly had given me many invitations to his house. The expedient succeeded: M. de Mairan was not in the way, and, happily, not being obliged to stop, I continued my journey without being spoken to by anybody.

The moment I was within the territory of Berne, I ordered the postillion to stop; I got out of my carriage, prostrated myself, kissed the ground, and exclaimed in a transport of joy: "Heaven, the protector of virtue, be praised, I touch a land of liberty!" Thus, blind and unsuspecting in my hopes, have I ever been passionately attached to that which was to make me unhappy. The man thought me mad. I got into the carriage, and a few hours afterwards I had the pure and lively satisfaction of feeling myself pressed within the arms of the respectable Roguin. Ah! let me breathe for a moment with this worthy host! It is necessary I should gain strength and courage before I proceed further. I shall soon find that in my way which will give employment to them both. It is not without reason that I have been diffuse in the recital of all the circumstances I have been able to recollect. Although they may seem uninteresting, yet, when once the thread of the conspiracy is got hold of, they may throw some light upon the progress of it; and, for instance, without giving the first idea of the problem I am going to propose, afford some aid in resolving it.

Suppose that, for the execution of the conspiracy of which I was the object, my absence was absolutely necessary, everything tending to that effect could not have happened otherwise than it did; but if without suffering myself to be alarmed by the nocturnal embassy of Madam de Luxembourg, I had continued to hold out, and, instead of remaining at the castle, had returned to my bed and quietly slept until morning, should I have equally had an order of arrest made out against me? This is a great question upon which the solution of many others depends, and for the examination of it, the hour of the comminatory decree of arrest, and that of the real decree may be remarked to advantage. A rude but sensible example of the importance of the least detail in the exposition of facts, of which the secret causes are sought for to discover them by induction.

BOOK XII

BOOK XII

[*1762*]

HERE commences the work of darkness, in which I have for the last eight years been enveloped, though it has not by any means been possible for me to penetrate the dreadful obscurity. In the abyss of evil into which I am plunged, I feel the blows reach me, without perceiving the hand by which they are directed or the means it employs. Shame and misfortune seem of themselves to fall upon me. When in the affliction of my heart I suffer a groan to escape me, I have the appearance of a man who complains without reason, and the authors of my ruin have the inconceivable art of rendering the public, unknown to itself, or without its perceiving the effects of it, accomplice in their conspiracy. Therefore, in my narrative of circumstances relative to myself, of the treatment I have received, and all that has happened to me, I shall not be able to indicate the hand by which the whole has been directed, nor assign the causes, while I state the effect. The primitive causes are all given in the preceding books; and everything in which I am interested, and all the secret motives pointed out. But it is impossible for me to explain, even by conjecture, that in which the different causes are combined to operate the strange events of my life. If amongst my readers one even of them should be generous enough to wish to examine the mystery to the bottom, and discover the truth, let him carefully read over a second time the three preceding books, afterwards at each fact he shall find stated in the books which follow, let him gain such information as is within his reach, and go back from intrigue to intrigue, and from agent to agent, until he comes to the first mover of all. I know where his researches will terminate; but in the meantime I lose myself in the crooked and obscure subterraneous path through which his steps must be directed.

During my stay at Yverdon, I became acquainted with all the family of my friend Roguin, and amongst others with his niece, Madam Boy de la Tour, and her daughters, whose father, as I think I have already observed, I formerly knew at Lyons. She was at Yverdon, upon a visit to her uncle and his sister; her eldest daughter, about fifteen years of age, delighted me by her fine understanding and excellent disposition. I conceived the most tender friendship for the mother and the daughter. The latter was destined by M. Roguin to the colonel, his nephew, a man already verging towards the decline of life, and who showed me marks of great esteem and affection; but although the heart of the uncle was set upon this marriage, which was much wished for by the nephew also, and

I was greatly desirous to promote the satisfaction of both, the great disproportion of age, and the extreme repugnancy of the young lady, made me join with the mother in postponing the ceremony, and the affair was at length broken off. The colonel has since married Mademoiselle Dillan, his relation, beautiful, and amiable as my heart could wish, and who has made him the happiest of husbands and fathers. However, M. Roguin has not yet forgotten my opposition to his wishes. My consolation is in the certainty of having discharged to him, and his family, the duty of the most pure friendship, which does not always consist in being agreeable, but in advising for the best.

I did not remain long in doubt about the reception which awaited me at Geneva, had I chosen to return to that city. My book was burned there, and on the 18th of June, nine days after an order to arrest me had been given at Paris, another to the same effect was determined upon by the republic. So many incredible absurdities were stated in this second decree, in which the ecclesiastical edict was formally violated, that I refused to believe the first accounts I heard of it, and when these were well confirmed, I trembled lest so manifest an infraction of every law, beginning with that of common-sense, should create the greatest confusion in the city. I was, however, relieved from my fears; everything remained quiet. If there was any rumor amongst the populace, it was unfavorable to me, and I was publicly treated by all the gossips and pedants like a scholar threatened with a flogging for not having said his catechism.

These two decrees were the signal for the cry of malediction, raised against me with unexampled fury in every part of Europe. All the gazettes, journals, and pamphlets, rang the alarm-bell. The French especially, that mild, generous, and polished people, who so much pique themselves upon their attention and proper condescension to the unfortunate, instantly forgetting their favorite virtues, signalized themselves by the number and violence of the outrages with which, while each seemed to strive who should afflict me most, they overwhelmed me. I was impious, an atheist, a madman, a wild beast, a wolf. The continuator of the Journal of Trévoux was guilty of a piece of extravagance in attacking my pretended Lycanthropy, which was no mean proof of his own. A stranger would have thought an author in Paris was afraid of incurring the animadversion of the police, by publishing a work of any kind without cramming into it some insult to me. I sought in vain the cause of this unanimous animosity, and was almost tempted to believe the world was gone mad. What! said I to myself, the editor of the *Paix perpétuelle,* spread discord; the publisher of the *Vicaire Savoyard,* impious; the writer of the *Nouvelle Héloïse,* a wolf; the author of *Emile,* a madman! Gracious God! what then should I have been had I published the treatise of *l'Esprit,* or any similar work? And yet, in the storm raised against the author of that book, the public, far from joining the cry of his persecutors, revenged him of them by eulogium. Let his book and mine, the receptions the two works met with, and the treatment of the two authors in the different countries of Europe, be compared; and for the difference let causes satisfactory to a man of sense be found, and I will ask no more.

I found the residence of Yverdon so agreeable that I resolved to yield to the solicitations of M. Roguin and his family, who were desirous of keeping me there. M. de Moiry de Gingin, bailiff of that city, encouraged me by his goodness to remain within his jurisdiction. The colonel pressed me so much to accept for my habitation a little pavilion he had in his house between the court and the garden, that I complied with his request, and he immediately furnished it with everything necessary for my little household establishment.

The banneret Roguin, one of the persons who showed me the most assiduous attention, did not leave me for an instant during the whole day. I was much flattered by his civilities, but they sometimes importuned me. The day on which I was to take possession of my new habitation was already fixed, and I had written to Thérèsa to come to me, when suddenly a storm was raised against me in Berne, which was attributed to the devotees, but I have never been able to learn the cause of it. The senate, excited against me, without my knowing by whom, did not seem disposed to suffer me to remain undisturbed in my retreat. The moment the bailiff was informed of the new fermentation, he wrote in my favor to several of the members of the government, reproaching them with their blind intolerance, and telling them it was shameful to refuse to a man of merit, under oppression, the asylum which such a numerous banditti found in their states. Sensible people were of opinion the warmth of his reproaches had rather embittered than softened the minds of the magistrates. However this may be, neither his influence nor eloquence could ward off the blow. Having received an intimation of the order he was to signify to me, he gave me a previous communication of it; and that I might wait its arrival, I resolved to set off the next day. The difficulty was to know where to go, finding myself shut out from Geneva and all France, and foreseeing that in this affair each state would be anxious to imitate its neighbor.

Madam Boy de la Tour proposed to me to go and reside in an uninhabited but completely furnished house, which belonged to her son in the village of Motiers, in the Val-de-Travers, in the county of Neuchâtel. I had only a mountain to cross to arrive at it. The offer came the more opportunely, as in the states of the King of Prussia I should naturally be sheltered from all persecution, at least religion could not serve as a pretext for it. But a secret difficulty, improper for me at that moment to divulge, had in it that which was very sufficient to make me hesitate. The innate love of justice, to which my heart was constantly subject, added to my secret inclination to France, had inspired me with an aversion to the King of Prussia, who, by his maxims and conduct, seemed to tread under foot all respect for natural law and every duty of humanity. Amongst the framed engravings, with which I had decorated my alcove at Montmorency, was a portrait of this prince, and under it a distich, the last line of which was as follows:

*Il pense en philosophe, et se conduit en roi.**

This verse, which from any other pen would have been a fine eulogium, from mine had an unequivocal meaning, and too clearly explained the verse by which it was preceded. The distich had been read by everybody who came to see me, and my visitors were numerous. The Chevalier de Lorenzi had even written it down to give it to D'Alembert, and I had no doubt but D'Alembert had taken care to make my court with it to the prince. I had also aggravated this first fault by a passage in Emilius, where, under the name of Adrastus, king of the Daunians, it was clearly seen whom I had in view, and the remark had not escaped critics, because Madam de Boufflers had several times mentioned the subject to me. I was, therefore, certain of being inscribed in red ink in the registers of the King of Prussia, and besides, supposing his majesty to have the principles I had dared to attribute to him, he, for that reason, could not but be displeased with my writings and their author; for everybody knows

* *He thinks like a philosopher, and acts like a king.*

the worthless part of mankind, and tyrants have never failed to conceive the most mortal hatred against me, solely on reading my works, without being acquainted with my person.

However, I had presumption enough to depend upon his mercy, and was far from thinking I ran much risk. I knew none but weak men were slaves to the base passions, and that these had but little power over strong minds, such as I had always thought his to be. According to his art of reigning, I thought he could not but show himself magnanimous on this occasion, and that being so in fact was not above his character. I thought a mean and easy vengeance would not for a moment counterbalance his love of glory, and putting myself in his place, his taking advantage of circumstances to overwhelm with the weight of his generosity a man who had dared to think ill of him, did not appear to me impossible. I therefore went to settle at Motiers, with a confidence of which I imagined he would feel all the value, and said to myself: When Jean-Jacques rises to the elevation of Coriolanus, will Frederic sink below the General of the Volsci?

Colonel Roguin insisted on crossing the mountain with me, and installing me at Motiers. A sister-in-law to Madam Boy de la Tour, named Madam Girardier, to whom the house in which I was going to live was very convenient, did not see me arrive there with pleasure; however, she with a good grace put me in possession of my lodging, and I ate with her until

Thérèsa came, and my little establishment was formed.

Perceiving at my departure from Montmorency I should in future be a fugitive upon the earth, I hesitated about permitting her to come to me and partake of the wandering life to which I saw myself condemned. I felt the nature of our relation to each other was about to change, and that what until then had on my part been favor and friendship, would in future become so on hers. If her attachment was proof against my misfortunes, to this I knew she must become a victim, and that her grief would add to my pain. Should my disgrace weaken her affections, she would make me consider her constancy as a sacrifice, and instead of feeling the pleasure I had in dividing with her my last morsel of bread, she would see nothing but her own merit in following me wherever I was driven by fate.

I must say everything; I have never concealed the vices either of my poor mamma or myself; I cannot be more favorable to Thérèsa, and whatever pleasure I may have in doing honor to a person who is dear to me, I will not disguise the truth, although it may discover in her an error, if an involuntary change of the affections of the heart be one. I had long perceived hers to grow cooler towards me, and that she was no longer for me what she had been in our younger days. Of this I was the more sensible, as for her I was what I had always been. I fell into the same inconvenience as that of which I had felt the effect with mamma,

and this effect was the same now I was with Thérèsa.
Let us not seek for perfection, which nature never produces; it would be the same thing with any other
woman. The manner in which I had disposed of my
children, however reasonable it had appeared to me,
had not always left my heart at ease. While writing
my *Traité de l'Education,* I felt I had neglected duties
with which it was not possible to dispense. Remorse
at length became so strong that it almost forced from
me a public confession of my fault at the beginning of
my Emilius, and the passage is so clear, that it is
astonishing any person should, after reading it, have
had the courage to reproach me with my error. My
situation was however still the same, or something
worse, by the animosity of my enemies, who sought
to find me in a fault. I feared a relapse, and unwilling
to run the risk, I preferred abstinence to exposing
Thérèsa to a similar mortification. I had besides remarked that a connection with women was prejudicial to my health; this double reason made me form
resolutions to which I had sometimes but badly kept,
but for the last three or four years I had more constantly adhered to them. It was in this interval I had
remarked Thérèsa's coolness; she had the same attachment to me from duty, but not the least from
love. Our intercourse naturally became less agreeable,
and I imagined that, certain of the continuation of
my cares wherever she might be, she would choose to
stay at Paris rather than to wander with me. Yet she
had given such signs of grief at our parting, had re-

quired of me such positive promises that we should meet again, and, since my departure, had expressed to the Prince de Conti and M. de Luxembourg so strong a desire of it, that, far from having the courage to speak to her of separation, I scarcely had enough to think of it myself; and after having felt in my heart how impossible it was for me to do without her, all I thought of afterwards was to recall her to me as soon as possible. I wrote to her to this effect, and she came. It was scarcely two months since I had quitted her; but it was our first separation after an union of so many years. We had both of us felt it most cruelly. What emotion in our first embrace! O how delightful are the tears of tenderness and joy! How does my heart drink them up! Why have not I had reason to shed them more frequently?

On my arrival at Motiers I had written to Lord Keith, marshal of Scotland, and governor of Neu-châtel, informing him of my retreat into the states of his Prussian majesty, and requesting of him his protection. He answered me with his well-known generosity, and in the manner I had expected from him. He invited me to his house. I went with M. Martinet, lord of the manor of Val-de-Travers, who was in great favor with his excellency. The venerable appearance of this illustrious and virtuous Scotchman, powerfully affected my heart, and from that instant began between him and me the strong attachment, which on my part still remains the same, and would be so on his, had not the traitors, who have deprived me of all the consolations of life, taken advantage of my absence to deceive his old age and depreciate me in his esteem.

George Keith, hereditary marshal of Scotland, and brother to the famous General Keith, who lived gloriously and died in the bed of honor, had quitted his country at a very early age, and was proscribed on account of his attachment to the house of Stuart. With that house, however, he soon became disgusted by the unjust and tyrannical spirit he remarked in the ruling character of the Stuart family. He lived a long time in Spain, the climate of which pleased him exceedingly, and at length attached himself, as his brother had done, to the service of the King of Prussia, who knew men and gave them the reception they merited. His majesty received a great return for this reception, in the services rendered him by Marshal Keith, and by what was infinitely more precious, the sincere friendship of his lordship. The great mind of this worthy man, haughty and republican, could stoop to no other yoke than that of friendship, but to this it was so obedient, that with very different maxims he saw nothing but Frederic the moment he became attached to him. The king charged the marshal with affairs of importance, sent him to Paris, to Spain, and at length, seeing he was already advanced in years, let him retire with the government of Neuchâtel, and the delightful employment of passing there the remainder of his life in rendering the inhabitants happy.

The people of Neuchâtel, whose manners are trivial, know not how to distinguish solid merit, and suppose wit to consist in long discourses. When they saw a sedate man of simple manners appear amongst them, they mistook his simplicity for haughtiness, his candor for rusticity, his laconism for stupidity, and rejected his benevolent cares, because, wishing to be useful, and not being a sycophant, he knew not how to flatter people he did not esteem. In the ridiculous affair of the minister Petitpierre, who was displaced by his colleagues, for having been unwilling they should be eternally damned, my lord, opposing the usurpations of the ministers, saw the whole country of which he took the part, rise up against him, and when I arrived there the stupid murmur had not entirely subsided. He passed for a man influenced by the prejudices with which he was inspired by others, and of all the imputations brought against him it was the most devoid of truth. My first sentiment on seeing this venerable old man, was that of tender commiseration, on account of his extreme leanness of body, years having already left him little else but skin and bone; but when I raised my eyes to his animated, open, noble countenance, I felt a respect, mingled with confidence, which absorbed every other sentiment. He answered the very short compliment I made him when first I came into his presence by speaking of something else, as if I had already been a week in his house. He did not bid us sit down. The stupid chatelain, the lord of the manor, remained standing. For my part I at first sight saw in the fine and piercing eye of his lordship something so conciliating that, feeling myself entirely at ease, I without ceremony, took my seat by his side upon the sofa. By the familiarity of his manner I immediately perceived the liberty I took gave him pleasure, and that he said to himself: This is not a Neuchâtelois.

Singular effect of the similarity of characters! At an age when the heart loses its natural warmth, that of this good old man grew warm by his attachment to me to a degree which surprised everybody. He came to see me at Motiers under the pretense of quail shooting, and stayed there two days without touching a gun. We conceived such a friendship for each other that we knew not how to live separate; the castle of Colombier, where he passed the summer, was six leagues from Motiers; I went there at least once a fortnight, and made a stay of twenty-four hours, and then returned like a pilgrim with my heart full of affection for my host. The emotion I had formerly experienced in my journeys from the Hermitage to Eaubonne was certainly very different, but it was not more pleasing than that with which I approached Colombier.

What tears of tenderness have I shed when on the road to it, while thinking of the paternal goodness, amiable virtues, and charming philosophy of this respectable old man! I called him father, and he called me son. These affectionate names give, in some measure, an idea of the attachment by which we were united, but by no means that of the want we felt of each other, nor of our continual desire to be together. He would absolutely give me an apartment at the castle of Colombier, and for a long time pressed me to take up my residence in that in which I lodged during my visits. I at length told him I was more free and at my ease in my own house, and that I had rather continue until the end of my life to come and see him. He approved of my candor, and never afterwards spoke to me on the subject. Oh, my good lord! Oh, my worthy father! How is my heart still moved when I think of your goodness? Ah, barbarous wretches! how deeply did they wound me when they deprived me of your friendship! But no, great man, you are and will ever be the same for me, who am still the same. You have been deceived, but you are not changed.

My lord maréchal is not without faults; he is a man of wisdom, but he is still a man. With the greatest penetration, the nicest discrimination, and the most profound knowledge of men, he sometimes suffers himself to be deceived, and never recovers his error. His temper is very singular and foreign to his general turn of mind. He seems to forget the people he sees every day, and thinks of them in a moment when they least expect it; his attention seems ill-timed; his presents are dictated by caprice and not by propriety. He gives or sends in an instant whatever comes into his head, be the value of it ever so small. A young Genevese, desirous of entering into the service of Prussia, made a personal application to him; his lordship, instead of giving him a letter, gave him a little bag of peas, which he desired him to carry to the king. On receiving this singular recommendation his majesty gave a commission to the bearer of it. These elevated geniuses have between themselves a language which the vulgar will never understand. The whimsical manner of my lord maréchal, something like the caprice of a fine woman, rendered him still more interesting to me. I was certain, and afterwards had proofs, that it had not the least influence over his sentiments, nor did it affect the cares prescribed by friendship on serious occasions, yet in his manner of obliging there is the same singularity as in his manners in general. Of this I will give one instance relative to a matter of no great importance. The journey from Motiers to Colombier being too long for me to perform in one day, I commonly divided it by setting off after dinner and sleeping at Brot, which is half way. The landlord of the house where I stopped, named Sandoz, having to solicit at Berlin a favor of importance to him, begged I would request his excellency to ask it in his behalf. "Most willingly," said I, and took him with me. I left him in the antechamber, and mentioned the matter to his lordship, who returned me no answer. After passing with him the whole morning, I saw as I crossed the hall to go to dinner, poor Sandoz, who was fatigued to death with waiting. Thinking the governor had forgotten what I had said to him, I again spoke of the business before we sat down to table, but still received no answer. I thought this manner of making me feel I was importunate rather severe, and, pitying the poor man in waiting, held my tongue. On my return the next day I was much surprised at the thanks he returned me for the good dinner his excellency had given him after receiving his paper. Three weeks afterwards his lordship sent him the rescript he had solicited, dispatched by the minister, and signed by the king, and this without having said a word either to myself or Sandoz concerning the business, about which I thought he did not choose to give himself the least concern.

I could wish incessantly to speak of George Keith; from him proceeds my recollection of the last happy moments I have enjoyed; the rest of my life, since our separation, has been passed in affliction and grief of heart. The remembrance of this is so melancholy and confused that it was impossible for me to observe the least order in what I write, so that in future I shall be under the necessity of stating facts without giving them a regular arrangement.

I was soon relieved from my inquietude arising from the uncertainty of my asylum, by the answer from his majesty to the lord marshal, in whom, as it will readily be believed, I had found an able advocate. The king not only approved of what he had done, but desired him, for I must relate everything, to give me twelve louis. The good old man, rather embarrassed by the commission, and not knowing how to execute it properly, endeavored to soften the insult by transforming the money into provisions, and writing to me that he had received orders to furnish me with wood and coal to begin my little establishment; he moreover added, and perhaps from himself, that his majesty would willingly build me a little house, such a one as I should choose to have, provided I would fix upon the ground. I was extremely sensible of the kindness of the last offer, which made me forget the weakness of the other. Without accepting either, I considered Frederic as my benefactor and protector, and became so sincerely attached to him, that from that moment I interested myself as much in his glory as until then I had thought his successes unjust. At the peace he made soon after, I expressed my joy by an illumination in a very good taste: it was a string of garlands, with which I decorated the house I inhabited, and in which, it is true, I had the vindictive haughtiness to spend almost as much money as he had wished to give me. The peace ratified, I thought as he was at the highest pinnacle of military and political fame, he would think of acquiring that of another nature, by reanimating his states, encouraging in them commerce and agriculture, creating a new soil, covering it with a new people, maintaining peace amongst his neighbors, and becoming the arbitrator, after having been the terror, of Europe. He was in a situation to sheath his sword without danger, certain that no sovereign would oblige him again to draw it. Perceiving he did not disarm, I was afraid he would profit but little by the advantages he had gained, and that he would be great only by halves. I dared to write to him upon the subject, and with a familiarity of a nature to please men of his character, conveying to him the sacred voice of truth, which but few kings are worthy to hear. The liberty I took was a secret between him and myself. I did not communicate it even to the lord marshal, to whom I sent my letter to the king sealed up. His lordship forwarded my dispatch without asking what it contained. His majesty returned me no answer, and the marshal going soon after to Berlin, the king told him he had received from me a scolding. By this I understood my letter had been ill received, and that the frankness of my zeal had been mistaken for the rusticity of a pedant. In fact, this might possibly be the case; perhaps I did not say what was necessary, nor in the manner proper to the occasion. All I can answer for is the sentiment which induced me to take up my pen.

Shortly after my establishment at Motiers, Travers having every possible assurance that I should be suffered to remain there in peace, I took the Armenian habit. This was not the first time I had thought of doing it. I had formerly had the same intention, particularly at Montmorency, where the frequent use of probes often obliging me to keep my chamber, made me more clearly perceive the advantages of a long robe. The convenience of an Armenian tailor, who frequently came to see a relation he had at Montmorency, almost tempted me to determine on taking this new dress, troubling myself but little about what the world would say of it. Yet, before I concluded upon the matter, I wished to take the opinion of M. de Luxembourg, who immediately advised me to follow my inclination. I therefore procured a little Armenian wardrobe, but on account of the storm raised against me, I was induced to postpone making use of it until I should enjoy tranquillity, and it was not until some months afterwards that, forced by new attacks of my disorder, I thought I could properly, and without the least risk, put on my new dress at Motiers, especially after having consulted the pastor of the place, who told me I might wear it even in the temple without indecency. I then adopted the waistcoat, caffetan, fur bonnet, and girdle; and after having in this dress attended divine service, I saw no impropriety in going in it to visit his lordship. His excellency, on seeing me clothed in this manner, made me no other compliment than that which consisted in saying *"Salaam alek,"* i.e., "Peace be with you;" the common Turkish salutation; after which nothing more was said upon the subject, and I continued to wear my new dress.

Having quite abandoned literature, all I now thought of was leading a quiet life, and one as agreeable as I could make it. When alone, I have never felt weariness of mind, not even in complete inaction; my imagination filling up every void, was sufficient to keep up my attention. The inactive babbling of a private circle, where, seated opposite to each other, they who speak move nothing but the tongue, is the only thing I have ever been unable to support. When walking and rambling about there is some satisfaction in conversation; the feet and eyes do something; but to hear people with their arms across speak of the weather, of the biting of flies, or what is still worse, compliment each other, is to me an insupportable torment. That I might not live like a savage, I took it into my head to learn to make laces. Like the women, I carried my cushion with me when I went to make visits, or sat down to work at my door, and chatted with passers-by. This made me the better support the emptiness of babbling, and enabled me to pass my time with my female neighbors without weariness. Several of these were very amiable and not devoid of wit. One in particular, Isabelle d'Yvernois, daughter of the attorney-general of Neuchâtel, I found so estimable as to induce me to enter with her into terms of particular friendship, from which she derived some advantage by the useful advice I gave her, and the services she received from me on occasions of importance, so that now a worthy and virtuous mother of a family, she is perhaps indebted to me for her reason, her husband, her life, and happiness. On my part, I received from her gentle consolation, particularly during a melancholy winter, throughout the whole of which, when my sufferings were most cruel, she came to pass with Thérèsa and me long evenings, which she made very short to us by her agreeable conversation, and our mutual openness of heart. She called me papa, and I called her daughter, and these names, which we still give to each other, will, I hope, continue to be as dear to her as they are to me. That my laces might be of some utility, I gave them to my young female friends at their marriages, upon condition of their suckling their children; Isabella's eldest sister had one upon these terms, and well deserved it by her observance of them; Isabella herself also received another, which, by intention, she as fully merited. She has not been happy enough to be able to pursue her inclination. When I sent the laces to the two sisters, I wrote each of them a letter; the first has been shown about in the world; the second has not the same celebrity: friendship proceeds with less noise.

Amongst the connections I made in my neighborhood, of which I will not enter into a detail, I must mention that with Colonel Pury, who had a house upon the mountain, where he came to pass the summer. I was not anxious to become acquainted with him, because I knew he was upon bad terms at court, and with the lord marshal, whom he did not visit. Yet, as he came to see me, and showed me much attention, I was under the necessity of returning his visit; this was repeated, and we sometimes dined with each other. At his house I became acquainted with M. du Perou, and afterwards too intimately connected with him to pass his name over in silence.

M. du Perou was an American, son to a commandant of Surinam, whose successor, M. le Chambrier, of Neuchâtel, married his widow. Left a widow a second time, she came with her son to live in the country of her second husband.

Du Perou, an only son, very rich, and tenderly beloved by his mother, had been carefully brought up, and his education was not lost upon him. He had acquired much knowledge, a taste for the arts, and piqued himself upon his having cultivated his rational faculty: his Dutch appearance, yellow complexion, and silent and close disposition, favored this opinion. Although young, he was already deaf and gouty. This rendered his motions deliberate and very grave, and although he was fond of disputing, he in general spoke but little because his hearing was bad. I was struck with his exterior, and said to myself, this is a thinker, a man of wisdom, such a one as anybody would be happy to have for a friend. He frequently addressed himself to me without paying the least compliment, and this strengthened the favorable opinion I had already formed of him. He said but little to me of myself or my books, and still less of himself; he was not destitute of ideas, and what he said was just. This justness and equality attracted my regard. He had neither the elevation of mind, nor the discrimination of the lord marshal, but he had all his simplicity; this was still representing him in something. I did not become infatuated with him, but he acquired my attachment from esteem; and by degrees this esteem led to friendship, and I totally forgot the objection I made to the Baron Holbach: that he was too rich.

For a long time I saw but little of Du Perou, because I did not go to Neuchâtel, and he came but once a year to the mountain of Colonel Pury. Why did not I go to Neuchâtel? This proceeded from a childishness upon which I must not be silent.

Although protected by the King of Prussia and the lord marshal, while I avoided persecution in my asylum, I did not avoid the murmurs of the public, of municipal magistrates and ministers. After what had happened in France it became fashionable to insult me; these people would have been afraid to seem to disapprove of what my persecutors had done by not imitating them. The *classe* of Neuchâtel, that is, the ministers of that city, gave the impulse, by endeavoring to move the council of state against me. This attempt not having succeeded, the ministers addressed themselves to the municipal magistrate, who immediately prohibited my book, treating me on all occasions with but little civility, and saying, that had I wished to reside in the city I should not have been suffered to do it. They filled their Mercury with absurdities and the most stupid hypocrisy, which, although it made every man of sense laugh, animated the people against me. This, however, did not prevent them from setting forth that I ought to be very grateful for their permitting me to live at Motiers, where they had no authority; they would willingly have measured me the air by the pint, provided I had paid for it a dear price. They would have it that I was obliged to them for the protection the king granted me in spite of the efforts they incessantly made to deprive me of it. Finally, failing of success, after having done me all the injury they could, and defamed me to the utmost of their power, they made a merit of their impotence, by boasting of their goodness in suffering me to stay in their country. I ought to have laughed at their vain efforts, but I was foolish enough to be vexed at them, and had the weakness to be unwilling to go to Neuchâtel, to which I yielded for almost two years, as if it was not doing too much honor to such wretches, to pay attention to their proceedings, which, good or bad, could not be imputed to them, because they never act but from a foreign impulse. Besides, minds without sense or knowledge, whose objects of esteem are influence, power, and money, are far from imagining even that some respect is due to talents, and that it is dishonorable to injure and insult them.

A certain mayor of a village, who for sundry malversations, had been deprived of his office, said to the lieutenant of Valde-Travers, the husband of Isabella: *"I am told this Rousseau has great wit; bring him to me that I may see whether he has or not."* The disapprobation of such a man ought certainly to have no effect upon those on whom it falls.

After the treatment I had received at Paris, Geneva, Berne, and even at Neuchâtel, I expected no favor from the pastor of this place. I had, however, been recommended to him by Madam Boy de la Tour, and he had given me a good reception; but in that country where every new-comer is indiscriminately flattered, civilities signify but little. Yet, after my solemn union with the reformed church, and living in a Protestant country, I could not, without failing in my engagements, as well as in the duty of a citizen, neglect the public profession of the religion into which I had entered; I therefore attended divine service. On the other hand, had I gone to the holy table, I was afraid of exposing myself to a refusal, and it was by no means probable, that after the tumult excited at Geneva by the council, and at Neuchâtel by the *classe* (the ministers), he would, without difficulty, administer to me the sacrament in his church. The time of communion approaching, I wrote to M. de Montmollin, the minister, to prove to him my desire of communicating, and declaring myself heartily united to the Protestant church; I also told him, in order to avoid disputing upon articles of faith, that I would not hearken to any particular explanation of the point of doctrine. After taking these steps, I made myself easy, not doubting but M. de Montmollin would refuse to admit me without the preliminary discussion to which I refused to consent, and that in this manner everything would be at an end without any fault of mine. I was deceived: when I least expected anything of the kind, M. de Montmollin came to declare to me not only that he admitted me to the communion under the condition which I had proposed, but that he and the elders thought themselves much honored by my being one of their flock. I never in my whole life felt greater surprise or received from it more consolation. Living always alone and unconnected, appeared to me a melancholy destiny, especially in adversity. In the midst of so many proscriptions and persecutions, I found it extremely agreeable to be able to say to myself: I am at least amongst my brethren; and I went to the communion with an emotion of heart, and my eyes suffused with tears of tenderness, which perhaps were the most agreeable preparation to Him to whose table I was drawing near.

Sometime afterwards his lordship sent me a letter from Madam de Boufflers, which he had received, at least I presumed so, by means of D'Alembert, who was acquainted with the maréchal. In this letter, the first that lady had written to me after my departure from Montmorency, she rebuked me severely for having written to M. de Montmollin, and especially for having communicated. I the less understood what she meant by her reproof, as after my journey to Geneva, I had constantly declared myself a Protestant, and had gone publicly to the Hôtel de Hollande without incurring the least censure from anybody. It appeared to me diverting enough, that Madam de Boufflers should wish to direct my conscience in matters of religion. However, as I had no doubt of the purity of her intention, I was not offended by this singular sally, and I answered her without anger, stating to her my reasons.

Calumnies in print were still industriously circulated, and their benign authors reproached the different powers with treating me too mildly. For my part, I let them say and write what they pleased, without giving myself the least concern about the matter. I was told there was a censure from the Sorbonne, but this I could not believe. What could the Sorbonne have to do in the matter? Did the doctors wish to know to a certainty that I was not a Catholic? Everybody already knew I was not one. Were they desirous of proving I was not a good Calvinist? Of what consequence was this to them? It was taking upon themselves a singular care, and becoming the substitutes of our ministers. Before I saw this publication I thought it was distributed in the name of the Sorbonne, by way of mockery: and when I had read it I was convinced this was the case. But when at length there was not a doubt of its authenticity, all I could bring myself to believe was, that the learned doctors would have been better placed in a madhouse than they were in the college.

I was more affected by another publication, because it came from a man for whom I always had an esteem, and whose constancy I admired, though I pitied his blindness. I mean the mandatory letter against me by the archbishop of Paris. I thought to return an answer to it was a duty I owed myself. This I felt I could do without derogating from my dignity; the case was something similar to that of the King of Poland. I have always detested brutal disputes, after the manner of Voltaire. I never combat but with dignity, and before I deign to defend myself I must be certain that

he by whom I am attacked will not dishonor my re-
tort. I had no doubt but this letter was fabricated by
the Jesuits, and although they were at that time in
distress, I discovered in it their old principle of crushing the wretched. I was therefore at liberty to follow
my ancient maxim, by honoring the titulary author,
and refuting the work, which I think I did completely.

I found my residence at Motiers very agreeable,
and nothing was wanting to determine me to end my
days there, but a certainty of the means of subsistence.
Living is dear in that neighborhood, and all my old
projects had been overturned by the dissolution of my
household arrangements at Montmorency, the establishment of others, the sale or squandering of my furniture, and the expenses incurred since my departure.
The little capital which remained to me daily diminished. Two or three years were sufficient to consume
the remainder without my having the means of renewing it, except by again engaging in literary pursuits: a pernicious profession which I had already
abandoned. Persuaded that everything which concerned me would change, and that the public, recovered from its frenzy, would make my persecutors
blush, all my endeavors tended to prolong my resources until this happy revolution should take place,
after which I should more at my ease choose a resource
from amongst those which might offer themselves.
To this effect I took up my Dictionary of Music, which
ten years' labor had so far advanced as to leave noth-

ing wanting to it but the last corrections. My books, which I had lately received, enabled me to finish this work; my papers sent me by the same conveyance, furnished me with the means of beginning my memoirs to which I was determined to give my whole attention. I began by transcribing the letters into a book, by which my memory might be guided in the order of facts and time. I had already selected those I intended to keep for this purpose, and for ten years the series was not interrupted. However, in preparing them for copying I found an interruption at which I was surprised. This was for almost six months, from October, 1756, to March following. I recollected having put into my selection a number of letters from Diderot, De Leyre, Madam d'Epinay, Madam de Chenonceaux, etc., which filled up the void and were missing. What was become of them? Had any persons laid their hands upon my papers whilst they remained in the Hotel de Luxembourg? This was not conceivable, and I had seen M. de Luxembourg take the key of the chamber in which I had deposited them. Many letters from different ladies, and all those from Diderot, were without date, on which account I had been under the necessity of dating them from memory before they could be put in order, and thinking I might have committed errors, I again looked them over for the purpose of seeing whether or not I could find those which ought to fill up the void. This experiment did not succeed. I perceived the vacancy to be real, and that the letters had certainly been taken away. By whom and for what purpose? This was what I could not comprehend. These letters, written prior to my great quarrels, and at the time of my first enthusiasm in the composition of *Héloïse,* could not be interesting to any person. They containing nothing more than cavilings by Diderot, jeerings from De Leyre, assurances of friendship from M. de Chenonceaux, and even Madam d'Epinay, with whom I was then upon the best of terms. To whom were these letters of consequence? To what use were they to be put? It was not until seven years afterwards that I suspected the nature of the theft. The deficiency being no longer doubtful, I looked over my rough drafts to see whether or not it was the only one. I found several, which on account of the badness of my memory, made me suppose others in the multitude of my papers. Those I remarked were that of the *Morale Sensitive,* and the extract of the adventures of Lord Edward. The last, I confess, made me suspect Madam de Luxembourg.

La Roche, her valet de chambre, had sent me the papers, and I could think of nobody but herself to whom this fragment could be of consequence; but what concern could the other give her, any more than the rest of the letters missing, with which, even with evil intentions, nothing to my prejudice could be done, unless they were falsified? As for the maréchal, with whose real friendship for me, and invariable integrity, I was perfectly acquainted, I never could suspect him for a moment. The most reasonable supposition, after long tormenting my mind in endeavoring to discover the author of the theft, that which imputed it to D'Alembert, who, having thrust himself into the company of Madam de Luxembourg, might have found means to turn over these papers, and take from amongst them such manuscripts and letters as he might have thought proper, either for the purpose of endeavoring to embroil me with the writer of them, or to appropriate those he should find useful to his own private purposes. I imagined that, deceived by the title of *Morale Sensitive*, he might have supposed it to be the plan of a real treatise upon materialism, with which he would have armed himself against me in a manner easy to be imagined. Certain that he would soon be undeceived by reading the sketch, and determined to quit all literary pursuits, these larcenies gave me but little concern. They besides were not the first the same hand had committed * upon me without having complained of these pilferings. In a very little time I thought no more of the trick that had been played me than if nothing had happened, and began to collect the materials I had left for the purpose of undertaking my projected confessions.

I had long thought the company of ministers, or

* *I had found in his Elemens de Musique (Elements of Music) several things taken from what I had written for the Encyclopedie, and which were given to him several years before the publication of his elements. I know not what he may have had to do with a book entitled Dictionaire des Beaux Arts (Dictionary of the Fine Arts), but I found in it articles transcribed word for word from mine, and this long before the same articles were printed in the Encyclopedie.*

at least the citizens and burgesses of Geneva, would remonstrate against the infraction of the edict in the decree made against me. Everything remained quiet, at least to all exterior appearance; for discontent was general, and ready, on the first opportunity, openly to manifest itself. My friends, or persons calling themselves such, wrote letter after letter exhorting me to come and put myself at their head, assuring me of public separation from the council. The fear of the disturbance and troubles which might be caused by my presence, prevented me from acquiescing with their desires, and, faithful to the oath I had formerly made, never to take the least part in any civil dissension in my country, I chose rather to let the offense remain as it was, and banish myself forever from the country, than to return to it by means which were violent and dangerous. It is true, I expected the burgesses would make legal remonstrances against an infraction in which their interests were deeply concerned; but no such steps were taken. They who conducted the body of citizens sought less the real redress of grievances than an opportunity to render themselves necessary. They caballed but were silent, and suffered me to be bespattered by the gossips and hypocrites set on to render me odious in the eyes of the populace, and pass upon them their boistering for a zeal in favor of religion.

After having, during a whole year, vainly expected that some one would remonstrate against an illegal proceeding, and seeing myself abandoned by my fellow-citizens, I determined to renounce my ungrateful country in which I never had lived, from which I had not received either inheritance or services, and by which, in return for the honor I had endeavored to do it, I saw myself so unworthily treated by unanimous consent, since they, who should have spoken, had remained silent. I therefore wrote to the first syndic for that year, to Mr. Favre, if I remember right, a letter in which I solemnly gave up my freedom of the city of Geneva, carefully observing in it, however, that decency and moderation, from which I have never departed in the acts of haughtiness which, in my misfortunes, the cruelty of my enemies have frequently forced from me.

This step opened the eyes of the citizens, who feeling they had neglected their own interests by abandoning my defense, took my part when it was too late. They had wrongs of their own which they joined to mine, and made these the subject of several well-reasoned representations, which they strengthened and extended, as the refusal of the council, supported by the ministry of France, made them more clearly perceive the project formed to impose on them a yoke. These altercations produced several pamphlets which were undecisive, until that appeared entitled *Lettres écrites de la Campagne,** a work written in favor of the council, with infinite art, and by which the remonstrating party, reduced to silence, was crushed for a time. This production, a lasting monument of

* *Letters written from the Country.*

the rare talents of its author, came from the Attorney-General Tronchin, a man of wit and an enlightened understanding, well versed in the laws and government of the republic. *Siluit terra.*

The remonstrators, recovered from their first overthrow, undertook to give an answer, and in time produced one which brought them off tolerably well. But they all looked to me, as the only person capable of combating a like adversary with hope of success. I confess I was of their opinion, and excited by my former fellow-citizens, who thought it was my duty to aid them with my pen, as I had been the cause of their embarrassment, I undertook to refute the *Lettres écrites de la Campagne,* and parodied the title of them by that of *Lettres écrites de la Montagne,** which I gave to mine. I wrote this answer so secretly, that at a meeting I had at Thonon, with the chiefs of the malcontents to talk of their affairs, and where they showed me a sketch of their answer, I said not a word of mine, which was quite ready, fearing obstacles might arise relative to the impression of it, should the magistrate or my enemies hear of what I had done. This work was, however, known in France before the publication; but government chose rather to let it appear, than to suffer me to guess at the means by which my secret had been discovered. Concerning this I will state what I know, which is but trifling: what I have conjectured shall remain with myself.

I received, at Motiers, almost as many visits as at

* *Letters written from the Mountain.*

the Hermitage and Montmorency; but these, for the most part, were a different kind. They who had formerly come to see me were people who, having taste, talents, and principles, something similar to mine, alleged them as the causes of their visits, and introduced subjects on which I could converse. At Motiers the case was different, especially with the visitors who came from France. They were officers, or other persons who had no taste for literature, nor had many of them read my works, although, according to their own accounts, they had traveled thirty, forty, sixty, and even a hundred leagues to come and see me, and admire the illustrious man, the very celebrated, the great man, etc. For from the time of my settling at Motiers, I received the most impudent flattery, from which the esteem of those with whom I associated had formerly sheltered me. As but few of my new visitors deigned to tell me who or what they were, and as they had neither read nor cast their eye over my works, nor had their researches and mine been directed to the same objects, I knew not what to speak to them upon: I waited for what they had to say, because it was for them to know and tell me the purpose of their visit. It will naturally be imagined this did not produce conversations very interesting to me, although they, perhaps, were so to my visitors, according to the information they might wish to acquire; for as I was without suspicion, I answered, without reserve, to every question they thought proper to ask me, and they commonly went away as well informed as my-self of the particulars of my situation.

I was, for example, visited in this manner by M. de Feins, equerry to the queen, and captain of cavalry, who had the patience to pass several days at Motiers, and to follow me on foot even to La Ferrière, leading his horse by the bridle, without having with me any point of union, except our acquaintance with Made-moiselle Fel, and that we both played at *bilboquet*.*

Before this I had received another visit much more extraordinary. Two men arrived on foot, each leading a mule loaded with his little baggage, lodging at the inn, taking care of their mules and asking to see me. By the equipage of these muleteers they were taken for smugglers, and the news that smugglers were come to see me was instantly spread. Their manner of addressing me sufficiently showed they were persons of another description; but without being smugglers they might be adventurers, and this doubt kept me for some time on my guard. They soon removed my apprehensions. One was M. de Montauban, who had the title of Comte de la Tour-du-Pin, gentleman to the dauphin; the other, M. Dastier de Carpentras, an old officer, who had his cross of St. Louis in his pocket, because he could not display it. These gentlemen, both very amiable, were men of sense, and their man-ner of traveling, so much to my own taste, and but little like that of French gentlemen, in some measure, gained them my attachment, which an intercourse

* *A kind of cup and ball.*

with them served to improve. Our acquaintance did not end with the visit; it is still kept up, and they have since been several times to see me, not on foot, that was very well for the first time; but the more I have seen of these gentlemen the less similarity have I found between their taste and mine; I have not discovered their maxims to be such as I have ever observed, that my writings are familiar to them, or that there is any real sympathy between them and myself. What, therefore, did they want with me? Why came they to see me with such an equipage? Why repeat their visit? Why were they so desirous of having me for their host? I did not at the time propose to myself these questions; but they have sometimes occurred to me since.

Won by their advances, my heart abandoned itself without reserve, especially to M. Dastier, with whose open countenance I was more particularly pleased. I even corresponded with him, and when I determined to print the Letters from the Mountain, I thought of addressing myself to him, to deceive those by whom my packet was waited for upon the road to Holland. He had spoken to me a good deal, and perhaps purposely, upon the liberty of the press at Avignon; he offered me his services should I have anything to print there: I took advantage of the offer and sent him successively by the post my first sheets. After having kept these for some time, he sent them back to me, "Because," said he, "no bookseller dared to undertake them;" and I was obliged to have recourse to Rey, taking care to send my papers, one after the other, and not to part with those which succeeded until I had advice of the reception of those already sent. Before the work was published, I found it had been seen in the office of the ministers, and D'Escherny, of Neuchâtel, spoke to me of a book, entitled, *De l'Homme de la Montagne,** which D'Holbach had told him was by me. I assured him, and it was true, that I never had written a book which bore that title. When the letters appeared he became furious, and accused me of falsehood, although I had told him truth. By this means I was certain my manuscript had been read; as I could not doubt the fidelity of Rey, the most rational conjecture seemed to be, that my packets had been opened at the post-house.

Another acquaintance I made much about the same time, but which was begun by letters, was that with M. Laliaud of Nimes, who wrote to me from Paris, begging I would send him my profile; he said he was in want of it for my bust in marble, which Le Moine was making for him to be placed in his library. If this was a pretense invented to deceive me, it fully succeeded. I imagined that a man who wished to have my bust in marble in his library had his head full of my works, consequently of my principles, and that he loved me because his mind was in unison with mine. It was natural this idea should seduce me. I have since seen M. Laliaud. I found him very ready to render me many trifling services, and to concern himself in

* *Of the Man of the Mountain.*

my little affairs, but I have my doubts of his having, in the few books he ever read, fallen upon any one of those I have written. I do not know that he has a library, or that such a thing is of any use to him; and for the bust he has a bad figure in plaster, by Le Moine, from which has been engraved a hideous portrait that bears my name, as if it bore to me some resemblance.

The only Frenchman who seemed to come to see me, on account of my sentiments, and his taste for my works, was a young officer of the regiment of Limousin, named Séguier de St. Brisson. He made a figure in Paris, where he still perhaps distinguishes himself by his pleasing talents and wit. He came once to Montmorency, the winter which preceded my catastrophe. I was pleased with his vivacity. He afterwards wrote to me at Motiers, and whether he wished to flatter me, or that his head was turned with *Emile,* he informed me he was about to quit the service to live independently, and had begun to learn the trade of a carpenter. He had an elder brother, a captain in the same regiment, the favorite of the mother, who, a devotee to excess, and directed by I know not what hypocrite, did not treat the youngest son well, accusing him of irreligion, and what was still worse, of the unpardonable crime of being connected with me. These were the grievances, on account of which he was determined to break with his mother, and adopt the manner of life of which I have just spoken, all to play the part of the young *Emile.* Alarmed at this petulance, I immediately wrote to him, endeavoring to make him change his resolution, and my exhortations were as strong as I could make them. They had their effect. He returned to his duty, to his mother, and took back the resignation he had given to the colonel, who had been prudent enough to make no use of it, that the young man might have time to reflect upon what he had done. St. Brisson, cured of these follies, was guilty of another less alarming, but, to me, not less disagreeable than the rest: he became an author. He successively published two or three pamphlets which announced a man not devoid of talents, but I have not to reproach myself with having encouraged him by my praises to continue to write.

Some time afterwards he came to see me, and we made together a pilgrimage to the island of St. Pierre. During this journey I found him different from what I saw of him at Montmorency. He had, in his manner, something affected, which at first did not much disgust me, although I have since thought of it to his disadvantage. He once visited me at the hotel de St. Simon, as I passed through Paris on my way to England. I learned there what he had not told me, that he lived in the great world, and often visited Madam de Luxembourg. Whilst I was at Trie, I never heard from him, nor did he so much as make inquiry after me, by means of his relation Mademoiselle Séguier, my neighbor. This lady never seemed favorably disposed towards me. In a word, the infatuation of M. de St. Brisson ended suddenly, like the connection of M.

de Feins: but this man owed me nothing, and the former was under obligations to me, unless the follies I prevented him from committing were nothing more than affectation; which might very possibly be the case.

I had visits from Geneva also. The Delucs, father and son, successively chose me for their attendant in sickness. The father was taken ill on the road, the son was already sick when he left Geneva; they both came to my house. Ministers, relations, hypocrites, and persons of every description came from Geneva and Switzerland, not like those from France, to laugh at and admire me, but to rebuke and catechise me. The only person amongst them, who gave me pleasure, was Moultou, who passed with me three or four days, and whom I wished to retain much longer; the most persevering of all, the most obstinate, and who conquered me by importunity, was a M. d'Ivernois, a merchant at Geneva, a French refugee, and related to the attorney-general of Neuchâtel. This man came from Geneva to Motiers twice a year, on purpose to see me, remained with me several days together from morning to night, accompanied me in my walks, brought me a thousand little presents, insinuated himself in spite of me into my confidence, and intermeddled in all my affairs, notwithstanding there was not between him and myself the least similarity of ideas, inclination, sentiment, or knowledge. I do not believe he ever read a book of any kind throughout, or that he knows upon what subject mine are written.

When I began to herbalize, he followed me in my botanical rambles, without taste for that amusement, or having anything to say to me or I to him. He had the patience to pass with me three days in a public house at Goumoins, whence, by wearying him and making him feel how much he wearied me, I was in hopes of driving him. I could not, however, shake his incredible perseverance, nor by any means discover the motive of it.

Amongst these connections, made and continued by force, I must not omit the only one that was agreeable to me, and in which my heart was really interested: this was that I had with a young Hungarian who came to live at Neuchâtel, and from that place to Motiers, a few months after I had taken up my residence there. He was called by the people of the country the Baron de Sauttern, by which name he had been recommended from Zurich. He was tall, well made, had an agreeable countenance, and mild and social qualities. He told everybody, and gave me also to understand, that he came to Neuchâtel for no other purpose, than that of forming his youth to virtue, by his intercourse with me. His physiognomy, manner, and behavior, seemed well suited to his conversation, and I should have thought I failed in one of the greatest duties had I turned my back upon a young man in whom I perceived nothing but what was amiable, and who sought my acquaintance from so respectable a motive. My heart knows not how to connect itself by halves. He soon acquired my friendship,

and all my confidence, and we were presently inseparable. He accompanied me in all my walks, and became fond of them. I took him to the maréchal, who
received him with the utmost kindness. As he was yet
unable to explain himself in French, he spoke and
wrote to me in Latin, I answered in French, and this
mingling of the two languages did not make our conversations either less smooth or lively. He spoke of his
family, his affairs, his adventures, and of the court of
Vienna, with the domestic details of which he seemed
well acquainted. In fine, during two years which we
passed in the greatest intimacy, I found in him a mildness of character proof against everything, manners
not only polite but elegant, great neatness of person,
an extreme decency in his conversation, in a word, all
the marks of a man born and educated a gentleman,
and which rendered him in my eyes too estimable not
to make him dear to me.

At the time we were upon the most intimate and
friendly terms, D'Ivernois wrote to me from Geneva,
putting me upon my guard against the young Hungarian who had taken up his residence in my neighborhood; telling me he was a spy whom the minister
of France had appointed to watch my proceedings.
This information was of a nature to alarm me the
more, as everybody advised me to guard against the
machinations of persons who were employed to keep
an eye upon my actions, and to entice me into France
for the purpose of betraying me.

To shut the mouths, once for all, of these foolish

advisers, I proposed to Sauttern, without giving him the least intimation of the information I had received, a journey on foot to Pontarlier, to which he consented. As soon as we arrived there I put the letter from D'Ivernois into his hands, and after giving him an ardent embrace, I said: "Sauttern has no need of a proof of my confidence in him, but it is necessary I should prove to the public that I know in whom to place it." This embrace was accompanied with a pleasure which persecutors can neither feel themselves, nor take away from the oppressed.

I will never believe Sauttern was a spy, nor that he betrayed me; but I was deceived by him. When I opened to him my heart without reserve, he constantly kept his own shut, and abused me by lies. He invented I know not what kind of story, to prove to me his presence was necessary in his own country. I exhorted him to return to it as soon as possible. He set off, and when I thought he was in Hungary, I learned he was at Strasbourgh. This was not the first time he had been there. He had caused some disorder in a family in that city; and the husband knowing I received him in my house, wrote to me. I used every effort to bring the young woman back to the paths of virtue, and Sauttern to his duty.

When I thought they were perfectly detached from each other, they renewed their acquaintance, and the husband had the complaisance to receive the young man at his house; from that moment I had nothing more to say. I found the pretended baron had imposed upon me by a great number of lies. His name was not Sauttern, but Sauttersheim. With respect to the title of baron, given him in Switzerland, I could not reproach him with the impropriety, because he had never taken it; but I have not a doubt of his being a gentleman, and the marshal, who knew mankind, and had been in Hungary, always considered and treated him as such.

He had no sooner left my neighborhood, than the girl at the inn where he ate, at Motiers, declared herself with child by him. She was so dirty a creature, and Sauttern, generally esteemed in the country for his conduct and purity of morals, piqued himself so much upon cleanliness, that everybody was shocked at this impudent pretension. The most amiable women of the country, who had vainly displayed to him their charms, were furious: I myself was almost choked with indignation. I used every effort to get the tongue of this impudent woman stopped, offering to pay all expenses, and to give security for Sauttersheim. I wrote to him in the fullest persuasion, not only that this pregnancy could not relate to him, but it was feigned, and the whole a machination of his enemies and mine. I wished him to return and confound the strumpet, and those by whom she was dictated to. The pusillanimity of his answer surprised me. He wrote to the master of the parish to which the creature belonged, and endeavored to stifle the matter. Perceiving this, I concerned myself no more about it, but I was astonished that a man who could stoop so low should have been sufficiently master of himself to deceive me by his reserve in the closest familiarity.

From Strasbourgh, Sauttersheim went to seek his fortune in Paris, and found there nothing but misery. He wrote to me, acknowledging his error. My compassion was excited by the recollection of our former friendship, and I sent him a sum of money. The year following, as I passed through Paris, I saw him much in the same situation; but he was the intimate friend of M. de Laliaud, and I could not learn by what means he had formed this acquaintance, or whether it was recent or of long standing. Two years afterwards Sauttersheim returned to Strasbourgh, whence he wrote to me and where he died. This, in a few words, is the history of our connection, and what I know of his adventures; but while I mourn the fate of the unhappy young man, I still, and ever shall, believe he was the son of people of distinction, and that the impropriety of his conduct was the effect of the situations to which he was reduced.

Such were the connections and acquaintance I acquired at Motiers. How many of these would have been necessary to compensate the cruel losses I suffered at the same time!

The first of these was that of M. de Luxembourg, who, after having been long tormented by the physicians, at length became their victim, by being treated for the gout, which they would not acknowledge him to have, as for a disorder they thought they could cure.

According to what La Roche, the confidential

servant of Madam de Luxembourg, wrote to me relative to what had happened, it is by this cruel and memorable example that the miseries of greatness are to be deplored.

The loss of this good nobleman afflicted me the more, as he was the only real friend I had in France, and the mildness of his character was such as to make me quite forget his rank, and attach myself to him as my equal. Our connection was not broken off on account of my having quitted the kingdom; he continued to write to me as usual.

I nevertheless thought I perceived that absence, or my misfortune, had cooled his affection for me. It is difficult to a courtier to preserve the same attachment to a person whom he knows to be in disgrace with courts. I moreover suspected the great ascendancy Madam de Luxembourg had over his mind, had been unfavorable to me, and that she had taken advantage of our separation to injure me in his esteem. For her part, notwithstanding a few affected marks of regard, which daily became less frequent, she less concealed the change in her friendship. She wrote to me four or five times into Switzerland, after which she never wrote to me again, and nothing but my prejudice, confidence, and blindness, could have prevented my discovering in her something more than a coolness towards me.

Guy the bookseller, partner with Duchesne, who, after I had left Montmorency, frequently went to the hotel de Luxembourg, wrote to me that my name was in the will of the maréchal. There was nothing in this either incredible or extraordinary, on which account I had no doubt of the truth of the information. I deliberated within myself whether or not I should receive the legacy. Everything well considered, I determined to accept it, whatever it might be, and to do that honor to the memory of an honest man, who, in a rank in which friendship is seldom found, had had a real one for me. I had not this duty to fulfill. I heard no more of the legacy, whether it were true or false; and in truth I should have felt some pain in offending against one of the great maxims of my system of morality, in profiting by anything at the death of a person whom I had once held dear. During the last illness of our friend Mussard, Leneips proposed to me to take advantage of the grateful sense he expressed for our cares, to insinuate to him dispositions in our favor. "Ah! my dear Leneips," said I, "let us not pollute by interested ideas the sad but sacred duties we discharge towards our dying friend. I hope my name will never be found in the testament of any person, at least not in that of a friend." It was about this time that my lord marshal spoke to me of his, of what he intended to do in it for me, and that I made him the answer of which I have spoken in the first part of my memoirs.

My second loss, still more afflicting and irreparable, was that of the best of women and mothers, who, already weighed down with years, and overburthened with infirmities and misery, quitted this vale of tears for the abode of the blessed, where the amiable remembrance of the good we have done here below is the eternal reward of our benevolence. Go, gentle and beneficient shade, to those of Fenelon, Bernex, Catinat, and others, who in a more humble state have, like them, opened their hearts to true charity; go and taste of the fruit of your own benevolence, and prepare for your son the place he hopes to fill by your side. Happy in your misfortunes that Heaven, in putting to them a period, has spared you the cruel spectacle of his! Fearing, lest I should fill her heart with sorrow by the recital of my first disasters, I had not written to her since my arrival in Switzerland; but I wrote to M. de Conzié, to inquire after her situation, and it was from him I learned she had ceased to alleviate the sufferings of the afflicted, and that her own were at an end. I myself shall not suffer long; but if I thought I should not see her again in the life to come, my feeble imagination would less delight in the idea of the perfect happiness which I there hope to enjoy.

My third and last loss, for since that time I have not had a friend to lose, was that of the lord marshal. He did not die, but tired of serving the ungrateful, he left Neuchâtel, and I have never seen him since. He still lives, and will, I hope, survive me: he is alive, and thanks to him, all my attachments on earth are not destroyed. There is one man still worthy of my friendship; for the real value of this consists more in what we feel than in that which we inspire; but I have lost the pleasure I enjoyed in his, and can rank him in the number of those only whom I love, but with whom I am no longer connected. He went to England to receive the pardon of the king, and acquired the possession of the property which formerly had been confiscated. We did not separate without an intention of again being united, the idea of which seemed to give him as much pleasure as I received from it. He determined to reside at Keith Hall, near Aberdeen, and I was to join him as soon as he was settled there: but this project was too flattering to my hopes to give me any of its success. He did not remain in Scotland. The affectionate solicitations of the King of Prussia induced him to return to Berlin, and the reason of my not going to him there will presently appear.

Before this departure, foreseeing the storm which my enemies began to raise against me, he of his own accord sent me letters of naturalization, which seemed to be a certain means of preventing me from being driven from the country. The community of the Convent of Val de Travers followed the example of the governor, and gave me letters of *Communion,* gratis, as they were the first. Thus, in every respect, become a citizen, I was sheltered from legal expulsion, even by the prince; but it has never been by legitimate means, that the man who, of all others, has shown the greatest respect for the laws, has been persecuted. I do not think I ought to enumerate, amongst the number of my losses at this time, that of the Abbé Mably. Having lived some time at the house of his mother, I have been acquainted with the abbé, but not very intimately, and I have reason to believe the nature of his sentiments with respect to me changed after I required a greater celebrity than he already had. But the first time I discovered his insincerity was immediately after the publication of the *Letters from the Mountain*. A letter attributed to him, addressed to Madam Saladin, was handed about in Geneva, in which he spoke of this work as the seditious clamors of a furious demagogue.

The esteem I had for the Abbé Mably, and my great opinion of his understanding, did not permit me to believe this extravagant letter was written by him. I acted in this business with my usual candor. I sent him a copy of the letter, informing him he was said to be the author of it. He returned me no answer. This silence astonished me: but what was my surprise when by a letter I received from Madam de Chenonceaux, I learned the abbé was really the author of that which was attributed to him, and found himself greatly embarrassed by mine. For even supposing for a moment that what he stated was true, how could he justify so public an attack, wantonly made, without obligation or necessity, for the sole purpose of overwhelming, in the midst of his greatest misfortunes, a man to whom he had shown himself a well-wisher, and who had not done anything that could excite his enmity? In a short time afterwards the Dialogues of Phocion, in which I perceived nothing but a compilation, without shame or restraint, from my writings, made their appearance.

In reading this book I perceived the author had not the least regard for me, and that in future I must number him among my most bitter enemies. I do not believe he has ever pardoned me for the Social Contract, far superior to his abilities, or the Perpetual Peace; and I am, besides, of opinion that the desire he expressed that I should make an extract from the Abbé de St. Pierre, proceeded from a supposition in him that I should not acquit myself of it so well.

The further I advanced in my narrative, the less order I feel myself capable of observing. The agitation of the rest of my life has deranged in my ideas the succession of events. These are too numerous, confused, and disagreeable to be recited in due order. The only strong impression they have left upon my mind is that of the horrid mystery by which the cause of them is concealed, and of the deplorable state to which they have reduced me. My narrative will in future be irregular, and according to the events which, without order, may occur to my recollection. I remember about the time to which I refer, full of the idea of my confessions, I very imprudently spoke of them to everybody, never imagining it could be the wish or interest, much less within the power of any person whatsoever, to throw an obstacle in the way of this undertaking, and had I suspected it, even this would not have rendered me more discreet, as from the nature of my disposition it is totally impossible for me to conceal either my thoughts or feelings. The knowledge of this enterprise was, as far as I can judge, the cause of the storm that was raised to drive me from Switzerland, and deliver me into the hands of those by whom I might be prevented from executing it.

I had another project in contemplation which was not looked upon with a more favorable eye by those who were afraid of the first: this was a general edition of my works. I thought this edition of them necessary to ascertain what books, amongst those to which my name was affixed, were really written by me, and to furnish the public with the means of distinguishing them from the writings falsely attributed to me by my enemies, to bring me to dishonor and contempt. This was besides a simple and an honorable means of insuring to myself a livelihood, and the only one that remained to me. As I had renounced the profession of an author, my memoirs not being of a nature to appear during my lifetime; and as I no longer gained a farthing in any manner whatsoever, and constantly lived at a certain expense, I saw the end of my resources in that of the produce of the last things I had written. This reason had induced me to hasten the finishing of my Dictionary of Music, which still was incomplete. I had received for it a hundred louis and a life annuity of three hundred livres; but a hundred louis could not last long in the hands of a man who annually expended upwards of sixty, and three hundred livres a year was but a trifling sum to one upon whom parasites and beggarly visitors lighted like a swarm of flies.

A company of merchants from Neuchâtel came to

undertake the general edition, and a printer or book-seller of the name of Reguillat, from Lyons, thrust himself, I know not by what means, amongst them to direct it. The agreement was made upon reasonable terms, and sufficient to accomplish my object. I had in print and manuscript, matter for six volumes in quarto. I moreover agreed to give my assistance in bringing out the edition. The merchants were, on their part, to pay me a thousand crowns down, and to assign me an annuity of sixteen hundred livres for life.

The agreement was concluded but not signed, when the Letters from the Mountain appeared. The terrible explosion caused by this infernal work, and its abominable author, terrified the company, and the under-taking was at an end.

I would compare the effect of this last production to that of the letter on French Music, had not that letter, while it brought upon me hatred, and exposed me to danger, acquired me respect and esteem. But after the appearance of the last work, it was matter of astonishment at Geneva and Versailles, that such a monster as the author of it should be suffered to exist. The little council, excited by Resident de France, and directed by the attorney-general, made a declaration against my work, by which, in the most severe terms, it was de-clared to be unworthy of being burned by the hands of the hangman, adding, with an address which bor-dered upon the burlesque, there was no possibility of speaking of or answering it without dishonor. I would here transcribe the curious piece of composition, but unfortunately I have it not by me. I ardently wish some of my readers, animated by the zeal of truth and equity, would read over the Letters from the Mountain: they will, I dare hope, feel the stoical moderation which reigns throughout the whole, after all the cruel outrages with which the author was loaded. But unable to answer the abuse, because no part of it could be called by that name, nor to the reasons because these were unanswerable, my enemies pretended to appear too much enraged to reply: and it is true, if they took the invincible arguments it contains for abuse, they must have felt themselves roughly treated.

The remonstrating party, far from complaining of the odious declaration, acted according to the spirit of it, and instead of making a trophy of the Letters from the Mountain, which they veiled to make them serve as a shield, were pusillanimous enough not to do justice or honor to that work, written to defend them, and at their own solicitation. They did not either quote or mention the letters, although they tacitly drew from them all their arguments, and by exactly following the advice with which they conclude, made them the sole cause of their safety and triumph. They had imposed on me this duty: I had fulfilled it, and unto the end had served their cause and the country. I begged of them to abandon me, and in their quarrels to think of nobody but themselves. They took me at my word, and I concerned myself no more about their affairs, further than constantly to exhort them to peace, not doubting, should they continue to be obstinate, of their being crushed by France; this however did not happen; I know the reason why it did not, but this is not the place to explain what I mean.

The effect produced at Neuchâtel by the Letters from the Mountain was at first very mild. I sent a copy of them to M. de Montmollin, who received it favorably, and read it without making any objection. He was ill as well as myself; as soon as he recovered he came in a friendly manner to see me, and conversed on general subjects. A rumor was however begun: the book was burned I know not where. From Geneva, Berne, and perhaps from Versailles, the effervescence quickly passed to Neuchâtel, and especially to Val de Travers, where, before even the ministers had taken any apparent steps, an attempt was secretly made to stir up the people. I ought, I dare assert, to have been beloved by the people of that country in which I have lived, giving alms in abundance, not leaving about me an indigent person without assistance, never refusing to do any service in my power, and which was consistent with justice, making myself perhaps too familiar with everybody, and avoiding, as far as it was possible for me to do it, all distinction which might excite the least jealousy. This, however, did not prevent the populace, secretly stirred up against me by I know not whom, from being by degrees irritated against me, even to fury, nor from publicly insulting me, not only in the country and upon the road, but in the street. Those to whom I had rendered the greatest services became most irritated against me, and even people who still continued to receive my benefactions, not daring to appear, excited others, and seemed to wish thus to be revenged of me for their humiliation, by the obligations they were under for the favors I had conferred upon them. Montmollin seemed to pay no attention to what was passing, and did not yet come forward. But as the time of communion approached, he came to advise me not to present myself at the holy table, assuring me, however, he was not my enemy, and that he would leave me undisturbed. I found this compliment whimsical enough; it brought to my recollection the letter from Madam de Boufflers, and I could not conceive to whom it could be a matter of such importance whether I communicated or not. Considering this condescension on my part as an act of cowardice, and moreover, being unwilling to give to the people a new pretense under which they might charge me with impiety, I refused the request of the minister, and he went away dissatisfied, giving me to understand I should repent of my obstinacy.

He could not of his own authority forbid me the communion: that of the Consistory, by which I had been admitted to it, was necessary, and as long as there was no objection from that body I might present myself without the fear of being refused. Montmollin procured from the *Classe* (the ministers) a commission to summon me to the Consistory, there to give an account of the articles of my faith, and to excommunicate me should I refuse to comply. This excommunication could not be pronounced without the aid of the Consistory also, and a majority of the voices. But the peasants, who under the appellation of elders, composed this assembly, presided over and governed by their minister, might naturally be expected to adopt his opinion, especially in matters of the clergy, which they still less understood than he did. I was therefore summoned, and I resolved to appear.

What a happy circumstance and triumph would this have been to me could I have spoken, and had I, if I may so speak, had my pen in my mouth! With what superiority, with what facility even, should I have overthrown this poor minister in the midst of his six peasants! The thirst after power having made the Protestant clergy forget all the principles of the reformation, all I had to do to recall these to their recollection and reduce them to silence, was to make comments upon my first Letters from the Mountain, upon which they had the folly to animadvert.

My text was ready, and I had only to enlarge on it, and my adversary was confounded. I should not have been weak enough to remain on the defensive; it was easy to me to become an assailant without his even perceiving it, or being able to shelter himself from my attack. The contemptible priests of the *Classe,* equally careless and ignorant, had of themselves placed me in the most favorable situation I could desire to crush them at pleasure. But what of this? It was necessary I should speak without hesitation, and find ideas, turn of expression, and words at will, preserving a presence of mind, and keeping myself collected, without once suffering even a momentary confusion. For what could I hope, feeling, as I did, my want of aptitude to express myself with ease? I had been reduced to the most mortifying silence at Geneva, before an assembly which was favorable to me, and previously resolved to approve of everything I should say. Here, on the contrary, I had to do with a caviller who, substituting cunning to knowledge, would spread for me a hundred snares before I could perceive one of them, and was resolutely determined to catch me in an error let the consequence be what it would. The more I examined the situation in which I stood, the greater danger I perceived myself exposed to, and feeling the impossibility of successfully withdrawing from it, I thought of another expedient. I meditated a discourse which I intended to pronounce before the Consistory, to exempt myself from the necessity of answering. The thing was easy. I wrote the discourse and began to learn it by memory, with an inconceivable ardor. Thérèsa laughed at hearing me mutter and incessantly repeat the same phrases, while endeavoring to cram them into my head. I hoped, at length, to remember what I had written: I knew the chatelain, as an officer attached to the service of the prince, would be present at the Consistory, and that notwithstanding the maneuvers and bottles of Montmollin, most of the elders were well disposed towards me. I had, moreover, in my favor, reason, truth, and justice, with the protection of the king, the authority of the council of state, and the good wishes of every real patriot, to whom the establishment of this inquisition was threatening. In fine, everything contributed to encourage me.

On the eve of the day appointed, I had my discourse by rote, and recited it without missing a word. I had it in my head all night: in the morning I had forgotten it. I hesitated at every word, thought myself before the assembly, became confused, stammered, and lost my presence of mind. In fine, when the time to make my appearance was almost at hand, my courage totally failed me. I remained at home and wrote to the Consistory, hastily stating my reasons, and pleaded my disorder, which really, in the state to which apprehension had reduced me, would scarcely have permitted me to stay out the whole sitting.

The minister, embarrassed by my letter, adjourned the Consistory. In the interval, he, of himself, and by his creatures, made a thousand efforts to seduce the elders, who, following the dictates of their consciences, rather than those they received from him, did not vote according to his wishes, or those of the class. Whatever power his arguments drawn from his cellar might have over these kind of people, he could not gain one of them, more than the two or three who were already devoted to his will, and who were called his *ames damnées*.* The officer of the prince, and the Colonel Pury, who, in this affair, acted with great zeal, kept

* *Damned Souls.*

the rest to their duty, and when Montmollin wished to proceed to excommunication, his Consistory, by a majority of voices, flatly refused to authorize him to do it. Thus reduced to the last expedient, that of stirring up the people against me, he, his colleagues, and other persons, set about it openly, and were so successful, that notwithstanding the strong and frequent rescripts of the king, and the orders of the council of state, I was at length obliged to quit the country, that I might not expose the officer of the king to be himself assassinated while he protected me.

The recollection of the whole of this affair is so confused, that it is impossible for me to reduce to or connect the circumstances of it. I remember a kind of negotiation had been entered into with the class, in which Montmollin was the mediator. He feigned to believe it was feared I should, by my writings, disturb the peace of the country, in which case, the liberty I had of writing would be blamed. He had given me to understand that if I consented to lay down my pen, what was past would be forgotten. I had already entered into this engagement with myself, and did not hesitate in doing it with the class, but conditionally and solely in matters of religion. He found means to have a duplicate of the agreement upon some change necessary to be made in it, the condition having been rejected by the class; I demanded back the writing, which was returned to me, but he kept the duplicate, pretending it was lost. After this, the people, openly excited by the ministers, laughed at the rescripts of the king, and the orders of the council of state, and shook off all restraint. I was declaimed against from the pulpit, called antichrist, and pursued in the country like a mad wolf. My Armenian dress discovered me to the populace; of this I felt the cruel inconvenience, but to quit it in such circumstances, appeared to me an act of cowardice. I could not prevail upon myself to do it, and I quietly walked through the country with my caffetan and fur bonnet in the midst of the hootings of the dregs of the people, and sometimes through a shower of stones. Several times as I passed before houses, I heard those by whom they were inhabited call out: "Bring me my gun, that I may fire at him." As I did not on this account hasten my pace, my calmness increased their fury, but they never went further than threats, at least with respect to fire-arms.

During this fermentation I received from two circumstances the most sensible pleasure. The first was my having it in my power to prove my gratitude by means of the lord marshal. The honest part of the inhabitants of Neuchâtel, full of indignation at the treatment I received, and the maneuvers of which I was the victim, held the ministers in execration, clearly perceiving they were obedient to a foreign impulse, and the vile agents of people, who, in making them act, kept themselves concealed; they were moreover afraid my case would have dangerous consequences, and be made a precedent for the purpose of establishing a real inquisition.

The magistrates, and especially M. Meuron, who

had succeeded M. d'Ivernois in the office of attorney-general, made every effort to defend me. Colonel Pury, although a private individual, did more, and succeeded better. It was the colonel who found means to make Montmollin submit in his Consistory, by keeping the elders to their duty. He had credit, and employed it to stop the sedition; but he had nothing more than the authority of the laws, and the aid of justice and reason, to oppose to that of money and wine: the combat was unequal, and in this point Montmollin was triumphant. However, thankful for his zeal and cares, I wished to have it in my power to make him a return of good offices, and in some measure discharge a part of the obligations I was under to him. I knew he was very desirous of being named a counselor of state; but having displeased the court by his conduct in the affair of the minister Petitpierre, he was in disgrace with the prince and governor. I however undertook, at all risks, to write to the lord marshal in his favor: I went so far as even to mention the employment of which he was desirous, and my application was so well received that, contrary to the expectations of his most ardent well wishers, it was almost instantly conferred upon him by the king. In this manner fate, which has constantly raised me to too great an elevation, or plunged me into an abyss of adversity, continued to toss me from one extreme to another, and whilst the populace covered me with mud I was able to make a counselor of state.

The other pleasing circumstance was a visit I received from Madam de Verdelin with her daughter, with whom she had been at the baths of Bourbonne, whence they came to Motiers and stayed with me two or three days. By her attention and cares, she at length conquered my long repugnancy; and my heart, won by her endearing manner, made her a return of all the friendship of which she had long given me proofs. This journey made me extremely sensible of her kindness: my situation rendered the consolations of friendship highly necessary to support me under my sufferings. I was afraid she would be too much affected by the insults I received from the populace, and could have wished to conceal them from her that her feelings might not be hurt, but this was impossible; and although her presence was some check upon the insolent populace in our walks, she saw enough of their brutality to enable her to judge of what passed when I was alone. During the short residence she made at Motiers, I was still attacked in my habitation. One morning her chambermaid found my window blocked up with stones, which had been thrown at it during the night. A very heavy bench placed in the street by the side of the house, and strongly fastened down, was taken up and reared against the door in such a manner as, had it not been perceived from the window, to have knocked down the first person who should have opened the door to go out. Madam de Verdelin was acquainted with everything that passed; for, besides what she herself was witness to, her confidential servant went into many houses in the village, spoke to everybody, and was seen in conversation with Montmollin. She did not, however, seem to pay the least attention to that which happened to me, nor never mentioned Montmollin nor any other person, and answered in a few words to what I said to her of him. Persuaded that a residence in England would be more agreeable to me than any other, she frequently spoke of Mr. Hume, who was then at Paris, of his friendship for me, and the desire he had of being of service to me in his own country. It is time I should say something of Hume.

He had acquired a great reputation in France amongst the Encyclopedists by his essays on commerce and politics, and in the last place by his history of the House of Stuart, the only one of his writings of which I had read a part, in the translation of the Abbé Prévot. For want of being acquainted with his other works, I was persuaded, according to what I heard of him, that Mr. Hume joined a very republican mind to the English paradoxes in favor of luxury. In this opinion I considered his whole apology of Charles I. as a prodigy of impartiality, and I had as great an idea of his virtue as of his genius. The desire of being acquainted with this great man, and of obtaining his friendship, had greatly strengthened the inclination I felt to go to England, induced by the solicitations of Madam de Boufflers, the intimate friend of Hume. After my arrival in Switzerland, I received from him, by means of this lady, a letter extremely flattering; in which, to the highest encomiums on my genius, he subjoined a pressing invitation to induce me to go to England, and the offer of all his interest, and that of his friends, to make my residence there agreeable. I found in the country to which I had retired, the lord marshal, the country-man and friend of Hume, who confirmed my good opinion of him, and from whom I learned a literary anecdote, which did him great honor in the opinion of his lordship and had the same effect in mine. Wallace, who had written against Hume upon the subject of the population of the ancients, was absent whilst his work was in the press. Hume took upon himself to examine the proofs, and to do the needful to the edition. This manner of acting was according to my own way of thinking. I had sold at six sols (three pence) a piece, the copies of a song written against myself. I was, therefore, strongly prejudiced in favor of Hume, when Madam de Verdelin came and mentioned the lively friendship he expressed for me, and his anxiety to do me the honors of England; such was her expression. She pressed me a good deal to take advantage of this zeal and to write to him. As I had not naturally an inclination to England, and did not intend to go there until the last extremity, I refused to write or make any promise; but I left her at liberty to do whatever she should think necessary to keep Mr. Hume favorably disposed towards me. When she went from Motiers, she left me in the persuasion, by every-thing she had said to me of that illustrious man, that he was my friend, and she herself still more his.

After her departure, Montmollin carried on his

maneuvers with more vigor, and the populace threw off all restraint. Yet I still continued to walk quietly amidst the hootings of the vulgar; and a taste for botany, which I had begun to contract with Doctor d'Ivernois, making my rambling more amusing, I went through the country herbalizing, without being affected by the clamors of this scum of the earth, whose fury was still augmented by my calmness. What affected me most was, seeing families of my friends,* or of persons who gave themselves that name, openly join the league of my persecutors; such as the D'Ivernois, without excepting the father and brother of my Isabelle Boy de la Tour, a relation to the friend in whose house I lodged, and Madam Girardier, her sister-in-law. This Peter Boy was such a brute; so stupid, and behaved so uncouthly, that, to prevent my mind from being disturbed, I took the liberty to ridicule him; and, after the manner of the *Petit Prophete,* I wrote a pamphlet of a few pages, entitled, *la Vision de Pierre de la Montagne dit let Voyant,*†

---

* *This fatality had begun with my residence at Yverdon: the banneret Roguin dying a year or two after my departure from that city, the old papa Roguin had the candor to inform me with grief, as he said, that in the papers of his relation, proofs had been found of his having been concerned in the conspiracy to expel me from Yverdon and the state of Berne. This clearly proved the conspiracy not to be, as some persons pretended to believe, an affair of hypocrisy; since the banneret, far from being a devotee, carried materialism and incredulity to intolerance and fanaticism. Besides, nobody at Yverdon had shown me more constant attention, nor had so prodigally bestowed upon me praises and flattery as this banneret. He faithfully followed the favorite plan of my persecutors.*

† *The vision of Peter of the Mountain, called the Seer.*

in which I found means to be diverting enough on the miracles which then served as the great pretext for my persecution. Du Peyrou had this scrap printed at Geneva, but its success in the country was but moderate; the Neuchâtelois, with all their wit, taste but weakly attic salt or pleasantry when these are a little refined.

In the midst of decrees and persecutions, the Genevese had distinguished themselves by setting up a hue and cry with all their might; and my friend Vernes amongst others, with an heroical generosity, chose that moment precisely, to publish against me letters in which he pretended to prove I was not a Christian. These letters, written with an air of self-sufficiency, were not the better for it, although it was positively said the celebrated Bonnet had given them some correction: for this man, although a materialist, has an intolerant orthodoxy the moment I am in question. There certainly was nothing in this work which could tempt me to answer it; but having an opportunity of saying a few words upon it in my Letters from the Mountain, I inserted in them a short note sufficiently expressive of disdain to render Vernes furious. He filled Geneva with his furious exclamations, and D'Ivernois wrote me word he had quite lost his senses. Sometime afterwards appeared an anonymous sheet, which instead of ink seemed to be written with the water of Phelethon. In this letter I was accused of having exposed my children in the streets, of taking about with me a soldier's trull, of being worn out with debaucheries, and other fine things of a like nature. It was not difficult for me to discover the author. My first idea on reading this libel, was to reduce to its real value everything the world calls fame and reputation amongst men; seeing thus a man who was never in a brothel in his life, and whose greatest defect was his being as timid and shy as a virgin, treated as a frequenter of places of that description; and in finding myself charged with being eaten up by the pox. I, who not only never had the least taint of any venereal disease, but, according to the faculty, was so constructed as to make it almost impossible for me to contract it. Everything well considered, I thought I could not better refute this libel than by having it printed in the city in which I longest resided, and with this intention I sent it to Duchesne to print it as it was with an advertisement, in which I named M. Vernes and a few short notes by way of eclaircissement. Not satisfied with printing it only, I sent copies to several persons, and amongst others one copy to the Prince Louis of Wirtemberg, who had made me polite advances, and with whom I was in correspondence. The prince, Du Peyrou, and others, seemed to have their doubts about the author of the libel, and blamed me for having named Vernes upon so slight a foundation. Their remarks produced in me some scruples, and I wrote to Duchesne to suppress the paper. Guy wrote to me he had suppressed it: this may or may not be the case; I have been deceived on so many occasions that there would be nothing extraordinary in my being so on this, and, from the time of which I speak, was so enveloped in profound darkness that it was impossible for me to come at any kind of truth.

M. Vernes bore the imputation with a moderation more than aſtonishing in a man who was supposed not to have deserved it, and after the fury with which he was seized on former occasions. He wrote me two or three letters in very guarded terms with a view, as it appeared to me, to endeavor by my answers to discover how far I was certain of his being the author of the paper, and whether or not I had any proofs againſt him. I wrote him two short answers, severe in the sense, but politely expressed, and with which he was not displeased. To this third letter, perceiving he wished to form with me a kind of correspondence, I returned no answer, and he got D'Ivernois to speak to me. Madam Cramer wrote to Du Peyrou, telling him she was certain the libel was not by Vernes. This however did not make me change my opinion. But as it was possible I might be deceived, and as it is certain that if I were, I owed Vernes an explicit reparation, I sent him word by D'Ivernois that I would make him such a one as he should think proper, provided he would name to me the real author of the libel, or at leaſt prove that he himself was not so. I went further: feeling that, after all, were he not culpable, I had no right to call upon him for proofs of any kind, I ſtated, in a memoir of considerable length, the reasons whence I had inferred my conclusion, and determined to submit them to the judgment of an arbitrator, against whom Vernes could not except. But few people would guess the arbitrator of whom I made choice. I declared at the end of the memoir, that if, after having examined it, and made such inquiries as should seem necessary, the council pronounced M. Vernes not to be the author of the libel, from that moment I should be fully persuaded he was not, and would immediately go and throw myself at his feet, and ask his pardon until I had obtained it. I can say with the greatest truth that my ardent zeal for equity, the uprightness and generosity of my heart, and my confidence in the love of justice innate in every mind, never appeared more fully and perceptible than in this wise and interesting memoir, in which I took, without hesitating, my most implacable enemies for arbitrators between a calumniator and myself. I read to Du Peyrou what I had written: he advised me to suppress it, and I did so. He wished me to wait for the proofs Vernes promised, and I am still waiting for them; he thought it best I should in the meantime be silent, and I held my tongue, and shall do so the rest of my life, censured as I am for having brought against Vernes a heavy imputation, false and unsupported by proof, although I am still fully persuaded, nay, as convinced as I am of my existence, that he is the author of the libel. My memoir is in the hands of Du Peyrou. Should it ever be published my reasons will be found in it, and the heart of Jean-Jacques, with which my contemporaries would not be acquainted, will I hope be known.

I have now to proceed to my catastrophe at Motiers, and to my departure from Val de Travers, after a residence of two years and a half, and an eight months suffering with unshaken constancy of the most unworthy treatment. It is impossible for me clearly to recollect the circumstances of this disagreeable period, but a detail of them will be found in a publication to that effect by Du Peyrou, of which I shall hereafter have occasion to speak.

After the departure of Madam de Verdelin the fermentation increased, and, notwithstanding the reiterated rescripts of the king, the frequent orders of the council of state, and the cares of the chatelain and magistrates of the place, the people, seriously considering me as antichrist, and perceiving all their clamors to be of no effect, seemed at length determined to proceed to violence; stones were already thrown after me in the roads, but I was however in general at too great a distance to receive any harm from them. At last, in the night of the fair of Motiers, which is in the beginning of September, I was attacked in my habitation in such a manner as to endanger the lives of everybody in the house.

At midnight I heard a great noise in the gallery which ran along the back part of the house. A shower of stones thrown against the window and the door which opened to the gallery fell into it with so much noise and violence, that my dog, which usually slept there, and had begun to bark, ceased from fright, and ran into a corner gnawing and scratching the planks to endeavor to make his escape. I immediately rose, and was preparing to go from my chamber into the kitchen, when a stone thrown by a vigorous arm crossed the latter, after having broken the window, forced open the door of my chamber, and fell at my feet, so that had I been a moment sooner upon the floor I should have had the stone against my stomach. I judged the noise had been made to bring me to the door, and the stone thrown to receive me as I went out. I ran into the kitchen, where I found Thérèsa, who also had risen, and was tremblingly making her way to me as fast as she could. We placed ourselves against the wall out of the direction of the window to avoid the stones, and deliberated upon what was best to be done; for going out to call assistance was the certain means of getting ourselves knocked on the head. Fortunately the maid-servant of an old man who lodged under me was waked by the noise, and got up and ran to call the chatelain, whose house was next to mine. He jumped from his bed, put on his robe de chambre, and instantly came to me with the guard, which, on account of the fair, went the round that night, and was just at hand. The chatelain was so alarmed at the sight of the effects of what had happened that he turned pale, and on seeing the stones in the gallery, exclaimed, "Good God! it is a regular quarry!" On examining below stairs, the door of a little court was found to have been forced, and there was an appearance of an attempt having been made to get into the house by the gallery. On inquiring the reason why the guard had neither prevented nor perceived the disturbance, it came out that the guards of Motiers had insisted upon doing duty that night, although it was the turn of those of another village.

The next day the chatelain sent his report to the council of state, which two days afterwards sent an order to inquire into the affair, to promise a reward and secrecy to those who should impeach such as were guilty, and in the meantime to place, at the expense of the king, guards about my house, and that of the chatelain, which joined to it. The day after the disturbance, Colonel Pury, the Attorney-General Meuron, the Chatelain Martinet, the Receiver Guyenet, the Treasurer d'Ivernois and his father, in a word, every person of consequence in the country, came to see me, and united their solicitations to persuade me to yield to the storm, and leave, at least for a time, a place in which I could no longer live in safety nor with honor. I perceived that even the chatelain was frightened at the fury of the people, and apprehending it might extend to himself, would be glad to see me depart as soon as possible, that he might no longer have the trouble of protecting me there, and be able to quit the parish, which he did after my departure. I therefore yielded to their solicitations, and this with but little pain, for the hatred of the people so afflicted my heart that I was no longer able to support it.

I had a choice of places to retire to. After Madam de Verdelin returned to Paris, she had, in several letters, mentioned a Mr. Walpole, whom she called my lord, who, having a strong desire to serve me, proposed to me an asylum at one of his country houses, of the situation of which she gave me the most agreeable description; entering, relative to lodging and subsistence, into a detail which proved she and Lord Walpole had held particular consultations upon the project. My lord marshal had always advised me to go to England or Scotland, and in case of my determing upon the latter, offered me there an asylum. But he offered me another at Potsdam, near to his person, and which tempted me more than all the rest. He had just communicated to me what the king had said to him upon my going there, which was a kind of invitation to me from that monarch, and the Duchess of Saxe-Gotha depended so much upon my taking the journey that she wrote to me, desiring I would go to see her in my way to the court of Prussia, and stay some time before I proceeded farther; but I was so attached to Switzerland that I could not resolve to quit it so long as it was possible for me to live there, and I seized this opportunity to execute a project of which I had for several months conceived the idea, and of which I have deferred speaking, that I might not interrupt my narrative.

This project consisted in going to reside in the island of St. Pierre, an estate belonging to the Hospital of Berne, in the middle of the lake of Bienne. In a pedestrian pilgrimage I had made the preceding year with Du Peyrou we had visited this isle, with which I was so much delighted that I had since that time incessantly thought of the means of making it my place of residence. The greatest obstacle to my wishes arose from the property of the island being vested in the people of Berne, who three years before had driven me from amongst them; and besides the mortification of returning to live with people who had given me so unfavorable a reception, I had reason to fear they would leave me no more peace in the island than they had done at Yverdon. I had consulted the lord marshal upon the subject, who thinking as I did, that the people of Berne would be glad to see me banished to the island, and to keep me there as a hostage for the works I might be tempted to write, had founded their dispositions by means of M. Sturler, his old neighbor at Colombier. M. Sturler addressed himself to the chiefs of the state, and, according to their answer, assured the marshal the Bernois, sorry for their past behavior, wished to see me settled in the island of St. Pierre, and to leave me there at peace. As an additional precaution, before I determined to reside there, I desired the Colonel Chaillet to make new inquiries. He confirmed what I had already heard, and the receiver of the island having obtained from his superiors permission to lodge me in it, I thought I might without danger go to the house, with the tacit consent of the sovereign and the proprietors; for I could not expect the people of Berne would openly acknowledge the injustice they had done me, and thus act contrary to the most inviolable maxim of all sovereigns.

The island of St. Pierre, called at Neuchâtel the island of La Motte, in the middle of the lake of

Bienne, is half a league in circumference; but in this
little space all the chief productions necessary to subsistence are found. The island has fields, meadows,
orchards, woods, and vineyards, and all these, favored
by variegated and mountainous situations, form a distribution of the more agreeable, as the parts, not being
discovered all at once, are seen successively to advantage, and make the island appear greater than it really
is. A very elevated terrace forms the western part of it,
and commands Gleresse and Neuveville. This terrace
is planted with trees which form a long alley, interrupted in the middle by a great saloon, in which, during the vintage, the people from the neighboring
shores assemble and divert themselves. There is but
one house in the whole island, but that is very spacious
and convenient, inhabited by the receiver, and situated
in a hollow by which it is sheltered from the winds.

Five or six hundred paces to the south of the island
of St. Pierre is another island, considerably less than
the former, wild and uncultivated, which appears to
have been detached from the greater isle by storms: its
gravelly soil produces nothing but willows and persi-
caria, but there is in it a high hill well covered with
greensward and very pleasant. The form of the lake
is an almost regular oval. The banks, less rich than
those of the lake of Geneva and Neuchâtel, form a
beautiful decoration, especially towards the western
part, which is well peopled, and edged with vineyards
at the foot of a chain of mountains, something like
those of Cote-Rotie, but which produce not such ex-

cellent wine. The bailiwick of St. Jean, Neuveville, Berne, and Bienne, lie in a line from the south to the north, to the extremity of the lake, the whole interspersed with very agreeable villages.

Such was the asylum I had prepared for myself, and to which I was determined to retire after quitting Val de Travers.* This choice was so agreeable to my peaceful inclinations, and my solitary and indolent disposition, that I consider it as one of the pleasing reveries, of which I became the most passionately fond. I thought I should in that island be more separated from men, more sheltered from their outrages, and sooner forgotten by mankind: in a word, more abandoned to the delightful pleasures of the inaction of a contemplative life. I could have wished to have been confined in it in such a manner as to have had no intercourse with mortals, and I certainly took every measure I could imagine to relieve me from the necessity of troubling my head about them.

The great question was that of subsistence, and by the dearness of provisions, and the difficulty of carriage, this is expensive in the island; the inhabitants are besides at the mercy of the receiver. This difficulty was removed by an arrangement which Du Peyrou

* *It may perhaps be necessary to remark that I left there an enemy in M. du Teneaux, mayor of Verrieres, not much esteemed in the country, but who has a brother, said to be an honest man, in the office of M. de St. Florentin. The mayor had been to see him sometime before my adventure. Little remarks of this kind, though of no consequence in themselves, may lead to the discovery of many underhand dealings.*

made with me, in becoming a substitute to the company which had undertaken and abandoned my general edition. I gave him all the materials necessary, and made the proper arrangement and distribution. To the engagement between us I added that of giving him the memoirs of my life, and made him the general depositary of all my papers, under the express condition of making no use of them until after my death, having it at heart quietly to end my days without doing anything which should again bring me back to the recollection of the public. The life annuity he undertook to pay me was sufficient to my subsistence. My lord marshal having recovered all his property, had offered me twelve hundred livres a year, half of which I accepted. He wished to send me the principal, but this I refused on account of the difficulty of placing it. He then sent the amount to Du Peyrou, in whose hands it remained, and who pays me the annuity according to the terms agreed upon with his lordship. Adding therefore to the result of my agreement with Du Peyrou, the annuity of the marshal, two-thirds of which were reversible to Thérèsa after my death, and the annuity of three hundred livres from Duchesne, I was assured of a genteel subsistence for myself, and after me for Thérèsa, to whom I left seven hundred livres a year, from the annuities paid me by Rey and the lord marshal; I had therefore no longer to fear a want of bread. But it was ordained that honor should oblige me to reject all these resources which fortune and my labors placed within my reach, and that I should die as poor as I had lived. It will be seen whether or not, without reducing myself to the last degree of infamy, I could abide by the engagements which care has always been taken to render ignominious, by depriving me of every other resource to force me to consent to my own dishonor. How was it possible anybody could doubt of the choice I should make in such an alternative? Others have judged of my heart by their own.

My mind at ease relative to subsistence was without care upon every other subject. Although I left in the world the field open to my enemies, there remained in the noble enthusiasm by which my writings were dictated, and in the constant uniformity of my principles, an evidence of the uprightness of my heart, which answered to that deducible from my conduct in favor of my natural disposition. I had no need of any other defense against my calumniators. They might under my name describe another man, but it was impossible they should deceive such as were unwilling to be imposed upon. I could have given them my whole life to animadvert upon, with a certainty, notwithstanding all my faults and weaknesses, and my want of aptitude to support the lightest yoke, of their finding me in every situation a just and good man, without bitterness, hatred, or jealousy, ready to acknowledge my errors, and still more prompt to forget the injuries I received from others; seeking all my happiness in love, friendship, and affection, and in everything carrying my sincerity even to imprudence and the most incredible disinterestedness.

I therefore in some measure took leave of the age in which I lived and my contemporaries, and bade adieu to the world, with an intention to confine myself for the rest of my days to that island; such was my resolution, and it was there I hoped to execute the great project of the indolent life to which I had until then consecrated the little activity with which Heaven had endowed me. The island was to become to me that of Papimanie, that happy country where the inhabitants sleep

*Ou l'on fait plus, ou l'on fait nulle chose.**

This *more* was everything for me, for I never much regretted sleep; indolence is sufficient to my happiness, and provided I do nothing, I had rather dream waking than asleep. Being past the age of romantic projects, and having been more stunned than flattered by the trumpet of fame, my only hope was that of living at ease, and constantly at leisure. This is the life of the blessed in the world to come, and for the rest of mine here below I made it my supreme happiness.

They who reproach me with so many contradictions will not fail here to add another to the number. I have observed the indolence of great companies made them unsupportable to me, and I am now seeking solitude for the sole purpose of abandoning myself to inaction. This however is my disposition; if there be

* *Where they do more: where they do nothing.*

in it a contradiction, it proceeds from nature and not from me; but there is so little that it is precisely on that account that I am always consistent. The indolence of company is burdensome because it is forced. That of solitude is charming because it is free, and depends upon the will. In company I suffer cruelly by inaction, because this is of necessity. I must there remain nailed to my chair, or stand upright like a picket, without stirring hand or foot, not daring to run, jump, sing, exclaim, nor gesticulate when I please, not allowed even to dream, suffering at the same time the fatigue of inaction and all the torment of constraint; obliged to pay attention to every foolish thing uttered, and to all the idle compliments paid, and constantly to keep my mind upon the rack that I may not fail to introduce in my turn my jest or my lie. And this is called idleness! It is the labor of a galley slave.

The indolence I love is not that of a lazy fellow who sits with his arms across in total inaction, and thinks no more than he acts, but that of a child which is incessantly in motion doing nothing, and that of a dotard who wanders from his subject. I love to amuse myself with trifles, by beginning a hundred things and never finishing one of them, by going and coming as I take either into my head, by changing my project at every instant, by following a fly through all its windings, in wishing to overturn a rock to see what is under it, by undertaking with ardor the work of ten years, and abandoning it without regret at the end of ten minutes; finally, in musing from morning until night without order or coherence, and in following in everything the caprice of a moment.

Botany, such as I have always considered it, and of which after my own manner I began to become passionately fond, was precisely an idle study, proper to fill up the void of my leisure, without leaving room for the delirium of imagination or the weariness of total inaction. Carelessly wandering in the woods and the country, mechanically gathering here a flower and there a branch; eating my morsel almost by chance, observing a thousand and a thousand times the same things, and always with the same interest, because I always forgot them, were to me the means of passing an eternity without a weary moment. However elegant, admirable, and variegated the structure of plants may be, it does not strike an ignorant eye sufficiently to fix the attention. The constant analogy, with, at the same time, the prodigious variety which reigns in their conformation, gives pleasure to those only who have already some idea of the vegetable system. Others at the sight of these treasures of nature feel nothing more than a stupid and monotonous admiration. They see nothing in detail because they know not for what to look, nor do they perceive the whole, having no idea of the chain of connection and combinations which overwhelms with its wonders the mind of the observer. I was arrived at that happy point of knowledge, and my want of memory was such as constantly to keep me there, that I knew little enough to make the whole new to me, and yet everything that was necessary to make me sensible of the beauties of all the parts. The different soils into which the island, although little, was divided, offered a sufficient variety of plants, for the study and amusement of my whole life. I was determined not to leave a blade of grass without analyzing it, and I began already to take measures for making, with an immense collection of observations, the *Flora Petrinsularis.*

I sent for Thérèsa, who brought with her my books and effects. We boarded with the receiver of the island. His wife had sisters at Nidau, who by turns came to see her, and were company for Thérèsa. I here made the experiment of the agreeable life which I could have wished to continue to the end of my days, and the pleasure I found in it only served to make me feel to a greater degree the bitterness of that by which it was shortly to be succeeded.

I have ever been passionately fond of water, and the sight of it throws me into a delightful reverie, although frequently without a determinate object.

Immediately after I rose from my bed I never failed, if the weather was fine, to run to the terrace to respire the fresh and salubrious air of the morning, and glide my eye over the horizon of the lake, bounded by banks and mountains, delightful to the view. I know no homage more worthy of the divinity than the silent admiration excited by the contemplation of His works, and which is not externally expressed. I can easily comprehend the reason why the inhabitants of great cities, who see nothing but walls, and streets, have but little faith; but not whence it happens that people in the country, and especially such as live in solitude, can possibly be without it. How comes it to pass that these do not a hundred times a day elevate their minds in ecstasy to the Author of the wonders which strike their senses? For my part, it is especially at rising, wearied by a want of sleep, that long habit inclines me to this elevation which imposes not the fatigue of thinking. But to this effect my eyes must be struck with the ravishing beauties of nature. In my chamber I pray less frequently, and not so fervently; but at the view of a fine landscape I feel myself moved, but by what I am unable to tell. I have somewhere read of a wise bishop who in a visit to his diocese found an old woman whose only prayer consisted in the single interjection "Oh!" "Good mother," said he to her, "continue to pray in this manner; your prayer is better than ours." This better prayer is mine also.

After breakfast, I hastened, with a frown on my brow, to write a few pitiful letters, longing ardently for the moment after which I should have no more to write. I busied myself for a few minutes about my books and papers, to unpack and arrange them, rather than to read what they contained; and this arrangement, which to me became the work of Penelope, gave me the pleasure of musing for a while. I then grew weary, and quitted my books to spend the three or four hours which remained to me of the morning in the study of botany, and especially of the system of

Linnæus, of which I became so passionately fond, that, after having felt how useless my attachment to it was, I yet could not entirely shake it off. This great observer is, in my opinion, the only one who, with Ludwig, has hitherto considered botany as a naturalist and a philosopher; but he has too much studied it in herbals and gardens, and not sufficiently in nature herself. For my part, whose garden was always the whole island, the moment I wanted to make or verify an observation, I ran into the woods or meadows with my book under my arm, and there laid myself upon the ground near the plant in question, to examine it at my ease as it stood. This method was of great service to me in gaining a knowledge of vegetables in their natural state, before they had been cultivated and changed in their nature by the hands of men. Fagon, first physician to Louis XIV., and who named and perfectly knew all the plants in the royal garden, is said to have been so ignorant in the country as not to know how to distinguish the same plants. I am precisely the contrary. I know something of the work of nature, but nothing of that of the gardener.

I gave every afternoon totally up to my indolent and careless disposition, and to following without regularity the impulse of the moment. When the weather was calm, I frequent went immediately after I rose from dinner, and alone got into the boat. The receiver had taught me to row with one oar; I rowed out into the middle of the lake. The moment I withdrew from the bank, I felt a secret joy which almost made me leap, and of which it is impossible for me to tell or even comprehend the cause, if it were not a secret congratulation on my being out of the reach of the wicked. I afterwards rowed about the lake, sometimes approaching the opposite bank, but never touching at it. I often let my boat float at the mercy of the wind and water, abandoning myself to reveries without object, and which were not the less agreeable for their stupidity. I sometimes exclaimed, "O nature! O my mother! I am here under thy guardianship alone; here is no deceitful and cunning mortal to interfere between thee and me." In this manner I withdrew half a league from land; I could have wished the lake had been the ocean. However, to please my poor dog, who was not so fond as I was of such a long stay on the water, I commonly followed one constant course: this was going to land at the little island where I walked an hour or two, or laid myself down on the grass on the summit of the hill, there to satiate myself with the pleasure of admiring the lake and its environs, to examine and dissect all the herbs within my reach, and, like another Robinson Crusoe, build myself an imaginary place of residence in the island. I became very much attached to this eminence. When I brought Thérèsa, with the wife of the receiver and her sisters, to walk there, how proud was I to be their pilot and guide! We took there rabbits to stock it. This was another source of pleasure to Jean-Jacques. These animals rendered the island still more interesting to me. I afterwards went to it more frequently, and with greater pleasure, to observe the progress of the new inhabitants.

To these amusements I added one which recalled to my recollection the delightful life I led at the Charmettes, and to which the season particularly invited me. This was assisting in the rustic labors of gathering of roots and fruits, of which Thérèsa and I made it a pleasure to partake, with the wife of the receiver and his family. I remember a Bernois, one M. Kirkeberguer, coming to see me, found me perched upon a tree with a sack fastened to my waist, and already so full of apples that I could not stir from the branch on which I stood. I was not sorry to be caught in this and similar situations. I hoped the people of Berne, witnesses to the employment of my leisure, would no longer think of disturbing my tranquillity but leave me at peace in my solitude. I should have preferred being confined there by their desire: this would have rendered the continuation of my repose more certain.

This is another declaration upon which I am previously certain of the incredulity of many of my readers, who obstinately continue to judge of me by themselves, although they cannot but have seen, in the course of my life, a thousand internal affections which bore no resemblance to any of theirs. But what is still more extraordinary is, that they refuse me every sentiment, good or indifferent, which they have not, and are constantly ready to attribute to me such bad ones as cannot enter the heart of man: in this case they find it easy to set me in opposition to nature, and to make of me such a monster as cannot in reality exist. Nothing absurd appears to them incredible, the moment it has a tendency to blacken me, and nothing in the least extraordinary seem to them possible, if it tends to do me honor.

But, notwithstanding what they may think or say, I will still continue faithfully to state what J. J. Rousseau was, did, and thought; without explaining, or justifying, the singularity of his sentiments and ideas, or endeavoring to discover whether or not others have thought as he did. I became so delighted with the island of St. Pierre, and my residence there was so agreeable to me that, by concentrating all my desires within it, I formed the wish that I might stay there to the end of my life. The visits I had to return in the neighborhood, the journeys I should be under the necessity of making to Neuchâtel, Bienne, Yverdon, and Nidau, already fatigued my imagination. A day passed out of the island seemed to me a loss of so much happiness, and to go beyond the bounds of the lake was to go out of my element. Past experience had besides rendered me apprehensive. The very satisfaction that I received from anything whatever was sufficient to make me fear the loss of it, and the ardent desire I had to end my days in that island, was inseparable from the apprehension of being obliged to leave it. I had contracted a habit of going in the evening to sit upon the sandy shore, especially when the lake was agitated. I felt a singular pleasure in seeing the waves break at my feet. I formed of them in my

imagination the image of the tumult of the world contrasted with the peace of my habitation; and this pleasing idea sometimes softened me even to tears. The
repose I enjoyed with ecstasy was disturbed by nothing but the fear of being deprived of it, but this inquietude was accompanied with some bitterness. I
felt my situation so precarious as not to dare to depend
upon its continuance. "Ah! how willingly," said I to
myself, "would I renounce the liberty of quitting this
place, for which I have no desire, for the assurance of
always remaining in it. Instead of being permitted to
stay here by favor, why am I not detained by force!
They who suffer me to remain may in a moment drive
me away, and can I hope my persecutors, seeing me
happy, will leave me here to continue to be so? Permitting me to live in the island is but a trifling favor.
I could wish to be condemned to do it, and constrained
to remain here that I may not be obliged to go elsewhere." I cast an envious eye upon Micheli du Crêt,
who, quiet in the castle of Arbourg, had only to determine to be happy to become so. In fine, by abandoning myself to these reflections, and the alarming
apprehensions of new storms always ready to break
over my head, I wished for them with an incredible
ardor, and that instead of suffering me to reside in
the island, the Bernois would give it me for a perpetual prison: and I can assert that had it depended
upon me to get myself condemned to this, I would
most joyfully have done it, preferring a thousand

times the necessity of passing my life there to the danger of being driven to another place.

This fear did not long remain on my mind. When I least expected what was to happen, I received a letter from the bailiff of Nidau, within whose jurisdiction the island of St. Peter was; by his letter he announced to me from their excellencies an order to quit the island and their states. I thought myself in a dream. Nothing could be less natural, reasonable, or foreseen than such an order: for I had considered my apprehensions as the result of inquietude in a man whose imagination was disturbed by his misfortunes, and not to proceed from a foresight which could have the least foundation. The measures I had taken to insure myself the tacit consent of the sovereign, the tranquillity with which I had been left to make my establishment, the visits of several people from Berne, and that of the bailiff himself, who had shown me such friendship and attention, and the rigor of the season in which it was barbarous to expel a man who was sickly and infirm, all these circumstances made me and many people believe that there was some mistake in the order, and that ill-disposed people had purposely chosen the time of the vintage and the vacation of the senate suddenly to do me an injury.

Had I yielded to the first impulse of my indignation, I should immediately have departed. But to what place was I to go? What was to become of me at the beginning of the winter, without object, preparation, guide, or carriage? Not to leave my papers and effects at the mercy of the first comer, time was necessary to make proper arrangements, and it was not stated in the order whether or not this would be granted me. The continuance of misfortune began to weigh down my courage. For the first time in my life I felt my natural haughtiness stoop to the yoke of necessity, and, notwithstanding the murmurs of my heart, I was obliged to demean myself by asking for a delay. I applied to M. de Graffenried, who had sent me the order, for an explanation of it. His letter, conceived in the strongest terms of disapprobation of the step that had been taken, assured me it was with the greatest regret he communicated to me the nature of it, and the expressions of grief and esteem it contained seemed so many gentle invitations to open to him my heart: I did so. I had no doubt but my letter would open the eyes of my persecutors, and that if so cruel an order was not revoked, at least a reasonable delay, perhaps the whole winter, to make the necessary preparations for my retreat, and to choose a place of abode, would be granted me.

Whilst I waited for an answer, I reflected upon my situation, and deliberated upon the steps I had to take. I perceived so many difficulties on all sides, the vexation I had suffered had so strongly affected me, and my health was then in such a bad state, that I was quite overcome, and the effect of my discouragement was to deprive me of the little resource which remained in my mind, by which I might, as well as it was possible to do it, have withdrawn myself from my melancholy situation. In whatever asylum I should take refuge, it appeared impossible to avoid either of the two means made use of to expel me. One of which was to ſtir up against me the populace by secret maneuvers; and the other to drive me away by open force, without giving a reason for so doing. I could not, therefore, depend upon a safe retreat, unless I went in search of it farther than my ſtrength and the season seemed likely to permit. These circumſtances again bringing to my recollection the ideas which had lately occurred to me, I wished my persecutors to condemn me to perpetual imprisonment rather than oblige me incessantly to wander upon the earth, by successively expelling me from the asylums of which I should make choice; and to this effect I made them a proposal. Two days after my firſt letter to M. de Graffenried, I wrote him a second, desiring he would ſtate what I had proposed to their excellencies. The answer from Berne to both was an order, conceived in the moſt formal and severe terms, to go out of the island, and leave every territory, mediate and immediate of the republic, within the space of twenty-four hours, and never to enter them again under the most grievous penalties.

This was a terrible moment. I have since that time felt greater anguish, but never have I been more embarrassed. What afflicted me most was being forced to abandon the project which had made me desirous to pass the winter in the island. It is now time I should relate the fatal anecdote which completed my disasters, and involved in my ruin an unfortunate people whose rising virtues already promised to equal those of Rome and Sparta. I had spoken of the Corsicans in the *Contrat Social* as a new people, the only nation in Europe not too worn out for legislation, and had expressed the great hope there was of such a people if it were fortunate enough to have a wise legislator. My work was read by some of the Corsicans, who were sensible of the honorable manner in which I had spoken of them; and the necessity under which they found themselves of endeavoring to establish their republic, made their chiefs think of asking me for my ideas upon the subject. M. Buttafuoco, of one of the first families in the country, and captain in France, in the Royal Italians, wrote to me to that effect, and sent me several papers for which I had asked to make myself acquainted with the history of the nation and the state of the country. M. Paoli, also, wrote to me several times, and though I felt such an undertaking to be superior to my abilities, I thought I could not refuse to give my assistance in so great and noble a work, the moment I should have acquired all the necessary information. It was to this effect I answered both these gentlemen, and the correspondence lasted until my departure.

Precisely at the same time, I heard that France was sending troops to Corsica, and that she had entered into a treaty with the Genoese. This treaty and sending of troops gave me uneasiness, and, without imagining I had any further relation with the business, I thought it impossible and the attempt ridiculous, to labor at an undertaking which required such undisturbed tranquillity as the political institution of a people in the moment when perhaps they were upon the point of being subjugated. I did not conceal my fears from M. Buttafuoco, who rather relieved me from them by the assurance that, were there in the treaty things contrary to the liberty of his country, a good citizen like himself would not remain as he did in the service of France. In fact, his zeal for the legislation of the Corsicans, and his connections with M. Paoli, could not leave a doubt on my mind respecting him; and when I heard he made frequent journeys to Versailles and Fontainebleau, and had conversations with M. de Choiseul, all I concluded from the whole was, that with respect to the real intentions of France he had assurances which he gave me to understand, but concerning which he did not choose openly to explain himself by letter.

This removed a part of my apprehensions. Yet, as I could not comprehend the meaning of the transportation of troops from France, nor reasonably suppose they were sent to Corsica to protect the liberty of the inhabitants, which they themselves were very well able to defend against the Genoese, I could neither make myself perfectly easy, nor seriously undertake the plan of the proposed legislation, until I had solid proofs that the whole was serious, and that the parties meant not to trifle with me. I much wished for an interview with M. Buttafuoco, as that was certainly the best means of coming at the explanation I wished. Of this he gave me hopes, and I waited for it with the greateſt impatience. I know not whether he really intended me any interview or not; but had this even been the case, my misfortunes would have prevented me from profiting by it.

The more I considered the proposed undertaking, and the further I advanced in the examination of the papers I had in my hands, the greater I found the necessity of ſtudying, in the country, the people for whom inſtitutions were to be made, the soil they inhabited, and all the relative circumstances by which it was necessary to appropriate to them that inſtitution. I daily perceived more clearly the impossibility of acquiring at a diſtance all the information necessary to guide me. This I wrote to M. Buttafuoco, and he felt it as I did. Although I did not form the precise resolution of going to Corsica, I considered a good deal of the means necessary to make that voyage. I mentioned it to M. Daſtier, who having formerly served in the island under M. de Maillebois, was necessarily acquainted with it. He used every effort to dissuade me from this intention, and I confess the frightful description he gave me of the Corsicans and their country, considerably abated the desire I had of going to live amongſt them.

But when the persecutions of Motiers made me think of quitting Switzerland, this desire was again ſtrengthened by the hope of at length finding amongſt these islanders the repose refused me in every other place. One thing only alarmed me, which was my unfitness for the active life to which I was going to be condemned, and the aversion I had always had to it. My disposition, proper for meditating at leisure and in solitude, was not so for speaking and acting, and treating of affairs with men. Nature, which had endowed me with the first talent, had refused me the last. Yet I felt that, even without taking a direct and active part in public affairs, I should as soon as I was in Corsica, be under the necessity of yielding to the desires of the people, and of frequently conferring with the chiefs. The object even of the voyage required that, instead of seeking retirement, I should in the heart of the country endeavor to gain the information of which I stood in need. It was certain that I should no longer be master of my own time, and that, in spite of myself, precipitated into the vortex in which I was not born to move, I should there lead a life contrary to my inclination, and never appear but to disadvantage. I foresaw, that, ill supporting by my presence the opinion my books might have given the Corsicans of my capacity, I should lose my reputation amongst them, and, as much to their prejudice as my own, be deprived of the confidence they had in me, without which, however, I could not successfully produce the work they expected from my pen. I was certain that, by thus going out of my sphere, I should become useless to the inhabitants, and render myself unhappy.

Tormented, beaten by storms from every quarter,

and, for several years past, fatigued by journeys and persecution, I strongly felt a want of the repose of which my barbarous enemies wantonly deprived me: I sighed more than ever after that delicious indolence, that soft tranquillity of body and mind, which I had so much desired, and to which, now that I had recovered from the chimeras of love and friendship, my heart limited its supreme felicity. I viewed with terror the work I was about to undertake; the tumultuous life into which I was to enter made me tremble, and if the grandeur, beauty, and utility of the object animated my courage, the impossibility of conquering so many difficulties entirely deprived me of it.

Twenty years of profound meditation in solitude would have been less painful to me than an active life of six months in the midst of men and public affairs, with a certainty of not succeeding in my undertaking.

I thought of an expedient which seemed proper to obviate every difficulty. Pursued by the underhand dealings of my secret persecutors to every place in which I took refuge, and seeing no other except Corsica where I could in my old days hope for the repose I had until then been everywhere deprived of, I resolved to go there with the directions of M. Buttafuoco as soon as this was possible, but to live there in tranquillity; renouncing, in appearance, everything relative to legislation, and, in some measure to make my hosts a return for their hospitality, to confine myself to writing in the country the history of the Corsicans, with a reserve in my own mind of the intention of secretly acquiring the necessary information to become more useful to them should I see a probability of success. In this manner, by not entering into an engagement, I hoped to be enabled better to meditate in secret and more at my ease, a plan which might be useful to their purpose, and this without much breaking in upon my dearly beloved solitude, or submitting to a kind of life which I had ever found insupportable.

But the journey was not, in my situation, a thing so easy to get over. According to what M. Daʃtier had told me of Corsica, I could not expe& to find there the most simple conveniences of life, except such as I should take with me; linen, clothes, plate, kitchen furniture, and books, all were to be conveyed thither. To get there myself with my gouvernante, I had the Alps to cross, and in a journey of two hundred leagues to drag after me all my baggage; I had also to pass through the ʃtates of several sovereigns, and according to the example set to all Europe, I had, after what had befallen me, naturally to expe& to find obstacles in every quarter, and that each sovereign would think he did himself honor by overwhelming me with some new insult, and violating in my person all the rights of persons and humanity. The immense expense, fatigue, and risk of such a journey made a previous consideration of them, and weighing every difficulty, the firʃt ʃtep necessary. The idea of being alone, and, at my age, without resource, far removed from all my acquaintance, and at the mercy of these semi-barbarous and ferocious people, such as M. Daſtier had described them to me, was sufficient to make me deliberate before I resolved to expose myself to such dangers. I ardently wished for the interview for which M. Buttafuoco had given me reason to hope, and I waited the result of it to guide me in my determination.

Whilſt I thus hesitated came on the persecutions of Motiers, which obliged me to retire. I was not prepared for a long journey, especially to Corsica. I expeſted to hear from Buttafuoco; I took refuge in the island of St. Pierre, whence I was driven at the beginning of winter, as I have already ſtated. The Alps, covered with snow, then rendered my emigration impraſticable, especially with the promptitude required from me. It is true, the extravagant severity of a like order rendered the execution of it almoſt impossible; for, in the midſt of that concentered solitude, surrounded by water, and having but twenty-four hours after receiving the order to prepare for my departure, and find a boat and carriages to get out of the island and the territory, had I had wings, I should scarcely have been able to pay obedience to it. This I wrote to the bailiff of Nidau, in answer to his letter, and hastened to take my departure from a country of iniquity. In this manner was I obliged to abandon my favorite projeſt, for which reason, not having in my oppression been able to prevail upon my persecutors to dispose of me otherwise, I determined, in consequence of the invitation of my lord marshal, upon a journey to Berlin, leaving Thérèsa to pass the winter in the island of St. Pierre, with my books and effects, and depositing my papers in the hands of M. du Peyrou. I used so much diligence that the next morning I left the island and arrived at Bienne before noon. An accident, which I cannot pass over in silence, had here well nigh put an end to my journey.

As soon as the news of my having received an order to quit my asylum was circulated, I received a great number of visits from the neighborhood, and especially from the Bernois, who came with the most detestable falsehood to flatter and soothe me, protesting that my persecutors had seized the moment of the vacation of the senate to obtain and send me the order, which, said they, had excited the indignation of the two hundred. Some of these comforters came from the city of Bienne, a little free state within that of Berne, and amongst others a young man of the name of Wildremet, whose family was of the first rank, and had the greatest credit in that little city. Wildremet strongly solicited me in the name of his fellow-citizens to choose my retreat amongst them, assuring me that they were anxiously desirous of it, and that they would think it an honor and their duty to make me forget the persecutions I had suffered! that with them I had nothing to fear from the influence of the Bernois, that Bienne was a free city, governed by its own laws, and that the citizens were unanimously resolved not to hearken to any solicitation which should be unfavorable to me.

Wildremet perceiving all he could say to be in-effectual, brought to his aid several other persons, as well from Bienne and the environs as from Berne; even, and amongst others, the same Kirkeberguer, of whom I have spoken, who, after my retreat to Swit-zerland had endeavored to obtain my esteem, and by his talents and principles had interested me in his favor. But I received much less expected and more weighty solicitations from M. Barthes, secretary to the embassy from France, who came with Wildremet to see me, exhorted me to accept his invitation, and surprised me by the lively and tender concern he seemed to feel for my situation. I did not know M. Barthes; however I perceived in what he said the warmth and zeal of friendship, and that he had it at heart to persuade me to fix my residence at Bienne. He made the most pompous eulogium of the city and its inhabitants, with whom he showed himself so intimately connected as to call them several times in my presence his patrons and fathers.

This from Barthes bewildered me in my conjec-tures. I had always suspected M. de Choiseul to be the secret author of all the persecutions I suffered in Swit-zerland. The conduct of the resident of Geneva, and that of the ambassador at Soleure but too much con-firmed my suspicion; I perceived the secret influence of France in everything that happened to me at Berne, Geneva, and Neuchâtel, and I did not think I had any powerful enemy in that kingdom, except the Duke de Choiseul. What therefore could I think of the visit of Barthes and the tender concern he showed for my welfare? My misfortunes had not yet destroyed the confidence natural to my heart, and I had still to learn from experience to discern snares under the appearance of friendship. I sought with surprise the reason of the benevolence of M. Barthes; I was not weak enough to believe he had acted from himself; there was in his manner something ostentatious, an affectation even, which declared a concealed intention, and I was far from having found in any of these little subaltern agents that generous intrepidity which, when I was in a similar employment, had often caused a fermentation in my heart. I had formerly known something of the Chevalier Beauteville, at the castle of Montmorency; he had shown me marks of esteem; since his appointment to the embassy he had given me proofs of his not having entirely forgotten me, accompanied with an invitation to go and see him at Soleure. Though I did not accept this invitation, I was extremely sensible of his civility, not having been accustomed to be treated with such kindness by people in the place. I presumed M. de Beauteville, obliged to follow his instructions in what related to the affairs of Geneva, yet pitying me under my misfortunes, had by his private cares prepared for me the asylum of Bienne, that I might live there in peace under his auspices. I was properly sensible of his attention, but without wishing to profit by it, and quite determined upon the journey to Berlin, I sighed after the moment in which I was to see my lord marshal, persuaded I should in future find real repose and lasting happiness nowhere but near his person.

On my departure from the island, Kirkeberguer accompanied me to Bienne. I found Wildremet and other Biennois, who, by the water side, waited my getting out of the boat. We all dined together at the inn, and on my arrived there my first care was to provide a chaise, being determined to set off the next morning. Whilst we were at dinner, these gentlemen repeated their solicitations to prevail upon me to stay with them, and this with such warmth and obliging protestations, that notwithstanding all my resolutions, my heart, which has never been able to resist friendly attentions, received an impression from theirs; the moment they perceived I was shaken they redoubled their efforts with so much effect that I was at length overcome, and consented to remain at Bienne, at least until the spring.

Wildremet immediately set about providing me with a lodging, and boasted, as of a fortunate discovery, of a dirty little chamber in the back of the house, on the third story, looking into a courtyard, where I had for a view the display of the stinking skins of a dresser of chamois leather. My host was a man of a mean appearance, and a good deal of a rascal; the next day after I went to his house I heard that he was a debauchee, a gamester, and in bad credit in the neighborhood. He had neither wife, children, nor servants, and shut up in my solitary chamber, I was in the midst of one of the most agreeable countries in Europe, lodged in a manner to make me die of melancholy in the course of a few days. What affected me most was, that, notwithstanding what I had heard of the anxious wish of the inhabitants to receive me amongst them, I had not perceived, as I passed through the streets, anything polite towards me in their manners, or obliging in their looks. I was, however, determined to remain there; but I learned, saw, and felt, the day after, that there was in the city a terrible fermentation, of which I was the cause. Several persons hastened obligingly to inform me that on the next day I was to receive an order, conceived in most severe terms, immediately to quit the state, that is the city. I had nobody in whom I could confide; they who had detained me were dispersed. Wildremet had disappeared; I heard no more of Barthes, and it did not appear that his recommendation had brought me into great favor with those whom he had styled his patrons and fathers. One M. de Van Travers, a Bernois, who had an agreeable house not far from the city, offered it me for my asylum, hoping, as he said, that I might there avoid being stoned. The advantage this offer held out was not sufficiently flattering to tempt me to prolong my abode with these hospitable people.

Yet, having lost three days by the delay, I had greatly exceeded the twenty-four hours the Bernois had given me to quit their states, and knowing their severity, I was not without apprehensions as to the manner in which they would suffer me to cross them,

when the bailiff of Nidau came opportunely and relieved me from my embarrassment. As he had highly
disapproved of the violent proceedings of their excellencies, he thought, in his generosity, he owed me
some public proof of his taking no part in them, and
had courage to leave his bailiwick to come and pay
me a visit at Bienne. He did me this favor the evening before my departure, and far from being incognito he affected ceremony, coming *in fiocchi* in his
coach with his secretary, and brought me a passport
in his own name that I might cross the state of Berne
at my ease, and without fear of molestation. I was
more flattered by the visit than by the passport, and
should have been as sensible of the merit of it, had
it had for object any other person whatsoever. Nothing makes a greater impression upon my heart than
a well-timed act of courage in favor of the weak unjustly oppressed.

At length, after having with difficulty procured a
chaise, I next morning left this barbarous country,
before the arrival of the deputation with which I was
to be honored, and even before I had seen Thérèsa,
to whom I had written to come to me, when I thought
I should remain at Bienne, and whom I had scarcely
time to countermand by a short letter, informing her
of my new disaster. In the third part of my memoirs,
if ever I be able to write them, I shall state in what
manner, thinking to set off for Berlin, I really took
my departure for England, and the means by which
the two ladies who wished to dispose of my person,

after having by their maneuvers driven me from Switzerland, where I was not sufficiently in their power, at last delivered me into the hands of their friends.

[I added what follows on reading my memoirs to M. and Madam, the Countess of Egmont, the Prince Pignatelli, the Marchioness of Mesme, and the Marquis of Juigné.

"I have written the truth: if any person has heard of things contrary to those I have just ſtated, were they a thousand times proved, he has heard calumny and falsehood; and if he refuses thoroughly to examine and compare them with me whilſt I am alive, he is not a friend either to juſtice or truth. For my part, I openly, and without the leaſt fear declare, that whoever, even without having read my works, shall have examined with his own eyes my disposition, charaƈter, manners, inclinations, pleasures, and habits, and pronounce me a dishoneſt man, is himself one who deſerves a gibbet."

Thus I concluded, and every person was silent; Madam d'Egmont was the only person who seemed affeƈted: she visibly trembled, but soon recovered herself, and was silent like the reſt of the company. Such were the fruits of my reading and declaration.]

END OF THE SECOND PART